vol. 1 c. 1

Eyewitness Accounts of the American Revolution

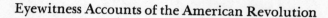

Diary of the
American Revolution
Frank Moore

The New York Times & Arno Press

DIARY

OF THE

AMERICAN REVOLUTION.

Eng.^d by A.H. Ritchie

Willm Moultrie

DIARY

OF THE

AMERICAN REVOLUTION.

FROM

NEWSPAPERS AND ORIGINAL DOCUMENTS.

BY

FRANK MOORE.

VOL. I.

NEW YORK:
CHARLES SCRIBNER, GRAND STREET.
LONDON:
SAMPSON LOW, SON & COMPANY.
MDCCCLX.

PREFACE.

THE materials of these volumes are taken from Whig and Tory newspapers, published during the American Revolution, private diaries, and other cotemporaneous writings. They present to the student of this day the same view the readers of the revolutionary period enjoyed—the manners and customs of the people, and the moral and religious, as well as political features of the time.

As far as practicable, the language of the writers has been preserved. For every assertion presented the reader will find an authority which must be his guide in ascertaining its value in an historical point of view; while, at the same time, he must keep in mind the truth that the errors and lampoons of a period belong as much to its history as the facts and flatteries.

Among the newspapers from which the editor has drawn his material, no one requires an especial notice in this place; a history of the periodical writers of

the last century would in itself. exceed the limits of
these volumes. Such a work would prove an interesting and important addition to the literature of America.

In conclusion, the editor acknowledges his obligations for the many favors and facilities extended to him
by the various Historical Societies of the United States,
most especially to the officers of the New York Historical Society, from whom he has received the most
valuable assistance.

New York, October, 1859.

LIST OF AUTHORITIES USED IN THIS WORK.

Newspapers and other Printed Material.

BAILEY'S FREEMAN'S JOURNAL.
BROADSIDES—NEW YORK HISTORICAL SOCIETY.
BOSTON NEWS LETTER.
BOSTON INDEPENDENT CHRONICLE.
BOSTON WEEKLY ADVERTISER.
BOSTON GAZETTE AND COUNTRY JOURNAL.
CONSTITUTIONAL GAZETTE.
CONNECTICUT COURANT.
CONNECTICUT GAZETTE.
CONNECTICUT JOURNAL.
ESSEX GAZETTE.
FREEMAN'S JOURNAL AND NEW HAMPSHIRE GAZETTE.
GEORGIA GAZETTE.
GAINE'S NEW YORK GAZETTE.
    "   WEEKLY MERCURY.
LONDON EVENING POST.
LONDON GAZETTE.
LONDON MORNING POST.
LONDON PUBLIC ADVERTISER.
MASSACHUSETTS SPY.
MARYLAND GAZETTE.
MARYLAND JOURNAL.
MIDDLESEX JOURNAL.
NEW ENGLAND CHRONICLE.
NEW ENGLAND GAZETTE.
NEW HAMPSHIRE GAZETTE.
NEW LONDON GAZETTE.
NEW JERSEY GAZETTE.
NEW JERSEY JOURNAL.
NEWPORT MERCURY.
NEW YORK PACKET.
NEW YORK JOURNAL.
NEW YORK GAZETTE.
PENNSYLVANIA GAZETTE.
PENNSYLVANIA JOURNAL.
PENNSYLVANIA LEDGER.
PENNSYLVANIA PACKET.

PENNSYLVANIA EVENING POST.
PINCKNEY'S VIRGINIA GAZETTE.
PROVIDENCE GAZETTE.
RIVINGTON'S ROYAL GAZETTE.
SOUTH CAROLINA GAZETTE.
ST. JAMES' CHRONICLE.
THE UNIVERSAL INTELLIGENCER.
UPCOTT COLLECTION OF NEWSPAPER EXTRACTS—
     NEW YORK HISTORICAL SOCIETY.
VIRGINIA GAZETTE.

Manuscripts.

LETTERS OF CAPTAIN ISRAEL CARVER.
         "   EDWARD CHURCHILL.
         "   JONATHAN CHURCHILL.
         "   GENERAL HORATIO GATES.
         "   L. W. ELLIOTT.
DIARY OF CAPTAIN SMYTHE, OF THE ROYAL ARMY.
         "   ELKANAH GOULD.
         "   SOLOMON E. CLIFT.
         "   JOHN V. MASON.
         "   JOHN PARKS.

LIST OF MAPS AND PLATES.

PORTRAIT OF WILLIAM MOULTRIE (*Frontispiece.*)	.	VOL. I.	PAGE
MAP OF LAKE CHAMPLAIN AND LAKE GEORGE .	.	—	78
VIEW OF BOSTON	.	—	97
VIEW OF QUEBEC .	.	—	185
MAP OF BOSTON AND VICINITY .	.	—	212
VIEW OF NEW YORK	.	—	311
PORTRAIT OF GUY CARLETON	.	—	454
PLAN OF THE OPERATIONS OF THE BRITISH AND REBEL ARMY, 1777	—	494
PORTRAIT OF GENERAL BURGOYNE	.	—	513
PORTRAIT OF SIR HENRY CLINTON (*Frontispiece.*)	.	VOL. II.	
PORTRAIT OF HENRY LEE	.	—	209
PLAN OF THE SIEGE OF SAVANNAH	.	—	224
PLAN OF THE SIEGE OF CHARLESTON	.	—	258
VIEW OF CHARLESTON	.	—	273
PORTRAIT OF MAJOR ANDRE	.	—	336
PORTRAIT OF JAMES RIVINGTON	.	—	448
MAP OF NEW YORK .	.	—	498
PORTRAIT OF CORNWALLIS .	.	—	512

DIARY OF THE REVOLUTION.

CHAPTER I.

JANUARY 1.—THE chief troubles of our Israel[1] are the Philantrops, the Hazlerods, the Sir Froths, the Tims, the Bens, and the Bobs. These are men, who, for large shares in the American plunder, have sold themselves to do wickedly. The barbarians who have been aiding and assisting bad governors and abandoned ministers, in all their attempts to subjugate and enslave these once happy colonies: the hireling prostitutes who have been constantly representing to ministry that the friends of liberty were a small, insignificant, divided faction; that the people had not virtue to sacrifice any parts of the profits of their trade, or the luxury of their living for the sake of their country; or spirit to withstand the least exertion of power. These are traitors who were for none but licensed town-meetings,[2] and gave administration the outlines of the execrable Boston Port Bill and the other detestable bills for destroying the charter,[3] and those sacred compacts which Americans once thought were of some value, the faith of kings being the security. These are the unblushing advocates for pensioned governors, dependent judges, hired attorneys, and sheriff created jurors, that the people might, under color of law, be stript of their property, without their consent, and suitably punished if they should dare to complain: the odious rebels, who, for the support of these hateful measures, have invited the troops and ships, that are now distressing the inhabitants of Boston, and alarm-

Causes of trouble in Boston.

[1] The town of Boston. [2] See the Governor's proclamation.
[3] Of Massachusetts Bay.

ing not only a single province, but a whole continent. And when almost every event has turned out contrary to their predictions, and when it might be reasonably expected that the union of the colonies, the resolutions of the Continental Congress, and the late associations and preparations to withstand all hostile attempts upon our persons or properties, might lead administration to suspect at least the policy or safety of pushing this people to extremities; we find this infamous cabal playing over the old game of ministerial deception, and Timothy Ruggles[1] with a gravity peculiar to himself and an owl,

Timothy Ruggles' assertion.

asserting in the public prints—"that though many of the people had for some time past been arming, their numbers would not appear in the field so large as imagined, before it was known that independency was the object in contemplation;"[2] and further, that since that time, many associated in divers parts of the province, to support what he calls "Government."—But the views and designs of these pensioned prostitutes of Massachusetts,—in all that they say or write, are perfectly kenned by the most short-sighted amongst us. In vain are their scare-crows, raw-head and bloody bones, held up to deter us from taking the most effectual means for our security. The little scribbling, illiberal

[1] The Chief Justice of the province of Massachusetts Bay. See statement and plan of association, published by Judge Ruggles in most of the Boston papers, Dec. 23–27, 1774, and reprinted in Gaines' New York Gazette, Jan. 9, 1775.

[2] An assertion as false as it is impudent and injurious, first uttered by a hireling priest,* in the *New York Freeholder*, who at the same time declared that he had rather be under the government of Roman Catholics than Dissenters—a declaration truly characteristic of the doctor, and his little club of malignants.—The people of Massachusetts have hitherto acted purely on the defensive; they have only opposed those new regulations which were instantly to have been executed, and would have annihilated all our rights. For this absolutely necessary and manly step they have received the approbation of the Continental Congress, one of the most respectable assemblies in the world. They aim at no independency, nor any thing new, but barely the preservation of their old rights. They have referred their cause to the whole continent, and are determined to act only in free consultation, and close union with their brethren. This is indeed the safety of all.—*Editor of the Journal.*

* Dr. Myles Cooper, the President of King's, now Columbia, College, a vigorous writer in favor of the crown.

pieces, which have disgraced the Massachusetts Gazettes, will not lessen the Continental Congress in our esteem; or retard the measures they have recom- *The Gazettes.* mended, notwithstanding the sums paid to effect it. These writers, and their attempts to encourage or mislead, are treated with ineffable contempt by their countrymen. It has, however, been unhappy for both countries that the represen- tations and projects of such men as these have been heeded and adopted on the other side of the Atlantic; men whose very livings have depended upon the continuation of those measures which Americans have so long complained of, and sought to have redressed. If these *unnaturals* should succeed in their present misleading attempts, to the preventing a speedy close to our differences, we shall then have good reason to conclude that *blindness* has happened to Britons, that the *fulness* of American Liberty might come in.[1]

JANUARY 3.—THIS morning, Mr. John Case, an old man of near sixty years of age, from Long Island, was entreated by an acquaintance of his to go to the house of Jasper Drake, tavern- keeper near Beckman's Slip, where he was told Captain McD——l,[2] Captain S——s,[3] and others wanted to converse with him on politics. He went, and soon entered into conver- sation with Captain McD——l, who attempted to convince him that he was in an error, but not being able to effect it, politely left him. Captain S——s, with several *Captain Sears* other persons, then attacked him with the force *and John Case.* of their eloquence and noise, but Case said he was an un- learned man, and but of few words,—that he could not reply to above one. That he judged, however, the fairest way to come at the truth would be to recur to the origin of the pres- ent contest between Great Britain and the Colonies, and to trace from the time of the stamp act, the encroachments of ministerial power, and the increasing demands for provincial privileges. This was objected to by Captain S——s, as it would require too much time and attention to discuss. He

[1] Pennsylvania Journal, Jan. 25. [2] Alexander Mac Dougall.
[3] Isaac Sears, afterwards called by the loyalists, King Sears.

said that he would question him a little, and asked Case
whether the king had not violated his coronation oath ?   Mr.
Case replied, that he thought he had not, and reasoned on this
and other matters in as cool a manner as possible, in order not
to irritate Captain S——s, who, however, soon grew warm,
and branded Case with the appellation of Tory, and told him
that if he was in Connecticut government he would be put to
death.   S——s then demanded of Case whether, if the Bos-
tonians were to take up arms, he would fight for the king?
Case answered, that if he fought on either side, he would certainly fight for no one else, as he conceived King George to
be his lawful sovereign, for the minister a few days before
prayed for our rightful sovereign Lord King George the Third,
on which S——s replied he was sorry that he had turned
churchman, where such prayers were used ; Case replied,
these expressions were delivered the preceding Sunday by
Dr. Rodgers[1] at the Presbyterian meeting, for he himself was
a Presbyterian.   After a few more queries and replies of a
similar nature, S——s told him that he would not suffer a
Tory to sit in company with gentlemen, placed a chair in the
chimney corner, caught Case by the arm, and forced him into
it.   He then called for a negro boy, who belonged to the
house, and ordered him to sit along with him ; for that he
(Case) was only fit to sit in company with slaves ; but the
negro had too much understanding to comply.   Mr. Case then
called for some wine, and offered it to the company, but
S——s refused to accept of it, pushed him down in the chair
where he before had placed him, and ordered the rest not to
drink with a Tory ; and further, that whoever spoke to Case,
should forfeit a bowl of toddy, which was exacted by him
from two persons who happened to disobey his mandates.
S——s then told Case that his age protected him, for if he
was a young man, he would have placed him on a red-hot
gridiron ; and after he had detained this old man as long as
he thought proper, he dismissed him.[2]

[1] John Rodgers, D. D., pastor of the Wall street church.
[2] This account was published in Rivington's Gazette, Jan. 12, in the form of a
deposition, witnessed by Mr. Case.

JANUARY 5.—THE professorship lately instituted by our most gracious sovereign, at King's College in New York, is to be held by a tutor of the college, at the same time a clergyman. His business, besides teaching, will King's College. be to deliver annual lectures in defence of the Christian, and on the principles of natural religion. His title, the Regius Professor of Divinity, with a salary from the Crown. An incontestable evidence this, of his Majesty's desire of supporting the Christian religion in America, as it is in England, by annual lectures in its defence.[1]

JANUARY 8.—A LETTER from London of a late date, says, Lord North behaves with the greatest firmness and composure, and is resolutely determined to carry his point Lord North continues firm. with the colonies, and smiles with contempt upon any tales of congresses and combinations in America. The Duke of Richmond has positively declared his The Duke of Richmond's opinion. opinion, that the colonies have proceeded to such unjustifiable lengths, their pretensions cannot any longer be supported ; and that the constitutional authority of Parliament over them must be maintained ; and that this is the language of most people of England.[2]

JANUARY 9.—A WRITER in England gives the following advice to administration with respect to America : "Let authority give way to prudence; dignity is supported Advice to the Ministry. best by justice; the bread of at least one hundred thousand manufacturers is of more importance than a shadowy authority ; the lives of our fellow-subjects, descended from ourselves, and though born in a distant climate, are dear to us. One passionate resolve may sacrifice a million of British subjects, and subject this nation and its dependencies to ruin, and those who framed it to everlasting infamy. More is at stake than many comprehend ; those who say otherwise are ignorant, or foes in disguise."[3]

---

[1] Gaines' New York Gazette, Jan. 9.   [2] The same.
[3] Supplement to Holt's New York Journal, Jan. 5.

JANUARY 10.—THIS evening was married by the Reverend
Doctor Auchmuty, Mr. Joseph Dillon, son of Captain Dillon,
Joseph Dillon
married.   commander of His Majesty's packet, the Mercury,
to Miss Joanna Van Horne, daughter of Mr. Gar-
ret Van Horne, late an eminent merchant of this city ; a very
amiable and truly deserving young lady.[1]

THE people of Marblehead, Massachusetts, met to-day and
resolved, that, as a great number of the inhabitants of that
Motion in Marble-
head, Mass. town may soon be called forth, to assist in defending the charter and constitution of that province,
as well as the rights and liberties of all America, in order
thereto it is necessary that they should be properly disciplined and instructed in the art of war ; they also ordered that
a committee of fifteen be appointed to attend to the conduct
of the ministerial tools and Jacobites in that town, and to report their names to the town, that effectual measures may be
taken to silence them in the future, or expel them from the
community.[2]

JANUARY 12.—THIS day, his Majesty's frigate, the Kingfisher, Captain Montague, went up to Turtle Bay to lay there
for the winter season.[3]

AT a late meeting of exotics, styled The Sons of Liberty, in
New York, the pamphlet entitled " Farmer A. W.'s View of
the controversy between Great Britain and the Colonies," &c.,
published last week by Mr. Rivington, was introduced by one
of the mushrooms, and after a few pages being read to the
company, they agreed *nem. con.* to commit it to the flames,
without the benefit of clergy ; though many, very many indeed, could neither write nor read ; however, their common
executioner immediately threw it into the fire, where it was
consumed, and its spiritual part ascended in vapor, to the

[1] Gaines' Mercury, Jan. 16.   [2] Upcott, iv. 295.
[3] New York Gazette, Jan. 16.

upper regions; whither not one of the company durst aspire, even in idea.[1]

JANUARY 17.—THE Provincial Congress of South Carolina met on the 11th instant, and have continued in session, Sundays not excepted, until to-day. They have shut up the courts of law; no process is to issue in civil cases, and all proceedings had, since the return day, September 20, 1774, are to be staid. This is such a step as no other province has yet taken.[2]

A CORRESPONDENT says:—"The violent party in Philadelphia are greatly crest-fallen; they see with inexpressible chagrin the numbers of their former adherents which they lose every day. The Pennsylvania Farmer, a gentleman of great discernment, and possessed of a very large estate, has deserted them, greatly alarmed at the length our committee are carrying matters; he has declared he will not meet them any more, and he does not declare alone."[4]

ANOTHER writer observes, that the cause of the enemies of American liberty must needs be in a most desperate condition, since they have recourse to the most infamous acts and falsehoods to carry their point. Of these he instances a long catalogue, among which are the following:—That the people in several colonies are deserting the cause of their country and joining its enemies to enslave it. That several of the most eminent patriots had deserted the cause, particularly the Philadelphia farmer—who remains the same invariable friend he has ever been to his country and mankind, and is now one of the delegates for the province of Pennsylvania, to meet next May in general Congress."[5]

JANUARY 19.—THE Governor of Connecticut called his counsel together on the 4th instant; their deliberations are kept very secret; but we are told they have ordered three

[1] Rivington's Gazette, Jan. 12.   [2] Gaines' Mercury, Feb. 6.   [3] John Dickinson.
[4] Extract of a letter from Philadelphia, in Rivington's Gazette, Jan. 19.
[5] Holt's Journal, Feb. 9.

hundred barrels of gunpowder, and lead in proportion, to be purchased at the public expense. The militia in the whole colony is mustered every week, and in most towns they have a deserter from his Majesty's forces, by way of drill sergeant. Nothing but a spirit of independence would suffer matters to be carried to such extremities, as make all prudent inhabitants fear that our parchment will soon totter.[1]

JANUARY 20.—A LITTLE after ten o'clock this evening, two young men passing down Milk street, near the entrance into Long Lane, they were accosted by an officer, not in the English, but as they supposed in another language, which they did not understand; they asked him what he meant; he replied he meant to tell them to go about their business. They had not gone far before the officer called to them to stop. They stopped till he came up to them, and angry words ensued. The young men, however, parted from him the second time, and went on their way towards their homes. The officer followed and overtook them near the head of the lane, and stopped them again, telling them he supposed they were stiff Americans; to which one of them said he gloried in the character. Here again words ensued, and the officer drew his sword, flourished it and struck one of the young men on the arm, who immediately seized him. At this juncture, three or four of the town watch, who were upon the patrol, came up and separated them, advising them to go home. The two young men did so, but the officer refused, saying he was prisoner of the watch and would go with them; they told him he was not their prisoner, but might go where he pleased, and if he desired it, they would see him safe home: but he insisted upon it that he was their prisoner. The watchmen went down the lane towards their head-quarters in King street, where they had been going before, and the officer accompanied them. In the way they met with several persons, whom they took to be servants of officers, who, supposing the officer to be in custody of the watch, attempted to rescue him,

Disturbance at Boston.

---

[1] Extract of a letter from Hartford, Jan. 13; Rivington's Gazette, Jan. 19.

but he insisted upon being a prisoner, and said the watchmen were his friends, and he *would* go with them. They then went forward, and in Quaker Lane, which leads into King street, they were met and assaulted by more than twenty officers of the army, who took several of their watch poles from them, and wounded some of them.[1]

JANUARY 23.—THIS morning a detachment of about one hundred and twenty soldiers from the army in Boston, under the command of Captain Balfour, were embarked in armed vessels for Marshfield, about forty miles from that place. We are at a loss for the occasion of this extraordinary manœuvre, as all of our accounts from Marshfield

Balfour visits Marshfield.

---

[1] Edes and Gills' account, as published in Rivington's Gazette, Feb. 9. The same paper contains the following "Other Side of the Question:"—You have read in that fund of lies and sedition, Edes and Gill,* of a "high-handed riot." There have been five field officers on a court of inquiry, to inspect into the conduct of the officers concerned on that occasion. It commenced by Lieutenant Myers, 38th Regiment, being, without the smallest cause, insulted by two townspeople, who not only called him a Tory, rascal, scoundrel, &c., but damned the king, governor, army, and every friend to government; the former he put up with, the latter resented, by knocking the person down. He was immediately surrounded by the watch; and though he immediately surrendered, and gave his sword to a Mr. Winslow, who came up at the time, (a private gentleman,) and informed them, and this gentleman, of the cause of the quarrel, they treated him with every indignity possible; not only allowed the two men to knock him down in the midst of them, but they themselves kicked and beat him all the way to the watch-house, a little short of a quarter of a mile. The noise about the watch-house brought together a few officers, whom Mr. Myers requested not to interfere, concealed from them the cruel treatment he had met with, and insisted on remaining in custody. The insolence of the watch to those gentlemen occasioned a fresh riot, when the interposition of a party from the main guard prevented any bad consequences. Immediately after, Myers was released, by order from the governor. Complaints were immediately lodged against the officers, and bail is to be given to-morrow for their appearance. I cannot quit this subject without observing, that the high-flyers are much disappointed in the event of this riot; not only at the little mischief done, but at the ready submission of every officer concerned, to the laws of the country.

The spirit of the people here seems to subside a little; and we have every reason to believe, that, in order to keep it up, the vagabonds of the town are employed to insult the troops, which they do daily, in hopes of bringing about another massacre.

* The publishers of the Boston Gazette and Country Journal.

agree that the people in that vicinity were peaceable, and no injury had been offered any of the Tories. A few persons there, it is said, who have rendered themselves disagreeable and contemptible to their neighbors, have taken it into their heads to make complaint to General Gage for military protection. In this they have engaged a number of idle young fellows, and some negroes to join them. The letters from thence state that the numbers and quality of the petitioners are despicable. Some inhabitants not unfriendly to the Tory cause, signified their disapprobation of this measure. The sending soldiers alarms and irritates the country ; but what service the Tory cause is to receive from this step, time will discover.[1]

JANUARY 25.—A DESPICABLE pamphlet lately published in Boston, now commonly called the " *Grey Maggot*," has asserted, " That the only apology which could be made for the conduct of the Continental Congress in adopting the Suffolk resolves, was that they came into this vote immediately after drinking thirty-two bumpers of Madeira, of which the next morning, when their heads were cool, they were ashamed, and then prudently determined not to do the business till after dinner for the future ! " If it would not offend the characters of that truly august assembly to take so much notice of this most impudent and false assertion, as seriously to contradict it, we would say, that it appears from the minutes of the Congress, that as they sat till late in the afternoon, they never did any business after dinner, and that the Suffolk resolves were acted upon Saturday, in the forenoon. From this instance the public may see to what an astonishing height of unblushing falsehood and the basest calumny against the most respectable characters, the enemies of our common rights have now attained ; and how ready they are to perform any dirty drudgery for the sake of procuring or preserving a titled or lucrative place.[2]

The Grey Maggot.

SATURDAY last, after a few days' illness, died at Philadelphia, in the fifty-fourth year of his age, universally lamented,

---

[1] Pennsylvania Journal, Feb. 8.   [2] The same paper.

Thomas Lawrence, Esq., Vendue Master, one of the aldermen, and for some time mayor of that city, which Thomas Lawrence died. offices he filled with unsullied reputation. In short, benevolence marked his character, and virtue in him wore her most amiable dress, being constantly exercised in love towards his family, uprightness in his dealings, sincerity in his friendships, cheerfulness in his conversation, and an earnest desire to promote peace and happiness around him. This day his remains were deposited in the family vault in Christ' church burying-ground, attended by a very large number of respectable citizens. The funeral was conducted agreeable to the resolves of the Continental Congress.[1]

" THOSE who have turned the least part of their attention to history," says a writer in England, " will find a strong similitude between us at the present time and the English and Romans. Romans in their declension. The latter at that period were more luxurious, dissipated, and fanciful in dress, equipage, arts, &c., than at any other time—*so are we.* Suicide more peculiarly marked that era—*so it does ours.* Their emperors held the dignity of government in such open contempt that they frequently made their horses consuls. Ours, in this last point, goes beyond them, by making asses senators ; yet with all this, the *form* of government was supported. —Alas! ours at present is nothing but a form."[2]

JANUARY 27.—In the town of Plymouth, Massachusetts, eleven persons were chosen to observe the actions of the Tories, and make report from time to time, what they can hear and observe.[3]

JANUARY 28.—YESTERDAY the house, barn, and barrack of Jacob Van Binschola, of Poughkeepsie, Dutchess County, was

---

[1] Gaines' Mercury, Jan. 30.—On the 20th October, 1774, the Continental Congress, in their Articles of Association, resolved that, " on the death of any relation or friend, none of us, or any of our families, will go into any further mourning-dress than a black crape or ribbon on the arm or hat, for gentlemen ; and a black ribbon and necklace for ladies ; and we will discontinue the giving of gloves and scarfs at funerals."—*Journals of Congress.*

[2] Holt's Journal, Feb. 9.   [3] New York Journal, Feb. 16.

burnt to the ground, together with every thing therein contained.
The villainous action was perpetrated by a negro fellow belonging to the family, who some time before had been corrected
by his master. Confessing his guilt, he has been tried and
burnt to-day.[1]

FEBRUARY 1.—THIS day the Provincial Congress of Massachusetts, met at Cambridge, and the Hon. John Hancock was
chosen president.[2]

FASTING and prayer, appointed by authority, throughout
the colony of Connecticut, " to implore the divine mercy at this
dark and critical time." A number of Tories be-

Connecticut To-ries.

longing to the town of Stamford, in that colony,
met at a certain tavern to spend the day in regaling themselves,
and, as their manner commonly is upon such occasions, testifying their loyalty to the king, by disobeying the proclamation of his Governor. They received intelligence of some casks
of powder, which a carman was entrusted with, for the use of
the colony. Of this they gave immediate information to an
under officer of the customs, who seized the powder, and
ordered it to his own house.[3]

FEBRUARY 3.—A NUMBER of men from a distant town
having heard of the seizure of the powder at Stamford, went
in a body to that town ; proceeded in an orderly

Affair at Stamford.

manner to the house where the powder was
lodged, which they entered without opposition, and having
found it, rode off with the casks, without any bad consequences, saving a plentiful discharge of Billingsgate from the
mortified disappointed faction, and the no small consternation
of the informers, who upon the first news of the company's
approach, ran off with great trepidation, and hid themselves
until all was over.[4]

[1] Gaines' Mercury, Feb. 13.   [2] New York Gazette, Feb. 13.
[3] Holt's Journal, Feb. 16.
[4] Holt's Journal, Feb. 16.—Rivington, in his Gazette of the 9th Feb., pub-
lishes the following: One day last week, seven half barrels of gunpowder were

FEBRUARY 9.—YESTERDAY some gentlemen were dining together at a house in New York, and in the course of the conversation, one of the company frequently used the word *Tory;* the gentleman at whose house Definition of a Tory. they dined, asked him, 'Pray, Mr. ——, what is a Tory?' He replied, 'A Tory is a thing whose head is in England, and its body in America, and its neck ought to be stretched.'[1]

FEBRUARY 16.—ON Thursday morning, the 2d instant, the ship JAMES, Captain Watson, arrived at New York from Glasgow, with a cargo of coals and dry goods, but as she did not arrive within the time prescribed The ship James at Sandy Hook. by the tenth article of the association of the Continental Congress,[2] a strict watch was constantly kept, by some of the sub-committee, and a number of inhabitants, to prevent the landing of any goods, in a clandestine manner; and the captain was requested to procure such necessaries as he might stand in need of, and immediately quit the port. With this request,

seized by William Hubbard, Esq., at Stamford, in Connecticut, on its way from New York to New Haven, over land.

We have just received advice, that the house of the collector of Stamford was, the day after the seizure of the gunpowder, attacked by a number of Liberty lads, who took possession of the powder, and carried it off on horses to Fairfield. They were headed by one Bartram, a quondam sergeant in the provincial service. A party from Hartford, with Colonel Wyllys, Captain Alcott, two of the Messrs. Bull, thirty of them in all, marched to Fairfield, took possession of the powder, and lodged it in the loyal town of Hartford.

[1] New York Journal, Feb. 9.

[2] Association, Article 10.—In case any merchant, trader, or other person, shall import any goods or merchandise, after the first day of December, and before the first day of February next, the same ought forthwith, at the election of the owner, to be either re-shipped, or delivered up to the committee of the county or town wherein they shall be imported, to be stored at the risk of the importer, until the non-importation agreement shall cease, or be sold under the direction of the committee aforesaid; and in the last-mentioned case, the owner or owners of such goods shall be reimbursed out of the sales, the first cost and charges, the profit, if any, to be applied towards relieving and employing such poor inhabitants of the town of Boston, as are immediate sufferers by the Boston Port Bill; and a particular account of all goods so returned, stored, or sold, to be inserted in the public papers; and if any goods or merchandise shall be imported after the said first day of February, the same ought forthwith to be sent back again, without breaking any of the packages thereof.—*Journals of Congress.*

he seemed rather unwilling to comply, and was encouraged to hope from the assurances of a number of ministerial tools, who promised to support him, that his cargo would be landed ; for which purpose they employed a few vagrants to go on board the ship, which then lay in the harbor, and bring the colors on shore, with a view of raising a posse, to assist in landing the goods ; but the banditti that were collected for this purpose were soon suppressed by the inhabitants, who are for supporting the association, and who began to assemble in great numbers ; upon which the captain, conceiving the ship to be in great danger, sent the mate on shore, requesting assistance to get her under sail, as the seamen refused to do that duty. This request being complied with, they immediately got her under weigh, and fell down about four miles below the city, where she remained, attended by a boat, with a member of the committee and some of the townsmen on board, till last Thursday night (9th), when she was again brought into the harbor, by an officer and a number of men belonging to his Majesty's ship King Fisher ; which ship it is supposed came down from Turtle Bay expressly for the purpose of protecting her, and intimidating the inhabitants.

As soon as it was known that the ship was coming up again, the people, highly exasperated, began to assemble together in great numbers, and immediately went to the captain's lodgings ; seized him, and after conducting him through many of the principal streets, attended by a prodigious concourse of people, he was, without suffering the least hurt or injury, put on board a boat, with some hands to row him, and sent off. His ship then lying at anchor ten miles below the town, he went on board the man-of-war, which lay in the harbor, where his own ship did not arrive until the next morning, when she came to anchor under the cannon of the King Fisher. In this situation matters remained until Saturday, when they began to unmoor the ship, intending to get under sail, but were prevented by the lieutenant of the man-of-war, who hailed the ship, and demanded if they had a clearance. Being assured in the negative he ordered them not to unmoor. This obstruction greatly exasperated a number of people that were

collected to see her get under sail, who went in quest of the
captain of the King Fisher, to know by what authority he
detained the ship, but they could not meet with him; he was,
however, soon after waited upon, by one of the gentlemen to
whom the ship was consigned, and on being informed of the
lieutenant's conduct, and asked his reasons for detaining her,
he replied that he had nothing to do with her, and immediately gave orders to let her pass.   Accordingly she got
under sail the next morning about ten o'clock, accompanied
by a boat, with two of the committee and a number of inhabitants on board ; which boat, after taking out the pilot, left her
at two o'clock P. M., about a league to the southward of Sandy
Hook, with a fresh gale, and at half-past four o'clock she was
out of sight.

As every artifice has been used, and a variety of manœuvres
put in practice, by a set of ministerial hirelings, to procure the
landing of the cargo of this ship, it must give real pleasure to
every lover of his country to observe that the good people of
New York are determined to support the association of the
general Congress at all events.[1]

IT appears that the inhabitants of Maryland are all in
motion ; forming county meetings, choosing committees of
observation to carry into effectual execution,   Maryland in
without fear, favor, or partiality, the measures   motion.
recommended by the grand Continental Congress, and forming
companies to learn the art military.   Anne Arundel county,
including the citizens of Annapolis, have resolved that every
person who should refuse to contribute to the purchase of
arms and ammunition for the use of that county, before the
first of this month (Feb.), shall be deemed an enemy to
America, and his name published in the Maryland Gazette.
The General Assembly of New Jersey have approved of the
proceedings of the Continental Congress, and instructed their
delegates to propose and agree to every reasonable and constitutional measure for the accommodation of the unhappy differences at present subsisting between the mother country and
the colonies.[2]

[1] Holt's New York Journal, Feb. 16.   [2] Upcott, iv. 297.

The members of the Philadelphia committee of correspondence deny the rumors reflecting on their patriotism.[1]

WHILE the county delegates were in session at Fairfield, Connecticut, the day before yesterday, the following toast was drank by a company of gentlemen in that town :—Addition to Whigs; Subtraction to Tories; Multiplication to the friends of Liberty, and Division to the enemies of America.[2]

<small>Arithmetical Toasts.</small>

FEBRUARY 17.—IT is said that at least three-fourths of the people in Cortlandt's manor, New York, have declared their unwillingness to enter into the Congressional measures,[3] that a great number of the peo-

<small>Cortlandt's Manor Disaffected.</small>

---

[1] Gaines' Mercury, March 13.

[2] Holt's Journal, Feb. 23.—At the meeting of the delegates, every town in the county was represented except Ridgefield and Newton. In the evening of the day the meeting was held, " two of the inhabitants of a place *lately known and called by the name of Ridgefield*, put up at a public house in Weathersfield, Conn., and entering into conversation, boldly justified the vote of the said *late town of Ridgefield*, in disapproving of the doings of the Continental Congress; and proceeded far in supporting Court doctrines of passive obedience to Parliament, &c. This was taken notice of by a number of gentlemen present, who considered it, in effect, as a direct breach of the Association of the said Congress, and therefore voted, that, 'in their opinion, it was proper that those persons should be returned the way from whence they came, under safe conduct, from town to town, *to the said place lately known by the said name of Ridgefield :*' and, that all honest and true men to this country might know and avoid them, proper persons were appointed instantly to attend them on their return as far as Farmington, and there to acquaint the inhabitants of their behavior, and leave them to their further transportation, as is usual; and as by law is provided, in cases of strolling idiots, lunatics, &c. A letter was accordingly written to the gentlemen at Farmington, representing their unhappy and desperate situation, which was signed by the principal gentlemen present; and the unhappy men, properly escorted, set off at nine o'clock, amidst the hisses, groans, &c., of a respectable concourse of people, the populace following them out of town, beating a dead march."—*Clift's Diary, and Holt's Journal*, Jan. 23.

[3] This rumor is denied by " a gentleman of undoubted veracity," as follows : " There are not any of the landholders in said manor, except one C——y, a miller, at Peekskill, and a few interlopers of his kidney, that are of that perverse sentiment. The proprietors of the manor of Cortlandt, together with all the other landholders, except the above miller and his few adherent Tories, are unanimous in favor of the Congress measures."—*Holt's Journal*, March 2.

ple in general in Westchester county are preparing to do the like, and that the association against the Continental Congress has been signed by three hundred persons in the neighborhood of Poughkeepsie only. Many lists are sent about Dutchess county, on which also many hundreds have subscribed.[1]

On Friday last, at Messrs. Sharp and Curtenius's furnace, in New York, a cylinder was cast for the steam-engine of the waterworks now in course of erection in that city. This is the first performance of the kind ever attempted in America, and allowed by judges to be extremely well executed.[2]

February 18.—A few days ago a riot occurred at Elizabethtown in Jersey. The scene opened between twelve and one o'clock, with seizing a poor Staten Islander, for *Elizabethtown riot.* no other crime than because some people of that ever loyal island were supposed to have been ready to assist in landing some goods from Captain Watson's Scotch ship, which lately left New York, and is departed with his cargo for Jamaica, having arrived at New York after the first of February, the day limited by the Congress for the importation of goods. The man's boat was dragged ashore, and his oysters distributed to the hungry vagabonds, who were visibly headed in the centre of the town, by Jonathan *Judge Hampton.* Hampton, a Justice of the Peace, a Judge of the county court, and chairman of the committee. Hampton was the man who attempted lately to obstruct the passage of his Majesty's royal regiment of Ireland, over the ferries, and prevented wagons from carrying their baggage; this same Hampton was the man who raised a riot lately in Sussex county, attacked a peddler, and destroyed his property. About four o'clock, when the mob discharged the poor oyster man, they proceeded to abuse all the people in the town who were known to be well affected to the constitution; they erected a gallows, in order more particularly to insult them, and fixed up a liberty pole in the middle of the town. It must be observed, that the worshipful Judge, Jonathan Hampton, was,

[1] Upcott, iv. 297.   [2] Rivington's Gazette, Feb. 16.

as usual, completely drunk when the riot commenced. For the honor of the police, it must be recorded, that two of the aldermen, Messrs. Blanchard and Dayton, exerted themselves greatly to suppress those violences, but they were only able to check them. Two of the *Delegates* contributed towards a collection that was made for their ever-staunch friends the *mob*. Mr. Alderman Blanchard ordered the gallows to be demolished, after it had existed two hours; and their deity, the liberty pole, was struck by an order from the committee, without the consent of that exemplary and able guarantee of American freedom, the righteous and immaculate Judge Jonathan Hampton.

This was a glorious day to the sons of licentiousness; and it was also a glorious day to the sons of loyalty; for it has made in Elizabethtown more proselytes to the side of order and government, than all the other endeavors that have been exerted to abate the fever of the times.[1]

LAST night, Mr. John Schoonmaker, being in bed at his house in Ulster county, New York, overheard the follow-
Negro Plot in Ulster Co. ing conversation between his own negro York, and a negro named Joe, belonging to Mr. Johannes Schoonmaker. "*York*. How many?—*Joe*. A great many.— *York*. From where?—*Joe*. From Keyserick, Hurley, and Kingstown.— *York*. How much powder have they?—*Joe*. Two pounds.— *York*. That is not enough, they should have more to get through with it, and drums enough to prevent hearing the cries. They will begin two at your house, two at John De Puis, and in proportion, more at other houses. It will be put in execution between this and Wednesday night. When once begun we must go through with it. We are to set fire to the houses, and stand at the doors and the windows to receive the people as they come out."[2]

[1] Rivington's Gazette, March 2.

[2] Gaines' Mercury, March 6.—This account having been deposed before a magistrate, the two negroes were committed to gaol, and, together with several other negroes, examined before four magistrates who met for that purpose, but no further discoveries could be made.

Another account names Marbletown, as well as the three above mentioned;

FEBRUARY 20.—THE Provincial Congress of Massachusetts Bay has resolved : that the great law of self-preservation calls upon the inhabitants of that colony, immediately to prepare against every attempt that may be made to attack them by surprise. And, upon serious deliberation, most earnestly recommended to the militia in general, as well as the detached part of it in minute-men, that they spare neither time, pains, nor expenses, at so critical a juncture, in perfecting themselves forthwith in military discipline; and that skilful instructors be provided for those companies which are not already provided therewith. It also recommends to the towns and districts in that colony, that they encourage such persons as are skilled in the manufactory of fire-arms and bayonets, diligently to apply themselves there for supplying such of the inhabitants as shall be deficient.

Massachusetts Resolutions.

They have since adjourned to the twenty-second of next month, then to meet at Concord, an inland town, about eighteen miles from Boston.[1]

FEBRUARY 23.—SOME time ago a Presbyterian minister, not far distant from North Haven, Connecticut, applied to a lieutenant of the militia to step into the market and give him the words of command, in order to his performing the manual exercise ; the officer declined it, but being repeatedly pressed to a compliance, consented. The minister declared he had practised the military exercises with an intention of going to Boston against the King's troops, if there should be occasion for his service. Having taken post in the market, he shouldered, faced, marched, and performed all the motions with much exactness, to the great delight of a

A Patriotic Minister.

and that the negroes were to be divided into parties, to fire the houses, cry *Me!* and kill the people as they came out. The motive for this conspiracy was the recovery of their freedom. A large quantity of powder and ball was found with several negroes ; and besides this, there are said to be advices in town, that besides the two negroes before mentioned, seventeen or eighteen have been committed to gaol.

A report has likewise been current, that these negroes were to be joined by five or six hundred Indians; but it does not appear that there is any good foundation for the report.—*Pennsylvania Journal*, March 8.

[1] Gaines' Mercury, Feb. 27.

turbulent Hibernian, who was about eighteen years ago sold in this part of the world,[1] and on all occasions insults the name and government of our most gracious sovereign, and bids defiance to the law. This republican thanked the divine for his fine performance, applauded his gallant resolutions, and conducted him to enjoy a mug of flip, at his own house. A gentleman passing by, whilst the puritan was exhibiting à la militaire, asked him if he had quite forsaken his spiritual for a soldier's profession, on which the crowd menaced him with the discipline of tar and feathers, but the former secured himself by a precipitate retreat.[2]

IT appears that the upper House of the Georgia Assembly, though they say they disapprove of some of the measures of the other colonies, are heartily disposed to maintain their rights and liberties ; while the lower House declare, " they should be insensible not to feel their numerous grievances and wish them redressed, and that they only contend for the enjoyment of their constitutional rights and liberties, which soften every care of life, and render existence itself desirable."[3]

Sentiments of Georgia.

FEBRUARY 27.—SOME time ago, Dr. Clarke, of Reading, a gentleman distinguished by a firm attachment to the king and the constitution, was seized in the township of Hartford, Connecticut, and to the indelible disgrace of their police, carried upon a rail about the parish, under which cruelty he several times fainted. When dismissed by his tormentors, and examined by Dr. Tidmarsh, he was found to be injured in a manner unfit for description. The doctor was menaced with the same treatment for his humanity to the sufferer, whose only crime was speaking in terms of respect of the king, and of his government.[4]

Dr. Clarke, of Reading.

---

[1] This probably refers to the custom of selling a man for the commission of a crime.

[2] Rivington's Gazette, Feb. 23.   [3] Holt's Journal, March 2.

[4] Gaines' Mercury, Feb. 27.

FEBRUARY 28.—LAST Sunday an attempt was made by a
regiment of the king's troops, under Colonel Leslie, to seize
some brass cannon which General Gage had
heard was deposited at or near Salem, Massachu- *Leslie at Salem.*
setts. The troops were sent to Marblehead in a transport, apparently manned as usual. Between two and three o'clock
in the afternoon, as soon as the people had gone to meeting,
the decks were covered with soldiers, who having loaded, and
fixed their bayonets, landed with great despatch; and instantly
marched off. Some of the inhabitants suspecting they were
bound to Salem, to seize some materials there preparing for an
artillery, despatched several messengers to give information of
it. These materials were on the north side of the North River,
and to come at them it was necessary to cross a bridge, one
part of which was made to draw up to let vessels pass. The
inhabitants kept a look out for the appearance of the troops.
The vanguard arrived, and took their route down town as far
as the long wharf; perhaps to decoy the inhabitants thither,
away from the place to which the main body was destined.
The main body arrived soon after and halted a few minutes by
the town-house. It is said inquiry was immediately made by
some of the officers, for a half-brother of Colonel Browne,[1] the

[1] Colonel John Sargent. He was a merchant of Salem. His name is at the
head of those who addressed Governor Gage on his arrival in Salem, in June,
1774; in which address they acknowledge they "are deeply sensible of His
Majesty's paternal care and *affection* to this Province in the appointment of a person of His Excellency's experience, wisdom, and *moderation* in these troublesome
and difficult times." This was pronounced a most contemptible "Tory production," which disgraced the public prints. Sargent was a notorious Tory, and was
proscribed in the banishment act of 1778, and went to England.

Colonel William Browne was one of the most prominent inhabitants of Salem,
and previous to the troubles which led to the Revolution, enjoyed great popularity; but by espousing the cause of the mother country, he forfeited all claim to
the favorable consideration of the people. He was one of the "infamous seventeen" rescinders in 1768,—signed the address to Governor Hutchinson in 1774, and
accepted office under Governor Gage. Upon the breaking out of the Revolution
he became a refugee, and was included in the act of banishment of 1778, and the
conspiracy act of 1779. His landed estates, which were numerous and valuable,
were all confiscated to the use of the Government; and in 1779 his homestead, in
Salem, was sold to the late Elias Hasket Derby, senior, where, in 1799, he erected
his princely mansion at an expense of eighty thousand dollars, which was taken

mandamus counsellor. Be this as it may, he was soon whispering in the Colonel's ear, in the front of the regiment, and when he parted from the Colonel, the regiment marched with a quick pace towards the north bridge; just before their entering upon which the bridge was pulled up. The regiment, however, pushed on till they came to the bridge, not observing (as it seemed) that it was drawn up. The Colonel expressed some surprise, and turning about, ordered an officer to face his company to a body of men standing on the wharf on the other side of the drawbridge, and to fire. One of the townsmen[1] (who had kept along side of the colonel from the time he marched from his own house) told him he had better not fire, that he had no right to fire, without further orders, and if you do fire (said he) you will all be dead men. The company neither faced nor fired.

The Colonel then retired to the centre of his regiment, assembled his officers, and held a consultation; which being ended, he advanced a little, and declared he would maintain his ground, and go over the bridge if it was a month first. The same townsman replied, he might stay there as long as he pleased, no one cared for that. The half-brother before mentioned (it is said) made towards the bridge, but seeing the drawbridge up, he said, "It is all over with us." He has since disappeared. Meanwhile two large gondolas that lay aground (for it was low water) were scuttled, lest they should cross the channel in them. But whilst one gentleman with his assistants was scuttling his own gondola, a party of about twenty soldiers jumped into it, and with their bayonets charged against the unarmed townsmen (some of whom they pricked), and compelled them to quit it; but before this a sufficient hole was made in the bottom. This attack of the soldiers, and some other occurrences, occasioned a little bicker-

down in 1815, and near its site now stands the City Market House. Colonel Browne, after leaving the country, was appointed Governor of Bermuda, and died in England in 1802, aged sixty-five. He was a graduate of Harvard College, of the class of 1755.—*Endicott's Account.*

[1] Capt. John Felt.

ing, but by the interposition of some of the inhabitants, the disputes subsided.

At length some gentlemen asked the Colonel what was his design in making this movement, and why he would cross the bridge? He said he had orders to cross it, and he would cross it if he lost his life with the lives of all his men ; and asked why the king's highway was obstructed? He was told it was not the king's road, but the property of the inhabitants, who had a right to do what they pleased with it. Finally the Colonel said he must go over ; and if the bridge was let down so as he might pass, he pledged his honor he would not march above thirty rods beyond it, and then immediately return.

The regiment had now been at the bridge about an hour and an half, and every thing being secured, the inhabitants directed the bridge might be let down. The regiment immediately passed over, marched a few rods, returned, and with great expedition went back to Marblehead,[1] where they went on board the transport without delay.[2]

[1] "There were eighty military companies in Marblehead at that time, comprising nearly the whole male population, between sixteen and sixty years of age. They were all promptly assembled under Colonel Orne, and ordered to station themselves behind the houses and fences along the road, prepared to fall upon the British on their return from Salem, if it should be found that hostile measures had been used by them ; but if it should appear that no concerted act of violence upon the persons or property of the people had been committed, they were charged not to show themselves, but to allow the British detachment to return unmolested to their transport.—*John Howard's Account : Upham's Address.*

[2] The following " translation " appeared in the Massachusetts Spy, March 2 :— " Cæsar, though celebrated for an heroic mind, was liable to be betrayed by the villainous toad-eaters at his table, into *low freaks ;* in the prosecution of which he would sometimes disgrace even his most worthy officers,—for such undoubtedly was *Caius Lessala.* This brave, sensible, polite man, was despatched from Castellinum *two hours after sunset,* on the 5th of the Kalends of March, (answering to our 25th of February,) with *near* 300 *picked men* in a galley, under verbal orders to land at Marmoreum, and proceed to Saleminum, while the inhabitants of both places were engaged in celebrating a solemn institution. *Lessala* was not to open his written instructions till he reached the causeway. He conducted the affair with a despatch and propriety worthy of his character, expecting to find he had been sent to surprise one of *Pompey's* fortified magazines. But great indeed was his chagrin, when he read that his errand was only to *rob* a private enclosure in the North-Fields of that village. He suddenly returned to Castellinum, mentioned some obstruction of a Fly-Bridge, and with not a little resentment in his

It is regretted that an officer of Colonel Leslie's acknowledged worth should be obliged, in obedience to his orders, to
come upon so pitiful an errand. Various reports

Danvers militia. were spread abroad respecting the troops; the
country was alarmed, and one company arrived in arms from
Danvers, just as the troops left the town. Messengers were
immediately despatched to the neighboring towns, to save them
the trouble of coming in; but the alarm flew like lightning (and fame, doubtless, magnified the first simple reports),
so that great numbrs were in arms, and some on their march,
before the messengers arrived.[1]

A correspondent says:—" You may be assured there is a
most amazing change of sentiments in the people of the
province of Pennsylvania. The Quakers, high and low Dutch,
the Baptists, &c., are warmly opposed in their opinions to the
violent and independent measures lately adopted, and wish for
others more moderate, prudent, and rational. And there is
the greatest prospect, that in a little time that province will
recover its at present lost character for wisdom, moderation,
and firmness." [2]

MARCH 1.—THE following " Petition" came to my hand by
accident; whether it is to be presented to the Assembly now

Old Women's Petition. sitting at Philadelphia, the next Congress or
Committee, I cannot say. But it is certainly
going forward, and must convince every thinking person
that the measures of the late Congress were very weak,
wicked, and foolish, and that the opposition to them is much
more considerable and respectable than perhaps many have
imagined:

The PETITION of divers OLD WOMEN of the city of Philadelphia; humbly sheweth:—That your petitioners, as well spin-

eyes, told Cæsar that the 'geese were flown.' The base courtiers enjoyed the
HUM, which they had contrived against the veteran; and laid their heads together
for a new scheme to dupe Cæsar.—Vi. Cæs. Eds. Americ. Fol. 1775."

[1] Essex Gazette, Feb. 28, and Pennsylvania Packet, March 13.
[2] Rivington's Gazette, March 2.

sters as married, having been long accustomed to the drinking of tea, fear it will be utterly impossible for them to exhibit so much patriotism as wholly to disuse it. Your petitioners beg leave to observe, that, having already done all possible injury to their nerves and health with this delectable herb, they shall think it extremely hard not to enjoy it for the remainder of their lives. Your petitioners would further represent, that coffee and chocolate, or any other substitute hitherto proposed, they humbly apprehend from their heaviness, must destroy that brilliancy of fancy, and fluency of expression, usually found at tea tables, when they are handling the conduct or character of their absent acquaintances. Your petitioners are also informed, there are several old women of the other sex, laboring under the like difficulties, who apprehend the above restriction will be wholly insupportable; and that it is a sacrifice infinitely too great to be made to save the lives, liberties, and privileges of any country whatever. Your petitioners, therefore, humbly pray the premises may be taken into serious consideration, and that they may be excepted from the resolution adopted by the late Congress, wherein your petitioners conceive they were not represented; more especially as your petitioners only pray for an indulgence to those spinsters, whom age or ugliness have rendered desperate in the expectation of husbands; those of the married, where infirmities and ill behavior have made their husbands long since tired of them, and those *old women* of the *male gender* who will most naturally be found in such company. And your petitioners as in duty bound shall ever pray, &c.[1]

MARCH 2.—IT is said that some people in Dutchess county, New York, and others on the opposite side of Hudson river, are engaged in a scheme for establishing a port _{Dutchess County} in that part of the country. They have a place _{Port of Entry} in contemplation, where they say a few hundred pounds, properly bestowed, in building docks and quays, will accommodate fifty top-sail vessels. This plan, it seems, was projected

---

[1] Communicated by " E. B." to the Pennsylvania Journal, March 1.

some years ago, but was neither prosecuted nor made public. A suspicion, that the misconduct of the city merchants, under the influence of the Congress, may soon cause the only port of the province to be shut up, has now revived it. Should we bring upon ourselves this punishment, it is imagined there will be no difficulty in obtaining the privilege of a custom house for the river ; the consequence of which will be, that all the country beyond it will be much benefited, and all the estates within twenty miles of it will be vastly increased in their value, and New York will finally and irrecoverably lose one-half of its commerce. A large majority of the inhabitants of the upper counties are well affected to government, and it is thought that the above-mentioned scheme will soon make proselytes of all the rest.[1]

NOTHING has surprised people more than the Virginians and Marylanders joining, with so much warmth, with the New England Republicans, in their opposition to the ancient constitution, which has been the glory of an Englishman in every part of the world. As there are certainly no nations under the heavens more opposite to each other than the inhabitants of these colonies, it would be very difficult to account for it on the principles of religion or sound policy, had not the Virginians plainly discovered their indifference to both ; so highly revered by their illustrious ancestors.[2]

North and South.

MARCH 2.—NEW YORK, after being one of the most refractory cities on the continent, is become the most submissive and obedient, for the people have not only built excellent barracks for the army, but also supply the troops with every necessary of life. Lately the Assembly voted money for the current year, and, notwithstanding the passing the Stamp Act, and duties on paper, glass, painters'

New York loyal.

---

[1] " L. W." in Rivington's Gazette, March 2.

[2] Remarks on the late manœuvres in America, by a real friend to his King and country ; and an American.—*Rivington*, March 2.

colors, and on tea, and their assembly annihilated by tyranny, yet that very assembly, when afterwards suffered to meet, immediately granted fifteen hundred pounds to be invested in an equestrian statue of his Majesty, on the arrival of which it was erected on a square near the fort.[1] Yesterday being the anniversary day of its erection, Governor Colden, with his wretched council and assembly, the mayor, and aldermen, with the military, went in procession to the spot, where, after surrounding the leaden horse and his rider, the common crier made proclamation for the whole company to be uncovered, when an oration was made by the town clerk, in which he recited the many blessings they enjoy under this pious reign, after which they drank his Majesty's health, and returned to their respective homes amidst the hisses of the people.

The wretches above mentioned met in council and assembly, have by a majority voted not to obey the General Congress resolution, but to protest against and oppose all the continent of America, who are making so noble a stand in defence of their liberty, while the people wish to do the same. But they are unhappily in the hands of dependent placemen, contractors, informers, a refugee Roman Catholic family, and others, the veriest reptiles on earth. New York, therefore, is the only colony on which the British junto must rely to enslave America.[2]

A few days ago, as the thirty-eighth regiment were marching out of Boston, by way of exercising their men, a countryman drove his horses right across the street in front of the ranks. One of the officers (Lieutenant House) putting his hand to the horses' heads to turn them, the countryman made a blow at him, missed him, and struck one of the soldiers. On their march back, the soldier seeing the same man, returned his compliment with the soft end of his firelock, upon which the fellow, bleeding like a pig, roared out, " Gentlemen, you see what I suffer for the cause of liberty."[3]

[1] Bowling Green.   [2] Upcott, iv. 299.
[3] Rivington's Gazette, March 9.

MARCH 4.—LAST evening a number of persons who disapprove of the proposal made by the committee for the city and county of New York,[1] met at the house of widow

New York Loyalists.

De la Montagnie, in that place, and after choosing Mr. John Thurman chairman, proposed attempting to get the business intended for next Monday, postponed until the twentieth of April; and published a hand-bill desiring those who were of their sentiments to meet them there on Monday the sixth instant, at ten o'clock, and to proceed from thence to the Exchange. A number of the friends of constitutional liberty, hearing of the manœuvre, and apprehending a scheme was on foot to defeat the design of sending delegates to the Congress, met this evening and determined to support the committee, of whose virtue and patriotism they have had ample experience.[2]

MARCH 6.—THIS day[3] the old South Meeting-house in Boston was crowded with mobility and some gentlemen. The selectmen with Adams, Church, Hancock, Cooper, and

Warren's Oration.

others, assembled in the pulpit, which was covered with black, and we all sat gaping at one another above an hour expecting! At last a single horse chair stopped at the apothecary's opposite the meeting, from which descended the orator of the day, (Warren,) and entering the shop, was

---

[1] The following is the advertisement referred to:—"To the freeholders and freemen of the city and county of New York: As the last Congress held at Philadelphia, recommended that another Congress should be convened at the same place on the tenth day of May next, and the election of delegates ought not to be longer delayed, most of the other colonies having already appointed them: And as the committee has no power, without the approbation of their constituents, to take any measures for that purpose: They therefore request that the freeholders and freemen of the city and county of New York, will be pleased to assemble at the Exchange on Monday, the sixth instant, at twelve o'clock, to signify their sense of the best method of choosing such delegates; and whether they will appoint a certain number of persons to meet such deputies as the counties may elect for that purpose, and join with them in appointing, out of their body, delegates for the next Congress.—*Holt's Journal*, March 2.

[2] Holt's Journal, March 9.

[3] The anniversary of the Boston Massacre occurring this year on Sunday, the commemoration of it was postponed until the next day, the 6th.

followed by a servant, with a bundle, in which were the Cice-
ronian Toga, &c. Having robed himself, he proceeded across
the street to the meeting, and being received into the pulpit,
was announced by one of his fraternity to be the person appointed to declaim on the occasion. He then, putting himself
into a Demosthenian posture, with a white handkerchief in his
right hand, and his left in his breeches, began and ended without action. He was applauded by the mob, but groaned at
by the people of understanding. One of the pulpiteers
(Adams) then got up, and proposed the nomination of another
to speak next year, on the Bloody Massacre, (the first time
that expression was mentioned to the audience,) when some
officers cried, Oh fie, fie, fie! The gallerians apprehending
fire, fire, bounced out of the windows, and swarmed down the
gutters, like rats, into the street. The forty-third regiment returning accidentally from exercise, with drums beating, threw
the whole body into the utmost consternation. There were
neither pageantry, exhibitions, processions, or bells tolling as
usual, and to-night is remarked for being the quietest these
many months past.[1]

EARLY this morning preparations were made for the meeting at the Exchange in New York. A union flag with a red
field was hoisted on the liberty-pole, where at   New York Union
nine o'clock the friends of freedom assembled, and   Flag.
having got into proper readiness, about eleven began their
march to the Exchange. They were attended by music, and
two standard-bearers carrying a large union flag, with a blue
field, on which were the following inscriptions: On one side,
GEORGE III. REX, AND THE LIBERTIES OF AMERICA ; NO POPERY.
On the other, THE UNION OF THE COLONIES, AND THE MEASURES
OF THE CONGRESS.
    Some time after they had arrived at the Exchange, came
also another company who had met at the widow De la Montagnie's, among whom were some officers of the army and
navy, several of his Majesty's council, and those members of

---

[1] " A Spectator," in Rivington's Gazette, March 16.

the House of Representatives who had refused taking into
consideration the proceedings of the Congress; together with
the officers of the customs, and other dependents on the court.
Soon after the parties met, some confusion arose, but it subsided without any bad consequences.[1] The chairman of the
committee then proceeded to explain the design of the meeting; after which he proposed the following questions: First,
Whether a certain number of persons shall be appointed and
authorized to meet such deputies as the counties may elect,
and join with them for the *sole* purpose of appointing out of
their body on the twentieth of April next, delegates for the
next Congress?   Second, Whether this meeting will authorize
the committee to nominate eleven deputies for their approbation?   Both of which were carried in the affirmative.[2]

The meeting and the majority which determined these
questions are supposed to have been the most numerous and
Meeting at the   respectable ever known in New York, on the de-
Exchange.   cision of any public proposal. The business of
the day being finished, the friends of freedom paraded
through one of the principal streets, to the liberty pole, and
then dispersed in the most quiet and orderly manner.[3]

Tнıs afternoon, at New York, as William Cunningham and

[1] Dr. Gordon says of this meeting: "When assembled in a body, there was a
confused cry of 'Congress or no Congress?' After much altercation, the Tories
had a recourse to compulsive reasoning, and began dealing about their blows.
The Whigs were in the worst situation, not being provided with similar arguments,
till two of their party repaired to an adjoining cooper's yard, from whence they
drew forth to the assistance of their friends a number of hoop-sticks, which they
reduced to a proper length, and forwarded to the combatants. The Whigs, being
thus supplied, soon carried the day by club law, and beat their opponents off the
ground. The Tories being worsted, and not a little terrified, lest the fury of Captain Sears (whom they termed, in a way of reproach, 'King') should lead him
to head a mob, and do them some capital injury, promoted a provincial convention,
which otherwise would not have existed."—*Hist. Amer. Revolution*, vol. i. p. 318.

[2] The following are the names of the gentlemen nominated by the committee:
Philip Livingston, John Jay, James Duane, John Alsop, Isaac Low, Francis Lewis,
Abraham Walton, Abraham Brasher, Alexander McDougall, Leonard Lispenard,
and Isaac Roosevelt.—*Upcott*, iv. 299.

[3] Pennsylvania Packet, March 13.

John Hill, were coming from the North river, they stopped
Affair at New York. near the liberty-pole, to see a boxing match, but
had not stood long, when Cunningham was struck
at by Smith Richards, James Vandyke, and several others;
called Tory, and used in a most cruel manner by a mob of
above two hundred men. Mr. Hill coming up to his assistance, was beaten and abused most barbarously, though neither of them gave the least offence, except being on the king's
side of the question at the meeting this morning. The leaders
of this mob brought Cunningham under the liberty pole, and
told him to go down on his knees and damn his Popish king
George, and they would then set him free; but on the contrary, he exclaimed, "God bless King George." They then
dragged him through the green, tore the clothes off his back,
and robbed him of his watch. They also insisted on Hill's
damning the king, but he refusing, was used in the same manner, and were it not for some of the peace officers, viz., Captain Welsh, John Taylor, William Dey, and Joseph Wilson,
together with —— Goldstream, who rescued them from the
violence of this banditti, and brought them to the jail, for the
security of their persons from further injuries, they would
inevitably have been murdered.[1]

MARCH 8.—A WRITER in Boston[2] addresses the Provincial
Congress of Massachusetts as follows:—

"Your assuming the government of Massachusetts Bay,
makes it unnecessary for me to make any apology for address-
To the Massachu- setts Congress. ing you in this public manner, further, than by
acquainting you that it is to represent to you the
distresses of some of those people, who, from a sense of their
duty to the king, and a reverence for his laws, have behaved
quietly and peaceably; and for which reason they have been
deprived of their liberty, abused in their persons, and suffered
such barbarous cruelties, insults, and indignities, besides the
loss of their property, by the hands of lawless mobs, and riots,

[1] Article in Rivington's Gazette, March 9, signed by William Cunningham and
John Hill. See page 45.
[2] Under the signature of "Plain English."

as would have been disgraceful even for savages to have committed. The courts of justice being shut up in most parts of the province, and the justices of those courts compelled by armed force, headed by some who are members of your Congress, to refrain from doing their duties, at present it is rendered impracticable for those sufferers to obtain redress, unless it be by your interposition, or the aid of military force, which will be applied for in case this application fails. A particular enumeration of all the instances referred to, is apprehended unnecessary, as many of your members are personally knowing to them, and for the information of any of you who may pretend ignorance of them, the following instances are here mentioned. In August last, a mob in Berkshire forced the justices of the court of Common Pleas from their seats, and shut up the court-house. They also drove David Ingersoll from his house, and damaged the same, and he was obliged to leave his estate; after which his enclosures were laid waste. At Taunton, Daniel Leonard[1] was driven from his house, and bullets fired into it by the mob, and he obliged to take refuge in Boston, for the supposed crime of obeying his Majesty's requisition as one of his council for this province. Colonel Gilbert, of Freetown, a firm friend to government, in August last being at Dartmouth, was attacked at midnight by a mob of about an hundred, but by his bravery, with the assistance of the family where he lodged, they were beaten off. The same night Brigadier Ruggles was also attacked by another party, who were routed after having painted and cut the hair off of one of his horse's mane and tail. Afterwards he had his arms taken from his dwelling-house in Hardwick, all of which are not yet returned. He had at another time a very valuable English horse, which was kept as a stallion, poisoned, his family disturbed, and himself obliged to take refuge in Boston, after having been insulted in his own house, and twice on his way, by a mob. The chief justice of the province in Middleborough, was threatened to be stopped on the highway in going to Boston court, but his firmness and known resolution,

---

[1] Author of a series of articles in defence of the Crown, under the signature, *Massachusettensis.*

supporting government in this as well as many other instances, intimidated the mob from laying hands on him; he
was also threatened with opposition in going into court, but
the terror of the troops prevented. The whole bench were
hissed by a mob as they came out of court. In September,
Mr. Sewall, his Majesty's Attorney-General for Massachusetts
Bay, was obliged to repair to Boston for refuge. His house
at Cambridge was attacked by a mob, and his windows were
broken, but the mob was beaten off by the gallant behavior
and bravery of some young gentlemen of his family. About
the same time the Lieutenant-Governor Oliver, president of
his Majesty's council, was attacked at Cambridge, by a mob
of about four thousand, and was compelled to resign his seat
at the board, since which, upon further threats, he has been
obliged to leave his estate, and take refuge with his family in
Boston. At Worcester, a mob of about five thou-
sand collected, prevented the court of Common   Mob at Worcester.
Pleas from sitting, (about one thousand of them had fire-arms,)
and all drawn up in two files, compelled the judges, sheriffs,
and gentlemen of the bar, to pass them with cap in hand, and
read their disavowal of holding courts under the new acts of
parliament, not less than thirty times in their procession.
Daniel Oliver, Esq., of Hardwick, was disarmed by a mob,
and has been obliged to take refuge in Boston, to the total loss
of his business. Colonel Phips, the very reputable and highly
esteemed sheriff of the county of Middlesex, by a large mob
was obliged to promise not to serve any processes of courts,
and to retire to Boston for protection from further insults.
Colonel Saltonstall, the very humane sheriff of the county of
Essex, has been obliged to take refuge in Boston, to screen himself from the violence of the mob. The court of Common Pleas
was forbidden to sit at Taunton, by a large mob, with a justice
acting as one of their committee. At Middleborough, Peter
Oliver, Esq., was obliged to sign a paper, not to execute his
office, under the new acts. At Springfield, the   Courts closed at
courts of Common Pleas and General Sessions of   Springfield.
the peace, were prevented sitting by a large mob, who kept the
justices from entering the court-house, and obliged them, the

sheriff, and gentlemen of the bar, to desist, with their hats off, from holding any courts. Colonel Edson, one of his Majesty's council, has been driven from his house in Bridgewater, and kept from it ever since last August, for being a friend to government, and accepting his Majesty's appointment as counsellor.

"The courts of General Session of the Peace and inferior courts of Common Pleas for the county of Plymouth, have been shut up. In August, Colonel Putnam of Worcester, a firm friend to Government, had two fat cows stolen and taken from him, and a very valuable grist-mill burnt, and was obliged to leave a fair estate in Worcester, and retire to Boston, where he has been ever since, for his protesting against riots, &c. Colonel Murray, of Rutland, one of his Majesty's council, has been obliged to leave a large estate in the country, and repair to Boston to save himself from being handled by the mob, and compelled to resign his seat at council board. His house has been attacked, his family put in fear. Colonel Vassall, of Cambridge, from intolerable threats, and insolent treatment by mobs of his friends and himself, has left his elegant seat there, and retired to Boston, with his amiable family, for protection. John Borland, Esq., is in the same predicament with Colonel Vassall. Honorable John Chandler, Esq., judge of probate, &c., for the county of Worcester, has been obliged to retreat to Boston for protection, and leave his business, and a numerous family of hopeful youths behind him, with great reluctance, and who, before he came away, was ordered by the mob to hold his office till further orders.

"The Plymouth protesters, addressers, and military officers, were compelled by a mob of two thousand, collected from Plymouth and Barnstable counties, to recant and resign their military commissions. Thomas Foster, Esq., an ancient gentleman, was obliged to run into the woods, and had like to have been lost, and the mob, although the justices, with Mr. Foster, were sitting in the town, ransacked his house, and damaged his furniture. He was obnoxious as a friend to government, and for that reason they endeavored to deprive him of his business, and to prevent even his taking the acknowledgment of a deed. Richard Clark, Esq., a consignee of the tea, was

obliged to retire from Salem to Boston, as an asylum; and
his son Isaac went to Plymouth to collect debts, but in the
night was assaulted by a mob and obliged to get out of town
at midnight. Jesse Dunbar, of Halifax, in Plymouth county,
bought some fat cattle of Mr. Thomas the counsellor, and
drove them to Plymouth for sale; one of the oxen being
skinned and hung up, the committee came to him, and finding
he bought it of Mr. Thomas, they put the ox into a cart, and
fixing Dunbar in his belly, carted him four miles, and there
made him pay a dollar, after taking three more cattle and a
horse from him. The Plymouth mob delivered him to the
Kingston mob, which carted him four miles further, and forced
from him another dollar, then delivered him to the Duxbor-
ough mob, who abused him by throwing the tripe in his face,
and endeavoring to cover him with it to the endangering his
life. They then threw dirt at him, and after other abuses
carried him to said Thomas's house, and made him pay another
sum of money, and he not taking the beef, they flung it in the
road and quitted him. Daniel Dunbar, of Halifax, an ensign
of militia there, had his colors demanded by the mob, some of
the selectmen being the chief actors. He refused; they broke
into his house, took him out, forced him upon a rail, and after
keeping him for two or three hours in such abuses, he was
forced to give his colors up to save his life. A constable of
Hardwick, for refusing to pay his collections, directly contrary
to the oath of his office, was bound and confined six and thirty
hours, and threatened with being sent to Simsbury mines.[1]
His wife being dangerously ill, he was released after signing a
something which one of the mob had prepared for him. The
mob committee of the county of York, ordered that no one
should hire any of Sir William Pepperell's estates, buy no
wood of him, or pay any debts due to him. In February, at
Plymouth, a number of ladies attempted to divert themselves
at their assembly room, but the mob collected, (the committee
having met previous thereto,) and flung stones which broke
the shutters and windows, and endangered their lives. They

[1] In Connecticut.

were forced to get out of the hall, and were pelted and abused to their own homes. After this the ladies diverted themselves by riding out, but were followed by a mob, pelted and abused, with the most indecent Billingsgate language. These things happened at the time when some of the people of Plymouth, in conjunction with the committee men from other towns in that county, aided and assisted by four dissenting clergymen, were presenting to General Gage, by their memorial, the peaceable state they were in before the arrival of a party of soldiers[1] at Marshfield, in that county.

"The Honorable Israel Williams, Esq., one who was appointed of his Majesty's new council, but had declined the office through infirmity of body, was taken from his house by the mob in the night, carried several miles, put into a room with a fire, the chimney at the top, the doors of the room closed, and kept there for many hours in the smoke, till his life was in danger; then he was carried home, after being forced to sign what they ordered, and a guard placed over him to prevent his leaving the house.

"To recount the suffering of all from mobs, rioters, and trespassers, would take more time and paper than can be spared for that purpose. It is hoped the foregoing will be sufficient to put you upon the use of proper means and measures for giving relief to all that have been injured by such unlawful and wicked practices."[2]

MARCH 9.—COLONEL LESLIE's ridiculous expedition to Salem, Massachusetts, on the twenty-sixth of last month, occasioned such an alarm, that the people of all the neighboring towns, as well as those of thirty and forty miles distant, were mustering, and great numbers actually on their march for that place; so that it is thought that not less than twelve or fifteen thousand men would have been assembled in that town within twenty-four hours after the alarm, had not the precipitate retreat of the troops from the drawbridge prevented it.[3]

[1] Balfour's party.
[2] Rivington's Gazette, March 9, and Curwen's Journal, pp. 449 et seq.
[3] Pennsylvania Packet, March 20.

A LETTER in Messrs. Mill's and Hick's paper,[1] signed, " A Son of New England," appears to be the produce of a distempered brain, which, like many others in Boston and the neighboring towns, are raving after liberty; a word they have got by rote like a parrot, without knowing the meaning of it; and when Massachusettensis,[2] or any other unprejudiced writer, endeavors to make them sensible of their error, and clearly prove it is not liberty but licentiousness they are running after, they immediately fly into abuse, calling them the enemies of their country, not considering that they themselves, the imaginary supporters of liberty, are the real enemies of this country, by spiriting up the people, by every delusive method, to forfeit every thing that is dear to them in this world, and to merit the curses of their children from generation to generation. **New England.**

It is to be hoped that there are very few who think that the fate of Britain depends on the liberties of America, or that the mother country will ever suffer the colonies to dictate to her. She has been long tender of the rod, but be assured the time approaches when she will exercise it with severity, and show the stubborn sons of New England that she will not any longer bear with their degenerate behavior. If every man had thought for himself, and not been led by the nose by a Cooper[3] or an Adams,[4] all might have been happy; but these inconsiderate people have made themselves idols, viz., liberty trees, newspapers, and congresses, which by blindly worshipping have so engrossed their minds, that they give not the least attention to their several occupations, but attend at taverns, where they talk politics, get drunk, damn king, ministers, and taxes, and vow they will follow any measures proposed to them by their demagogues, however repugnant to religion, reason, and common sense.

It is a remark that the high sons of liberty consist but of two sorts of men. The first are those who by their debauch-

---

[1] The Boston Weekly Advertiser of Jan. 30.

[2] Daniel Leonard, of Taunton, Mass., author of a series of articles under that signature.

[3] Samuel Cooper, D. D., of Boston.   [4] Samuel Adams.

eries and ill conduct in life, are reduced almost to poverty, and are happy in finding a subsistence, though it is even on the destruction of their country ; for on the turbulence of the times, and the heated imaginations of the populace, depends their existence. The latter are the ministers of the gospel, who, instead of preaching to their flocks meekness, sobriety, attention to their different employ-ments, and a steady obedience to the laws of Britain, belch from the pulpit liberty, independence, and a steady perse-verance in endeavoring to shake off their allegiance to the mother country. The independent ministers have ever been, since the first settling of this colony, the instigators and abet-tors of every persecution and conspiracy.[1]

New England Clergy.

MARCH 9.—As the populace of Boston have thought fit to repeal the tarring and feathering act, the king's troops have thought fit to revive the said statute; and in consequence of such a determination, to-day they gave us a specimen of a royal mob. The soldiers have been encouraged by their officers to take every method of tricking the unwary. Yesterday, an honest countryman was inquiring for a firelock, when a soldier hearing him, said he had one he would sell. Away goes the ignoramus, and after paying the soldier very honestly for the gun, (which was only an old one without a lock,) was walking off when half a dozen seized him and hurried the poor fellow away under guard, for a breach of the act against trading with the soldiers. After keeping him in duress all night, this morning, instead of carrying him before a magistrate, who on complaint would have fined him, (as has been the case in several instances,) the officers con-demned him without a hearing, to be tarred and feathered, which sentence has been executed.

A Royal Mob.

After stripping him naked and covering him with tar and feathers, they mounted him on a one-horse truck, and surround-

----

[1] Rivington's Gazette, March 9.—This piece was published with the following note :—" Mr. Rivington : Sir,—By inserting the following letter in your paper, which was refused admittance in a paper in Boston, you will much oblige your humble servant, *Belisarius*."

ing the truck with a guard of twenty soldiers with fixed bayonets, accompanied with all the drums and fifes of the regiment, (forty-seventh,) and a number of officers, negroes, and sailors, exhibited him as a spectacle through the principal streets of
the town.   They fixed a label on the man's back, on which was
written AMERICAN LIBERTY, OR A SPECIMEN OF DEMOCRACY ; and
to add to the insult they played Yankee Doodle :—Oh Britain,
how art thou fallen!   Is it not enough that British troops,
who were once the terror of France and Spain, should be made
the instruments of butchering thy children! but must they
descend also to exploits too infamously dirty for any but the
meanest of the mobility to practice?   What a wretched figure
will the Boston expedition hereafter make in the historic page![1]

MARCH 10.—AMONG numerous misrepresentations in Mr.
Rivington's Gazetteer of yesterday, are many notorious ones,
mixed with sundry absolute falsehoods, in a para- Affair at the
graph to which the names of William Cunning- Liberty Pole.
ham and John Hill are affixed as subscribers.   In this extraordinary paragraph, above two hundred men of New York are
represented as having united in abusing those two inoffensive
gentlemen, and in that disorderly, riotous company, two inhabitants of that city[2] are particularly mentioned by name, and
positively charged, not only with abusing the two harmless
innocents before mentioned, but with robbery and high
treason.
    On reading this account we were naturally led, by several
circumstances, to inquire into the characters of the two persons accused, and of their accusers.   The two first we find to
be citizens, bred if not born in New York, peaceable, inoffensive men of property, and of irreproachable characters.   The
two last strangers here, (especially Cunningham,) almost entirely unknown, except by the little specimens they have
lately exhibited of their characters, which are not much in
their favor.   As to Hill, we have heard, and therefore shall
say but little about him.   He has brought himself upon the

---

[1] Holt's Journal, March 30.   [2] Smith Richards and James Van Dyck.

stage as a companion, an associate of Cunningham, and a volunteer with him in the glorious expedition, wherein their defeat has afforded them an opportunity of making conspicuous figures in Rivington's Gazetteer. As to Cunningham, his former character is unknown to us, but we may reasonably suppose it was not inconsistent with the specimen he has given us during the short space of time we have been favored with his company. His first exhibition was in the character of a *Son of Liberty;* that is, *a friend and asserter of the rights of the people, and the English Constitution, a warm patriot, and opposer of the tyrannical acts and pretensions of the British Parliament.* But in a few days, touched, not with Ithuriel's spear, but with an impulse from a spirit of a quite opposite nature, he starts up at once in his true character, a finished emissary of tyranny, officiously distinguishing and thrusting himself forward, to execute the orders and promote the designs of the enemies of his country, to destroy its constitution, and reduce it to a state of slavery.

His first appearance that we have heard of, was to interpose in preventing the departure of the Scotch ship, and thereby cause a violation of the solemn association of the British American colonies, agreed on last year by the delegates in general Congress at Philadelphia. But in this being unable to effect any thing, except showing his principles and disposition, *fame* had little to say of him, till this exploit in the fields, except that he has often been heard blustering in behalf of the ministry, and that his behavior had recommended him to the favor of several men of eminence, both in the military and civil departments—that he has often been seen, on a footing of familiarity, at their houses, and parading the streets on a horse belonging to one of the gentlemen, who, doubtless, is not displeased with the conduct of the rider.

We did not know until we saw this account in Rivington's paper that these same gentlemen helped to make up the group of woful countenances of the minor party at the Exchange on the memorable sixth of March; a day which our heroes doubtless intended to make as famous by their achievements in the afternoon, as it was by the defeat in the morning of the party under which they enlisted. And this may reasonably account for their conduct at the liberty-pole, as well as their design in going there, where they say they were so cruelly attacked by a mob of about two hundred men.

Messrs. Hill and Cunningham appeared and made part of the minority at the Exchange on the sixth. Their business was to prevent the execution of the measures recommended by the Continental Congress for the preservation of our constitutional rights and liberties, and consequently to promote the designs of the British Ministry, in subjecting America and all the British empire to a despotic government. And these men for thus appearing, or perhaps bullying a little, have the modesty to pretend that they appeared on the king's side, though opposed to the very principles on which he holds his crown. As a further proof of their modesty they call upwards of two hundred men, assembled at the liberty-pole, who were probably part of the respectable majority from the Exchange, a mob.[1]

A great body of the majority from the Exchange returned to the liberty-pole, when Cunningham and Hill came among them. The behavior of this majority at the Exchange demonstrated their peaceable disposition; and having succeeded in all they intended, they were in high good humor, and less disposed to quarrel than before. It is therefore highly improbable that they should have been the aggressors in quarrelling with Cunningham and Hill, or have used them in the unfair, abusive manner they have represented. These two men, on the contrary, having shared in the disappointment of their party, were probably soured in their temper, and went among the other party with a design to quarrel and raise disturbance. When upon such an occasion and in such a company they began a quarrel, it is no wonder they were roughly treated, but rather that they escaped so well. They have, in their improbable, inconsistent account, expressly charged two of the company with robbing them of a watch, and requiring them

---

[1] What they might be when these two gentlemen came amongst them, we shall not pretend to say; but before that, we believe they deserved a more respectful appellation.—*Author of the Article.*

to curse the king; for which scandalous assertions, under their hand, it is said suits are commenced against them, and ample damages will doubtless be recovered; as from a great number of depositions of creditable persons who were present, it appears that the report against Messrs. Richards and Van Dyck is entirely groundless. It is said that Cunningham has declared that he should not have published the account, if he had not been urged to it by one or more gentlemen of the minor party.[1]

MARCH 11.—This day the "freeholders of Botetourt," in Virginia, instructed their representatives[2] as follows: "We require you to represent us with hearts replete with the most grateful and loyal veneration for the race of Brunswick, for they have been truly our fathers; and at the same time the most dutiful affection for our sovereign, of whose honest heart we cannot entertain any diffidence, but sorry we are to add, that in his councils we can no longer confide. A set of miscreants unworthy to administer the laws of Britain's empire, have been permitted impiously to sway. How unjustly, cruelly, and tyrannically they have invaded our rights we need not now put you in mind.

Botetourt Instructions.

"We only say, and we assert it with pride, that the subjects of Britain are *one*, and when the honest man of Boston, who has broken no law, has his property wrested from him, the hunter of the Alleghanies must take the alarm, and as a freeman of America, he will fly to the representatives, and thus instruct them: 'Gentlemen, my gun, my tomahawk, my life, I desire you to tender to the honor of my king and country; but my LIBERTY to range these woods upon the same terms my father has done, is not mine to give up. It was not purchased by me, and purchased it was. It is entailed upon my son, and the tenure is sacred. Watch over it, gentlemen, for to him it must descend unviolated, if my arm can defend it; but if not, if wicked power is permitted to prevail against me,

[1] Holt's Journal, March 23. See Rivington's account, March 6.
[2] Colonel Andrew Lewis and Mr. John Bowyer.

the original purchase was blood, and mine shall seal the surrender.'

"That our countrymen, and the world may know our disposition, we choose that this be published. And we have one request to add, that is, that the SONS OF WORTH AND FREEDOM, who appeared for us at Philadelphia, will accept our most ardent grateful acknowledgments. And we hereby plight them our faith, that we will religiously observe their resolutions, and obey their instructions, in contempt of power and temporary interest; and should the measures they have wisely calculated for our relief fail, *we will stand prepared for every contingency.*" [1]

A TRIAL about a disputed horse race that has been run on Rye flats, came on to-day before Peter Guion, Esq., at Besley's tavern, at New Rochelle. One of the parties demanded a jury, and the justice accordingly issued   Patriotic Jury.
a process. A number of the inhabitants were summoned and appeared, but unanimously refused to be sworn, declaring that as horse-racing was contrary to the Association of the Congress,[2] they would never serve as jurors in any such cause, and that if the judge thought proper to commit them, they would go to jail. In short, the justice was obliged to try the cause himself.[3]

MARCH 13.—A FEW days ago, a certain Byrns, a young man lately from England, who has acted in the capacity of a tax-gatherer, near Georgetown, Pennsylvania, but   Byrn's Adventure.
who lately sold his commission, and probably
spent the money, stopped two wagons, on their way from Duck Creek, Cross Roads, to the head of Chester, and seized them as forfeited to the king, for reasons best known to himself, and made their drivers follow him with them to Downes, tavern. Stepping in there to get a drink, he presently came

---

[1] Published in Williamsburg, Va., March 11, and republished in Holt's Journal, March 30.
[2] See Article 8th of the Association of Congress, in Journals of Congress, Oct. 20, 1774.   [3] Holt's Journal, April 6.

out, and missing the wagons, pushed after, soon overtook them, and was returning, when several young men met him, knocked up his heels, and then took his gun, laid it in the road, and made the wagons drive over it twice or thrice, till they had rendered it entirely useless. They then tied a grape vine, provided for that purpose, about his neck, and dragged him to a mill, not far distant, where they primed him over a little, not having a sufficient quantity of varnish to give him a complete gloss, then gently sprinkling the feathers of an old pillow over that, they led him into Georgetown, where they drenched him with Newberry rum and water, taken from a duck-hole, until it began to work unpleasantly. They then led him like a victim, unto a duck-hole, where they launched him in with such swiftness, that the other shore brought him up. In this situation they had him some time; at last they made him fast with a grape vine, and brought him to a confession. He damned Bute, North, and all their brethren and followers, and said that the Americans were a generous, spirited, and much injured people. They then gave him a terrestrial absolution on condition that he would immediately transport himself to Europe, and there speak the sentiments now delivered; which being agreed to, he set out the same evening for Boston.[1]

MARCH 14.—YESTERDAY afternoon several riotous and disorderly persons, to the number of between eighty and ninety,

Westminster Massacre. assembled at Westminster, Cumberland county, in the province of New York.[2] They took possession of the court house, with an avowed intent of preventing the court from being held. Many of them had arms, and those who were unprovided for, collected arms and ammunition with all possible despatch. Many of the magistrates being present, it was thought advisable that the sheriff should make the usual proclamation against riotous assemblies, and demand possession of the court house and jail, which being refused several times, about nine o'clock at night a party as-

---

[1] New York Gazette, March 27.   [2] Now in the State of Vermont.

sembled in order to disperse the rioters. These proceeded with
the sheriff and some magistrates to the court house, where
proclamation was again made by the sheriff for the rioters to
disperse, and sundry attempts were made to get in, without
using fire-arms, but this proving ineffectual, three guns were
fired over the door, in hopes the rioters would be intimidated
and retire ; but so determined were they in their undertaking,
that the fire was immediately returned from the court house,
by which one of the magistrates was slightly wounded, and
another person shot through his clothes. The magistrates
seeing the imminent danger they were in, so well exerted
themselves that they forced the front door, and after a very
smart engagement, wherein one of the rioters was killed,[1] and
many persons on both sides wounded, the court house was
cleared, and proper measures were taken to preserve the
peace. This morning all was tumult and disorder ; the judges,
however, opened the court at the usual hour, and adjourned
till three o'clock this afternoon ; but by that time the body of
rioters beginning to assemble in large parties, from New
Hampshire and places adjacent, and particularly from Bennington, in the neighboring county of Albany, with a hostile
appearance, the court, foreseeing no probability of being able
to proceed to business, adjourned till next June term. The
body of rioters, which soon amounted to upwards of five
hundred, surrounded the court house, took the judges, the
justices, the sheriffs, the clerk, and as many more of their
friends as they could find, into close custody, and sent parties

---

[1] William French. The following record may be seen at this day (1859) upon
a simple slate stone, in the old burial-ground at Westminster, Vermont :

> "In Memory of WILLIAM FRENCH,
> Son to Mr. Nathaniel French, who
> Was Shot at Westminster, March ye 13th,
> 1775, by the hands of Cruel Ministereal tools,
> of Georg ye 3d, in the Corthouse at a 11 o' Clock
> at Night in the 22d, year of his Age.
>
> HERE WILLIAM FRENCH his Body lies,
> For Murder his Blood for Vengance cries.
> King Georg the third his Tory crew
> tha with a bawl his head Shot threw.
> For Liberty and his Country's Good,
> he Lost his Life his Dearest Blood."

out, who are returning with more prisoners. The roads and passages are guarded with armed men, who indiscriminately lay hold of all passengers, against whom any of the party intimates the least suspicion, and the mob, stimulated by their chief leaders to the utmost fury and revenge, breathe nothing but blood and slaughter against the unfortunate persons in their power; the only thing which suspends their fate, is a difference of opinion as to the manner of destroying them. And from the violence and inhumanity of the disposition apparent in the rioters, it is greatly to be feared that some of the worthy men in confinement will fall a sacrifice to the brutal fury of a band of ruffians, before timely aid can be brought to their assistance.[1]

MARCH 16.—A WRITER in England says: "This is the important crisis which will determine the fate of America. The bold resolves of your Congress have pushed matters to an extremity, and render a complete decision of the dispute inevitable. Whether America shall be independent of, or subordinate to Parliament, is now the question. I wish the prospect was clearer of an amicable settlement. The leaders of government were heartily disposed to fall in with any proposals of accommodation which might have secured your liberties and preserved the sovereignty in the British legislature, which is essential to the welfare of the empire; but hot men among you have extended your claims so far as to make it impossible for Parliament to comply, without relinquishing every shadow of its authority. The merchants have met on the subject. They are to petition Parliament for redress; but are neither to find fault with the late measures, nor to propose any mode for your relief, but to submit it entirely to Parliament. This intelligence is from two respectable merchants, who are of the committee.

What particular measures will be adopted by Parliament,

[1] Essex Gazette, March 21; New York Journal, March 23; Gaines' Gazette, March 27. The persons taken into custody were conveyed to the jail at Northampton, Mass.; but upon their application to the Chief Justice of New York, they were released from confinement, and returned home.—*Jones's Narrative.*

on its ensuing meeting, no one can precisely determine; but this may be depended on, that there will be no relaxation with respect to Boston.

The strongest hope which we have yet left, is, that the assembly of New York will firmly and dutifully state their grievances, unembarrassed with points foreign to the subject, and free from an undistinguishing approbation of the measures of others. Such a petition will assuredly be honorably received, and in all probability open the way for a lasting accommodation of the present differences. How little do they seem sensible of the uncertainty and miseries of a civil war, which would plunge headlong into violence rather than sacrifice a punctilio![1]

MARCH 19.—SINCE the army have found the season has passed for nature's forming a bridge from Boston, they become abusive and insulting. They are now finishing their fortifications on the Neck, by picketing each [Affairs in Boston.] side. Thursday last being recommended by the Provincial Congress to be a day of fasting and prayer, on the morning of that day the society at the west end of Boston were greatly disturbed by a party of officers and soldiers of the fourth or the king's own regiment. When the people were assembling, they brought two marquee tents, and pitched them within ten yards of the meeting house, then sent for three drums and three fifes, and kept them beating and playing till the service was over.

In the evening of the next day, Colonel Hancock's elegant seat, situated near the common, was attacked by a number of officers, who, with their swords, cut and hacked the fence before his house in a most scandalous manner, and behaved very abusively, by breaking people's windows, and insulting almost every person they met.

Yesterday the Neck guard seized a quantity of musket cartridges with ball, (we suppose through the information of some dirty scoundrel, many of which we now have among us,) and about three thousand pounds of ball, which were being

[1] Extract of a letter from London, in Rivington's Gazetteer, March 16.

carried into the country. This was private property. The owner applied to the General first, but he absolutely refused to deliver it. They abused the teamster very much, and run a bayonet into his neck. The same evening a number of officers heated with liquor, (as it is said,) with drawn swords ran through the streets, like what they really were, madmen, cutting every one they met. The stage coach just arrived from Providence, passing by, they attacked it, broke the glass, and abused the passengers. The driver being a smart fellow, jumped off his seat, caught one of them, Captain G.,[1] and some blows passed, when the officer retired not much to his credit.

To-day Colonel Hancock was again much insulted by a number of inferior officers and privates, who entered his inclosures, and refused to retire after his requesting them so to do; telling him that his house, stables, &c., would soon be theirs, and then they would do as they pleased. However, on his application to the General, he immediately sent one of his aide-de-camps to the officer of the guard at the bottom of the common, to seize any officer or private who should molest Colonel Hancock, or any inhabitant, in their lawful calling.[2]

MARCH 20.—It is said that General Gage has four hundred of Rivington's papers regularly sent him every week by the post, which are distributed among the army, navy, and such others as are thought most proper to promote the infamous plan of enslaving this country. These papers are, doubtless, paid for out of the American revenue. Thus, Americans, you already begin to see your own money employed for enslaving yourselves and your children.[3]

Rivington's Papers.

WE are constantly agitated by hearing complaints from different persons of the more than savage barbarity of the soldiers in Boston, encouraged and often joined and headed by the officers. They are now become so insolent that it is hardly safe to walk the streets at noonday, and there seems to be no

[1] Captain Gore, of the Fifth Regiment.   [2] Upcott, iv. 301.
[3] Supplement to Holt's Journal, March 30.

check or control. But they are rather countenanced and encouraged by their superiors, in their lawless outrages. They appear to be a banditti of lawless freebooters, just let loose upon us, for the innocent and laudable purposes of robberies, rapes, and murders; nor can we at present see any prospect of avoiding these calamities, but by a general evacuation of the town. The late news seems to increase their insolence, which was barely tolerable before. The reason is obvious. The common soldiers and their wives have frequently and loudly complained of the fallacy and injustice of the officers, who promised them fine houses, rich plunder, and a thousand other gratifications, which they hoped to be in possession of long before this. These expectations have undoubtedly prevented the desertion of hundreds. But they grow more and more impatient, so that we fear violence will, sooner or later, take place, let what will be the determinations in England, unless some method can be adopted to prevent or restrain them, tantamount to leaving the town, as the people in general do not seem inclined to go out.[1]

MARCH 21.—A FEW friends of liberty at Poughkeepsie, New York, met at the house of Mr. John Bailey, about three miles out of that town, and erected a pole on his land, with a flag on it, bearing on one side, THE KING, and on the other, THE CONGRESS AND LIBERTY; but the sheriff of Dutchess county, attended by a judge of the inferior court, and two of his Majesty's justices of the peace, and a constable, with some others, friends to constitutional liberty and good order, cut the same down as a public nuisance.[2]

Flag of Poughkeepsie.

THE method lately used in New York to post up inflammatory handbills, was the same used in England at the time of the Pretender. It was done by a man who carried a little boy in a box like a magic lantern, and while he leaned against the wall, as if to rest himself, the boy

Bill Posting in New York.

---

[1] Extract of a letter from Boston.—*Newport Mercury*, April 3, *and Pennsylvania Journal*, April 12.

[2] Holt's Journal, April 6.

drew back the slide, pasted on the paper, and shutting himself up again, the man took the proper occasion to walk off to another resting place.[1]

MARCH 28.—THIS evening was. married, at the White Plains, Westchester County, New York, Mr. Gabriel Purdy, youngest son of Mr. Samuel Purdy, to the agreeable Miss Charity Purdy, daughter of Mr. Joseph Purdy, both of that loyal town. What particularly is remarkable in the affair, is this, the guests consisted of forty-seven persons; thirty-seven of whom were Purdys, and not a single Whig among them.[2]

BY the late proceedings in Boston, it seems that those sent over to repeal, or make null and void, the good and wholesome law of tarring and feathering, and to establish a new-fangled form of government in the Massachusetts Bay, strange to tell, have adopted the very laws they were sent to abolish! Is it possible that the omnipotent King, Lords, and Commons of Great Britain should send a powerful fleet and army, three thousand miles, at the expense of millions of money, *only* for the purpose of tarring and feathering a poor, harmless countryman?[3]

ON the report of a design to form an army in Canada, to join the king's regular forces in fighting against, and enslaving the other British colonies, the Canadians were greatly alarmed, and took the best method in their power to secure themselves from the service. And as, by the laws of France, married men cannot be compelled to serve in the militia, the Canadians considered marriage as a protection, to which, since their new laws, they have so universally had recourse, that, it is said, there is hardly an unmarried man to be found in all the country.[4]

MARCH 30.—THIS morning at daylight, the troops at Bos-

[1] Parks' Diary.   [2] Rivington, April 20.
[3] Supplement to Holt's Journal, March 30. See March 9, *ante*.
[4] Holt's Journal, April 6.

ton beat to·arms, and five regiments marched out, with Earl
Percy at their head.   It was supposed they were   Earl Percy's
going to Concord, where the Provincial Congress   Excursion.
is now sitting.   A quantity of provisions and warlike stores
are lodged there.   Several expresses were immediately sent
away to give notice of their marching.   Important consequences were apprehended ; but, happily, they only went a
few miles out, and then returned.   The town and country
were alarmed, and many of them got equipped for a march.
It has given such uneasiness, that committees from twelve of
the near towns have met upon it ; and intend sending a petition to the Provincial Congress, representing this affair to
them, and desiring they will take up the matter, and remonstrate with the General upon it.   The troops went out of the
common road, marched over the people's land, where their
grain was sown, and through their gardens; broke down their
fences, walls, &c., and did other injuries.   It is thought such
proceedings will bring on bad consequences, if not prevented.

The late conduct of the regulars in Boston, in tarring and
feathering a countryman, headed by one of their colonels, and
other officers, and the spirited remonstrance it occasioned from
the selectmen of the town of Billerica, to General Gage, has
made much talk.[1]   The military spirit and resolution prevail-

[1] The following is the remonstrance presented to General Gage :—May it
please your Excellency :—We the selectmen of the town of Billerica, beg leave to
remonstrate to your Excellency, that on the Eighth of March last, one Thomas
Ditson, an inhabitant of said town of Billerica, was tarred and feathered and
very much abused by a party of His Majesty's forty-seventh regiment, under the
command of Lieut.-Col. Nesbitt.   As guardians for said town, and from a regard
for the liberties and properties of its inhabitants, we cannot but resent this pro-
cedure.   Your Excellency must be sensible that this· act is a *high infraction* on
that personal security which every Englishman is entitled to; and without which
his boasted constitution is but a name.   It is sufficiently unhappy for us that we find
troops quartered among us for the purpose of enforcing obedience to acts of Parliament, in the highest sense iniquitous, cruel, and unjust.   It is still more unhappy,
if these troops, instead of preserving the character which British troops once had,
should pour in additional insult, and be guilty of the most brutal outrages. * * *
Lieutenant-Colonel Nesbitt is an officer under your Excellency's command.   Of
you, therefore, we DEMAND satisfaction for the insult committed by him.   We
think it is in your power.   We beg your Excellency that the breach now too wide
between Great Britain and this Province, may not by such brutality still be in-

ing in this province, in support of their liberties and constitution, is astonishing. We hope we shall soon have some good news from home, to prevent any breaking out, which we begin to fear, especially if the troops continue their marchings out. It is said that forty or fifty of the troops were so fatigued by their march, that they could not keep up with their fellow-soldiers, on their return. It is also said they are intending to go out again soon.[1]

It has been intimated to some considerable merchants in England, that the "ministry will be ready to meet any conciliatory measures that may be proposed with respect to America."—It is nonsense to talk of proposing conciliatory measures. The Americans have no terms to propose, nor can they hear any. They only insist upon the enjoyment of their inherent rights, and cannot give up a tittle of them, without being absolute slaves, which they are determined never to be, so long as they have hearts to feel, and hands to fight.[2]

The sloop Charming Peggy, Captain Tilley, sailed for Bristol. In this vessel was transmitted by the Honorable the General Assembly of New York, an humble, firm, dutiful, and loyal petition to his Majesty; as also a memorial to the Lords, and a representation and remonstrance to the Commons of Great Britain, requesting their mutual endeavors for a settlement of the present disputes subsisting between the mother country and the colonies.[3]

creased. We assure you, sir, it always has been, and still is, our sentiment and prayer, that harmony may be restored, and that we may not be driven to the last distress of nations:—But may it please your Excellency, we must tell you, we are determined, if the innocent inhabitants of our country towns must be interrupted by soldiers, in their lawful intercourse with the town of Boston, and treated with the most brutish ferocity, we shall hereafter use a different style from that of petition and complaint. If the grand bulwarks of our constitution are thus violently torn away, and the powers on earth prove unfriendly to the cause of virtue, liberty, and humanity, we are still happy. We can appeal to Him who judgeth righteously; and to Him we cheerfully leave the event.—*Holt's Journal*, March 30.

    [1] Extract of a letter from Boston, dated April 1st.—*Pennsylvania Journal*, April 12.

    [2] Supplement to Holt's Journal, March 30.   [3] Pennsylvania Packet, April 10.

CHAPTER II.

APRIL 3.—THIS day the committee at New York received a letter from the general committee of South Carolina, in which they say : " The present struggle seems to us most glorious and critical. We seem to ourselves to stand upon the very division line between all the blessings of freedom, and the most abject vassalage. The very idea of an earthly power, which shall bind the present and future millions of America, in all cases whatsoever; in the direction of which we are to have no more voice than our oxen, and over which we can have no constitutional control, fills us with horror. To hold not only our liberty and property at will, but our lives also, as well as the lives of all our posterity ! To be absolutely dependent for the air in which we breathe, and the water which we drink, upon a set of men at the distance ; who, even when they abuse that power, are out of the reach of our vengeance, is a proposal which this colony hears with indignation, and can only submit to when there is no possible remedy. By the late detestable acts of the British Parliament respecting America, all mankind will judge whether that body may be safely entrusted with such a power. We have now appealed to the remaining justice of the nation ; we have endeavored to arouse them to a sense of their own dangers ; we have appealed to their mercantile interests for our defence. Our hopes of success are not yet damped by any thing but the possibility of disunion among ourselves. We have the pleasure to inform you, that in this colony, the association takes place as effectually as law itself. Sundry vessels from England have been already obliged to return

South Carolina.

with their merchandise, or have thrown it overboard as common ballast.[1]

" We may assure you of our fixed determination to adhere to the resolutions at all hazards, and that ministerial opposition is here obliged to be silent ; we wish for the day when it shall be silenced among you likewise.   And whatever noise is made by the friends of arbitrary rule, about the design of those proceedings in your House of Assembly, we cannot, and will not believe that you intend to desert the cause.   We feel ourselves bound to you by the closest ties of interest and affection.   We consider this season as big with American glory, or with American infamy, and, therefore, most ardently wish you the direction and aid of that Almighty Being, who presides over all.

" We confidently expect to meet you in General Congress at Philadelphia, with hearts full of zeal in our country's cause, and full of mutual confidence in the integrity of each other."

APRIL 4.—A LETTER from London says, that " despatches have been sent from here by a sloop-of-war to General Gage, containing, among other things, a royal proclamation, declaring the inhabitants of Massachusetts Bay, and some others in the different colonies, actual rebels, with a blank commission to try and execute such of them as he can get hold of.   With this is sent a list of names to be inserted in the commission, as he may judge expedient. Messrs. Samuel Adams, John Adams, Robert Treat Paine, and John Hancock, of Massachusetts Bay ; John Dickinson, of Philadelphia ; Peyton Randolph, of Virginia ; and Henry Middleton, of South Carolina, are particularly named, with several others.   This black list the General will no doubt

Gage's Black List.

---

[1] Lately arrived at Charleston, S. C., Captain William Carter, of the snow Lively, from Falmouth and Teneriffe, having imported two tons of potatoes, which fell under the last clause of the tenth article of the Continental Association. Rather than endanger the health of his people by carrying them back, he chose to throw them overboard into the river, which he did in presence of the Committee of Observation.—*Pennsylvania Packet*, April 8.

[2] This letter was signed by Charles Pinckney as chairman and published in the Pennsylvania Packet, April 10.

keep to himself, and unfold it gradually as he finds it convenient.[1] Every mark of power is preparing to be shown to
the Americans. Three general officers are appointed to go
with the next troops. They are Generals Burgoyne, Clinton,
and Howe. A considerable number of men are drafted from
the three regiments of guards, and ordered to hold themselves
in readiness to embark for America immediately. Four regiments from Ireland, one of them light dragoons, are under
sailing orders for Boston, with several capital ships of war,
and six cutters, to obstruct the American trade, and prevent
all European goods from going there, particularly arms and
ammunition.—Oh, poor America!"[2]

APRIL 7.—LAST Tuesday, Governor Martin met the Assembly of North Carolina, at Newbern, and addressed them
in a high-flying, abusive, anti-American speech,
in which he spoke hard things of all the colonies,   *North Carolina.*
congresses, committees, and people on this continent, except
those of his own stamp, and begged of his assembly not to
approve of sending delegates to the Congress in May. To
this the Assembly returned a truly noble answer, and to-day
they have passed the following resolution : " That the House
do highly approve of the proceedings of the Continental Congress lately held at Philadelphia, and that they are determined, as members of the community in general, that they
will strictly adhere to the said resolutions, and will use the
influence they have to induce the same observance by every
individual of this colony."[3]

APRIL 11.—THIS morning a very respectable number of
freeholders and inhabitants of the county of Westchester,[4]
assembled at the White Plains, agreeable to no-   *Meeting at White*
tice given, that their sentiments might be known   *Plains.*
concerning the choice of a committee, to meet other committees in the city of New York, for the purpose of choosing
delegates to the next Continental Congress.

[1] Pennsylvania Packet, April 17.　　[2] Holt's Journal, April 13.
[3] Holt's Journal, April 27.　　[4] New York.

The friends to order and government met at the house of Captain Hatfield. Those who were for a committee, put up at another public house in the town. About twelve o'clock, word was brought to the gentlemen at Captain Hatfield's, that the opposite party had already entered upon the business of the day; upon which they immediately walked down to the court-house, although not half of their friends who were expected had yet appeared; where they found the other company collected in a body. The numbers on each side seemed to be nearly equal, and both together might amount to two hundred, or, at most, to two hundred and fifty. The friends to government then declared, that as they had been unlawfully called together, and for an unlawful purpose, they did not intend to contest the matter with them by a poll, which would be tacitly acknowledging the authority that had summoned them, but that they came only with a design to protest against all such disorderly proceedings, and to show their detestation of all unlawful committees and congresses. They then declared their determined resolution to continue steadfast in their allegiance to their gracious and merciful sovereign, King George the Third; to submit to lawful authority, and to abide by and support the only true representatives of the people of the colony, the General Assembly. Then giving three huzzas, they returned to Captain Hatfield's, singing, as they went, with a loyal enthusiasm, the grand and animating song of

> "God save great George our King,
> Long live our noble King," &c.

At their return, finding that many of their friends had arrived during their absence, and that many still kept coming in, they proceeded to draw up, and sign a *declaration*,[1] which they

---

[1] The following is the declaration:—"We, the subscribers, freeholders and inhabitants of the county of Westchester, having assembled at the White Plains, in consequence of certain advertisements, do now declare that we met here to express our honest abhorrence of all unlawful congresses and committees, and that we are determined, at the hazard of our lives and properties, to support the King and Constitution, and that we acknowledge no representatives but the General Assembly, to whose wisdom and integrity we submit the guardianship of our rights, liberties, and privileges."—This was signed by a large body of the residents of Westchester county. See *Rivington* April 20—May 15.

seemed to do with as much patriotic zeal as ever warmed the hearts of true and faithful subjects.[1]

APRIL 12.—THIS afternoon John Sullivan and John Langdon, Esqs., delegates for the province of New Hampshire, arrived at New York. They are on their way to the grand Continental Congress, to be held at Philadelphia on the tenth of next month. At the same time, the Kingfisher sloop-of-war weighed anchor and proceeded to the North River, in order to protect two transports, which lately arrived from Boston, to take in necessaries for carrying on the siege of that place.[2]

APRIL 18.—THE grenadiers and light infantry companies are all drafted from the several regiments in Boston, and put under the command of an officer. Most of the transports and other boats are put together, and fitted up for immediate service. We suspect that some formidable expedition is intended by the soldiery; but what or where we cannot determine. The town watches in Boston, Charlestown, Cambridge, and other towns, are all ordered to look well to the landing places.[3]

APRIL 19.—ABOUT ten o'clock last night, the troops in Boston were discovered to be in motion in a very secret manner, and it was found they were embarking in boats which they had privately brought to the place in the evening at the lower end of the common. Expresses set off immediately to alarm the country, that they might be on their guard. When they were passing about a mile beyond Lexington, they were stopped by a party of officers who came out of Boston in the afternoon of that day, and were seen lurking in bye-places in the country until after dark. One of the expresses immediately fled, and was pursued a long distance by an officer, who, when he had overtaken him, presented a pistol and cried out, " You're a dead man if you don't stop!" but he kept on until he gained a

Battle of Lexington.

[1] Rivington's Gazette, April 20.   [2] Holt's Journal, April 13.
[3] Pennsylvania Journal, May 24.

house, when, stopping suddenly, he was thrown from his horse; and having the presence of mind to call out to the people of the house, "Turn out! turn out! I've got one of them!" the officer immediately retreated as fast as he had pursued. The other express,[1] after undergoing a strict examination, was allowed to depart.

The body of the troops, in the mean time, under the command of Lieutenant-Colonel Smith, had crossed the river and landed at Phipps' farm. They proceeded with great silence to Lexington, six miles below Concord. A company of militia, numbering about eighty men, had mustered near the meeting-house. Just before sunrise the king's troops came in sight, when the militia began to disperse. The troops then set out upon the road, hallooing and huzzaing, and coming within a few rods of them, the commanding officer cried out in words to this effect, "Disperse, you damned rebels! damn you, disperse!" upon which the troops again huzzaed, and at the same time one or two officers discharged their pistols, which were instantaneously followed by the firing of four or five of the soldiers, and then there seemed to be a general discharge from the whole. It is to be noticed, they fired upon the militia as they were dispersing agreeably to their command, and that they did not even return the fire. Eight of our men were killed, and nine wounded. The troops then laughed, and damned the Yankees, and said they could not bear the smell of gunpowder.

Soon after this action, the troops renewed their march to Concord, where they divided into parties, and went directly to the several places where the province stores were deposited. Each party was supposed to have a Tory pilot.[2] One body

---

[1] Paul Revere.

[2] "A young man, unarmed, who was taken prisoner by the enemy at Lexington, and made to assist in carrying off their wounded, says, he saw a barber who lives in Boston, thought to be one Warden, with the troops, and that he heard them say he was one of their pilots. He likewise saw said barber fire twice upon our people, and heard Earl Percy order the troops to fire the houses. He also says that several British officers were among the wounded, who were carried into Boston, where our informant was dismissed. They took two of our men prisoners, and they are now confined in the barracks."—*Massachusetts Spy*, May 3.

went into the jail yard, and spiked and otherwise damaged the cannon belonging to the province, and broke and set fire to the carriages. They then entered a store and rolled out about a hundred barrels of flour, which they unheaded, and emptied about forty into the river.[1] Some took possession of the town-house, which was soon after discovered to be on fire, but which was extinguished without much damage. Another party took possession of the North Bridge. About one hundred and fifty of the militia, who had mustered upon the alarm, coming towards the bridge, were fired upon by the troops, and two were killed upon the spot. Thus did the troops of Britain's king fire FIRST at two several times upon his loyal American subjects, and put a period to ten lives before one gun was fired upon them! Our people THEN returned the fire, and obliged the troops to retreat, who were soon joined by their other parties, but finding they were still pursued, the whole body moved back to Lexington, both troops and militia firing as they went.

During this time an express was sent to General Gage, who despatched a reinforcement under the command of Earl Percy, with two field-pieces. Upon the arrival of this reinforcement at Lexington, just as the retreating party had reached there, they made a stand, picking up their dead, took all the carriages they could find, and put their wounded thereon. Others of them—to their eternal disgrace be it spoken—were robbing and setting houses on fire, and discharging their cannon at the meeting-house.

[1] "The shrewd and successful address of Capt. Timothy Wheeler, on this occasion, deserves notice. He had the charge of a large quantity of provincial flour, which, together with some casks of his own, was stored in his barn. A British officer demanding entrance, he readily took his key and gave him admission. The officer expressed his pleasure at the discovery, but Capt. Wheeler, with much affected simplicity, said to him, putting his hand on a barrel, 'This is my flour. I am a miller, sir; yonder stands my mill; I get my living by it. In the winter I grind a great deal of grain, and get it ready for market in the spring. This,' pointing to one barrel, 'is the flour of wheat; this,' pointing to another, 'is the flour of corn; this is the flour of rye; this,' putting his hand on his own casks, 'is *my* flour; this is *my* wheat; this is *my* rye; this is *mine*.' 'Well,' said the officer, 'we do not injure private property;' and withdrew, leaving this important discovery untouched."—*Holmes' Annals*.

While this was transacting a party of the militia at Menotomy,[1] attacked a party of twelve of the enemy, who were carrying stores and provisions, killed one of them and took possession of their arms and stores, without any loss.

The troops having halted about an hour at Lexington, found it necessary to make a second retreat, carrying with them many of their dead and wounded. This they continued from Lexington to Charlestown, with great precipitation, the militia closely following them, firing till they reached Charlestown Neck, where they arrived a little after sunset.[2] Passing

[1] This party was led by the Rev. Phillips Payson, D. D.,* to whom the following extract refers:—"The Rev. Mr. Payson, of Chelsea, in Massachusetts Bay, a mild, thoughtful, sensible man, at the head of a party of his own parish, attacked a party of the regulars, killed some and took the rest prisoners. This gentleman has been hitherto on the side of government, but oppression having got to that pitch beyond which even a wise man cannot bear, he has taken up arms in defence of those rights, civil and religious, which cost their forefathers so dearly. The cruelty of the King's troops, in some instances, I wish to disbelieve. They entered one house in Lexington where were two old men, one a deacon of the church, who was bed-ridden, and another not able to walk, who was sitting in his chair; both these they stabbed and killed on the spot, as well as an innocent child running out of the house."—*Pennsylvania Journal*, August 2.

[2] "In this action the regulars have lost in all, sixty-five killed, one hundred and eighty wounded, and twenty-eight made prisoners. Of the provincials, fifty have been killed, thirty-four wounded, and four are missing. The following officers and gentlemen are of the number:—Justice Isaac Gardner, of Brookline; Capt. Isaac Davis, of Acton; Captain Jonathan Wilson, of Bedford; Lieut. John Brown, and Sergt. Elisha Mills, of Needham; and Deacon Josiah Haynes, of Sudbury, killed; Capt. Eleazer Kingsbury, of Needham; Captain Samuel Williams, of Cambridge; Captains Charles Mills, Nathaniel Barrett, and George Minot, of Concord; Capt. Oliver Barnes, and Deacon Aaron Chamberlain, of Chelmsford, wounded.

"Captains John Ford and Oliver Barrow, and Deacon Davis, all of Chelmsford, distinguished themselves in the course of the day. It can be fully proved that Captain Ford killed five regulars. James Howard, a private in the Acton company, and a regular, coming out of a house, caught sight of each other, and discharged their pieces at the same instant; both shots taking effect, the last dropped down dead, and the first expired a few hours after. A big boy joined in the chase of the retreating troops and was very expert in firing at them; at length a ball from the enemy grazed his head, and produced a flesh wound; he soon recovered the shock, bound up his head with a handkerchief, and renewed his pursuit."—*Gordon's American Revolution*, vol. i., p. 326.

* Dr. Payson was born at Walpole, Massachusetts, on the 18th of January, 1736. He graduated at Harvard College in 1754, and from the time of his ordination (three years after) until his death, he was constantly and zealously engaged in the service of the church. During the Revolution, he boldly advocated the cause of the Colonists. He died January 11, 1801.

over the Neck the enemy proceeded up Bunker Hill and encamped for the night.[1]

APRIL 20.—ONE Mansfield, a breeches maker in Boston, who went out with the troops yesterday, was in the skirmish fired at by the regulars through mistake—they taking him to be one of the provincials. The ball entered his neck and came out of his mouth. Wretches like him often meet their just reward.

SOME officers in the king's army, it is said, have sworn that the Americans fired first. Their method of cheating the devil, we are told, has been by some means brought about. They procured three or four traitors to their God and country, born among us, and took with them; and *they* first fired upon their countrymen, which was immediately followed by the regulars. It is said also that these wretches were dressed in soldier's clothing.

YESTERDAY, when the second brigade, under Earl Percy, marched out of Boston, to reinforce the first, nothing was played by the fifes and drums but Yankee Doodle, (which had become their favorite tune ever since that notable exploit, which did so much honor to the troops of Britain's king, of tarring and feathering a poor countryman in Boston, and parading with him through the principal streets, under arms, with their bayonets fixed.) Upon their return to Boston, one asked his brother officer how he liked the tune now. "D—n them!" returned he—"they made us dance it till we were tired!" Since which Yankee Doodle sounds less sweet in their ears.[2]

A DESERTER from Boston says that Gen. Gage has written

---

[1] Pennsylvania Journal, May 24:—"The British officers and soldiers have done ample justice to the bravery and conduct of the Massachusetts militia—they say that no troops ever behaved with more resolution. A soldier who had been in the action, being congratulated by a fellow-soldier on his safe return to Boston, declared, 'That the militia had fought like bears, and that he would as soon attempt to storm hell, as to fight against them a second time.'"—*Pennsylvania Packet*, May 1.

[2] Pennsylvania Journal, May 24.

home since the battle of Lexington, that the Americans load
their rifle-barrel guns with a ball slit almost in four quarters,
which when firing out of those weapons, breaks into four
pieces and *generally* does great execution.[1]

THE first stand made by the country in the late engagement was with only two hundred men at Concord Bridge,
Battle of Lexington. which the soldiers were endeavoring to pull up.
The soldiers gave the first fire, and killed three
or four. It was returned with vigor by the country people,
and the regulars began soon to retire. The country people immediately lined the roads, which are secured with stone walls,
and their numbers hourly increasing, they annoyed the regulars exceedingly, allowing them to halt but two or three
times, and then in open plains for a few minutes.

A considerable body of provincials formed an ambuscade
near Cambridge for the troops on their return; but the bridge
having been destroyed by the first brigade in their march out,
the troops took their route through Charlestown, and by that
means avoided a total overthrow. The number of the regulars
when the two brigades joined, is said to have been at least
eighteen hundred. It does not appear that they were attacked
by more than six hundred provincials until they got near to
Charlestown, when a very strong reinforcement from the towns
of Marblehead and Salem fell in with them, and gave them
two severe fires. This quickened their pace to Bunker Hill,
where they took refuge, formed in order, and remained until
reinforced by the third brigade sent over from Boston to secure their retreat. This was effected without further loss.

A gentleman, who mixed with the soldiers at Charlestown
ferry, says he saw at least two officers and soldiers brought
over wounded in an hour. It is impossible at this time to ascertain the number of the killed and wounded on either side.
A young gentleman who was within twelve miles of the field
of battle informs us that the country had buried one hundred
and ninety soldiers, and it is supposed a great number must
have been carried off and burnt on Bunker Hill by their com-

[1] MSS. letter from Hunnewell to Gould.

rades. General Haldiman and Lord Percy are both returned
safe, having been enclosed on all sides by their soldiers, during the retreat. Mr. Paul Revere, who left Boston to acquaint
Messrs. Hancock and Adams of the design against them, was
taken prisoner, but got clear again by a stratagem. Colonel
Murray's son,[1] who conducted the first brigade to Concord, is a
prisoner, and not killed as reported. Upon the whole, Lord
North's troops have had a severe drubbing ; and when we consider the disparity of numbers and discipline, and the sudden
and unexpected attack against the country, we have reason to acknowledge the interposition of Heaven on that memorable day.[2]

YESTERDAY the ship Samson arrived at New York from
England. Accounts by this vessel mention that the forces
destined for, and on their way to America, are eleven regiments
of foot, and two of light horse, on board ninety-five transports,
with seventeen men-of-war, all victualled for twelve months ;
other accounts reduce the forces and ships to about half the
above number. All, however, agree, that the design of their
coming is to dragoon the British colonies into a surrender of their
liberty and property, and to destroy the English constitution :
—*They who refuse to fight for their liberty deserve to be slaves.*

A letter from London received by the captain of the Samson says, " The friends of America, on the arrival of the packet,
were much alarmed at a report that New York
was disaffected to the common cause, and had   The Fishery Bill.
determined to break the resolves of the Congress, especially
that of non-importation. However, we had the pleasure, from
the best accounts, to find it otherwise. I have now to inform
you that notwithstanding all we could do, the Fishery Bill[3]

---

[1] Samuel Murray, a graduate of Harvard College in 1772, proscribed in 1778,
and died in 1785.

[2] Pennsylvania Packet, May 1.

[3] " THE BLACK ACT."—A bill to restrain the trade and commerce of the Provinces of Massachusetts Bay and New Hampshire; the colonies of Connecticut and
Rhode Island, and Providence Plantation, in North America, to Great Britain,
Ireland, and the British Islands in the West Indies; and to prohibit such provinces and colonies from carrying on any fishery on the Banks of Newfoundland,
or other places therein mentioned, under certain conditions, and for a time to be
limited.—*Holt's Journal*, April 20.

was yesterday (March 1) read the third time, and passed the House of Commons, whereby a stop is to be put to all the fisheries on the first of July, except the whale fishery, which is to be continued until the first of November. Every impartial man must in his heart condemn a bill so replete with inhumanity and cruelty. It will be an everlasting stain on the annals of our *pious* sovereign, who, from the best accounts, is the grand promoter of these proceedings. We hope the firmness of your countrymen will evince to all the world, your just sense of measures so unjust; and will, in due season, retort them with vengeance on the guilty heads of the enemies of the British empire.[1]

APRIL 23.—A WRITER in Wethersfield, in a letter to New York, says: "The eyes of America are on New York. The

Wethersfield to New York.

ministry have certainly been promised by some of your leading men, that your province would desert us; but you will be able to form a better judgment when you see how this intelligence is relished. Take care of yourselves! We have more than men enough to block up the enemy at Boston; and if we are like to fall by treachery, by heaven, we will not fall unavenged on the traitors. If balls, or swords, will reach them, they shall fall with us. It is no time now to dally or be merely neutral. He that is not for us is against us, and ought to feel the first of our resentment. You must now declare, most explicitly, one way or the other, that we may know whether we are to go to Boston or New York. If you desert, our men will as cheerfully attack New York as Boston, for we can but perish, and that we are determined upon, or be free. I have nothing to add."[2]

APRIL 24.—THE communication between Boston and the country is entirely stopped up, and not a soul permitted to go in or out without a pass. This day the Governor has disarmed all the inhabitants, after giving them his word and honor that the soldiers should not molest nor plunder them. Cambridge

[1] Holt's Journal, April 20.   [2] Holt's Journal, April 27.

is the head-quarters of the provincials, and they are commanded by General Putnam. They are entrenching themselves at
Roxbury, and erecting batteries to play on the lines.[1]

THE following anecdote, we are assured, is authentic. It
was communicated by a gentleman from the neighborhood of
Boston :—An American soldier who had received a wound in
his breast, in pursuing General Gage's troops on the nineteenth
of April, supported his body against a tree, when a brother
soldier came up to him and offered him his assistance. " I am
beyond your assistance, (said the wounded man,) pursue the
enemy." With these words on his lips, he fell back and died.[2]

A GENTLEMAN who travelled lately through Connecticut,
informs us that he met with an old gentlewoman who told
him that she had fitted out and sent five sons and eleven
grandsons to Boston, when she heard of the engagement between the provincials and regulars. The gentleman asked
her if she did not shed a tear at parting with them ? " No,"
said she, " I never parted with them with more pleasure."
" But suppose," said the gentleman, " they had all been killed."
" I had rather (said the noble matron) this had been the case,
than that ONE of them had come back a coward." [3]

APRIL 29.—THE following association was set on foot in
New York to-day, and signed by above one thousand of the
principal inhabitants. It is to be transmitted through all the
counties in the province, where, we make no doubt, it will be
signed by all ranks of people :

" Persuaded that the salvation of the rights and liberties of
America, depends, under God, on the firm union of its inhabitants, in a vigorous prosecution of the　　New York
measures necessary for its safety, and convinced　Association.
of the necessity of preventing the anarchy and confusion which
attend a dissolution of the powers of government; we, the
freemen, freeholders, and inhabitants of the city and county

[1] Extract of a letter from Boston, in the New York Gazette, May 1.
[2] Pennsylvania Packet, June 12.　　　[3] Virginia Gazette, June 24.

of New York, being greatly alarmed at the avowed design of the ministry to raise a revenue in America, and shocked by the bloody scene now acting in the Massachusetts Bay, do, in the most solemn manner, resolve never to become slaves; and do associate under all the ties of religion, honor, and love to our country, to adopt and endeavor to carry into execution, whatever measures may be recommended by the Continental Congress, or resolved upon by our provincial convention, for the purpose of preserving our constitution and opposing the execution of several arbitrary and oppressive acts of the British Parliament, until a reconciliation between Great Britain and America, on constitutional principles, (which we most ardently desire,) can be obtained; and that we will, in all things, follow the advice of our general committee, respecting the purposes aforesaid, the preservation of peace and good order, and the safety of individuals and private property." [1]

MAY 1.—IT is said that several letters written by General Gage were intercepted last week on their way to New York;

Congress to be Seized. which contain matters of a very serious and alarming nature. It is expected the public will soon be made acquainted with the contents of the General's letters, which are now in possession of the patriots of New York. Some believe that the Congress are to be seized, and sent to England, and this belief is strengthened by letters from London. It therefore becomes the duty of every man to prepare for such a ministerial attempt, and to be ready, at an hour's notice, to defend the Congress.

ON Saturday last a meeting of the military associators was held in Philadelphia, when it was determined that each

Associations in Philadelphia. ward should be formed into one or more companies; the officers to be chosen in the respective wards. Two troops of light-horse are now raising there. Two companies of expert riflemen, and two companies of artillerymen are forming. They have six pieces of brass ar-

---

[1] Rivington's Gazetteer, May 4.

tillery and several light iron ones. Their provincial arms, powder, and equipments, are all secured. Three provincial magazines are forming. In short, *Mars* has established his empire .in that city ; and it is not doubted but they will have in a few weeks from this date, four thousand men well equipped for their own defence, or for the assistance of their neighbors.

Several gentlemen who measured the ground on which the people stood at the meeting on Saturday, are of the opinion that their number amounted to eight thousand.[1]

MAY 2.—A CORRESPONDENT at Paris, says :—" I find the French are extremely attentive to our American politics, and to a man, strongly in favor of us. Whether mostly from ill-will to Britain, or friendship to the colonies, may be matter of doubt ; but they profess it to be upon a principle of humanity, and a regard to the natural rights of mankind. They say that the Americans will be either revered or detested by all Europe, according to their conduct at the approaching crisis. They will have no middle character ; for in proportion as their virtue and perseverance will render them a glorious, their tame submission will make them a despicable people." [2]

MAY 4.—THE post having been interrupted, the postmaster, who has hitherto without legal authority been appointed from home, and as a conveniency, permitted here un-questioned, has discharged the riders, the expense of which he has no longer a fund to support. An office for this necessary business will doubtless be put under proper regulations by the Continental Congress, and no more be permitted to return to the rapacious hands of unauthorized intruders ; since it would be the most contemptible pusillanimity to suffer a revenue to be raised from our property, to defray the expense of cutting our throats. It is said, Mr. William Goddard, who has been a great sufferer, with many others, by the mal-practices of an illegal holder of this office, is now on a journey, in order to put the business under proper regulations to be laid before the Congress.[3]

The Post Office.

[1] Pennsylvania Packet, May 1.   [2] Gaines' Mercury, July 10.
[3] Holt's Journal, May 4.

DIARY OF THE REVOLUTION.

RIVINGTON, in his paper of this morning, offers the following to the public :—" As many publications have appeared from *Rivington Apologizes.* my press which have given great offence to the colonies, and particularly to many of my fellow-citizens, I am therefore led by a most sincere regard for their favorable opinion, to declare to the public, that nothing which I have ever done, has proceeded from any sentiments in the least unfriendly to the liberties of this continent, but altogether from the ideas I entertained of the liberty of the press, and of my duty as a printer. I am led to make this free and public declaration to my fellow-citizens, which I hope they will consider as a sufficient pledge of my resolution for the future to conduct my press upon such principles as shall not give offence to the inhabitants of the colonies in general, and of this city in particular, to which I am connected by the tenderest of all human ties, and in the welfare of which I shall consider my own as inseparably involved." [1]

MAY 5.—THIS evening arrived at Philadelphia, Captain Osborne, from London, in whom came passenger the worthy Dr. Benjamin Franklin, agent for Massachusetts government, and the province of Pennsylvania.

Welcome! once more,
To these fair western plains—thy native shore;
Here live beloved, and leave the tools at home,
To run their length, and finish out their doom.
Here lend thine aid to quench their brutal fires,
Or fan the flame which Liberty inspires,
Or fix the grand conductor, that shall guide
The tempest back, and 'lectrify their pride.
Rewarding Heaven will bless thy cares at last,
And future glories glorify the past.

Why staid apostate Wedderburn behind,
The scum—the scorn—the scoundrel of mankind? [2]

[1] Rivington's Gazetteer, May 4
[2] Referring to Wedderburn's attack on Dr. Franklin in the Privy Council, in ıgland, January, 1774.

> Whose heart at large to every vice is known,
> And every devil claims him for his own ;
> Why came he not to take the large amount
> Of all we owe him, due on thine account ? [1]

MAY 6.—THIS afternoon, arrived at New York from the eastward, on their way for Philadelphia, to attend the Continental Congress, the Hon. John Hancock and Thomas Cushing, Esqs. ; Samuel Adams and Robert Treat Paine, Esqs., delegates for the province of Massachusetts Bay ; and the Hon. Eliphalet Dyer, Roger Sherman, Esq., and Silas Deane, Esq., delegates for the colony of Connecticut. They were met a few miles out of town by a great number of principal gentlemen of that place, in carriages and on horseback, and escorted into the city by near a thousand men under arms. The roads were lined with a greater number of people than were ever known on any occasion before. Their arrival was announced by the ringing of bells, and other demonstrations of joy. They have double sentries placed at the doors of their lodging.[2]

YESTERDAY there was a meeting at Williamsburg, Virginia, of the committee and part of the militia of King William county ; when the contents of the second express from the northward was communicated. It had such an effect on the minds of the people, that near two hundred pounds was immediately subscribed for the use of our brethren now fighting in the common cause. Most of the principal gentlemen subscribed ten pounds each, and as not half the country were present, there is no doubt it will be nearly doubled.[3]

---

[1] Pennsylvania Packet, May 8.   [2] Rivington's Gazetteer, May 11.

[3] Virginia Gazette, May 6 :—The first express with the news of the Battle of Lexington reached Williamsburg on the morning of the twenty-ninth of April. The express leaving Watertown on the morning of the battle, passed through Worcester, Mass., Brookline, Norwich, New London, Lyme, Saybrook, Killingworth, East Guilford, Guilford, Branford, and New Haven, and arrived at Fairfield, (on the 22d.) It arrived at New York on Sunday, (23d,) and was immediately forwarded to Philadelphia, by Isaac Low, chairman of the New York Committee, and reached that place at four o'clock in the afternoon of the next day, (24th.) On the arrival of the news at Baltimore, the inhabitants seized upon the Provincial magazine, containing fifteen hundred stands of arms.—*Pennsylvania Journal*, April 24 ; *Virginia Gazette*, April 29 ; *Holt's Journal*, June 1.

MAY 8.—THIS morning the delegates from the eastward, together with Philip Livingston, James Duane, John Alsop, and Francis Lewis, delegates for New York city; Colonel William Floyd for Suffolk, and Simon Boerum for Kings county, in New York, set out for Philadelphia attended by a great train, to the North River ferry, where two or three sloops and a number of other vessels were provided. It is said about five hundred gentlemen crossed the ferry with them, among whom were two hundred militia under arms.[1]

MAY 9.—THE committee of Bucks county, Pennsylvania, met yesterday and recommended the people to asssociate into
Bucks county, Pennsylvania.
companies, and learn the military exercise of arms. Some townships have already begun, and many others, animated with the same zeal for the welfare of their country, readily fall in with the plan, a knowledge of which, we have great reason to fear, we shall be soon called upon to give a proof of. The unanimity, prudence, spirit and firmness, which appeared in the deliberations of yesterday, do honor to Bucks county, and will, we hope, in some measure, wipe off those aspersions they too deservedly lay under. A large number of the inhabitants assembled, and the resolves of the day being made public, testified their highest approbation of the conduct of the committee, and unanimously voted them the thanks of the county. A disciple of that species of creatures called *tories* being formally introduced to a tar-barrel, of which he was repeatedly pressed to smell, thought prudent to take leave abruptly, lest a more intimate acquaintance with it should take place.[2]

MAY 10.—THE commanding officer at Cambridge has given leave to the regulars who were taken prisoners, either to go to Boston and join their respective regiments, or have liberty to work in the country for those who will employ them. In consequence of which, those who were confined in Worcester, Massachusetts, fifteen in number, heartily requested to be

[1] Holt's Journal, May 11.   [2] Pennsylvania Packet, May 15.

employed by the people, not choosing to return to their regiments to fight against their American brethren, though some of
them expressed their willingness to spill their blood in defence
of their king in a righteous cause. They all set out yesterday
for different towns.[1]

To-DAY the eastern delegates arrived at Philadelphia. They
were met about six miles out by the officers of all the companies in the city, and by many other gentlemen on horseback,
in all amounting to five hundred. When they came within
two miles of the city they were met by the company of riflemen, and a company of infantry, with a band of music, who
conducted them through the most public streets of the city to
their lodgings, amidst the acclamations of near fifteen thousand
spectators.[2]

THE proceedings of April nineteenth have united the colonies
and continent, and brought in New York to act as vigorously
as any other place whatsoever, and has raised an Effect of the Battle
army in an instant, which are lodged in the sev- of Lexington.
eral houses of the towns round Boston, till their tents are
finished, which will be soon. All that is attended to, besides
ploughing and planting, is making ready for fighting.
The non-importations and non-exportations will now take place
from necessity, and traffic give place to war. We have a fine
spring, prospects of great plenty ; there was scarce ever known
such a good fall of lambs ; we are in no danger of starving,
through the cruel acts against the New England governments ;
and the men who had been used to fishery, a hardy generation
of people, Lord North has undesignedly kept in the country
to give strength to our military operations, and to assist as
occasion may require. Thanks to a superior wisdom for his
blunders. The General is expecting reinforcements, but few
have arrived as yet, the winds, contrary to the common run
this season, instead of being easterly, have been mostly the
reverse. When the reinforcement arrives, and is recovered of

Pennsylvania Journal, May 24.   [2] Virginia Gazette, May 27.

the voyage, the General will be obliged in honor to attempt dislodging the people, and penetrating the country. Both soldiers and inhabitants are in want of fresh provisions, and will be like to suffer much, should the provincial army be able to keep the town shut up on all sides, excepting by water, as at present.[1]

MAY 17.—THIS evening arrived at Philadelphia, John Brown, Esq., from Ticonderoga, express to the General Congress, from whom we learn that on the beginning of this instant, a company of about fifty men from Connecticut, and the western part of Massachusetts, joined by upwards of one hundred from Bennington, in New York government, and the adjacent towns, proceeded to the eastern side of Lake Champlain, and on the night before the tenth current, crossed the lake with eighty-five men, not being able to obtain craft to transport the rest, and about day-break invested the fort, whose gate, contrary to expectation, they found shut, but the wicker open, through which, with the Indian war-whoop, all that could, entered one by one, others scaling the wall on both sides of the gate, and instantly secured and disarmed the sentries, and pressed into the parade, where they formed the hollow square; but immediately quitting that order, they rushed into the several barracks on three sides of the fort, and seized on the garrison, consisting of two officers, and upwards of forty privates,[2] whom they brought out, disarmed, put under guard, and have since sent prisoners to Hartford in Connecticut. All this was performed in about ten minutes, without the loss of life, or a drop of blood on our side, and but very little on that of the king's troops.

In the fort were found about thirty barrels of flour, a few barrels of pork, seventy odd chests of leaden ball, computed at three hundred tons, about ten barrels of powder in bad condition, near two hundred pieces of ordnances of all sizes, from eighteen-pounders downwards, at

Ticonderoga taken.

Crown Point.

<hr />

[1] Dr. Gordon in Gaines' Mercury, June 19.

[2] A party of the 26th, commanded by Capt. De la Place, who was surprised in his bed.

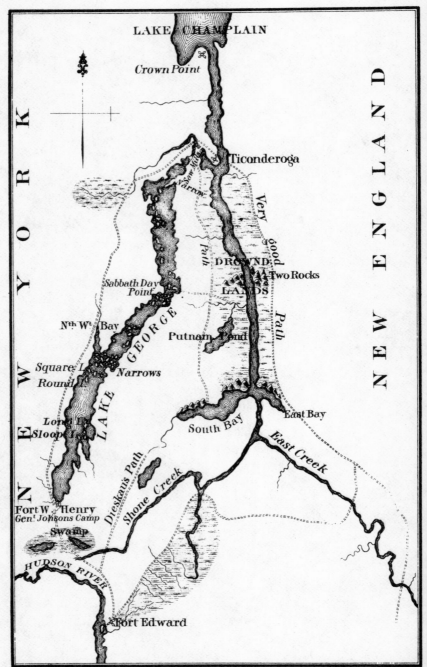

LAKE CHAMPLAIN

Crown Point

Ticonderoga

NEW YORK

NEW ENGLAND

Narrow

Very good

DROWND
LANDS

Two Rocks

Path

Sabbath Day
Point

Nth Wt Bay

LAKE GEORGE

Putnam Pond

Square I.
Round I.

Narrows

Long I.
Sloop I.

South Bay

East Bay

East Creek

Dieskau's Path

Shone Creek

Fort W. Henry
Genl Johnsons Camp
Swamp

HUDSON RIVER

Fort Edward

Ticonderoga and Crown Point, which last place, being held only by a corporal and eight men, falls of course into our hands.

By this sudden expedition, planned by some principal persons in the four neighboring colonies, that important pass is now in the hands of the Americans, where, we trust, the wisdom of the grand Continental Congress will take effectual measures to secure it, as it may be depended on, that administration means to form an army in Canada, composed of British regulars, French, and Indians, to attack the colonies on that side.

Mr. Brown brought intercepted letters from Lieutenant Malcom Fraser, to his friends in New England, from which it appears that General Carleton has almost unlimited powers, civil and military, and has issued orders for raising a Canadian regiment, in which, Mr. Fraser observes, the officers find difficulty, as the common people are by no means fond of the service. He likewise remarks, that all the king's European subjects are disaffected at the partial preference given to the late converts to loyalty, as he phrases it, to their utter exclusion from all confidence, or even common civility. Matters are indeed in such a situation, that many, if not most of the merchants, talk of leaving the province.

Mr. Brown also relates that two regular officers of the 26th regiment, now in Canada, applied to two Indians, one a head warrior of the Caughanawaga tribe, to go out with them on a hunt to the south and east of the rivers St. Lawrence and Sorel, and pressing the Indians farther and farther on said course, they at length arrived at Cohass,[1] where, the Indians say, they were stopped and interrogated by the inhabitants, to whom they pretended they were only on a hunt, which the inhabitants (as the Indians told Mr. Brown) replied must be false, as no hunters used silver (bright) barrelled guns. However, the Cohass people dismissed them all, and when they returned into the woods, the Indian warrior insisted on knowing what their real intention was, and they told him that it was to reconnoitre the woods, to find a passage for an army to

[1] Northern New Hampshire.

march to the assistance of the king's friends at Boston. The Indian asked, where they would get the army? They answered, in Canada, and that the Indians in the upper castles would join them. The chief on this expressed resentment that he, being one of the head men of the Caughanawaga tribe, should never have been consulted in the affair. But Mr. Brown presumes the aversion of this honest fellow and his friends to their schemes, was the reason of their being kept from their knowledge.

The conductors of this grand expedition are to be Monsieur St. Luke le Corne, the villain who let loose the Indians on the prisoners at Fort William Henry, and one of his associates.

Oh George, what tools art thou obliged to make use of ! [1]

MAY 18.—WE hear from Halifax, that the people have at last shown they have spirit. It seems the agents for procuring forage for the expected regiment of dragoons had taken without consent of the owner, and were shipping for Boston, a great quantity of hay, upon which the people set fire to, and wholly destroyed it; and when that work was finished, they attempted the like by the king's magazines, which they several times fired, but they were extinguished by the people from the ships of war lying there, who made a brisk fire on the people, and prevented them from

Whigs in Halifax.

[1] Pennsylvania Journal, May 24; see also the following authentic account of the taking of the fortresses of Ticonderoga and Crown Point, by a party of the Connecticut forces:—

"Captain Edward Mott, and Captain Noah Phelps, set out from Hartford, on Saturday, the 29th of April, in order to take possession of the fortress of Ticonderoga and the dependencies thereunto belonging; they took with them from Connecticut, 16 men unarmed, and marched privately through the country till they came to Pittsfield, without discovering their design to any person till they fell in company with Col. Ethan Allen, Col. Easton, and John Brown, Esq., who engaged to join themselves to said Mott and Phelps, and to raise men sufficient to take the place by surprise, if possible. Accordingly, the men were raised, and proceeded as directed by said Mott and Phelps. Col. Ethan Allen commanding the soldiery, on Tuesday they surprised and took the fortress, making prisoners the commandant and his party. On Wednesday morning they possessed themselves of Crown Point, taking possession of the ordnance stores, consisting of upwards of 200 pieces of cannon, 3 mortars, sundry howitzers, and 50 swivels, &c."—*Rivington's Gazetteer*, May 18.

effecting their design. The fugitives from Boston are gone
for Halifax, but the people say, no d—d Tories shall be allowed
to breathe in their air, so that those d—ls can't find a resting
place there, which was the only place on the continent that
they even dared to hope they might stay in.[1]

THEY had a great fire in Boston last night. It appeared to
be between King street and the market; it continued all
night, and is not yet extinguished. What has really happened, is to us uncertain as yet.[2]

MAY 21.—A CORRESPONDENT writing from Boston, says:—
" As to the inhabitants removing, they are suffered to go out
under certain restrictions. This liberty was obtained after many town-meetings, and several con-   Boston.
ferences between their committee and General Gage. The
terms mutually agreed to were: ' That the inhabitants should
deliver up all their arms to the selectmen.' This was generally done, though it took up some days. On this condition
the inhabitants were to have had liberty to move out of town,
with their effects, and during this to have free egress and re-

---

[1] Holt's Journal, May 18, and the Virginia Gazette, June 24.

[2] Rivington's Gazetteer, May 25. The fire began in the barracks, under the
arch formerly improved by Benjamin Davis, about half after eight o'clock, 17th
May. The soldiers were receiving some cartridges, by which means one took fire,
and communicated to many more, which immediately set fire to the room. The
following is a list of the stores burnt, with the owners' names prefixed:—
John Hancock, 1 store and shed; Thomas Fayerweather, 1 store; Benjamin
Andrews, 2 ditto; Edward Gray, 2 ditto; Joseph Barrel, 1 ditto; John Head, 1
ditto; John Williams, 1 ditto, with 50 barrels of flour, donation; Heyslop and
Co., 1 ditto; Andrew Black, 1 ditto; Nathaniel Carey, 1 ditto and shed; Alexander Hill, 1 ditto and shed; James Russel, impost office; John Soley, 1 store;
John Sweetser, 1 ditto; three ditto at the town dock; six stores, and a cooper's
shop, owned by Eliakim Hutchinson; adjoining the town dock, improved for barracks, one store by Elias Thomas, sailmaker; two stores leading down to the
barracks, improved by Grant Webster and William Blair. Instead of ringing the
bells as usual, the soldiers beat to arms, by which the people were in great confusion, not being used to such signals in time of fire.
N. B. The inhabitants took particular care to save the goods in Mr. Hancock's store.*

* Holt's Journal, June 1.

gress. But mark the event. The arms being delivered, orders were issued by the general, that those who inclined to remove, must give in their names to the selectmen, to be by them returned to the military town major, who was then to write a pass for the person or family applying, to go through the lines or over the ferry. But all merchandise was forbid; after a while, all provisions were forbid; and now, all merchandise, provisions, and medicine. Guards are appointed to examine all trunks, boxes, beds, and every thing else to be carried out; these have proceeded to such extremities, as to take from the poor people a single loaf of bread and half a pound of chocolate; so that no one is allowed to carry out a mouthful of provisions; but all is submitted to quietly. The anxiety indeed is so great to get out of town, that even were we obliged to go naked, it would not hinder us. But there are so many obstructions thrown in the way, that I do not think those who are most anxious, will be all out in less than two or three months. Vastly different from what was expected; for the general at first proposed, unasked, to procure the admiral's boats to assist the inhabitants in the transportation of their effects, which is not done, and there are but two ferry boats allowed to cross. They have their designs in this, which you may easily guess at. We suffer much for want of fresh meat. The transports, with the marines, are all arrived." [1]

MAY 24.—THIS day, Dr. Myles Cooper, president of King's College in New York, sailed for Bristol, in the Exeter, having remained for near two weeks on board the King Fisher, commanded by Captain Montague, where he thought fit to shelter himself from the resentment of a people who consider him as the writer of several pieces highly injurious to the liberties of America. The Rev. Dr. Chandler, and the Rev. Mr. Cook, go passengers with him. [2]

It having been thought highly expedient, at this exigency of our public affairs, that every person among us who is known to be an enemy to the rights and privileges of this country,

---

[1] Pennsylvania Journal, June 7.   [2] Pennsylvania Journal, May 31.

and has been aiding and abetting the cursed plans of a tyrannical ruler, and an abandoned ministry, should be disarmed
and rendered as incapable as possible of doing fur-   Tories disarmed
ther material mischief, the Tories in Worcester,   at Worcester.
Massachusetts, were notified to appear with their arms and
ammunitions on Monday last. They accordingly appeared,
and after surrendering their arms to the committee of correspondence, and being strictly ordered not to leave the town, or
to meet together without a permit, were dismissed.[1]

THE people of New Jersey have taken possession of the
treasury of that province, in which was the amount of between
twenty and thirty thousand pounds; which money is to be appropriated to the payment of the troops now raising in that
province, for the defence of the liberties of America.[2]

MAY 25.—THE man-of-war Cerberus arrived at Boston, with
the three generals Howe, Clinton, and Burgoyne, together
with about seven hundred marines and two hundred drafts.[3]

---

[1] Pennsylvania Packet, June 5.   [2] Holt's Journal, June 1.

[3] Holt's Journal, June 8:—A storm of thunder and lightning that occurred
on the day the generals embarked from England, gave rise to the following lines,
which were published under the signature of HAMDEN:

> The chiefs embark, and clouds involve the skies,
> Storms sweep the sea, and blusterous winds arise;
> The heav'ns themselves, red with uncommon ire,
> Their thunders hurl, and flash indignant fire.
> Oh Thou! who rules the earth, and guides the flood,
> Have mercy on the innocent and good.
> Oh! spare the land, and let thy vengeance fall,
> On those who dare whole nations to enthrall;
> Send thy own thunders on the guilty head,
> And, to appease thy wrath, strike the vile monsters dead.
> But, oh! restrain the hand of civil war
> And let thy favor'd nations cease to jar.
> Establish firm the American's rights and laws,
> And may this land resound with their applause;
> Then shall our vows in all thy temples rise,
> And praise ascend in incense to the skies.
>   *Pennsylvania Packet*, June 26.

MAY 26.—LAST Sabbath[1] about ten o'clock A. M., an express arrived at General Thomas's quarters at Roxbury, Massachusetts, informing him that four sloops, two of
Skirmish at   them armed, had sailed from Boston to the
Grape Island.
south shore of the bay, and that a number of soldiers were
landing at Weymouth. General Thomas ordered three companies to march to the support of the inhabitants. When
they arrived, they found the soldiers had not attempted to
land at Weymouth, but had landed on Grape Island, from
whence they were carrying off hay on board the sloops. The
people of Weymouth assembled on a point of land next to
Grape Island, but the distance from Weymouth shore to said
island was too great for small arms to do much execution.
Nevertheless, our people frequently fired. The fire was returned from one of the vessels with swivel guns, but the shot
passed over our heads, and did no mischief. Matters continued in this state for several hours, the soldiers poling the
hay down to the waterside, our people firing at the vessel, and
they now and then discharging swivel guns. The tide was
now come in, and several lighters which were aground were
got afloat, upon which our people, who were ardent for battle,
got on board, hoisted sail, and bore directly down upon the
nearest point of the island. The soldiers and sailors immediately left the barn, and made for their boats, and put off
from one end of the island, whilst our people landed on the
other. The sloops hoisted sail with all possible expedition,
whilst our people set fire to the barn, and burnt seventy or
eighty tons of hay, then fired several tons which had been
poled down to the water side, and brought off the cattle.[2] As
the vessels passed Horse-Neck, a sort of promontory which
extends into Germantown, they fired their swivels and small
arms at our people very briskly, but without effect, though
one of the bullets from their small arms, which passed over
our people, struck against a stone with such force, as to take
off a large part of the bullet. Whether any of the enemy were
wounded, is uncertain, though it is reported three of them

---

[1] May 21.   [2] Virginia Gazette, June 17.

were. It is thought that they did not carry off more than one
or two tons of hay.[1]

MAY 28.—YESTERDAY a party of the American army at
Cambridge, to the number of between two and three hundred
men, had orders to drive off the live stock from Battle of
Hog and Noddle's islands. In attempting to carry Hog Island.
out these orders, they were attacked by the king's troops.
The combat began on Hog island about five o'clock in the afternoon, and continued almost incessantly till midnight. The
attack was made with cannon, swivels, and small arms, from
an armed schooner, sloop, and eight or ten barges, upon our
people, who had small arms only, but were very advantageously posted by Colonel Putnam, who got to them just in
season to station and command them properly. He placed
them in a ditch up to their wastes in water, and covered by
the bank, to their necks. The schooner, sloop, and boats full
of men, came within twelve or fifteen rods of them, and gave
our people a fine opportunity to place their shot well. About
midnight the fire ceased a little, and our people retreated to
the main land, where they were soon after joined by Captain
Foster with two field-pieces, which were planted on the way of
Winnesimit ferry. At daylight this morning, the combat was
renewed, and as the schooner passed the ferry way, she was
briskly attacked by our people, with the field-pieces and small
arms, which soon clearing her deck, she drifted on shore,
where our people set fire to her, and she blew up, notwithstanding the utmost endeavors of the people in the boats to
tow her off, and save her from destruction. In this they exposed themselves much to our fire, and suffered greatly.
When they found the schooner was lost, they with difficulty
towed off the sloop, much disabled, and retired to their den ;
and thus ended the combat. This afternoon our people got
out of the wreck twelve four-pounders, six swivels, and every
thing else that was valuable, without molestation ; they afterwards destroyed or removed from both the islands all the

[1] Rivington's Gazetteer, June §.

stock, a large quantity of hay, and burned all the barns and houses.

All this was done in sight, and as we may say, under the noses of the whole fleet and army at Boston without molestation. The killed of the enemy (General Gage's crew of enemies to the English constitution) they themselves allow to be more than one hundred, besides wounded ; others, who have good opportunity to know, say their killed and wounded exceed three hundred, and I believe they have suffered as much as in their precipitate flight from Lexington on the memorable 19th of April. Our killed none ! wounded three ! Heaven apparently, and most evidently, fights for us, covers our heads in the day of battle, and shields our people from the assaults of our common enemies. What thanks can speak our gratitude !

These interpositions, and our determined resolutions, may perhaps make our haughty enemies glad to quit their unjust professions for a cooler and more calm retreat, in some distant quarter of the globe ; and leave us peaceably to enjoy those rights and liberties which God in our nature has given us, as our inalienable right, and which they are most unjustly endeavoring to wrest from us by violence.[1]

A correspondent gives the following etymology of the word Yankee :—" When the New England colonies were first settled, the inhabitants were obliged to fight their way against many nations of Indians. They found but little difficulty in subduing them all, except one tribe who were known by the name of Yankoos, which signifies *invincible*. After much waste of blood and treasure, the Yankoos were at last subdued by the New England men. The remains of this nation (agreeably to the Indian custom) transferred their name to their conquerors. For a while they were called Yankoos, but from a corruption, common to names in all languages, they got through time the name of Yankees. A name which we hope will soon be equal to that of a Roman, or an ancient Englishman.[2]

[1] Virginia Gazette, June 24, and Pennsylvania Journal, June 21.
[2] Clift's Diary, and the Virginia Gazette, June 10.

MAY 30.—A CAPTAIN who was lately seized by Admiral Greaves and taken into Boston, has just come out; he says he was at the wharf at Noddle's island when the battle began. The master of the Diana schooner *Noddle's Island.* told him, that guns were never better served than the Americans'; that not a shot missed him.[1] One man was carried on board for dead, but the next morning he came to, and had not the least wound about him; others were frightened almost to death. There is an amazing difference in the looks and behavior of the enemy since the battle, from what there was before; before there was nothing but noise and confusion, now all is still and quiet, insomuch that one can hardly perceive that there is any fleet or army there. From the general down to the common soldier, they seem to be in a great panic, and are afraid to go to bed for fear the Yankees will kill them before morning.[2]

JUNE 1.—THE synod of New York and Philadelphia, at their late meeting in the former city, appointed the last Thursday in June to be observed by all the congregations under their care, as a day of fasting and *General Fast.* prayer, on account of the alarming state of our public affairs. Should the Continental Congress appoint a fast, the synod have directed that to be observed in preference to the day appointed by themselves, provided that it is not more than four weeks distant from the last Thursday of June; if at a greater distance, they have ordered both days to be kept. They also recommend to all the congregations in their charge, to spend

---

[1] General Putnam, by his ingenious invention and invincible courage, having nearly expended his cannon ball before the king's schooner, took this method to get more from the Somerset in Boston harbor: He ordered parties consisting of about two or three of his men, to show themselves on the top of a certain sandy hill, near the place of action, in sight of the man-of-war, but at a great distance, in hopes that the captain would be fool enough to fire at them. It had the desired effect, and so heavy a fire ensued from this ship and others, that the country round Boston thought the town was attacked. By this he obtained several hundred balls, which were easily taken out of the sand, and much sooner than he could have sent to head-quarters for them.—*Constitutional Gazette*, Sept. 23.

[2] Pennsylvania Journal, June 28.

the afternoon of the last Thursday in every month in public prayer, during the continuance of our present troubles.[1]

THE martial spirit which prevails among the inhabitants of Somerset county, in New Jersey, truly merits the attention of the public. We have certain intelligence that they are forming themselves into companies, and daily exercising, to become complete masters of the military discipline; and particularly, that the township of Bridgewater, in said county, met at Rariton, the sixth instant, and chose Mr. Abraham Ten Eyck, captain, under whose command eighty-five volunteers immediately enlisted, to be in readiness at an hour's warning, to march for the assistance of any neighboring colony, on any emergency. Their pay and other necessaries are provided by said township. The other counties and townships, it is hoped, will follow their example, as it may be necessary to repel force by force, in order to secure our national rights and privileges.[2]

Somerset, New Jersey.

A PARLIAMENTARY youngster opening one day unseasonably, an old sportsman, who sat next him, whispering in his ear, reminded him, that when a young dog was faulty, it was customary to couple him with one better trained, and whose experience might correct his error; true, replied the boy archly, when young dogs run counter, I know it is usual to couple them; but when *old dogs* run counter, we *hang them up*.[3]

JUNE 4.—YESTERDAY morning a detachment of cavalry from the Williamsburg[4] volunteers, in their uniforms, well mounted and equipped, with a wagon containing their baggage and provisions, set out in a regular military procession, to meet the Hon. PEYTON RANDOLPH, Esq., late president of the Grand Continental Congress, on the way from Philadelphia, his presence being requisite at the general assembly now sitting. To-day about noon, the troop of horse met that gentleman at Ruffin's ferry, accompanied by

Peyton Randolph.

[1] Holt's Journal, June 1.   [2] Rivington's Gazetteer, June 1.
[3] Pennsylvania Packet, June 12.   [4] In Virginia.

Colonel Carter Braxton, and escorted them to Williamsburg, after having been joined by a company of infantry, who marched out the distance of two miles for the same purpose. They arrived about sunset, and were attended to the hon. gentleman's house by the whole body of cavalry and infantry, whose very martial appearance gave great satisfaction to the spectators. The bells began to ring as our worthy delegate entered the city, and the unfeigned joy of the inhabitants, on this occasion, was visible in every countenance; there were illuminations in the evening, and the volunteers, with many other respectable gentlemen, assembled at the Raleigh, spent an hour or two in harmony and cheerfulness, and drank several patriotic toasts.[1]

JUNE 6.—This being the day agreed on for the exchange of prisoners, between twelve and one o'clock, Dr. Warren[2] and Brigadier-General Putnam, in a phaeton, together with Major Dunbar, and Lieut. Hamilton of the 64th, on horseback, Lieut. Potter, of the marines, in a chaise; John Hilton of the 47th, Alexander Campbell of the 4th, John Tyne, Samuel Marcy, Thomas Perry, and Thomas Sharp of the marines, wounded men in two carts; the whole escorted by the Weathersfield company, under the command of Captain Chester, entered the town of Charlestown, and marching slowly through it, halted at the ferry, where, upon a signal being given, Major Moncrief landed from the Lively man-of-war in order to receive the prisoners and see his old friend General Putnam.[3] Their meeting was truly cordial and affectionate. The wounded privates were soon sent on board the Lively, but Major Moncrief and the other officers returned with General Putnam and Dr. Warren to the house of Dr. Foster, where an entertainment was provided for them. About three o'clock a signal was made by the Lively, that they were ready to deliver up our prisoners, upon which General Putnam and Major Moncrief went to the ferry, where they received Messrs.

Exchange of Lexington Prisoners.

---

[1] Postscript to Pennsylvania Packet, June 19.   [2] Joseph Warren.
[3] Major Moncrief and General Putnam served throughout the French war in the same regiment.

John Peck, James Hews, James Brewer, and Daniel Preston, of Boston; Messrs. Samuel Frost and Seth Russell, of Cambridge; Mr. Joseph Bell, of Danvers; Mr. Elijah Seaver, of Roxbury; and Cæsar Augustus, a negro servant of Mr. Tileston, of Dorchester, who were conducted to the house of Captain Foster and there refreshed; after which the general and major returned to their company, and spent an hour or two in a very agreeable manner. Between five and six o'clock Major Moncrief, with the officers that had been delivered to him, were conducted to the ferry, where the Lively's barge received them, after which General Putnam, with the prisoners that had been delivered to him, returned to Cambridge, escorted in the same manner as before. The whole was conducted with the utmost decency and good humor, and the Weathersfield company did honor to themselves, their officers, and their country. The regular officers expressed themselves as highly pleased; those who had been prisoners politely acknowledged the genteel kind treatment they had received from their captors; the privates, who were all wounded men, expressed in the strongest terms their grateful sense of the tenderness which had been shown them in their miserable situation; some of them could do it only by their tears. It would have been to the honor of the British arms if the prisoners taken from us could with justice have made the same acknowledgment. It cannot be supposed that any officers of rank, or common humanity, were knowing to the repeated cruel insults that were offered them; but it may not be amiss to hint to the *upstarts* concerned, two truths of which they appear to be wholly ignorant, viz. : That compassion is as essential a part of the character of a truly brave man as daring, and that insult offered to the person completely in the power of the insulter, smells as strong of cowardice as it does of cruelty.[1]

JUNE 8.—THIS forenoon, Laughlin Martin and John Dealy were carried through the principal streets of Charleston, South Carolina, in complete suits of tar and feathers. The very

---

[1] Virginia Gazette, July 1.

indecent and daring behavior of the two culprits, in several instances, occasioned their being made public spectacles of. After having been exhibited for about half an hour, and having made many acknowledgments of Tarring at Charleston. their crime, they were conducted home, cleaned, and quietly put on board of Captain Lasley's ship, lying wind bound for Bristol. Upon the intercession of Martin's friends, and his promises of future good behavior, he is allowed to come on shore and follow his business as usual.[1]

This morning the three battalions of the city and liberties of Philadelphia, consisting of fifteen hundred men, the artillery company of one hundred and fifty, (with two twelve and four six-pound brass field-pieces,) a Philadelphia Battalions. troop of light horse, several companies of light infantry, rangers, and riflemen, in the whole above two thousand men, marched to the commons, and having joined in brigade, went through the manual exercise firings and manœuvres, (with a dexterity scarcely to have been expected from such short practice,) in the presence of the honorable members of the Continental Congress, and several thousand spectators; among whom were a great number of the most respectable inhabitants of this city.[2]

The New York Provincial Congress have desired the General Assembly of Connecticut to send sufficient force to hold the important fortresses of Ticonderoga and Crown Point, until that province can raise troops for the purpose, and they will

---

[1] Gaines' Mercury, July 3.

[2] Rivington's Gazetteer, June 15:—Colonel John Hancock was asked to review the battalions, which gave rise to the following lines:—

> While Freedom's daughters all their aid afford,
> And deck the warrior with the gorgeous sword;
> Do thou, great Hancock, all their ranks inspire
> With patriot virtues, and the hero's fire.
> Form'd by thy blest example—they shall claim
> The fair one's fondness, and the conqueror's fame.
>
> *Pennsylvania Packet*, June 12.

reimburse the expense, those fortresses being within the limits
of that province.[1]

The grand American army at Cambridge is nearly completed. Great numbers of the Connecticut, New Hampshire,
and Rhode Island troops are arrived there. Among the latter
there is a fine company of artillery, with four excellent field-
pieces. Many large pieces of battering cannon are expected
soon from different places. Twelve pieces, eighteen and
twenty-four-pounders, with a quantity of ordnance stores, are
already arrived from Providence.[2]

Colonel Skeene, governor of Ticonderoga and Crown Point,
is at Philadelphia upon his parole of honor, to keep within
eight miles of the city between the Delaware and Schuylkill,
and not to correspond with any person on political subjects.
This gentleman concealed the circumstance of his being an
officer, from the captain with whom he came a passenger.
But a few days before they made the capes of Delaware, they
spoke a New England vessel, who informed them of the taking
of Ticonderoga. The Colonel instantly declared he would
march with five thousand men from Canada, and retake it;
and manifested such warmth on the occasion that the captain
of the ship discovered the quality of his passenger, and after
reprimanding him for the imposition he had practised upon
him, thought it prudent, upon his arrival at Philadelphia, to
deliver him up. The Colonel had taken care, however, to
destroy his despatches, and now finds how ineffectual is his
commission to tamper with the members of the Congress, in
the way that an immaculate ministry procure the sanction of
an immaculate Parliament.[3]

June 12.—To-day General Gage has issued a proclamation,
offering pardon in the king's name to all those, excepting
Samuel Adams and John Hancock, who will forthwith lay down their arms, and return to their
usual occupations. Those who do not accept the mercy he

Gage's
Proclamation.

[1] Rivington's Gazetteer, June 8.   [2] Park's Diary.
[3] Virginia Gazette, July 8.

offers, and who give protection to those gentlemen, or assist them in any way, are to be treated as rebels and traitors. Martial law is also declared, "for so long a time as the present unhappy occasion shall necessarily require." A correspondent says :—"The proclamation is replete with consummate impudence, the most abominable lies, and stuffed with daring expressions of tyranny as well as rebellion against the established constitutional authority both of Great Britain and of the American States."

TOM GAGE'S PROCLAMATION;

Or blustering denunciation
(Replete with defamation)
Threatening devastation,
And speedy jugulation,
Of the new English nation.—
Who shall his pious ways shun?

WHEREAS the rebels hereabout,
Are stubborn still, and still hold out;
Refusing yet to drink their tea,
In spite of Parliament and me ;
And to maintain their bubble, Right,
Prognosticate a real fight;
Preparing flints, and guns, and ball,
My army and the fleet to maul;
Mounting their guilt to such a pitch,
As to let fly at soldiers' breech;
Pretending they design'd a trick,
Tho' ordered not to hurt a chick ;
But peaceably, without alarm,
The men of CONCORD to disarm ;
Or, if resisting, to annoy,
And every magazine destroy :—
All which, tho' long obliged to bear,
Thro' want of men, and not of fear;
I'm able now by augmentation,
To give a proper castigation ;
For since th' addition to the troops,
Now reinforc'd as thick as hops ;
I can, like Jemmy at the Boyne,
Look safely on—fight you, Burgoyne ;
And mow, like grass, the rebel Yankees,
I fancy not these doodle dances :—

Yet, e'er I draw the vengeful sword,
I have thought fit to send abroad,
This present gracious proclamation,
Of purpose mild the demonstration,
That whosoe'er keeps gun or pistol,
I'll spoil the motion of his systole ;
Or, whip his ——, or cut his weason,
As haps the measure of his treason :—
But every one that will lay down
His hanger bright, and musket brown,
Shall not be beat, nor bruis'd, nor bang'd,
Much less for past offences hang'd ;
But on surrendering his toledo,
Go to and fro unhurt as we do :—
But then I must, out of this plan, lock
Both SAMUEL ADAMS and JOHN HANCOCK ;
For those vile traitors (like debentures)
Must be tucked up at all adventures ;
As any proffer of a pardon,
Would only tend those rogues to harden :—
But every other mother's son,
The instant he destroys his gun,
(For thus doth run the king's command,)
May, if he will, come kiss my hand.—
And to prevent such wicked game, as
Pleading the plea of ignoramus ;
Be this my proclamation spread
To every reader that can read :—
And as nor law nor right was known
Since my arrival in this town ;
To remedy this fatal flaw,
I hereby publish martial law.
Meanwhile, let all, and every one
Who loves his life, forsake his gun ;
And all the council, by mandamus,
Who have been reckoned so infamous,
Return unto their habitation,
Without or let or molestation.—
Thus graciously the war I wage,
As witnesseth my hand,—TOM GAGE.

By command of MOTHER CARY,
    Thomas Flucker, Secretary.[1]

IT is said that there are no less than three German princes
upon their travels incog. in New England. This looks not a

—————
[1] Pennsylvania Journal, June 28.

little suspicious; certain it is, that there is not a Court in Germany, that would not send their best generals to the assistance of the Americans.[1]

THE following paragraph is extracted from some remarks on *Gage's* account of the battle at Lexington, which is published in the London Gazette of to-day. The miserable Gazette writer concludes his narrative Gage's Account of Lexington. by informing the public that General Gage says, "*that too much praise cannot be given to Lord Percy for his remarkable activity the whole day.*" The public will think this a very singular compliment! The preceding part of the narrative has told us a story about the troops marching, or in plainer English, retreating from Lexington. They did not halt, but continued their retreat for fifteen miles. What then are we to understand by the remarkable activity of Lord Percy? His personal bravery is too well known to leave room for suspicion that he would show "remarkable activity" in retreating; yet the account in the Gazette leaves the compliment so ambiguous, that an invidious reader might suppose Lord Percy made it, like the swift-footed Achilles, with *a light pair of heels.* It is not surprising that Gage should wish to pay his court to Northumberland house; but when he pays another compliment, as he cannot write himself, he should entrust a better hand than the pensioned compiler of the Gazette.[2]

JUNE 14.—A FEW days ago returned to New York from the eastward, Mr. William Goddard, who has been indefatigable in soliciting the establishment of post-offices on constitutional principles, in which he has at The Post-Office. last succeeded. The matter has been taken up by the committees, provincial Congresses, or assemblies, in the colonies of New Hampshire, Massachusetts Bay, Rhode Island, and Connecticut, throughout which, offices, postmasters, riders, and rates of postage have been established and are to be laid before the Continental Congress, there to be approved or altered as

---

[1] Extract from a London paper in the Constitutional Gazette, August 26.
[2] Constitutional Gazette, August 26.

shall be thought expedient. It is hoped New York and the other governments will adopt similar measures. The rates of postage have been continued as before.[1]

JUNE 15.—THE Continental Congress elected Colonel George Washington, a delegate from Virginia, general and commander-in-chief of all the American forces.[2]—It was last year reported that Sir Jeffery Amherst had said, that with five thousand English regulars he would engage to march from one end to the other of the continent of North America. This being spoken of publicly in a coffee-house in North America, Colonel Washington, who was present, declared, that with one thousand Virginians he would engage to stop Sir Jeffery Amherst's march. It is the fashion at St. James' to despise the Americans, to call them cowards, poltroons, &c., and the resolution seems to be taken to put their courage to the proof. The very able, spirited, and prudent conduct of this gallant officer when he covered and preserved the remains of the English army after one of their defeats in the last war in North America,[3] has endeared him to every brave man, and stamped him with the name of being a most noble officer.[4]

IT is said that all the men-of-war which were in the harbors near Boston, have been called to that place, and that every method is taken to strengthen the town. The intrenchment

[1] Holt's Journal, June 15:—Mr. Holt announces a "Constitutional Post-Office," as kept in his printing office, in his paper of June 22.

[2] Journals of Congress.—The following is the staff appointed by the Continental Congress:—George Washington, Esq., of Virginia, General and Commander-in-Chief of all the American forces; Artemas Ward, Esq., of Massachusetts Bay, Charles Lee, Esq., Philip Schuyler, Esq., of Albany, in New York Province, Israel Putnam, Esq., to be Major-Generals; and Horatio Gates, Esq., Adjutant-General.

General Washington has appointed Thomas Mifflin, Esq., of Philadelphia, to be his aide-de-camp; and Major-General Lee has appointed Samuel Griffin, Esq., of Virginia, to be his aide-de-camp.*

[3] Braddock's Expedition.

[4] Extract from a London paper of April 15, 1775, republished in the Pennsylvania Packet, June 12.

* Rivington's Gazetteer, June 29.

BOSTON IN 1775.

Eng. by W.E. Tucker.

at the fortification is now extended quite across the Neck, by which the town is become an island. Some of the transports from Cork have arrived at Boston, and the grenadiers and infantry appear to be in motion. General Gage by his late conduct, seems to be greatly alarmed.[1]

JUNE 17.—LAST night a detachment from the camp at Cambridge, marched to Charlestown, and there took possession of Breed's Hill, about half a mile from the ferry. Their intrenching tools not coming up in season, Battle of Breed's Hill. it was twelve o'clock before they began their work. At daylight this morning they were discovered from Boston, when the men-of-war at the ferry, the battery from Cop's Hill, and the floating batteries, kept up a continual cannonading and bombarding, which fortunately did but little execution, although their intrenchments were very far from being completed. This continued till about two o'clock, when a large army, under the command of General Howe, landed in Charlestown, and after plundering it of all its valuable effects, set fire to it in ten different places. Then, dividing the army, part of it marched up in the front of the provincial intrenchments and began an attack at long shot; the other part marched round the town of Charlestown under cover of the smoke occasioned by the fire of the town. The provincial sentries discovered the regulars marching upon their left wing, and gave notice to the Connecticut forces posted there. Captain Knowlton,[2] of Ashford, with four hundred of said forces, immediately repaired to, and pulled up, a post and rail fence, and carrying the posts and rails to another fence, put them together for a breastwork. He then gave orders to the men not to fire until the enemy were got within fifteen rods, and then not till the word was given. The word being given, the regulars fell surprisingly; it was thought by spectators who stood at a distance that the provincials did great execution.

The action continued about two hours, when the regulars on the right wing were put into confusion and gave way. The

<hr/>

[1] Virginia Gazette, July 1.
[2] Thomas Knowlton:—See Battle of Harlem Plains, September, 1776.

Connecticut troops closely pursued them, and were on the point of pushing their bayonets, when orders were received from General Pomeroy, for those who had been in action for two hours to fall back, and their places to be supplied by fresh troops. These orders being mistaken for a direction to retreat, the troops on the right wing began a general retreat, which was handed to the left, the principal place of action, where Captains Knowlton, Chester, Clark, and Putnam, had forced the regulars to give way, and being warmly pursuing them, were, with difficulty, persuaded to retire; but the right wing by mistaking the orders having already retreated, the left, to avoid being encircled, were obliged to retreat with the main body. They retreated with precipitation across the causeway to Winter's Hill, in which retreat they were exposed to the fire of the enemy from their shipping and floating batteries.

The provincials sustained their principal loss in passing the causeway. The regulars pursued the provincials to Winter's Hill, where the latter being reinforced by General Putnam, renewed the battle, repulsed the regulars with great slaughter, and pursued them till they got under cover of their cannon on the shipping. The regulars then returned to Bunker's Hill, and the provincials to Winter's Hill, where they are now intrenching and erecting batteries.

In this action fell our worthy and much lamented friend, Doctor Warren, with as much glory as Wolfe, after performing many feats of bravery, and exhibiting a coolness and conduct which did honor to the judgment of his country in appointing him a few days before one of our major generals.[1]

The number of regulars which first attacked the provincials, was not less than two thousand. The number of the provincials was only fifteen hundred, who, it is supposed would soon have gained a complete victory had it not been for the unhappy mistake already mentioned. The regulars were afterwards re-

[1] Joseph Warren was born in Roxbury, Massachusetts, on the eleventh of June, 1741. He graduated at Harvard College in 1759, and studied medicine under Dr. James Lloyd. Four days previous to the battle of Breed's Hill, he received his commission as Major-General, and fell just as the retreat of the provincials commenced.—*Gordon.*

inforced with a thousand men. It is uncertain how great a number of them were killed or wounded, but all agree that their loss is more than one thousand. General Howe says, "you may talk of your Mindens and Fontenoys, but I never saw nor heard of such a carnage in so short a time." [1]

JUNE 18.—YESTERDAY evening, his excellency the Right Honorable Lord William Campbell, governor-in-chief of South Carolina, with his lady and family, arrived at Charleston in the Scorpion man-of-war from England. His Lordship was saluted on his arrival by the Tamar man-of-war, by Fort Johnson, and the several forts in town ; and about one o'clock to-

----

[1] Gaines' Mercury, July 3 ; Pennsylvania Packet, June 26. Another account of this battle is given by a gentleman in Providence, Rhode Island, to his friend in New York, as follows :—" On the evening of the 16th, Col. Putnam took possession of Bunker's Hill with about two thousand men, and began an intrenchment, which they had made some progress in. At eight in the morning, a party of regulars landed at Charlestown, and fired the town in divers places. Under cover of the smoke, a body of about five thousand men marched up to our intrenchments, and made a furious and sudden attack ; they were driven back three times ; and when they were making the third attack, one of our people imprudently spoke aloud that their powder was all gone, which being heard by some of the regular officers, they encouraged their men to march up to the trenches with fixed bayonets, and entered them ; on which our people were ordered to retreat, which they did with all speed, till they got out of musket-shot. They then formed, but were not pursued. In the mean time six men-of-war and four floating batteries were brought up, and kept up a continual fire on the causeway that leads on to Charlestown. Our people retreated through the fire, but not without the loss of many of the men. The brave Doctor Warren is among the killed, and Colonel Gardner is wounded. We left six field-pieces on the hill. Our people are now intrenched on Pleasant Hill, within cannon shot of Bunker's Hill. The loss of the King's troops must be very considerable ; the exact number we cannot tell.* Among the slain is Major Pitcairn.† If our people had been supplied with ammunition they would have held possession most certainly. Our people are in high spirits, and are very earnest to put this matter on another trial."— *Rivington's Gazetteer*, June 29.

* Of the regulars, two hundred and twenty-six were killed, and eight hundred and twenty wounded. Of the provincials, one hundred and thirty-nine were killed, and three hundred and fourteen missing.

† Lieutenant Pitcairn, son to Major, was standing by his father when that noble officer fell, and expired without uttering a word. He looked very wishfully at the lieutenant, who kneeled down and cried out, "My father is killed, I have lost my father." This slackened the firing of the regulars for some minutes, many of the men echoing the words, "We have all lost a father."—*Upcott*, iv. 313.

day his Lordship landed at Champney's wharf, where he was received by several gentlemen, and also by the grenadier company and the regiment of militia under arms. From the wharf his Lordship walked in procession, preceded by the grenadier company, to the state-house, where his commission was read and published in the council chamber, in the presence of some of the members of his majesty's council. From this place he returned in the same order to the Exchange, where his commission was again read; after which his Lordship and the whole company repaired to the state-house, where a genteel entertainment was provided.[1]

JUNE 20.—THIS morning the three battalions of Philadelphia, and the liberties, together with the artillery company, a troop of lighthorse, several companies of light infantry, rangers, and riflemen, in the whole about two thousand, marched out to the commons, and having joined in brigade, were reviewed by General Washington, who is appointed commander-in-chief of all the North American forces by the honorable Continental Congress. They went through the manual exercise, firings, and manœuvres with great dexterity and exactness.

This evening Thomas Jefferson, Esq., arrived here from Virginia, to attend the Congress, agreeable to his election, in the room of the Hon. Peyton Randolph, Esq. He is attended by Doctor M'Clurg.[2]

JUNE 22.—THE Provincial Congress of South Carolina broke up, after three weeks of unremitted application. They have requested, by public advertisement, that men of every denomination and persuasion will carry with them to all places of divine worship, loaded fire-arms. This, on Sunday last, was almost generally complied with.[3]

JUNE 23.—ONE of the surgeons attending the military hospital at Boston, has written home, that the provincials in the late engagement, "had either exhausted their ball, or were

[1] Virginia Gazette, July 8.   [2] Rivington's Gazetteer, June 29.
[3] Pennsylvania Journal, July 12.

determined that every wound should prove fatal. Their muskets were charged with old nails and angular pieces of iron,
and from most of the men being wounded in the legs, I am inclined to believe it was their design, not wishing to kill the
men, to leave them as burdens on us, to exhaust the provisions, as well as to intimidate the rest of the soldiery." [1]

JUNE 24.—YESTERDAY morning General Washington and
General Lee set off from Philadelphia to take command of the
American army at Massachusetts Bay. They were accompanied
a few miles from town by the troop of lighthorse, and by all
the officers of the city militia on horseback. They parted
with our celebrated commanders, expressing the most ardent
wishes for their success over the enemies of our liberty and
country.

Major Thomas Mifflin is appointed aide-de-camp to General
Washington, and accompanies the general to the camp near
Boston. The active and successful part which this gentleman
has taken in the civil and military affairs of the province of
Pennsylvania, has endeared him so much to his fellow-citizens
that few men have ever left us more universally beloved or
regretted. [2]

JUNE 25.—THIS afternoon at four o'clock, General Washington, attended by Generals Lee and Schuyler, and the light-
horse of Philadelphia, on the way for the American camp at
Cambridge, landed at Colonel Lispenard's seat, about a mile
above New York, from whence they were conducted into the
city, by nine companies of foot, in their uniforms, and a
greater number of the principal inhabitants of that city than
ever appeared on any occasion before. [3]

THE ship Juliana, Captain Montgomery, arrived at Sandy
Hook last night, from London, in which vessel his excellency
Governor Tryon came passenger. He landed at New York at
eight o'clock this evening, and was conducted to the house of

[1] Upcott, iv. 313.   [2] Rivington's Gazetteer, June 29.
[3] Pennsylvania Journal, June 28.

the Hon. Hugh Wallace, Esq., by an immense number of the principal people of that city.[1]

JUNE 26.—THE Massachusetts occasional newspaper of to-day, gives the following account of the action at Boston on the seventeenth :—" This town was alarmed at break of day, by a firing from the Lively ship-of-war ; and a report was immediately spread that the provincials had broke ground, and were raising a battery on the heights of the peninsula of Charlestown, against the town of Boston. They were plainly seen, and in a few hours a battery of six guns played upon their works. Preparations were instantly made for the landing a body of men ; and some companies of grena-diers and light infantry, with some battalions, and field artil-lery, amounting in the whole to about two thousand men, under the command of Major-General Howe and Brigadier-General Pigot, were embarked with great expedition, and landed on the peninsula without opposition, under cover of some ships-of-war and armed vessels.

British Account of the Battle of Breed's Hill.

The troops formed as soon as landed ; the provincials on the heights were perceived to be in great force, and strongly posted. A redoubt thrown up on the 16th at night, with other works full of men, defended with cannon, and a large body posted in the houses of Charlestown, covered their right ; and their left was covered by a breastwork, part of it cannon proof, which reached from the left of the redoubt to the Mystic river.

Besides the appearance of the provincials' strength, large columns were seen pouring in to their assistance ; but the king's troops advanced. The attack began by a cannonade, and notwithstanding various impediments of fences, walls, &c., and the heavy fire they were exposed to, from the vast num-ber of provincials, and their left galled from the houses of Charlestown, the troops made their way to the redoubt, mount-ed the works and carried it. The provincials were then forced from other strongholds, and pursued till they were driven clear of the peninsula, leaving five pieces of cannon behind them. Charlestown was set on fire during the engagement, and most part of it consumed. The loss they sustained must have been considerable, from the vast number they were seen to carry off during the action, exclusive of what they suffered from the shipping. About a hundred were buried the next day after, and thirty found wounded on the field, some of whom are since dead. About one hundred and seventy of the king's troops were killed and since dead of their wounds; and a great many were wounded.

This action has shown the bravery of the king's troops, who under every disadvantage, gained a complete victory over three times their number, strongly posted, and covered by breast-works.[1]

[1] Rivington's Gazetteer, July 13:—Another account from Boston mentions, that the provincials occupied a post at Charlestown on a commanding ground, which overlooked Boston, at 1,500 yards distance, which works they had constructed in the night. It consisted of a redoubt, with cannons mounted, and a continued intrenchment to a drained swamp on one side and defended by the houses in Charlestown on the other, which were filled with provincial troops. On the approach of day, the British artillery began to fire on the provincials' works, from a battery of six 24-pounders, and a howitzer from Copp's hill towards the north end, which played principally upon the redoubt. About two o'clock in the afternoon, the grenadiers and light infantry, consisting of twenty companies, with the 5th, 38th, 43d, and 52d regiments, embarked, and were landed on Charlestown point, about six hundred and fifty yards from the provincials' works, which, being formed, the boats returned for the 63d and 47th regiments, the marines, and ten pieces of artillery, the whole under the command of Major-General Howe, who had a low swampy land to pass, and to surmount a higher piece of ground, formed by nature for defence. The fire of six field-pieces and a heavy one of musketry from the provincials continued without intermission, on the British troops, and they still poured in fresh men from Cambridge, from the moment the forces marched from the encampment; signals being made by three guns from Roxbury church, and smoke from hill to hill, and the bells ringing, so that before the action was over, they were reinforced with a large body of men. At last, after an obstinate attack of an hour, reaching the summit very gradually, the British troops stormed the redoubt, and the provincials retired. They were cautiously pursued until another rising ground was obtained, which entirely commands the whole peninsula, but more immediately the neck of land.

The loss in killed and wounded of the provincials cannot be accurately ascertained. Five field-pieces and four hundred intrenching tools, with twenty-nine prisoners, fell into the hands of the British troops.

One armed ship, two sloops, and five floating batteries fired on the neck, but they did not altogether answer the end intended, as they neither prevented reinforcing or retreating.—*Rivington's Gazetteer*, July 13.

JUNE 27.—YESTERDAY afternoon General Washington with his suite, attended by the several New York militia companies,

Washington leaves New York. a troop of gentlemen of the Philadelphia light-horse, commanded by Captain Markoe, and a number of the inhabitants of New York, set out for the provincial camp at Cambridge, near Boston. Last night he rested at King's Bridge, and this morning proceeded on his journey.[1]

JUNE 29.—A CORRESPONDENT at Charleston, South Carolina, writes :—" Our place has rather the appearance of a garrison town than a mart for trade ; one company keeps guard all day, and two every night. In our situation we cannot be too watchful and may require much strength, for our negroes have all high notions of their liberty, and we lately learnt by intercepted letters and other ways, that there have been endeavors to set the Indians on us. Mr. Stuart, the superintendent of Indian affairs, is accused of being the person who has forwarded this wicked design, and he has fled for safety.

"The Tories in Georgia are now no more. That province is almost universally on the right side, and is about to choose delegates to send to the Congress." [2]

---

[1] Pennsylvania Journal, July 5 :—Before the general's departure, the provincial congress of New York presented him with an address, in which, after expressing their gratification at his appointment, they say:—" In you, sir, and in the worthy generals under your command, we have the most flattering hopes of success in the glorious struggle for American liberty, and the fullest assurances, that, whenever this important contest shall be decided by that fondest wish of every American soul, an accommodation with our mother country, you will cheerfully resign the important deposit committed into your hands, and reassume the character of our worthiest citizen."

The general, after declaring his gratitude for the regard shown him, added, " May your warmest wishes be realized in the success of America at this important and interesting period, and be assured that every exertion of my worthy colleagues and myself, will be equally extended to the re-establishment of peace and harmony between the mother country and these colonies. As to the fatal but necessary operations of war, when we assumed the soldier, we did not lay aside the citizen, and we shall most sincerely rejoice with you in that happy hour, when the establishment of American liberty, on the most firm and solid foundations, shall enable us to return to our private stations in the bosom of a free, peaceful, and happy country."—*Pennsylvania Journal*, July 5.

[2] New York Gazette, July 24.

JUNE 29.—YESTERDAY General Wooster, with seven companies of his regiment, and Colonel Waterbury, with his regiment complete, both consisting of about eighteen hundred men, arrived at New York from Connecticut. They appear to be a healthy, hearty body of men, and are now encamped about two miles out of town.[1]

THE reports from the northward are various; it is thought from the best accounts, that the Canadians will be very reluctant to enter into the service against the colonies, and it is pretty certain that General Carleton *Canada.* has hanged two or three of them for refusing, and speaking discouraging to others; so that it is on the whole believed that through all the stratagems of tyranny, Carleton will dragoon a number of the Canadians and Indians into the service. It is generally believed he is making preparation to come against us; but some think otherwise, and that he is only fortifying at St. John's to prevent any incursion from us. Doubtless a short time will discover which of those is the truth. We have certain intelligence that Guy Johnson is making all the interest possible to raise the Indians about the Lakes and Oswegatcha against us.[2]

JULY 1.—GENERAL PUTNAM, who commanded the Connecticut troops, is a veteran soldier of great experience. He served during the whole of the last war against the *General Putnam.* French, and was wounded fifteen different times in the service of his country. He was once taken prisoner by the Indians, who first scalped, then tied him to a tree, and were about to make a stroke at his head, which would have put an end to his existence, when a French officer happening at the instant to pass by, saved his life.

When he heard of the battle of Lexington, he was following his plough. As soon as he was satisfied of the truth of the news, he took one of his horses out of the plough, and bid his servant take the other and follow him with his arms to Boston.

[1] Rivington's Gazetteer, July 6.   [2] Gaines' Mercury, July 17.

Should the boasting General Burgoyne ridicule the simplicity of our American Cincinnatus, and be asked at the same time where *his* master's orders found *him* when he was commanded to repair to Boston, the answer would most probably be, " in a gambling house or brothel." [1]

July 3.—A writer in London says:—"Though the American soldiery perhaps may not be so regularly disciplined as the king's troops, yet it must be considered that there is a very material difference between a man who fights for his natural liberty, and the man who only fights because he is paid for it. The former defends himself in a just cause; the latter is the mere dupe of power. The former is animated by the zeal of his attachments to the public weal; the latter has no attachments at all, except to his pay for slaughter and bloodshed." [2]

This night died of the wounds he received in the battle of the seventeenth of June, the amiable, the gallant Colonel Thomas Gardner, of Cambridge, Massachusetts. [3]

None of the men who have been raised by the several colonies, are, in future, to be distinguished as the troops of any particular colony, but as the forces of " The United Colonies of North America," into whose joint service they have been taken by the Continental Congress, and are to be paid and supported accordingly. [4]

Colonel Lasher's battalion was reviewed at New York by Major-General Schuyler, accompanied by the Brigadier-Generals Montgomery and Wooster, in the presence of a very respectable number of the principal gentlemen and ladies. They went through the exercises and evolutions with the greatest order, alertness, and decorum. That country can never be enslaved, whose rights are defended by the hands of its citizens. [5]

[1] Pennsylvania Packet, July 3, and Virginia Gazette, August 12.
[2] New York Gazette, July 3.   [3] Gaines' Mercury, July 17.
[4] Letter from Dr. Leonard to John Murray.— *Winslow.*
[5] New York Gazette, July 10.

JULY 4.—THE Provincial Congress of New York, being informed by a number of the freeholders of the city, that the corporation had prepared and intended to present an address to Governor Tryon, congratulating him on his return to government, the Congress unanimously voted, that they disapproved of the same, and ordered that the secretary serve a copy of the above vote on the mayor, which was done accordingly.[1]

JULY 5.—GENERAL WOOSTER, and the officers of the Connecticut forces at New York, dined at Mr. Samuel Frances, in the Fields, where an elegant entertainment was pro- Dinner to vided by the members of the New York Military General Wooster. Club. The day was spent in the utmost harmony, every thing conspiring to please, being all of one mind, and one heart. The following loyal toasts were drank :—1. The king—better counsellors to him. 2. The hon. Continental Congress. 3. General Washington, and the army under his command. 4. The several provincial congresses and committees in the confederated colonies. 5. A speedy union on constitutional principles between Great Britain and America. 6. Conquest and laurels to all those heroes who draw their swords in support of freedom. 7. Confusion and disappointment to the friends of despotism and the enemies of America. 8. May the disgrace of the rebels against the constitution be as *conspicuous* as that of the rebels against the house of Hanover. 9. All those worthies in both Houses of Parliament, who stood forth advocates of America and the rights of mankind. 10. The Lord Mayor, and worthy citizens of London. 11. The glorious memory of King William. 12. The immortal memory of Hampden, Sydney, and every patriot who fell in defence of liberty. 13. May the enemies of America be turned into salt-petre, and go off in hot blasts. 14. May Great Britain see her error before America ceases in affection. 15. May America ever be the dread and scourge of tyrants. 16. The daughters of America in the arms of their brave defenders *only*. 17.

[1] Upcott, iv. 317.

Death and jack-boots, before dishonor and wooden shoes. 18. The glorious nineteenth of April, when the brave Americans convinced General Gage and the friends of tyranny, that they dare fight and conquer also.[1]

JULY 7.—IT is said that Governor Martin, of North Carolina, has issued a proclamation,[2] " tending to persuade, seduce, and intimidate the good people of that province from taking measures to preserve those rights and that liberty, to which, as subjects of a British king, they have the most undoubted claim," and that " the committee of the counties of New Hanover, Brunswick, Bladen, Dublin, and Orslow, in order to prevent the pernicious influence of the said proclamation, have unanimously resolved that, in their opinion, his excellency Josiah Martin, Esq., hath, by the said proclamation and by the whole tenor of his conduct since the unhappy disputes between Great Britain and her colonies, discovered himself to be an enemy to the happiness of that colony in particular, and to the freedom, rights, and privileges of America in general." [3]

Martin's Proclamation.

JULY 8.—THIS forenoon, a trumpeter came from the regular's army, with a letter from General Burgoyne to General Lee; and was conducted blindfolded by the guards, to the head-quarters, in Cambridge.   After delivering the letter he was permitted to return. The contents of this letter has occasioned much speculation and is variously reported ; but we hear the substance of it is nothing more than this : That General Burgoyne laments being obliged to act in opposition to a gentleman for whom he formerly entertained a great veneration ; but that his conduct proceeds from principle, and doubts not that General Lee is actuated by the same motive ; he wishes affairs may be accommodated, and desires to have a conference with General Lee.[4]

Burgoyne and Lee

This has been proposed to the general officers, and to the Provincial Congress, but they declare against it, as it has given

---

[1] Rivington's Gazetteer, July 6.
[2] Dated Fort Johnston, June 15.
[3] Pennsylvania Packet, July 31.
[4] New York Gazette, July 24.

rise to suspicions and jealousies among the men, who are not
ignorant that a politeness of this kind one hour, is quite consistent with cutting throats the next.[1]

JULY 9.—YESTERDAY morning, about half-past two o'clock,
we were called up and informed that the regulars had attacked
the lines at Roxbury. We heard distinctly the firing of small
arms and artillery on Roxbury Neck, and soon discovered a
great fire in that quarter, but two hours elapsed before we
knew the cause, which was as follows :

Two hundred volunteers, from the Rhode Island and Massachusetts forces, undertook to burn a guard-house of the regulars on the Neck, within three hundred yards of their
principal works. They detached six men, about   Skirmish on
ten o'clock in the evening, with orders to cross on   Roxbury Neck.
a marsh up to the rear of the guard-house, and there to watch
an opportunity to fire it. The remainder of the volunteers
secreted themselves in the marsh on each side of the Neck,
about two hundred yards from the house. Two pieces of brass
artillery were drawn softly on the marsh within three hundred
yards, and upon a signal from the advanced party of six men,
two rounds of cannon shot were fired through the guard-house.
Immediately the regulars, who formed a guard of forty-five or
fifty men, quitted the house and were then fired on by the
musketry, who drove them with precipitation into their lines.
The six men posted near the house set fire to it, and burnt it
to the ground. After this they burnt another house nearer
the lines, without losing a man. They took two muskets and
accoutrements, a halbert, &c., all which were bloody, and
showed evident marks of loss on the part of the regulars. The
houses have been a long while made use of by the regulars as
an advanced post, and has given them an opportunity of discovering our operations at Roxbury.[2]

JULY 10.—A GENTLEMAN who came out of Boston to-day,

[1] Markoe to Clift, July 9 ; also Holt's Journal, July 27.
[2] Extract of a letter from the Camp at Cambridge, July 9, in Holt's Journal,
July 27.

says the inhabitants have been numbered, and amount to six
Affairs in Boston. thousand five hundred and seventy-three. The
soldiers number, women and children, thirteen
thousand six hundred. Three hundred Tories are chosen to
patrol the streets; forty-nine at night. It is very sickly
there; from ten to thirty funerals in a day, and no bells allowed to toll; Master Lovell[1] has been taken up and put in
jail, in consequence of some letters found in Dr. Warren's
pockets.

The regular officers say : " Damn the rebels, they will not
flinch." A great number of floating batteries are building,
and five transports and three sloops are sailed for hay and
wood to the eastward.

This gentleman also says, that the officers and soldiers
triumph very much at the death of Dr. Warren, saying, it is
better to them than five hundred men.[2]

THE following instructions for the officers of the several
regiments of the Massachusetts Bay forces, who are immediately
Massachusetts to go upon the recruiting service, were issued this
Recruiting Orders. morning at Cambridge, by General Gates :—" You
are not to enlist any deserter from the ministerial army, nor
any stroller, negro, or vagabond, or person suspected of being
an enemy to the liberty of America, nor any under eighteen
years of age.

" As the cause is the best that can engage men of courage
and principle to take up arms ; so it is expected that none but
such will   accepted by the recruiting officer. The pay, provision, &c., being so ample, it is not doubted but that the
officers sent upon this service will, without delay, complete
their respective corps, and march the men forthwith to camp.

" You are not to enlist any person who is not an American
born, unless such person has a wife and family, and is a settled
resident in this country. The persons you enlist must be provided with good and complete arms." [3]

[1] James Lovell, the schoolmaster.   [2] Pennsylvania Journal, July 26.
[3] Gaines' Mercury, July 24.

JULY 11.—A CORRESPONDENT informs us that one of the gentlemen appointed to command a company of riflemen, to be raised in one of the frontier counties of Pennsylvania, had so many applications from the people in his neighborhood, to be enrolled for the service, that a greater number presented than his instructions permitted him to engage, and being unwilling to give offence to any, thought of the following expedient. He, with a piece of chalk, drew on a board the figure of a nose of the common size, which he placed at the distance of one hundred and fifty yards, declaring that those who should come nearest the mark should be enlisted. Sixty odd hit the object.—General Gage, take care of *your* nose.[1]

Pennsylvania Riflemen.

THE regulars are situated on Bunker's and Breed's Hills, both on the peninsula, where the late town of Charlestown stood, and within reach and under the cover of the guns, from the batteries in the town of Boston, and the ships in the harbor, and of a number of floating batteries, which they have built, that carry two guns in their bows, two in their sterns, and one on each side. The Americans are situated near Charles river, about two hundred rods below Harvard College, where they have a redoubt, which begins the line; then about sixty rods from that another redoubt, and lines continued near one hundred rods. At Charlestown road, on the west side of the road, at the foot of Prospect Hill, another redoubt, and strong fortification. On Prospect Hill, is *Putnam's* post, a very strong fortification; and between that and Winter Hill a redoubt. On Winter Hill, a strong citadel, and lines over Charlestown road, to Mystic; then in Mr. Temple's pasture, a strong redoubt, that commands to Mystic river, so that they have a complete line of circumvallation from Charles river to Mystic river. The Americans' main fortress is on Prospect Hill; the regulars on Bunker's Hill, within cannon shot of each other. A hill between these two posts, a little to the eastward of Prospect Hill,

The Armies at Boston.

[1] Virginia Gazette, July 22.

called *Cobble Hill*, will soon create a *squabble* as to which shall have it. It will not be many days before a contest begins, which will probably bring on a general engagement. In four or five days more, the Americans will be well prepared, and won't care how soon the regulars come ; the sooner the better. At Roxbury side the regulars have dug across the neck, and let the water through, and the Americans in turn, have intrenched across the outer end of the neck, and are strongly fortified there, and on the hill by the meeting-house ; so strong, that it is believed every man in Boston, and at Bunker's and Breed's Hills must fall, before they can force a passage that way into the country.[1]

JULY 12.—THIS afternoon, at fifty-five minutes past three o'clock, there was a violent shock of an earthquake at Jessup-borough, twelve miles southwest of Lake George.[2] The earth was much agitated, with small tossing, agile waves, and the noise thereof as loud as thunder ; and it was with difficulty that some people that were building a house could sit on the timber. At fifty-one minutes after six, and forty-one minutes after seven, were two small shocks with less noise.[3]

Earthquake at Lake George.

DURING a severe cannonade at Roxbury, last week, a bomb, thirteen inches in diameter, fell within the American lines, and burnt furiously, when four of the artillerymen ran up, and one kicked out the fuse, saved the bomb, and probably some lives —a stroke of heroism worthy of record. The regulars have so hardened the provincials by their repeated firing, that a cannonading is just as much minded as a common thunder shower. All things look well. The provincials are now strongly posted, as are the regulars. Neither side are willing to attack each other in their lines.

We have just got over land from Cape Cod, a large fleet of whale boats ; in a day or two we shall man them in Cambridge

[1] Holt's Journal, July 27.   [2] In New York.
[3] Pennsylvania Journal, August 9:—The first shock was considerable at Ticonderoga, Fort Edward, and was felt by some people in Albany.

and Mystic rivers, and try to keep the regulars' boats from
insulting us.[1]

JULY 16.—As to intelligence from Boston, it is seldom we
are able to collect any that may be relied on ; and to repeat
the vague flying rumors would be endless. We   Suffering in
heard yesterday by one Mr. Rolston, a goldsmith,   Boston.
who got out from Boston in a fishing schooner, that the distress
of the troops increases fast, their beef is spent, their malt and
cider all gone ; all the fresh provisions they can procure, they
are obliged to give to the sick and wounded ; that thirteen of
the provincials who were in jail, and were wounded at Charlestown, are dead ; that no man dared to be seen talking to his
friend in the street ; that they are obliged to be within every
evening at ten o'clock according to martial law, nor can any
inhabitant walk the streets after that time without a pass from
Gage ; that Gage has ordered all the molasses to be distilled
into rum for the soldiers ; that he has taken away all licenses
for selling of liquors, and given them to his creatures ; that he
has issued an order that no one else shall sell under a penalty
of ten pounds ; that the spirit which prevails among the soldiers is that of malice and revenge ; that there is no true
courage to be observed among them ; that their duty is hard,
always holding themselves in readiness for an attack, which
they are in continual fear of ; that Doctor Eliot[2] was not on
board of a man-of-war as was reported ; Mr. Lovel, with many
others, is certainly in jail ; that last week a poor milch cow
was killed in town and sold for a shilling sterling a pound ;
that the transports from Ireland and New York arrived last
week, but every additional man adds to their distress.[3]

JULY 19.—WEDNESDAY evening last, a number of ladies and
gentlemen collected at a place called East Farms, in Connecticut, where they had a needless entertainment, and made
themselves extremely merry with a good glass of wine. Such

---

[1] Extract of a letter from Cambridge in the New York Gazette, July 31.
[2] Andrew Eliot, D. D., pastor of the new church in Boston.
[3] Pennsylvania Journal, August 2.

entertainments and diversions can hardly be justified upon any occasion; but at such a day as this, when every thing around us has a threatening aspect, they ought to be discountenanced, and every good man should use his influence to suppress them. And are not such diversions and entertainments a violation of the eighth article of the Association of the Continental Congress? And is it not expected that the Committee of Inspection will examine into such matters, and if they find any persons guilty of violating said Association, that they treat them according as the rules of it prescribe?[1]

Last Monday night, two men belonging to the Swan, Captain Ayscough, being on shore, at Newport, Rhode Island, saw fit to attempt an escape from their old and detested habitation. The next morning two or three of the ferry boats which pass between Newport and Conanicut were fired upon and brought to, an event so singular that two respectable members of the committee waited upon Captain Ayscough to know the reason. He told them that two of his men the night before were sent on shore upon some errand, and had not returned, and added, that he was confident the inhabitants knew where they were, and that they were detained by them purposely. The two gentlemen declared themselves ignorant of the matter, and believed the whole town to be. However, to pacify Captain Ayscough, they assured him that they would summon the committee together, inquire into the matter, and, at the same time, desired Captain Ayscough to write a letter to the committee, stating his grievance. This he did, and they promised to wait on him in the afternoon with an answer. As the captain's letter was rather in the threatening style, the committee could not help inquiring what he meant thereby, and assured him in their reply, that they were not to be intimidated, and did not think themselves by any means accountable for the desertion of any of his men. Captain Ayscough read the letter with considerable composure, folded it up and then gave it to Wallace, captain of the Rose; Ayscough, at this time, being on board

Alarm at Newport.

---

[1] Barber's Historical Collections of Connecticut, page 175.

Wallace's ship. Captain Wallace immediately flew into a most terrible passion, threw the letter down in a violent fit of rage, damned the committee and the Congress, and swore at Ayscough for writing to such a parcel of damned rebels, and declared that if he knew the two gentlemen who were then present to be of the committee they never should go on shore again. They endeavored to pacify him, but in vain. He swore, repeatedly, that if there was a God in heaven, the town should be destroyed before morning; that he was the king's officer and would not be insulted. Hereupon the two gentlemen left the ship. A signal gun was instantly discharged, and the three pirates in the harbor and their tender immediately weighed anchor and came close in with the town. Their tomkins were taken out, the marines on board beat to arms, and all the hostile preparations imaginable going forward against a defenceless seaport, consisting (exclusive of the men) of not less than six thousand women and children. About half-past nine in the evening, a cannon was discharged from the Rose, when many really thought the firing on the town was begun. Several women fainted away; others went into fits, and a few absolutely miscarried by the fright.

This morning about one or two o'clock, one of the Swan's men returned, and in order, it is supposed, to save himself from a flogging, as it was necessary for him to give some account of himself, he invented the following lie, and swore to it upon the Holy Evangelist, namely : "That the Rhode Island rebels had taken him and his companion, and wanted that they should enlist among them to fight against the king, but that they refused, and because they did, the rebels gagged them and then carried them to Providence jail, but that he broke away and travelled thirty miles to get on board again;" with much of the same stuff.

The captains of the pirates either believed this gross and inconsistent falsehood, or fain would make the inhabitants think so; accordingly it was taken down in writing, sent on shore, and satisfaction demanded, or the town should certainly be laid in ashes that very day. Another cannon was now discharged, four ferry boats and two wood sloops seized, quantities of tar and other inflammatory and combustible matter put into the same, in order to set on fire and send into the wharves, as a more expeditious way of destroying the town than by cannon only ; the cannon at the same time were to be fired on every part of the town. The court-house, Doctor Stiles'[1] meeting-house, and the printing office were first of all to feel the effects of this horrid plot. The most terrible parade was kept up by these low ministerial tools till near two o'clock this afternoon, when two persons of undoubted veracity (farmers within two or three miles of the town) went on board the Swan. One of these gentlemen assured the captains of the three ships, that he saw the stragglers, for whose desertion such terrible confusion had ensued,· in his corn-field yesterday morning, and described them ; the other gentleman declared that he saw them in the afternoon near where he was making hay, and likewise described them. After fully proving that they knew the men, by pointing out the one who had returned, notwithstanding four others were first produced in order to deceive them, they came on shore ; when, all at once, the boats and prisoners were dismissed, the ships weighed anchor and stood up the river.

Let every honest American rise up in opposition to such inhuman, and must we add, *when speaking of Britons too*, worse than savage cruelty. To prepare, after so hostile a manner, to destroy thousands of lives and ruin vast estates, merely because two drunken wretches had fled from a ship under the command of a petty tyrant, is what will make a considerable figure in some future page, when our many trials are handed down to posterity by some able historian.[2]

A WRITER says that General Gage's army is now divided into three companies. "The first company is under ground ;
Gage's Army.   the second is above ground ; the third is in the hospital ; and the general has received express orders from home for the second and third companies to march and follow the first."[3]

[1] Ezra Stiles, D. D., of the Second Congregational Church in Newport.
[2] Pennsylvania Packet, August 7.   [3] Constitutional Gazette, Oct. 11.

YESTERDAY morning, according to orders issued the day before by Major-General Putnam, all the continental troops under his immediate command assembled on Prospect Hill, when the declaration of the Continental Congress[1] was read, after which an animated and pathetic address to the army was made by the Reverend Mr. Leonard,[2] chaplain to General Putnam's regiment, and succeeded by a pertinent prayer; when General Putnam gave the signal, and the whole army shouted their loud amen by three cheers; upon which a cannon was fired from the fort, and the standard lately sent to General Putnam was exhibited, flourishing in the air, bearing on one side this motto, AN APPEAL TO HEAVEN, and on the other side, QUI TRANSTULIT SUSTINET. The whole was conducted with the utmost decency, good order, and regularity, and to the universal acceptance of all present. And the PHILISTINES on Bunker's Hill heard the shout of the ISRAELITES, and, being very fearful, paraded themselves in battle array.[3]

A REPORT is current, that the troops will not winter at Boston, but the province they are to remove to is not clear. Some say Rhode Island will be the head-quarters, others New York, with Long Island, as it lies so contiguous. It is to be remarked, that either of these provinces is a more desirable and proper climate for troops to winter in than Boston, and at Boston no good can be expected from the winter campaign, whereas there is a chance of doing something on new ground, and among new people, not so expert in arms or so inured to the field. What adds to the probability of the report is, that such a measure would embarrass the Provincials more than any other whatever, for the men, who still look on themselves as trained militia only, would think they had a right to be discharged when they had no enemy to oppose, and the peace of their province as it were totally restored. Whereas, according to the principles and spirit of the leaders of that unfortunate town and province, they must by all means

Troops to remove from Boston.

---

[1] The declaration of the Continental Congress, setting forth the causes and necessity of their taking up arms.—See American Eloquence, vol. i., p. 286.

[2] Abiel Leonard, D.D.   [3] Virginia Gazette, August 12.

persuade the men to follow the regulars to any distant province, in order to stir up the same spirit of opposition there, that has reigned in Boston; for it is an undoubted fact, that if government gains any one province over to its side, the business is done, and the others would soon follow.   Another thing in favor of the troops moving is, that it would probably alarm the Congress so much, that that august and respectable assembly would soon break up, there being a great deal of difference between holding such meeting with a body of troops in the neighborhood, and in having no forces near them for hundreds of miles.[1]

JULY 21.—YESTERDAY, agreeably to the recommendation of the delegates in the hon. Continental Congress, was observed with the utmost solemnity, by fasting, abstinence, and devotion.   In all the churches in New York were large congregations, and excellent discourses, delivered from the several pulpits, expressive of the truly calamitous situation of this unhappy continent.[2]

Fast Day.

At New Castle, in Delaware, the Reverend Æneas Ross delivered a discourse in the morning, from Deut. 23, 9th verse, "When the host goeth forth against the enemy, then keep thee from every wicked thing!" And in the afternoon, the Reverend Joseph Montgomery preached from Deut. 29th chap., 9th and 10th verses transposed, "Ye stand this day all of you before the Lord your God; your captains of your tribes, your elders and your officers, with all the men of Israel; keep therefore the words of this covenant and do them, that ye may prosper in all that ye do!" Both of the services were attended by all the militia, with their proper officers in their uniform, and a numerous concourse of the other inhabitants.[3]

JULY 24.—By authentic accounts from South Carolina, we are informed that the colony of Georgia has appointed delegates to the Continental Congress now in Philadelphia, where they may be expected daily to arrive.   The same accounts

[1] Upcott, vol. iv., p. 319.   [2] New York Gazette, July 24.
[3] Pennsylvania Packet, July 24.

inform, that the people of Carolina have taken into their possession about one hundred and thirty barrels of gunpowder
imported in the ship ——, Captain Maitland, from London,
on Government account.[1]

JULY 25.—CAPTAIN DOWDLE, with his company of riflemen,
from Yorktown, Pennsylvania, arrived at Cambridge about
one o'clock to-day, and since has made proposals   Dowdle's Rifle-
to General Washington to attack the transport   men.
stationed at Charles river. He will engage to take her with
thirty men. The general thinks it best to decline it at present;
but at the same time commends the spirit of Captain Dowdle
and his brave men, who, though they just came a very long
march, offered to execute the plan immediately.[2]

JULY 28.—A DESERTER from Boston says, that, yesterday
morning, General Gage surrendered in the orders of the day,
his command of the army to General Howe, and   Rumor of Gage's
now acts only as a Civil Governor; that he is   Resignation.
lampooned and despised by the whole army; that Howe is
much censured for his mode of attack on our lines last month;
that their artillery was wretchedly served; and, what is more
strange, that all their spare cartridges which they brought out,
were twelve-pounders, and they took only nine-pounders cannon, so that when the Americans were obliged to quit their
lines, the regulars had not one round of artillery.[2]

JULY 30.—LAST Friday the regulars cut several trees, and
were busy all night in throwing up a line, and   Skirmish on
abbatis in front of it. In the evening orders were Charlestown Neck.
given to the York County Riflemen to march down to our

---

[1] Holt's Journal, July 27. Last night arrived at Philadelphia, the Georgia
Packet, from Georgia, in which came passengers the Hon. John Houston, Archibald Bullock, Noble Wimberly Jones, Lyman Hall, and Doctor Zubly, delegates
appointed to represent that colony in the Continental Congress.—*Pennsylvania
Packet*, August 14.

[2] Extract of a letter from Cambridge, Massachusetts, July 25, in the Pennsylvania Journal, August 9.

[3] Pennsylvania Packet, Postscript, August 14.

advanced post on Charlestown Neck, to endeavor to surround the advanced guard, and to bring off some prisoners, from whom we expected to learn their design in throwing up the abbatis on the Neck. The rifle company divided, and executed their plan in the following manner : Captain Dowdle, with thirty-nine men, filed off to the right of Bunker's Hill, and creeping on their hands and knees, got into the rear without being discovered. The other division of forty men under Lieutenant Miller, were equally successful in getting behind the sentinels on the left, and were within a few yards of joining the division on the right, when a party of regulars came down the hill to relieve their guard, and crossed our riflemen under Captain Dowdle, as they were lying on the ground in an Indian file. The regulars were within twenty yards of our men before they saw them, and immediately fired. The riflemen returned the salute, killed several, brought off two prisoners, and their arms, with the loss of Corporal Creuse, who is supposed to be killed, as he has not been heard of since the affair.

In return for this the regulars alarmed us last night in their turn. At one o'clock this morning, a heavy firing of small arms and cannon occasioned our drums to be beat to arms, and the corps were immediately ordered to their posts. The firing continued in three different quarters, Roxbury, Sewell's Point at the mouth of Cambridge river, and at the advanced post at Charlestown Neck. Some hours elapsed before we knew the design of the enemy, which was this : We had surrounded some of their out-guard the night before, which induced them to serve our sentinels in like manner.

They sent two flat-bottomed boats to Sewell's Point to attack our redoubt there. The boats, after a useless fire of several hours, retired. The picquet guard of the enemy on Charlestown Neck, attacked and drove in our advanced guard, who, being reinforced by General Lee's orders, recovered their ground and beat the enemy, killed several, and brought off seven muskets without losing a man, although our men engaged them under their guns, within point blank shot of their lines.[1]

¹ Constitutional Gazette, August 12.

CHAPTER III.

AUGUST 4.—THE good people of Virginia now consider Lord Dunmore as their mortal enemy, and will no longer brook the many gross insults they have received from him, which are daily repeated ; and the d—d shirtmen, as they are emphatically called by some of his minions, it is more than probable, will make some of them rue, before long, their ill-timed, base, and ungenerous conduct.[1]

AN officer in General Gage's army says :—" The reason that so many more of the king's troops were wounded than killed in the late action in New England, is, that the Americans use a small shot, called *buck shot*, which is much smaller than the soldiers' bullets." [2]

LAST Sabbath, a child of Colonel Robinson, of Dorchester, Massachusetts, was baptized by the Reverend Mr. Dunbar,[3] of Stoughton, by the name of GEORGE WASHINGTON.[4]

AUGUST 7.—ON Friday evening last, arrived at Lancaster, Pennsylvania, on their way to the American camp, Captain Cresap's company of riflemen, consisting of one hundred and thirty active, brave young fellows ; Cresap's Riflemen. many of whom have been in the late expedition under Lord Dunmore, against the Indians. They bear in their bodies visible marks of their prowess, and show scars and wounds which

---

[1] Pennsylvania Journal, August 16.   [2] Samuel Dunbar, D. D.
[3] Gaines' Mercury, August 14   [4] Constitutional Gazette, August 23.

would do honor to Homer's Iliad. They show you, to use the poet's words :—

"Where the gor'd battle bled at every vein!"

One of these warriors, in particular, shows the cicatrices of four bullet holes through his body. These men have been bred in the woods to hardships and dangers from their infancy. They appear as if they were entirely unacquainted with, and had never felt the passion of fear. With their rifles in their hands, they assume a kind of omnipotence over their enemies. One cannot much wonder at this, when we mention a fact which can be fully attested by several of the reputable persons who were eye-witnesses of it. Two brothers in the company took a piece of board five inches broad and seven inches long, with a bit of white paper, about the size of a dollar, nailed in the centre, and while one of them supported this board perpendicularly between his knees, the other, at the distance of upwards of sixty yards, and without any kind of rest, shot eight bullets through it successively, and spared a brother's thigh ! Another of the company held a barrel stave perpendicularly in his hands with one edge close to his side, while one of his comrades, at the same distance, and in the manner before mentioned, shot several bullets through it, without any apprehension of danger on either side. The spectators appearing to be amazed at these feats, were told that there were upwards of fifty persons in the same company who could do the same thing ; that there was not one who could not plug nineteen bullets out of twenty, as they termed it, within an inch of the head of a tenpenny nail. In short, to evince the confidence they possessed in their dexterity at these kind of arms, some of them proposed to stand with apples on their heads, while others at the same distance, undertook to shoot them off ; but the people who saw the other experiments declined to be witnesses of this. At night a great fire was kindled around a pole planted in the Court House Square, where the company, with the captain at their head, all naked to the waist, and painted like savages, (except the captain, who was in an Indian shirt,) indulged a vast concourse of people with a perfect exhi-

bition of a war-dance, and all the manœuvres of Indians, holding council, going to war, circumventing their enemies by de-
files, ambuscades, attacking, scalping, &c.   It is said by those
who are judges, that no representation could possibly come
nearer the original.   The captain's expertness and agility, in
particular, in these experiments astonished every beholder.
This morning they will set out on their march for Cambridge.[1]

AUGUST 8.—THE riflemen on their way from the southern
colonies through the country, administer the new-fashioned
discipline of tar and feathers to the obstinate and refractory
Tories that they meet on their road, which has a very good
effect.   Those whose crimes are of a more atrocious nature,
they punish by sending them to General Gage.   They took a
man in New Milford, Connecticut, a most incorrigible Tory,
who called them d—d rebels, &c., and made him walk before
them to Litchfield, which is twenty miles, and carry one of his
own geese all the way in his hand.   When they arrived there,
they tarred him, and made him pluck his goose, and then
bestowed the feathers on him, drummed him out of the company, and obliged him to kneel down and thank them for their
lenity.[2]

AUGUST 9.—THIS morning the following appeal was posted
in the city of Philadelphia :—" To the SPINNERS in this city,
the suburbs, and country :—Your services are now wanted to
promote the AMERICAN MANUFACTORY, at the corner of Market
and Ninth streets, where cotton, wool, flax, &c., are delivered
out ; strangers, who apply, are desired to bring a few lines, by
way of recommendation, from some respectable person in their
neighborhood.

One distinguishing characteristic of an excellent woman,
as given by the wisest of men, is, " That she seeketh wool and
flax, and worketh willingly with her hands to the spindle, and
her hands holdeth the distaff."   In this time of public distress,

[1] Virginia Gazette, September 9, and Pennsylvania Journal, August 23
[2] Barber's Historical Collections of Connecticut, page 480.

you have now, each of you, an opportunity not only to help to sustain your families, but likewise to cast your mite into the treasury of the public good. The most feeble effort to help to save the state from ruin, when it is all you can do, is as the widow's mite, entitled to the same reward as they who, of their abundant abilities, have cast in much."[1]

THE riflemen from York County[2] have annoyed the regulars very much. By a gentleman who left Boston yesterday, we hear that Captains Percival and Sabine, of the marines, Captain Johnson of the royal Irish, and Captain Le Moine of the Train, were killed on Monday. Captain Chetwyn, son of Lord Chetwyn, is mortally wounded. The number of privates killed this week we have not heard. The regulars have thrown up a breastwork across the neck at the foot of Bunker's Hill, to secure their sentries and advanced guards. Yesterday Captain Morgan arrived from Virginia with his company of riflemen; but they are grown so terrible to the mercenaries, that nothing is to be seen from their breastworks but a hat. General Gage has built thirteen boats, which will carry sixty men each, and they have been several days practising the men to row them about in Boston harbor, from which we may suppose some party is to be made by water.[3]

AUGUST 10.—YESTERDAY the Falcon sloop-of-war, under the command of Captain Lindzee, hove in sight of Gloucester, Cape Ann,[4] and seemed to be in quest of two schooners from the West Indies, bound to Salem, one of which he soon brought too; the other taking advantage of a fair wind, put into Gloucester harbor; but Lindzee having made a prize of the first, pursued the second into the harbor, and brought the first with him. He anchored, and sent two barges with fifteen men in each, armed with muskets and swivels. These were attended by a whale boat, in which was the lieutenant and six privates, with orders to seize the loaded schooner, and carry

Attack on Gloucester.

---

[1] Pennsylvania Journal, August 9.   [2] Pennsylvania.
[3] Extract of a letter from Cambridge, August 9; Pennsylvania Journal, August 16.   [4] Massachusetts.

her under the Falcon's bow. The militia and other inhabitants were alarmed at this dangerous attempt, and prepared for a vigorous opposition. The barge men, under the command of the lieutenant, boarded the schooner at the cabin windows, which provoked a smart fire from the people on the shore, by which three of the enemy were killed, and the lieutenant wounded in the thigh, who thereupon returned to the man-of-war. Upon this Lindzee sent the other schooner and a small cutter he had to attend him, well armed, with orders to fire upon the damned rebels, wherever they could see them, and that he would in the mean time cannonade. He immediately fired a broadside upon the thickest settlements, and stood with a diabolical pleasure to see what havoc his cannon might make. "Now," said he, "my boys, we will aim at the damned Presbyterian church. Well! my brave fellows, one shot more and the house of God will fall before you." While he was thus venting his hellish rage, and setting himself as it were against heaven, the Almighty was on our side. Not a ball struck or wounded an individual person, although they went through our houses in almost every direction when filled with women and children. Under God our little party at the water-side performed wonders, for they soon made themselves masters of both the schooners, the cutter, the two barges, the boat, and every man in them, and all that pertained to them. In the action, which lasted several hours, we have lost but one man, two others wounded, one of whom is since dead, the other very slightly wounded. We took, of the men-of-war's men, thirty-five; several are wounded, and one since dead; twenty-four are sent to head-quarters. The remainder being impressed from this and the neighboring towns, are permitted to return to their friends. This morning Captain Lindzee warped off with but one-half of his men, with neither a prize boat nor tender, except a small skiff the wounded lieutenant returned in.

Among the prisoners taken, is one Budd, gunner of the Falcon sloop-of-war, who was some time ago at Machias with a number of others, and carried to Worcester, and upon being released from close confinement, took an opportunity of running off with a few of the Tory gentry, and got on board the

Falcon again. It is hoped this fellow, if re-taken, will be better secured.[1]

LAST evening, returned to Boston, after about three weeks' cruise, twelve transports, having on board about a thousand ministerial butchers, under convoy of three men-of-war. During their cruise they plundered and pillaged about two thousand sheep, and upwards of one hundred head of cattle, from Gardiners' and Fishers' Islands, near New London, Connecticut, though it is said, after they were secured, they tendered payment. They also took and carried in with them, an outward bound vessel, with about forty head of cattle and thirty sheep. With this trophy of victory, on their arrival at Boston, the bells were set to music, to the no small joy and rejoicing of the Tories there.

How is the glory of Britain departed! Her army which not long since was the terror of many nations, is now employed in cutting the throats of his majesty's loyal subjects, and SHEEP STEALING! Felons, indeed![2]

AUGUST 12.—A WRITER in Plymouth, England, says:— "The whole country here is in great consternation about the fire kindled in America, and it is thought that the assistance of our pious and reverend fathers in the church, will be much wanted there, to quench the flames of zeal for liberty, and to spirit up the soldiery, as Father O'Neil did in Ireland, 'Declaring that all who died in their country's cause, should sup with him in Paradise that night.' But the king getting the better of the action, Father O'Neil clapped spurs to his horse and made off; which one of his party observing, cried out, 'Oh father, will you not stay and sup with us to-night?' To which the pious father answered, 'That it was a fast day with him.' We might expect the same answer from our pious fathers; they would sooner fast, if called upon, than go over to America."[3]

---

[1] Virginia Gazette, September 16.   [2] Constitutional Gazette, August 23 and 30.
[3] Pennsylvania Journal, August 16.

August 14.—This day being the anniversary of the ever memorable 14th of August, 1765, when an opposition to the ministerial plan to enslave the Americans was first made, it was celebrated by the field-officers of the sixth brigade, under the command of Colonel James Frye, at the House of Jonathan Hastings, Esq., in Cambridge, Massachusetts, where the following toasts were drank, viz. :
1. The Continental Congress. 2. Success to our undertakings. 3. The memorable 14th of August, 1765. 4. May American valor ever prove invincible to the attempt of ministerial tyranny to oppress them. 5. The twelve united colonies. 6. All our friends in Great Britain. 7. Liberty without licentiousness. 8. A speedy and happy conclusion to the present unhappy disputes. 9. The 19th of April, 1775. 10. A speedy entrance, possession, and opening of the town of Boston. 11. The President of the Continental Congress. 12. General Washington, and the other general officers of the American army. 13. A speedy export to all the enemies of America, without any drawback. 14. Immortal honor to that patriot and hero, Doctor Joseph Warren, and the brave American troops, who fought the battle at Charlestown, on the 17th of June, 1775.[1]

Intelligence was received this morning, at Williamsburg, Virginia, that a brig which was lately taken, laden with provisions, and carried into Boston by ministerial pirates, returned from thence to Norfolk last Wednesday, having on board seven officers of the regular army. We do not hear that any soldiers are come with them, or are to follow, but it is certain that the Earl of Dunmore's ship is now completed for an expedition ; and that his lordship has fitted up thirteen field-pieces for service. It is apprehended he intends to commence hostilities upon York, or James river very soon.[2]

Last night, arrived at the camp in Cambridge, Swashan the chief, with four other Indians of the St. Francis tribe, conducted

---

[1] Gaine's Mercury, August 28.   [2] Constitutional Gazette, August 26.

by Mr. Reuben Colburn, who has been honorably recompensed for his trouble. The above Indians came to offer their services in the cause of American liberty, have been kindly received, and are now entered the service. Swashan says he will bring one-half of his tribe, and has engaged four or five other tribes, if they should be wanted. He says the Indians of Canada, in general, and also the French, are greatly in favor of the Americans, and are determined not to act against them.[1]

AUGUST 17.—THIS morning, at East Hartford, Connecticut, sallied from the Lyon Tavern and its dependencies, a corps of
Female Infantry.   female infantry, of twenty rank and file, with a flank guard of three chosen spirits of the male line, and marching westward about one mile in martial array and excellent order, saving stride and gabble, these attacked and carried, without opposition from powder, law, or conscience, Mr. Pitkin's store, in which was lodged a quantity of sugar designed for the army, of which they plundered and bore away in triumph two hundred and eighteen pounds. A travelling gentleman falling in with the rear, whom they mistook for the owner of the spoils, was attacked and drove with great fury ; but being well mounted, made his escape. The whole was completed in two hours, and without loss of blood, except from a few accidental scratches of side arms, underslung without scabbards.

That so unexampled a spirit of heroism may not want due notice and encouragement, it is proposed that this corps be augmented by voluntary enlistment to a battalion, for the ranging service in the northern department, to be in the uniform of rifle frocks, and the snug Scotch kilt, and allowed, besides perquisites and plunder, a generous bounty on scalps, and a fine new standard with an elegant device of a lady inverted, and to be commanded by the celebrated *Madame de la Mell Hobb Greg Scratch.*[2]

AUGUST 21.—WE hear from Cecil county, in the province

Pennsylvania Journal, August 30.
[2] Connecticut Courant, September 10, and Barber's Connecticut Collections, p. 75.

of Maryland, that Mr. Elihu Hall, jr., a young gentleman of family, fortune, and character, in said county, last Sabbath had his first-born son baptized JOHN HANCOCK, as well to express his esteem of the New England bravery in general, as in particular honor of the great American PATRIOT of that name, who now, under God, presides in the honorable Continental Congress.[1]

CAPTAIN ROSS, with his company of riflemen and the stores, arrived at Cambridge on Friday last. There has not a random shot of a rifleman done any execution lately, worth mentioning. A letter from a selectman in Boston to his son in our camp, advises him to quit it, as there was to be some very important stroke made in a few days; we do not pay much regard to it, as it is very improbable he should know any thing of what they intend. Our lines are so strong we have nothing to fear but a surprise. There have been letters passing between the Generals Washington and Gage, on his treatment of our officers who are in jail in Boston. Our letter was in very mild terms, carefully avoiding any epithets that might be deemed unpolite. Gage's answer was in a different strain, directed to "George Washington, Esq.," calling us rebels and usurpers, and what not, affecting great clemency in having forborne to hang our prisoners. General Washington gave him a suitable reply; and so it stands :—We broke a Colonel Gerish yesterday, for cowardice on Bunker's Hill, the 17th of June.[2]

AUGUST 28.—THE Provincial Congress of New York having resolved that the cannon should be removed from the battery in the city, a number of the citizens collected New York fired for that purpose last Wednesday evening; and upon. part of the provincial artillery, under the command of Captain John Lamb, were posted on the battery to prevent the landing of any party from the Asia man-of-war, to annoy them while at work. When they marched down, which was about eleven

[1] Pennsylvania Packet, August 21.
[2] Extract of a letter from the Camp at Cambridge, August 21; Gaine's Mercury, September 11.

o'clock, they observed one of the above ship's barges lying at
some distance from the shore, where she continued upwards of
an hour; then she got under sail, and fired a musket at the men
that were posted on the Battery. This was immediately returned
by a smart fire of musketry from the artillery, and a few of the
Independent light infantry belonging to Colonel Lasher's battalion, that were likewise posted there for the above purpose.
Soon after this the Asia fired three cannon, when the drums
beat to arms, which alarmed the inhabitants. When they had
assembled she began a heavy and smart fire, of nine, eighteen,
and twenty-four-pounders, and some grape shot, succeeded by
a discharge of musketry from the marines, but without doing
any other mischief than damaging the upper part of several
houses near the fort and Whitehall, and wounding three men.
Notwithstanding the fire from the Asia, the citizens effected
their purpose, and carried off twenty-one pieces of cannon,
being all that were mounted on carriages. Since this disturbance the women and children have been continually moving
out of town, with their most valuable effects.[1]

THIS evening was married, at the seat of Thaddeus Burr,
Esq., at Fairfield, Connecticut, by the Reverend Mr. Elliot,
the Hon. John Hancock, Esq, President of the Continental
Congress, to Miss Dorothy Quincy, daughter of Edmund
Quincy, Esq., of Boston. Florus informs us, that "in the
second Punic war, when Hannibal besieged Rome and was
very near making himself master of it, a field upon which part
of his army lay, was offered for sale, and was immediately purchased by a Roman, in a strong assurance that the Roman
valor and courage would soon raise the siege." Equal to the
conduct of that illustrious citizen was the marriage of the
Honorable John Hancock, Esq., who, with his amiable lady,
has paid as great a compliment to *American* valor, and discovered equal patriotism, by marrying now while all the
colonies are as much convulsed as Rome when Hannibal was
at her gates.[2]

---

[1] Gaine's Mercury, August 28.   [2] New York Gazette, September 4.

AUGUST 31.—YESTERDAY morning a tender chased into Stonington harbor two small sloops, which had a number of people on board bound to Block Island. They had but just time to get on shore before the tender came in, which after making a tack came close alongside of Captain Denison's wharf, discharged a full broadside into the stores and houses, and sailing out again, in a little time returned with the Rose man-of-war and another tender. As soon as the Rose could get her broadside to bear on the town, she began a very heavy fire, also the tenders, who were under sail, and continued firing the whole day, with very little intermission. During the time a flag was sent off from the shore, desiring Captain Wallace, commander of the Rose, to let them know what he meant by firing on the town. His answer was, that he did it in his own defence. We have one man mortally wounded, and the houses, stores, &c., very much shattered. This morning they sailed out and anchored at the north side of the west end of Fisher's Island, where they remain. There were five or six people killed on board the tenders, by the inhabitants, who assembled, and were under arms the whole day. They have carried off a schooner loaded with molasses, belonging to Patuxet, near Providence, from the West Indies, and the two small sloops that landed the people.[1]

SEPTEMBER 1.—THE enemies to liberty and America, headed by Tom Gage, lately gave a notable specimen of their hatred to the very name of liberty. A party of Boston Liberty
Tree cut down. them, of whom Job Williams was the ringleader, a few days since repaired to a tree at the south end of Boston, known by the name of Liberty Tree, and armed with axes, &c., made a furious attack upon it. After a long spell of laughing, and grinning, sweating, swearing, and foaming with malice diabolical, they cut down a tree, because it bore the name of liberty. Be it known to this infamous band of traitors, that the GRAND AMERICAN TREE OF LIBERTY, planted in the centre of the united colonies of North America, now flourishes with unrivalled, increasing beauty ; and bids fair in a short time to

---

[1] New York Gazette, September 11.

afford under its wide-spreading branches, a safe and happy retreat for all the sons of liberty, however numerous and dispersed.[1]

SEPTEMBER 5.—ON Monday last, died at Brunswick, New Jersey, in the sixty-third year of his age, on his way to New York, the Hon. James Habersham, Esq., president of his Majesty's council of Georgia. He was a man of great probity, integrity, and honor; an able counsellor, an affectionate and tender parent, and well acquainted with the delicacies of true friendship. In his life he was greatly beloved, esteemed, and honored by all his friends; and his death is equally regretted by all who had the honor of his acquaintance. His remains were on Thursday evening interred in the family vault of Nathaniel Marston, Esq., in Trinity Church-yard, at New York.[2]

James Habersham.

THE following remarkable piece was distributed in a handbill, through the city of London, last July:

Lieutenant-General Bastwick's beating orders for free American Volunteers:—" All gentlemen volunteers, natives of Great Britain, friends to the liberty of America, who are willing to serve their sovereign by saving their country, and to succor and support their injured brethren, inhabitants and possessors of the great Western hemisphere, suffering by the murderous orders of an unoffended but implacable man, have now the singular honor paid them of being solicited to stand forward in a cause, where their own character, their conscience, and even their interests should urge them to the most conspicuous exertions. Let all such, of all sizes from three feet nine to six feet three, and the shorter the better, who can feel no wounds but the wounds of the constitution, who bleed already at every pore for the distresses of the oppressed Americans, whose lungs are panting for the fame they are going to enjoy by relieving them, whose hearts lie in the right places, and are ready to burst within their breasts, for

Bastwick's Beating Orders.

---

[1] Constitutional Gazette, September 9.   [2] Rivington's Gazetteer, Sept. 7.

want of vent to the vengeance they wish to take. Let all
such repair to the Castle and Falcon Inn, Aldergate street,
where they will be honorably entertained by Lieutenant-General Jedediah Bastwick, and may enter into present pay and
quarters. Entrance money, fifty acres of land in the Alleghany
Mountains, or their value payable at the Royal Exchange.
Bringers will be proportionally rewarded. No persons well
and alive will be refused. A fine fifty gun ship lies ready at
the Nore, to waft the brave adventurers in military heroism to
the real scenes of action in America, to the scenes of glory,
victory, and triumph. Now is your time for making your
fortunes. Who is there afflicted whom I will not relieve?
The ends of the world are come upon us, and we shall soon
possess them for our own. The completion of the scripture is
at hand. ' Come unto me, all ye that are heavy laden, and I
will relieve you.' Your armor is but light. A rifle barrel,
or a tomahawk, is all you have to bear ; and you have now
your choice of joining with myriads of brave partakers in the
same glorious warfare, by entering into one of the following
regiments : Ticonderoga Pioneers, Schenectady Scalpers, Mohawks, Missalago Hatchetmen, Ohio Scouts, Massachusetts
Minute Men, Scarondarona Split Shirts, Lake Champlain
Pikes, Lake Ontario Jacks, Concord Riflemen, or the General's own Regiment of Alleghany Mountaineers. GOD SAVE
AMERICA ! " [1]

AMERICA is determined and unanimous, a very few Tories
excepted, who will probably soon export themselves. Britain,
at the expense of three millions, has killed one hundred and
fifty Yankees this campaign, which is twenty thousand pounds
a head, and on Bunker's Hill she gained a mile of ground, half
of which she has since lost by not having post on Ploughed
Hill; during the same time sixty thousand children have been
born in America. From this data ——'s excellent mathemati-
cal head will easily calculate the time and expense requisite
to kill us all, and conquer our whole territory.[2]

[1] Constitutional Gazette, September 23.   [2] Clift's Diary.

A JUNTO SONG.[1]

'Tis money makes the member vote
   And sanctifies our ways;
It makes the patriot turn his coat,
   And money we must raise.
        And a taxing we will go, we'll go.

More taxes we must sure impose,
   To raise the civil list;
Also pay our ayes and noes,
   And make opposers hist.

One single thing untaxed at home,
   Old England could not show,
For money we abroad did roam,
   And thought to tax the *new.*

The power supreme of Parliament,
   Our purpose did assist,
And taxing laws abroad were sent,
   Which rebels do resist.

Shall we not make the rascals bend
   To Britain's supreme power?
The sword shall we not to them send,
   And leaden balls a shower?

Boston we shall in ashes lay,
   It is a nest of knaves:
Will make them soon for mercy pray,
   Or send them to their graves.

But second thoughts are ever best,
   And lest our force should fail,
What fraud can do, we'll make a test,
   And see what bribes avail.

Each colony, we will propose,
   Shall raise an ample sum;
Which well applied, under the rose,
   May bribe them—as at home.

We'll force and fraud in one unite,
   To bring them to our hands;
Then lay a tax on the sun's light,
   And king's tax on their lands.[2]

[1] To the tune of "*A begging we will go, will go,*" &c.   [2] Holt's Journal, Sept. 7.

SEPTEMBER 8.—IT is reported and generally believed, that Lord Dunmore is called home, with what view we have not yet learned, but probably it is to render an account of his sagacious and spirited conduct in Virginia, which can hardly fail to attract the attention of Lord North, and the Butonian Junto, so as to have his eminent services recompensed with some higher department in the state, perhaps Lord Dartmouth's. His lordship has this satisfaction upon his departure, that he will leave Virginia with the universal consent of the inhabitants of all ranks and denominations.[1]

SEPTEMBER 11.—THE people of New Hampshire are building a strong fort at Pierce's Island, in Piscataqua river, in order to prevent their capital, the town of Portsmouth, from being attacked by the piratical ships-of-war which now infest this coast.

In the late exploit of cutting down the Liberty Tree in Boston by Gage's men, a soldier in attempting to dismantle it of one of its branches, fell on the pavement, by which he was instantly killed.

General Gage, it is said, has hanged three of the provincials, for breaking open and plundering some of the houses in Boston evacuated by the inhabitants; so that the great thieves, it seems, begin to hang the little ones. O! glorious times indeed! But what then? Why, then the fate of these petty rogues is, in some respects, like that of the little fish that are occasionally devoured to fatten and keep alive the larger ones. Besides, administration have herein verified the ancient aphorism, viz.: *set a rogue to catch a rogue.* Well, what next? Why the next thing is, a short but fervent petition, that Jack Ketch, Esq., might go forward in the business of hanging with despatch, till the world is filled with great thieves as well as little ones.[2]

ONE of the royal sloops at anchor near Norfolk, was lately kept in constant alarm a whole night; with her matches burning, tomkins out, guns loaded with grape shot and all hands

[1] Pennsylvania Journal, Sept. 20.   [2] Constitutional Gazette, Sept. 16.

at their quarters, till day-light discovered the formidable enemy which had caused such terrible apprehensions, to be only one of the neighbors with his negroes catching mullets. The governor, it is said, was sent for, to assist with his sage advice at the council of war that was held on this mighty occasion.[1]

SEPTEMBER 15.—AN officer in Boston, writes thus to his father in London : " Why should I complain of hard fate ? General Gage and his family have for this month past, lived upon salt provisions. Last Saturday, General Putnam in the true style of military complaisance, which abolishes all personal resentment and smooths the horrors of war when discipline will permit, sent a present to the General's lady of a fine fresh quarter of veal, which was very acceptable, and received the return of a very polite card of thanks." [2]

IN a late hurricane at Virginia, it seems Lord Dunmore fared but indifferently, as by some accident or other, occasioned by the confusion in which the sailors were, his lordship fell overboard, and was severely ducked. But according to the old saying : " Those who are born to be hanged, will never be drowned." [3]

SEPTEMBER 17.—LAST week the Reverend Doctor Morrison received a call to the elegant new church in Brattle street, in Boston, vacated by the flight of Doctor Cooper ; and to-day he delivered an excellent discourse to a genteel audience. His discourse tended to show the fatal consequences of sowing sedition and conspiracy among parishioners, which this pulpit has been most wickedly practising ever since the corner-stone was laid.[4]

SEPTEMBER 18.—WE are much astonished at the behavior

---

[1] Pennsylvania Journal, September 13.

[2] Extract from a London paper in the Constitutional Gazette, September 16.

[3] Constitutional Gazette, September 30.

[4] From Draper's Boston News Letter; republished in the Virginia Gazette, of October 28.

of some of those captains of men-of-war, who are stationed upon our coasts. They seem greedily to antici- pate the horror of blood shedding; and although The British Navy. war is not yet proclaimed, nor any hostilities ordered by Parliament against the colonies in general, yet confiding in their strength, they daringly assault our towns, and destroy lives upon the least provocation whatever.

When Porto Bello was restored to the Spaniards, it was agreed that the English should have a free trade there; before some of the people of the town destroyed one of the English vessels there in the night, and murdered the men on board her. When this was known, ships were sent to demand satisfaction, which was refused. Orders were then given to beat down the town. The commander in that service sent a boat on shore to inform the inhabitants of his business, and desire the women and children to remove out of the city. He allowed them a whole day for the purpose—sent ashore again to see if it was done, and then battered down only some of the houses, and a church or two, and that in the day time. Such was the true old British spirit, even when dealing with Spaniards and executing positive orders! How different from this is the conduct of those inhuman commanders now upon our coasts! How detestable their character! A Wallace and an Ayscough disgraced humanity and brought reproach upon the British Navy by wantonly employing it to terrify women and children. But the conduct of a Vandeput is more surprising and cruel than even theirs. They only threatened Captain Vandeput. —he actually fired upon a defenceless town, and his previous preparations showed that he was not actuated by a sense of duty, but by the cold-blooded barbarity of an assassin. He acknowledges in his first letter that he was informed of the design of taking away the cannon from the battery; why then did he not, by a letter to the magistrates, let the city know he esteemed it his duty to defend those guns? In that case the town, apprised of his determination, might have thought it more prudent to desist than to provoke him. But upon his own principle of protecting the battery, what right had he to elevate his guns, and fire heavy balls at random upon the city, a great part of whose inhabitants must consist of children and women. Surely the blood of innocents will rise in judgment against him. It was not owing to his wishes or endeavors, but only to the goodness of Almighty God, that hundreds of men, totally ignorant of what was doing at the battery, were not murdered. O! had this happened in the days of good old King George, that father of his people, it would have cost Vandeput not only his character and his ship, but his head would atone for his horrid barbarity.[1]

SEPTEMBER 19.—THIS morning the mayor of New York informed the committee of safety, that Governor Tryon acquainted him he had received a letter from Lord Dartmouth, informing him that orders had been given to the commanders of his majesty's ships in America, that in case any more troops should be raised, or any fortifications erected, or any of his majesty's stores taken, the commanders of the ships-of-war should consider such cities or places in a state of rebellion.[2]

LAST Saturday night, in Duchess County, New York, James Smith, Esq., a judge of the Court of Common Pleas for that county, was very handsomely tarred and feathered, for acting in open contempt of the resolves of the county committee, as was Coen Smith, of the same place, for the like behavior. They were carted five or six miles into the country. The judge undertook to sue for, and recover the arms taken from the Tories by order of said committee, and actually committed one of the committee, who assisted at disarming the Tories, which enraged the people so much, that they rose and rescued the prisoner, and poured out their resentment on this villanous retailer of the law.[3]

Affair in Duchess County.

THE besieged army in Boston have pulled down a number of houses between the Haymarket and the old fortification;

---

[1] Extract of a letter from Annapolis, Maryland, in the Constitutional Gazette, September 20.

[2] Constitutional Gazette, September 20.   [3] Upcott, iv. 327.

but whether from the want of fuel, or to make room for erecting any new defence, or digging a canal, we have not been able to learn. One of the impressed seamen, who had the good fortune to make their escape from Boston. there last night, says that the sailors on board the men-of-war are very sickly, and almost all of them very feeble and greatly emaciated, owing to bad provisions.

LAST war, thirteen brothers, sons of one woman in the colony of Connecticut, each of them six feet high, all went into the war in defence of their country, and were all brave men. This perhaps is the most remarkable instance of the kind any country hath produced. The name of this prolific and heroic family is HUNTLY.[1]

SEPTEMBER 20.—A SYSTEM of justice similar to that adopted against the devoted town of Boston, is likely to be established in Virginia, by the renowned commander[2] of the Hampton Shipping Seized. fleet there. He has in the course of this week, as a reprisal for the loss of a tender, seized every vessel belonging to Hampton that came within his reach, and thereby rendered himself the terror of all the small craft and fishing boats in this river, especially the latter, having brought some of them under his stern, by a discharge of his cannon at them. He has likewise seized a vessel belonging to the Eastern shore, and having honored the passengers so far with his notice, as to receive them on board his own vessel, took the liberty of sending one of their horses as a present to Lord Dunmore. This act of generosity, we doubt not, will gain him considerable interest with his lordship, it being an instance of his industry in distressing a people, who have of late become obnoxious to his excellency for their spirited behavior. We hope that those who have lived under and enjoyed the blessings of the British Constitution, will not continue tame spectators of such flagrant violations of its most salutary laws in defence of private property. The crimes daily committed by this plunderer, we would not willingly brand with the odious name of piracy,

[1] Gaine's Mercury, October 2.   [2] Captain Squires, of the Otter.

but we are confident they come under those offences to which the English laws have denied the benefit of clergy.[1]

TO THE BOSTON WOMEN.

O Boston wives and maids, draw near and see
Our delicate Souchong and Hyson tea,
Buy it, my charming girls, fair, black, or brown,
If not, we'll cut your throats, and burn your town.[2]

SEPTEMBER 22.—THIS week will ever be remembered as the most remarkable epoch in the annals of this country, for the discovery of the grand repository and dark depositum of Governor Martin's infernal magazine, which in cool deliberation he intended to deal out in weapons of death to the good people of North Carolina.   In the Palace Garden, at Newbern, and under a fine bed of cabbages, was discovered and dug up, a barrel containing about three bushels of gunpowder; in the palace cellar was also dug up, two quarter casks of the same commodity, the casks quite new, and marked, " R. B." In the Palace Garden was also dug up, about one thousand pounds of musket balls, lately cast, and about five hundred pounds of iron swivel balls, a large quantity of small shot, lead, iron worms for the cannon, with swabs, rammers, artillery, boxes, matches, and the whole apparatus for his park artillery which he would certainly have mounted at the palace, had not the appearance of the people of the town of Newbern, on his attempting to move the palace guns, driven him from the trenches before he had made them quite tenable.   'Tis said his excellency, the night before he took his precipitate flight from the palace, buried those engines of death, that they might remain in places of safety till he or his creatures might have an opportunity of using them. The palace cannon were spiked up after his excellency left the palace, by a person who no doubt will be obliged to answer for his conduct.   As it is improbable the governor could procure these deadly weapons without assistance, the committee of

Governor Martin's Magazine.

---

[1] Virginia Gazette, September 23.
[2] From the St. James' Chronicle; Upcott, iv. 339.

the town and county are using their utmost endeavors to discover the authors of so black a treachery.[1]

THE following droll affair lately happened at Kinderhook,
New York. A young fellow, an enemy to the liberties of
America, going to a quilting frolic, where a num-
ber of young women were collected, and he the   Affair at Kinderhook, N. Y.
only man in company, began his aspersions on Congress, as
usual, and held forth some time on the subject, till the girls,
exasperated at his impudence, laid hold of him, stripped him
naked to the waist, and instead of tar, covered him with molasses, and for feathers took the downy tops of flags, which
grow in the meadows, and coated him well and then let him
go. He has prosecuted every one of them, and the matter has
been tried before Justice S——. We have not as yet heard his
worship's judgment. It is said Parson Buel's[2] daughter is
concerned in the affair.[3]

IT is whispered that government has ordered General Gage
to offer five thousand pounds to any person or persons, who

[1] Constitutional Gazette, October 28.
[2] "Parson Buel, during his residence at Southhold, Long Island, was on friendly
and intimate terms with Gov. Tryon, and from his lively disposition, ready wit,
and fondness for the chase, was a favorite with Sir William Erskine, and often
had it in his power to soften the severity of war. Sir William, one Saturday, said
to Mr. Buel, 'I have ordered the people of your parish to appear with their teams
at Southampton to-morrow.' Mr. B. replied, 'I know it, but I, as commander-in-
chief on the Sabbath, have annulled the order.' Sir William did not insist.
"Mr. Buel frequently joined the parties of the British officers, which he en-
livened by humorous anecdotes and agreeable conversation. Once when he was
behind the appointed time for a deer hunt, Sir William had detained the party.
Tired of waiting they had now mounted, when seeing his friend Buel approaching,
he ordered his men to dismount to receive him. Lord Percy, an aid, while im-
patiently pacing the floor, was introduced to Mr. Buel, who thereupon asked him
what portion of his majesty's forces he had the honor to command? 'A legion
of devils just from hell.' 'Then,' said Mr. Buel, with a low bow, 'I suppose I
have the honor of addressing Beelzebub, the prince of devils!' His lordship
put his hand on his sword. This was rebuked by Sir William, and the laugh
turned on Percy, who after a while was restored to good humor by the marked
attention of the parson."—*Holmes' Annals.*
[3] Gould's Diary; Gaine's Mercury, October 2.

will bring him General Putnam's head; this has been privately communicated to most of the royalists in and about Boston, who can be confided in.[1]

A few days since the authority of Portsmouth, in New Hampshire, disarmed all those persons in that town called *Tories disarmed in Portsmouth, N. H.* Tories, including crown officers, who would not declare their readiness to use their arms in the present contest in favor of the United Colonies. The Sandamanians[2] urged their religious principles in excuse for their not taking up arms, which as tending to affect a revolution they could not conscientiously do; but declared their intention of peaceably submitting to whatever government might be established.

September 30.—That grand rebel to his king and country, Thomas Gage, and his desperate band of traitors and military butchers, intends raising a regiment of " loyal fencible Americans; " the command of which is already given to one Gorham, who served last war in America. We are told that some head Tories, a few negroes, and convicts, have already enlisted. Whether a regiment of such beings can be called " loyal fencible Americans," the world can judge. We are likewise informed by a Boston paper, that regiments similar to the above are forming in the other colonies. Yes, ye Judases! for your consolation we would inform you that (exclusive of our army in camp) regiments of truly " loyal fencible Americans," are now raising in all the colonies from Nova Scotia to the Floridas, who are determined to defend their liberties and properties; and to resist, whilst life lasts, the tyranny of your master, the devil, whose chief vicegerents in the British dominions are Bute and North. Rebels! remember, that Americans revere their king while he governs righteously—they love

---

[1] Constitutional Gazette, October 4.

[2] The followers of Robert Sandeman, a native of Perth, in Scotland, who came to America in the fall of 1764, and settled at Danbury, Connecticut, where he gathered a church in July of the year following. He was the author of the answer to Hervey's Theron and Aspasia.

their country, and are ready to bleed in its behalf. But ye, ye butchers! disgrace your king, and millions yet unborn will curse your memory.[1]

THIS afternoon, between two and three o'clock, an officer at the head of a party of marines and sailors landed at the County Wharf, in Norfolk, in Virginia, under cover of the men-of-war, who made every appearance of firing on the town, should the party be molested, and marched up the main street to Mr. Holt's printing-office, from whence they carried off the types, and sundry other printing implements, with two of the workmen, and, after getting to the water-side with their booty, gave three cheers, in which they were joined by a crowd of rascally negroes. A few spirited gentlemen in Norfolk, justly incensed at so flagrant a breach of good order and the constitution, and highly resenting the conduct of Lord Dunmore and the navy gentry, who have now commenced to be downright pirates and banditti, ordered the drums to beat to arms, but were joined by very few; so that it appears Norfolk is, at present, a very insecure place for the life or property of any individual, and is consequently deserted daily by numbers of the inhabitants, with their effects.

Lord Dunmore is exceedingly offended with the Virginia printers, for presuming to furnish the public with a faithful relation of occurrences, and now and then, making a few strictures upon his lordship's own conduct, as well as that of some of his delightful associates, such as Dicky Squire and little white-headed Montagu.[2] Some of their actions have certainly deserved the severest reprehension, to say no more; for which the printers appeal to the whole world, even Freddy North himself, and the immaculate Johnny Bute. It seems his lordship has it much at heart to destroy every channel of public intelligence that is inimical to his designs upon the liberties of this country, alleging that they poison the minds of the people; or, in other words, lay open to them the tyrannical de-

[1] Constitutional Gazette, October 7.
[2] Commanders of the British ships at Virginia.

signs of a wicked ministry, which hath been supported in character by most of their slavish dependents. It is to be hoped, however, that neither his lordship, nor any other person, however dignified, will have it in his power to succeed in so diabolical a scheme, only fit to be accomplished among Turks, and never could have been devised but by a person of the most unfriendly principles to the liberties of mankind.[2]

THE following is said to be the plan which will be put in execution for reducing America:—Ten thousand Hanoverians are to be taken into British pay, the expenses to be defrayed out of duties to be laid by parliament, and levied in America. This body of men is to be stationed in several parts of that continent, and to be kept on foot in peace as well as in war. Fortresses are to be built in the provinces of New England, New York, Pennsylvania, and Virginia, in which those foreign mercenaries are to be stationed, and accommodated with barracks, firing, etc., at the expense of the several colonies in which they shall happen to be quartered. Besides this, a fleet of five ships of the line and twenty frigates are always to be stationed in that service, both to prevent smuggling, and, in case of any disturbance, to be ready to co-operate in reducing the rebellious or disaffected to obedience. Every Hanoverian soldier, who shall have served seven years with the approbation of his superior officer or officers, shall have a portion of ground, not more than fifty nor less than twenty acres, rent free, forever. The expense of raising a proper habitation, furnishing same, purchasing implements of husbandry, etc., to be defrayed by the colony in which he shall be then resident. The whole expense of recruiting to be provided for in like manner—that is to say, fifty pounds for every soldier, and one hundred for every trooper, rating his horse at fifty and himself at as much more. This mercenary army is to consist of thirty battalions of infantry, of five hundred men each, and four regiments of cavalry; twenty battalions and two regiments of which are always to be stationed in the four New England provinces, and the remaining ten battalions and two regiments at New York, Philadelphia, and Williamsburg in Virginia, and their neighborhoods. On the whole, as the Germans are known to be a very prolific people, it is supposed that by the beginning of the year 1800, there will be no less than a million of that nation, including their offspring, within the four New England provinces alone.[1]

OCTOBER 2.—THIS evening were married at Union Hill, in the borough of Westchester, New York, John Watts, junior, Esq., recorder of New York, to Miss Jane De Lancey; and Thomas H. Barclay, Esq., to Miss Susanna De Lancey, daughters of the late Peter De Lancey, Esq.

> "Round their nuptial beds,
> Hovering with purple wings, th' Idalian boy
> Shook from his radiant torch, the blissful fires
> Of innocent desires,
> While Venus scatter'd myrtles."[2]

THIS evening arrived in the Piscataqua river a ship from England intended for Boston. It appears that yesterday she was in company with the Raven man-of-war, bound to the same place, but parted with her in the night. Meeting a fisherman at the eastward of Cape Ann, the captain inquired the course to Boston. The honest fisherman, pointing towards the Piscataqua, said, "There is Boston." The crew shaped their course accordingly, and soon found themselves under the guns of a battery lately erected by the people of New Hampshire. The commander of the battery, with a number of men, very humanely went on board to pilot the ship up to Portsmouth. "I cannot go there," said the captain of the ship, "I am bound to Boston." "But you must," replied the other. Then he ordered her to get under way, and soon carried her safe alongside a wharf, where she is taken proper care of. She has been out eleven weeks from Bristol, in England, and has on board eighteen hundred bar-

Piscataqua Prize.

[1] Constitutional Gazette, September 30.   [2] Rivington's Gazetteer, Oct. 5.

rels, and four hundred half barrels, of flour, intended for the use of the besieged army in Boston.[1]

THE AMERICAN EXPEDITION.

Our political wrongheads, to show themselves frantic,
Would extend the excise laws beyond th' Atlantic;
Those they sent were oppos'd with American rage,
For a general excise is a General Gage.
But though gaging did plainly appear their intentions,
They were quite unacquainted with foreign dimensions;
As different as English and Frenchmen's apparels,
For instead of *plain casks* they were all *rifle barrels*,
With such potent contents, as their parties deploring,
For it's laid them at rest, *where they sleep without snoring.*
Keep! Putnam! one peal of Bostonian thunder!
That some here may atone for the national plunder.
Do thou, Lord of hosts! send such surgeons to bleed 'em,
And deal thus with the foes to American freedom.
This, this is the prayer of all virtuous, good men,
And the venal alone will refuse their Amen.

OCTOBER 3.—THE thanks of the worthy New York Sons of Liberty, in solemn congress assembled, were this night voted, and unanimously allowed to be justly due to Mr. Jacob Vredenburgh, *barber*, for his firm, spirited, and *patriotic* conduct in refusing to complete an operation vulgarly called SHAVING, which he had begun on the face of Captain John Croser, commander of the Empress of Russia, one of his Majesty's transports, now lying in the river; but most fortunately and providentially was informed of the identity of the gentleman's person when he had about half finished the job.

Vredenburgh the Barber.

It is most devoutly to be wished that all gentlemen of the razor will follow this wise, prudent, interesting, and praiseworthy example, so steadily, that every person who pays due allegiance to his Majesty, and wishes peace, happiness, and unanimity to the colonies, may have his beard to grow as long as ever was king Nebuchadnezzar's.[3]

[1] Holt's Journal, October 12.
[2] From the London Evening Post, republished in Holt's Journal, October 5.
[3] Upcott, iv. 333.

WE are not a little cheered to hear our grievances exciting sympathy in England. At a dinner given by the Lord Mayor to the freeholders of Middlesex, at the George, at Cheswick, several loyal toasts were drank, among English Sympathy which were the following: "General Putnam and all those American heroes who, like men, nobly prefer death to slavery and chains."—"To him who risks his life in support of a good government, and would in opposition to a bad one."—"Messrs. Hancock and Adams, and all our worthy fellow-subjects in America, who are nobly contending for our rights with their own." [1]

THE DILEMMA.

In ev'ry civil war this hazard's run :
" Conquer thou'rt ruin'd ; conquer'd thou'rt undone."
Who gives the advice, shows wondrous want of skill,
But those who follow it are weaker still.
Of understanding is not he bereft,
Whose right hand is employed to maim his left? [3]

OCTOBER 4.—A CORRESPONDENT at London says, " It is under consideration to form a parliament, or general council, for all the provinces in America, something similar to that of Ireland; the governors and some partic- An American Parliament. ular officers to form an upper house."—With due thanks to our aged mother, now debilitated in her mental faculties, for her solicitude in forming a government for us; we would desire her to spare herself that trouble. We, being now of age to manage our own business, shall take care to form a government for ourselves, in which we want no one to interpose, though we shall always have a dutiful regard to our mother, desire to be upon good terms with her, and render her all the help that is consistent with the necessary care of our freedom and interest—which is as much as any reasonable, affectionate mother can expect or desire. [3]

---

[1] Pennsylvania Journal, October 4.   [2] Constitutional Gazette, October 4.
[3] Holt's Journal, October 5.

OCTOBER 6.—THE infamous Dr. Kearsley of Philadelphia, not content with his late triumphal procession for his enmity to this country, has made a further attempt to injure it, but to-day was happily discovered.

Doctor Kearsley.

Some letters of his were intercepted in a vessel bound from here to London, which were filled with the most villanous invectives and scandalous misrepresentations of the first characters in this country, and the public proceedings.

This so enraged the people in general, that if it had not been for the humanity of some gentlemen who conducted him to gaol, he would possibly have been very roughly handled. He is as sulky as when exalted on the cart, glories in the mischief he still hopes to do this country, and refuses to give any satisfaction.

This ungrateful son of Galen has acquired a considerable fortune by his practice in Philadelphia, and in manufacturing Keyser's Pills, which are sold for genuine by a certain Tory bibliopolist[1] in a neighboring province.[2]

OCTOBER 8.—YESTERDAY afternoon appeared in sight of Bristol harbor[3] a very formidable fleet, consisting of sixteen sail, viz. : three men-of-war, one bomb ketch, and other armed vessels, all of which, excepting the Glasgow, which ran ashore at Papaquash point, drew up in a line of battle from one end of the town to the other. Soon after they had moored, a barge came from the Rose to the head of a wharf, with the lieutenant, who asked if there were any gentlemen on the wharf? William Bradford being present, answered yes ; whereupon the lieutenant informed him Captain Wallace had a demand to make on the town, and desired that two or three of the principal men, or magistrates, of the town, would go on board his ship, within an hour, and hear his proposals ; otherwise hostilities would be commenced against the

Bristol Bombarded.

---

[1] Hugh Gaine, the publisher of the New York Gazette and Weekly Mercury.

[2] Constitutional Gazette, October 14 and 21 :—We hear Dr. John Kearsley is sentenced to be imprisoned for a limited time in the back counties of Pennsylvania, for high crimes against this country.

[3] In Rhode Island.

town. The above gentleman replied, as a magistrate, that, in his opinion, Captain Wallace was under a greater obligation to come ashore and make his demands known to the town, than for the magistrates to go on board his ship to hear them ; and added, that if Captain Wallace would come to the head of the wharf the next morning, he should be treated as a gentleman, and the town would consider of his demands. With this answer the lieutenant returned on board the Rose. The inhabitants being made acquainted with the above association, repaired to the wharf and waited with the utmost impatience for a reply from Captain Wallace, till an hour had expired, when the whole fleet began a most heavy cannonading, and the bomb vessel to bombard and heave shells and carcases into the town ; which continued, without intermission an hour and a half.

In the mean time, Colonel Potter, in the hottest of the fire, went upon the head of the wharf, hailed the Rose, went on board, and requested a cessation of hostilities, till the inhabitants might choose a committee to go on board and treat with Captain Wallace ; which request was complied with ; and six hours were allowed for the above purpose. Colonel Potter returned and made a report to the committee of inspection, who chose a select committee to hear Captain Wallace's demands, which, after they had gone on board, Captain Wallace informed them were a supply of two hundred sheep and thirty fat cattle. This demand, the committee replied, it was impossible to comply with ; for the country people had been in and driven off their stock, saving a few sheep and some milch cows.

After some hours had expired, during the negotiation, without coming to any agreement, Captain Wallace told them : " I have this one proposal to make : if you will promise to supply me with forty sheep, at or before twelve o'clock, I will assure you that another gun shall not be discharged." The committee, seeing themselves reduced to the distressing alternative, either to supply their most inveterate enemy with provisions, or to devote to the flames the town, with all the goods, besides near one hundred sick persons, who could not be removed without the utmost hazard of their lives ; I say, seeing themselves reduced to this dreadful dilemma of two evils, reluctantly chose the least, by agreeing to supply them with forty sheep at the time appointed, which was punctually performed.

The Reverend Mr. John Burt, having been confined to his house by the camp distemper, when the cannonading began, left his habitation to seek some place of safety, and to-day was found dead in a neighboring field.[1] It is conjectured that, being overcome with fear and fatigue, he fell down and was unable to raise himself up, and so expired. A child of Captain Timothy Ingraham, having been removed in the rain, is also dead.

What equally challenges our admiration and gratitude to God is, that no more lives were lost, or persons hurt, by such an incessant and hot fire ; the streets being full of men, women, and children, the whole time. The shrieks of the women, the cries of the children, and groans of the sick, would have extorted a tear from even the eye of a Nero.[2]

LORD WILLIAM CAMPBELL, Governor of South Carolina, has fled with the utmost precipitation on board the man-of-war in the harbor ; the committee of Charleston having

Lord William Campbell.

very fortunately discovered that his excellency had employed one Cameron, an Indian commissary in the interior parts of that province, to engage the Indians in the ministerial service. He had actually enlisted six hundred of them, and furnished them with every necessary in order to butcher the inhabitants of the back country. This plan was discovered by a gentleman who seized the express on its way from said Cameron to the Governor, whom he knew to be disaffected to the American cause, and conveyed the despatches

---

[1] The Reverend Mr. Burt was born in Boston, and received a liberal education at Harvard College, graduating from that institution in 1736. He was, on the 13th of May, 1741, ordained pastor of the Congregational Church in Bristol, where he labored in the work of the ministry thirty-four years. He was a gentleman of a respectable character.—*Gaine's Mercury*, October 23.

[2] Extract of a letter from Bristol, in the New York Gazette, October 23.

to the provincial committee. The gentleman disguised himself in a drover's habit, and attended the express to the governor's house, heard the conversation between them, and then discovered the whole plot to the committee.[1]

OCTOBER 12.—LAST Tuesday, one of the privateers from Beverly, Massachusetts, having been on a cruise in the bay, was followed, on her return into port, by the Nautilus man-of-war. The privateer ran aground *Beverly Privateers.* in a cove a little without Beverly harbor, where the people speedily assembled, stripped her, and carried her guns, etc., ashore. The man-of-war was soon within gun-shot, when she also got aground; she, however, let go an anchor, and bringing her broadside to bear, began to fire upon the privateer. The people of Salem and Beverly soon returned the compliment from a number of cannon on shore, keeping up a warm and well-directed fire on the man-of-war for two or three hours, and it is supposed did her considerable damage, and probably killed and wounded some of her men; but before they could board her, which they were preparing to do, the tide arose (about eight o'clock in the evening), when she cut her cable and got off. Some of her shot struck one or two buildings in Beverly; but no lives were lost, and the privateer damaged very little, if any.[2]

IT is said General Gage has actually sailed from Boston for England:—General Howe, since he took command of the *butchering army*, in order to show his skill in the art *militaire*, on Friday last began a smart cannonade, when ninety-three shot were fired from the several batteries at Boston on the army at Roxbury, without doing any other damage than wounding one man in the arm and killing two cows.[3]

A PARTY of young men in London lately went to one of the temporary cook-shops in Covent Garden, when one of them

---

[1] Gaine's Mercury, October 9.   [2] Rivington's Gazetteer, October 19.
[3] Holt's Journal, October 19, and Pennsylvania Journal, October 18.

said to his companions :—" I'll show you how the Americans intend to serve Boston. You must suppose that pan over the charcoal fire to be the town, and the sausages in it to be General Gage and the king's troops ; and then," says he, " they will be served thus "—when he threw a paper with some gunpowder in it under the pan, which immediately blew the sausages, etc., into the air. " There," cries he, " now you may see where Boston is, and also how the Americans will leave General Gage and his soldiers to fly without wings ! " He then gave the woman a guinea for the loss of her goods, and left her very well satisfied about the matter.[1]

OCTOBER 19.—YESTERDAY, at New York, departed this life, of a fever, Michael Cresap, Esq., eldest son of Colonel Thomas
Death of Captain Cresap, of Potomac, in Virginia, in the twenty-
Cresap. eighth year of his age. He was captain of a rifle company now in the continental army before Boston. He served as a captain under the command of Lord Dunmore, in the late expedition against the Indians, in which he eminently distinguished himself, by his prudence, firmness, and intrepidity, as a brave officer ; and in the present contest between the parent state and the colonies, gave proofs of his attachment to the rights and liberties of his country. He has left a widow and four children to deplore the loss of a husband and a father ; and by his death his country is deprived of a worthy and esteemed citizen. To-day he was interred at Trinity Church. His funeral was attended from his lodgings by the independent companies of militia, and the most respectable inhabitants, through the principal streets to the church. The grenadiers of the first battalion fired three volleys over his grave. The whole was conducted with great decency, and in military form.[2]

BY accounts from Canada we learn, that on the twenty-fifth of September last, Colonel Ethan Allen, prompted by ambi-
Allen taken tion, had imprudently, without orders, crossed
Prisoner. over from Longueuil with thirty of his own men

---

[1] Virginia Gazette, October 28.
[2] Rivington's Gazetteer, October 26, and Constitutional Gazette, October 23.

and fifty Canadians, in order to get possession of Montreal. Colonel Prescot, hearing of his coming, engaged a number of people from the suburbs, at half a joe per man, to join a party of regulars from the garrison, and to go out against him. They met about two miles from the town, when a smart engagement ensued, which lasted upwards of two hours. The enemy had two field-pieces. After a long engagement, the Americans were obliged to retire. Colonel Allen and two or three of his men were taken prisoners, and about as many were wounded; the rest returned to their friends. By the best accounts we learn that a considerable number of the regulars were killed and wounded.[1]

THIS morning news came in from Marblehead, that a small vessel, sent from Boston to New Providence, in the Bahamas, for fruit and turtle, and having one hundred and twenty of the latter on board, came either accidentally or designedly to Marblehead, where they were all seized, and are now on the road to Cambridge. What a baulk to the poor regulars, and what vexation to them to think the Yankees should regale on what they themselves had already feasted on in imagination.[2]

AN English paper says: "As every rebel who is taken prisoner in America has incurred the pain of death by the law martial, it is said government will charter several transports, after their arrival in Boston, to convey the culprits to the East Indies for the Company's service; as it

Punishment for the Rebels.

---

[1] New York Gazette, October 23:—A correspondent says, "The expedition was a thing of the colonel's own head, without orders from the general; * and from whom, as well as others, he receives much censure. If they had been apprised of it, they could have put him in a situation to have succeeded without much danger. But Allen is a high flying genius, pursues every scheme on its first impression, without consideration, and much less judgment. It was with the utmost difficulty, and through the greatest entreaty, that General Schuyler permitted him to go with the army, knowing his natural disposition; and, indeed, his fears have proved not groundless, and though trifling our loss, and the detachment, yet it gives a check to our progress."—New England Chronicle, November 2.

[2] Pennsylvania Journal, October 18.

* General Montgomery.

is the intention of the government to punish only the ringleaders and commanders *capitally*, and to suffer the inferior rebels
to redeem their lives by entering into the East India Company's
service. This translation will only render them more useful
subjects than in their native country."—How these traitors ar-
rogantly presume upon the execution of their schemes of villany, as if they possessed a real omnipotence, and could command future events.[1]

THE London Morning Chronicle,[2] contains the following
lines, on taking the fort and stores at Ticonderoga by the provincials :

> BRAVE race of men ! that lately shewed,
> The British fire in you renewed ;
> May God your land secure defend !
> (Your constant guardian, your best friend,)
> Unite your hearts, your counsels bless,
> And grant your just designs success.[3]

OCTOBER 24.—LAST Sunday, died of an apoplectic stroke,
at Philadelphia, in the sixty-third year of his age, the Hon.
Peyton Randolph, Esq., of Virginia, late President of the Continental Congress, and Speaker of
the House of Burgesses in Virginia ; a gentleman who possessed
the virtues of humanity in an eminent degree, and, joining
with them the strongest judgment, was the delight of his
friends in private life, and a most valuable member of society ;
having long filled, and with great ability and integrity discharged, the most honorable public trusts. To the truth of
this his family, his friends, and his country bear mournful testimony. This afternoon his remains were removed from Mr.
Benjamin Randolph's to Christ Church, where an excellent
sermon on the mournful occasion was preached by the Rev.
Mr. Duche, after which the corpse was carried to the burial-
ground, and deposited in a vault till it can be conveyed to
Virginia.[4]

Death of Peyton Randolph.

[1] Holt's Journal, October 19.   [2] Of July 14, 1775.
[3] Virginia Gazette, October 28.   [4] Pennsylvania Journal, October 25.

OCTOBER 28.—CAPTAIN BARNES'S sloop, one of the four prizes taken by the Viper sloop-of-war, some time ago, has been retaken by the following stratagem : A midshipman and four men from the Viper were put on board, Barnes's Sloop. with two of Captain Barnes's crew, and the master of another vessel, lately taken by the enemy, was shipped as a pilot. Their orders were to carry the vessel to Boston, but, if separated from the others, to take her into Newport. They parted the first night, and the night following made Rhode Island. The pilot was carrying her in at the east side, and on the midshipman's expressing his surprise at not seeing the lighthouse, he was informed that the sons of liberty had burned it. They soon came to an anchor at Howland's ferry ; the midshipman inquired for the man-of-war, when the pilot, pointing to the lights on the shore, told him they were the ships. Early next morning the pilot, assisted by Captain Barnes, nailed up the companion door, and beckoned a number of people on board from the shore, who released the pirates from their confinement, and conducted them to head-quarters on the island ; from whence they were carried to Providence and safely lodged in gaol.[1]

AFTER Lord Dunmore, with his troops and navy, had been for several weeks seizing the persons and property of his Majesty's peaceable subjects in Virginia, on Wednesday night last (25th) a party from an armed tender Hampton, Va., threatened. landed near Hampton, and took away a valuable negro man slave and a sail from the owner ; next morning there appeared off the mouth of Hampton river a large armed schooner, a sloop, and three tenders, with soldiers on board, and a message was received at Hampton from Captain Squires, on board the schooner, that he would that day land and burn the town ; on which a company of regulars and a company of minute men, who had been placed there in consequence of former threats denounced against that place, made the best disposition to prevent their landing, aided by a body of militia who were suddenly called together on the occasion. The enemy accordingly

---

[1] Constitutional Gazette, November 8.

attempted to land, but were retarded by some boats sunk across the channel for that purpose; upon this they fired several small cannon at the provincials, without any effect, who, in return, discharged their small arms so effectually, as to make the enemy move off, with the loss of several men, as it is believed; but they had, in the mean time, burnt down a house belonging to a Mr. Cooper, on that river.

On intelligence of this reaching Williamsburg, about nine at night, a company of riflemen were despatched to the aid of Hampton, and the colonel of the second regiment sent to take the command of the whole; who with the company, arrived about eight o'clock next morning. The enemy had, in the night, cut through the sunken boats and made a passage for their vessels, which were drawn up close to the town, and began to fire upon it soon after the arrival of the party from Williamsburg; but as soon as our men were so disposed as to give them a few shot, they went off so hastily that our people took a small tender with five white men, a woman, and two slaves, six swivels, seven muskets, some small arms and other things, a sword, pistols, and several papers belonging to a Lieutenant Wright, who made his escape by jumping overboard and swimming away, with Mr. King's negro man. They are on shore, and a pursuit, it is hoped, may overtake them. There were in the vessel two men mortally wounded; one is since dead and the other near his end; besides which, nine men were seen to be thrown overboard from one of the vessels. We had not a man even wounded. The vessels went over to Norfolk, and the whole force from thence is intending to visit Hampton to-day. If they come, we hope our brave troops will be prepared for them.[1]

"The memory of the just is blessed."

ON the morning of the twenty-fourth instant, departed this life, at Philadelphia, in the seventy-second year of her age, in certain hope of a joyful resurrection, Sarah Morris, an eminent minister among the people called Quakers.

[1] Rivington's Gazetteer, November 9.

Her life and conversation were uniformly consistent with her Christian profession, adorning the doctrine she preached. Cheerful without gaiety, serious without austerity, and pious without affectation, she was an ornament to society and the delight of her friends and acquaintance, whose affliction for their loss can only be alleviated by an assurance that it is her great gain. A long and painful illness she bore with the fortitude and resignation becoming a Christian, whose expectations of enduring happiness were fixed on that foundation which standeth sure.[1]

A short time before the skirmish at Concord, Massachusetts, the officers of the army, being highly incensed by the inhabitants of Boston, from the many insults which had been offered them, and exasperated by the many inflammatory preachings and orations delivered from the pulpit, resolved privately to take an opportunity to seize the promoters of these discourses, the principals of which were Adams, Hancock, and Doctor Warren. The scheme was now laid, and the young man fixed upon to carry it into execution was an ensign in the army, who was to give the signal to the rest, distributed about the church, by throwing an egg at Doctor Warren in the pulpit. However, this scheme was rendered abortive, in the most whimsical manner, for he who was deputed to throw the egg fell in going to the church, dislocated his knee, and broke the egg, by which means the scheme failed, and the skirmish at Concord happening within a few days, these worthy patriots of their country retired to Roxbury.[2]

[1] Pennsylvania Packet, October 30.
[2] Extract from a London paper in the Virginia Gazette, December 2.—See page 34, ante.

CHAPTER IV.

NOVEMBER 1.—COLONEL ALLEN's misfortune happened by
reason of his not being joined by four hundred men, which,
undoubtedly, would have enabled him to have
withstood the party that attacked him, they being
only three hundred strong. Colonel Allen withstood them an
hour and a quarter, with only about forty men, exclusive of
seventy Canadians. When the party from Montreal was
marching down to give Colonel Allen battle, he retreated to an
advantageous spot of ground, where he made a stand, and soon
saw a party of men filing off to surround him, whereupon he
sent off about half his men, under the command of Captain
Youngs, to annoy them; but neither Youngs nor any of his
party ever fired a gun, for reasons best known to themselves,
and Allen was left with about thirty-five men, as most of the
Canadians left him on the first fire from the enemy. Allen
had but one man killed in the skirmish—seventeen of the enemy were killed; among whom are Major Carden, who commanded the party, and several principal Tory merchants of
Montreal. Several Canadians were taken prisoners with Colonel Allen, whom the regular officers said they would put to
death; on which Allen stepped up, opened his breast, and said
the Canadians were not to blame; that he brought them there,
and if anybody must be murdered, let it be him. This got
him great credit with all the officers at Montreal, and Carleton
himself said it was a pity a man of Allen's spirit should be
engaged in so bad a cause, as he calls it. Colonel Allen is
prisoner on board the Gaspee brig, before Montreal. General

Ethan Allen.

Schuyler has offered to give up any officer he has, in exchange for him, but has not yet received an answer.[1]

NEARLY all the people belonging to Cape Ann, in Massachusetts, have evacuated the town, and have proceeded so far in removing their effects, as to take away the glass windows from the meeting-house and many Cape Ann. of the dwelling-houses. Lieutenant-colonel Mason, of the artillery, has been down from Cambridge to give directions in fortifying the harbor, where two batteries are already erected, and other measures taken for giving the enemy a proper reception.

WE hear that Mr. Samuel Hodgdon, within a month past, had a child baptized in *Boston*, by the Rev. Dr. Mather, by the name of SAMUEL ADAMS; and last Sabbath was baptized, by the Rev. Mr. French, at Andover, a child of Nathanael Appleton, Esq., by the name of George Washington.[2]

NOVEMBER 7.—THE province of New Hampshire has asked advice of the Congress relative to assuming government. The Congress advised the Provincial Convention to New Hampshire
asks Advice. grant warrants for a free and full election of representatives of the colony, who, if they think it necessary, are to choose such a form of government as they, in their judgment, shall think will best promote the happiness of the people, and preserve peace and good order during the present dispute with Great Britain. The same advice was given to South Carolina, and in a few months we hope every colony will be perfectly free.[3]

THIS day Lord Dunmore[4] issued the following proclamation,

[1] Extract of a letter from camp before St. John's, in the Constitutional Gazette, November 29.

[2] New England Chronicle, November 2.

[3] Extract of a letter from Philadelphia, in the Constitutional Gazette, December 6.

[4] His title was JOHN, EARL OF DUNMORE, his Majesty's Lieutenant and Governor-General of the colony and dominion of Virginia, and Vice-Admiral of the same.

from his retreat on board the war-ship William, now at anchor
Dunmore's   off Norfolk, Virginia. It at once shows the
Proclamation. baseness of his heart, his malice and treachery
against the people who were once under his government, and
his officious violation of all law, justice, and humanity ; not to
mention his arrogating to himself a power which neither he
can assume, nor any power upon earth invest him with.

> Not in the legions
> Of horrid hell, can come a devil more damned,
> In evils, to top Dunmore!

" A PROCLAMATION :—As I have ever entertained hopes that
an accommodation might have taken place between Great
Britain and this colony, without being compelled, by my duty,
to this most disagreeable, but now absolutely necessary step ;
rendered so by a body of armed men, unlawfully assembled,
firing upon his Majesty's tenders ; and the formation of an
army, and that army now on their way to attack his Majesty's
troops and destroy the well-disposed subjects of this country.
To defeat such treasonable purposes, and that all such traitors and their abettors may be brought to justice, and that the
peace and good order of this colony may be again restored,
which the ordinary course of the civil law is unable to effect ;
I have thought fit to issue this, my proclamation, hereby declaring, that until the aforesaid good purposes can be obtained,
I do, in virtue of the power and authority to me given by his
Majesty, determine to execute martial law, and cause the same
to be executed throughout this colony ; and to the end that
peace and good order may the sooner be restored, I do require
every person capable of bearing arms to resort to his Majesty's
STANDARD, or be looked upon as a traitor to his crown and
government, and thereby become liable to the penalty the law
inflicts upon such offences, such as forfeiture of life, confiscation of lands, etc., etc. And I do hereby further declare all
indentured servants, negroes, or others, appertaining to rebels,
FREE, that are willing and able to bear arms ; they joining his
Majesty's troops, as soon as may be, for the purpose of re-

ducing this colony to a proper sense of their duty to his Majesty's crown and dignity.   I do further order and require, all his Majesty's liege subjects to retain their quit rents, or any other taxes due, or that may become due, in their own custody, till such time as peace be again restored to this at present most unhappy country, or demanded of them, for their former salutary purposes, by officers properly authorized to receive the same." [1]

It is necessary, for the welfare of two sorts of people, that the appearance of this proclamation should be attended with some comment.   Such as have mixed much in society, and have had opportunities of hearing the subject of the present unnatural contest discussed, will be but little startled at the appellation of *rebel*, because they will know it is not merited.   But others there may be, whose circumstances may, in a great measure, have excluded them from the knowledge of public matters, who may be sincerely attached to the interest of their country, and who may yet be frightened to act against it, from the dread of incurring a guilt which, by all good men, is justly abhorred.   To these, it may be proper to address a few remarks upon this proclamation; and, as a part of it respects the negroes, and seems to offer something very flattering and desirable to them, it may be doing them, as well as the country, a service, to give them a just view of what they are to expect, should they be so weak and wicked as to comply with what Lord Dunmore requires.   Those, then, who are afraid of being styled *rebels*, we would beg to consider, that although Lord Dunmore, in this proclamation, insidiously mentions his having till now entertained hopes of an accommodation, yet the whole tenor of his conduct, for many months past, has had the most direct and strongest tendency to widen the unhappy breach, and render a reconciliation more difficult.   ·For what other purpose did he write his false and inflammatory letters to the ministers of state?   Why did he, under cover of the night, take from us our powder, and render useless the arms of our public magazine?   Why did he secretly and treacherously lay snares for the lives of our unwary

Remarks on Lord Dunmore's Proclamation.

---

[1] Pennsylvania Journal, December 6.

brethren ; snares that had likely to have proved but too effectual ? [1] Why did he, under idle pretences, withdraw himself from the seat of government, where alone he could, had he been willing, have done essential service to our country? Why, by his authority, have continual depredations been since made upon such of our countrymen as are situated within the reach of ships-of-war and tenders? Why have our towns been attacked, and houses destroyed? Why have the persons of many of our most respectable brethren been seized upon, torn from all their connections, and confined on board of ships? Was all this to bring about a reconciliation? Judge for yourselves, whether the injuring of our persons and properties be the readiest way to gain our affections. After insulting our persons, he now presumes to insult our understandings also. Do not believe his words, when his actions so directly contradict them. If he wished for an accommodation ; if he had a desire to restore peace and order, as he professes, it was to be upon terms that would have been disgraceful, and, in the end, destructive of every thing dear and valuable.

Consider, again, the many attempts that have been made to enslave us. Nature gave us equal privileges with the people of Great Britain : we are equally, with them, entitled to the disposal of our own property ; and we have never resigned to them those rights, which we derived from nature. But they have endeavored, unjustly, to rob us of them. They have made acts of parliament, in which we in no manner concurred, which dispose of our property ; acts which abridge us of liberties we once enjoyed, and which impose burdens and restraints upon us too heavy to be borne. Had we immediately taken

[1] In the night of Saturday, (June 3, 1775,) some young men got into the public magazine in Williamsburg, Virginia, intending to furnish themselves with arms, but were soon surprised by the report of a gun, which was so artfully placed, (said to be contrived by Lord Dunmore,) that upon touching a string that was in their way, it went off, and wounded three persons, but not mortally. One of them was terribly hurt by several small balls that entered his arm and shoulder ; another, by the loss of two fingers of his right hand, rendered incapable of following his profession for subsistence ; the other wounded very slightly. There were two guns prepared for this horrid purpose, one of which was brought out the next morning and found to be double charged.—*Holt's Journal*, June 22.

up arms to assert our rights, and to prevent the exercise of unlawful power, though our cause would have been just, yet our
conduct would have been precipitate, and, so far, blamable.
We might then, with some shadow of justice, have been
charged with *rebellion*, or a disposition to rebel. But this was
not the way we behaved. We petitioned once and again, in
the most dutiful manner; we hoped the righteousness of
our cause would appear, that our complaints would be heard
and attended to; we wished to avoid the horrors of a civil
war, and so long proceeded in this fruitless track, that our not
adopting a more vigorous opposition seemed rather to proceed
from a spirit of meanness and fear than of peace and loyalty;
and all that we gained was, to be more grievously oppressed.
At length we resolved to withhold our commerce from Great
Britain, and, by thus affecting her interest, oblige her to redress our grievances. But in this also we have been disappointed. Our associations have been deemed unlawful combinations, and opposition to government. We have been entirely
deprived of our trade to foreign countries, and even amongst
ourselves, and fleets and armies have been sent to reduce us to
a compliance with the unjust and arbitrary demands of the
British minister and corrupt parliament. Reduced to such
circumstances, to what could we have recourse but to arms?
Every other expedient having been tried and found ineffectual,
this alone was left, and this we have, at last, unwillingly
adopted. If it be *rebellion* to take up arms in such a cause as
this, rebellion, then, is not only justifiable, but an honorable
thing.

But let us not be deceived with empty sounds. They who
call us rebels cannot make us so. Rebellion is open, and
avows opposition to lawful authority; but it is usurped and
arbitrary power which we have determined to oppose. Societies
are formed and magistrates appointed, that men may the better enjoy the blessings of life. Some of the rights which they
have derived from nature they part with, that they may the
more peaceably and safely possess the rest. To preserve the
rights they have reserved, is the duty of every member of society; and to deprive a people of these is *treason*, is *rebellion*

against the state. If this doctrine, then, be right, which no one, we believe, will venture to deny, we are dutiful members of society; and the persons who endeavor to rob us of our rights, *they are the rebels,—rebels to their country and to the rights of human nature.* We are acting the part of loyal subjects, of faithful members of the community, when we stand forth in opposition to the arbitrary and oppressive acts of any man, or set of men. Resort not, then, to the standard which Lord Dunmore has set up; and, if any of you have been so mistaken in your duty as to join him, fly from his camp as an infected place, and speedily rejoin your virtuous, suffering countrymen; for be you well assured, that the time will come when these invaders of the rights of human kind will suffer the punishment due to their crimes; and when the insulted and oppressed Americans will, if they preserve their virtue, triumph over all their enemies.

The second class of people, for whose sake a few remarks upon this proclamation seem necessary, is the negroes. They
The Slaves. have been flattered with their freedom, if they be able to bear arms, and will speedily join Lord Dunmore's troops. To none, then, is freedom promised, but to such as are able to do Lord Dunmore service. The aged, the infirm, the women and children, are still to remain the property of their masters; masters who will be provoked to severity, should part of their slaves desert them. Lord Dunmore's declaration, therefore, is a cruel declaration to the negroes. He does not even pretend to make it out of any tenderness for them, but solely on his own account; and, should it meet with success, it leaves by far the greater number at the mercy of an enraged and injured people. But should there be any among the negroes weak enough to believe that Dunmore intends to do them a kindness, and wicked enough to provoke the fury of the Americans against their defenceless fathers and mothers, their wives, their women and children, let them only consider the difficulties of effecting their escape, and what they must expect to suffer if they fall into the hands of the Americans. Let them farther consider what must be their fate, should the English prove conquerors in this dispute. If we can judge of

the future from the past, it will not be much mended. Long
have the Americans, moved by compassion, and actuated by
sound policy, endeavored to stop the progress of slavery. Our
assemblies have repeatedly passed acts laying heavy duties upon
imported negroes, by which they meant altogether to prevent
the horrid traffic ; but their humane intentions have been as
often frustrated by the cruelty and covetousness of a set of
English merchants, who prevailed upon the king to repeal our
kind and merciful acts, little indeed to the credit of his humanity. Can it then be supposed that the negroes will be better
used by the English, who have always encouraged and upheld
this slavery, than by their present masters, who pity their condition, who wish, in general, to make it as easy and comfortable as possible, and who would willingly, were it in their
power, or were they permitted, not only prevent any more negroes from losing their freedom, but restore it to such as have
already unhappily lost it ?

No ; these ends of Lord Dunmore and his party being answered, they will either give up the offending negroes to the
rigor of the laws they have broken, or sell them in the West
Indies, where every year they sell many thousands of their
miserable brethren, to perish either by the inclemency of the
weather, or the cruelty of barbarous masters. Be not then, ye
negroes, tempted by this proclamation to ruin yourselves.
We have given you a faithful view of what you are to expect ;
and declare, before God, in doing it, we have considered your
welfare as well as that of the country. Whether you will profit
by the advice, we cannot tell ; but this we know, that whether
we suffer or not, if you desert us, *you* most certainly will.[1]

NOVEMBER 9.—IN South Carolina they have two thousand
men in actual pay, and five hundred horse on the frontiers.
Colonel Gadsden, commander-in-chief, and Colo-   Affairs in
nel Isaac Huger, second colonel, first regiment.   South Carolina.
Second regiment, Colonel Moultrie, Isaac Mott, lieutenant-colonel, late of the Royal Americans. Fort Johnson fortified, and

---

[1] Virginia Gazette, November 25.

garrisoned with four hundred and fifty men. Mount Pleasant fortified with four cannon, two hundred men stationed to prevent the shipping taking water. No provisions allowed the king's ships. Two schooners fitted out, mounting fourteen and twelve guns, and full manned as cruisers. The three forts in Charleston and the first bastion, fortified with cannon. An intrenchment, about four miles from town, laid out ; tools made and men ready to begin the intrenchment when the express came away. Women and children almost all moved out of town, and barracks built for them in the country. They have twenty tons of powder, and the quantity daily increasing. Two thousand men in uniforms, blue faced with red. Light horse, five hundred, blue faced with white, and well furnished. The militia in the country in fine order ; drill sergeants having been sent among them many months past. The regulators in the back country, who were under oath, have entered into a treaty to remain neuter ; Thomas Fletcher and Patrick Cunningham, their chiefs, are now in Charleston. The people are under no apprehensions from their negroes. The Honorable William Henry Drayton, the worthy judge of the superior court, has made a treaty with the Cherokees to assist the inhabitants in case of necessity.[1]

NOVEMBER 10.—YESTERDAY a party of regulars from Boston, amounting to four or five hundred men, embarked in a number of barges from Charlestown Point, about one o'clock, P. M., when the tide was at a high flood, and landed upon Lechmere's Point, under cover of a man-of-war and a floating battery, where they seized a sentinel who was drunk and asleep upon his post. The other sentinels fired upon them, and then gave the alarm to the camp upon Prospect Hill. Lechmere's Point is a piece of high land surrounded by marsh, and when the tide is up is entirely an island. This circumstance the regulars knew, and intended to take advantage of it. Their purpose was to steal the sheep and cattle that were feeding there. They effected a landing without op-

Fight on Lechmere's Point.

[1] Rivington's Gazetteer, November 9.

position (as indeed there were none at that time on the ground
to oppose them), and began to drive the cattle to their boats.
His excellency [1] ordered Colonel Thompson and his regiment
of Pennsylvania riflemen to turn out immediately, and they
obeyed with cheerfulness.   Colonel Thompson and Colonel
Mifflin [2] headed them, and passed the morass up to their
breasts in water.   When they were all over and formed under
cover of a hill, they marched forward.   Colonel Thompson
gave the Indian yell, which was re-echoed back from the
whole regiment, who immediately rushed out from their ambuscade, and poured in whole volleys upon the regulars, who
returned the fire in great confusion, and retreated with the
greatest precipitation on board their boats, firing at random
upon our men, who kept up a heavy fire upon them, notwithstanding the constant blaze from the man-of-war, floating battery, and boats, which latter mounted six patteraroes, or swivels, each.   The event of the skirmish is yet uncertain : doubtless they must have lost a number of men, as our shot were
well planted.   We fired a few shot at them from Prospect Hill,
and a field-piece, we had planted for the purpose, in the valley
below.   Some of our men are badly wounded, but we hear of
none of them who were killed.   When the enemy saw they
were likely to be prevented in accomplishing their purpose,
with a villanous malice, characteristic of the tools of despotism, they stabbed the poor dumb cattle.   During the engagement twenty-two large ships hove in sight, with troops from
England and Ireland. [3]

This day three dead bodies have floated along shore, supposed to be drowned by the sinking of a barge, which our
field-pieces stove.   The enemy had cannon placed at the
water's edge, along Charlestown Point, which, together with
the large artillery from Bunker Hill, made an incessant roar,
with grape-shot, chain-shot, &c., but to no purpose.   The riflemen drove them like a herd of swine down a steep place,
where some of them were killed, drowned, or scared to death,

---

[1] General Washington.   [2] Thomas Mifflin.
[3] Rivington's Gazetteer, November 23.

in sight of their brethren in iniquity, who covered the tops of Fort Beacon and Bunker Hill to view the noble exploit of cow-stealing. The general has since ordered all the stock to be driven off the peninsula of Dorchester.

Captain Adams, of Beverly, Mass., in a privateer, has taken two prize schooners, and a sloop, laden with fish and oil from Halifax, for the besieged army in Boston ; and has also retaken a sloop, off Marblehead, with two officers, six seamen, and two marines, prisoners, who were put on board to pilot her into Boston.

Captain Coit, in a privateer from Plymouth in Massachu-setts, has taken two prizes laden with fish, flour, hogs, sheep, cattle, potatoes, cheese, and all kinds of poultry, from Halifax, for the use of the hungry crew in Boston. The vessels were brought safe into Plymouth, where Captain Coit (a humorous genius) made the prisoners land upon the same rock our ancestors first trod when they landed in America, where they gave three cheers, and wished success to American arms.[1]

Captain Coit.

THE QUARREL WITH AMERICA.

Rudely forced to drink tea Massachusetts in anger
Spills the tea on John Bull—John falls on to bang her,
Massachusetts enrag'd, calls her neighbors to aid,
And gives Master John a severe bastinade!
Now, good men of the law! pray who is in fault,
The one who begins, or resists the assault?[2]

NOVEMBER 13.—A GENTLEMAN who lately came out of Boston assures, that the rebels in Boston, by order of their general, Howe, have taken down the pulpit, and all the pews in the Old South meeting-house, and are using it for a riding school. This he saw. Thus we see the

The Old South Church.

[1] Extract of a letter from Roxbury, Massachusetts, in the Pennsylvania Journal, November 29.
[2] Familiarly stated by a London paper, republished in the Constitutional Gazette, November 25.

house once set apart for true worship and service of God, turned into a den for thieves![1]

THE PAUSING AMERICAN LOYALIST.

To sign, or not to sign?   That is the question,
Whether 'twere better for an honest man
To sign, and so be safe; or to resolve,
Betide what will, against associations,
And, by retreating, shun them.   To fly—I reck
Not where: And, by that flight, t' escape
Feathers and tar, and thousand other ills
That loyalty is heir to: 'Tis a consummation
Devoutly to be wished.   To fly—to want—
To want?   Perchance to starve: Ay, there's the rub!
For, in that chance of want, what ills may come
To patriot rage, when I have left my all—
Must give me pause :—There's the respect
That makes us trim, and bow to men we hate.
For, who would bear th' indignities o' th' times,
Congress decrees, and wild convention plans,
The laws controll'd, and inj'ries unredressed,
The insolence of knaves, and thousand wrongs
Which patient *liege men* from vile *rebels* take,
When he, *sans* doubt, might certain safety find,
Only by flying?   Who would bend to fools,
And truckle thus to mad, mob-chosen upstarts,
But that the dread of something after flight
(In that blest country, where, yet, no moneyless
Poor wight can live) puzzles the will,
And makes ten thousands rather sign—and eat.
Than fly—to starve on loyalty.—
Thus, dread of want makes rebels of us all:
And thus the native hue of loyalty
Is sicklied o'er with a pale cast of *trimming;*
And enterprises of great pith and virtue,
But unsupported, turn their streams away,
And never come to action.[2]

NOVEMBER 17.—A LETTER from England by the last packet, says :—The prevailing toast in every company of true Englishmen, is, " Victory to America! and re-establishment to the British Constitution."

---

[1] Pennsylvania Journal, Nov. 29.   [2] Middlesex Journal, January 30, 1776.

Can any one read with a grave face the high sounding additions newly granted to General Gage, (vide the public prints.) To appoint a man governor over a country as large as China, whilst he remains " in durance vile," in a little nook, scarce a mile and a half in diameter, and cannot obtain a *pig* from *Hog Island*, nor a truss of hay from Noddle Island, though both within three miles of him, puts him much in the condition of a Moorfield's monarch, who, with a crown and sceptre, pretends to give laws to mighty nations.—The renowned governor of Barataria was forbidden by his physicians to taste any delicate food. The viceroy in North America is compelled to a similar diet. In vain he wishes for venison, poultry, and even fresh meat; salt beef and rusty bacon are pronounced to be fittest for him, by those who are empowered to prescribe; he must take them or fast. Decide, ye casuists, *if ye can*, which is the greatest object of pity, the faithful squire of the English Don, or the trusty arms bearer of English Quixotry.[1]

COLONEL HENRY[2] received an express yesterday morning, at Williamsburg, Virginia, with the following intelligence, viz. :

Virginia.

that Lord Dunmore having received advice that about two hundred of the militia[3] were on their march to join the troops destined for the protection of the lower parts of the country, marched from Norfolk last Tuesday, about one o'clock in the afternoon, with about three hundred and fifty men, consisting of regular soldiers, sailors, runaway negroes, and Tories, to intercept them; who, not having the last intelligence of his lordship's approach, were obliged to engage under every disadvantage, both as to the enemy's superiority in point of numbers, and the situation of the ground, being hemmed in by a fence. Our people fought a considerable time, and it is thought did great execution; but were at last overpowered, and forced to retreat, with the loss of Mr. John Ackiss, in the minute service, killed on the spot;

[1] Constitutional Gazette, November 25.   [2] Patrick Henry.
[3] Of Princess Anne County, Virginia.

and Colonel Joseph Hutchings, and one Mr. Williams wounded, who were taken prisoners with seven others. The public,
no doubt, will be exceedingly incensed, on finding that Lord
Dunmore has taken into his service the very scum of the country, to assist him in his diabolical schemes, against the good
people of this government, all well attached to his Majesty,
but mortal enemies to his infamous ministry and their subordinate tools ; but it is to be hoped his sphere of mischief will
soon be circumscribed within narrow bounds, as Colonel Woodford, with about eight hundred as brave troops as the world
can produce, are now on their march to Norfolk ; and, should
his lordship incline to give them battle, we have not the
smallest doubt they will give a very satisfactory account of
him.[1]

NOVEMBER 21.—THIS morning the following address to
the worthy officers and soldiers in the American army, was
distributed in the camp at Cambridge, Roxbury, and elsewhere:[2]

Honor will Crown every Defender of Liberty.

Your exertions in the cause of freedom, guided by wisdom
and animated by zeal and courage, have gained you the love
and confidence of your grateful countrymen ; and Address to the
they look to you, who are EXPERIENCED VETERANS,   Army.
and trust that you will still be the GUARDIANS OF AMERICA.
As I have the honor to be an American, and one among the
Free Millions, who are defended by your valor, I would pay
the tribute of thanks, and express my gratitude, while I solicit
you to continue in your present honorable and important station. I doubt not America will always find enough of her
sons ready to flock to her standard, and support her freedom ;
but experience proves that *experienced* soldiers are more capable of performing the duties of the camp, and better qualified
to face the enemy, than others ; and therefore every friend of
America will be desirous that most of the gentlemen who

[1] New York Gazette, December 4.   [2] Mason's Journal.

compose the present army may continue in the service of their country until " LIBERTY, PEACE, AND SAFETY " are established. Although your private concerns may call for your assistance at home, yet the voice of your country is still louder, and it is painful to heroic minds to quit the field when LIBERTY calls, and the voice of *injured millions* cries " To arms! to arms! " Never was a cause more important or glorious than that which you are engaged in; not only your wives, your children, and distant posterity, but humanity at large, the world of mankind, are interested in it; for if tyranny should prevail in this great country, we may expect LIBERTY will expire throughout the world. Therefore, more human glory and happiness may depend upon your exertions than ever yet depended upon any of the sons of men. He that is a soldier in defence of such a cause, needs no title; his post is a post of honor, and although not an emperor, yet he shall wear a crown—of glory—and blessed will be his memory!

The savage and brutal barbarity of our enemies in burning Falmouth,[1] is a full demonstration that there is not the least remains of virtue, wisdom, or humanity, in the
Independence. British court; and that they are fully determined with fire and sword, to butcher and destroy, beggar and enslave the whole American people. Therefore we expect soon to break off all kind of connection with Britain, and form into a GRAND REPUBLIC of the AMERICAN UNITED COLONIES, which will, by the blessing of heaven, soon work out our salvation, and perpetuate the liberties, increase the wealth, the power and the glory of this Western world.

Notwithstanding the many difficulties we have to encounter, and the rage of our merciless enemies, we have a glorious prospect before us, big with every thing good and great. The further we enter into the field of independence, our prospects will expand and brighten, and a complete Republic will soon complete our happiness. " Blindness seems to have happened to Britain, that the fulness of America might come in;" and we have every encouragement to " stand

---

[1] Falmouth was destroyed by Captain Mowatt, on the 18th of October.

fast in the liberties wherewith heaven hath made us free."
Persevere, YE GUARDIANS OF LIBERTY! May success be your
constant attendant, until the enemies of freedom are no more,
and all future generations, as they successively tread the stage
of time, and taste the JOYS OF LIBERTY, will rise up and call
YOU blessed.[1]

WE hear the Earl of Dunmore has composed a most elab-
orate and profound treatise on the Art of Government, with
which his lordship intends soon to favor the pub-
lic ; and that is the true reason of the printing   Lord Dunmore.
press in Virginia being carried on shipboard.   In twenty-two
years will be published, dedicated (without permission) to his
Excellency Governor Martin, in fifty volumes, folio, a nar-
cotic work, entitled " The Yawnings of Tautology," or " The
Gapings of Prolixity," with this motto " Brevis esse laboro.
Hor.," with a soporific but friendly admonition to " Messrs.
Caswell, Ashe, Howes, alias Howe," &c., by the Lady Dow-
ager Threadbare Spintext, of Drowsy Hall, in the county of
Laudanum.[2]

NOVEMBER 29.—ON the twentieth of this month, sixteen
respectable inhabitants of New Haven, Connecticut, in company with Captain Sears, set out from that place   Rivington's Press
to East and West Chester, in the province of   Destroyed.
New York, to disarm the principal Tories there, and secure the
persons of Parson Seabury,[3] Judge Fowler, and Lord Under-

[1] Article under the signature of " A Freeman," in the New England Chronicle,
November 23.

[2] Constitutional Gazette, November 25.

[3] Samuel Seabury, D. D., first Bishop of the Episcopal Church in the United
States. He was born in 1728; graduated at Yale College in 1751, and visited
England to study medicine, but relinquished that study for that of the ministry.
He was first settled at Brunswick, (New Jersey,) then at Jamaica, on Long Island,
and afterwards in Westchester, New York. After the commencement of the war,
he fled to New York city, where he remained until the declaration of peace. In
November, 1784, he was consecrated as bishop of the Episcopal Church of Con-
necticut, and for many years after discharged the duties of the office at New
London, in Connecticut. He died in 1796.

hill.[3] On their way thither they were joined by Captains Richards, Sillick, and Mead, with about eighty men. At Mamaroneck they burnt a small sloop, which was purchased by government, for the purpose of carrying provisions on board the " Asia." At East Chester they seized Judge Fowler, then repaired to West Chester and secured Seabury and Underhill. Having possessed themselves of these three caitiffs, they sent them to Connecticut under a strong guard. The main body, consisting of seventy-five, then proceeded to New York, where they entered at noonday on horseback, bayonets fixed, in the greatest regularity, went down the main street, and drew up in close order before the printing office of the infamous James Rivington. A small detachment entered it, and in about three-quarters of an hour brought off the principal part of his types, for which they offered to give an order on Lord Dunmore.[2] They then faced and wheeled to the left, and marched out of town to the tune of *Yankee Doodle*. A vast concourse of people assembled at the Coffee House, on their leaving the ground, and gave them three very hearty cheers.

On their way home they disarmed all the Tories that lay on their route, and yesterday arrived at New Haven, escorted by a great number of gentlemen from the westward, the whole making a very grand procession. Upon their entrance into town they were saluted with the discharge of two cannon, and received by the inhabitants with every mark of approbation and respect. The company divided into two parts, and concluded the day in festivity and innocent mirth. Captain Sears returned in company with the other gentlemen, and proposes to spend the winter at New Haven, unless public business should require his presence at New York. Seabury, Underhill, and Fowler, three of the dastardly protesters against the proceedings of the Continental Congress, and who it is believed had concerted a plan for kidnapping Captain Sears, and conveying him on board the Asia man-of-war,

[1] Nathaniel Underhill, Mayor of Westchester.
[2] See account of the seizure of Holt's types, &c., at Virginia; ante.

are (with the types and arms) safely lodged in New Haven, where it is expected Lord Underhill will have leisure to form the scheme of a lucrative lottery, the tickets of which cannot be counterfeited; and Parson Seabury sufficient time to compose sermons for the next Continental fast.[1]

DECEMBER 1.—A WRITER in England says:—The blood of the unfortunate Stuarts, some of which crept into Brunswick veins, and fouled the purer sources of that illustrious family, received a grand addition to its own original stain, from an intermarriage with the House of Tudor. *King's Evil versus People's Evil.* Tyranny could never be more completely inoculated. A political contagion ensued, which neither the petition nor the bill of rights have been effectual to purge. Horrid tumors of uncontrollable authority, have for ages swelled the mind political of some of our sovereigns. Tumors, these, incurable by the English physic of Magna Charta. The King's Evil is justly esteemed a dreadful disease, but the people's evil is a disorder of much higher importance. Brutus and Hampden were the only state chirurgeons who, in former times, attempted a cure. Hancock and Adams are the persons from whom, in our times, the Americans expect relief. Neither alteratives nor palliatives will avail. It is from surgery, not physic, we must call for aid. The lancet, not the phial, can relieve us.[2]

---

[1] Pennsylvania Journal, December 6:—The following recantation of Judge Fowler is printed in the same paper:—Whereas I, Jonathan Fowler, Esq., one of his Majesty's Judges of the Inferior Court for the County of Westchester, in the Province of New York, did some time ago sign a protest against the Honorable Continental Congress, which inconsiderate conduct I am heartily sorry for, and do hereby promise for the future not to transgress in the view of the people of this continent, nor in any sense to oppose the measures taken by the Continental Congress.

I do also certify, that some time past being at Court at the White Plains, I heard a person say, whom several people present believed to be a lieutenant or midshipman of the Asia, man-of-war, that the captain of the Asia intended to take Captain Sears up, and that there soon would be delivered (gratis) from on board the man-of-war, great quantities of paper money in imitation of Continental currency, which would be printed with the types taken from Mr. Holt, of Virginia. As witness my hand, JONATHAN FOWLER.

[2] Constitutional Gazette, December 20.

GENERAL GAGE, on his arrival in England, is to be created
Lord Lexington Baron of Bunker's Hill. This honor will
prove but a poor counterbalance for the disgrace
which is sure to be thrown on him by the people,
as well as for the hardships he has endured in the town of
Boston, when being cooped up to fatten on salt provisions and
peas, he has had the mortification to reflect that his troops
never once sallied out on a successful expedition. It is to be
hoped that General Burgoyne will have better luck, for should
he be either shot, or chance to die of the scurvy, how can the
ministry expect forgiveness of the literary world, which was so
highly entertained last year by that truly classical performance
—*The Maid of the Oaks.*[1]

General Gage.

GARDNER'S GHOST.[2]

Let *little* villains conscience gor'd,
  Their sable vigils keep!
George on his downy pillow snor'd:
  (How royal villains sleep!)

An hour ere day began to break,
  There Gardner's spectre stood:[3]
The curtain shook—it cried "Awake,
  Awake—thou log of wood.

[1] General Burgoyne wrote three dramas, *Bon Ton*, *The Heiress*, and *The Maid of the Oaks.*

[2] "A prophetic ballad found in Merlin's Cave, Richmond," and published in the sixty-fourth number of a publication entitled "The Crisis: to be continued weekly during the present bloody civil war in America." *

[3] Colonel Thomas Gardner, "a gentleman of a most amiable character and respectable family in Massachusetts Bay," who was wounded in the action of the 17th of June last, and died on the evening of the 3d of July following.

* The Crisis was published in England, and was discontinued on the publication of the ninetieth number, with the following "address from the authors to the public:"—We have carried on the Crisis near two years from the most disinterested principles, for the honor and interest of our country; with a view to expose the horrid deformity of tyranny, rapine, and lawless power, and to show the blessings and advantages of liberty. We have braved every danger with a spirit and resolution which, we flatter ourselves, few men would have done. We have attacked vice, corruption, and folly in whomsoever they were found. We now lay down this paper with grateful thanks to the public, and as liberty and virtue have taken their flight to America, the only asylum for freemen, we are determined to follow, and not longer struggle in vain to animate our dastardly degenerate countrymen with the noble spirit of their forefathers, against the ingratitude of a tyrant, whose barefaced system of despotism and blood must soon end in the ruin of England, and the slavery of the present *bastard* race of Englishmen.

"Thy veins hath apathy congealed,
    Unthawed by pity's tear,
One spark a flinty heart may yield,
    Struck with the steel of fear!

"Yes,—know that head so proud in crest,
    Sunk on the cygnet's plume,
Shall for an axe and block be dress'd,
    Shall meet a Charles's doom.

"Or crouched in abject, care-worn plight
    Beneath its sorrows low,
Its bread by day—its rest by night,
    To Bourbon's mercy owe.

"Speak tyrant, which of Stuart's race
    Could match thy bloody work?
Go read when Stafford was in place,
    A Jeffries and a Kirk.[1]

"Then sailing history's modern page,
    Skilled in her ancient lore,
Tell us if Nero in this age,—
    Or Borgia could do more?

"Monster, dismiss your [2] white rose clans,
    The impious task forbear!
Nor in their blood embrue those hands,
    Who placed a sceptre there!

"That liberty you now invade,
    Gave you your *only* right,
Thus in their sons our sires are paid,
    While you for Scotchmen fight.

"Satan for thee sunk deep in hell,
    Shall forge his hotted tongs:
And friends who guard his inmost cell,
    Twine scorpions round their thongs.

"But hark!—I hear th' ill-omen'd cock,
    The Gallic sun shall rise,
Lo [3] *commerce founders on yon rock,*
    The British lion dies."

[1] General Kirk, that master-piece of inhumanity.
[2] *Query:* Are these of the *white* or the *red* rose rebels?
[3] The prophecy.

George felt the dream, fetch'd many a shriek,
   And tho' the ghost is gone,
Starts from his bed,—still hears it speak,
   A cold damp sweat comes on.

With that, like Gloster, in his tent,
   He casts him on the ground,
And by these words seems to repent,
   " Boston, bind up my wound.

" Just Heaven give back the blood I've spilt,
   My subjects' lives restore."
He wakes, and to atone his guilt,
   Bids GAGE go butcher more.

DECEMBER 6.—AT Quibbletown, New Jersey, Thomas Randolph, cooper, who had publicly proved himself an enemy to
Affair at Quibbletown. his country, by reviling and using his utmost
endeavors to oppose the proceedings of the conti-
nental and provincial conventions, in defence of their rights
and liberties ; and being judged a person not of consequence
enough for a severer punishment, was ordered to be stripped
naked, well coated with tar and feathers, and carried in a
wagon publicly around the town—which punishment was accordingly inflicted. As soon as he became duly sensible of
his offence, for which he earnestly begged pardon, and promised to atone, as far as he was able, by a contrary behavior for
the future, he was released and suffered to return to his house,
in less than half an hour. The whole was conducted with
that regularity and decorum that ought to be observed in all
public punishments.[1]

SOME time ago some boys in the Queen's County, Long Isl-
and, having caught several *cats*, went to the plain, with their
The Queen's County Cat. dogs, to have the pleasure of hunting them. A
cat being let out of the bag was pursued by the
dogs ; and the lads, who were on horseback, followed in full
chase. The cat led them towards Hempstead, and just at
that instant they were seen by an assembly man, whose imag-

[1] Holt's Journal, December 28.

ination converted them into Yankees. He set off immediately post haste to alarm the people, who had for some time dreaded a visit from their friends in New England, and a great part of the country were thrown into the utmost consternation. Some betook themselves to flight for safety ; others thought to shelter in recluse and solitary places, and waiting trembling in retirement, until they found their property remained unhurt, when they returned home, and were informed that all the confusion was occasioned by a few boys hunting some cats. A justice of the peace was absent from home three days on this occasion.[1]

DECEMBER 9.—THIS morning, after reveille beating, two or three great guns and some muskets were discharged from the enemy's fort near Great Bridge,[2] which, as it was not an unusual thing, was little regarded by Colonel Woodford.[3] However, soon after he heard a call to the soldiers to stand to their arms ; upon which, with all expedition, he made the proper disposition to receive the enemy.   In

Battle of the Great Bridge.

[1] Constitutional Gazette, December 30.

[2] As the scene of action is but little known to the generality of people, it may be necessary to give some description of it, that the relation may be more clear and satisfactory. The Great Bridge is built over what is called the southern branch of Elizabeth River, twelve miles above Norfolk. The land on each side is marshy to a considerable distance from the river, except at the two extremities of the bridge, where are two pieces of firm land, which may not improperly be called islands, being surrounded entirely by water and marsh, and joined to the mainland by causeways. On the little piece of firm ground on the farther or Norfolk side, Lord Dunmore had erected his fort in such a manner that his cannon commanded the causeway on his own side, and the bridge between him and us, with the marshes around him. The island on this side of the river contained six or seven houses, some of which were burnt down (the nearest to the bridge) by the enemy, after the arrival of our troops ; in the others, adjoining the causeway on each side, were stationed a guard every night by Colonel Woodford, but withdrawn before day, as they might not be exposed to the fire of the enemy's fort in recrossing the causeway to our camp, this causeway being also commanded by their cannon. The causeway on our side was in length, about one hundred and sixty yards, and on the hither extremity our breastwork was thrown up. From the breastwork ran a street, gradually ascending, about the length of four hundred yards, to a church, where our main body was encamped.—*Pinkney's Virginia Gazette*, December 20.

[3] Colonel William Woodford, commander of the Virginia Militia.

the mean time the enemy had crossed the bridge, fired the remaining houses on the island, and some large piles of shingles,
and attacked our guard in the breastwork.   Our men returned
the fire, and threw them into some confusion, but they were
instantly rallied by Captain Fordyce, and advanced along the
causeway with great resolution, keeping up a constant and
heavy fire as they approached.   Two field-pieces, which had
been brought across the bridge and planted on the edge of
the island, facing the left of our breastwork, played briskly at
the same time upon us.   Lieut. Travis, who commanded in the
breastwork, ordered his men to reserve their fire till the enemy came within the distance of fifty yards, and then they
gave it to them with terrible execution.   The brave Fordyce
exerted himself to keep up their spirits, reminded them of
their ancient glory, and, waving his hat over his head, en-
couragingly told them the day was their own.   Thus pressing
forward he fell within fifteen steps of the breastwork.[1] His
wounds were many, and his death would have been that of a
hero, had he met it in a better cause.   The progress of the
enemy was now at an end ; they retreated over the causeway
with precipitation, and were dreadfully galled in the rear.
Hitherto on our side only the guard, consisting of twenty-five,
and some others, upon the whole not amounting to more than
ninety, had been engaged.   Only the regulars of the 14th
regiment, in number one hundred and twenty, had advanced
upon the causeway, and about two hundred and thirty Tories
and negroes had, after crossing the bridge, continued upon the
island.   The regulars, after retreating along the causeway,
were again rallied by Captain Leslie, and the two field-pieces
continued to play upon our men.   It was at this time that Colonel Woodford was advancing down the street to the breastwork with the main body, and against him was now directed
the whole fire of the enemy.   Never were cannon better
served ; but yet, in the face of them and the musketry which

---

[1] The unfortunate Fordyce was a captain of grenadiers in the fourteenth regiment.   "As he was a brave and gallant officer," said Colonel Woodford, "I
promised to bury him with all the military honors due to his great merit."—*Letter
from Col. Woodford to Edmund Pendleton in New York Packet*, January 4. 1776.

kept up a continual blaze, our men marched on with the utmost intrepidity. Colonel Stevens, of the Culpeper battalion, was sent around to the left to flank the enemy, which was done with such activity and spirit that a rout immediately ensued. The enemy fled into their fort, leaving behind them the two field-pieces, which, however, they took care to spike up with nails. Many were killed and wounded in the flight, but Colonel Woodford very prudently restrained his troops from urging their pursuit too far. From the beginning of the attack till the repulse from the breastwork might be about fourteen or fifteen minutes; till the total defeat, upwards of half an hour. It is said that some of the enemy preferred death to captivity, from a fear of being scalped, which Lord Dunmore inhumanly told them would be their fate should they be taken alive. Thirty-one killed and wounded fell into our hands, and the number borne off was much greater. Through the whole of the engagement every officer and soldier behaved with the greatest courage and calmness. The conduct of our sentinels we cannot pass over in silence. Before they quited their stations, they fired at least three rounds as the enemy were crossing the bridge, and one of them, who was posted behind some shingles, kept his ground till he had fired eight times; and after receiving a whole platoon, made his escape over the causeway into our breastwork. The scene was closed with as much humanity as it had been conducted with bravery. The work of death being over, every one's attention was directed to the succor of the unhappy sufferers, and it is an undoubted fact that Captain Leslie was so affected with the tenderness of our troops towards those who were yet capable of assistance, that he gave signs from the fort of his thankfulness for it.[1] What is not to be paralleled in history,

---

[1] The soldiers showed the greatest humanity and tenderness to the wounded prisoners. Several of them ran through a hot fire to lift up and bring in some that were bleeding, and whom they feared would die if not speedily assisted by the surgeon. The prisoners expected to be scalped, and called out, "For God's sake do not murder us." One of them who was unable to walk, calling out in this manner to one of our men, was answered by him, "Put your arm about my neck, and I'll show you what I intend to do." Then taking him, with his arm over his neck, he walked slowly along, bearing him up with great tenderness to the breast-work.—*Pennsylvania Evening Post*, January 6.

and will scarcely appear credible, except to such as acknowledge a Providence over human affairs, this victory was gained
at the expense of no more than a slight wound in a soldier's
hand ; and one circumstance which renders it still more amazing is, that the field-pieces raked the whole length of the
street, and absolutely threw double-headed shot as far as the
church ; and afterwards, as our troops approached, cannonaded
them heavily with grape-shot.[1]

LAST week General Howe gave orders for taking down the
Old North meeting-house, the first, and, for some time, the only
place of worship in Boston, and one hundred
wooden houses, for firewood ; another meeting-
house is turned into barracks ; and a third into a riding
school. What they will do with it now, the horses being sent
away, we cannot tell ; but the regulars, alias ministerialists,
have a particular spite against meeting-houses. The wooden
houses were taken down to supply some vessels with fuel, that
are gone to England with about eight hundred invalids.

The Old North Church destroyed.

General Gage, in one of his letters to the ministry, falsely
accuses the troops of the Continental Congress of fighting like
savages ; but like what do the regular troops of a Christian
prince fight, who wantonly destroy inoffensive towns by fire,
and invade the rights of religious worship, contrary to the
practice of all civilized nations ? Even infidels have held
churches sacred ; nor will history afford an example of an
enemy perverting them to unworthy uses. Let Britain blush
for the degeneracy of her sons ![2]

DECEMBER 26.—THIS morning, about four hundred of the
militia of Sussex County, New Jersey, under the command of
Colonel Ephraim Martin and Marsh Thompson, assembled at
Newtown, and from thence proceeded in good order and regularity, in quest of Tories, a considerable number of whom, in-

[1] Pennsylvania Evening Post, January 6.
[2] Constitutional Gazette, December 16 and 30.

habitants of that county, had entered into a combination and agreement not to comply with any Congress measures. We hear about forty are taken, most of whom have recanted, signed the association, and profess themselves true sons of liberty, being fully convinced of their error. Two or three, who remain incorrigible, are to be sent to the Congress to be dealt with.[1]

LAST Monday, General Lee arrived from Cambridge, at Newport, Rhode Island, attended by his guard, a party of riflemen, and the cadet company of Providence. While there he called before him a number of obnoxious persons, to whom he tendered an oath of fidelity to the country, which was taken by all of them excepting Colonel Joseph Warton, Jr., Nicholas Lechmere, and Richard Beale, the two last custom-house officers, who refused taking it; upon which, they were put under guard and sent to Providence.[2]

General Lee's Oath

The following copy of the oath imposed by General Lee, is submitted to the public, who will judge how far it is consistent with that liberty, independence, and right of private judgment, which the Americans pretend they are contending for:[3]

"I, ——, here, in the presence of Almighty God, as I hope for ease, honor, and comfort in this world, and happiness in the world to come, most earnestly, devoutly, and religiously do swear, that I will neither directly nor indirectly assist the wicked instruments of ministerial tyranny and villany, commonly called the king's troops and navy, by furnishing them with provisions and refreshments of any kind, unless authorized by the Continental Congress or Legislature, at present established in this particular colony of Rhode Island. I do also swear, by the tremendous and Almighty God, that I will neither directly nor indirectly convey any intelligence, nor give any advice to the aforesaid enemies described; and that I pledge myself, if I should by any accident get knowledge of

[1] Holt's Journal, December 28.   [2] Pennsylvania Evening Post, January 16.
[3] Middlesex Journal, February 15, 1776.

such treasons, to inform immediately the committee of safety
And, as it is justly allowed that when the rights and sacred lib
erties of a nation or community are invaded, neutrality is no
less base and criminal than open and avowed hostility, I d
further swear and pledge myself, as I hope for eternal salva
tion, that I will, whenever called upon by the voice of th
Continental Congress, or by the Legislature of this particula
colony under their direction, take up arms, and subject mysel
to military discipline in defence of the common rights and lib
erties of America. So help me God." [1]

THE great Queen Elizabeth acquired more true glory b
her piety than by her victories, of which there is a strong in

Good Fortune.

stance in the universal admiration of her mott
on the medal, struck on the occasion of the de
struction of the Spanish Armada : " He blew with his winds
and they were scattered."

If the hand of heaven was only seen and to be acknowl
edged in these great events which concern kings and prince
kings and princes would only have to acknowledge the protec
tion of a Divine Providence. But we see in matters of les

---

[1] GENERAL LEE, on his arrival at New York, despatched Isaac Sears to Lon
Island, to administer the oath to the Tories residing there. The following fir
report made by Sears to Lee, is taken from George H. Moore's work on th
" Treason of Major-General Charles Lee," now in course of preparation :

JAMAICA, March 17th, 1776.

SIR,—It is a duty that I owe to my Comman[r] to aquaint him of my procee
ings in execut[s] the order he gave me. Yesterday afternoon I arived at Newtow
and tendered the oath to four of the grate Torries, which they swallowed as ha
as if it was a four pound shot, that they ware trying to git down. On this day
11 o'clock, I came here, whare I sent out scouting parties, and have ben able
ketch but five Torries, and they of the first rank, which swallowed the oath. Th
houses are so scatering it is impossible to ketch many without hosses to rid aft
thim. But I shall exert myself to ketch the gratest part of the ringledors, ar
beleve I shell effect it, but not less then five days from this time. I can asu
your honor they are a set of villins in this country, and beleve the better half
them are wateing for soport and intend to take up arms against us. And it is n
oppinion nothing else will do but removeing the ringledors to a place of secuert[y]

From your most ob[t] Hum[le] Sir[t]

ISAAC SEARS.

QUEBEC IN 1775.

Eng d by A.H.Ritchie.

importance, such as concern the people, the care of heaven is
displayed, of which I beg leave to mention the following instance : " It was agreed to fit out a number of ships-of-war
for our defence ; a particular kind of lanthorns, called Mus-
covy lights, was necessary for the powder rooms, to prevent
the danger arising from the common lanthorns. They were
not to be had, nor could one be made, on this extensive continent ; perhaps one of the kind had never been before imported
into America. At the very juncture in which they were
wanted, a transport is taken by one of our cruisers, and in
her there is found, not only the kind of lanthorns which we so
much wanted, but the exact number we wanted, and not one
more or less. Surely we may, without being charged with
superstition, be permitted to say, " The Lord hath done this,
and it is marvellous in our eyes." [1]

DECEMBER 31.—THE Americans have made an unsuccessful
attack upon the town of Quebec. General Montgomery finding his cannon too light to effect a breach, and
that the enemy would not hearken to terms of Attack on Quebec.
capitulation, formed a design of carrying the town by esca-
lade. In this he was encouraged by the extensiveness of the
works, and the weakness of the garrison. When every thing
was prepared, while he was awaiting the opportunity of a
snow-storm to carry his design into execution, several of his
men deserted to the enemy. His plan, at first, was to have
attacked the upper and lower town at the same time, depend-
ing principally for success upon the upper town. But discovering, from the motions of the enemy, that they were apprised
of his design, he altered his plan, and, having divided his small
army into four detachments, ordered two feints to be made
against the upper town, one by Colonel Livingston [2] at the head
of the Canadians, against St. John's gate, the other by Captain Brown, at the head of a small detachment, against Cape
Diamond, reserving to himself and Colonel Arnold, the two
principal attacks against the lower town.

[1] Constitutional Gazette, December 14.   [2] Henry Livingston.

At five o'clock this morning, the hour appointed for the attack, the general, at the head of the New York troops, advanced against the lower town. Being obliged to take a circuit, the signal for the attack was given and ·the garrison alarmed before he reached the place. However, pressing on, he passed the first barrier, and was just opening the at-

Montgomery
Killed.

tempt on the second, when, by the first fire from the enemy, he was unfortunately killed,[1] together with his aide-de-camp, Captain J. McPherson, Captain Cheesman, and two or three more. This so dispirited the men, that Colonel Campbell, on whom the command devolved, found himself under the disagreeable necessity of drawing them off.

In the meanwhile Colonel Arnold, at the head of about three hundred and fifty of those brave troops, (who with unparalleled fatigue had penetrated Canada under his command,) and Captain Lamb's company of artillery, had passed through St. Roques' gate, and approached near a two-gun battery, picketed in, without being discovered. This he attacked, and

Arnold Wounded.

though it was well defended for about an hour, carried it, with the loss of a number of men. In this attack, Colonel Arnold had the misfortune to have his

---

[1] RICHARD MONTGOMERY was born in the north of Ireland, in the year 1737. He entered the English army, and was with General Wolfe at Quebec in 1759. Quitting the army in 1772, he settled in America, where he married a daughter of R. R. Livingston. On the commencement of the difficulties between the colonies and Great Britain, he warmly espoused the cause of the colonists, and, in the fall of 1775, was connected with General Schuyler in the command of the expedition against Canada. In October, owing to the indisposition of General Schuyler, the chief command of the army devolved upon Montgomery. The progress of his troops from Ticonderoga to the redoubts before Quebec, was marked with bravery and success. They took Chamblee on the 18th of October, St. John's on the 3d of November, and on the 12th he led them into Montreal. In December, he joined General Arnold, who had come from the camp at Cambridge, through the wilderness of Maine, and they together marched to Quebec.

Every mark of distinction was shown to the corpse of General Montgomery, who was interred in Quebec on the 2d of January, 1776.* In 1818, his body was removed, in accordance with an act of the New York Legislature, and re-interred at St. Paul's church-yard, in New York city.

* Pennsylvania Evening Post, January 25.

leg splintered by a shot, and was obliged to be carried to the hospital. After gaining the battery, his detachment passed on to a second barrier, which they took possession of. By this time the enemy, relieved from the other attack, by our troops being drawn off, directed their whole force against this detachment, and a party sallying out from Palace gate, attacked them in the rear. These brave men sustained the whole force of the garrison for three hours, but finding themselves hemmed in, and no hopes of relief, they were obliged to yield to numbers, and the advantageous situation the garrison had over them.

After this unfortunate repulse, the remainder of the army retired about eight miles from the city, where they have posted themselves advantageously, and are continuing the blockade, waiting for the reinforcements which are now on their march to join them.[1]

[1] New York Packet, February 1, 1776.

CHAPTER V.

JANUARY 1.—THE virtue of the British court seems to have swallowed up all the virtue of the island of Great Britain.

State of the Country.
The common people are lost in a night of ignorance. They annex no ideas to slavery but wooden shoes and soup meagre. Even the Roman Catholic religion has now no terrors in it to Englishmen.

The American colonies are just beginning to emerge from Egyptian darkness, with respect to the rights of human nature. About two hundred years ago, the human heart discovered its folly and depravity upon the theatre of religion; about one hundred years they both appeared through the medium of science. We are shocked at our species, when we read the history of the human understanding at these memorable periods. The present age shows equal absurdities and vices upon the theatre of politics. Here we discover in other forms every thing for which we condemn our ancestors. Posterity will tread most heavily upon our ashes, as the principles of government are more simple than the principles of religion and science. They will wonder whether we were men or brutes.

There has always been such a mixture of monarchy and aristocracy in republics, that they never have had fair play in the world. We can say but little from experience of their expediency or duration. Most of the free states in the world have been formed by men just emerged from a state of slavery. No wonder, therefore, they have been liable to disorders, and a speedy dissolution. What sort of government would the negroes in the southern colonies form, if they were suddenly set at liberty? Almost all the blood that has been shed in contests for liberty, has been to shake off a subjection to foreign states.

The British constitution, with all its imperfections, even absolute monarchy itself, would insure more happiness to the colonies than they can expect (according to the usual operation of moral and natural causes) from a union with the people, or a dependence upon the ministry of Great Britain.[1]

It is wonderful how happily the Americans have been preserved. From Bunker's Hill fight to the present day, the regulars have fired, on the Cambridge side, about a thousand balls, bombs, and carcases ; and, on the Roxbury side, better than two thousand, and have killed, including those who have died of their wounds, on the Cambridge side, seven, and in Roxbury, five.

Yesterday the new Admiral Shuldam, arrived at Boston, with several ships, which occasioned great firing most of the day.[2]

JANUARY 2.—YESTERDAY, at about quarter after three o'clock, the British fleet lying off Norfolk, Virginia, commenced a cannonade against that town, from upwards of one hundred pieces of cannon, and continued till nearly ten o'clock at night, without intermission. It then abated a little, and continued till two this morning. Under cover of their guns, the regulars landed and set fire to the town in several places near the water, though our men strove all in their power to prevent them. The houses being chiefly of wood, took fire immediately, and the fire spread with amazing rapidity. It is now become general, and the whole town will probably be consumed in a day or two. Expecting that the fire would throw the Americans into confusion, the enemy frequently landed, but were every time repulsed. The burning of the town has made several avenues through which the enemy may now fire with greater effect.

Norfolk Burnt.

[1] "Seasonable Thoughts," in the Pennsylvania Journal, January 3.
[2] Constitutional Gazette, January 13.

The tide is now rising, and we expect, at high water, another cannonade. May it be as ineffectual as the last, for we have not one man killed, and but a few wounded.[1]

DEACON WHITCOMB, of Lancaster, Massachusetts, (who was a member of the assembly of Massachusetts Bay, till the present war commenced, had served in former wars and been in different engagements,) had served as a Colonel in the Continental army; but, on account of his age, was left out upon the new regulation. His men highly resented it, and declared they would not enlist again after their time was out. The Colonel told them he did not doubt there were sufficient reasons for the regulation, and was satisfied with it. He then blamed them for their conduct, and said he would enlist as a private. A Colonel Brewer heard of it, and offered to resign in favor of Colonel Whitcomb. The whole coming to General Washington's ears, he allowed of Colonel Brewer's resignation in favor of Colonel Whitcomb, appointed the former barrack-master till he could further promote him, and acquainted the army with the whole affair in general orders. Let antiquity produce a more striking instance of true greatness of mind.[2]

A CORRESPONDENT in London says: "Several contractors have set off for Rome for a fresh supply of Jesuit's bark; as tea does not agree with an American stomach, being apt to produce the heartburn. There is a rumor the new parliament intends to force the bark upon the Yankees, especially as Doctor Bute recommend it as a great specific for the fever of rebellion, for which, no doubt, they will have gratitude enough to thank the doctor, by heartily wishing he may very soon experience the quintessence of the axe, the halter, or the syrup of gun flints.[3]

"Colonel Allen is now chained and kept close in Pendennis Castle, in Cornwall, England. He was brought over to be

---

[1] New York Packet, January 25, and Pennsylvania Evening Post, January 16.
[2] Constitutional Gazette, December 13.   [3] New York Packet, January 4.

tried by the act which passed last session, and which was repealed two days before the unhappy prisoner arrived." [1]

WE hope our countrymen will not be at all dispirited at the destruction of Norfolk, but rather rejoice that half the mischief our enemies can do us is done already. They have destroyed one of the first towns in America, and the only one (except two or three) in Virginia, which carried on any thing like a trade. We are only sharing part of the sufferings of our American brethren, and can now glory in having received one of the keenest strokes of the enemy, without flinching. They have done their worst, and to no other purpose than to harden our soldiers, and teach them to bear without dismay, all the most formidable operations of a war carried on by a powerful and cruel enemy; to no other purpose than to give the world specimens of British cruelty and American fortitude, unless it be to force us to lay aside that childish fondness for Britain, and that foolish, tame dependence on her. We had borne so long with the oppressions of an ungenerous restriction of our trade—of a restriction, in some instances, which seemed calculated merely as badges of our subjection, and had been contented so long with barely refusing to purchase commodities which they had taxed for the purpose of raising a revenue in America, that our patience and moderation served but to encourage them to proceed to greater lengths. To greater lengths they have proceeded, as far as the proudest tyrant's lust of despotism, stimulated by cruelty, a rancorous malice, and an infernal spirit of revenge, could hurry them. How sunk is Britain! Could not Britons venture to wage war with America till they were told that Americans were cowards—till they had disarmed them, or had, as they thought, put it out of their power to procure arms; nor even then without the assistance of Roman Catholics and Indians, and endeavoring to raise amongst us a domestic enemy? Was this like a brave and generous nation? If they were lost to all the feelings of Britons, for men con-

To the Virginians.

---

[1] Middlesex Journal, January 4.

tending for the support of the British constitution, if they
were determined to conquer America, why did they not attempt it like Britons?   Why meanly run about to the different powers of Europe, entreating them not to assist us?   Why
make use of every base and inhuman stratagem, and wage a
savage war unknown amongst civilized nations?   Surely who
ever has heard of Carleton's, Connolly's, and Dunmore's plots
against us, cannot but allow that they must have been authorized by a higher power; and whoever believes this cannot but
wish to be instantly and forever removed from under such a
power, and to be guarded most effectually against it.   Most
freely would we cut the gordian knot which has hitherto so
firmly bound us to Britain, and call on France and Spain for
assistance against an enemy who seem bent on our destruction, but who, blessed be the God of Hosts, have been baffled
in most of their attempts against us, been chastised in all, and
have made many attacks against us without being able to kill
a single man.[1]

JANUARY 7.—THIS morning, the sixth daughter of Captain
Bancroft, of Dunstable, Massachusetts, was baptized by the
name of MARTHA DANDRIDGE, the maiden name of his Excellency General Washington's lady.   The child was dressed in
buff and blue, with a sprig of evergreen on its head, emblem-
atic of his Excellency's glory and provincial affection.[2]

As Lord North has owned in Parliament that the ministry
have been misled and deceived by American informers, it is
but justice that the public should know them.
American
Informers.   Here they are: Wentworth, Governor of New
Hampshire; Hutchinson, late governor of Boston, pensioner
on Ireland, £1,000 a year; Benj. Hallowell, a commissioner of
customs at Boston, £600 a year; Ruggles, one of the council
of Boston, £200 a year pension; Oliver, lieutenant-governor,
made such by Hutchinson; Moffat, custom-house officer at

[1] "An American" in the Virginia Gazette, January 5.
[2] Essex Gazette, January 18.

New London, £300 a year; William Smith, an attorney at New York, and a counsellor; James Delancey, a captain in the army; John Watts, a contractor with Harley and Oliver Delancey; Stockden, an attorney and king's counsellor at New Jersey; Franklin, governor of New Jersey, son of Benjamin; Dulany, an attorney and commissary at Maryland; Dunmore, Governor of Virginia; Martin, brother to Target, governor of North Carolina; Jonathan Sewall, a school-master at Boston, judge of the admiralty, £600 a year; Auchmuty, a priest.[1]

JANUARY 8.—THIS evening, Major Knowlton was despatched with a hundred men, to make an incursion into Charlestown. He crossed the mill dam, which lies between Cobble Hill and Bunker's Hill, about nine o'clock, and immediately proceeded down the street, on the westerly side of Bunker's Hill. A part of the men, under the command of Captain Keyes, at the same time were ordered to take post on the east side of the street, just under the hill, in order to intercept any person who might escape from the houses in the street, some of which were occupied by the enemy. These houses, which are a little without the compact part of the town, the enemy suffered to remain, in June last, for their own convenience.

Knowlton's visit to Charlestown.

They were now surrounded and set fire to by our men. In one of them they found six soldiers, and one woman, all of whom, except one refractory fellow who was killed, were brought off. In another of the houses, according to the information of the prisoners, lived seventeen of the enemy's carpenters. The woman says she went to this house in order to borrow something, just before our men arrived; but seeing no light, and not being able to get into that part of the house where they kept, she concluded they were all asleep. As it is very certain no one escaped from the house, and as our men set the building on fire very suddenly, it is thought the whole seventeen perished in the flames. We burnt ten houses, and

[1] "A Clerk," in the Middlesex Journal, January 13.

brought off six or seven muskets. Three or four houses are still standing. The whole was performed in less than an hour, without the loss of a single man, either killed or wounded. The regulars in the fort on Bunker's Hill did not act with that regularity which those gentlemen who labor hard to show the superiority of red coats over brown coats, would persuade us that regulars always do ; for they kept a hot and close fire on absolutely nothing at all : that is, they fired without an object. Our people calmly executed their purpose, laughed in security, and in security returned to their camp.[1]

JANUARY 17.—THOUGH much has been said of late about WHIG and TORY, few persons are acquainted with their ori-

Origin of Whig and Tory.

gin :—In the year 1679, King Charles the Second fell sick in the summer, upon which the Duke of York, his brother, an avowed papist, returned immediately to court, without the king's leave, with a view to secure the succession of the crown to himself, as his Majesty had no legitimate issue. This alarmed the Protestants, and made them eager for the sitting of parliament, and gave rise to sundry petitions, signed by great numbers of hands, both in city and country, which was very displeasing to his Majesty. That arbitrary tyrant told the petitioners, that he was judge of what was fit to be done. "You would not take it well," said he, "if I should meddle with your affairs, and I desire you will not meddle with mine."—Upon this, counter-addresses were promoted by the influence of the court over all the nation, expressing a detestation and abhorrence of the practice of the petitioners, and referring the sitting of the parliament absolutely to the king's pleasure, by which they obtained the name of *abhorrers ;* which occasioned a great ferment among the people, so that sundry of the privy council deserted their stations at court.

The petitioners for the sitting of parliament, and their adversaries, the abhorrers of such petitions, gave rise to the two grand parties, which have since divided the nation under the distinguishing names of WHIG and TORY. The Whigs, or low-

---

[1] Pennsylvania Evening Post, January 23 and 30.

churchmen, so called from moderation about the hierarchy and their charity for their fellow-Christians of other denominations, were the more zealous Protestants, declared enemies to Popery, and willing to remove to a further distance from the superstitions of the Church of Rome. They were firm to the British constitution and the liberties of their country. The clergy of this persuasion were eminent for their candor and charity, so that they were far from confining salvation to their own communion. Their laity were remarkable for their zeal in promoting the famous bill for excluding the Popish Duke of York from the crown, as the best expedient to secure the Protestant establishment. They were for confining the royal prerogative within the compass of law, for which reason their adversaries charged them with republican principles, and gave them the reproachful name of *Whig*, or sour milk, a name first given to the Presbyterians in Scotland, when they were persecuted by the high church, because, when they were forced to flee from their habitations, hungry and thirsty, they often drank butter-milk whig, or whey, when they came to any friend's house that would shelter and entertain them.

The Tories, or high-churchmen, stood on the side of the prerogative, and were for setting the king above law. They went into all the arbitrary measures of the court, and adopted into our religion (says Dr. Welwood) a Mahometan principle, under the names of non-resistance and passive obedience; which, since the times of that impostor who first broached it, has been the means of enslaving a great part of the world. These gentlemen leaned more to a coalition with the Papists, than with the Presbyterians. They cried up the name and authority of the church, and being men of little tenderness and conscience themselves, paid no regard to the consciences of others. They were for forcing the non-conformists to come into the church by all kinds of coercive measures, as fines, imprisonments, gibbets, &c. But with all their zeal about the church, they were, generally, persons of lax and dissolute morals, and would risk the whole Protestant religion, rather than go into any measures of exclusion or limitation. Most of the high-church clergy were for raising money without Parlia-

ment; one or two court bishops giving measures to the rest,
and they to their clergy. No men did more to enslave the
nation and introduce Popery, than they. Their adversaries
therefore gave them the name of Tories; a name first given to
Irish robbers or highwaymen, who lived upon plunder, and
were prepared for any daring or villanous enterprise. The
non-conformists fell in unanimously with the Whigs, or low-
churchmen, in all points relating to liberty and the civil constitution, as they must do always, if they are consistent with
themselves.

Whig and Tory, then, are names used only with allusion to
their originals, from whence they are borrowed—*sour milk* and
highway robber. Such as trust to our common dictionaries for
an explanation, will only deceive themselves; and they should
know, that they only discover their ignorance in history,
when they profess they are not Tories, because they are not
Irish robbers.[1]

MR. WASHINGTON is just such another character as my Lord
Essex, the Parliament's general in King Charles the First's
time. Putnam may very well be compared to
Ireton. Hancock is one of the greatest desperadoes living. Adams generally sleeps with the memoirs of the
Cardinal de Retz under his pillow. The slow and lenient
measures of the British Government have been interpreted by
our rulers into fear. We poor, distressed Americans, make a
fine joke of your pity. Do not imagine we desire peace, even
upon those terms we seem to solicit it. Were you to agree to
those terms, behold some new demands without satisfaction
for which we cannot think of laying down our arms. The
king must dismiss and punish those servants who have so
highly offended us. After King Charles had granted the Rebel Parliament all they could ask, for want of a better pretence, they declared they could not trust him, and so began
the Civil War. Let somebody remember, that the Congress has
amused you with proposals of accommodation, merely to gain

Letter of a Virginian.

---

[1] New York Packet, January 18.

time; it has answered their end, and they were tolerably well prepared by the latter end of the summer. This winter some of their grand schemes are to be put in execution. They have had amazing success; for all Canada is in their hands already. The Canadians have used General Carleton extremely ill. Montreal was taken almost without a blow. Troops are now marching for Nova Scotia, and you may expect to hear of the surrender of Halifax some time in February. The American cruisers have had as good luck with your transports; indeed the country is so well provided for defence, that every town looks like a store-house, filled with all kinds of warlike necessaries. All people, both high and low, seem as unanimous, as easy, and composed as if engaged in the most safe and justifiable undertaking in the world.[1]

THE following lines were spoken extempore by an American lady, on hearing that the *conquering hero*, General Gage, was on his passage home to England :

> From Boston comes the frighted cow,[2]
> The ruins left to hapless Howe!
> Clinton, a Russ in mind and body,
> Is almost drowned in Boston toddy:
> Burgoyne, like Wedderburne or Meredith,
> Is seeking pelf through Britain's very death.
> Earl Percy there, as well as here,
> The ladies think is very queer!
> They give him tea and keep him warm,
> For surely *he* can do no harm.
>
> Oh Putnam, Ward, and martial Lee!
> The fair's best wishes are for ye,
> The guardians of dear Liberty![3]

JANUARY 20.—SCYLURUS the Scythian, having fourscore sons,

[1] Letter from "A Virginian," to the editor of the Middlesex Journal, published in that paper, January 23.
[2] It is observable that she has never got over the panic with which she was struck at Braddock's defeat! But at all appearances of danger, her hair is observed to rise and stand on end. This is not a fault, but a very great misfortune.
[3] From the London Public Advertiser, republished in the Pennsylvania Evening Post, February 3.

desired nothing so much as to bring them up in the love of each other, and to show them how invincible concord would render them, as he lay on his death-bed, he called them around him, and giving to each of them a bundle of javelins, bade them try if they could break the bundles. The young men having attempted and declaring it impracticable, Scylurus untied the bundles in their presence, broke the javelins one by one, with the greatest ease, and from thence took occasion thus to address his children : " Behold, my sons, your strength, whilst linked together in the bonds of amity ; on the contrary, how weak, and what an easy prey you must be, when separated in your interests by discord and sedition." [1]

Union.

JANUARY 23.—THE Jersey boys are scouring Long Island. They have taken Justice French and some more ringleaders, and a great many arms.   No opposition is made to them.   The people curse their leaders, say they deceived them, promised to support them, and in the time of danger left them.   They will never trust them again.   An officer in this expedition says : " We set out from Woodbridge on Wednesday the seventeenth instant, with about six hundred militia, and were joined at New York with a detachment from Lord Stirling's battalion, consisting of near three hundred.   On Friday morning we crossed, with all our troops, at Horn's Hook, near Hell Gate, and met with no opposition ; we then proceeded on our way towards Jamaica, took in custody some of the principal persons proscribed ; sent out parties, and brought in many of those who voted against sending delegates ; disarmed them and required them to sign an obligation we had drawn up, in which we enjoin them not to oppose either the Continental or Provincial Congresses, but to be subject to them, and not to aid or assist the ministerial troops in the present contest.   From Jamaica we went to Hampstead town, where we expected the warmest opposition, but were disappointed, as the inhabitants came in and brought their arms voluntarily, for two days, as fast as we could receive them.   We have about three

Tory Hunting.

[1] New York Packet, January 25.

hundred stand of arms and a considerable quantity of powder and lead. We are now on our way to Oyster Bay, and shall scour the country as we go, and exert ourselves to discharge the trust enjoined on us. Colonel Heard sent his detachment home last Tuesday, as he thought the militia sufficient. He is indefatigable in discharging his duty ; treats the inhabitants with civility and the utmost humanity. The delinquents express themselves well pleased that a detachment of Jerseymen, and not of New England, were sent to disarm them. Many of those who are proscribed as principals, have either fled or secreted themselves ; several we have in custody. Some others, I believe, are yet to be had, but by some means or other they procured a list of the persons pointed out as principals before our arrival. We are making inquiry how they got their intelligence, but are not yet informed. Those that have come in, and surrendered their arms, are much irritated with those who have led them to make opposition, and have deserted them in the day of difficulty. I conceive they will be as safe if not safer in our custody, than at present among their neighbors, of whom some of them seem very apprehensive, and complain that they have met with insults already." [1]

JANUARY 25.—WE hear that the enemy, in Boston, the evening on which our troops burnt the houses at Charlestown, were entertaining themselves at the exhibition of a play, which they called the Blockade of Boston ; in the midst of which a person appeared before the audience, and with great earnestness, declared that the Yankees were attacking Bunker's Hill. The deluded wretches, at first, took this to be merely *farcical*, and intended as a part of their diversion. But soon convinced that the actor meant to represent a solemn *reality*, the whole assembly left the house in confusion, and scampered off with great precipitation. [2]

[1] Pennsylvania Evening Post, January 25 and February 3.
[2] Another account of Major Knowlton's expedition is given by an officer in the king's army :—On the 8th instant, between eight and nine o'clock at night, we were alarmed by some of the enemy, who came over a small neck of land by a mill upon Charlestown side, and came into some houses that were not destroyed

Lately, we have had several deserters from the enemy. One of them stationed at Charlestown mills, pitched his companion over the dam, and then ran for Cobble Hill.

Last Friday, General Clinton, with a considerable number of grenadiers and light infantry, sailed from Boston, and were supposed to be bound for Virginia.[2]

THE Whigs in South Carolina, are in high spirits. They have large supplies of powder and arms; and having resolutely refused the men-of-war provisions or water, they were obliged to quit the coast. The Tamer (on board of which is Lord William Campbell, late Governor of South Carolina) having taken a sloop from Bermuda, with two hundred and sixty half johannesses, the property of a house in Charleston, the convention granted the injured an order to

South Carolina.

on the 17th of June, where they surprised and took one sergeant and three private men prisoners, who belonged to a wooding party, after which they set fire to the houses, and retreated under a heavy fire of cannon and musketry from one of our redoubts. Among the rest they had got a stout fellow of ours (a grenadier) prisoner, who pretended to be lame, and could walk but slowly, upon which they made him deliver up his arms; and the rebel captain who commanded the party told his men to retreat, saying, "I swear I will take this serpent of a regular under my charge;" but upon his going over the neck of land, the grenadier struck the captain a severe blow on his face with his fist, took him up in his arms, pitched him headlong into the mud, and then ran off. But what is most extraordinary, a new farce was that night to have been acted at Boston, called The Blockade of Boston; the play was just ended and the curtain going to be drawn up for the farce, when the actors heard from without that an attack was made on the heights of Charlestown, upon which one of them came in, dressed in the character of a Yankee sergeant (which character he was to play) desired silence, and informed the audience the alarm guns were fired; that the rebels had attacked the town, and were at it tooth and nail over at Charlestown. The audience thinking this was the opening of the new piece, clapped prodigiously; but soon finding their mistake, a general scene of confusion ensued. They immediately hurried out of the house to their alarm posts; some skipping over the orchestra, trampling on the fiddles, and every one making his most speedy retreat. The actors (who were all officers) calling out for water to wash the smut and paint from off their faces; women fainting, and, in short, the whole house was nothing but one scene of confusion, terror, and tumult. I was upon guard at the advance lines before the town of Roxbury, and we expected a general attack that night, but the rebels were not so forward, for in a few hours every thing was quiet.—*Extract of a genuine letter from Boston, in the Middlesex Journal*, February 27.

[1] New England Gazette, January 25.

sell as much of his lordship's goods and chattels as would repay the money, &c., stolen from them ; on which they sold his coach, horses, &c., and have written him, that they have a balance of thirty pounds, which they are ready to pay to his order. His lordship has stolen sixty or seventy negroes.— How is England fallen ; when its king is a butcher, his ministers knaves, and its nobles negro thieves![1]

JANUARY 30.—A PARAGRAPH in a late number of the London Packet, says : *The public may depend upon the authenticity of the following articles.*—" By a letter from Boston, we learn that the army now have plenty of provisions, and are in much better health and spirits than of late. General Lee, a few days before the letter writer sent his information, had a mutinous soldier in his corps, upon whom he drew his sword, and, running it through his body, instantly despatched him. It is thought that General Lee is not now alive, in consequence of this violence."[2]

Paragraphs from England.

Mr. Washington, we hear, is married to a very amiable lady, but it is said that Mrs. Washington, being a warm loyalist, has separated from her husband since the commencement of the present troubles, and lives, very much respected, in the city of New York.[3]

FEBRUARY 1.—THE plan which Lord George Germaine has laid down for the operations of the next campaign in North America, is for the main army to take the march along the line of coast, and utterly to destroy every city, town, and village, on both sea and great rivers, to which a ship of any burden can come up, which will entirely cut off all the naval designs of the Americans, and perhaps prove the most effective means of putting an end to the war. Several members of the cabinet seconded the opinion, and it is imagined it will prove the prevailing one.—Lord North is against it.

Germaine's Plan.

Letters by the packet declare, that on an epilogue being

[1] Essex Gazette, February 1.
[2] Pennsylvania Evening Post, January 30.   [3] Upcott, iv. 341.

spoken by Ridesdale, after the Beggar's Opera, which was acted in Dublin for a public charity, the audience were so much offended at a line in it, where the Americans were styled rebels, and made so great a disturbance, that the major thought it prudent to omit the exceptionable passage, when he spoke the epilogue again a few nights afterwards.[1]

FEBRUARY 4.—THIS afternoon, between two and three o'clock, General Lee arrived at New York, from the eastward.

Lee at New York. He was escorted into town by Captain Leary's troop of light horse, and a great number of the inhabitants. About the same time General Clinton arrived from Boston, in the ship-of-war Mercury, in company with a transport brig. The committee of safety met immediately, and we expected something like a commencement of hostilities, but the mayor went on board the Mercury, where the general assured him that not a man is to be landed. Clinton is going to the southward, probably Virginia. Lee says he will send word on board the man-of-war, that if they set a house on fire in consequence of his coming, he will chain one hundred of their friends together by the neck, and make the house their funeral pile.[2]

FEBRUARY 6.—THE Virginia forces, under Colonel Howe, abandoned Norfolk this morning, after removing the poor in-

Norfolk Abandoned. habitants, with such effects as they could carry along with them, and demolishing the intrenchments, which Lord Dunmore threw up a little before he fled on board the fleet, now lying before that place. What few houses remained after the late bombardment were likewise destroyed, after being valued, to prevent the enemy's taking shelter in them. Thus, in the course of five weeks, has a town which contained upwards of six thousand inhabitants, many of them in affluent circumstances, a place that carried on an extensive trade and commerce, consequently affording bread to many thousands, been reduced to ashes, and become desolate, through

[1] Middlesex Journal, February 23 and 29.
[2] Pennsylvania Evening Post, February 6.

the wicked and cruel machinations of Lord North and the junto, aided by their faithful servants, my Lord Dunmore, with his motley army, and the renowned Captain Bellew, commodore of his Britannic Majesty's fleet in Virginia, and his generous and valiant crew.   Truly may it be now said,

> " Never can true reconcilement grow
>   Where wounds of deadly hate have pierc'd so deep."

The troops are now stationed at Kemp's Landing, the Great Bridge, and in and about Suffolk.[1]

A FABLE.

Some mice deep intrench'd in a rich Cheshire cheese,
  Grimalkin long wish'd to devour,
Secure from their numbers, they lived at their ease,
  And bravely defied his power.

In vain all the day he sat watching their holes,
  All his tricks and his force were in vain ;
Each effort convinced him the vermin had souls,
  Determined their cheese to maintain.

Grimalkin, deep versed in political schools,
  Affected the siege to give o'er,
Supposing the mice were such ignorant fools,
  They would venture abroad as before.

But, as he retreated, a spirited mouse,
  Whom time had bedappled with grey,
Cried, " All your finesse we don't value a sous,
  No more to your cunning a prey.

" This cheese by possession we claim as our own,
  Fair freedom the claim doth approve ;
Our wants are but few, and her blessings alone,
  Sufficient those wants to remove.

" No cat will we own ; with ambition run mad,
  For our king — so move off in a trice ;
If we find from experience a king must be had,
  That king shall be made by the mice."[2]

[1] Constitutional Gazette, February 28.
[2] "R. R.," in the Pennsylvania Evening Post, February 17.

FEBRUARY 10.—SOME people among us seem alarmed at the
name of Independence, while they support measures and propose plans that comprehend all the *spirit* of it.

Independence.

Have we not made laws, created courts of judica-
ture, established magistrates, made money, levied war, and
regulated commerce, not only without his Majesty's intervention,
but absolutely against his will? Are we not as criminal in the
eye of Britain for what we have done as for what we can yet
do? If we institute any government at all, for heaven's sake
let it be the best we can. We shall be as certainly hanged for
a bad as a good one, for they will allow nothing for the waver-
ings of filial tenderness. It will all be placed to the account of
blundering ignorance. If, therefore, we incur the danger, let
us not decline the reward. In every other instance, *Independence* raises an idea in the mind that the heart grasps at with
avidity, and a feeling soul never fails to be stricken and depressed with the very sound of dependence. If in a private
family the children, instead of being so educated as to take
upon them the functions of good citizens, should be brought to
years of maturity under the apparel, food and discipline of infancy, what laws, natural or civil, would acquit the parents of
the child of infamy and criminality? A set of great lounging
infants tied to mamma's apron at two-and-twenty, with long
bibs and pap-spoons, would put a Sybarite to the blush.

Now, as every moral virtue or vice is vastly enhanced
when considered in relation to a community as well as individuals, I insist upon it that he who would keep a community in
a state of infantile dependence, when it became a fit member
of the great republic of the world, would be vastly more
criminal and infamous than the imaginary family mentioned
before. Whenever I have been an advocate for dependence, I
have felt a conscious want of public virtue. I own it arises from
laziness in me. I was willing to brush through life as I began
it, and to leave the rooting out the thorns and thistles, as well
as the harvest of the laurels, to posterity, and this, I think, was
the case of most of us; but now that we have gone through
the rough work, to desert the glorious prospect it opens
to us, would be heretical, damnable, and abominable, even to

a sensible Pope. It is a duty of much moment to us as men, and of the last degree of magnitude as citizens, to maintain, at every risk, a perfect independence of every thing but good sense, good morals, good laws, good government, and our good Creator.[1]

FEBRUARY 11.—LAST night, about eleven o'clock, intelligence was received at Elizabethtown, New Jersey, that the man-of-war, transports, and tenders, which fell down on Sunday, from the harbor of New York, A False Alarm. to the watering-place, with two hundred marines on board, intended to commit depredations on Staten Island, and furnish themselves with live stock. General Livingston[2] ordered three hundred of the militia to march forthwith to prevent the intended robbery; and having despatched the necessary orders, and a party to reconnoitre the south side of the island, and to procure all possible intelligence of the motions of the enemy, marched himself about three in the morning. The several detachments met at Ward's, in sight of the light-house, and were there joined by a company of light horse, under the command of Captain Blanchard; but, learning that the fleet had left the Hook the day before, the greater part of the troop, still on their march, were ordered back, and a proper number directed to guard the coast, under the command of Colonel Thomas, (lest the departure of the enemy might prove a feint,) to give instant notice of their return.

The alacrity with which the men entered into the service, is truly laudable, and worthy that spirit which ought to animate every honest American.[3]

FEBRUARY 14.—ABOUT four o'clock this morning, a large party of ministerial butchers, supposed to be about one thousand, were discovered crossing the ice from Boston Attack at Dorchester. Neck to Dorchester Neck. The sentry immediately discharged his piece at them, and ran for the guard house to

---

[1] Extract of a letter from a member of the Virginia Convention—*New York Packet*, April 3.
[2] William Livingston.   [3] New York Packet, February 22.

inform Captain Barnes, (commander of the guard,) who had
already taken the alarm by the sentries firing their pieces ; and,
from information he could get of the course they were steering,
judged their design was to cut off the retreat of the guard,
which consisted only of sixty men. Captain Barnes immediately marched his guard off the neck to the edge of the marsh,
and just escaped them, and lest the guns that had just been
fired should not alarm the camp, he sent off several messengers.
The enemy marched along with two field-pieces, and posted
themselves in so advantageous a manner, that Captain Barnes
could not attack them with the least hope of success, and he
was obliged to wait for the arrival of reinforcements. In the
mean time the cut-throats improved every minute of their time
in setting fire to the buildings on Dorchester Neck, while they
still moved toward the castle, where boats were ready to receive
them. But our troops were so close upon them, that they put
out the fire of six or seven of the buildings, and gained the
point next to the castle, before the sons of Belial had reached
their lines. They made prisoners of six of the guard and one
old man, an inhabitant.[1]

FEBRUARY 16.—THIS evening, Captain Souder arrived at
Philadelphia from Grenada. On his passage, he spoke a vessel from Cork, the master of which informed him
The
Commissioners. that twenty-five transports, with four thousand
troops on board, had sailed from Cork for America. Captain
Souder says, that before he left Grenada, a London paper of the
thirtieth of last November arrived there, in which was a list
of the thirty-nine commissioners appointed to *treat with the
Congress*, among whom were Lord Howe and Governor Johnston.[2]

FEBRUARY 19.—THIS day, the ship Hope, from Bristol, in
England, arrived at Annapolis. By her we learn, that Lord

[1] Pennsylvania Journal, March 6 :—It is about two miles from the encampment
at Dorchester, over the causeway, &c., to said guard house, and one mile from
thence to the point next the castle.
[2] Pennsylvania Evening Post, February 17.

Cornwallis, with five regiments, was to sail about the middle of December last, to rendezvous in Virginia, and a part or all of his forces to proceed to South Carolina. Cornwallis is to resign the command when at Williamsburg (if he ever arrives there) to General Clinton, and is there to act under that officer, or command a detachment, as the exigency of affairs may require.

The commissioners would sail about the middle of January, and were to be followed by as large an armament of ships and troops as was possible for Britain to raise in her present state. The ministry breathe nothing but murder, and it is thought that the commissioners are only sent out as a stop-gap, while they have time to raise troops or try the arts of corruption. Among the commissioners, it is said, are Lord Howe, Lord Littleton, Captain Barrington, Governor Pownal, Governors Johnston and Gage, who are all to come out in an eighty or ninety gun ship.[1]

FEBRUARY 20.—THE blockade of Quebec is kept up completely, and the Americans are receiving frequent deserters from the town. The regulars have been seen breaking up the vessels in the harbor for firewood. This absolutely does great honor to General Arnold and his little party. They will now get ease, as troops are coming in pretty fast. One company of Pennsylvania troops arrived yesterday with some American manufactured gunpowder, and many of the New England volunteers. We now have about fifteen hundred men before Quebec, but before the reinforcement arrived, the blockade was kept up by five hundred men, exclusive of a few Canadians, in whom little or no dependence could at that time be put, nor indeed at any time, without a greater force of continental troops.[2]

FEBRUARY 23.—WHATEVER may be reported by the ministerial agents spread through the country, rest assured that the accounts of American weakness contain not one syllable of truth. The Congress have in nothing taken greater pains than

[1] Constitutional Gazette, March 2.   [2] Upcott, iv. 347.

in making themselves perfect masters of the resources of the whole continent; they know that matter completely,
State of America. and having gained it, upon the very best author-
ity, have rejected the offers they have certainly received, both from France and Spain.   It is no secret at Philadelphia that such offers were made; the agents were known, and they had several repeated conferences upon the offers they brought from the house of Bourbon, to become mediators in the quarrel between England and her colonies.   What the answer precisely was, is not known ; but the offers were certainly civilly refused for the present, till the further conduct of the mother country should be experienced.   Certain it is there is no apprehension in any part of America, of not being able to resist the whole force of Great Britain ; and this confidence is founded on the determination to sacrifice every city of America to the same fate which Norfolk has experienced, rather than to submit to political permanent evils, esteemed much worse evils than any that can accrue from the passing mischiefs of burning and destroying.   They have certainly objects at stake of much greater consideration than houses and towns, and they will defend them upon that idea.   Besides, if government was to be successful in conquering, in what manner are the Americans to be kept in subjection ?   Nothing less than an army, almost equal to that which effects the conquest, could do this ; and what would be the benefit of these provinces to Great Britain, kept in such a manner and at such an expense ?   No truth appears clearer to the best informed people in all parts of America, than the absurdity of the conduct of the British Parliament and Ministry.[1]

FEBRUARY 27.—THE pamphlet entitled " Common Sense,"[2]

[1] Extract of a letter from New York, in the Middlesex Journal, March 30.

[2] This pamphlet, by Thomas Paine, was first published on the 9th of January. It was addressed to the INHABITANTS OF AMERICA, on the following interesting subjects:—1. The origin and design of government in general, with concise remarks on the English constitution.   2. Of monarchy and hereditary succession.   3. Thoughts on the present state of American affairs.   4. Of the present ability of America, with some miscellaneous reflections.   *Man knows no master, save creating heaven, or those whom choice and common good ordain.*

is indeed a wonderful production. It is completely calculated
for the meridian of North America.—The author   Paine's
introduces a new system of politics, as widely dif- "Common Sense."
ferent from the old, as the Copernican system is from the
Ptolemaic. The blood wantonly spilt by the British troops at
Lexington, gave birth to this extraordinary performance, which
contains as surprising a discovery in politics as the works of
Sir Isaac Newton do in philosophy. This animated piece dis-
pels, with irresistible energy, the prejudice of the mind against
the doctrine of independence, and pours in upon it such an in-
undation of light and truth, as will produce an instantaneous
and marvellous change in the temper—in the views and feelings of an American. The ineffable delight with which it is
perused, and its doctrines imbibed, is a demonstration that the
seeds of independence, though imported with the troops from
Britain, will grow surprisingly with proper cultivation in the
fields of America. The mind indeed exults at the thought of a
final separation from Great Britain, whilst all its prejudices
and enchanting prospects in favor of a reconciliation, like the
morning cloud, are chased away by the heat and influence of
this rising luminary, and although the ties of affection and
other considerations have formerly bound this country in a
threefold cord to Great Britain, yet the connexion will be dissolved, and the gordion knot be cut. "For the blood of the
slain, the voice of weeping nature cries it is time to part." [1]

THIS morning, the North Carolina minute men and militia,
under the command of Brigadier-General James Moore, had
an engagement with the Tories, at Widow Moore's   Battle of
Creek bridge.[1] At the break of day, an alarm   Moore's Creek.
gun was fired, immediately after which, scarcely leaving the
Americans a moment to prepare, the Tory army, with Captain
McCloud at their head, made their attack on Colonels Caswell
and Lillington, posted near the bridge, and finding a small
intrenchment vacant, concluded that the Americans had aban-

[1] Constitutional Gazette, February 24.
[2] Moore's Creek runs from North to South, and empties into South River, about
eighteen miles above Wilmington, North Carolina.

VOL I.—14

doned their post. With this supposition, they advanced in a most furious manner over the bridge. Colonel Caswell had very wisely ordered the planks to be taken up, so that in passing they met with many difficulties. On reaching a point within thirty paces of the breastworks, they were received with a very heavy fire, which did great execution. Captains McCloud and Campbell were instantly killed, the former having nine bullets and twenty-four swan shot through and into his body. The insurgents retreated with the greatest precipitation, leaving behind them some of their wagons, &c. They cut their horses out of the wagons, and mounted three upon a horse. Many of them fell into the creek and were drowned. Tom Rutherford ran like a lusty fellow :—both he and Felix Keenan were in arms against the Carolinians, and they by this time are prisoners, as is Lieutenant-Colonel Cotton, who ran at the first fire. The battle lasted three minutes. Twenty-eight of the Tories, besides the two captains, are killed or mortally wounded, and between twenty and thirty taken prisoners, among whom is his Excellency General Donald McDonald. This, we think, will effectually put a stop to Toryism in North Carolina.[1]

MARCH 1.—WHEN the last transport that arrived at New York was off Sandy Hook, the little piratical schooner belonging to the "Protectors of our Trade" in the harbor, was sent down with a pilot to bring her up, but the captain of the transport, taking her to be a New England privateer, and being unprepared for fighting, having but eighteen men, six muskets, and two swivels on board, stood off to sea again, and the schooner followed her. The captain of the transport seeing it impossible to escape, hove to, in order to let her come up. The schooner, seeing this, took her also to be a privateer, and imagined this only to be a manœuvre to decoy her, and so, in her turn, began to run away, and after mutually chasing each other for about two hours, the transport came up with, and hailed her, which soon rectified the mistake, to the great joy of

[1] New York Packet, March 28, and Pennsylvania Evening Post, March 23.

both the heroic commanders. This intelligence was received from a person who was on board the transport at the time.

A CORRESPONDENT in London says :—Lord Howe is to go first commissioner, in the new, idle, ridiculous commission that is to be made out, to treat with America. His lordship is not to be, nor to act as commander of any force, but in a civil capacity only.

Discerning men already say this commission scheme will not succeed. America will not treat with those men, nor with any persons (however otherwise respectable) sent by those who advised the late barbarous bloody measures against her.

First remove Lord Mansfield, and the tools of Lord Bute, and then, and not till then, America and England will believe the court are truly desirous of peace.[1]

MARCH 9.—LAST Saturday night, the artillery at the fortresses of Cobble Hill and Lechmere's Point, below Cambridge, and at Lamb's dam in Roxbury, bombarded and cannonaded the town. The following night, the same was continued with great briskness ; and the whole of Monday night, the artillery from all the above fortresses played incessantly. The shot and shells were heard to make a great crashing in the town, but we have not learnt any of the particulars of the execution done thereby. The regulars returned the fire from their batteries at West Boston, and from their lines on the Neck, very vigorously. They threw many shells into the battery at Lechmere's Point, one into the fort on Prospect Hill, and one or two as far as fort "number two," within a quarter of a mile of the College.[2]

Dorchester Heights taken.

The grand object of the Americans was, to draw off the attention of the British from Dorchester Heights, until they could take possession of that position on Monday night. This was accomplished by three thousand men, under General Thomas.[3] The men worked with such alertness, that by morn-

---

[1] Constitutional Gazette, March 2 and 6.   [2] Harvard.
[3] John Thomas.

ing they were in a condition to sustain any attack of the enemy. On Tuesday, the whole army were assembled at their proper posts, to act as circumstances required. It was expected and hoped that General Howe would send out such a force as he thought competent, to dislodge the Americans from Dorchester Hill; that being the case, they were prepared to push into Boston, from Cambridge, with four thousand men. We are since informed that Lord Percy was detached, with three thousand men in transports, to the castle, in order to land on Wednesday from that quarter. On Tuesday night there was such a high gale of wind, which continued part of next day, that, glad of a plea for not attacking, they returned to Boston, and have been busy ever since, in carrying off their best effects from Boston on board their ships; and by their movements, which we can plainly discover, they are now busy in dismantling their fortifications and in getting ready to go off. This is confirmed by the captain of one of their transport vessels, who escaped from them the night before last, with all his crew. He says, on Tuesday morning, our works being discovered from the shipping, the Admiral immediately sent word of it to General Howe, informing him at the same time, that unless he could dispossess the Americans of that post, there was no safety for the fleet, and he should immediately fall down to Narraganset Road. We longed for nothing so much as their coming, but they are too prudent. It is reduced to the greatest moral certainty, that they are now preparing with all despatch, to abandon the town. This does not slacken, but rather increases the ardor of our troops to push on their works on Dorchester Hill, so that by the middle of the week, we may expect to have constructed such a battery there, as will command both the town and shipping, and if they don't leave it before, will oblige them to hasten their departure, and, we hope, compel them to abandon many valuable articles they wish to take off with them.[1]

MARCH 14.—THE common topic of conversation, since last

---

[1] Pennsylvania Journal, March 20.

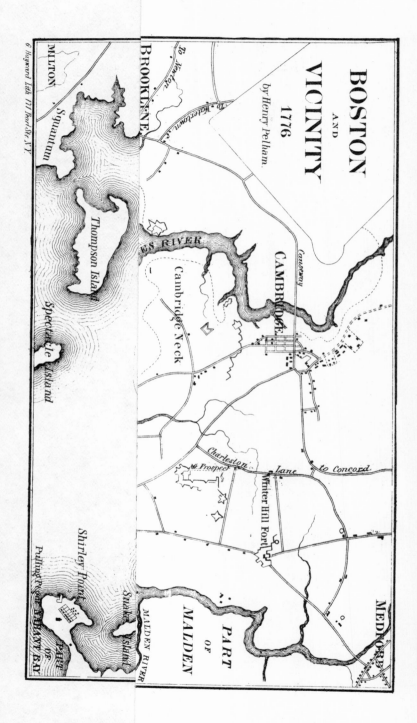

BOSTON
AND
VICINITY
1776
by Henry Pelham.

G. Hayward Lith 171 Pearl St., N.Y.

MILTON

Squantum

BROOKLINE

To Newton

To Watertown.

Thompson Island

Spectacle Island

ES RIVER

Cambridge Neck

CAMBRIDGE

Causeway

Charleston Lane to Concord.

to Prospect

Winter Hill Fort

MEDFORD

PART
OF
MALDEN

MALDEN RIVER

Shirley Point

Snake Island

PART OF NAHANT BAY

Palmers Point

Friday, has been the evacuation of the town of Boston by King George's plundering, murdering army, under General Howe. On that day, a paper was brought out by a flag of truce, to which was affixed the names of sundry inhabitants, among which were some of the selectmen, advising that they were permitted by General Howe, in behalf of the town, to notify our army, that if the firing into the place was discontinued, the British troops would leave the same in three or four days, without destroying it. Though the enemy might really be preparing to leave the town, this paper was thought worthy of little attention, as being nothing more than a mere finesse, to induce a relaxation in our proceedings. Sundry persons, since the above paper came out, have escaped from the town, and inform that the enemy are very busy in shipping their effects on board the transports, and that there is great appearance of their going off very speedily. Yesterday it was reported that they were plundering the town, breaking and destroying every thing they cannot carry away.[1]

THE ministry have boasted much of their *regular*, their *disciplined* troops, which they fancied capable of beating all the *irregulars* in the world. One would wonder how men of any attention to what has passed, could deceive themselves into such an opinion, when so many FACTS within the memory of men not very old, evince the contrary.

Regulars and Irregulars.

The following *Yankee* song gives us a pretty little collection of those facts, and is printed for the encouragement of our militia ; for though it is not safe for men too much to despise their enemies, it is of use that they should have a good opinion of themselves, if just, when compared with those they are to fight with.

If we search for the cause of this superior bravery in the *people* of a country, compared with what are called *regular troops*, it may be found in these particulars : that the men who compose a European regular army, are generally such as have

[1] Constitutional Gazette, March 23.

neither property nor families to fight for, and who have no principle, either of honor, religion, public spirit, regard for liberty, or love of country, to animate them.   They are therefore only pressed on to fight by their officers, and had rather be anywhere else than in a battle.   Discipline only gives the officers the power of actuating them ; and superior discipline may make them superior to other troops of the same kind not so well disciplined.   Thus discipline seems to supply, in some degree, the defect of principle.   But men equally armed, and animated by principle, though without discipline, are always superior to them when only equal in numbers ; and when principle and discipline are united on the same side, as in our present militia, treble the number of mere unprincipled mercenaries, such as the regular armies commonly consist of, are no match for such a militia.

Let us, however, not be presumptuously careless in our military operations, but mix caution with courage, and take every prudent measure to guard against the attempts of our enemies ; it being as advantageous to defeat their designs as their forces.

THE KING'S OWN REGULARS.[1]

Since you all will have singing, and won't be said nay,
I cannot refuse, when you so beg and pray ;
So I'll sing you a song,—as a body may say,
'Tis of the King's Regulars, who ne'er ran away.
    O! the old soldiers of the King, and the King's own Regulars.

At Prestonpans we met with some rebels one day,
We marshalled ourselves all in comely array ;
Our hearts were all stout, and bid our legs stay,
But our feet were wrongheaded and took us away.

At Falkirk we resolved to be braver,
And recover some credit by better behavior :
We wouldn't acknowledge feet had done us a favor,
So feet swore they would stand, but—legs ran however.

[1] "And their triumph over the Irregulars; a new song, to the tune of '*An old courtier of the Queen's, and the Queen's old courtier ;*' which is a kind of recitation, like the chanting of the prose psalms in cathedrals."

No troops perform better than we at reviews,
We march and we wheel, and whatever you choose,
George would see how we fight, and we never refuse,
There we all fight with courage—you may see 't in the news.

To Monongahela, with fifes and with drums,
We marched in fine order, with cannon and bombs;
That great expedition cost infinite sums,
But a few irregulars cut us all into crumbs.

It was not fair to shoot at us from behind trees,
If they had stood open, as they ought, before our great guns, we
      should have beat them with ease,
They may fight with one another that way if they please,
But it is not *regular* to stand, and fight with such rascals as these.

At Fort George and Oswego, to our great reputation,
We show'd our vast skill in fortification;
The French fired three guns;—of the fourth they had no occasion;
For we gave up those forts, not through fear, but mere persuasion.

To Ticonderoga we went in a passion,
Swearing to be revenged on the whole French nation;
But we soon turned tail, without hesitation,
Because they fought behind trees, which is not the *regular* fashion.

Lord Loudon, he was a regular general, they say;
With a great regular army he went on his way,
Against Louisburg, to make it his prey,
But returned—without seeing it,—for he didn't *feel bold* that day.

Grown proud at reviews, great George had no rest,
Each grandsire, he had heard, a rebellion suppressed,
He wish'd a rebellion, looked round and saw none,
So resolved a rebellion to make—of his own.

The Yankees he bravely pitched on, because he thought they
      wouldn't fight,
And so he sent us over to take away their right;
But lest they should spoil our review clothes, he cried braver and
      louder,
For God's sake, brother kings, don't sell the cowards any powder.

Our general with his council of war did advise
How at Lexington we might the Yankees surprise;
We march'd—and re-march'd—all surprised—at being beat;
And so our wise general's plan of *surprise*—was complete.

For fifteen miles, they follow'd and pelted us, we scarce had time to
  pull a trigger;
But did you ever know a retreat performed with more vigor?
For we did it in two hours, which saved us from perdition ;
'Twas not in *going out*, but in *returning*, consisted our EXPEDITION.

Says our general, "We were forced to take to our *arms* in our own
  defence,
(For *arms* read *legs*, and it will be both truth and sense,)
Lord Percy, (says he,) I must say something of him in civility,
And that is—'I can never enough praise him for his great—agility.'"

Of their firing from behind fences, he makes a great pother;
Every fence has two sides, they made use of one, and we only forgot
  to use the other;
That we turned our backs and ran away so fast; don't let that disgrace us,
'Twas only to make good what Sandwich said, that the Yankees—
  could not face us.

As they could not get before us, how could they look us in the face?
We took care they shouldn't, by scampering away apace.
That they had not much to brag of, is a very plain case;
For if they beat us in the fight, we beat them in the race.[1]

MARCH 16.—THIS day, Governor Tryon, now on board the
ship Duchess of Gordon, lying in the North River, sent the
following message to the inhabitants of the colony of New York :—" Notwithstanding prejudice,
delusion, and faction, have hitherto, among too many, usurped
the seat of reason and reflection, and every exhortation I have
offered to the inhabitants of this province (in whose affection I
have been taught to be happy) has been reviled and treated
with neglect, yet as my wishes for their prosperity, and feelings
for their calamities, cannot easily be suppressed even towards
the disobedient, I cannot but repeat my endeavors to recall
those who have revolted from their allegiance to a sense of
their duty, and to comfort those who have been the objects of
oppression, for their zealous attachment to our happy constitution, and their steady obedience to the sovereignty of the British empire.

Tryon's Message.

[1] Pennsylvania Evening Post, March 30.

"It is in the clemency and authority of Great Britain only, under God, that we can look for happiness, peace, and protection, and I have it in command, from the king, to encourage by every means in my power, the expectations in his Majesty's well-disposed subjects in this government, of every assistance and protection the state of Great Britain will enable his Majesty to afford them, and to cherish every appearance of a disposition, on their part, to withstand the tyranny and misrule which accompany the acts of those who have but too well hitherto succeeded in the total subversion of legal government. Under such assurances, therefore, I exhort all the friends to good order and our justly admired constitution, still to preserve that constancy of mind, which is inherent in the breasts of virtuous and loyal citizens, and I trust a very few months will relieve them from their present oppressed, injured, and insulted condition.

"England, Scotland, Ireland, and Wales have united to place their whole strength, power, and confidence in his Majesty's hands. The numerous addresses from all parts of the king's dominions in Europe, speak the loyalty and zeal with which his subjects there engage to support his Majesty, in asserting and maintaining the just sovereignty of the British empire over all its members.

"The British state moves not by sudden and violent sallies, nor wantonly oppresses. She has lenity for her basis, and is distinguished for moderation and forbearance; but when her just indignation is roused, the experience of other nations can testify her weight and force. It cannot be sufficiently lamented, that the conduct of this country has called for so severe a rod. May a timely and dutiful submission avert its stroke.

"I have the satisfaction to inform you, that a door is still open to such honest, but deluded, people as will avail themselves of the justice and benevolence which the supreme legislature has held out to them, of being restored to the king's grace and peace, and that proper steps have been taken for passing a commission for that purpose, under the great seal of Great Britain, in conformity to a provision in a late act of Parliament, the Commissioners, thereby to be appointed, having also power to inquire into the state and condition of the colonies for effecting a restoration of the public tranquillity." [1]

A few days ago, a sloop, bound from Hispaniola to Philadelphia, the property of Mr. Beveridge, a merchant in that city, and commanded by Captain Forrester, was taken by a tender belonging to the Roebuck man-of-war; and one Roger, a midshipman, with five seamen, was put on board to conduct her to Norfolk, Virginia, at the same time taking out all the hands, except the mate and a boy.

Forrester's Adventure.

On her voyage there, one of the casks of wine in the hold, by some accident becoming leaky, the midshipman and his party went down to stop the leak, when the mate and boy, with great heroism, shut down the hatches and secured the prisoners, and then pushed for the Eastern shore with the vessel and cargo, the latter worth at least four thousand pounds sterling.

Captain Hammond, on hearing of this affair, ordered Captain Forrester, who was on board the Roebuck, up to the prison ship at Norfolk, in a pilot boat, under the escort of a midshipman and six hands; but the vessel running aground on an oyster bank two miles below Dunmore's ship, the midshipman ordered one of the seamen into a canoe to do something for the relief of the vessel, when Captain Forrester, seizing the opportunity and leaping into the canoe, cut the painter with a jack leg knife, on which he swung off with the tide; then turning to the seaman, swore he would cut his throat if he offered to obstruct his escape. His menace quieted the fellow, till Captain Forrester had paddled about one hundred yards, when finding his escape practicable, he pulled with his might, and both got safely ashore, amidst a cloud of curses and imprecations from the midshipman and sailors. The captain and his comrade, whom he has taken, have gone to Accomack to look after the vessel and to dispose of the cargo to the best advantage.

Captain Forrester says that the Kingfisher has gone round to Boston to bring a number of ships-of-war up the Delaware

[1] Constitutional Gazette, March 20.

River, to prevent the Philadelphians from making any further preparations for the defence of their city; it being determined upon, it seems, that the grand attack shall be made upon Philadelphia as soon as the fleet and troops arrive from England, but we hope will prove equally abortive with the rest of the cursed ministerial schemes to enslave America.[1]

THE following odd affair happened at Stratford, in Connecticut, a few days ago:—A child of Mr. Edwards, of that place, was baptized by the Rev. Mr. ——, of Norwalk, and named Thomas Gage. This alarmed the neighborhood, and one hundred and seventy young ladies formed themselves into a battalion, and with solemn ceremony appointed a general and the other officers to lead them on. The petticoat army then marched in the greatest good order to pay their compliments to Thomas Gage, and present his mother with a suit of tar and feathers; but Thomas's sire having intelligence of their expedition, *vi et armis*, kept them from entering his house, so that the female soldiers returned to head-quarters without effecting what they intended, and disbanded themselves.[2]

MARCH 17.—THIS morning the British army in Boston, under General Howe, consisting of upwards of seven thousand men, after suffering an ignominious blockade for many months past, disgracefully quitted all their strongholds in Boston and Charlestown, fled from before the army of the United Colonies, and took refuge on board their ships. The most material particulars of this signal event are as follows:—About nine o'clock, a body of the regulars were seen to march from Bunker's Hill, and, at the same time, a very great number of boats, filled with troops, put off from Boston, and made for the shipping, which lay chiefly below the castle. On the discovery of these movements, the continental army paraded; several regiments embarked in boats and proceeded down the river from Cambridge. About the same time two men were sent to Bunker's Hill, in order to make discoveries.

       Boston
       Evacuated.

---

[1] New York Packet, April 11.   [2] New England Gazette, May 30.

They proceeded accordingly, and, when arrived, making a signal that the fort was evacuated, a detachment was immediately sent down from the army to take possession of it. The troops on the river, which were commanded by General Putnam, landed at Sewall's Point, where they received intelligence that all the British troops had left Boston, on which a detachment was sent to take possession of the town, while the main body returned up the river. About the same time, General Ward, attended by about five hundred troops from Roxbury, under the command of Colonel Ebenezer Learned, who embarked and opened the gates, entered the town on that quarter, Ensign Richards carrying the standard.

The command of the whole being then given to General Putnam, he proceeded to take possession of all the important posts, and thereby became possessed, in the name of the Thirteen United Colonies of North America, of all the fortresses in that large and once populous and flourishing metropolis, which the flower of the British army, headed by an experienced general, and supported by a formidable fleet of men-of-war, had, but an hour before, evacuated in the most precipitate and cowardly manner. God grant that the late worthy inhabitants, now scattered abroad, may speedily re-occupy their respective dwellings, and never more be disturbed by the cruel hand of tyranny ; and may the air of that capital be never again contaminated by the foul breath of Toryism.

The joy of our friends in Boston, on seeing the victorious and gallant troops of their country enter the town almost at the heels of their barbarous oppressors, was inexpressibly great. The mutual congratulations and tender embraces which soon afterwards took place, between those of the nearest connections in life, for a long time cruelly rent asunder by the tyranny of our implacable enemies, surpasses description. From such a set of beings, the preservation of property was not expected. And it was found that a great part of the evacuated houses had been pillaged, the furniture broken and destroyed, and many of the buildings greatly damaged. It is worthy of notice, however, that the buildings belonging to the honorable John Hancock, Esq., particularly his elegant mansion house, are left in good order. All the linen and woollen goods, except some that may be secreted, are carried off,[1] and all the salt and molasses is destroyed. The regulars have also destroyed great quantities of effects belonging to themselves, which they could not carry away, such as gun carriages and other carriages of various kinds, house furniture, &c., together with a quantity of flour and hay. All their forts, batteries, redoubts, and breastworks remain entire and complete. They have left many of their heaviest cannon mounted on carriages, and several of them charged, all of which are either spiked, or have a trunnion beaten off. They have also left several of their largest mortars; quantities of cannon shot, shells, numbers of small arms, and other instruments of war, have been found, thrown off the wharves, concealed in vaults or broken in pieces. In the fort on Bunker's Hill, several hundred good blankets were found. It is said about fifteen or twenty of the king's horses have also been taken up in the town; and it is thought that about the same number of Tories remain behind.

We are told that the Tories were thunder-struck when orders were issued for evacuating the town, after being many hundred times assured, that such reinforcements would be sent, as to enable the king's troops to ravage the country at pleasure. Thus are many of those deluded creatures, those vile traitors to their country, obliged at last, in their turn, to abandon their once delightful habitations, and go they know not where. Many of them, it is said, considered themselves as undone, and seemed, at times, inclined to throw themselves on the mercy of their offended country, rather than leave it. One

---

[1] On the 10th of March, a week previous to the evacuation of Boston, General Howe issued the following proclamation:—" As linen and woollen goods are articles much wanted by the rebels, and would aid and assist them in their rebellion, the commander-in-chief expects that all good subjects will use their utmost endeavors to have all such articles conveyed from this place. Any who have not opportunity to convey their goods under their own care, may deliver them on board the Minerva, at Hubbard's wharf, to Crean Brush, Esq., marked with their names, who will give a certificate of their delivery, and will oblige himself to return them to the owners, all unavoidable accidents excepted. If after this notice any person secretes or keeps in his possession such articles, he will be treated as a favorer of the rebels."—*Pennsylvania Evening Post*, April 16.

or more of them, it is reported, have been left to end their lives by the unnatural act of suicide.

The British, previous to their going off, scattered great numbers of crows' feet on Boston Neck, and in the streets, in order to retard our troops in case of a pursuit; and with such silence and precaution did they embark, that a great part of the inhabitants did not know it until after they were gone.

To the wisdom, firmness, intrepidity and military abilities of our amiable and beloved general, his Excellency George Washington, Esq.,* to the assiduity, skill, and bravery of the other worthy generals and officers of the army, and to the hardiness and gallantry of the soldiery, is to be ascribed, under God, the glory and success of our arms, in driving from one of the strongest holds in America, so considerable a part of the British army as that which last week occupied Boston.[1]

This afternoon, a few hours after the British retreated, the

---

[1] New York Packet, March 28:—A British officer gives the following account of the bombardment and evacuation of Boston:—"About three weeks ago the rebels opened a heavy cannonade and bombardment on the town of Boston, from the neighboring heights, which they continued for several successive nights. On the 6th instant, General Howe held a council of war, wherein it was determined that next morning the enemy should be attacked on Dorchester Neck, and a large detachment from our army was embarked on board of transports and flat-bottomed boats for that purpose; but when they were about to land, the wind blew so hard as rendered the disembarkation impossible. When the day dawned, it was perceived that the enemy were so numerous and so strongly fortified and intrenched, even beyond belief, that it was judged prudent to desist from the attempt. Had we proceeded, the affair must have been very bloody; no less than twelve thousand of the rebels were ready prepared to defend their redoubts; however, our disposition was such as would, in all human probability, have insured victory. The grenadiers were to have attacked in columns, with fixed bayonets, and had strict orders not to fire a shot. The light infantry were to have covered the flanks of the grenadiers' columns, who were to have been supported by several regiments.

"On this day se'nnight, the general was pleased to order a retreat, which was effected with the utmost regularity. Nor did the rebels enter the town for above an hour after it was evacuated. We have brought off all our cannon, all our artillery stores, all our provisions, and every thing else which could be of any use to the rebels. Our army, together with the women and children, and almost all the friends of government who were in town, are now on board transports. Our destination is not yet made known."—*Middlesex Journal*, May 12.

Reverend Mr. Leonard[1] preached at Cambridge an excellent sermon, in the audience of his Excellency the General, and others of distinction, well adapted to the interesting event of the day, from Exodus xiv. 25: "And took off their chariot wheels, that they drave them heavily; so that the Egyptians said, Let us flee from the face of Israel, for the Lord fighteth for them against the Egyptians."[2]

MARCH 22.—YESTERDAY, about noon, an effigy was exhibited through the principal parts of New York city, attended by a great concourse of the inhabitants, and others, with the following labels:

"William Tryon, late Governor of this province, but now a professed rebel and traitor to its dearest rights and privileges, as well as to his native country, who, in order to extinguish every spark of American liberty, and recommend himself to the favor of a brutal tyrant, and an insidious court, did illegally, unjustly, and cruelly, shed the blood of an innocent and worthy citizen, when he had the command in North Carolina.[3] For which, and his numberless traitorous practices against the liberties of this country, he is to suffer the just demerits of his atrocious villany, as a warning to all others,

Tryon's Effigy at New York.

> 'Calm thinking villains, whom no faith can fix,
>   Of crooked counsels, and dark politics.'

"Secondly.—Behold the bloody tool of a sanguinary despot, who is using his utmost efforts to enslave you!—'With how secure a brow, and specious form he gilds the secret traitor!'

"Thirdly.—Tories take care!!!"

After it had been sufficiently exposed, it was hung on a gallows, which had been prepared in the middle of the parade, where, after having received the contempt of an oppressed, insulted, and incensed people, it was cut down and destroyed, the whole being conducted without any manner of injury to

---

[1] Chaplain to Gen. Putnam's command.   [2] Penn. Evening Post, March 30.
[3] Thomas Whitehurst, killed in a stamp riot in 1766.

any person whatever, unless it was the person who kept the sign of Tryon's Arms, which were taken down by some of the procession. In one hand of the effigy was placed Tryon's late address to the inhabitants of this province.[1]

Lord Dunmore has made an excellent use of Mr. Holt's press, which he moved by violence out of Norfolk on board his
Informers in Virginia. ship; publishing a weekly paper in two half sheets which he calls the " *Virginia Gazette*," and sends to such tools as he would choose to work with him; and this is done at the expense of the crown!

His behavior shows how necessary it is to put a stop to all communication with him; and from the quick intelligence his lordship has of every intelligence in this city, it becomes highly so to endeavor to discover who are the spies amongst us. It may not be amiss to warn such persons of their danger, and to remind them how severe a punishment may be inflicted on them by the law of nature and nations. They will not be held up to contempt, which was the punishment that was adapted to offences before the war broke out; but death, inflicted by the sentence of a court-martial, or by the just indignation of our enraged people, is the punishment due to their crimes.[2]

His Majesty has been pleased to present Mr. Peter Johnson, son of the late Sir W. Johnson, Bart., to a pair of colors
Ethan Allen. in the twenty-sixth regiment. This young gentleman distinguished himself greatly during the late campaign in Canada, particularly in an action with a party of rebels, commanded by Colonel Ethan Allen, in the neighborhood of Montreal. The latter had formed a design to surprise and take possession of that city; on which a party of the Royalists and some Indians went out and attacked them. In the engagement, Major John Carden, a brave veteran, late of the sixtieth regiment, was mortally wounded by Allen. Presently after, an encounter happened between him and the above-mentioned Mr. Johnson. Allen fired at him without effect; on

---

[1] Constitutional Gazette, March 23.   [2] Pennsylvania Evening Post, April 2.

which, the latter marched up with his fuzee presented, and
demanded of Allen to surrender, who instantly complied, by
laying down his arms, exclaiming, "that his piece had never
before failed him." The Indians presently finding Mr. Johnson had taken this famous leader, proposed sacrificing him to
the manes of Major Carden, but Mr. Johnson humanely interposed, and with much difficulty saved Allen's life; since he
had already generously given him quarter.[1]

MARCH 25.—YESTERDAY being the Lord's day, the Reverend
Mr. Bridge,[2] of Chelmsford, in Massachusetts, preached a most
animating discourse from these words, 2 Kings vii. 7: "Wherefore they arose and fled in the twilight, and left their tents and
their horses, and their asses, even the camp as it was, and fled
for their lives."

This passage of Scripture is a good description of the late
flight of our ministerial enemies from Boston, for they left
their tents and their horses, and a number of *Tories* for *asses!*[3]

THE Tory General McDonald,[4] lately taken prisoner at the
defeat of the Tories in North Carolina, was in rebellion in the
year 1745, against his lawful sovereign, and headed many of the same clan and name, who are
now his followers. These emigrants, from the charity and benevolence of the assembly of North Carolina, received large
pecuniary contributions; and, to encourage them in making
their settlements, were exempted from the payment of taxes
for several years. It is a fact that numbers of that ungrateful
people, who have been lately in arms, when they arrived in
Carolina, were without the necessaries of life—their passages
even paid by the charitable contributions of the inhabitants.

Donald McDonald.

[1] Middlesex Journal, April 2, 1776.
[2] Rev. Ebenezer Bridge was a native of Boston, Massachusetts. He graduated
at Harvard College in 1736, and soon after entered the ministry. He was ordained at Chelmsford in 1741, and continued in the discharge of his sacred duties
over fifty years. He died October 1, 1792.
[3] New York Packet, April 6.
[4] See battle of Moore's Creek, February 27, **ante.**

they have since, under every encouragement that the province of North Carolina could afford them, acquired fortunes very rapidly, and thus they requite their benefactors.[1]

NOTWITHSTANDING the various reports of the fate of Colonel Allen, who was taken and sent to England in irons by General Prescott, we are assured that he has been seen in England, confined in a loathsome jail, and suffering under a heavy load of irons. How different the situation of Allen and Prescott :[2] the first, taken fighting for life, liberty, and property, is treated as a villain ; while the other, taken fighting to support the cruel edicts of a tyrannical ministry, whose aim is to rob and enslave, is lodged at a first-rate tavern in Philadelphia, and fed with the best the markets afford. Oh ! George ! who are the savages ? After this can any man blame the Americans. should they retaliate ?

A correspondent, upon hearing that the *real* errand of the commissioners coming from England was to grant pardons from the king, asked, " whether it would be featherable for a man to be detected with one of them in his pocket." [3]

MARCH 28.—THIS day, the Thursday lecture, which was established and has been observed from the first settlement of
The Thursday Lecture. Boston, without interruption until within these few months past,[4] was opened by the Rev. Dr. Eliot. His Excellency Gen. Washington, and the other general officers and their suites, having been previously invited, met in the council chamber, from whence, preceded by the sheriff with his wand, attended by the members of the council, who have had the small-pox, the committee of the House of Represent-

---

[1] Constitutional Gazette, March 30.

[2] Prescott was taken prisoner by Colonel Easton, near the mouth of the Sorel, in Canada, a short time after Allen was sent to England.

[3] New England Gazette, April 4.

[4] We hear that the Thursday lecture, which has been held in Boston for upwards of one hundred and thirty years, without any interruption, was closed about a fortnight since, by the Rev. Dr. Eliot, who delivered a discourse well adapted to the occasion.—*Pennsylvania Evening Post*, January 16, 1776.

atives, the selectmen, the clergy, and many other gentlemen, they repaired to the old brick meeting-house, where an excellent and well-adapted discourse was delivered from those words in the 33d chap. of Isaiah and 20th verse.

After divine service was ended, his Excellency, attended and accompanied as before, returned to the council chamber, from whence they proceeded to the Bunch of Grapes tavern, where an elegant dinner was provided at the public expense; after which many proper and pertinent toasts were drank. Joy and gratitude sat in every countenance, and smiled in every eye.[1]

MARCH 29.—THERE is a report that General Clinton is arrived at Cape Fear, North Carolina, with the troops he brought with him from Boston, and that he has been since joined by twelve or fifteen hundred from England, or the West Indies. We likewise hear that the Provincial troops are in motion, and marching from all quarters to attack him, so that we may soon expect to hear of another battle in that province, which we hope will prove equally glorious to the American arms as that which was, but a few weeks ago, so successfully fought by the brave Colonel Caswell, at Moore's Creek.[2]

THIS afternoon, Captain Jolly Allen, late a shop-keeper in Boston, with some other Tories, besides women and children, in a sloop, ran ashore on the back of Cape Cod, thinking they had got into the harbor of Halifax. This is a valuable prize, being laden with piece goods and some cash.[3]

[1] Pennsylvania Evening Post, April 9.
[2] Pennsylvania Journal, April 10.   [3] Constitutional Gazette, April 17.

CHAPTER VI.

APRIL 3.—YESTERDAY afternoon, five battalions of the Continental troops now stationed at New York, were reviewed by his Excellency General Heath, on the green, near the liberty pole. They made a martial appearance, being well armed, and went through their exercise much to the satisfaction of a great concourse of the inhabitants of the city.

New York.

In the evening a number of Americans visited and set fire to all the buildings on Bedlow's Island, where the British men-of-war were intrenching and fortifying it as an asylum for the Tory refugees; burnt and brought off all their intrenching tools, with a large number of white shirts and great coats; likewise an abundance of poultry of all sorts. The Asia fired on them, but not a man was killed or wounded. About the same time, a barge full of men, supposed to be from the men-of-war, landed and endeavored to set fire to the air furnace; but they were timely discovered before much damage was done. It is best to keep a good look-out for the rogues.[1]

THEY are very weak, who flatter themselves that in the state to which things have come, the colonies will be easily conquered by force alone. The persons who now govern the resolutions of what they call the Continental Congress, feel in themselves, at this moment, a degree of importance, which, perhaps, the greatest subjects in Europe

An English View.

[1] New York Packet, April 4.

scarce feel. From shop-keepers, tradesmen, and attorneys, they are become statesmen and legislators, and are employed in contriving a new system of government for an extensive empire, which they flatter themselves will become, and which, indeed, seems very likely to become, one of the greatest and most formidable that ever was in the world. Five hundred different people, perhaps, who in different ways act immediately under the Continental Congress ; and five hundred thousand, perhaps, who act under those five hundred, all feel, in the same manner, a proportionable rise in their own importance. Almost every individual of the governing party in America, fills at present, in his own fancy, a station superior not only to what he had ever filled before, but to what he had ever expected to fill ; and unless some new object of ambition is presented, either to him or to his leaders, if he has the ordinary spirit of a man, he will die in defence of that station.[1]

APRIL 8.—THIS day the remains of the brave General Warren were re-interred at Boston. Colonel Phinney's regiment marched first, with drums and fifes, in mourning, then the freemasons, the remains, the relations, General Warren. friends, and town's people. They repaired to the King's chapel ; Dr. Cooper prayed ; Mr. Morton[2] delivered a funeral oration ; closed with a solemn funeral dirge. The general's remains were found on the fourth instant, about three feet under ground on Bunker's Hill. They were known by two artificial teeth fastened in with gold wire, and by being found under the remains of a person buried in trowsers, agreeable to the account given by one who was well acquainted with that circumstance.[3]

GENERAL PUTNAM arrived at New York, from the camp at Cambridge, last Wednesday evening. On Friday he issued

---

[1] Middlesex Journal, April 6, 1776.

[2] Perez Morton. His oration is published in Niles' Principles and Acts of the Revolution.

[3] Constitutional Gazette, April 24.

an order, enjoining the soldiers to retire to their barracks and quarters at tattoo-beat, and to remain there until the reveille
Putnam
at New York. is beaten. He also desired the inhabitants to ob-
serve the same rule, and to-day, he says that it
has become absolutely necessary that all communication between the fleet and the shore should immediately be stopped,
and, for that purpose, has given positive orders that the
ships shall no longer be furnished with provisions. Any inhabitants or others who shall be taken, that have been on
board, near any of the ships, or going on board after the publication of the order, will be considered as enemies, and treated
accordingly. These are hard times for quiet people. Putnam
has appointed Jerry Alner superintendent of arrivals and
departures, under the new rules; and, as he will have full
sway among the Jersey oystermen, it is probable he will have
a way of giving the oysters, as well as the dealers, a fair clearance. *Confiscate if you can't pay;* that's his rule.[1]

CAPTAIN VANDEPUT, of the Asia man-of-war, having heard
at Boston that Lord Percy had received the king's leave
Earl Percy. to come home, and intended to accept it, waited
on his lordship and told him what he had heard;
adding, that he wished the Asia might have the honor to
afford him a passage; to which his lordship returned the
following answer: " 'Tis true I have the king's leave to
return when I please, but upon my honor, whilst there is a
grain of powder to be burnt in America for old England,
Lord Percy will not leave it." Read this, ye Macaronies and
Scavoir Vivres, warriors who strut in parks, and frequent mas-
querades, operas, &c., but are ready to resign in the hour of
danger, when your country's welfare is at stake.[2]

APRIL 16.—DAY before yesterday, as the Asia man-of-war
was passing through the Narrows, she was hailed by the rifle-

---

[1] MS. letter from Samuel Hawke to Job Winslow; see also New York Packet, April 11.

[2] Middlesex Journal, April 11.

men on Staten Island side, and desired to haul too. Some of
the Asia's people on deck asked " for what ? " " Because,"
answered the riflemen, " our orders are to suffer no boats to
pass without a permit from General Putnam." The Asia still
keeping under way, the riflemen fired upwards of forty shots
at her, which the Asia returned by firing two pieces from her
upper tier.[1]

FRANCE declares, she will not assist the American colonies
until they dissolve their connection with Great Britain. Should
that event take place, France would probably involve England
in a war with Germany. America was conquered in that
country in the last war. In the present war she might, in the
same country, be restored to liberty. The whole of the troops
sent by England to America (where so much was at stake) did
not amount to fifteen thousand men. The colonies at one time
had twenty-five thousand in pay, who bore the heat and burden of the war, but shared in no part of its glory or advantages. Americans, beware of reconciliation ! Ye can protect
yourselves.[2]

APRIL 18.—A CORRESPONDENT in London says : " To-morrow, the nineteenth, being Saint Yankie's day, (as tutelar
saint of North America,) and also anniversary of
the famous battle of Lexington ! the same will be   St. Yankie's Day.
most honorably observed by all the true and loyal friends t—
government from that country. There will be a grand procession from the Crown and Anchor, the place of rendezvous
in the Strand, to Saint Dunstan's, where a sermon suitable to
the occasion will be preached by the Rev. Mr. Coriolanus, from
New York. The procession, first being joined by the Reverend Band of Martyrs, (from their place of meeting in Saint
Paul's church-yard,) will move a little before eleven o'clock, in
the following order :

[1] Mason's Journal, and Constitutional Gazette, April 20.
[2] Addressed to the friends of the American army, in the Pennsylvania Journal,
April 17.

Governor Hutchinson, in his speckled velvet, as a representative of Saint Yankie, with Machiavel's works richly gilt and lettered, in his right hand, and supported by Governor Bernard and Governor Gage, both of them in armor; the cord and the feather on crimson cushions, carried by their two secretaries; the Mandamus counsellors in their best apparel, two and two; the admiralty judges in their parti-colored robes, two and two; the fugitive clergy in their canonicals, two and two; the American commissioners of the revenue, with scarfs and cypress leaves in their caps, two and two; their commission and seal of office on a black cushion, carried by their secretary; the fugitive colonels of the militia, in yellow, with wooden swords, two and two; the under officers of the American revenue in harlequin dresses, two and two; the author of the Calm Address, Taxation no Tyranny, the Plain Question,[1] and other writers in favor of American taxation, two and two; such North American merchants as, at the time they publicly went up to the throne with a petition in favor of the Americans, were privately soliciting ministry to indemnify any loss they might sustain by sending over cargoes of goods, in order to defeat the non-importation agreement, two and two; Messieurs Knox, Mauduit, and other agents for the friends of government in North America, two and two; Governor Pownal, with the best map, that is extant, of that country in one hand, and a typographical description of it (especially of his own province) in the other; the many respectable gentlemen who, from time to time, have been tarred and feathered for their loyalty and attachment to the constitution, to appear in that dress, two and two; all those prudent knowing ones, who, by refinement or duplicity, have in some measure persuaded the colonists (say rebels) to think them their friends, but are now lately come over to give private information, and to avail themselves of something beneficial from the general confusion, to appear in their parti-colored dominoes, with black crapes over their faces, two and two. The procession will be preceded by the Doctor of

Dr. Johnson.

Music, from Rhode Island, with his newly raised band of Highland bagpipers; and the whole to move upon the quick step, to the tune of Yankie Doodle. After the sermon is over, the procession will return, in the same order, to the place from whence it came, where an elegant entertainment will be ready at four o'clock, and the ceremony, it is expected, will conclude with great festivity in the evening.

N. B.—The nobility and others, who honor the procession with their attendance, are requested to give orders to their coachmen not to stop up the passage in the narrow part of the Strand.[1]

APRIL 19.—BY a late arrival from England we have the following, which are but the *old lies renewed :*—Government proposes to have in America, in the spring, *foreign troops*, consisting of Hessians, Brunswickers, Hanoverians, and Waldeckers, seventeen thousand ; British troops, sixteen thousand. Press warrants are sent out to Admiral Greaves, to press all American seamen. Press warrants are expected to be issued out soon, as the captains of all the outward bound ships have been very solicitous to procure protections. Orders have been sent to Plymouth for all the guardships there to take on board their full complement of men, as in time of war. Orders have been sent to all the outposts to be very cautious and strict in examining all persons and vessels, &c., that may be judged the least suspicious. Orders are given for a quantity of beef and pork, sufficient for ten ships of the line for six months, to be got ready as soon as possible.

"Old Lies Renewed."

A compact was lately signed between the court and three Northern powers, by which the latter have stipulated to furnish Great Britain between them, with 60,000 troops, the better to enable the latter to carry on the continental war. Government have sent over to Germany to engage 1,000 men called Jagers, people brought up to the use of the rifle barrel guns in boar hunting. They are amazingly expert. Every petty prince who hath forests, keeps a number of them, and they are

---

[1] Freeman's Journal, September 28.

allowed to take apprentices, by which means they are a numerous body of people. These men are intended to act in the next campaign in America, and our ministry plume themselves much in the thought of their being a complete match for the American riflemen.[1]

APRIL 20.—A WRITER gives the following reasons for a declaration of the independence of the American colonies :—1.
Reasons for Independence. The colonies will be delivered from two governments directly opposed to each other. 2. The colonies will be delivered from the disorders which arise from the unlimited, undescribed, and sometimes arbitrary power of conventions, committees of safety, and committees of inspection. 3. A criminal correspondence with the enemies of this country will be prevented, or punished, under the articles of high treason. 4. The colonies will be delivered from the danger of crown officers, whose apparent interest it will always be to remain inactive, or to co-operate with the enemies of America. 5. The British constitution may be immediately restored to each colony, with the great and necessary improvements of a governor and council chosen by the people. 6. France will immediately attack Britain in the most defenceless parts of her empire, and thus draw off her fleets and armies from our coasts. 7. All the powers of Europe will conceive such ideas of our union, love of freedom and military resources, that they will not be tempted to accept of a share in us, upon the condition of conquering us.[2]

THIS is not a time to trifle. Men who know they deserve nothing from their country, and whose hope is on the arm
Reconciliation Opposed. that hath sought to enslave ye, may hold out to you, as Cato[3] hath done, the false light of reconciliation. There is no such thing. 'Tis gone! 'Tis past! The grave hath parted us—and death, in the persons of the slain,

---

[1] Constitutional Gazette, April 20 and May 15.
[2] Pennsylvania Evening Post, April 20.
[3] The author of a series of letters to the people of Pennsylvania, favoring a reconciliation between the mother country and colonies, and against independence.

hath cut the thread of life between Britain and America. Conquest, and not reconciliation, is the plan of Britain. But admitting even the last hope of the Tories to happen, which is, that our enemies after a long succession of losses, wearied and disabled, should despairingly throw down their arms and propose a reunion. In that case, what is to be done? Are defeated and disappointed tyrants to be considered like mistaken and converted friends? Or would it be right to receive those for governors, who, had they been conquerors, would have hung us up for traitors? Certainly not. Reject the offer then, and propose another; which is, we will make peace with you as with enemies, but we will never reunite with you as friends. This effected, and ye secure to yourselves the pleasing prospect of an eternal peace. America, remote from all the wrangling world, may live at ease. Bounded by the ocean, and backed by the wilderness, who hath she to fear but her God?

Be not deceived. It is not a little that is at stake. Reconciliation will not now go down, even if it were offered. 'Tis a dangerous question, for the eyes of all men begin to open. There is now no secret in the matter; there ought to be none. It is a case that concerns every man, and every man ought to lay it to heart. He that *is* here, and he that was *born* here, are alike concerned. It is needless, too, to split the business into a thousand parts, and perplex it with endless and fruitless investigations. This unparalleled contention of nations is not to be settled like a school boy's task of pounds, shillings, pence, and fractions. The first and great question, and that which involves every other in it, and from which every other will flow, is *happiness.* Can this continent be happy under the government of Great Britain, or not? Secondly. Can she be happy under a government of our own? To live beneath the authority of those whom we cannot love, is misery, slavery, or what name you please. In that case there will never be peace. Security will be a thing unknown, because a treacherous friend in power is the most dangerous of enemies. The answer to the second question—can America be happy under a government of her own, is short and simple, viz.: As happy as she pleases ; she hath a blank sheet to write upon. Put it not off too long.

Painful as the task of speaking truth must sometimes be, yet we cannot avoid giving the following hint, because much, nay, almost every thing, depends upon it ; and that is, a thorough knowledge of the persons whom we trust. It is the duty of the public, at this time, to scrutinize closely into the conduct of their committee members, members of assembly, and delegates in Congress, to know what they do and their motives for so doing. Without doing this we shall never know who to confide in, but shall constantly mistake friends for enemies, and enemies for friends, till in the confusion of persons we sacrifice the cause.[1]

APRIL 22.—WE have all the debates in Parliament, by which it appears that the determination of the court is, first to *Movements of the Ministry.* conquer, and then to grant pardons to those they choose, and for this purpose only are the commissioners declared to be sent. This is the ostensible plan, but we are informed they are to bribe through thick and thin, to procure the betraying of America ; so that it behoves all men to watch, with the most attentive consideration, the conduct of those intrusted with the public concerns, whether colonial or continental. The last act of Parliament is a curious piece of retrospective injustice. After declaring the thirteen colonies in rebellion, and without his Majesty's protection, and our property made seizable wherever found on the water, it goes on to give legal sanction to all the violences and robberies, &c., that their people had committed previous to their passing that act. The Congress have, in consequence of this, recommended the fitting out privateers to cruise on British property.

It may be depended upon as fact, that the agents of the Scotch factors have been desired by the administration to make no noise about their debts in America ; for that they, the ministry, will see their debts paid by forfeiting American estates.

---

[1] "The Forrester," in the Pennsylvania Journal, April 24.

Thus we may account for the meaning of the intercepted letter lately published in the Virginia Gazette, wherein the factor is desired to make out a list of debts and send them to Scotland ; and thus these harpies, after having already pillaged a great part of the property of Virginia, are now making out accounts, under court auspices, by which all the remaining property of the country is to become theirs.[1]

THIS evening a paper printed in red letters, and called the American Gazette, was carried to the Plough Inn, at Sudbury, in England, and read before a number of tradesmen and others, who unanimously condemned it to the flames, it being calculated to stir up sedition against his Majesty's person and government. Some straw was immediately procured, and a fire made on Stour Hill, where the said paper was publicly burnt before a great number of spectators. While it was burning, a person solemnly repeated, " So may the schemes of America, that are formed against the government of Great Britain, fall to the dust." There were several kinds of fireworks exhibited on the occasion, and the evening concluded by drinking success to his Majesty's arms.[2]

The American Gazette.

APRIL 27.—THE essence of liberty consists in our having it in our power to choose our own rulers, and so far as we exercise this power we are truly free. Many advantages flow from such a plan of government. The following two have rarely been attended to, but every one will perceive them as soon as mentioned :

Effect of Elections.

A poor man has rarely the honor of speaking to a gentleman on any terms, and never with familiarity but for a few weeks before the election. How many poor men, common men, and mechanics, have been made happy within this fortnight, by a shake of the hand, a pleasing smile, and a little familiar chat with gentlemen who have not for these seven years past condescended to look at them. Blessed state which

[1] Pennsylvania Evening Post, May 14.   [2] Middlesex Journal, May 7.

brings all so nearly on a level! "What a clever man is Mr. ——," says my neighbor; "how agreeable and familiar! He has no pride at all! he talked as freely to me for half an hour as if he were neighbor —— there. I wish it were election time always. Thursday next he will lose all knowledge of ——, and pass me in the street as if he never had known me."

How kind and clever is the man who proposes to be sheriff, for two months before the election :—he knows everybody, smiles upon and salutes everybody, until the election is over; but then to the end of the year he has no time to speak to you, he is so engaged in seizing your property by writ of venditioni exponas, and selling your goods at vendue.

Thus the right of annual elections will ever oblige gentlemen to speak to you once a year, who would despise you forever, were it not that you can bestow something upon them.

Lying is so vulgar a failing that no gentleman would have any thing to say to it but at elections. Then, indeed, the greatest gentleman in the city will condescend to lie with the least of us. This year their humility is amazing, for they have stooped to the drudgery of going from house to house to circulate election lies about division of property. I cannot commend their policy herein, for such poor fellows as I am, with nothing more. However, it shows their willingness to come down a pin, which is such a favor that we ought to be truly thankful for it. In a word, electioneering and aristocratical pride are incompatible, and if ever we should have gentlemen to come down to our level, we must guard our right of election effectually, and not let the assembly take it out of our hands. Do you think even Mr. J—— would ever speak to you, if it were not for the May election? Be freemen, then, and you will be companions for gentlemen annually.[1]

A CORRESPONDENT in London says :—"His Majesty's right arm is lame, occasioned by a sprain from flourishing his sword over the heads of his new made knights.

[1] Pennsylvania Evening Post, April 27.

"The Rev. Mr. Peters,[1] from Lebanon, in Connecticut, has obtained his Majesty's leave to pick hops at 9d. per day, a penny more than the usual price, as a reward for his past faithful services; and by this lucrative business it is supposed he will soon acquire a fortune equal to that he left behind him.

"James Rivington,[2] of New York, is appointed cobweb sweeper of his Majesty's library. There are many other posts and rewards given to persons who have fled from the colonies, equal to the above mentioned."[3]

The Congress have struck a number of silver and copper medals, which are distributed among the officers of their army, and worn by them constantly. On one side are two vases swimming on the water, with the motto, *Frangimur si Collidimur;* on the other side is an emblematical device: four hands clinched together, and a dove over them; beneath them is a serpent cut in pieces.[4]

May 8.—Last week a certain Mr. Cable, in Fairfield, Connecticut, sent a load of provisions to the ministerial plunderers, and was loading a second time for the same purpose, but was discovered by a Tory, who was Fairfield Tories. concerned in the affair, and who made oath before a magistrate, of the scheme in agitation. The said Cable was observed to be sounding for deep water about the channel, which he found at a place called the Black Rock, and through which place he was to pilot a gang of cruel murderers, about one thousand in number, whose orders were to massacre men, women, and

---

[1] Samuel A. Peters, LL.D., an Episcopal clergyman, especially celebrated for a malicious and fabulous history of Connecticut. He was born in Hebron, Connecticut, December 12, 1735: graduated at Yale College in 1757, and afterwards took charge of the church of his native town, and one in Hartford. He was obliged to flee to England, in 1774. He returned to America in 1805, and died in New York, April 19, 1826.

[2] Rivington sailed from New York for London in the ship Samson, in company with Major Moncrieffe, and several loyalists, on the 10th January, 1776.— *New York Packet*, January 11.

[3] Constitutional Gazette, May 4.   [4] Middlesex Journal, May 2.

children. The signal of their landing was to be three cannon fired in the night.

This gang chiefly inhabited about Newtown, in Connecticut, and from that place all along to Dobb's ferry on the North River. Cable was on this discovery apprehended, and committed to Fairfield gaol, and also another villain named Pardelow, at Greenwich, who was detected enlisting men for the ministerial service, was examined before the committee of safety for Greenwich, and committed to gaol. Two more were apprehended, but discharged for want of sufficient proof. A list of the names of a number of them that had enlisted has been obtained, and a party of men are gone in pursuit of them.[1]

MAY 16.—THE Committee of Safety in Philadelphia having already made known to the inhabitants of that city, the pressing occasion there is for a large quantity of LEAD, to be employed in the defence of this country, and requested them to spare for the public use the various species of leaden weights in their respective families ; they have, as the most expeditious and easy method of procuring such LEAD, appointed Thomas Nevill, Frazer Kinsley, William Colliday, and John Darcy to go round the city and receive it at the several houses, they paying at the rate of sixpence per pound as formerly specified, it being understood that clock weights are not at present comprehended among them, as the iron weights to replace them are not yet made.

It is expected that every virtuous citizen will immediately and cheerfully comply with this requisition, but if any persons should be so lost to all sense of the public good as to refuse, a list of their names is directed to be returned to the committee.[2]

YESTERDAY is rendered memorable by a unanimous resolution of the Virginia convention,[3] now sitting at Williamsburg, to instruct their delegates in the Continental Congress

[1] Constitutional Gazette, May 8.
[2] Pennsylvania Evening Post, May 18.
[3] There were one hundred and twelve members present.

to move for a declaration of independence and freedom.   It is the result of the most mature deliberation, and we hope will be speedily ratified by the Congress.   Let the Virginia Votes
DOUBTERS read it: [1]—"Forasmuch as all the en- for Independence.
deavors of the United Colonies, by the most decent representations and petitions to the King and Parliament of Great Britain, to restore peace and security to America under the British government, and a reunion with that people upon just and liberal terms, instead of a redress of grievances, have produced, from an imperious and vindictive administration, increased insult, oppression, and a vigorous attempt to effect our total destruction.   By a late act, all these colonies are declared to be in rebellion, and out of the protection of the British crown, our properties subjected to confiscation, our people, when captivated, compelled to join in the murder and plunder of their relations and countrymen, and all former rapine and oppression of Americans declared legal and just.   Fleets and armies are raised, and the aid of foreign troops engaged to assist these destructive purposes.   The king's representative in this colony hath not only withheld all the powers of government from operating for our safety, but, having retired on board an armed ship, is carrying on a piratical and savage war against us, tempting our slaves, by every artifice, to resort to him, and training and employing them against their masters.   In this state of extreme danger, we have no alternative left but an abject submission to the will of those overbearing tyrants, or a total separation from the crown and government of Great Britain, uniting and exerting the strength of all America for defence, and forming alliances with foreign powers for commerce and aid in war.   Wherefore, appealing to the Searcher of Hearts for the sincerity of former declarations, expressing our desire to preserve the connection with that nation, and that we are driven from that inclination by their wicked councils, and the eternal laws of self-preservation.

"Resolved *unanimously*, That the delegates appointed to represent this colony in general Congress, be instructed to pro-

<hr/>

[1] Clift's Diary.

pose to that respectable body, TO DECLARE THE UNITED COLONIES FREE AND INDEPENDENT STATES, absolved from all allegiance to or dependence upon the crown or Parliament of Great Britain ; and that they give the assent of this colony to such declaration, and to whatever measures may be thought proper and necessary by the Congress, for forming foreign alliances, and a CONFEDERATION OF THE COLONIES, at such time, and in the manner as to them shall seem best. Provided, that the power of forming government for, and the regulations of the internal concerns of each colony, be left to the respective colonial legislatures.

" Resolved *unanimously*, That a committee be appointed to prepare a declaration of rights, and such a plan of government as will be most likely to maintain peace and order in this colony, and secure substantial and equal liberty to the people." [1]

The procuring of foreign assistance was the immediate object of this resolution, as the alternative of separation or submission was the assigned ground of it. But a political connection on any terms, with a people who have exerted against us every species of barbarity and insult, would have had few advocates.

In consequence of the resolution, universally regarded as the only path which will lead to safety and prosperity, some gentlemen made a handsome collection for the purpose of treating the soldiery, who to-day were paraded in Waller's grove, before Brigadier-General Lewis, attended by the gentlemen of the committee of safety, the members of the general convention, the inhabitants of the city, and others. The resolution being read aloud to the army, the following toasts were given, each of them accompanied by a discharge of the artillery and small arms, and the acclamations of all present :—
1. The American Independent States. 2. The grand Congress of the United States, and their respective Legislatures. 3. General Washington, and victory to the American arms.

The union flag of the American states waved upon the

---

[1] Edmund Pendleton, president, and John Tazewell, clerk of the convention.

capitol during the whole of this ceremony, which, being ended, the soldiers partook of the refreshment prepared for them by the affection of their countrymen, and the evening concluded with illuminations, and other demonstrations of joy. Every one seems pleased that the domination of Great Britain is now at an end, so wickedly and tyrannically has it been exercised for these twelve or thirteen years past, notwithstanding our repeated prayers and remonstrances for redress.[1]

TO VIRGINIA.

At length,—with generous indignation fir'd,
By freedom's noblest principles inspir'd,
The Continental spirit blazes high,
And claims its right of independence!
Virginia, hail! Thou venerable state!
In arms and councils still acknowledg'd great!
When lost Britannia in an evil hour
First[2] try'd the steps of arbitrary power,
Thy foresight then the Continent alarm'd,
Thy gallant temper ev'ry bosom warm'd.—

And now, when Britain's mercenary bands
Bombard our cities, desolate our lands,
(Our pray'rs unanswer'd, and our tears in vain,)
While foreign cut-throats-crowd th' ensanguin'd plain;
Thy glowing virtue caught the glorious flame,
And first renounc'd the cruel tyrant's name!
With just disdain, and most becoming pride,
Further dependence on the crown deny'd!

Whilst freedom's voice can in these wilds be heard,
Virginia's patriots shall be still rever'd.[3]

DOCTOR JOHNSON defines the word "expedient" as a thing necessary to be done, which implies that it cannot be expedient to do evil. Therefore the word "expedient" can only be applied to the promoting a good purpose; "Expedient." but you will find it frequently mentioned in the king's speeches; and, in Parliament, ministerialists make a monopoly of it, and apply it altogether to the use and service of his Majesty, to wit:

[1] Pennsylvania Journal, May 29. [2] The time of the Stamp Act.
[3] Freeman's Journal, July 27.

"It is become expedient to shut up the American ports;" "it is expedient to destroy their trade;" "quite expedient to take their vessels;" "expedient to bring them under our feet;" "expedient to humble them;" and highly "expedient to reduce them to absolute submission." General Gage found it expedient to fire upon a few unarmed peasants, and kill eight of them; he found it expedient to burn Charlestown, &c.; Lord Dunmore found it expedient to burn Norfolk, &c.; General Prescott thought it expedient to put Colonel Allen into irons, and transport him; and Governor Tryon thought it expedient to write to the Mayor of New York that "the commander of his Majesty's ships-of-war found it expedient to burn the pilot house;" and General Howe found it expedient to quit his stronghold at Boston, and escape from it, after he was out-generaled by General Washington; and some of his doctors found it expedient to mix a quantity of arsenic among the drugs they left behind, as a bait for the Yankee rats to nibble at, and all for the service of his Majesty; so that it seems to be a court favorite word, and become high treason for an American to use or apply it. What would the ministry or Parliament have done had there been no such word?

We hope the Americans will not adopt their language, and instead of the word "expedient," say "necessary;" and that it is now become highly necessary to oppose those ministerial grammarians, lest they should also attempt to defile our language, as they have defiled our land, with blood.[1]

MAY 23.—LAST Friday, the Continental armed schooner, Franklin, commanded by Captain Mugford, in sight of the British men-of-war, took, and carried into Boston,
Captain Mugford.
a ship from England, about three hundred tons burden, mounted with six carriage guns.

The enemy, intolerably vexed and chagrined that the prize should be taken and unloaded in their open view, formed a design of wreaking their vengeance on Captain Mugford. The Sunday following, he, in company with Captain Cunningham,

---

[1] Constitutional Gazette, May 18.

in the Lady Washington, a small privateer armed with swivels, blunderbusses, and muskets, fell down from Boston in order to go out in the bay. The enemy, observing their sailing, fitted out a fleet of boats for the purpose of surprising and taking them in the night; and the Franklin's running aground in the gut gave them a good opportunity of executing their plan.

The Lady Washington came to anchor near Captain Mugford; and between nine and ten o'clock he discovered a number of boats, which he hailed, and received for answer that they were from Boston. He ordered them to keep off, or he would fire upon them. They begged him, for God's sake, not to fire, for they were going on board him! Captain Mugford instantly fired, and was followed by all his men, and cutting his cable, brought his broadside to bear, when he discharged his cannon loaded with musket balls, directly in upon them. Before the cannon could be charged a second time, two or three boats were alongside, each of them supposed to have as many men as the Franklin on board—which had only twenty-one, including officers. By the best accounts they were not less than thirteen boats in all, many of them armed with swivels, and having on board, at the lowest computation, about two hundred men.

Captain Mugford and his men plied those alongside so closely with firearms and spears, and with such intrepidity, rapidity, and success, that two boats were soon sunk, and all the men either killed or drowned. But while the heroic Mugford, with outstretched arms, was righteously dealing death and destruction to our base and unnatural enemies, he received a fatal ball in the body, which in a few minutes put a period to his life, from which, had it been spared, his oppressed country would undoubtedly have reaped very eminent advantages.

After our brave men had maintained this unequal contest for about half an hour, the enemy thought proper to retire. The carnage among them must have been great, for besides the two boat loads killed and drowned, many were doubtless killed and wounded on board the others. Great execution was done by the spears. One man, with that weapon, is positive of having killed nine of the enemy!

The number of the boats which attacked the Franklin was about eight or nine. The remainder, to the number of four or five, at the same time attacked Captain Cunningham in the Lady Washington, who then had on board only six men besides himself. This brave little company gave the boats such a warm reception that they were soon glad to give over the contest, after suffering, it is thought, considerable loss.[1]

A WRITER in England says :—Dorchester Hill was taken in a very curious manner The rebels provided five hundred bundles of screwed hay, which they shoved before them, and under cover thereof mounted the heights, where they immediately fortified themselves, having brought the timber ready framed. They had also provided themselves with hogsheads and barrels filled with sand, and headed up, which they intended to have rolled down Dorchester Hill, in case the King's troops had attempted to mount the same.

A gentleman, after recapitulating the grievances of the Americans, summed them in the following words of scripture : " The fathers have eaten sour grapes, and the children's teeth are set on edge."[2]

MAY 25.—AT a time when tyranny bears fire in one hand, and instruments of death in the other, let us exert every nerve,

[1] Pennsylvania Evening Post, June 1 ; another account in the same paper, of May 28 :—Last Saturday night, (May 18,) the brave Captain Mugford, commander of the armed schooner Franklin, after seeing his prize safe in Boston harbor, was going out again, but the tide making against him, he came to anchor off Pudding Gut Point. The next morning, by daybreak, the sentry saw thirteen boats from the men-of-war making for them. They got ready to receive them before they could board the schooner; she sunk five of the boats, and the remainder attempting to board, they cut several of the crews' hands off as they laid them over the gunwale. The brave Captain Mugford making a blow at the people in the boats with a cutlass, received a wound in the breast, on which he called his lieutenant, and said, "I am a dead man; don't give up the vessel; you will be able to beat them; if not, cut the cable and run her on shore," and then expired in a few minutes. The lieutenant then ran her on shore, and the boats made off. The men that were taken up from the boats that sunk, say they lost at least seventy men. The schooner had but one man killed besides the captain.

[2] Middlesex Journal, May 23 and 25.

and, to our utmost, promote justice, equity, and good economy ; that by virtue, resolution, and union, we may break the monster's head, though he, Colossus-like, bestrides our harbors, shading the ocean with his lowering ^{To all Americans.} brow, and yawns with horrid jaws for the innocent blood of this continent.

But the most effectual way to prevent his blood-thirsty designs, and ward off devastation, will be to seize and confine, within the narrow circuit of a gaol or prison, the sons of this infernal monster. It is the part of a prudent man to confine the lion to his cage when in his power, though he should cease from roaring, or even feign himself a lamb ; and to break a serpent's head, though she, when caught, falsely pretended herself a dove. Let me tell you, words do not convert lions into lambs, serpents into doves, nor Tories into Sons of Liberty. Remember, as our Saviour was betrayed by one of his disciples, so is our country by her pretended friends.

But how ridiculous and destructive is this, to allow persons a right of property in any country, where they employ both their talents and properties to destroy its immunities, and even to sacrifice the blood of its inhabitants, to satisfy the wanton cravings of a greedy monster.

Let me say, to suffer those who contradict the true interest of their country at this important struggle to go unconfined, or to enjoy their former property, upon a slight confession or promise of reformation, is to give them the advantage to sport with our liberties, as well as to appear ridiculously stupid ourselves. I say, such folly as this cannot fail to give vice the laurel, whilst virtue sits in tears. There is a way to shun calamities of every kind, if rightly understood. The only one for us seems this : to discard the thought of riches, and seek for men of virtue, to serve the public cause. Virtue joined with knowledge will save a state from the greatest calamities ; while riches joined with avarice, like an impetuous torrent, drives headlong all within reach, and drowns them within its gloomy vortex.

My countrymen, when you are to employ a man for public

trust, consider, not who is most fond of such an office, or may like its profits best, but who is most fit, and who will serve his country best. He who gives his vote, being swayed by birth, fortune, or any thing beside the general good, sells his country. He who devotes his all to do it service, let his condition be what it may, is one of the noble columns upon which it stands. Those who prefer the favor of selfish persons, or their own private interest to the true interest of their country, do not long support their own or their country's cause; but being an insufficient basis for such a trust, by the assistance of avarice and luxury attempt the arduous task, till whatever they pretend to support falls, together with themselves, in one general ruin. Witness the British Parliament! There, virtue has long since been a crime; avarice hath taken the field, and entered the gates where the public councils are held; justice gives up the keys, and flies to seek an asylum in some propitious clime. And now behold what follows! How is the blood of her citizens sported with?—some living an ignoble life, others dying an inglorious death! Who can atone for such a crime as this? to sacrifice more than a thousand troops on death's grim altar, to gain what in reason's view was not their right, and what those who survived the bloody scene could not maintain.

Then to shun such horrid deeds, let us despise both avarice and avaricious men. Consider, I entreat you, that folly in a judge, a general, or a king, is folly indeed, and draws most aggravated ruin at its heels. O let virtue, prudence, and resolution, take the field! Let them possess the bench, the council chamber, and the senate.

Thus alone can a people be rendered happy, and a country glorious; but give me leave, my countrymen, as I both feel for ourselves and millions yet unborn, to warn you neither to suffer inattention to possess your minds or idleness your pens; and may each one within his own peculiar sphere, strive for the good of the whole. Then shall we, as individuals, be happy; as a people, terrible to our enemies; and as a country, glorious wherever fame shall celebrate the exploits of heroes, and just triumphs of virtuous deeds. And provinces and kingdoms, over which the Roman Eagle never flew, shall bow to the imperial sceptre of the free and independent States of America.[1]

MAY 31.—A CAPTAIN, lately arrived from St. Croix, says, that on the tenth instant, in latitude 34° longitude 67° 24', he fell in with a brig, the captain of which told him, that he sailed in company with a fleet of seventy sail of transports, under convoy of two sixty-four, four forty gun ships, and two bomb ketches, from which he parted on the fifth in a hard gale of wind. The fleet had on board a large number of Hessians, Brunswickers, and English troops, *all bound to Philadelphia*, "in order to disperse," as the captain expressed himself, "that hornet's nest the Congress, after which they were certain the continent would become a very easy prey." God grant that the patriots may be prepared to receive this armament.[2]

JUNE 1.—NOTWITHSTANDING the savage treatment we have met with from the King of Britain, and the impossibility of the colonies being ever happy under his government again, according to the usual operation of natural and moral causes, yet we still find some people wishing to be dependent once more upon the crown of Britain. I have too good an opinion of the human understanding, to suppose that there is a man in America who believes that we ever shall be happy again in our old connection with that crown. I, therefore, beg leave to oblige the advocates for dependence to speak for themselves in the following order :—

Views of the Dependants.

1. I shall lose my office.   2. I shall lose the honor of being related to men in office.   3. I shall lose the rent of my houses for a year or two.   4. We shall have no more rum, sugar, tea nor coffee, in this country, except at a most exorbitant price. 5. We shall have no more gauze or fine muslins imported among us.   6. The New England men will turn Goths and Vandals, and overrun all the Southern Colonies. N.B.—It is the fashion with the people who make this objection to independ-

---

[1] Addressed to all Americans who love liberty, and hold their country dear, by "Amicus Patriæ et Filius Libertatis."—*Providence Gazette*, May 25.

[2] Pennsylvania Evening Post, June 1.

ence, to despise the courage and discipline of the New England troops, and to complain that they are unwilling to fight out of their own colonies. 7. The church will have no king for a head. 8. The Presbyterians will have a share of power in this country. N. B.—These people have been remarked, ever since the commencement of our disputes with Great Britain, to prefer a Quaker or an Episcopalian, to one of their own body, where he was equally hearty in the cause of liberty. 9. I shall lose my chance of a large tract of land in a new purchase. 10. I shall want the support of the first officers of government, to protect me in my insolence, injustice, and villany. 11. The common people will have too much power in their hands. N. B.—The common people are composed of tradesmen and farmers, and include nine-tenths of the people of America.

Finally.—Sooner than submit to the chance of these probable evils, we will have our towns burnt, our country desolated, and our fathers, brothers, and children butchered by English, Scotch, and Irishmen; by Hanoverians, Hessians, Brunswickers, Waldeckers, Canadians, Indians, and Negroes. And, after all, such of us as survive these calamities, will submit to such terms of slavery as King George and his Parliament may impose upon us.[1]

JUNE 10.—To-DAY, the grand question of Independency was proposed to the first, second, fourth, and fifth battalions of associators of Philadelphia and suburbs; consisting of about two thousand officers and men. Against it, in the first battalions, four officers and twenty three privates—second, two privates—fourth and fifth unanimous for independence.

The lieutenant of the third battalion refusing to put the question, gave great umbrage to the men, one of whom replied to him in a genteel spirited manner.

" How our delegates in Congress may act," says a Pennsylvanian, " we know not, though we have a right to know, and intend to promote an inquiry for that purpose."—Take

---

[1] Article signed *Hutchinson, Cooper, Cato, &c.*, in the Pennsylvania Evening Post, June 1.

heed, Tories; you are at your last gasp! You have had many
warnings, and many kind invitations![1]

JUNE 14.—YESTERDAY, the inhabitants of the town of
Boston were made acquainted, by beat of drum, that an
expedition was to be undertaken against the
enemy's ships in Nantasket road, and for erecting   The Nantasket
proper fortifications in the lower harbor. Accordingly detachments from the colonial regiments, commanded by the Colonels
Marshall and Whitney, and the battalion of train, commanded
by Lieutenant-Colonel Crafts, were embarked on board boats
at the long wharf, together with cannon, ammunition, provision, intrenching tools, and every necessary implement, and
sailed for Pettick's Island and Hull, where they were joined
by some continental troops, and seacoast companies, so as to
make near six hundred men at each place. A like number
of the militia, from the towns in the vicinity of Boston harbor,
with a detachment from the train, and some field-pieces,
took post at Moon Island, Hoff's Neck, and Point Alderton.
At the same time, a detachment from the continental army,
under the command of Colonel Whitcomb, with two eighteen-
pounders, one thirteen-inch mortar, with the necessary
apparatus, intrenching tools, &c., were embarked for Long
Island to take post there. The troops, delayed by a calm, did
not arrive at their several places of destination till near daylight this morning. Notwithstanding this, however, such was
their activity and alertness, that they had the cannon planted,
and a line of defence hove up on Long Island and Nantasket
hill in a few hours, when a cannon-shot from Long Island
announced to the enemy our design. Soon after, a signal was
made for the whole fleet, consisting of eight ships, two snows,
two brigs, and one schooner, to unmoor and get under weigh.
The Commodore Banks bore our fire, and returned it with
spirit, till a shot from Long Island pierced the upper works
of his ship, when he immediately unmoored or cut his cables,
and got under sail, and happy for him that he did so, for in a

[1] Pennsylvania Evening Post, June 11.

small space of time afterwards, a shell from our works fell into the very spot he had but just before quitted. Unhappily, our cannon did not arrive at Pettick's Island and Nantasket as soon as might have been wished, but the fire from the latter place, being properly pointed against the commodore's ship, which came to in the Light House channel, is apprehended to have done considerable execution. However, the enemy were compelled once more to make a disgraceful precipitate flight; and we have it now in our power to congratulate our friends on our being in full possession of the lowest harbor of Boston; and, had the wind been to the eastward, we are confident we should have had the much greater pleasure of giving them joy on our being in the possession of many of the enemy's ships. Through Divine Providence, not one of our men were hurt.[1]

It is now certain, that there is not a ministerial troop in all New England, except such as are prisoners; nor is there a ministerial ship in any harbor in New England.[2] And it is worthy of special notice that the fourteenth day of June, 1774, was the last day allowed for trading vessels to leave or enter the port of Boston, through the cruelty of a British act of Parliament; and that the fourteenth of June, 1776, through the blessings of God upon the operations of a much injured and oppressed people, is the last day for British men-of-war, or ministerial vessels, to remain or enter within the said port, but as American prizes. Thus has Providence retaliated.[3]

June 17.—Rosy John Hancock has got frightened again, and has writ a letter to those plundering "Sons of Liberty,"
John Hancock. as they call themselves, all about an attempt our gracious king's troops are *going* to make on New York. He says the important hour is at hand that is to decide, not only the fate of the universe, but that of New York and the Congress in particular; and that he knows if their

[1] Pennsylvania Journal, June 26.   [2] New York Packet, June 27.
[3] Freeman's Journal, June 22.

feelings are at all like his, they'll do something brave.—They'll possibly do as he does, that is—keep out of harm's way, through a strict watch for the *reg'lars*, and, if requisite, a vigorous use of those gouty legs, that were so shamefully overworked on the morning the gallant Percy marched to Lexington.[1]

A CORRESPONDENT in Philadelphia, who signs himself a "determined independent," says: "The mild treatment which the Tories have met with, has only encouraged them in their disaffection, and, until an example is made of some of them, we shall always be exposed to private domestic dangers. Necessity, when self-preservation is the object, justifies severity. We have reasoned, we have pleaded with these men long enough, and all will not do. It signifies nothing meddling with the little and ignorant ones—their greatest error is want of knowledge ; but I would begin with the

Treatment for the Tories.

---

[1] Smythe's Journal, p. 38 :—The following, published in the Pennsylvania Evening Post, June 18, probably is the letter referred to :—

PHILADELPHIA, June 11, 1776.

GENTLEMEN:—The Congress have this day received advice, and are fully convinced, that it is the design of General Howe to make an attack upon the City of New York, as soon as possible. The attack, they have reason to believe, will be made within ten days.

I am, therefore, most earnestly to request, by order of Congress, to call forth your militia, as requested in my letter of the 4th instant, and to forward them with all despatch to the City of New York; and that you direct that they march in companies, or any other way that will hasten their arrival there.

The important day is at hand that will not only decide the fate of the City of New York, but in all probability of the whole Province. On such an occasion there is no necessity to use arguments with Americans. Their feelings, I well know, will prompt them to their duty, and the sacredness of the cause will urge them to the field.

The greatest exertions of vigor and expedition are requisite to prevent our enemies from getting possession of that town. I must, therefore, again most earnestly request you, in the name and by the authority of Congress, to send forward the militia, agreeable to the requisition of Congress, and that you will do it with all the despatch which the infinite importance of the cause demands.

I have the honor to be, Gentlemen,

Your most obedient humble servant,

JOHN HANCOCK, President.

heads and chiefs of them. It is time, it is high time to do it, if
we mean to live in safety. Matters are ripening very fast, and
either an independence must be declared, by which we can
legally punish the traitors, or the associators must, in my
opinion, be obliged to declare martial law for their own protection.[1]

JUNE 18.—THIS afternoon, the Provincial Congress of New
York gave an elegant entertainment to General Washington
Entertainment to and his suite ; the general and staff officers, and
Washington. the commanding officer of the different regiments
in and near the city. Many patriotic toasts were offered and
drank with the greatest pleasure and decency. After the toasts,
little Phil, of the Guard, was brought in to sing H——'s new
campaign song, and was joined by all the under officers, who
seemed much animated by the accompanying of Clute's drum-
sticks and Aaron's fife. Our good General Putnam got sick
and went to his quarters before dinner was over, and we missed
him a marvel, as there is not a chap in the camp who can lead
him in the *Maggie Lauder* song.[2]

A NEW SONG.[3]

When virtuous ardor, from motions sincere,
Nerves the arm of a soldier, what foe can he fear?
Undaunted he fights, and his glorious name
Immortal shall flourish through every campaign.

No horrible story of Briton or Hessian,
Can appal or incline him to quit a profession,
Which eager to follow, his soul's all in flame,
And burns for a part in the next brave campaign.

In fatigue, toil, and danger, he nobly delights,
No station alarms him, no terror affrights;
All the hardships of war, like a god, he sustains,
And thirsts for the glory of future campaigns.

---

[1] Constitutional Gazette, June 19.
[2] MS. letter from Captain Caleb Gibbs, of Washington's Guard, to his "Dear
Penelope."
[3] This probably is the song referred to by Captain Gibbs.

Though each of his foes were like Hercules brave,
While their efforts are tending a land to enslave,
With contempt he beholds th' unsoldierly stain,
And courts the fierce combat, and speedy campaign.

Should their number, the legions of Xerxes surpass;
Were their limbs of firm steel, and their bodies like brass,
He'd attempt to dissolve them with gunpowder flame,
And smile at the terrors of such a campaign.

The love of his country impassions his breast,
For its sake, with whole squadrons the field he'd contest,
Exert every nerve, and inflate every vein,
And a thousand times die in a single campaign.

Come then, each true soldier, thus let us behave,
Such motives are ours......and like him we'll be brave;
Let's disclose to the world from what heroes we came,
By the deeds of their sons, the ensuing campaign.

Let spirit and union dispel party strife,
While struggling for freedom and empire and life;
Ungenerous sentiments nobly disdain
Fir'd with the idea of such a campaign.

Then wreaths shall be twined of unfading renown,
Our brows to encircle and actions to crown;
And the clarion immortal, of sonorous fame,
Shall transmit to all ages, this glorious campaign.[1]

JUNE 24.—SINCE Friday last, a most barbarous and infernal plot has been discovered among the Tories in New York. Two of General Washington's guards are concerned,[2] a third whom they tempted to join them made the first discovery. The general report of their design is as

The Plot in New York.

[1] New York Packet, June 13.
[2] General Washington, in a letter to the President of Congress, dated New York, June 28, says:—"The plot had been communicated to some of the army, and part of my guard engaged in it. T—— H——,* one of them, has been tried, and, by the unanimous opinion of a court-martial, is sentenced to die, having enlisted himself and engaged others. The sentence, by the advice of the whole council of general officers, will be put in execution to-day, at eleven o clock. The others are not tried. I am hopeful this example will produce many salutary consequences, and deter others from entering into the like traitorous practices."—*Official Letters*, ed. 1795, v. i., p. 165.

* Thomas Hickey.

follows: upon the arrival of the British troops, they were to murder all the staff officers, blow up the magazines, and secure the passes of the town. Gilbert Forbes, a gunsmith, in the Broadway, was taken between two and three o'clock on Saturday morning, and carried before our Congress, who were then sitting. He refused to make any discovery, upon which he was sent to jail. The Reverend Mr. Livingston went to see him early in the morning, and told him he was very sorry to find he had been concerned, that his time was very short, not having above three days to live, and advised him to prepare himself. This had the desired effect; and he requested to be carried before the Congress again, promising to discover all he knew. Several have been since taken, between twenty and thirty, among them the mayor.[1] They are all now in confinement. Their party, it is said, consisted of about five hundred.[2]

JUNE 28.—THIS forenoon, was executed in a field between the Colonels M'Dougall and Huntington's camp, near the Bowry-lane, New York, in the presence of near twenty thousand spectators, a soldier belonging to his Excellency General Washington's guards, for mutiny and conspiracy; being one

[1] David Matthews was mayor at that time, as will appear from the following:— "New York, February 22.—Wednesday, se'night, his Excellency our governor was pleased to appoint Whitehead Hicks, Esq., one of the Judges of the Supreme Court of this province. Mr. Hicks having at the same time surrendered the office of mayor, his Excellency was pleased to appoint David Matthews, Esq., to that office; and last Friday they were both qualified to act in their respective stations."—*New York Packet*, February 22.

[2] Pennsylvania Journal, June 26. A further account in the same paper says:— "Yesterday, (23,) the mayor was examined twice, and returned prisoner under a strong guard. We have now thirty-four prisoners, and many more it is expected will be taken up. A party of our men went over to Long Island, Saturday last, to take up some of the Tories; they returned yesterday, and brought to town one Downing, who is charged with being in the hellish plot. They took six more prisoners and put them in Jamaica jail, on Long Island. The Tories made some resistance, and fired on our men in the woods; our people returned the fire, wounding one man mortally; they then called for quarter. This morning a party of three hundred men is ordered, but on what business is not known. The mayor acknowledges he paid Mr. Forbes, the gunsmith, who is one of the gang now in irons, £140, by order of Governor Tryon. Yesterday the general's housekeeper was taken up; it is said she is concerned."

of those who formed, and was soon to have put in execution, that horrid plot of assassinating the staff officers, blowing up the magazines and securing the passes of the town, on the arrival of the hungry ministerial myrmidons. It is hoped the remainder of those miscreants, now in our possession, will meet with a punishment adequate to their crimes.[1]

During the execution, Kip the moon-curser, suddenly sank down and expired instantly.[2]

JUNE 29.—OUR boys have pretty well thrashed Sir Peter Parker and all his forces. Yesterday morning, an attack was commenced by one of the small vessels of the *Attack on Sullivan's Island.* British fleet, on the fort at Sullivan's Island, and, notwithstanding our small number, a part of which was engaged in watching Clinton and Cornwallis, at the other (east) end of the island, we sustained it with the most complete success.[3]

A writer on board the fleet gives the following account of this action: "The signal for attacking was made by Sir Peter Parker, on the twenty-seventh of June, but the wind coming suddenly to the northward, the ships were obliged again to anchor. The troops had been encamped on Long Island since the fifteenth, and it was intended that General Clinton should pass the neck that divides Long Island from Sullivan's Island,[4] and attack by land, while Sir Peter Parker attacked by sea. General Lee had made such a disposition of masked batteries, troops, &c., that it is the opinion of all the officers of the army whom I have heard mention this circumstance, that if our troops had attacked, they must have been cut off; but this assertion does not satisfy the Navy, for they certainly expected great assistance from the army.

"On the morning of the twenty-eighth, the wind proved favorable, and it was a clear, fine day, but very sultry. The Thunder Bomb began the attack at half-past eleven, by throw-

---

[1] Pennsylvania Evening Post, July 2.
[2] Gywn's letter to Colonel Crafts.   [3] Clift's Diary.
[4] Sullivan's Island is situated on the northern side of Charleston harbor, about four miles from the city.

ing shells, while the ships were advancing. The ships that
advanced to attack the battery were the Bristol and Experiment,
two fifty-gun ships, the Solebay, Active, Actæon, and Syren
of twenty-eight guns, the Sphynx of twenty, and the Friendship, an armed ship of twenty-eight guns. With this force
what might not have been expected ? Unfortunately, the Bomb
was placed at such a distance, that she was not of the least
service. This, Colonel James, the principal engineer, immediately perceived ; to remedy which inconvenience, an additional quantity of powder was added to each mortar : the consequence was the breaking down the beds, and totally dis-
abling her for the rest of the day.

"The Bristol and Experiment suffered most incredibly : the
former very early had the spring of her cable shot away, and,
as she lay end on to the battery, was raked fore and aft ; she
lost upward of one hundred men, killed and wounded. Captain
Morris, who commanded her, lost his arm.[1] Perhaps an
instance of such slaughter cannot be produced. Twice the quar-
ter-deck was cleared of every person except Sir Peter, and he
was slightly wounded ;[2] she had nine thirty-two pounders in her
mainmast, which is so much damaged as to be obliged to be
shortened ; the mizzen had seven thirty-two pounders, and was
obliged, being much shattered, to be entirely cut away. It is
impossible to pretend to describe what the shipping suffered.
Captain Scott, of the Experiment, lost his right arm, and the
ship suffered exceedingly ; she had much the same number
killed and wounded as the Bristol. Our situation was rendered
very disagreeable, by the Actæon, Syren, and Sphynx running
foul of each other, and getting on shore on the middle ground.

[1] He died a week after, on board the Pigot.
[2] Sir Peter's breeches were torn off, his thigh and knee wounded, so that he
was able to walk only when supported on each side. These circumstances gave
rise to the following extempore, which appeared in the Constitutional Gazette,
soon after the action :—

> If "honor in the breech is lodged,"
>   As Hudibras has shown,
> It may from thence be fairly judged,
>   Sir Peter's honor's gone

The Sphynx disengaged herself by cutting away her bowsprit; and as it was not yet flood tide, she and the Syren fortunately warped off. The Actæon was burnt next morning by Captain Atkins, to prevent her falling into the hands of the Provincials.[1]

" Our ships, after lying nine hours before the battery, were obliged to retire with great loss. The Provincials reserved their fire until the shipping were advanced within point blank shot. Their artillery was surprisingly well served, it is said, under the command of a Mr. Masson and De Brahm. It was slow, but decisive indeed. They were very cool, and took great care not to fire except their guns were exceedingly well directed: but there was a time when the battery appeared to be silenced for more than an hour. The navy say, had the troops been ready to land at this time, they could have taken possession; how that is, I will not pretend to say.[2] I will

[1] While she was on fire, Mr. Millegan, one of the Carolina marine officers, and a party of men boarded her, brought off her colors, the ship's bell, and as many sails as three boats would contain.—*New York Gazette*, July 29.

[2] General Clinton was very much censured for not attempting to ford the shallow water (which was only three feet deep) between the east end of Sullivan's Island and Long Island, where he had been encamped, and attacking the Americans there. An English correspondent says:—" My wife is quite an American, and every conquest the Americans make, every battle they win, and every one of our ships they take, she says Providence is on their side, and it is only fighting against the wind to continue the contest. I am on the opposite side, and we have many interesting broils, or civil wars about it. She has it all in her head from the famous battle of Lexington, where our arms shone in their full lustre, to the siege of Sullivan's Island, where we came off with the worst; and this last affair, I must acknowledge, has almost set me wavering.

"One circumstance happened yesterday that fairly made me mad. My son Tommy being playing in the garden, in the middle of which is a small pond about three feet deep; his mother (I suppose on purpose to vex me) ordered Tommy to wade through the pond, which he refused, telling her he should be drowned, as it was too deep; orders were immediately given for Tommy to sound it, which he began preparing for, by taking a leather sucker and making it stick fast to a stone, tied about four feet of string to the end of a stick, and reached it as far as he was able, and he returned and told his mother it was as deep as a certain mark on the cord which he had made; which, on measuring, was found to be three feet, one inch, and seven-eighths; which, had he attempted, would have proved fatal to him.

"I well knew the design of this burlesque, so I threw down my pipe with a ven-

rather suppose it; but the fire became exceedingly severe when it was renewed again, and did amazing execution, after the battery had been supposed to have been silenced. This will not be believed when it is first reported in England. I can scarcely believe what I saw on that day; a day to me one of the most distressing of my life. The navy, on this occasion, have behaved with their usual coolness and intrepidity. One would have imagined that no battery could have resisted their incessant fire."[1]

geance, and secured a retreat, being fully sensible I could not, like the *brave* Sir Peter Parker, silence her battery. As soon as I came home last night, my enemy had the daring effrontery to present me with a print, neatly framed and glazed, called Troops fording a Brook; and with an air of exultation, asked me whether the officer on the grenadier's shoulders was not General Clinton?"—*Middlesex Journal*, September 7.

[1] Middlesex Journal, September 14.

CHAPTER VII.

JULY 1.—EVERY moment that I reflect on our affairs, the more I am convinced of the necessity of a formal declaration of Independence. Reconciliation is thought of now by none but knaves, fools, and madmen; and as we cannot offer terms of peace to Great Britian, until, as other nations have done before us, we agree to call ourselves by some name, I shall rejoice to hear the title of the UNITED STATES OF AMERICA, in order that we may be on a proper footing to negotiate a peace.

Thoughts on Independence.

Besides, the condition of those brave fellows who have fallen into the enemy's hands as prisoners, and the risk which every man runs, who bears arms either by land or sea in the American cause, makes a declaration of Independence absolutely necessary, because no proper cartel for an exchange of prisoners can take place while we remain dependants. It is some degree of comfort to a man, taken prisoner, that he belongs to some national power, is the subject of some state that will see after him. Oliver Cromwell would have sent a memorial as powerful as thunder to any king on earth, who dared to use prisoners in the manner which ours have been. What is it that *we* have done in this matter? Nothing. We are subjects of Great Britain and must not do these things! Shame on your cowardly souls that do them not! You are not fit to govern!

Were Britain to make a conquest of America, I would for my own part choose rather to be conquered as an independent state than as an acknowledged rebel. Some foreign powers might interpose for us in the first case, but they cannot in the latter, because the law of all nations is against us. Besides, the foreign European powers will not long be neutral, and unless we declare an independence, and send embassies to seek their friendship, Britain will be beforehand with us; for the moment that she finds she cannot make a conquest of America, by her own strength, she will endeavor to make an European affair of it. Upon the whole, we may be benefited by independence, but we cannot be hurt by it, and every man that is against it is a traitor.[1]

JULY 4.—THIS day, "after much deliberation, the Congress has adopted Independency, for the following reasons:"

WHEN in the course of human events, it becomes necessary for one people to dissolve the political bands which have connected them with another, and to assume among the powers of the earth, the separate and equal station to which the laws of nature and of Nature's God entitle them, a decent respect to the opinions of mankind requires that they should declare the causes which impel them to the separation.

Declaration of Independence.

We hold these truths to be self-evident, that all men are created equal, that they are endowed by their Creator with certain unalienable rights, that among these are life, liberty, and the pursuit of happiness.—That to secure these rights governments are instituted among men, deriving their just powers from the consent of the governed, that whenever any form of government becomes destructive of these ends, it is the right of the people to alter or to abolish it, and to institute new government, laying its foundation on such principles, and organizing its powers in such form, as to them shall seem most likely to effect their safety and happiness. Prudence, indeed, will dictate that governments long established, should not be changed for light and transient causes; and accordingly, all experience hath shown, that mankind are more disposed to suffer, while evils are sufferable, than to right

[1] "Republican," in the Pennsylvania Evening Post, June 29.

themselves by abolishing the form to which they are accustomed. But when a long train of abuses and usurpations, pursuing invariably the same object, evinces a design to reduce them under absolute despotism, it is their right, it is their duty, to throw off such government, and to provide new guards for their future security. Such has been the patient sufferance of these colonies; and such is now the necessity which constrains them to alter their former systems of government. The history of the present King of Great Britain is a history of repeated injuries and usurpations, all having in direct object the establishment of an absolute tyranny over these states. To prove this let facts be submitted to a candid world.

He has refused his assent to laws, the most wholesome and necessary for the public good.

He has forbidden his governors to pass laws of immediate and pressing importance, unless suspended in their operation till his assent should be obtained, and when so suspended, he has utterly neglected to attend to them.

He has refused to pass other laws for the accommodation of large districts of people, unless those people would relinquish the right of representation in the legislature, a right inestimable to them and formidable to tyrants only.

He has called together legislative bodies at places unusual, uncomfortable, and distant from the depository of their public records, for the sole purpose of fatiguing them into compliance with his measures.

He has dissolved representative houses repeatedly, for opposing with a manly firmness his invasions on the rights of the people.

He has refused for a long time, after such dissolutions, to cause others to be elected; whereby the legislative powers, incapable of annihilation, have returned to the people at large for their exercise; the state remaining in the mean time exposed to all the dangers of invasions from without, and convulsions within.

He has endeavored to prevent the population of these states; for that purpose obstructing the laws for naturalization of foreigners, refusing to pass others to encourage their migrations hither, and raising the conditions of new appropriations of lands.

He has obstructed the administrations of justice, by refusing his assent to laws for establishing judiciary powers.

He has made judges dependent on his will alone, for the tenure of their offices, and the amount and payment of their salaries.

He has erected a multitude of new offices, and sent hither swarms of officers to harass our people, and eat out their substance.

He has kept among us, in times of peace, standing armies without the consent of our legislatures.

He has affected to render the military independent of, and superior to the civil power.

He has combined with others to subject us to a jurisdiction foreign to our constitution, and unacknowledged by our laws; giving his assent to their acts of pretended legislation.

For quartering large bodies of armed troops among us.

For protecting them, by a mock trial, from punishment for any murders which they should commit on the inhabitants of these states.

For cutting off our trade with all parts of the world.

For imposing taxes on us without our consent.

For depriving us, in many cases, of the benefits of trial by jury.

For transporting us beyond seas to be tried for pretended offences.

For abolishing the free system of English laws in a neighboring province, establishing therein an arbitrary government, and enlarging its boundaries, so as to render it at once an example and fit instrument for introducing the same absolute rule into these colonies.

For taking away our charters, abolishing our most valuable laws, and altering fundamentally the forms of our governments.

For suspending our own legislatures, and declaring themselves invested with power to legislate for us in all cases whatsoever.

He has abdicated government here, by declaring us out of his protection and waging war against us.

He has plundered our seas, ravaged our coasts, burnt our towns, and destroyed the lives of our people.

He is, at this time, transporting large armies of foreign mercenaries to complete the works of death, desolation, and tyranny, already begun with circumstances of cruelty and perfidy, scarcely paralleled in the most barbarous ages, and totally unworthy the head of a civilized nation.

He has constrained our fellow-citizens, taken captive on the high seas, to bear arms against their country, to become the executioners of their friends and brethren, or to fall themselves by their hands.

He has excited domestic insurrections amongst us, and has endeavored to bring on the inhabitants of our frontiers, the merciless Indian savages, whose known rule of warfare is an undistinguished destruction of all ages, sexes, and conditions.

In every stage of these oppressions we have petitioned for redress in the most humble terms. Our repeated petitions have been answered only by repeated injury. A prince, whose character is thus marked by every act which may define a tyrant, is unfit to be the ruler of a free people.

Nor have we been wanting in attentions to our British brethren. We have warned them from time to time of attempts by their legislature to extend an unwarrantable jurisdiction over us. We have reminded them of the circumstances of our emigration and settlement here. We have appealed to their native justice and magnanimity, and we have conjured them by the ties of our common kindred to disavow these usurpations, which would inevitably interrupt our connections and correspondence. They too have been deaf to the voice of justice and of consanguinity. We must, therefore, acquiesce in the necessity which denounces our separation, and hold them, as we hold the rest of mankind, enemies in war, in peace, friends.

We, therefore, the representatives of the United States of America, in general congress assembled, appealing to the Supreme Judge of the world for the rectitude of our intentions,

do, in the name, and by the authority of the good people of
these colonies, solemnly publish and declare, that these
UNITED COLONIES are, and of right ought to be, FREE
AND INDEPENDENT STATES ; that they are absolved
from all allegiance to the British crown, and that all political
connection between them and the state of Great Britain, is and
ought to be totally dissolved ; and that as Free and Independent States, they have full power to levy war, conclude peace,
contract alliances, establish commerce, and to do all other acts
and things which Independent States may of right do. And
for the support of this declaration, with a firm reliance on the
protection of Divine Providence, we mutually pledge to each
other our lives, our fortunes, and our sacred honor.[1]

JULY 5.—THIS day, the Virginia Convention resolved, that
the following sentences in the morning and evening church
service shall be omitted :—" O Lord, save the
king, and mercifully hear us when we call upon
thee." That the fifteenth, sixteenth, seventeenth, and eighteenth sentences in the Litany, for the king's majesty, and the
Royal Family, &c., shall be omitted. That the two prayers
for the king's majesty, and the Royal Family, in the morning
and evening service, shall be omitted.

Change in the
Church Service.

That the prayers in the communion service, which acknowledge the authority of the king, and so much of the prayer for
the church militant as declares the same authority, shall be
omitted, and this alteration made in one of the above prayers
in communion service : " Almighty and everlasting God, we
are taught by thy holy word, that the hearts of all rulers are in
thy governance, and that thou dost dispose and turn them as it
seemeth best to thy goodly wisdom ; we humbly beseech thee to
dispose and govern the hearts of the magistrates of this commonwealth, that in all their thoughts, words, and works, they may
evermore seek thy honor and glory, and study to preserve thy

[1] Signed by order and in behalf of the Congress, John Hancock, President:
Attest, Charles Thomson, Secretary.*

* Pennsylvania Journal, July 10.

people committed to their charge in wealth, peace, and godliness.   Grant this, O Merciful Father, for thy dear Son's sake, Jesus Christ, our Lord, Amen."

That the following prayer shall be used instead of the prayer for the king's majesty, in the morning and evening service: " O, Lord, our heavenly Father, high and mighty, King of kings, Lord of lords, the only Ruler of the universe, who dost from thy throne behold all the dwellers upon earth, most heartily we beseech thee with thy favor to behold the magistrates of this commonwealth, and to replenish them with the grace of thy Holy Spirit, that they may always incline to thy will, and walk in thy way; endue them plenteously with heavenly gifts; strengthen them, that they may vanquish and overcome all their enemies; and finally, after this life, they may obtain everlasting joy and felicity, through Jesus Christ our Lord, Amen."

In the twenty-sixth sentence of the Litany use these words : "That it may please thee to endue the magistrates of this commonwealth with grace, wisdom, and understanding."

In the succeeding one, use these words : " That it may please thee to bless and keep them, giving them grace to execute justice and maintain truth."

Let every other sentence of the Litany be retained, without any alteration, except the above sentences recited.[1]

MARRIED, a short time since, in Mansfield, Connecticut, Mr. Luke Flint, of Windham, to Miss Mary Slate, daughter of Mr. Ezekiel Slate,—an agreeable and happy pair.   What deserves the public notice, and may serve to encourage the manufacturers of this country, is, that the entertainment, though served up with good wine, and other spirituous liquors, was the production of their fields and fruit gardens, assisted alone by a neighboring grove of spontaneous maples.

The bride and two of her sisters appeared in very genteel-like gowns, and others of the family in handsome apparel, with sundry silk handkerchiefs, &c., entirely of their own manufacture.[1]

---

[1] New York Gazette, July 29.   [2] Connecticut Gazette, July 11 * 18.

TITLES are the offspring of monarchical and arbitrary governments. While the object of the present war with Great Britain
was *reconciliation*, the titles of excellency, honorable, &c., were submitted to by the people of
America; but since the Declaration of Independence, the colonies have divorced monarchy forever, and become free, independent states. It becomes then necessary to adopt the simple
language of free governments.

Titles.

The Roman Senate in the height of its glory and happiness
had no other title than *Senatus populus que Romanus*, that is,
the senate and people of Rome. Scipio was addressed by the
name of Scipio, at the head of his army. Aristides was called
Aristides, in the councils and public streets of Athens. Let us
leave the titles of excellency and honorable to the abandoned
servants of a tyrant king,—the King of England, while we
satisfy ourselves with beholding our senators, governors, and
generals rich in real excellence and honor.[1]

DAY before yesterday, Governor Franklin, of New Jersey,
passed through Hartford, in Connecticut, on his way to Governor Trumbull, at Lebanon. Mr. Franklin is a
noted Tory, and ministerial tool, and has been exceedingly busy in perplexing the cause of liberty, and in
serving the designs of the British King and his minions. The
people of the Jerseys, on account of his principles, connections,
abilities, and address, viewed him as a mischievous and dangerous enemy in that province, and consequently thought it
expedient to remove him, under a strong guard, to Connecticut.
He is safely arrived, and will probably have leisure to reconnoitre his past life. He is son to Doctor Benjamin Franklin,[2]
the genius of the day, and the great patron of American Liberty.
If his excellency escapes the vengeance of the people, due to the
enormity of his crimes, his redemption will flow, not from his

William Franklin.

[1] Pennsylvania Evening Post, July 13.
[2] William Franklin, the last royal governor of New Jersey, was the natural
son of Dr. Franklin. He was born in 1731; was appointed governor in 1763,
and continued in office until he was sent to Connecticut. On his release he went
to England, where he died on the 17th of November, 1813.

personal merit, but from the high esteem and veneration which this country entertains for his honored father.[1]

JULY 8.—At twelve o'clock to-day, the Committees of Safety and Inspection of Philadelphia, went in procession to the State House, where the Declaration of the Independency of the United States of America was read to a very large number of the inhabitants of the city and county, and was received with general applause and heartfelt satisfaction. And, in the evening, our late king's coat-of-arms was brought from the hall in the State House, where the said king's courts were formerly held, and burned amidst the acclamations of a crowd of spectators.[2]

THE Declaration was received at Easton, in Pennsylvania, and proclaimed in the following order :—The Colonel and all the other field officers of the first battalion repaired to the court-house, the light infantry company marching there with their drums beating, fifes playing, and the standard, (the device for which is the Thirteen United Colonies,) which was ordered to be displayed. After that the Declaration was read aloud to a great number of spectators, who gave their hearty assent with three loud huzzas, and cried out, " May God long preserve and unite the FREE and INDEPENDENT States of America."[3]

AT Trenton, New Jersey, the Declaration was this day proclaimed, together with the new constitution of the colony, lately established, and the resolve of the Provincial Congress for continuing the administration of justice during the interim. The members of the Provincial Congress, the gentlemen of the committee, the officers and privates of the militia under arms, and a large concourse of the inhabitants, attended on this great and solemn occasion. The Declaration and other proceedings were received with loud acclamations.

The people now are convinced of what we ought long since

[1] Constitutional Gazette, July 13.   [2] Constitutional Gazette, July 17.
[3] Pennsylvania Evening Post, July 11.

to have known, that our enemies have left us no middle way
between perfect freedom and abject slavery. In the field, we
trust, as well as in council, the inhabitants of New Jersey will
be found ever ready to support the freedom and independence
of America.[1]

July 9.—This evening Nassau Hall, at Princeton, in New
Jersey, was grandly illuminated, and INDEPENDENCY proclaimed under a triple volley of musketry, and a universal acclamation for the prosperity of the United States. The ceremony
was conducted with the greatest decorum.[2]

On the late alarm at Elizabethtown, when an immediate
attack of the regulars was expected,[3] and every man, capable
of bearing arms, was summoned to defend it,
An Anecdote.
there were three or four young men (brothers)
going out from one house, when an elderly lady, mother or
grandmother to the young men, without betraying the least
signs of timidity, with a resolute calmness encouraged and
assisted them to arm. When they were ready to go, and just
setting out, she addressed them thus :—

"My children, I have a few words to say to you ; you are
going out in a just cause to fight for the rights and liberties of
your country. You have my blessing and prayers, that God
will protect and assist you. But if you fall ; his will be done.
Let me beg of you, my children, that if you fall, it may be like
men ; and that your wounds may not be in your back parts."[4]

July 10.—This afternoon the Declaration of Independence
was read at the head of each brigade of the Continental Army,
Independence posted at and in the vicinity of New York. It
Declared in
New York. was received everywhere with loud huzzas, and the
utmost demonstrations of joy ; and to-night the equestrian statue

---

[1] Pennsylvania Journal, July 17.
[2] Extract of a letter from Princeton, in the Pennsylvania Evening Post,
July 13.
[3] The regulars attempted an attack on the 3d of July.
[4] Pennsylvania Evening Post, August 10.

of George III., which Tory pride and folly raised in the year
1770, has, by the Sons of Freedom, been laid prostrate in the
dirt—the just desert of an ungrateful tyrant!   The lead wherewith the monument was made is to be run into bullets, to
assimilate with the brains of our infatuated adver-   Statue of George
saries, who, to gain a pepper-corn, have lost an   III. demolished.
empire.[1]   A gentleman who was present at this ominous fall
of leaden majesty, looking back to the original's hopeful beginning, pertinently exclaimed, in the language of the Angel to
Lucifer,

"If thou be'st he!   But ah, how fallen!   how changed!"

A few hours before the Declaration was read, the light
dragoon regiment of Connecticut troops arrived in the city,
and paraded on horseback through the streets, making a noble
and martial appearance.   Nothing could be more agreeable or
animating to all the true friends of their country, than the
sight of this corps, which is composed of the substantial yeo-
manry of a virtuous sister state.   Some of them assisted, in
their present uniforms, at the first reduction of Louisburg,
and their "lank, lean cheeks and war-worn coats," are viewed
with more veneration by their *honest* countrymen, than if they
were glittering nabobs from India, or bashaws with nine tails.[2]

[1] Lord Clare, in the House of Commons, declared that a pepper-corn, in acknowledgment of Britain's right to tax America, was of more importance than
millions without it.

[2] Pennsylvania Journal, July 17 ; also Captain Park's Diary :—In pursuance of
the Declaration of Independence, a general jail delivery, with respect to debtors,
took place in New York, on the same day it was read to the army.—*Pennsylvania
Evening Post*, July 16.

On the 18th of July, by order of the Convention of the State of New York, the
Declaration of the Independency of the United States of America was read at the
State House in New York, to a numerous and respectable body of the freeholders
and principal inhabitants of the city and county, and was received with general
applause and heartfelt satisfaction ; and, at the same time, our late king's coat of
arms was brought from the City Hall, where his courts were commonly held, and
burned, amidst the acclamations of thousands of spectators.

The same day, the Declaration "was proclaimed from the State House, in
Boston, Mass., amidst the acclamations of thousands, who assembled on the occasion."—*Pennsylvania Journal*, July 24, and *Pennsylvania Evening Post*, Aug. 3.

JULY 20.—THIS day, Lieutenant-Colonel Patterson, of the British army, came to New York, from Lord Howe's fleet, and landed near the main battery. He passed through a file of the Life Guards of General Washington, and had a private conference with him, at Colonel Knox's, for near half an hour.

Washington and
Col. Patterson.

After usual compliments, in which, as well as through the whole conversation, Colonel Patterson addressed General Washington by the title of Excellency, he entered upon the business by saying, that General Howe much regretted the difficulties which had arisen, respecting the address of the letters to General Washington,[1] and that it was deemed consistent with propriety, and founded upon precedents of the like nature by ambassadors and plenipotentiaries where disputes or difficulties of rank had arisen. He also said that General Washington might recollect he had, last summer, addressed a letter to General Howe, *To the Hon. William Howe, Esq.;* that Lord Howe and General Howe did not mean to derogate from the respect or rank of General Washington; that they held his person and character in the highest esteem, and that the direction, with the addition of &c., &c., &c., implied every thing that ought to follow. He then produced a letter, which he did not directly offer to General Washington, but observing that it was the same letter which had been sent, with a superscription To George Washington, &c., &c., &c., he laid it on the table. The general declined the letter, and said, that a letter directed to a person in a public character, should have some description or indication of it, otherwise it would appear a mere private letter; that it was true the &c., &c., &c., implied every thing, and they also implied any thing; that the letter to General Howe alluded to, was an answer to one received under a like

---

[1] On the 14th of July, Lord Howe sent up a flag, with the captain and lieutenant of the Eagle man-of-war. The adjutant-general met them after some little ceremony, but as their letter was directed for George Washington, Esq., he would not receive it. The officers insisted much on his receiving it, saying it was of a civil nature, his lordship being invested with unlimited powers, and was sorry he had not arrived a few days sooner.—*Pennsylvania Journal*, July 17.

address from him, which the officer on duty having taken, he did not think proper to return, but answered it in the same mode of address. He then said he should absolutely decline any letters directed to him as a private person, when it related to his public station.

Colonel Patterson then remarked, that General Howe would not urge his delicacy further, and repeated his assertions, that no failure of respect was intended. He then said that he would endeavor, as well as he could, to recollect General Howe's sentiments on the letter and resolves of Congress, sent him a few days before, respecting the treatment of our prisoners in Canada. "That the affairs of Canada were in another department, not subject to the control of General Howe, but that he and Lord Howe utterly disapproved of every infringement on the rights of humanity."[1]

Colonel Patterson then took a paper out of his pocket, and, after looking it over, said he had expressed nearly the words. General Washington then said that he had also forwarded a copy of the resolve to General Burgoyne.

To which Colonel Patterson replied, he did not doubt a proper attention would be paid to it, and that he (General Washington) was sensible that cruelty was not the characteristic of the British nation. Colonel Patterson then proceeded to say he had it in charge to mention the case of General Prescott, who they were informed was treated with such rigor, that under his age and infirmities, fatal consequences might be apprehended.

General Washington replied that General Prescott's treatment had not fallen under his notice; that all persons under his particular direction he had treated with kindness, and their situation was made as easy as possible; that he did not know where General Prescott was, but believed his treatment very different from their information.[2] General Washington then mentioned the case of Colonel Allen, and the officers who had been confined in Boston jail. As to the first, Colonel Patterson

[1] Referring to the barbarity of the Indians to some of the Americans in Canada.

[2] See page 226, ante.

answered, that General Howe had no knowledge of it but
by information from General Washington, and that the
Canada department was not under his direction or control;
that as to the other prisoners at Boston, whenever the state
of the army at Boston admitted it, they were treated with
humanity and even indulgence; that he asserted this
upon his honor, and should be happy in an opportunity to
prove it.

General Washington then observed, that the conduct of
several of the officers would well have warranted a different
treatment from what they had received; some having refused
to give any parole, and others having broken it when given,
by escaping or endeavoring so to do. Colonel Patterson
answered, that as to the first they misunderstood the matter
very much, and seemed to have mistook the line of propriety
exceedingly; and as to the latter, General Howe utterly
disapproved and condemned their conduct.

That if a remonstrance was made, such violations of good
faith would be severely punished; but that he hoped General
Washington was too just to draw public inferences from the
misbehavior of some private individuals; that bad men were
to be found in every class and society; that such behavior was considered as a dishonor to the British army.
Colonel Patterson then proceeded to say that the goodness
and benevolence of the king had induced him to appoint
Lord Howe and General Howe his commissioners to accommodate the unhappy dispute; that they had great powers,
and would derive the greatest pleasure from effecting an
accommodation; and that he (Colonel Patterson) wished to
have this visit considered as making the first advances to this
desirable object. General Washington replied he was not
vested with any powers on this subject, by those from whom
he derived his authority and power. But from what had
appeared or transpired on this head, Lord Howe and General
Howe were only to grant pardons; that those who had committed no fault wanted no pardon; that we were only defending
what we deemed our indisputable right. Colonel Patterson said
that would open a very wide field for argument. He then

expressed his apprehensions that an adherence to forms was likely to obstruct business of the greatest moment and concern.

He then observed, that a proposal had been formally made of exchanging Governor Skene for Mr. Lovell; that he now had authority to accede to that proposal. General Washington replied, that the proposition had been made by the direction of Congress, and having been then rejected, he could not now renew the business, or give any answer, till he had previously communicated it to them.

Colonel Patterson behaved with the greatest attention and politeness during the whole business, and expressed strong acknowledgments that the usual ceremony of blinding his eyes had been dispensed with. At the breaking up of the conference, General Washington strongly invited him to partake of a small collation provided for him, which he politely declined, alleging his late business, and an impatience to return to General Howe, though he had not executed his commission so amply as he wished. Finding he did not propose staying, he was introduced to the general officers, after which he took his leave, and was safely conducted to his own boat, which waited for him about four miles distant from the city.[1]

July 22.—Day before yesterday, the honorable the General Assembly of Rhode Island, being then sitting at the state house in Newport, at twelve o'clock, the brigade Independence declared at Newport, R. I. stationed there, under the command of Colonels William Richmond and Christopher Lippitt, marched from head-quarters, and drew up in two columns, on each side the parade, before the state house door. His honor the Governor and the members of the Assembly then marched through and received the compliments of the brigade; after which the secretary, at the head of the company, read a resolve of the assembly, concurring with the Congress in the Declaration of Independence. The Declaration was then read; next thirteen cannon were discharged at Fort Liberty, and then the brigade

[1] Pennsylvania Journal, July 31.

drew up and fired in thirteen divisions, from east to west, agreeable to the number and situation of the United States. The Declaration was received with joy and applause by all ranks, and the whole was conducted with great solemnity and decorum.[1]

ON INDEPENDENCE.

Come all you brave soldiers, both valiant and free,
It's for independence we all now agree ;
Let us gird on our swords, and prepare to defend
Our liberty, property, ourselves, and our friends.

In a cause that's so righteous, come let us agree,
And from hostile invaders set America free.
The cause is so glorious we need not to fear,
But from merciless tyrants we'll set ourselves clear.

Heaven's blessing attending us, no tyrant shall say
That Americans e'er to such monsters gave way,
But fighting we'll die in Americans' cause,
Before we'll submit to tyrannical laws.

George the Third of Great Britain, no more shall he reign,
With unlimited sway o'er these free states again ;
Lord North, nor old Bute, nor none of their clan,
Shall ever be honor'd by an American.

May heaven's blessings descend on our United States,
And grant that the union may never abate,
May love, peace, and harmony ever be found,
For to go hand in hand America round.

Upon our grand Congress, may heaven bestow
Both wisdom and skill our good to pursue,
On heaven alone, dependent we'll be,
But from all earthly tyrants we mean to be free.

Unto our brave generals may heaven give skill,
Our armies to guide and the sword for to wield ;
May their hands taught to war and their fingers to fight,
Be able to put British armies to flight.

[1] Pennsylvania Evening Post, August 1.

And now brave Americans, since it is so,
That we are independent we'll have them to know,
That united we are, and united we'll be,
And from all British tyrants we'll try to keep free.

May heaven smile on us in all our endeavors,
Safe guard our seaports, our towns, and our rivers,
Keep us from invaders by land and by sea,
And from all who'd deprive us of our liberty.[1]

JULY 30.—THE straggler from Howe's army at Staten Island, who was taken by our troops a few days ago, at Elizabethtown Point, was brought into camp at New York, this afternoon. He says he was pressed into the *Sir Peter Parker.* King's service early in September, of last year, and sent to England by Lord Dunmore; that he returned to Charleston with Sir Peter Parker, and was about the only sailor that was left whole, out of the entire fleet, after the fight at Sullivan's Island; that Sir Peter said he never saw such courage as Moultrie's men showed; and that in the hottest of the action a ball passed so near Sir Peter's coat tail as to tear it off, together with his clothes, clear to the buff, without drawing a spot of blood. * * * * He also says, that just before the thunder-storm we had week before last, the troops on Staten Island were preparing figures of Generals Washington, Lee, and Putnam, and Doctor Witherspoon, for burn- *Washington in Effigy.* ing in the night, but were prevented from finishing them by the great rain. The figures had all been erected on a pile of fagots, the generals facing the doctor, and he represented in the act of reading to them a late address. All of them, except General Washington, had been tarred and prepared for the feathers, when the storm came on and obliged the troops to find shelter. In the evening, when the storm was over, a large body of the soldiers gathered around the figures, which, being prepared, were set on fire, amidst the most terrible imprecations against *the rebels.* One of the party, seeing that Generals Putnam and Lee, and Doctor Witherspoon burnt furiously and were almost consumed, while General Washing-

[1] Freeman's Journal, August 17.

ton was still standing, with the tar burning off, ran away frightened, and was soon followed by most of his companions. The next morning, the figure was found as good as it ever was; a fact which caused a good deal of fear among the Hessian troops, most of whom are very superstitious, and it was not until after some of the officers told them the cause of its not burning, that they appeared contented. The reason was, that having no tar upon it before the rain commenced, it became saturated with water, and the tar only would burn.[1]

THE representatives of the State of Rhode Island and Providence plantations have passed a resolve, That if any person within that state shall, under pretence of preaching or praying, or in any other way or manner whatever, acknowledge or declare their late King to be their rightful lord or sovereign, or shall pray for the success of his arms, or that he may vanquish or overcome all his enemies, shall be deemed guilty of high misdemeanor, and therefore be presented by the grand jury of the county, where the offence shall be committed, to the superior court of the same county; and upon conviction thereof, shall forfeit and pay, as a fine, to and for the use of that state, the sum of one hundred thousand pounds lawful money, and pay all costs of prosecution, and shall stand committed to gaol until the same be satisfied.[2]

Rhode Island.

AUGUST 7.—THIS day was carried into Portsmouth, New Hampshire, by the Hancock privateer, which sailed from Philadelphia, a large three-decked ship, named the Reward, of between five and six hundred tons burden. She was a twenty-gun ship last war, in the service of the British King. She was from Tortola, bound to London, and had on board between ten and eleven hundred hogsheads of sugar, eighty-six hogsheads of rum, twelve bales of cotton,

Lord North's Turtles.

---

[1] Letter from Nathan Craig to Lemuel Clift:—In the Postscript of Gaine's Mercury, of October 21, is the following:—"Some time ago, General Washington and several other rebel worthies were burnt at the stake on Staten Island, by a party of the foreign troops."

[2] Constitutional Gazette, July 31.

and nine cannon, some of them brass. There were on board the ship a number of turtles, directed to Lord North, with his name cut in the shell, the best of which Captain Wingate Newman, master of the privateer, is determined to send to the Honorable John Hancock.[1]

THE committee of inspection for the county of Cumberland, in the State of New Jersey, the officers of the militia, and a great number of other inhabitants, having met at Bridgetown, went in procession to the court-house, where the declaration of independency, the constitution of New Jersey, and treason ordinance, were publicly read, and unanimously approved of. These were followed with a spirited address by Doctor Elmer, chairman of the committee, after which the peace officers' staves, on which were depicted the King's coat-of-arms, with other ensigns of royalty, were burnt in the street. The whole was conducted with the greatest decency and regularity.

Independence declared in Bridgetown.

The following is the substance of the before mentioned address : " Gentlemen of the Committee, Officers of the Militia, and Gentlemen Spectators :—From what has now been read, you see the long wished for, but much dreaded period has arrived, in which the connection between Great Britain and America is totally dissolved, and these colonies declared free and independent states. As this is an event of the greatest importance, it must afford satisfaction to every intelligent person to reflect that it was brought about by unavoidable necessity on our part, and has been conducted with a prudence and moderation becoming the wisest and best of men.

Elmer's Address.

With the independency of the American States, a new era in politics has commenced. Every consideration respecting the propriety or impropriety of a separation from Britain, is now entirely out of the question ; and we have now no more to do with the King and people of England, than we have with the King and people of France or Spain. No people under heaven

[1] Pennsylvania Evening Post, August 20.

were ever favored with a fairer opportunity of laying a sure foundation for future grandeur and happiness than we. The plan of government established in most states and kingdoms of the world, has been the effect of chance or necessity; ours of sober reason and cool deliberation. Our future happiness or misery, therefore, as a people, will depend entirely upon ourselves. If actuated by principles of virtue and genuine patriotism, we make the welfare of our country the sole aim of all our actions; if we intrust none but persons of ability and integrity with the management of our public affairs; if we carefully guard against corruption and undue influence in the several departments of government; if we are steady and zealous in putting the laws in strict execution, the spirit and principles of our new constitution, which we have just now heard read, may be preserved for a long time: but if faction and party spirit, the destruction of popular governments, take place, anarchy and confusion will soon ensue, and we shall either fall an easy prey to a foreign enemy, or some factious and aspiring demagogue possessed of popular talents and shining qualities. A Julius Cæsar, or an Oliver Cromwell, will spring up among ourselves, who, taking advantage of our political animosities, will lay violent hands on the government, and sacrifice the liberties of his country to his own ambitious and domineering humor. God grant that neither of these may ever be the unhappy fate of this, or any of the United States! To prevent which, while we are striving to defend ourselves against the unjust encroachments of a foreign and unnatural enemy, let us not neglect to keep a strict and jealous eye over our internal police and constitution. Let the fate of *Greece, Rome, Carthage,* and *Great Britain,* warn us of our danger; and the loss of liberty in all those states, for want of timely guarding against the introduction of tyranny and usurpation, be a standing admonition to us, to avoid the rock on which they have all shipwrecked.

Let us, as honest citizens and sincere lovers of our country, exert ourselves in the defence of our state, and in support of our new constitution; but, while we strive to vindicate the glorious cause of liberty, on the one hand, let us on the other hand, carefully guard against running into the contrary extreme of disorder and licentiousness.

In our present situation, engaged in a bloody and dangerous war with the power of Great Britain, for the defence of our lives, our liberties, our property, and every thing that is dear and valuable; every member of this state, who enjoys the benefits of its civil government, is absolutely bound, by the immutable law of self-preservation, the laws of God and of society, to assist in protecting and defending it. This is so plain and self-evident a proposition, that I am persuaded every person here present makes it the rule of his conduct on all occasions; and consequently, in a time of such imminent danger, will be extremely careful, at our ensuing election, not to trust any one with the management of our public affairs, who has not, by his vigilance and activity in the cause of liberty, proved himself to be a true friend to his country. The success, gentlemen, of our present glorious struggle wholly depends upon this single circumstance. For, though the situation and extent of the United States of America, and our numberless internal resources, are sufficient to enable us to bid defiance to all Europe; yet should we be so careless about our own safety, as to intrust the affairs of our state, while the bayonet is pointed at our breasts, to persons whose conduct discovers them to be enemies to their country, or whose religious principles will not suffer them to lift a hand for our defence, our ruin will inevitably follow.

As it is impossible for any one, possessed of the spirit of a man, who is a friend to the United States, and whose conscience does not furnish him with an excuse, to stand by, an idle spectator, while his country is struggling and bleeding in her own necessary defence; all such inactive persons ought, therefore, to be shunned as enemies or despised as cowards. And as I have reason to believe that many who plead conscience as an excuse, are sincere in their pretensions; and as every man's conscience ought to be free from compulsion, this single consideration should restrain us from forcing such into any of the departments of government. For to put such persons, at this time, in places of public trust, is actually to deprive them of liberty of conscience; for we thereby compel them either to betray the trust reposed in them, or to act contary to the dictates of their own consciences. A dilemma in which, act as they will, their conduct must be criminal. Besides, if we consulted only our own safety, it is plain, that to intrust the affairs of our government, at this juncture, to such people, is as dangerous as to intrust the management of a ship in a violent storm, to an infant, or an idiot.

As a friend to my country and a lover of liberty, I thought it my duty to address you on this occasion, and having now, as a faithful member of society, discharged my duty, I shall leave you to the exercise of your own judgment, and conclude with a request, that you would conduct yourselves this day in such a manner as to convince the public that your abhorrence of the cruel and bloody *Nero* of Britain, and his despicable minions of tyranny and oppression, arises, not from the mere impulse of blind passion and prejudice, but from sober reason and reflection; and while we rejoice in being formally emancipated from our haughty and imperious *Task-masters*, let us remember, that the final termination of this grand event is not likely to be brought about without shedding the blood of many of our dear friends and countrymen.[1]

A CORRESPONDENT in London says:—A certain popular preacher not far from town, last Sunday took his text from these words, Isaiah xxi. 15 : " For they fled from the sword— from the drawn sword and the bent bow, and from the grievousness of war ; " which words he thought to be highly descriptive of the inglorious retreat of the King's troops from Boston. And if it really was true, that these troops had ever turned a house of religious worship into a play house, he thought, go where they will, they can never expect success in any one enterprise, till by deep repentance they had conciliated the favor of heaven.

A most furious quarrel happened at the club in St. Paul's churchyard, between two of the fugitive clergy from North

America. The cause, it is said, was about who should be the bishop in that country, the idea of a suffragan being revived. Cooper[1] was much too many for Peters, and would, if Tucker and Vardil had not interposed, *Doctors Cooper and Peters quarrel.* not only have won the mitre, but have rendered his competitor totally unfit for any episcopal function. Alas! alas! these men in black are not all of them under the operation of grace.[2]

AUGUST 10.—AT Savannah, in Georgia, a declaration being received from the honorable John Hancock, Esq., by which it appeared that the Continental Congress, in the *Independence declared at Savannah.* name and by the authority of their constituents, had declared that the United Colonies of North America are, and of right ought to be, FREE AND INDEPENDENT STATES, and absolved from all allegiance to the British crown, his Excellency the President,[3] and the honorable the council, met in the council chamber and read the Declaration.

They then proceeded to the square before the assembly house, and read it to a great concourse of people, when the grenadier and light infantry companies fired a general volley. After this they proceeded in the following procession to the liberty pole : The grenadiers in front ; the provost-marshal, on horseback, with his sword drawn ; the secretary, with the Declaration ; his Excellency the President ; the honorable the council, and the gentlemen attending ; then the light infantry and the rest of the militia of the town and district of Savannah.

At the liberty-pole they were met by the Georgia battalion, who, after the reading of the Declaration, discharged their field-pieces, and fired in platoons. Upon this they proceeded to the

---

[1] See page 82, ante.   [2] Pennsylvania Evening Post, August 24.

[3] Archibald Bullock was elected president of the Executive Council of Georgia, in January, 1776. He was a native of Charleston, South Carolina, and on the commencement of the difficulties between the mother country and the colonies, he took a decided stand in favor of the latter. In 1775 he represented Georgia in the Continental Congress, and was very active in the cause of liberty. His speech to the Provincial Congress of his adopted State is marked with great strength and overflowing with patriotism. He died in less than a year after the Declaration of Independence.— *White's Hist. Coll. of Georgia,* p. 200.

battery, at the trustee's gardens, where the Declaration was read for the last time, and the cannon of the battery discharged.

His Excellency and council, Colonel Lachlan McIntosh, and other gentlemen, with the militia, dined under the cedar trees, and cheerfully drank to the UNITED, FREE, AND INDEPENDENT States of America. In the evening the town was illuminated, and there was exhibited a very solemn funeral procession, attended by the grenadier and light infantry companies, and other militia, with their drums muffled, and fifes, and a greater number of people than ever appeared on any occasion before, in that province, when George the Third was interred before the court-house in the following manner:

" Forasmuch as George the Third, of Great Britain, hath most flagrantly violated his coronation oath, and trampled on the constitution of our country, and the sacred rights of mankind: we, therefore, commit his political existence to the ground —corruption to corruption—tyranny to the grave—and oppression to eternal infamy, in sure and certain hope that he will never obtain a resurrection, to rule again over these United States of America. But, my friends and fellow-citizens, let us not be sorry, as men without hope, for *Tyrants* that thus depart—rather let us remember that America is free and independent; that she is, and will be, with the blessing of the Almighty, GREAT among the nations of the earth. Let this encourage us in well-doing, to fight for our rights and privileges, for our wives and children, for all that is near and dear unto us. May God give us his blessing, and let all the people say AMEN." [1]

AUGUST 12.—A CORRESPONDENT gives the following account of the capture of the privateer Yankee Hero :—Captain James

Privateer "Yankee Hero." Tracy sailed from Newburyport, in New Hampshire, on the seventh of June, in the Yankee Hero, for Boston, with twenty-six men only, including officers. This number was not a quarter of his complement; he was

---

[1] Universal Intelligencer, and Pennsylvania Evening Post, October 8.

provisioned for a six months' cruise, and was to take in the remainder of his men at Boston. The afternoon he went out, going round Cape Ann, he observed a sail in the offing, but in his situation did not think of looking after her. Two boats full, manned with their muskets, who had put out after the sail, came on board and informed him a number of transports had been close into the Cape that day, and fourteen men from the two boats joined him, and sent their boats on shore. He had now forty hands in the whole, (only a third of his complement,) and with these he put away for the sail, which bore E. S. E., about five leagues distance, the wind being then westerly. At six miles distance they perceived her to be a ship, and soon, from her management, to be a ship-of-war. As a contest with her must have been very unequal, Captain Tracy, who intended to make a harbor that night, ordered the brig to be put about for the shore, not then suspecting that the ship would come up with him. But he had not tacked ten minutes before the westerly wind died away, and the ship taking a fresh southerly breeze, came fast in, endeavoring to cut the brig off from the shore. After some time, the ship thus getting in the wake of the brig, the wind again came fresh to the westward, upon which the brig hauled to the wind in the best angle for the shore. The ship gave chase, and in an hour came up within half a mile, and began to fire her bow chasers, which the brig only answered with a swivel, Captain Tracy reserving his whole fire until the ship, keeping a constant fire, came up within pistol shot upon his lee quarter, when the brig gave her the best return they could make from their main and quarter deck guns, swivels, and small arms, and after kept up a constant fire. The ship was soon up alongside, and with twelve nine-pounders on a side, upon one deck, besides forecastle and quarter deck guns, and with her marines overlooking the brig as high as her leading blocks, kept up a continual fire. After some time, the ship hauled her wind so close (which obliged the brig to do the same) that Captain Tracy was unable to sight his lee guns. Upon this he backed under her stern, but the ship, which sailed much faster and worked as quick, had the advantage, and brought her broadside again upon him, which he could not evade. In this manner they lay, not a hundred feet from each other, yawing to and fro, for an hour and twenty minutes, the privateer's men valiantly maintaining their quarters against such a superior force. About this time, the ship's foremast guns beginning to slack fire, Captain Tracy tacked under her stern, and when clear of the smoke and fire, perceived his rigging to be most shockingly cut, yards flying about without braces, some of his principal sails shot to rags, and half his men, to appearance, dying and wounded.

Mr. Main, his first lieutenant, was among the first wounded, and Mr. Davis, one of the prize masters, fell in the last attack. In this situation they went to work to refit the rigging, and to carry the wounded below, the ship having then taken a broad sheer some way off, and none of her guns bearing. But before they could get their yards to rights, which they zealously tried for in hopes still to get clear of the ship, as they were now nearer in shore, or to part from her under the night, she again came up and renewed the attack, which obliged Captain Tracy to have recourse to his guns again, though he still kept some hands aloft to his rigging; but before the brig had again fired two broadsides, Captain Tracy received a wound in his right thigh, and in a few minutes he could not stand. He laid himself over the arm chest and barricade, determined to keep up the fire; but in a short time, from pain and loss of blood, he was unable to command, growing faint, and they helped him below. As soon as he came to, he found his firing had ceased, and his people round him wounded, and, not having a surgeon with them, in a most distressed situation, most of them groaning and some expiring.

Struck severely with such a spectacle, Captain Tracy ordered his people to take him up in a chair upon the quarter deck, and resolved again to attack the ship, which was all this time keeping up her fire. But after getting into the air, he was again so faint that he was for some time unable to speak, and finding no alternative, but they must be taken or sunk, for the sake of the brave men that remained, he ordered them to strike to the ship.

Thus was this action maintained upwards of two hours, in

a low single-decked vessel, with not half the metal the ship
had, against an English frigate, whose navy has been the dread
of nations, and by a quarter the number of people in the one
as in the other; yet the victors exulted as though they had
overcome a force as much superior as this was inferior to them.
The brig had four men killed and thirteen wounded, including
officers. The number in the Milford wounded is not known,
though there were some. The deprivation of these brave
officers and men is to be regretted by all friends to this country.

With justice to Captain Burr, of the Milford, it must be
acknowledged he treated with humanity and politeness the
officers and men that were wounded; but to the eternal disgrace of Britain, and the present King and Parliament, let it
be recorded, that in this very action above related, upwards of
thirty Americans, prisoners in the Milford, were forced, at the
forfeit of their lives, to fight against their countrymen; and
the officers and men of the Yankee Hero, that were not
wounded, are now detained in several of their ships, and may
meet with the same cruel fate; an exaction that even savages
have not been known to require. It is to the credit of the
Hero's men, that not one would enter upon the ship's books,
though not only urged by every persuasion, but by threats.[1]

AUGUST 14.—YESTERDAY, a number of women belonging to
Fishkill, in Duchess county, New York, collected together in
order to purchase some tea of Alderman Lefferts, Tea Troubles at
of New York, as he had a large quantity of it   Fishkill.
there, which he sent up last fall, to make a prey of the friends
of the United States by asking a most exorbitant price for
the same. Three gentlemen passing by the house where
they were assembled, the ladies saw them, sallied out from
the house, and entreated them, in the most humble manner,
to assist them. The gentlemen refusing to assist, obliged
the ladies to use means of force. After confining the gentlemen under guard, they proceeded to the choice of a committee of ladies, and chose three, and then chose a clerk and

---

[1] Essex Journal, August 9 * 22.

weigher. They then proceeded to open the boxes, and served out the same, and received six shillings for each pound, which the lady committee intended to remit to the general committee of the county.

The ladies offered for the tea, nine shillings per pound before they made the seizure, but upon Mr. Lefferts' refusing, they told him he must then take up with the continental price. The quantity taken was two boxes. Mrs. L——s hoped that none of the relations would assist in the mob, but the persons she mentioned were the first in fact.[1]

AUGUST 17.—A GENTLEMAN who lately escaped from New York, and joined the army on Staten Island, says :—" Every means of defence has been concerted to secure the city and whole island of New York from an attack of the royal army. Should General Howe succeed in that enterprise, his antagonist, Mr. Washington, has provided a magazine of pitch, tar, and combustibles, to burn the city before he shall retreat from his present station. The numbers of his men are daily diminishing ; they desert in large bodies, are sickly, filthy, divided, and unruly. Putrid disorders, the small-pox in particular, have carried off great numbers. When I left the city there were six thousand in their hospitals, to which use they have devoted King's College.

John Morin Scott is appointed Governor of New York, and Samuel Tucker, a cordwainer of Trenton, is exalted to that rank in New Jersey. The persecution of the loyalists continues unremitted. Donald M'Lean, Theophilus Hardenbrook, young Fueter, the silversmith, and Rem Rapelje, have been cruelly rode on rails, a practice most painful, dangerous, and, till now, peculiar to the humane republicans of New England. Mr. John Rapelje, of Brooklyn, and Mr. James Coggeshal, have been seized on their way to join General Howe, with a quantity of sheep in their possession ; however, the latter afterwards escaped, and found means to carry a number of fat wethers to the army.

Mr. John Foxcroft, postmaster-general, Mr. Dashwood,

[1] Constitutional Gazette, August 26.

Mr. Smith Ramage, Messrs. Hugh and Alexander Wallace, and Mr. Abraham Lott, the treasurer, are committed to gaol, having refused to take an oath of allegiance to the Congress; in short, every one suspected of an hostile disposition to that body, are disarmed and conducted into a d—nable durance, which was the case of the venerable chief justice Horsmanden, who, at eighty, was hurried into the country by a party of ruffians; but he proved so troublesome on the journey, that they chose to leave him on the road, without performing the injunctions of their demagogues.

Frequent have been the messages from General Howe to Mr. Washington, and Colonel Patterson has also been repeatedly in conference with the latter; but it seems that Mr. Washington's ultimatum was, that he would hearken to no propositions from the British commissioners. The Phœnix and Rose men-of-war, have passed up the North River about twenty-four miles, where they were attacked by row galleys and floating batteries, all which they either burnt or sunk, with a vast number of men. It was a dangerous service, and to the honor of Captain Hyde Parker and Captain James Wallace, most intrepidly and effectually performed. They are just returned, having expended all their ammunition.

On my arrival in General Howe's camp, I found Mr. Cortlandt Skinner appointed colonel, and Mr. John Morris, late of the 47th regiment, lieutenant-colonel of a corps consisting of fifteen hundred loyal Americans, and Major Rogers, the famous partisan in the last war, colonel of a corps of rangers. The Hessians arrived here on the 12th instant, full of health and ardor for immediate service. The guards, on their arrival, were ordered to land and refresh themselves after a tedious voyage, but they desired to be led on directly to action, in resentment of the atrocious insults to their King and country. Their impatience was beyond expressing, when they were told of some indignities lately offered to the statue of their royal sovereign in New York. I find the whole British army is now increased to between twenty-four and twenty-five thousand men, and not more than one hundred sick and disabled men among them.

Some people, lately arrived here from Philadelphia, tell us that Mr. J. Dickinson is employed by the Congress, in digesting a code of laws for the United States of America. We are informed that Mr. John Alsop, one of the New York delegates, has escaped from the Congress, and is on Long Island, on his way to join General Howe. Dr. Peter Middleton, Mr. Theophilus Bache, Mr. Philip John Livingstone, sheriff of Duchess county, Mr. John Watts, jun., recorder of New York, Mr. Augustus Van Cortlandt, and Messrs. Robert and Samuel Auchmuty, are lately arrived in this island, having narrowly escaped from their pursuers.

Lady Johnson is seized by order of General Schuyler, by way of reprisal for Sir John, her husband, who has taken an active and loyal part, at the head of his faithful Mohawks. These have declared that, should the least injury be done to her, they would desolate and extirpate every person and property belonging to this same general. A person just escaped from New York informs us, that there is again a fresh hunt for the friends of government, who are called Tories, and that Mr. Augustus Van Horne, Mr. Vincent Pearce Ashfield, Captain Haradd, Mr. John Roome, jun., Mr. John Stone Fairholme, and Captain Turnbull, late of the Royal Americans, are made prisoners; Captain Archibald Kennedy, of the royal navy, is confined in Morristown, and Governor Franklin, accompanied by that merry heart, David Mathews, Mayor of New York, now under sentence of death for eminent proofs of loyalty to his King and the old constitution, are removed into Connecticut government for the better security of their persons. Early this morning a *petiaugre*, with sixteen of the provincial soldiers, completely armed, arrived here. They found means to desert to us, and have each man received £3 currency for their firelocks; the general has disposed of them on board the men-of-war, to act as marines. Five guineas a man is given for recruits, who daily enter in great numbers. We are told by persons escaped from Jersey, that Lord Stirling, who commanded and was reconnoitring at Amboy, was killed by a cannon ball from our batteries, and that he was buried at that place. Colonel Guy Johnson is arrived here from England.

On the passage in a Halifax packet, a privateer engaged her; but after Captain Boulderson had gallantly defended his ship three glasses, the adventurer ended the contest by a retreat. On this occasion Dr. Constable received a wound, but is likely to do well. The episcopal churches in New York are all shut up, the prayer books burned, and the ministers scattered abroad in this and neighboring provinces.

It is now the Puritan's high holiday season, and they enjoy it with rapture all over the continent. Their behavior exactly assimilates the manners of the king-killing tribe during the English grand rebellion, but perhaps they may soon find an alteration in their spirits, from the execution of a plan for a general attack of the island of New York, &c., for which preparations are now making. The whole army is on ship board; General Clinton with the guards, Highlanders, and some other troops, is to land and attack the enemy's posts on Long Island. Lord Cornwallis is on the point of departure, with a considerable detachment of troops, round Long Island, and to land at New Rochelle, near West Chester; and General Howe, with the main body of the army, to proceed up the North River, and make a descent into West Chester county, as nearly opposite as possible to the place where Lord Cornwallis may secure a landing. Should General Howe succeed in this arrangement, it will be difficult for Mr. Washington to move from the island of New York, so that a general engagement may be expected.

We fancy that several days will elapse before the attack is made, to give time for Lord Cornwallis to get into the Sound, before General Howe attempts his landing in West Chester county. It is said that Mr. Washington's magazines are all in Cortlandt's Manor, and to get possession of them must surely be an object of General Howe's serious attention, and an additional inducement to attempt a landing in the rear of the provincial forces.[1]

A CORRESPONDENT wishes some able hand would undertake

---

[1] Extract of a letter, dated Staten Island; Upcott, iv. 383.

to describe General Lee's march from Boston to Charleston,
and would point out the remarkable circumstances of his meeting General Clinton at New York the day he arrived there;
of his finding him in Hampton Road when he came to Virginia; of Clinton's leaving Cape Fear just after
his arrival in North Carolina; and of his unlucky
meeting at Fort Sullivan. The world must have a high opinion
of General Lee's activity and vigilance, when they read of his
march of more than eleven hundred miles, and of the circumstances attending it throughout; and Clinton himself must look
on General Lee as his evil genius, thus haunting him along a
coast of such vast extent, and meeting him at last in Philippi.[1]

General Lee's Ubiquity.

So early as the reign of Charles the Sixth, of France, (the
time of our Henry the Fourth,) the French King (Charles)
gave a masquerade, in which himself and five
courtiers disguised their persons to imitate satyrs,
by covering their naked bodies with close linen habits, which
habits were then to be besmeared with rosin, on which down
was stuck all over. One of the company, in a frolic, touched
one of these satyrs with a lighted torch, as they were dancing
in a ring; the consequence was, all the six masques or satyrs
were enveloped in flames instantaneously. Four of the six
died immediately, and the King never recovered the fright and
disorder occasioned by the accident.[2]

Tar and Feathers.

AUGUST 20.—LAST Friday two fire-ships, commanded by
Captains Fosdyke and Thomas, gentlemen volunteers of rank
in the army of the United States, proceeded up
the North River with intent to give a suitable
warming to those piratical gentry that have infested it since
the 12th of July last.

Battle on the Hudson River.

The night was dark and favorable to the design, and the
enemy did not perceive our vessels till they were near aboard
of them. Captain Fosdyke grappled the Phœnix, but the fire

[1] Pennsylvania Evening Post, September 3.
[2] Middlesex Journal, August 20.

not communicating so soon as was expected, she disentangled
herself in about twenty minutes, after sustaining considerable
damage in her rigging.   Captain Thomas fell on board one of
the tenders, which was soon consumed ; and we are truly sorry
to inform the public this intrepid commander is yet missing.
This gallant enterprise struck so great a panic upon the enemy,
that they thought it prudent to quit their stations ; and yesterday, taking advantage of a fresh wind at S. E., attended with
considerable rain, they run the gauntlet, through a great number of well-directed shots from our batteries in and near New
York, which no doubt must have damaged them much.

Our galleys played smartly, and followed the ships a considerable distance into the bay.   The enemy's fire seemed to
be mostly directed upon the city, as the tops of the houses
were crowded with spectators ; but very little damage was
done to the buildings, nor any lives lost upon the occasion.[1]

AUGUST 22.—This night we have reason to expect the grand
attack from our barbarian enemies ; the reasons why, follow :
The night before last, a lad went over to Staten
Island, supped there with a friend, and got safe   Attack on New
                                                    York Expected.
back again undiscovered.   Soon after he went to General
Washington, and upon good authority reported, that the
English army, amounting to fifteen or twenty thousand, had
embarked and were in readiness for an engagement ; that
seven ships of the line, and a number of other vessels of war,
were to surround this city and cover their landing ; that the
Hessians, being fifteen thousand, were to remain on the island
and attack Perth Amboy, Elizabethtown. Point, and Bergen,
while the main body were doing their best at New York ; that
the Highlanders expected America was already conquered, and
that they were only to come over and settle on our lands, for
which reason they had brought their churns, ploughs, &c. ;
being deceived, they had refused fighting, upon which account
General Howe had shot one, hung five or six, and flogged many.

Last evening, in a violent thunder storm, Mr. —— (a very

---

[1] Pennsylvania Evening Post, August 20.

intelligent person) ventured over. He brings much the same
account as the above lad, with this addition :—that all the
horses on the island were by Howe's orders killed, barrelled up,
and put on board—the wretches thinking they could get no
landing at New York, and of consequence be soon out of
provision; that the Tories were used cruelly, and with the Highlanders were compelled to go on board the ships to fight in the
character of common soldiers against us. The British army are
prodigiously incensed against the Tories, and curse them as
the instruments of the war now raging. Mr. —— further informs, that last night the fleet was to come up, but the thunder storm prevented. The truth of this appears, from the circumstance of about three thousand red coats landing at ten
o'clock this morning on Long Island, where by this time it is
supposed our people are hard at it. There is an abundance of
smoke to-day on Long Island, our folks having set fire to stacks
of hay, &c., to prevent the enemy's being benefited in case
they get any advantage against us. All the troops in New
York are in high spirits, and have been under arms most of
the day, as the fleet have been in motion, and are now, as is
generally thought, only waiting for a change of tide. Forty-
eight hours or less, will determine it as to New York, one
way or the other.

The thunder storm of last evening was one of the most
dreadful we ever witnessed; it lasted from seven to ten o'clock.
Several claps struck in and about New York. Many houses
were damaged, and several lives lost. Three officers, a captain and two lieutenants, belonging to Colonel M'Dougal's
regiment, were struck instantly dead. The points of their
swords, for several inches, were melted, with a few silver dollars they had in their pockets; they (the persons) were seem-
ingly roasted. A dog in the same tent was also killed, and a
soldier near it struck blind, deaf, and dumb. One in the main
street was killed, as likewise ten on Long Island. Two or
three were much burnt, and greatly hurt. When God speaks,
who can but fear? [1]

¹ Pennsylvania Journal, August 28.

AUGUST 26.—TUESDAY last, a number of ships with troops on board, sailed from Staten Island out of the Narrows; next day they were followed by many more, and about ten o'clock Thursday morning, about ten thousand men landed between New Utrecht and Gravesend, on Long Island. Friday, a party of them came and took possession of Flatbush, which immediately brought on a very hot fire from the Americans, who are advantageously posted in the woods, and on every eminence round that place.

British Troops
land on Long
Island.

The advanced party of the regulars are encamped a little to the north-west of Flatbush church, and have a battery somewhat to the westward of Mr. Jeremiah Vanderbilts, from whence they continue to fire briskly on our people, who often approach and discharge their rifles within two hundred yards of their works. We have had only four men wounded since the enemy landed, but we were certain many of them fell; and a Hessian was killed last Friday. Several dollars were found in his pocket, and he had an excellent rifle. Many of the regulars are in rifle dresses.[1]

AUGUST 30.—ABOUT twelve o'clock last Monday night, (26th,) we were alarmed by the return of some of our scouting parties, who advised us that the English were in motion, and coming up the island, with several field-pieces. It was generally thought not to be the main body, but only a detachment, with a view to possess themselves of some advantageous heights. On which near three thousand men were ordered out, consisting chiefly of the Pennsylvania and Maryland troops, to attack them on their march. About sunrise the next morning, (27th,) we came up with a very large body of them.

Battle of Long
Island.

The Delaware and Maryland battalions made one party. Colonel Atlee with his battalion, a little before us, had taken post in an orchard and behind a barn; and, on the approach of the enemy, he gave them a very severe fire, which he bravely kept up for a considerable time, until they were near sur-

---

[1] Freeman's Journal, September 7.

rounding him, when he retreated to the woods. The enemy then advanced to us, upon which Lord Stirling, who commanded, drew us up in a line, and offered them battle in the true English taste. The British army then advanced within about three hundred yards of us, and began a very heavy fire from their cannon and mortars, for both the balls and shells flew very fast, now and then taking off a head. Our men stood it amazingly well—not even one of them showed a disposition to shrink.

Our orders were not to fire until the enemy came within fifty yards of us; but when they perceived we stood their fire so coolly and resolutely, they declined coming any nearer, although treble our number. In this situation we stood from sunrise till twelve o'clock, the enemy firing upon us the chief part of the time, when the main body of their army, by a route we never dreamed of, had entirely surrounded us and drove within the lines, or scattered in the woods all our men except the Delaware and Maryland battalions, who were standing at bay with double their number. Thus situated, we were ordered to attempt a retreat, by fighting our way through the enemy, who had posted themselves, and nearly filled every field and road between us and our lines. We had not retreated a quarter of a mile before we were fired upon by an advanced part of the enemy, and those upon our rear were playing upon us with their artillery. Our men fought with more than Roman virtue, and would have stood until they were shot down to a man. We forced the advanced party, which first attacked us, to give way, through which opening we got a passage down to the side of a marsh, seldom before waded over, which we passed, and then swam a narrow river, all the time exposed to the fire of the enemy. The companies commanded by Captains Ramsey and Scott were in the front, and sustained the first fire of the enemy, when hardly a man fell.

The whole of the right wing of our battalion, thinking it impossible to march through the marsh, attempted to force their way through the woods, where they were almost to a man killed or taken. The Maryland battalion has lost two hundred and fifty-nine men, amongst whom are twelve officers. Captains Veazey and Bowey, the first certainly killed; Lieutenants Butler, Sterret, Dent, Courley, Muse, Prawl, Ensigns Coats and Fernandes; who of them are killed or who prisoners, is yet uncertain. Many of the officers lost their swords and guns. We have since entirely abandoned Long Island, bringing off all our military stores.[1]

Generals Sullivan and Stirling are both prisoners; Colonels Atlee,[2] Miles, and Piper, are also taken. There are about a thousand men missing in all; we took a few prisoners. By a lieutenant we took, we understand they had about twenty-three thousand men on the island that morning. Most of our generals were on a high hill in our lines, viewing us with glasses. When we began our retreat, they could see the enemy we had to pass through, though we could not. Many of them thought we would surrender in a body, without firing. When we began the attack, General Washington wrung his hands, and cried out, "Good God, what brave fellows I must this day lose." Major Guest commanded the Maryland battalion, the colonel and lieutenant-colonel being both at York; Captains Adams and Lucas were sick. The major, Captain Ramsey, and Lieutenant Plunket, were foremost, and within forty yards of the enemy's muzzles, when they were fired upon by the enemy, who were chiefly under cover of an orchard, save a few

[1] General Washington called a council, and it was determined to retreat early in the evening of the 29th, but the strong tide and a furious wind from the east prevented it. About half-past eleven, however, the wind changed to the southerly, and the boats passed and repassed with perfect safety. In our suspense, we all prayed for relief, and surely the Lord was with us, for we were not only accommodated with a changing of the wind, but a fog overhung our army and concealed our redoubts, until the last soldier landed in New York. We all feel sore, but swear we'll do better in our next trial, which we are anxiously expecting.— *Letter from Ezekiel Cornell.**

[2] Samuel John Atlee commanded a Pennsylvania company in the French war. After his capture at Long Island, he remained a long period with the British, and soon after his release was appointed a commissioner to treat with the Indians. In 1780 he was elected to Congress, and was a member of the committee appointed to investigate the case of the mutiny of the Pennsylvania troops in 1781. He died at Philadelphia in November, 1786.

* Lieutenant-Colonel Cornell, of Scituate, in Massachusetts. He commanded the regiment in which Captain Stephen Olney served.—*See Mrs. Williams's Life of Olney.*

that showed themselves and pretended to give up, clubbing their firelocks until we came within that distance, when they immediately presented and blazed in our faces. They entirely overshot us, and killed some men away in the rear.[1] I had the satisfaction of dropping one of them the first fire I made; I was so near that I could not miss. I discharged my rifle seven times that day as deliberately as ever I did at a mark, and with as little perturbation.[2]

AUGUST 31.—A FEW days ago, a most infamous letter from

[1] Another account of this action is given as follows:—The great, the important day, big with the fate of America and liberty, seems to draw near. The British troops began to land on Long Island last Thursday, nearly their whole force, supposed to be more than twenty thousand British and foreign troops. They marched through the small town of Utrecht, on their way to Flatbush, another town about five miles from New York, near which they encamped; but were much harassed by our riflemen. Scouting parties were sent from our army to the adjacent woods, but were rather scanty in their numbers, considering the extent of ground they had to guard. The British forces, in three divisions, taking three different roads, and the advantage of the night, almost surrounded the whole of our out parties, who, though encircled with more than treble their numbers, bravely fought their way through the enemy, killing great numbers of them, and brought off some prisoners. The New York first battalion behaved with great bravery. Lord Stirling's brigade sustained the hottest of the enemy's fire; it consisted of Colonel Miles's two battalions, Colonel Atlee's, Colonel Smallwood's, and Colonel Hatch's regiments; they were all surrounded by the enemy, and had to fight their way through the blaze of their fire—they fought and fell like Romans! Lieutenant-Colonel Parry, of the Pennsylvania musketry, was shot through the head as he was giving orders to, and animating his men. The major part of Colonel Atlee's and Colonel Piper's regiments are missing. Doctor Davis and his mate were both taken prisoners as they were dressing a wounded person in the woods. Colonel Miles is missing, (a truly amiable character,) and supposed to be slain. General Parsons, with seven men, came in yesterday morning much fatigued, being for ten hours in the utmost danger of falling into the enemy's hands. Our killed, wounded, and missing, are imagined to be about one thousand; but for our encouragement the missing are hourly coming in. Our outguards have retreated to the main body of the army within the lines. The British army have two encampments about a mile from our lines, and by their manœuvres 'tis plain they mean to attack us by surprise, and storm our intrenchments. Our men show the greatest bravery, and wish them to come to action. The firing continued yesterday all the day.—*Pennsylvania Journal*, September 11.

[2] Extract of a letter from New York, September 1, in the Freeman's Journal, September 28.

Colonel Zedwitz to Tryon, the late governor of New York, was intercepted and fell into our hands.[1] After presenting his compliments in a formal manner to Lord Howe, and begging the contents of his letter ^Zedwitz's Letter.^ to be explained to him, Zedwitz proceeds to profess a consciousness that the world will censure him for his treachery in corresponding with the enemy of those in whose service he had engaged; but he apologizes for himself by appealing to the governor as a person who knew he had been forced to accept his commission for fear of ruin to himself and family; and as he had engaged through compulsion (*a most villanous lie, for he solicited for it*) from a rebellious mob, he infers that he can be under no obligation to conform to his engagements. Besides this, he observes that previous to his entrance in the continental army, he took the governor's advice on the occasion, and promised to do all he could in his new capacity, for his Majesty's service.

He next declares that ever since his return from Canada, he had been laying plans for the performance of his promise, and was in a fair way of doing something, when Forbes and the mayor were detected in their conspiracy,[2] which obliged him to lay aside his schemes; as Forbes had indiscreetly mentioned to the court on his trial a message from Governor Tryon to him, to wit: "that he would make his fortune if he would execute a certain commission." This, he says, rendered him suspected, and for the present frustrated his designs. However, as an instance that he was returning into favor, he informs the governor that General Washington had lately employed him to translate a paper into high German, which was to be printed and distributed among the Hessian troops. He advises to keep a good look-out.

In his next paragraph, he invents this abominable falsehood, that he had lately seen four villains at General W.'s house, with fourteen bottles of a mixture as black as ink, with which they were to poison the watering place on Staten Island, and were to receive a recompense of one thousand pounds each from the general.

---

[1] Clift's Diary.　　　　　[2] See page 255, ante.

He then informs, that a person always near the general, who was a friend to the King, though an interested one, had offered to furnish him with weekly returns of the strength and detail of the army till December, for the sum of four thousand pounds sterling, to be paid beforehand in hard gold; that he had proposed a reward of two thousand pounds sterling, which was agreed to, and he therefore desires (if the plan be agreeable) that the money might be immediately conveyed to him. He concluded with informing them that he shortly expected a full colonel's commission, with the command of the three forts up the North River.

The wickedness of this despicable man was discovered by the person whom he engaged to convey his letter. He endeavored to debauch one Steen, who, being a German, in but indifferent circumstances, and unemployed in our service, he imagined would be a proper instrument for his purpose. But Steen perceiving his intention, and being an honest man and a friend to the country, only amused him with a seeming compliance till he got his letter into his hands, and then, without delay, had it laid before the general.

Zedwitz, on his trial, acknowledged the letter to be his own, but pleaded that it was intended merely as a trick upon the enemy, to extract from them two thousand pounds sterling, in lieu of certain expenses he had put himself to in raising a regiment in Germany, at the request of the Marquis of Granby, for which he had never been reimbursed. The verdict of the court-martial is not yet known, but 'tis supposed he will suffer according to the merit of his crime.[1]

SEPTEMBER 3.—GENERAL HOWE gives the following account of the late action on Long Island:—On the twenty-second

Battle of Long Island. of last month, in the morning, the British, with Colonel Donop's corps of Chasseurs and Hessian grenadiers, disembarked near Utrecht on Long Island, without opposition, the whole being landed with forty pieces of cannon, in two hours and a half, under the direction of Commo-

---

[1] Pennsylvania Journal, September 4.

dore Hotham, Lieutenant-General Clinton commanding the first division of the troops.

The enemy had only small parties upon the coast, who, upon the approach of the boats, retired to the woody heights commanding a principal pass on the road from Flatbush to their works at Brooklyn. Lord Cornwallis was immediately detached to Flatbush with the reserve, two battalions of light infantry, and Colonel Donop's corps, with six field-pieces, having orders not to risk an attack upon the pass, if he should find it occupied; which proving to be the case, his lordship took post in the village, and the army extended from the ferry at the Narrows, through Utrecht and Gravesend, to the village of Flatland.

On the twenty-fifth, Lieutenant-General de Heister, with two brigades of Hessians from Staten Island, joined the army, leaving one brigade of his troops, a detachment of the 14th regiment from Virginia, some convalescents and recruits, under the command of Lieutenant-Colonel Dalrymple, for the security of that island.

On the twenty-sixth, Lieutenant-General de Heister took post at Flatbush, and in the evening Lord Cornwallis, with the British, drew off to Flatland. About nine o'clock, the same night, the van of the army, commanded by Lieutenant-General Clinton, consisting of light dragoons and brigade of light infantry, the reserve under the command of Lord Cornwallis, excepting the 42d regiment, which was posted to the left of the Hessians, the first brigade, and the 71st regiment, with fourteen field-pieces, began to move from Flatland across the country through the new lots, to seize a pass in the heights, extending from east to west along the middle of the island, and about three miles from Bedford, on the road to Jamaica, in order to turn the enemy's left, posted at Flatbush.

General Clinton being arrived within half a mile of the pass, about two hours before daybreak, halted and settled his dispositions for the attack. One of his patrols, falling in with a patrol of the enemy's officers, took them, and the general learning from their information that the rebels had

not occupied the pass, detached a battalion of light infantry
to secure it, and, advancing with his corps, upon the first
appearance of day, possessed himself of the heights, with such
a disposition as must have insured success, had he found the
enemy in force to oppose him.

The main body of the army, consisting of the guards, 2d,
3d, and 5th brigades, with ten field-pieces, led by Lord Percy,
marched soon after General Clinton, and halted an hour before
day in his rear. This column (the country not admitting of
two columns of march) was followed by the 49th regiment, with
four medium twelve-pounders, and the baggage closed the rear
with a separate guard.

As soon as these corps had passed the heights, they halted
for the soldiers to take a little refreshment, after which the
march was continued, and about half an hour past eight
o'clock, having got to Bedford, in the rear of the enemy's
left, the attack was commenced by the light infantry and
light dragoons upon large bodies of the rebels having cannon,
who were quitting the wood heights before mentioned, to return
to their lines, upon discovering the march of the army.
Instead of which, they were driven back, and the army still
moving on to gain the enemy's rear, the grenadiers and 32d
regiment being in front of the column, soon approached within
musket-shot' of the enemy's lines at Brooklyn, from whence
these battalions, without regarding the fire of cannon and
small arms upon them, pursued numbers of the rebels that
were retiring from the heights so close to their principal
redoubt, and with such eagerness to attack it by storm, that it
required repeated orders to prevail upon them to desist from
the attempt. Had they been.permitted to go on, it is my
opinion they would have carried the redoubt; but as it was
apparent the lines must have been ours at a very cheap rate,
by regular approaches, I would not risk the loss that might
have been sustained in the assault, and ordered them back to
a hollow way, in the front of the works, out of the reach of
musketry.

Lieutenant-General de Heister began soon after daybreak
to cannonade the enemy in his front, and, upon the approach

of our right, ordered Colonel Donop's corps to advance to the
attack of the hill, following himself at the head of the brigades.
The light infantry, about that time, having been reinforced by
the light company, the grenadier company, and two other
companies of the guards, who joined them with the greatest
activity and spirit, had taken three pieces of cannon, and were
warmly engaged with very superior numbers in the woods,
when, on the Hessians advancing, the enemy gave way, and
was entirely routed in that quarter.

On the left, Major-General Grant, having the fourth and
sixth brigades, the 42d regiment, and two companies of the
New York Provincials, raised by Governor Tryon in the spring,
advanced along the coast with ten pieces of cannon, to divert
the enemy's attention from their left. About midnight, he
fell in with their advanced parties, and at daybreak with a
large corps, having cannon and advantageously posted, with
whom there was skirmishing, and a cannonade for some hours,
until by the firing at Brooklyn, the rebels, suspecting their
retreat would be cut off, made a movement to their right, in
order to secure it across a swamp and creek, that covered the
right of their works; but being met in their way by a party of
2d grenadiers, who were soon after supported by the 71st
regiment, and General Grant's left coming up, they suffered
considerably. Numbers of them, however, did get into the
morass, where many were suffocated or drowned.

The force of the enemy detached from the lines where
General Putman commanded, was not less, from the best
accounts I have had, than ten thousand men, who were under
the orders of Major-General Sullivan, Brigadier-Generals Lord
Stirling and Woodhull. Their loss is computed to be about
thirty-three hundred killed, wounded, prisoners, and drowned,
with five field-pieces and one howitzer taken.

On the part of the King's troops, five officers, and fifty-six
non-commissioned officers and rank and file are killed; twelve
officers, and two hundred and forty-five non-commissioned
officers and rank and file are wounded; one officer and twenty
grenadiers of the marines taken, by mistaking the enemy for
the Hessians.

The Hessians had two privates killed, three officers, and twenty-three rank and file wounded. The wounds are in general very slight. Lieutenant-Colonel Monckton is shot through the body, but there are the greatest hopes of his recovery.

The behavior of both officers and soldiers, British and Hessians, was highly to their honor. More determined courage and steadiness in troops have never been experienced, or a greater ardor to distinguish themselves, as all those who had opportunity amply evinced by their actions.

In the evening of the 27th, the army encamped in front of the enemy's works. On the 28th, at night, broke ground six hundred yards distant from a redoubt upon their left, and on the 29th, at night, the rebels evacuated their intrenchments, and Red Hook, with the utmost silence, and quitted Governor's Island the following evening, leaving their cannon and a quantity of stores, in all their works. At daybreak on the 30th, their flight was discovered; the pickets of the line took possession, and those most advanced reached the shore opposite to New York, as their rear guard was going over, and fired some shot among them.

The enemy is still in possession of the town and island of New York, in force, and making demonstration to oppose us in their works on both sides of King's Bridge.

The inhabitants of Long Island, many of whom had been forced into rebellion, have all submitted, and are ready to take the oaths of allegiance.[1]

SEPTEMBER 4.—WE hear that the main body of our enemy's army are now encamped near Hellgate; to which place they
New York.   have transported a number of boats over land; and it is supposed they intend to cross and land a little above their encampment, and attack our army near King's Bridge, where we are making great preparations to receive them.

General Sullivan and Lord Stirling, who were both miss-

[1] Letter from General Howe to Lord George Germaine; Upcott, iv. 401.

ing after the battle of the 27th ult., are both alive and well; the former, on his parole, having obtained leave to go to Congress last Saturday, passed New York on his way to Philadelphia. It is said his business is to obtain an exchange of himself and Lord Stirling, for General Prescott, a prisoner in Pennsylvania, and General McDonald, a prisoner in North Carolina.

Since our troops have evacuated Long Island, the Tories and regulars treat the friends of their country with great severity and cruelty. Colonel Woodhull, late President of the New York Congress, for refusing to give up his side arms, was wounded on the head with a cutlass, and had a bayonet thrust through his arm.

By some people who left Huntingdon last Monday, we hear that the inhabitants of Suffolk county were to give up their arms yesterday.

Yesterday sixty-four women landed at Milford from Long Island, and we hear numbers are coming off daily to the continent.

Colonel Zedwitz has had his trial, and has been acquitted by a casting vote. He is yet held a prisoner.

A letter from New York mentions that when the Tories on Long Island went to congratulate General Howe on his success in driving the rebels from thence, he replied they ought rather to condole him on the loss of eighteen hundred brave men, and three generals.[1]

SEPTEMBER 6.—A MEETING of a large body of the inhabitants of Long Island, New York, was held, at which the following speech was delivered by an American re- cruiting officer in the Provincials, now raising for his Majesty's service, by order of his Excellency General Howe:—

Long Island Speech.

GENTLEMEN, FRIENDS, AND COUNTRYMEN :—Being appointed by his Excellency General Howe to raise a corps of Provincials for his Majesty's service, I readily engage in the attempt

---

[1] Freeman's Journal, September 14 and 28.

from principle, and in consequence of the fullest conviction that there are yet very many among us who still retain the most unshaken loyalty to our gracious sovereign, and zealous attachment to the blessings of the British constitution; who have long been anxious to wipe away from our country the reproach of a supposed universal revolt and disaffection of the Americans; and who are prompted as well by inclination, as by a sense of duty, to embrace the earliest opportunity of testifying by their conduct a continuance of their allegiance to his Majesty King George the Third, and a willing acknowledgment of the necessary and constitutional supremacy of the British legislature over the whole empire.

It is irksome to censure any collective bodies of our countrymen—we wish their conduct had been less culpable. I am confident we all hope that the sword of justice may be directed by the hand of compassion—that the guilty may be reclaimed, and that the deluded may be received with tenderness and mercy. But, gentlemen, now is the time to exert our endeavors if we wish to rescue ourselves from the evils of Republican tyranny, or our country from ruin. The misrule and persecutions of committees, conventions, and Congresses are no longer to be endured; they have become insupportable—they are too enormous for description. There are none of us but what have already either seen or felt the cruelty and oppression of their Republican despotism. Without effecting one salutary purpose, those self-created bodies have violated all the sacred ties of civil society, prostrated all law and government, and arbitrarily usurped an absolute control over the natural rights, the reason, and the consciences of their fellow-subjects. Instead of supporting constitutional liberty, and redressing public grievances, the special purposes of their original associations, they have denied their fellow-citizens the greatest and most valuable of all possible privileges: those of personal liberty, and freedom of speech. Instead of endeavoring, by dutiful representations in a constitutional method, for a reconciliation with the parent state, and thereby restoring to us the innumerable benefits and advantages of the former happy union between Great Britain and the colonies, they have most unjustifiably and perversely erected the standard of independency. This is not all. They have increased and multiplied the distresses of poverty and want among our poor. They have, moreover, deliberately involved their country in all the turbulence of faction, in all the evils of anarchy and licentiousness; and to complete the transcendent enormity of their crimes against the interest and prosperity of America, as well as the state to which we are united by the ties of nature, and bound by every civil, moral, and political obligation, they have disregarded the liberal and benevolent declaration of his Majesty's commissioners of peace, and with the most obdurate and unfeeling dispositions for the distresses of their countrymen, obstinately and wickedly precipitated the whole British continent of America into all the guilt of rebellion, and all the horrors and calamities of a civil war. In a few words, gentlemen, they have deluded the populace, they have betrayed their trust, they have forfeited the confidence of the public, they have ruined our country. Not to oppose them and their measures, were criminal. Not to join and assist the King's forces at this time would be at once unwise, unmanly, and ungrateful. And, gentlemen and countrymen, permit me to add, that the repeated assurances which have been given by the friends of government and good order, of their readiness to enter into his Majesty's service, leave me no room to doubt of the most immediate and honorable success. Your loyalty to your King, your duty to your country, your regard for your wives and children, the cause of violated justice and of injured majesty, all call aloud for your strenuous aid and united endeavors in assisting the royal army and navy in re-establishing the authority of his Majesty's government in the colonies, and with it a return to America of those happier days we all have seen, when the voice of peace and plenty was heard in our land, and we experienced, under the protection and benignity of the British State, the tranquil enjoyment of such constitutional and established liberties and privileges as were equal to our wishes, and known only to British subjects.[1]

---

[1] Gaine's Mercury, October 14.

SEPTEMBER 7.—SINCE our victory over Mr. Washington and his dirty pack of New England long-faces, we have received several challenges from the rebel camp, to fight man to man. Mr. Washington, who is one of the most capable men in the rebel army, don't seem to know that he might send his messages in by a flag, and therefore we receive most of them on the wind.[1]

THE following letter to Lord Viscount Howe, commander-in-chief of his Britannic Majesty's forces in North America, is published in the paper of to-day:[2]—My Lord: I am told there is great exultation among the English and mercenary troops under your lordship's command, on account of the late victory they obtained with an army of ten thousand men, (having a large train of artillery and many light horse to assist them in the work,) over three thousand Americans, having neither artillery nor horse to oppose their enemies with. Your army was commanded by a great many generals, colonels, &c., which, by superior cunning or generalship, had inclosed this handful of Americans, in full confidence of taking captive all that they spared alive; but the courage of these men baffled your hopes, who after laying great numbers of their enemies dead, that opposed their retreat, more than two-thirds reached their own lines in safety; therefore, we think you have no cause to exult.

My Lord, I assure you the Americans are not in the least dispirited at this unequal defeat; but, on the contrary, are much exasperated that you should act so cowardly in attacking three thousand men badly provided, with at least ten thousand of your veteran English troops, accompanied by thousands of orang-outang murdering brutes. The Americans wish for an opportunity to fight the invaders of their once happy land, on an equal footing, and let the fate of America rest on the issue of this conflict.

The mode we would propose is as follows, and which we

Letter to Lord Howe.

---

[1] MS. letter from John Hawk.
[2] Signed "Fairbattle," in the Pennsylvania Evening Post, September 7.

are anxious for your lordship to adopt; and, it being equitable, and your lordship being famed for generosity of sentiment, we have no doubt of succeeding to your wish. Let your lordship select ten thousand of your best troops and officers, with your lordship at their head; draw them up on the extensive plains of Long Island, where you will have every opportunity of displaying your great abilities. Arrange them in whatever manner you please; then let an equal number of Americans form themselves in battalia, and let each army be provided in all respects equal, with trains of artillery, and all other offensive weapons; then, on a given signal, begin the attack, and leave the issue to the God of armies. This is what the Americans have requested me to propose to Lord Howe; and the sooner he agrees to the proposal the better.

SEPTEMBER 9.—SINCE the retreat of our army from Long Island, the British have extended themselves a considerable length on the shore bordering the Sound, and on Tuesday a large number of them landed on Black- Armies
at New York. well's Island; but the shot from our batteries soon made them recross the river. On Wednesday, a ship from the fleet, supposed to be a frigate, passed between Governor's Island and Red Hook, and that evening reached a position in the Sound abreast of the island the enemy had been driven from; when, under cover of her guns, they, the next day, again came over to it in large bodies. This brought on a brisk cannonade for nearly two hours, in which the ship sustained so great a damage in her hull, as obliged her to move close in with the Long Island shore, for shelter from our shot and bombs. At the same time of attack, a firing also began from the enemy's batteries on Long Island, opposite New York, which was returned with such spirit by our people, in their fortresses at and about the ship yards, that they have given us little or no annoyance since, from that quarter.

Several men-of-war now lie within gun-shot of our main battery, and the greatest part of the fleet is stationed behind Governor's Island, though they have lately had very favorable winds to come up to New York; which gives us reason to think they do not mean to attack it by water, until they know the success of their forces in attempting to land on York island.

Last Thursday, a barge was seen in the East River, sounding the channel, where it is obstructed by scuttled vessels; but she soon made off, in consequence, it is supposed, of observing our people at the main fort, preparing to give her a suitable salutation.[1]

SEPTEMBER 16.—YESTERDAY morning, about eleven o'clock, the British troops, under cover of a tremendous fire from eight or ten ships-of-war, effected a landing near Mr. Stuyvesant's house in the Bowery, and in a few hours after took possession of the city of New York. About the same time, the Asia man-of-war and two other ships proceeded up the North River, but were very roughly handled by the American battery at Powle's Hook. This morning, at daylight, the Asia came down much faster than she went up, she and her consorts having narrowly escaped destruction by four of our fire ships that run in among them.[2]

British enter New York.

A PARTY from the enemy attacked the Americans, when a battle ensued, and continued about two hours, when the enemy gave way, and were pursued about two miles. In this action, the brave and intrepid Colonel Knowlton,[3] of Ash-

---

[1] Pennsylvania Evening Post, September 14.   [2] Freeman's Journal, Oct. 5.

[3] Thomas Knowlton was born in the town of Boxford, Massachusetts, in November, 1740, and when a child, removed with his parents to Ashford, in Connecticut. Before he was sixteen years old, he served as a private in the old French war, and, in 1760, he accompanied General Lyman at the siege of Havana. On his return to Ashford he married and became a farmer, in the employment of which he continued until the battle of Lexington. Soon after that occurrence, he was chosen captain of the Ashford militia company, and set off for the American camp, arriving there in time to take an important part in the battle of Breed's Hill.* He was present at the action on Long Island, and was actively engaged in the army until he received the fatal wound. After he was wounded he was removed from the field, and expired about sunset. In his death the country sustained a great loss. His gallantry, on all occasions, commanded the highest respect of Washington, who, in alluding to his death, said, "He would have been an honor to any country."—*See Washington's Official Letters*, vol. i., p. 248.

* See pages 97 and 193, ante.

ford, in Connecticut, was killed; and it is said Colonel Seldon, of Lyme, is among the slain. The loss the enemy sustained is said to have been very considerable. Our army is now between the nine and ten mile stones, (Harlem,) where they are strongly fortified and intrenched. The enemy's lines are about one mile and a half below them.[1]

SEPTEMBER 22.—YESTERDAY there was a terrible fire in New York. It broke out first at the most southerly part of the city, near White Hall, and was discovered be- tween twelve and one o'clock in the morning, the wind blowing very fresh from the south, and the weather exceeding dry. The rebel army having carried off all the bells of the city, the alarm could not be speedily communicated, and very few of the citizens were in town, most of them being driven out by the calamities of war, and several, of the first rank, sent prisoners to New England and other distant parts. A few minutes after the fire was discovered at White Hall, it was observed to break out in five or six other places, at a considerable distance.

Loyal account of the Fire in New York.

In this dreadful situation, when the whole city was threatened with destruction, Major-General Robertson, who had the chief command, sent immediately for two regiments that were encamped near the city, placed guards in several streets, and took every other precaution that was practicable to ward off the impending ruin. Lord Howe ordered the boats of the fleet to be manned, and after landing a large number of officers and seamen to assist us, the boats were stationed on each side of the city in the North and East Rivers, and the lines near the royal army were extended across the island, as it manifestly appeared the city was designedly set on fire.

The fire raged with inconceivable violence, and in its destructive progress swept away all the buildings between Broad street and the North River, almost as high as the City Hall; and from thence, all the houses between Broadway and

[1] Clift's Diary.

the North River, as far as King's College, a few only excepted. Long before the main fire reached Trinity church, that large, ancient, and venerable edifice was in flames, which baffled every effort to suppress them. The steeple, which was one hundred and forty feet high, the upper part wood, and placed on an elevated situation, resembled a vast pyramid of fire, exhibiting a most grand and awful spectacle. Several women and children perished in the fire. Their shrieks, joined to the roaring of the flames, the crush of falling houses, and the wide-spread ruin which everywhere appeared, formed a scene of horror great beyond description, which was still heightened by the darkness of the night. Besides Trinity church, the rector's house, the charity school, the old Lutheran church, and many other fine buildings, were consumed. St. Paul's church and King's College were directly in the line of fire, but saved with very great difficulty. After raging about ten hours, the fire was extinguished between ten and eleven o'clock this morning.

During this complicated scene of devastation and distress, at which the most savage heart might relent, several persons were discovered with large bundles of matches, dipped in melted rosin and brimstone, attempting to set fire to the houses. A New England man, who had a captain's commission under the Continental Congress, and in their service, was seized, having these dreadful implements of ruin. On being searched, the sum of five hundred pounds was found upon him. General Robertson rescued two of those incendiaries from the enraged populace, (who had otherwise consigned them to the flames,) and reserved them for the hand of deliberate justice. One White, a carpenter, was observed to cut the leather buckets which conveyed water; he also wounded, with a cutlass, a woman who was very active in handing water. This provoked the spectators to such a degree, that they instantly hung him up. One of those villains set fire to the college and was seized; many others were detected in the like crime and secured.

The officers of the army and navy, the seamen and soldiers, greatly exerted themselves, often with the utmost hazard to themselves, and showed all that alertness and activity for which they are justly celebrated on such occasions. To their vigorous efforts in pulling down such wooden buildings as would conduct the fire, it is owing, under Providence, that the whole city was not consumed; for the number of inhabitants was small, and the pumps and fire-engines were very much out of order. This last circumstance, together with the removal of our bells, the time and place of the fire's breaking out, when the wind was south, the city being set on fire in so many different places nearly at the same time, so many incendiaries being caught in the very act of setting fire to houses; these, to mention no other particulars, clearly evince, beyond the possibility of a doubt, that this diabolical affair was the result of a pre-concerted, deliberate scheme. Thus, the persons who called themselves our friends and protectors, were the perpetrators of this atrocious deed, which in guilt and villany, is not inferior to the Gun-powder Plot; whilst those who were held up as our enemies were the people who gallantly stepped forth, at the risk of their lives, to snatch us from destruction. Our distress was very great before, but this disaster has increased it tenfold. Many hundreds of families have lost their all, and are reduced from a state of affluence to the lowest ebb of want and wretchedness—destitute of shelter, food, and clothing.

Surely "there must be some chosen curse—some secret thunder in the stores of heaven, red with uncommon wrath to blast" the miscreants who thus wantonly sport with the lives, property, and happiness of their fellow-creatures, and unfeelingly doom them to inevitable ruin.[1]

---

[1] New York Mercury, September 30, 1776, and Freeman's Journal, January 7, 1777:—Mr. David Grim, a merchant in New York, who saw the conflagration, has left the following account of it:—It commenced in a small wooden house, on the wharf, near Whitehall slip, which was then occupied by a number of men and women of a bad character. The fire began late at night. There being but a few inhabitants in the city, in a short time it raged tremendously. It burned all the houses on the east side of Whitehall slip, and the west side of Broad street to Beaver street. A providential and happy circumstance occurred at this time; the wind was then southwesterly. About two o'clock in the morning the wind veered to the southeast; this carried the flames of the fire to the northwestward, and burned both sides of Beaver street to the east side of Broadway, then crossed

THIS day, one Hale,[1] in New York, on suspicion of being a spy was taken up and dragged without ceremony to the execution post, and hung up. General Washington has since sent in a flag, supposed to be on that account.

Broadway to Beaver lane, and burning all the houses on both sides of Broadway, with some few houses in New street to Rector street, and to John Harrison's, Esq., three-story brick house, which house stopped the fire on the east side of Broadway; from thence it continued burning all the houses in Lumber street, and those in the rear of the houses on the west side of Broadway to St. Paul's church, then continued burning the houses on both sides of Partition street, and all the houses in the rear (again) of the west side of Broadway to the North River. The fire did not stop until it got into Mortkile street, now Barclay street. The college yard and the vacant ground in the rear of the same, put an end to this awful and tremendous fire. Trinity church being burned, was occasioned by the flakes of fire that fell on the south side of the roof. The southerly wind fanned those flakes of fire in a short time to an amazing blaze, and it soon became out of human power to extinguish the same; the roof of this noble edifice being so steep that no person could go on it. St. Paul's church was in the like perilous situation. The roof being flat, with a balustrade on the eaves, a number of citizens went on the same, and extinguished the flakes of fire as they fell on the roof. Thus happily was this beautiful church saved from the destruction of this dreadful fire, which threatened the ruin thereof and that of the whole city. The Lutheran church being contiguous to the houses adjoining the same fire, it was impossible to save it from destruction. This fire was so furious and violently hot, that no person could go near it, and there were no fire engines to be had, at that time, in the city.—*Barber's New York*, p. 303.

A correspondent at Harlem, on the 26th wrote:—Friday last was discovered a vast cloud of smoke arising from the north part of the city, which continued till Saturday evening. The consequence was, that the Broadway from the new City Hall down to Whitehall is laid in ashes. Our friends were immediately suspected, and according to the report of a flag of truce who came to our lines soon after, those who were found on or near the spot were pitched into the conflagration; some hanged by the heels, and others by their necks with their throats cut. Inhuman barbarity!—*Freeman's Journal*, October 5.

[1] Nathan Hale was a descendant of John Hale, first minister of Banby, Massachusetts. He was the sixth child of Richard and Elizabeth Hale, and was born in Coventry, Connecticut. He graduated at Yale College in 1773, with distinguished honors. Of his private history little is known. The subjoined account was published some time after his execution.—*The following is a genuine specimen of Tory benevolence, and may be depended upon as real matter of fact :—*

"Samuel Hale, late of Portsmouth, in New Hampshire, after his elopement from thence, visited an uncle in Connecticut, where he was hospitably entertained; but as his uncle was a Whig, and had a son, a young gentleman of a liberal education and most amiable disposition, who strongly felt for his bleeding country, and being very active in the military way, was urged and prevailed upon to take

SEPTEMBER 29.—A few days ago one Dr. Hull, belonging to Wallingford, Connecticut, was drummed out of his regiment, at the American camp at Harlem, for selling soldiers certificates that they were unfit for duty. He charged eight pence for each man, and any one in his regiment might have had a certificate for that sum. He deserves to be advertised as a scoundrel as much as Wentworth.[1]

Doctor Hull.

SINCE the victory at Charleston, the inhabitants of the southern colonies are more unanimous and spirited in support of the cause of American Independence than they were before. A very artful speech made at Philadelphia by Samuel Adams (who is esteemed by all as one of the most subtle men in the Congress) to a very numerous body of the citizens, militia, &c., has almost irritated them to madness against Great Britain, and made them resolve to conquer or die in the cause they have espoused.[2]

Samuel Adams' Speech.

a commission in the Continental army; consequently Samuel was obliged to conduct with caution, and counterfeit, as well as he could, a whiggish phiz while he tarried, which, however, was but a short time, before he made his escape to General Howe in New York. Some time after this, Captain Hale, at the request of the general, went into New York in disguise, and having nearly accomplished his designs, whom should he meet but his aforesaid cousin Samuel, whom he attempted to shun, but Sam knew him too well. Captain Hale soon found he was advertised, and so particularly described that he could not get through Long Island; he therefore attempted to escape by the way of King's Bridge, and so far succeeded as to get to the outer guard, where he was suspected, apprehended, carried back and tried, and yet would have been acquitted had not his affectionate and grateful cousin Samuel appeared and made oath, that he was a captain in the Continental army, and that he was in there as a spy; in consequence of which he was immediately hung up. However, at the gallows he made a sensible and spirited speech, among other things told them they were shedding the blood of the innocent, and that if he had ten thousand lives, he would lay them all down, if called to it, in defence of this injured, bleeding country.

"The Printers throughout the continent are desired to exhibit this tragical scene to the public, that they may see what mercy they are to expect if they fall into the hands of Tories."—*Freeman's Journal*, February 18, 1777.

[1] Jonathan Wentworth, of New Hampshire.   [2] Upcott, iv. 397.

CHAPTER VIII.

OCTOBER 1.—A WRITER in the London Gazette, in a letter[1] to the lord mayor, says :—I was last week on board the American privateer called the Yankee, commanded by Captain Johnson, and lately brought into this port by Captain Ross, who commanded one of the West India sugar ships, taken by the privateer in July last; and, as an Englishman, I earnestly wish your lordship, who is so happily placed at the head of this great city, (justly famed for its great humanity even to its enemies,) would be pleased to go likewise, or send proper persons, to see the truly shocking, and I may say, barbarous and miserable condition of the unfortunate American prisoners, who, however criminal they may be thought to have been, are deserving of pity, and entitled to common humanity.

The Yankee Privateer.

They are twenty-five in number, and all inhumanly shut close down, like wild beasts, in a small, stinking apartment, in the hold of a sloop, about seventy tons burden, without a breath of air, in this sultry season, but what they receive through a small grating overhead, the openings in which are not more than two inches square in any part, and through which the sun beats intensely hot all day, only two or three being permitted to come on the deck at a time; and then they are exposed in the open sun, which is reflected from the decks and water like a burning glass.

I do not at all exaggerate, my lord ; I speak the truth ; and the resemblance that this barbarity bears to the memorable

[1] Dated August 6.

black hole at Calcutta, as a gentleman present on Saturday observed, strikes every one at the sight. All England ought to know that the same game is now acting upon the Thames on board this privateer, that all the world cried out against, and shuddered at the mention of in India, some years ago, as practised on Captain Hollowell, and other of the King's good subjects.

The putrid steams issuing from the hold are so hot and offensive, that one cannot, without the utmost danger, breathe over it, and I should not be at all surprised, if it should cause a plague to spread. The miserable wretches below look like persons in a hot bath, panting, sweating, and fainting for want of air; and the surgeon declares, that they must all soon perish in that situation, especially as they are almost all in a sickly state with bilious disorders.

The captain and surgeon, it is true, have the liberty of the cabin, (if it deserves the name of a cabin,) and make no complaints on their own account. They are both sensible, and well-behaved young men, and can give a very good account of themselves, having no signs of fear, and being supported by a consciousness of the justice of their cause. They are men of character, of good families in New England, and highly respected in their different occupations; but being stripped of their *all* by the burning of towns and other destructive measures of the present unnatural war, were forced to take the disagreeable method of making reprisals to maintain themselves and their children, rather than starve.

Numbers of gentlemen, and friends of government, who were on board at the same time, will confirm the truth of this my representation, being very sensibly touched themselves at the horrid sight.

English prisoners, taken by the Americans, have been treated with the most remarkable tenderness and generosity, as numbers who are safely returned to England most freely confess, to the honor of our brethren in the colonies. And it is a fact, which can be well attested in London, that this very surgeon on board the privateer, after the battle of Lexington, April nineteenth, 1775, for many days voluntarily and gen-

erously, without fee or reward, employed himself in dressing
the King's wounded soldiers, who but an hour before would
have shot him if they could have come at him, and in making a
collection for their refreshment, of wine, linen, money, &c.,
in the town where he lived. This is a real fact, of which the
most ample testimony may be had.

The capture of the privateer was solely owing to the ill-
judged lenity and brotherly kindness of Captain Johnson, who
not considering his English prisoners in the same light that he
would Frenchmen or Spaniards, put them under no sort of
confinement, but permitted them to walk the decks as freely
as his own people, at all times. Taking advantage of this
indulgence, the prisoners one day watching their opportunity,
when most of the privateer's people were below and asleep,
shut down the hatches, and making all fast, had immediate
possession of the vessel without using any force.

I shall conclude with saying, that though this letter is
addressed to your lordship, I hope that all who may read it,
and have any influence, will do all in their power to gain the
necessary relief; and it is humbly apprehended, that the well
disposed, who are blessed with affluence, could not better
bestow their bounty than upon those poor objects. Vegetables
and ripe fruits of all kinds, with porter, &c., must be very
useful, as well as the means to procure other necessaries.
The privateer lies opposite to Ratcliffe Cross, a mile and a
half below the Tower, and by asking for Captain Johnson,
admittance may be obtained.[1]

THE important day is come, big with the fate of millions,
and America now beckons to her sons to kindle all their
native fire, push into action every power, and
press to the seas or fields where Fame and Glory
call. The united wisdom of America in Congress has determined that it is necessary to the salvation of these States, that
an army be raised to serve during this war. The wisdom of
this measure must appear to all; therefore let us all promote

An Appeal.

----

[1] "Humanitas," in the Pennsylvania Journal, November 6.

it with our utmost power. He that enlists into this army of freemen, in defence of every thing good and great, enrolls his name in Fame's brightest temple, where it will shine (if not blotted by after misconduct) with growing lustre down applauding ages; while posterity rises through successive eras to taste the bliss of freedom handed down by US, their forefathers; and every infant tongue and hoary head will bless our memory; with rapture hail the day when we drew the sharpened steel against the Tyrant George, and with transports all their own, pass down the stream of time till time shall be no more!—How angelic the design to communicate felicity to all those millions who may rise after us, and inhabit these United States? "The blessings of future ages, which the conscious imagination anticipates," crowd together in the patriot's breast, and are the solid pleasures which delight his mind!

The history of mankind bleeds with the destruction which tyranny has made in all countries and nations; and while we weep over the "tragic pages stained with the blood of patriot citizens," they speak like a voice of thunder in the ears of Americans to guard against the execrable monster! Despotic kings, from the days of Nimrod to this hour, have deluged the world in blood, and have been the curses of mankind;— but in the whole catalogue of royal villains, has there been one of a more infernal character than *George the Third?* Do not our heroic ancestors, who fled from the tyranny of Britons, and subdued American wildernesses in spite of savage barbarity, speak to us from their celestial abodes, to defend the dear inheritance of Liberty, which they left us, while Posterity mingle their cries, reason and religion unite their voice in the pressing call! Imploring the assistance of Him, who gave us the rights of humanity, let us with a sacred ardor and unalterable firmness watch over and defend the rights of America, "nor pause to waste a coward thought on Life."

Every good mind must feel a glow of gratitude to heaven for the animating prospect of seeing America the asylum of liberty, the land of virtuous freedom, the seat of learning, of industry, manufactures, commerce, and husbandry; the nurse of heroes, the parent of science, the bosom of virtue, and the guardian of mankind. The whole series of divine dispensations, from the infant days of our fathers in America, are big with importance in her favor, and point to something great and good. If we look round the world, and view the nations with their various connections, interests, and dependencies, we shall see innumerable causes at work in favor of this growing country. Nature and art seem to labor, as it were, travail in birth, to bring forth some glorious events that will astonish mankind, and form a bright era in the annals of time.[1]

THE Hessians plunder all indiscriminately, Tories as well as Whigs; if they see any thing they want they seize it, and say, " Rebel good for Hesse man." A Tory complained to General Howe that he was plundered by the Hessians. The general said he could not help it—it was their way of making war. So the friends of government are protected ! This is great encouragement for the Tories. Lord Dunmore told Lord Stirling he was sorry he kept such company. His lordship replied, " My lord, I have kept whiter company than your lordship has of late."[2]

OCTOBER 8.—So vast a fleet was never before seen together in the port of New York, or perhaps in all America. The ships are
British Fleet. stationed up the East River or Sound, as far as Turtle Bay, and near the town. The multitude of masts carries the appearance of a wood. Some are moored up the North River, others in the bay between Red and Yellow Hook ; others, again, off Staten Island, and several off Powle's Hook, and towards the kills. The men-of-war are moored chiefly up New York Sound, and make, with the other ships, a very magnificent- and formidable appearance. Five men-of-war have been detached from the squadron into the North River, above Greenwich, probably to assist the operations of the army

---

Freeman's Journal, October 29.

[2] Alluding to his enlisting the Negroes of Virginia to fight against their masters.—*Freeman's Journal*, October 29.

against the rebels, who still remain on the northern extremity of the island, and on the heights above King's Bridge.

The savage burning of the city by the New England incendiaries will be a lasting monument of inveterate malice against the trade and prosperity of this colony, as well as rooted disaffection to British law and government. They had long threatened the performance of this villanous deed; and this is the best return that the people of property in this city, who have espoused their cause, are to expect for their heedless credulity.[1]

OCTOBER 14.—LATELY died, at his house upon Long Island, CADWALLADER COLDEN, Esq., for many years lieutenant-governor of New York, a man of great probity, knowledge, and steadiness, which he had occasion to show upon many occasions. When above ninety years of age, not all the threats of rebellious incendiaries could shake his undissembled loyalty to his sovereign, nor all their wiles seduce him from his attachment to the constitutional liberties of his country, in opposition to the republican system of popular tyranny. He died full of days, and had the satisfaction, before his departure, to know that the arms of his prince had prevailed, in a single instance, over the forces of the rebels. They who knew him best, will give his character that eulogium, which even a stranger will rejoice to pay to such distinguished merit.[2]

Cadwallader Colden.

IT has been observed that the British power, in the beginning of a war, generally makes but feeble, and oftentimes unsuccessful exertions; but that in the prosecution of hostilities, her force gradually increasing, like a gathered torrent, becomes almost irresistible. The last war is a striking evidence of the truth of this observation; and we have seen since the commencement of these troubles, the same line of conduct pursued towards these colonies. The first force

British Power.

[1] From the New York Mercury.—See Freeman's Journal, October 29.
[2] Gaine's Mercury, October 14.

VOL. I.—21

sent out was small, and employed with apparent reluctance—
we might have said, sent out with a wish that they might not
be employed at all.   This, instead of being imputed to its
proper motive, was construed into the weakness and (who could
have thought it!) into the timidity of Britain.   Our countrymen at home were stigmatized as cowards, while their brave
hearts only abhorred the idea of fighting against those who
claimed the title of brethren and friends.   Nothing but repeated insults and menaces against their King, their country,
and themselves, could have induced a persuasion in the army,
that the leaders of the sedition seriously meant nothing else
than to become rebels and enemies.   At last the British lion is
roused. We have seen, in the course of a summer, a powerful
army cross over the Atlantic, under the conduct of a gallant
fleet. We have heard of other considerable armaments arriving safely elsewhere upon this continent; and we have no
reason to doubt but that, if it were possible these should fail,
greater and greater would be sent out to reduce this country
to its indefeasible allegiance and duty.   To all this there are
only to be opposed the *wisdom* of a Congress consisting of men
either of new and doubtful characters, or of none at all; a
wretched paper currency which will only eat up the property
of the continent without adding an atom to it; and a vagabond
army of ragamuffins, with paper pay, bad clothes, and worse
spirits.   Is it reasonable to think that such a cause, with such
supporters, will ever be able to maintain itself against veteran
battalions of brave and loyal Britons, contending for British
honor and constitutional liberty?   Is it not strange that a people in such circumstances should be persuaded to reject all
overtures of reconciliation, by the machinations of an artful
and ambitious Congress?   It can only be accounted for by the
old adage, *Quos Deus vult perdere prius dementat.*[1]

OCTOBER 16.—THIS morning, at ten o'clock, the members of
his Majesty's council, the judges, and all the other well affected
citizens, who were not driven away by the hand of violence, or

[1] New York Gazette, October 14.

sent prisoners to other provinces, met at the City Hall in New
York, when a decent and respectful address to Lord Howe and
General Howe, the King's commissioners for re-   Meeting at New York.
storing peace to America, was read, representing
the firm attachment of the inhabitants to our rightful and
gracious sovereign, George the Third, and their sense of the
constitutional supremacy of Great Britain over these colonies;
lamenting the interruption of that harmony which formerly
subsisted between them, and praying that the city and county
might be restored to his Majesty's peace and protection. The
address was unanimously approved and adopted, and it was
agreed that the inhabitants should all sign it.   But the number assembled being too great to sign at that time, two respectable citizens were appointed to attend at a public house, adjoining the City Hall, from ten o'clock A. M., to two o'clock
P. M., every day, to take subscriptions till all had signed.   As
this measure was the first step which was necessary to be
taken on our part towards effecting a reconciliation with Great
Britain, joy was lighted up in every countenance, at the prospect of returning peace and union with the parent state.   The
populace expressed the feelings of their hearts by loud acclamations and shouts of applause.

After this, an affectionate address to his Excellency William Tryon, Esq., our worthy governor, was read, "requesting
him to present the above address to the commissioners, and
otherwise to exert himself that the prayer of it might be granted."   This address was also unanimously approved and agreed
to; and the honorable Mr. Chief Justice Horsmanden was
desired to sign and deliver it to his Excellency, in behalf of
the inhabitants.

The well-known humanity of the commissioners, and the
tender regard they have manifested for the welfare of America
in their several declarations, afford the most flattering hopes
that the address to them will be productive of the desired
effect.   And it is most devoutly to be wished, that the continent may follow the example of this city—that the Americans in general may avail themselves of his Majesty's clemency and paternal goodness, in offering to restore them to his

royal protection and peace. Those who continue deaf to such
benevolence, and thereby prolong the present destructive and
unnatural rebellion, will be utterly inexcusable in the sight of
God and man. Their obstinacy must be detested by the wise
and virtuous; the inevitable ruin attending it will be unpitied
by all, and posterity will execrate their memories.[1]

It is an observation of the celebrated Montesquieu, "that
individuals rarely incline to part with power—great bodies
never." The conduct of the Congress furnishes
another instance of the truth of this remark.

Loyal Strictures.

Though it is the grand interest of America to be reconciled to
Great Britain, and though it has been the constant and repeated profession of the several assemblies, that reconciliation
was their object; yet, when reconciliation was held out by
government, and commissioners were appointed to confer with
the colonies upon their own ground for that purpose, these
ambitious incendiaries, seeing that, upon such an event, all
their assumed consequence must be lost, had art enough to
hasten a declaration of absolute independence, before the desired commission could possibly arrive. The delegates had
perfect information of what was intended, and fearing that this
act of benevolence and conciliation might operate upon many
persons in the colonies, whose properties made it their interest
to solicit peace, resolved to put it out of the power of the several assemblies to listen to any overtures, by previously drawing them into an acquiescence with the avowal of independency. Thus the avarice of some indigent men, bankrupts
both in fortune and character, and the ambition of others who
lusted after power, has plunged this once happy country into
a flood of miseries, for which the lives and fortunes of these
parricides would, in the issue, make but a poor atonement.
'Tis easy to foresee that, so long as these demagogues have the
direction of affairs, no peace or settlement can be hoped for.
And it is not to be believed that the colonies can have had reconciliation sincerely in view, because they have hitherto em-

[1] New York Gazette, October 21.

ployed means which they must have known were exceptionable and offensive. Nor can it be supposed that they will ever be really desirous of it, till they have applied themselves, not through the medium of a Congress, but of their own respective assemblies, to the promoting of this salutary measure.[1]

LAST night, General Mercer passed over to Staten Island with part of the troops posted at Perth Amboy, New Jersey, and advanced within a few miles of Richmond Mercer's descent town, having been informed that a company of on Staten Island. British troops, one of Hessians, and one of Skinner's militia lay there. Colonel Griffin was detached with Colonel Patterson's battalion, and Major Clarke at the head of some riflemen, to fall in upon the east end of the town, while the remainder of the troops inclosed it on the other quarters. Both divisions reached the town by break of day this morning, but not before the enemy were alarmed. Most of them fled after exchanging a few shot with Colonel Griffin's detachment. Two of them were mortally wounded, and seventeen taken prisoners, with the loss only of two soldiers killed on our side. Colonel Griffin received a wound in the foot from a musket ball, and Lieutenant-Colonel Smith was slightly wounded in the arm. Amongst the prisoners taken in this action, are eight Hessians. Our troops brought off from Staten Island forty-five muskets, a number of bayonets, cutlasses, &c., and one standard of the British light horse.[2]

[1] New York Gazette, October 21.
[2] Pennsylvania Journal, October 23 ; Gaine, in his paper of October 21, says :— A body of the rebels skulked over from the New Jersey shore to Staten Island, and after cowardly setting fire to two or three farm houses, skulked back again to their former station. Probably, from their conduct, it may be judged that these were the people who, about the middle of last August, committed such an act of villanous barbarity as cannot be recited without indignation. A very little boy, belonging to an officer of the army, was playing by himself upon the shore of Staten Island, opposite the Jerseys, when about seven or eight of the riflemen or *ragged men*, came down slily, and discharged their muskets upon him. Immediately upon the poor creature's falling, they gave three cheers and retired. This was a most cruel, dastardly, and infamous murder upon a defenceless, innocent child. Such poltroons will always run away at the appearance and approach of men.

OCTOBER 22.—BEHOLD A COWARD!—The public is desired to take notice, that Daniel Pittee, ensign in Captain Timothy Stow's company, Colonel Wheelock's regiment, applied at head-quarters for a discharge, upon hearing the enemy were likely to attack our lines. He was refused, and next day deserted our camp. This infamous runaway belongs to the south parish of Dedham, in the county of Suffolk.[1]

OCTOBER 23.—FRIDAY morning last, we were alarmed by the drums beating to arms, and the enemy landed at Rodman's Point with their whole force. The brigade under the command of Colonel Glover, consisting of about seven hundred men, one regiment being absent for guard, marched down towards the place where the enemy were advancing, with a body of sixteen thousand, and a very large artillery. The first attack was made by a small party, on their advanced guard, which were effectually routed and forced to retreat to their main body, who, when they came up, were fired upon by two regiments, advantageously posted by Colonel Glover and Major Lee, (who behaved gallantly,) which brought many of them to the ground. Thus we continued fighting them and retreating the whole afternoon, until they came to a stand, where they now remain, stretching down along the Sound, towards Connecticut—we suppose for forage. Our men behaved like soldiers—conformed to the orders of the officers and retreated in grand order, which is the life of discipline. Our loss is about nine or ten killed, and about thirty wounded. The enemy, a deserter says, lost two hundred killed on the spot, and a great number wounded. People may think what they please of the regular and spirited behavior of the British troops, but I that day was an eye-witness to the contrary. I saw as great irregularity, almost, as in a militia; they would come out from their body and fire single guns. As to their courage, their whole body of sixteen thousand were forced to retreat by the fire of a single regiment, and many of them old troops. The fourth regiment was one that

Glover's Skirmish in Eastchester.

---

[1] Published by order, at Ticonderoga; Freeman's Journal, November 5.

run; and had we been reinforced with half their number, we might have totally defeated them; the shot from their artillery flew very thick about our heads.   The next day, General Lee (under whose command we are) came and publicly returned his thanks to Colonel Glover, and the officers and soldiers under his command, for their noble, spirited, and soldier-like conduct during the battle, and that nothing in his power should be wanting to serve those brave officers and men; and General Washington has since expressed himself much in the same words in his general orders.   General Lee says we shall none of us leave the army, but all stay and be promoted; but how that will be is uncertain.   Yesterday one of the corporals and two men in our regiment, by leave from the colonel, went out to see what they could pick up, and by going in the mouth of the enemy they brought off a number of fat cattle.   Flushed with their success, they went again this afternoon, and going directly in the rear of the Hessian camp, went into a house where they washed for the British officers, and were bringing off three tubs of shirts, but the man of the house informed the camp.   They turned out four hundred, who obliged our lads to retreat; but meeting with some of their comrades, they attacked and drove the Hessians, killed the major, took his commission and ten guineas out of his pocket, and have taken three of them prisoners, besides a number killed; many of our officers who saw them, say they are ugly devils.   They are now in camp.   The enemy have so far quitted York, that our people have been down as far as a place called Bowery Lane, which is but one mile from the extent of the city.[1]

> "What's human life?—to gaze upon the sun,
> And go the vulgar round of endless years?
> Or is it to be free?"—Taste Independence,
> Blissful moments; defend it till ye die!

By the favor of Providence we have reached that political point (which the wise have long seen to be the only foundation

---

[1] Extract of a letter from Mile Square, in Eastchester, New York.—*Freeman's Journal*, November 12.

of safety)—*Independence ;* our work is now plain before us—
to persevere to the end in supporting the Declaration we
have made to the world. To do this, every consideration urges
us; to retreat is death—is slavery, calamities of every name,
and all the gloomy horrors of the most odious and execrable
tyranny. Before us is all the glory of *Freedom*, pregnant with
every felicity our wishes can grasp, or human nature enjoy.
If we continue our exertions with that wisdom and magnanimity with which we began, *Liberty* will soon triumph, wealth
flow in through ten thousand channels, and America become
the glory of all lands. Tyranny is now exerting her utmost
power, and if resisted a little longer, George, and all his murderers, must bid adieu to America forever; then we shall
have the double happiness and honor of subduing the tyrants,
and enjoying liberty; the expense and dangers it has cost us
will sweeten the blessing. If we have not suffered enough yet
to make us duly prize the inestimable jewel, let us patiently
bear what is yet to come. But if we continue in the ways of
well-doing, we shall certainly succeed; for unerrring wisdom
has told us, "if we trust in the Lord and do good, we shall
dwell in the land and be fed;" therefore we have nothing to
do but to be faithful to God and our country, and the blessings
we contend for will be the portion of us and our children. The
price of liberty is not to be gained in a day, nor bought with a
small price, but is the reward of long labor and unremitting exertions; and a people are commonly made to realize their dependence on Heaven for so great a favor, before they are crowned
with complete success. The poor Dutch provinces were oppressed by a Spanish tyrant, like George of Britain, and
they (although poor and small in number, compared with the
States of America) resisted the tyrant who had at his command
a great and rich nation, and after a bloody contest of many
years, gloriously triumphed in the complete freedom of their
country. During the conflict, they were sometimes reduced
to such extreme difficulties as would have sunk any but free
minds into absolute despair; but they were blessed with a succession of heroes and statesmen, who wisely preferred liberty to
every thing else; and persevered through a long series of the

severest calamities of every kind, with undiminished fervor in the glorious cause, until they arrived at the blissful period of Independent States, and remain to this day a glorious monument of the supereminent virtue and valor of freemen. Let us imitate this bright example. With them we shall shine in the history of mankind, until the heavens are no more. The blood and treasure it may cost, will heighten the value of liberty, and brighten the future days of peace and glory, when we or posterity shall recount the noble exertions, and amazing intrepidity of those who were honored by Heaven as the instruments of saving this great people from infernal tyranny. It will add to the joys of prosperity, and sweeten the sacred triumphs of freemen, when encircled with the charms of peace, to look back upon the trying scenes of the present time, and review the difficulties surmounted through a series of conflicts, while each moment was big with importance, and the fate of thousands hung upon every hour.[1]

YESTERDAY, the Hessians, the Waldeckers, and other troops, debarked from their respective ships, at New York, and passed by the East River, in a multitude of flat-bottomed boats and other vessels, in the highest *Debarkation of Hessians.* spirits imaginable. It being a very fine day, the scene was rendered extremly beautiful by the crowds upon the water, cheering their military brethren and other spectators on shore, and making the hills resound with trumpets, French horns, drums and fifes, accompanied by the harmony of their voices. These have added an agreeable reinforcement to the British army, and they are, to all appearance, as fine troops as any in the world.

Nothing can exceed the unanimity and ardor of the seamen upon the present occasion. The sailor looks upon the soldier as his brother, and when a soldier has occasion to pass over water, rather than his uniform shall be damaged, hauls him away upon his shoulders from the boat to the shore; while the soldier welcomes the sailor on his part, and rejoices

[1] Addressed to the Independent sons of America, by a soldier.—*New Hampshire Gazette*, November 26.

to see the old British spirit for King and country, revived in in everybody about him. The very seamen on board the transports vie with the seamen of the men-of-war, in distinguishing themselves in actual service. One soul seems to animate them all; and it is confessed by many of the oldest officers, that such a spirit of harmony and military ardor was never seen to unite the two services of land and sea, so entirely before.[1]

LOST, an old black dog, of the American breed; answers to the name of PUTNAM;—had on a yellow collar with the following inscription, " *Ubi libertas ibi patriâ*, 1776. *Long Island:* " is an old domestic animal,— barks very much at the name of N(ort)h, and has a remarkable howl at that of Howe. Was seen in Long Island some time ago, but is supposed to have been alarmed.at some British troops who were exercising there, and ran off towards Hellgate. As he was a great favorite of the Washington family, they are fearful some accident has happened to him.[2]

General Putnam.

THE cowardly rebels, besides being very successful in the use of their legs, are the noisiest rascals in the world. Not sobered down by being driven from every post they have formed, they are now wasting their powder in celebrating the capture of a few cattle from Long Island. Yesterday morning, before daybreak, a party of them stole over from Eastchester, and carried off four old working oxen, a mangy dog and two kittens, and they are so rejoiced at this success of their arms, and the prospect of a good dinner, that Mr. Washington has ordered a *feu de joie*, and the usual complement of bad cider-rum.[3]

OCTOBER 27.—THIS morning, about seven o'clock, two frigates moved up the North River, and came to an anchor near Burdett's ferry, apparently with an intention to stop the ferry way and cut off the communication between Fort Lee and Fort Washington. The enemy at

Skirmish at Burdett's Ferry.

[1] New York Gazette, October 28.   [2] Middlesex Journal, December 3.
[3] MS. letter from S. Hawke.

the same time appeared on Harlem plain, and Colonel
Magaw, who commands on York Island, ordered the lines to
be manned. The ships endeavored to dislodge them by firing
on their flanks, but they fired to very little purpose. The
barbette battery, on the high hill on the left of the ferry,
opened on the frigates, and fired a considerable time without
doing them any, or but very little damage. Upon our ceasing
to fire, a gun from fort number one on York Island began
to play on them with great advantage, and hulled the one
highest up above twenty times. At this time two eighteen-
pounders, which were ordered down this side the river
opposite the ships, gave them so warm a salute that they
hoisted all sail; the foremost slipped her cable and appeared
to be in the greatest confusion; she could make no way
although rowed by two boats, till the lower one perceiving
her distress, sent two more barges to her assistance, who at
length dragged her out of the reach of our fire. It is very
probable that many of her men were killed; and she herself
extremely damaged; but the weather was so hazy that it was
impossible to see any thing distinctly at a distance. The
enemy by this time had begun a smart fire on the island with
field-pieces and mortars; our men returned the compliment.
They were out of their lines great part of the day. There
were but few discharges of small arms. Our men killed about
a dozen Hessians, and brought them off. We had one man
killed with a shell. This was the account at five o'clock;
it is now seven, and the firing has just ceased, but nothing
extraordinary has happened. We take this day's movement
to be only a feint; at any rate it is little honorable to the
red coats.

Yesterday, a party of the light horse and infantry took
possession of Phillip's Manor, between King's Bridge and our
main army; they continued there all night, but this morning
they retired.[1]

NOVEMBER 1.—DIED at Williamsburg, in Virginia, Colonel

---

[1] Extract of a letter from Fort Lee; Pennsylvania Journal, November 6.

Richard Bland, of Prince George, who lived universally
beloved, and died universally lamented. He was
Richard Bland.
more than thirty years a representative in
General Assembly for that county, and filled the trust with so
many shining abilities, so much unremitted attention, that
he gained the esteem and confidence of his constituents.
When his country called him forth to the arduous and important task of a delegate in the Continental Congress, he
approved himself an able and zealous friend and advocate
for the rights and liberties of his injured country. In a private
sphere of life he supported the character of a humane and
benevolent man, an affectionate, kind, indulgent husband and
parent, and, amongst his acquaintances, that of a warm and
steady friend.   In short, he possessed all the inestimable
qualifications that could render him dear to society,—all that
could form the virtuous, upright man.[1]

A WRITER in the Gazette offers the following explanations
and amendments to General Howe's late letters to Govern-
General Howe's ment, "in order to make the matter entirely clear
Letters explained. and intelligible:"—"The Mercury packet is
despatched to inform your lordship of the arrival of the
Halifax fleet, &c., at Sandy Hook, &c., where I met with
Governor Tryon on board of a ship, (*to which a most loyal
people obliged him to retire,*) and many gentlemen, fast friends
to government (*a few Scotchmen of no property nor probity*)
attending him, from whom I had the fullest information of
the state of the rebels, who are very numerous, and very
advantageously posted with a strong intrenchment, &c., with
more than one hundred pieces of cannon for the defence of
the town from the sea, and to obstruct the passage of the
fleet up the North River, (*so that we may sooner think of
snuffing the moon than doing execution here.*)
  "We passed the Narrows with three men-of-war, and the
first division, &c., landed the grenadiers, &c., to the great
joy of a most loyal people, (*who, because they are now left to*

our discretion, are exceeding loyal,) who (*as they pretend*) have
long suffered on that account, under the oppression of the
rebels stationed amongst them, who precipitately fled on the
approach of the shipping, (*and probably to entice us to pursue
them, in order to cut us to pieces ; but thanks to our profound
wisdom, we did not venture to stir an inch.*)

"In justice to Captain Raynor, who made the disposition
of the boats in landing the troops, and to Captain Curtis,
who was to superintend the execution, I must express my
entire satisfaction in the (*wise and spirited*) conduct of these
gentlemen, (*as I already mentioned the rebels fled, and there
was not a soul to hinder or harass our landing,*) and the
dependence to be placed upon their services in this line,
(*viz., in landing troops without the least opposition.*)

"I propose waiting here (*though there is hardly a possibility of staying without exposing my few troops to the utmost
danger*) for the English fleet, or for the arrival of Lieutenant-
General Clinton, in readiness to proceed, (*but by no means
much further,*) unless by some unexpected change of circumstances, (*and, entre nous, I expect that change every moment,*)
it should be found expedient to act with the present force,
(*to defend our retreat on board the ships.*)

"Vice Admiral Shuldham was joined on his voyage by
six transports, &c. There is no other intelligence of that
embarkation, (*that stands in need of being published,*) except
an account (*because of its being*) published in the New York
papers, that two transports of the fleet were taken by the
enemy's privateers, (*but in what manner, place, or time, your
lordship need not know, and suffice it ;*) that Major Menzies
was killed in the engagement, and that Lieutenant-Colonel
Campbell, with fifteen other officers, and about four hundred
and fifty of our men, were made prisoners, (*but how many men
were killed and wounded in the engagement I cannot tell, for
it was not published in the New York papers.*)

"Governor Franklin, who for a long time maintained his
ground in Jersey, (*I suppose under pretence of being a friend
to America, but now discovered,*) has been lately taken into
custody (*by a most loyal people*) at Amboy, and is now a prisoner at Connecticut.

" The mayor of New York was a few days ago confined on a
frivolous complaint, viz., of sending intelligence to Governor
Tryon, (*in order to destroy the main Provincial army of thirty
thousand men, and to betray the whole plan of the Congress
laid in defence of the glorious cause of Liberty,*) brought to
trial, and condemned to suffer death.

" Notwithstanding these violent proceedings, (*as we Tories
and Jacobites call it,*) I have the satisfaction to inform your
lordship (*in the same manner as all our governors did before ;
and should it turn out to the contrary, the minister can but
plead misinformation in the House of Commons*) that there is
great reason to expect a numerous body of inhabitants to join
the army from the provinces of New York, the Jerseys, and
Connecticut, who only wait for opportunities to give proofs of
their loyalty and zeal for government; (*witness that from the
above provinces, containing two hundred thousand inhabitants;*)
sixty men came over two days ago with a few arms, and I understand (*though I will not be positive*) that five hundred more
are ready to follow their example. This disposition of the
people (*viz., the five hundred men out of two hundred thousand, who are ready to join our ministerial army*) makes me
impatient for the arrival of Lord Howe, concluding the powers
with which he is furnished (*which, as I am informed, is to
treat with the Congress, and to make great condescensions*)
will have the best effect at this critical time.

" A naval force is preparing to be sent up the North River,
and orders are given for two of his Majesty's ships, one of
forty guns and the other of twenty, to proceed on that service;
(*but your lordship must look upon these two ships as good as
sunk already, as being exposed to the fire of the above-mentioned one hundred pieces of cannon of the rebels.*)

" Several men have, within these two days, come over to this
island, (*I believe I have mentioned that already,*) and to the
ships; and I am informed that the Continental Congress (*and
which your lordship must have known some months ago*) have
declared the United Colonies Free and Independent States." [1]

[1] Pennsylvania Journal, November 6.

LAST Monday we[1] received intelligence that the enemy, with
their whole body, were advancing towards us.   The army were
immediately alarmed, and part of General Wads-   Action at
worth's brigade, with some other regiments under   White Plains.
the command of General Spencer, consisting in the whole of
five or six hundred men, were sent out as an advance party,
to skirmish with the enemy, and harass them in their march.
We marched on to a hill about one mile and a half from our
lines, with an artillery company and two field-pieces, and
placed ourselves behind walls and fences, in the best manner
we could, to give the enemy trouble.   About half after nine
o'clock, our advance parties all came in, retreating before the
enemy; and the light parties of the enemy, with their advanced guard, consisting of two or three thousand, came in
sight, and marched on briskly towards us, keeping the high
grounds; and the light horse pranced on a little in the rear,
making a very martial appearance.   As our light parties
came on to the hills and discovered where we were, the enemy
began to cannonade us, and to fling shells from their hobits
and small mortars.   Their light parties soon came on, and we
firing upon them from the walls and fences, broke and scattered them at once; but they would run from our front and
get round upon our wings to flank us, and as soon as our fire
discovered where we were, the enemy's artillery would at
once begin to play upon us in the most furious manner.   We
kept the walls until the enemy were just ready to surround
us, and then we would retreat from one wall and hill to another, and maintain our ground there in the same manner, till
numbers were just ready to surround us.   Once the Hessian
grenadiers came up in front of Colonel Douglass's regiment,
and we fired a general volley upon them, at about twenty rods
distance, and scattered them like leaves in a whirlwind; and
they ran off so far that some of the regiment ran out to the
ground where they were when we fired upon them, and
brought off their arms and accoutrements, and rum, that the
men who fell had with them, which we had time to drink round

---

[1] The Americans at the White Plains, New York.

with before they came on again. They formed at a distance, and waited until their artillery and main body came on, when they advanced in solid columns upon us, and were gathering all around us, ten to our one. Colonel Douglass's and Silliman's regiments fired four or five times on them, as they were advancing, and then retreated, but not until the enemy began to fire on their flanks. Colonels Silliman, Douglass, and Arnold behaved nobly, and the men gained much applause. Colonels Webb's, Silliman's, and Douglass's regiments had the principal share in the action. Colonel Webb had four killed, and eight or ten wounded; Colonel Silliman lost six, and had ten or twelve wounded; Colonel Douglass had three killed, and six wounded. Colonels Brooks's, Smallwood's, and Ritzma's regiments, who were drawn up on the hill near the lines, suffered considerably. Our loss in the whole may be seventy or eighty killed or wounded. It is said by all the deserters and captains, who agree in their stories, that the enemy had about three hundred killed and wounded.

The scene was grand and solemn; all the adjacent hills smoked as though on fire, and bellowed and trembled with a perpetual cannonade and fire of field-pieces, hobits, and mortars. The air groaned with streams of cannon and musket shot; the hills smoked and echoed terribly with the bursting of shells; the fences and walls were knocked down and torn to pieces, and men's legs, arms, and bodies, mangled with cannon and grape-shot all around us. I was in the action, and under as good advantages as any one man, perhaps, to observe all that passed, and write these particulars of the action from my own observation.

No general action was designed on our part, and I believe one thousand men were never, at one time, engaged with the enemy. They came on to the hills opposite our lines, and halted; and after cannonading part of the lines a short time, they became very still and quiet.

Yesterday, (October 31st,) it was observed that they had near finished four or five batteries which they had erected against us; and as our ground, near the centre of the town at White Plains, was not good, being overlooked by neighboring hills, the generals, last night, drew off most of the troops from the lines there, and this morning the guards and sentries burned the town and forage all around it, and came off about nine o'clock.

We carried off all our stores, and planted our artillery on the hills about a mile and a half back of the centre of the town. The enemy advanced, this forenoon, on to the ground we left, but as soon as they came over the hill, we saluted them with our cannon and field-pieces, and they advanced no further. Their main body now lies over against us, and they have formed no lines across the country, as yet, below us. Their light horse may possibly scour across as far as the river, but how that is we cannot determine. All things seem to be quiet at Fort Washington.[1]

WANTED, by a gentleman fond of curiosities, who is shortly going to England, a parcel of Congress Notes, with which he intends to paper some rooms. Those who wish to make something of their stock in that commodity, shall, if they are clean and fit for the purpose, receive at the rate of one guinea per thousand for all they can bring before the expiration of the present month. Inquire of the printer. N. B.—It is expected they will be much lower.[2]

NOVEMBER 3.—THERE is a general curiosity in mankind to inquire into the character of those who arrive at stations of high trust and dignity. In the dreadful times of public commotion and civil discord, this laudable General Putnam. passion is most strongly excited. To satisfy this in part, an old friend of General Putnam's gives the following authentic account of that officer:

The general's paternal state consisted of a small farm in the colony of Connecticut, by the diligent cultivation of which, he supported himself till he entered the colony's service, during the late French war in America. The stories that have

Pennsylvania Evening Post, November 14.
[2] New York Gazette, October 28.

been repeatedly told, of his being a blacksmith and carpenter, are the contradictory effusions of ignorance and falsehood. When very young, he gave a proof of early courage, in following a fox that had plundered the poultry-yard into its den, creeping on his hands and knees, where, discovering it by the brightness of its own eyes, he destroyed it. This is not a very important fact, but it is a real one, well known to the people of Pomfret.

When a major of the rangers, in the year 1758, leading the van of a scouting party, he was overpowered and taken by a body of five hundred Indians and Canadians. During the latter part of the engagement, he was tied to a tree, and exposed to the fire of his own men. At last the enemy being forced to retreat, an Indian, in passing, struck him with the butt end of his musket, intending to kill him, but happened only to break one of his jaw-bones; immediately after a Canadian came up, cut the straps that fastened him to the tree, and led him off. He was carried to Ticonderoga, and soon after exchanged. A romantic account of this skirmish was given in the public prints some months ago, in which it was said that he had received a multitude of wounds, beside being scalped. All this is fiction; the blow above mentioned was the only one he received in that action.

In the colony service he considerably increased his estate. He has now a large, well-cultivated farm, and generally represents the town of Pomfret, in the colony assembly.

When the discontents in New England rose very high, in 1775, he was very much caressed by the American party; and, on a false rumor spreading through the country, of the King's troops having massacred five hundred inhabitants of Boston, he headed a large party of volunteers, in Connecticut, and marched to the relief of Boston, but soon returned home, on that intelligence being contradicted.

After the action at Concord, in April, 1775, he joined the Massachusetts troops, commanded by Warren.[1] He was then a colonel in rank. On June seventeenth, at one o'clock in the

---

[1] Major-General Joseph Warren.

morning, they took possession of Bunker's Hill, opposite to
Boston, where in a few hours they threw up a redoubt and intrenchment. When he saw the British troops embarking to
attack them, he advised Warren, who commanded in chief, to
retreat, and founded his opinion on the following reasons:—
" That he had often served with the King's troops; that although one-half or two-thirds of them should be killed, yet
those that remained would certainly storm their works; that
the moment the intrenchment was mounted, his countrymen,
whom he knew very well, would run; for though they would
fight as long as any troops whatever, while under cover, yet
they would never stand an open engagement, and the push of
the bayonet; that the spirit of veteran troops ought not to be
expected from them, who were raw men, badly disciplined,
and badly armed; that it would be highly injudicious to put
them, at first, to so severe a trial, as the check they would in
all probability receive, would tend greatly to dishearten them,
and have a very bad effect on all their future operations."

This salutary advice was rejected by Warren, who was very
opinionated, addicted to liquor, and in haste to distinguish
himself, this being the very first morning of his apprenticeship
in the art of war. He replied, " That they had been branded
as cowards, but would show the military they could fight as
well as themselves," and ordered the colonel to return to Cambridge, and bring on the rest of the men. Putnam obeyed.
On the march back, his men followed him with spirit enough
till they reached the fort of Bunker's Hill, when the heavy
firing, it being then the heat of the engagement, made them
shrink. (This he has often mentioned when speaking of that
day's service.) Whilst he was laboring fruitlessly in this
manner, the King's troops stormed the redoubt, and he was
instantly joined by the fugitives; upon which they all retreated over the neck as fast as possible. The colonel had frequently given it as his opinion that if but five hundred men
had pursued them, he could not have kept one man at Cambridge. But no pursuit being made, he took post there; and
as they heard from Boston that very night what dreadful havoc
they had made amongst the King's troops, the men immedi-

ately recovered their spirits. So much does success in war depend on the improvement of a single moment.

The colonel was now promoted to the rank of major-general, but his commission was hardly delivered to him, when it was debated, in the General Congress, to supersede him, and give his rank to Mr. Thomas,[1] a favorite of General Washington. He was only saved from this insult by the necessity they had for his services. During the summer and autumn, 1775, whilst Boston was blockaded, he was by far the most popular officer in the American camp; he was the first to take up the spade and the mattock, and to join the common men in all the fatigues of the day, which very naturally endeared him to them. His popularity, however, suffered a great shock, towards the latter end of the same year; for, at the request of the General Congress and the commander-in-chief, attempting to persuade the men, whose time of service was nearly expired, to continue in arms four months longer, till another army could be embodied, he raised a general clamor against himself. The men went off precisely at their time, and exclaimed against him over all the country, as an enemy to liberty. By this defection, in the space of six weeks in the middle of winter, there were not more than seven thousand men in the extensive lines round Boston. If General Howe had had good intelligence, he might have cleared the whole environs of that town in less than twenty-four hours; for such a small body of troops were very insufficient to defend a line of intrenchments and redoubts, that extended at least twelve or fourteen miles, from Mystic River all round the head of the Bay to Dorchester Point. Another raw army was at last drawn together, which made some semblance of attacking Boston, on which General Howe left it. Since the war has been moved into the territory of New York, we find General Putnam commanding in the lines, at the battle of Brooklyn. It is not surprising that new levies should be beat by veterans. After the defeat, the desertion of their lines was a wise measure, as their retreat might have been cut off by ships of war posted in the East River.

General John Thomas died at Sorel, in Canada, on the 2d of June, 1776.

There is no doubt but General Putnam wishes as sincerely for peace as any man on either side of the question; yet there is no man in either army will do his duty with greater bravery in the field. He never was a favorer of American Independency. As to his person, he is middle size, very strongly made, no fat, all bones and muscles; he has a lisp in his speech, and is now upwards of sixty years of age.[1]

NOVEMBER 8.—THIS day, a few of the common soldiers of the *third* and *fifth* Pennsylvania battalions, gave rise to a little skirmish, which, though trifling in itself, we cannot help relating it, as it seems to point out some of the effects of discipline.

Skirmish at Mount Washington.

The scene of this little rencontre lay on an eminence between the termination of Mount Washington and King's Bridge,[2] in a transverse line with, and under the full command of a height in possession of our Hessian enemy. Near the summit of this eminence, and facing some of our works, is a large rock or natural breastwork, where a small body of their men were posted. Two of our people had the boldness to advance up this hill without the least cover, in order, they said, to have a fairer shot at those planted behind the rocky barrier. These sustained the musketry of the Hessians, and the fire from a field-piece from the neighboring height. Some more of our men went up to their assistance. The fire upon the breastwork was now redoubled, and poured in upon our enemies, in such a close and well-managed succession as entirely silenced them.

The Hessian main guard, who were posted about four hundred yards from this place, seeing the danger of their sentries, turned out and marched to their relief. About fifty of the enemy were in motion. Our little body was now augmented to between fifteen and twenty. They were at but a very small distance from the breastwork, when, perceiving the route of the Hessians, they saw they must either give up the ground they had gained, or intimidate the approaching enemy. At this crit-

[1] A correspondent of the Middlesex Journal, December 21.
[2] Near New York.

ical juncture, I could see the brave fellows form with the utmost regularity and order; and then, as if under the command of the best officer, arrange into three divisions. The spectators on both sides, as if by mutual agreement, seemed willing to trust the issue of this little affair to those already in the field and in motion.

Two of our divisions immediately began a circuit around the bend of the hill, in order, as was supposed, to get on the rear of the enemy at the rocks, and oppose the main guard, who were coming on, whilst the centre division advanced towards the rock, keeping up, all the while, a regular fire. This little piece of instinctive, or, rather, mechanical generalship, had a most beautiful effect. The sentries, aware of their danger, precipitately retreated, carrying off two killed or wounded. Our men took possession of their post, burned their huts, and secured a rifle gun, a musket, and blanket, which we suppose belonged to those who were carried off. Upon gaining the contested ground, they gave three cheers for the Congress, which was returned by their flanking parties, and replied to by the Hessian artillery.

The divisions now united, and seemed, notwithstanding the enemy's field-pieces and superior force, which was advancing against them, resolved on defending the height they had so martially obtained. For this purpose we could see them dispose themselves along a rail fence that commanded the road, by which the Hessian guard must pass before they could make an advantageous attack. They were now reinforced with a few stragglers from other regiments.

Their fire was so very well directed and judiciously managed as to keep the Hessians at bay; and, at length, forced them to take shelter in an orchard, nearly opposite to our little line of adventurers. They held their ground till night, and then came off in good order, and with only one man wounded—a Sergeant Wright, of the third Pennsylvania regiment. He received a ball in advancing to the rocky breastwork.

I have been more particular in the detail of this little affair, as it seems to show, in some measure, the force and advantages of good discipline. Here, a few men, without any preconcerted plan, met together by chance, and without a leader to direct them, exhibited an epitome of generalship that would not have dishonored even Hannibal or Scipio. Examples of this kind show, more than any thing else, the importance and necessity of early and late inculcating the strictest forms of discipline. It is by no means improbable, that the beauty and order of most of the animal motions arise from repetition. This, particularly in the soldiery, begets habits which are often preferable to the greatest courage.[1]

NOVEMBER 9.—HITHERTO the achievements of our little army on York Island have been extremely fortunate. The genius that presides there seems to be of the enterprising kind. Last campaign it was thought a matter of great hardihood and praise to burn the enemy's guard house at Roxbury, on Boston Neck, and a few houses in Charlestown,[2] under cover of the night; but here such exploits are conducted in open day.

This morning, we found the enemy once more in possession of the rock from whence we had routed them yesterday. About eighty men, under the command of Colonel Penrose, of Philadelphia, and Major Hubley, (late an officer at the northward,) resolved to dislodge them a second time. As the men were in high spirits, and the barn and dwelling-house which the guard occupied at but a small distance, the colonel proposed storming them. We soon regained the rock, and, with surprising rapidity, the houses, notwithstanding an incessant fire from the enemy's artillery, main guard, and a small redoubt in an orchard adjoining the guard, that commanded the road. The Hessians were soon obliged to abandon their posts. We killed on the spot about ten, and the rest either escaped or were burned in the houses, which some of our men, without orders, immediately fired.

It is something remarkable that on our side we had only one man wounded. Perhaps the sally was so unexpected as to have entirely disconcerted and confused the enemy. As

[1] Pennsylvania Evening Post, November 21.   [2] See page 193, ante.

it is, no men ever behaved more resolutely or bravely than ours.[1]

NOVEMBER 13.—YESTERDAY the British decamped from Dobb's ferry, and marched as far as Phillip's manor, (five miles from King's Bridge,) where they halted and pitched their tents. They seem to be bending their course towards York Island, and it is apprehended they mean to attack Fort Washington. Yesterday we reinforced the garrison at that place with five hundred men, and we hope it is very tenable. Deserters inform us that they are resolved to take it this campaign, if they are obliged to invest it with their whole army. The three ships which went up the North River a few days ago, have fallen down within three miles of Fort Lee, and will push by the first fair wind.

Last night we went a Tory hunting with a party of fifty men, but the birds had flown before we arrived. However, we were repaid by a sight of the enemy's encampment, whose fires being very numerous and greatly extended, exhibited a delightful appearance.[2]

IT is very remarkable, says a correspondent, that the event of this unnatural war should so directly contradict Lord Sandwich's assertion in calling the Americans "cowards," and that his particular friends should suffer so essentially. Major Pitcairne re-echoed his lordship's opinion, and boasted, before he embarked at Portsmouth, that if he drew his sword but half out of the scabbard, the whole banditti (as he termed them) of Massachusetts Bay, would flee from him. Behold, he is slain, on the first time he appears in the field against them. Captain Howe, of the Glasgow, another of his lordship's friends, falls in with two or three ragamuffin privateers, and he brings his lordship an undeniable proof that the Americans are not cowards; and now we have a Gazette account that these cowards have beat two fifty-gun ships, four frigates, of twenty-eight guns each, and two others of twenty-eight guns each, making together two hundred and fifty-two guns.[1] How many had those cowardly Americans? Why, truly, nineteen. And though the King's ships had so many as two hundred and fifty-two well manned, to so few as nineteen, yet those cowardly Americans made those heroes and friends of Lord Sandwich, with his *boon companion* Sir Peter Parker, and a Scotch lord, confess that their attempt to take an insignificant fort "was impracticable, and that a further attempt would have been the destruction of many brave men, without the least probability of success." They certainly confided in Lord Sandwich's bare *ipse dixit*, and could not be otherwise convinced, without losing one of the King's ships, and having five more nearly battered to pieces, besides losing sixty-four killed, and one hundred and forty-one wounded.[2]

NOVEMBER 16.—ABOUT two o'clock this afternoon a large body of British troops from New York, with a body of Hessians from King's Bridge, made an attack upon the American lines at that place. At the same Fort Washington taken. time, a number of boats from the shipping came up Harlem River, and landed a party of men, who advanced forward with an intention to cut off our retreat, which in part they effected; but a part of our men taking advantage of a hill, got safe to the fort; the other part, being almost surrounded, were obliged to fight their way through the enemy, by which means the heaviest fire from our troops was directed against the Hessians, who were beat back, and obliged to be reinforced three several times by large detachments from their main body. In this manner our small army, under the command of Colonel Magaw, retreated, sustaining with unexampled resolution a continual fire of the cannon, field-pieces, and musketry of more than five to one in number, till they reached Fort Washington, when the engagement ceased. Soon after the engagement ended, the enemy made a demand of the fort, and Colonel Magaw finding it impossible to defend it, surrendered the same to the enemy about sunset.

[1] At Sullivan's Island.   [2] Pennsylvania Journal, November 27.

The number of our men who were killed in the above engagement is uncertain, but the whole loss in killed and taken prisoners, is upwards of two thousand. What loss the enemy sustained is likewise uncertain, but if we may believe the account given by a deserter who came to head-quarters since the engagement, the Hessians had between four and five thousand men killed on the spot.

Master James Lovel, of Boston, who has been a prisoner more than eighteen months, is now on his way from New York to Boston, having been exchanged for Governor Skeene, who was some time held a prisoner in Hartford.

We hear Colonel Ethan Allen is now on board a ship at New York; that he has been treated since his being taken a prisoner with the utmost barbarity, till lately, but the rigor of his oppressors has been a little softened, and he is now treated according to his rank; and we hope an exchange will soon take place, when he may again return into the bosom of his grateful country.[1]

John Hancock, Esq., President of the American Congress, is now more the object of pity than contempt. His fortune alone raised this very weak man to consideration in the political world, and with the diminution and loss of property, his power and influence have declined and fallen. Adams' conspiracy, like that of most others, was originally composed of persons destitute of property and the means of living. Mr. Hancock was therefore early admitted a most useful member, and with his name and credit, a system of sedition was undertaken and reared to a general rebellion and revolt, which, through the poverty and dishonest characters of the others, could not have been supported and propagated without these aids. They even found it necessary for some time to play him off as head of the league; and he not only contributed profusely towards the charges and expenses of the common cause, but advanced moneys for the discharge of the debts, and for the maintenance and subsistence

John Hancock.

[1] Freeman's Journal, December 3.

of his indigent friend Adams, who had no other visible means of freedom from a jail. He had in return the appearance of gratitude and respect, in being raised to the first honors in the election and gift of the people, and thought himself indebted to Adams for the promotion to the president's chair. But this person was too much a politician to have regard to his benefactor in these preferments; he made him only the stalking horse of his own ambition, and consulted his honor no further than was conducive to his own interest, and the designs of the confederacy. These could not long be promoted by Hancock, exhausted of his whole estate; and he has lately suffered repeated acts of mortifying neglect, and had many clear evidences of the wishes of his old friends, not so much for his ruin, which would little avail them, as for his retirement with Mr. Speaker Cushing, whom they had before laid aside as useless. His natural peevishness was irritated by these unexpected and ungrateful dispositions of his friends; he would least of all brook an injury from one so much obliged to him as Adams personally had been, and his resentment hurried him into an open opposition and contention with this insidious man, which probably before this time has terminated in his own fall and ruin. For it appears by the last advices from Philadelphia, in a channel of intelligence of great credibility, that this very Adams had made a motion in Congress for the expulsion of his benefactor Hancock, founded on the ostensible reason of holding principles incompatible with independency; in which, though he did not immediately and directly prevail, because it was not thought derogatory of the honor and prejudicial of the general interest of that body to depose and expel their president, yet it was not doubted that a more decent method would be taken to lay him aside.[1]

NOVEMBER 18.—By a person lately from the American camp, a gentleman of undoubted veracity, who was prisoner and enlarged by General Howe, we are informed that the

---

[1] "Cæsar," in the Middlesex Journal, December 26.

enemy lost before the lines of Fort Washington, seventeen hundred killed on the field, and ninety-six wagon loads of wounded, the most mortally; that our people behaved with the greatest intrepidity and resolution; that our loss was about three hundred killed and wounded.—This account may be depended on, as it came from divers of the British officers, with whom the gentleman was intimately acquainted.

Fort Washington.

The attack did not commence at the lines at Harlem, as has been reported, that post being at least six miles distant from Fort Washington, but at the outlines north of the fort, distant about a quarter of a mile; that the Hessians made the attack, and marched within point blank pistol shot of the lines, where they were kept at least two hours, and were, by the intrepidity and well-placed fire of our people, cut down in whole ranks. The brave Americans kept their post until a heavy column of British troops appeared in their rear; the lines there being entirely open, obliged them to retreat and endeavor to gain the fort; but the British troops being nearer the fort, cut off and obliged a considerable part to surrender prisoners. The fort was immediately summoned, but the commanding officer first pleaded for a term of five days; that being refused, plead for the honors of war, which was also denied, and the garrison was informed that unless they surrendered at discretion, the fort would be immediately invested, and they must abide the consequence. A council of war was immediately held, and it was decided that, as they had not any water, nor could get any at the places from which the garrison had been supplied with the article, they being in possession of the enemy, and that the fort was not capable of defence, agreed to surrender it and themselves at discretion. The commanding officer of the fort is a gentleman of great courage, and would have defended it as long as a single soldier remained to support it, had it been capable of defence. The highest honors are due to him, his gallant officers, and the brave soldiers who were under his command.[1]

---

[1] Freeman's Journal, December 10.

GEORGE SELWYN, the other evening, in one of the polite gaming houses in London, hearing a young gentleman speaking with great animation of the miraculous escape of General Howe, who was said to have been patting Lord Percy's charger, at the time the animal was shot under him, replied:—"You are right; and never was a more miraculous escape, or perhaps more temper shown upon any occasion, than by the two general officers, in that situation." "How was that? I did not hear any thing about it." "No!— why it seems they were disputing about the age of the horse, and had made a bet upon it;—Lord Percy said he was aged; Sir William said otherwise; and just as the latter was looking into his mouth, to satisfy his doubts, a nine pounder came from Fort Washington, and severed the horse's head from his body; upon which Sir William Howe, with great composure, took up the head and showed his lordship the mark in his mouth. Lord Percy, instantly dismounting, paid him the money, and then, with the greatest intrepidity, led his brigade to the walls of the fort." [1]

Anecdote of Selwyn.

THE PRUDENT GENERALS COMPARED.

> When Rome was urged by adverse fate,
>   On Cannæ's evil day,
> A Fabius saved the sinking state,
>   By *caution* and *delay*.

> "One only State!" reply'd a smart;
>   Why talk of such a dunce?
> When *Billy Howe*, by the same art,
>   Can save THIRTEEN at once. [2]

NOVEMBER 21.—AN officer in the British navy has written home, that the bravery of the King's troops cannot be too highly commended. He then says that every capital enterprise hitherto made by General Howe, has either been in the night or by break of day, our soldiers being taught to depend more upon their bayonets than their muskets; and about twilight is

---

[1] Middlesex Journal, January 4, 1777.   [2] Same, January 2.

found the best season for hunting the rebels in the woods, at which time their rifles are of very little use; and they are not found so serviceable in a body as musketry, a rest being requisite at all times; and before they are able to make a second discharge, it frequently happens that they find themselves run through the body by the push of a bayonet, as a rifleman is not entitled to any quarter.

He also says, that on the rebels first retreating, a clergyman at Westchester assembled the people, and, in a very pathetic and loyal address, advised them to repentance and submission, which had the desired effect. This conduct enraged the rebels against him exceedingly, and on their return they cut his throat, and afterwards mangled the dead body in a shocking manner. His wife and children were stripped almost naked, and driven round the rebel camp. They were treated in this cruel manner several days, and then sent to our camp. Notwithstanding these instances of savage cruelty, their prisoners with us are treated with the utmost humanity.[1]

YESTERDAY, a party of the British army landed near Dobb's ferry, and soon after took possession of Fort Lee. On the appearance of our troops, the rebels fled like scared rabbits, and in a few moments after we reached the hill near their intrenchments, not a rascal of them could be seen. They have left some poor pork, a few greasy proclamations, and some of that scoundrel Common Sense man's letters, which we can read at our leisure, now that we have got one of the "impregnable redoubts" of Mr. Washington's to quarter in. * * * * We intend to push on after the long-faces in a few days.[2]

Fort Lee taken.

IN the country dances published in London for next year, there is one called "Lord Howe's Jig," in which there is "cross over, change hands, turn your partner, foot it on both sides," and other movements admirably depictive, says a correspondent, of the present war in America.[3]

[1] Middlesex Journal, December 31.
[2] Markoe to Oswald. *
[3] Pennsylvania Journal, March 12.

AFTER the late battle of the White Plains, the provincial officers who were taken prisoners, being dispersed in different parts of the regular army, were occasionally asked to dine at the tables of our general officers. General De Heister. It happened one day that a party of them dined with General De Heister, the Hessian General, who, as soon as the cloth was taken away, drank "the King." Some of the provincials drank the toast, others drank their wine and said nothing. At last, one who had more plain dealing about him than the rest, refused drinking it, giving it as a reason, with many apologies, "that if it had been a favorite toast with him, he would not then be in the situation he was at present." This occasioned some confusion, and in particular brought on an altercation between him and the general, which in the end terminated in the latter so far forgetting himself as to strike the former with his cane. This no doubt is nothing more than what is common in the German discipline, yet, though it may be thought advisable for us to want their assistance as soldiers, it is to be hoped British generals will reprobate such feelings and manners.[1]

THERE is very good intelligence that the British intend to make a push for Philadelphia. We hear part of their force is embarked, either to go up the Delaware, and make their attacks on both sides at once, or else to amuse the Southern States, and prevent their sending any assistance to Philadelphia. We have not force enough to oppose their march by land. We look to New Jersey and Pennsylvania for their militia, and on their spirit depends the preservation of America. If in this hour of adversity they shrink from danger, they deserve to be slaves indeed! If the freedom that success will insure us, if the misery that awaits our subjection, will not rouse them, why let them sleep till they awake in bondage.[2]

NOVEMBER 27.—YESTERDAY afternoon, at the review of the militia for the city of Philadelphia and liberties, nothing could

---

[1] Upcott, iv. 419.   [2] Pennsylvania Journal, November 27.

exceed the zeal and ardor of the men, who unanimously turned out volunteers, to serve their country at this important juncture. So laudable an example, it is hoped, will be followed in the other parts.

At eleven o'clock this forenoon, a very large and general town meeting was held in the State House yard. The members of the General Assembly and the Council of Safety were present; Mr. Rittenhouse, vice-president of the council, being in the chair. The intelligence which has been received of the probability of General Howe having it in contemplation to invade the State, was laid before the citizens, and they were informed that the Congress requested the militia of the city, and several of the counties, and part of the militia of each of the other counties, to march into New Jersey. The people expressed their cheerful approbation of the measure, by the most unanimous acclamations of joy ever observed on any occasion, and the militia are ordered to be reviewed to-morrow, at two o'clock in the afternoon. General Mifflin addressed his fellow-citizens in a spirited, animating, and affectionate address, which was received by them with marks of approbation, which showed their esteem for, and confidence in, the general.[1]

Meeting at Philadelphia.

NOVEMBER 30.—This day, the Howes have issued a proclamation commanding all persons whatsoever, who are assembled together in arms against his Majesty's government, to disband themselves, and return to their dwellings, there to remain in a peaceable and quiet manner. They also charge and command all such other persons as are assembled together under the name or names of general or provincial Congresses, committees, conventions, or other associations, by whatever name or names known and distinguished, or who, under color of any authority from any such Congress, committee, convention, or other association, take upon them to issue or execute any orders for levying money, raising troops, fitting out armed ships or vessels, imprisoning and otherwise

Proclamation of the Howes.

---

[1] Freeman's Journal, December 24.

molesting his Majesty's subjects, to desist and cease from all
such treasonable actions and doings, and to relinquish all such
usurped power and authority, so that peace may be restored;
a speedy remission of past offences quiet the apprehensions
of the guilty, and all the inhabitants of the said colonies be
enabled to reap the benefit of his Majesty's paternal goodness,
in the preservation of their property, the restoration of their
commerce, and the security of their most valuable rights, under
the just and moderate authority of the crown and parliament
of Great Britain.   And they further declare and make known
to all men, that every person who, within sixty days, shall appear before the governor, or any other officer in his Majesty's
service, having the command of any detachment or parties of
his Majesty's forces, or before the admiral or commander-
in-chief of his Majesty's fleets, or any officer commanding any
of his Majesty's ships-of-war, or any armed vessel in his Majesty's service, within any of the ports, havens, creeks, or
upon the coast of America, and shall claim the benefit of this
proclamation, and, at the same time, testify his obedience to
the laws by subscribing a declaration in the words following:

"I, A. B., do promise and declare that I will remain in a
peaceable obedience to his Majesty, and will not take up arms
in opposition to his authority," shall and may obtain a full and
free pardon of all treasons, misprisons of treason by him
heretofore committed or done, and of all forfeitures, attainders,
and penalties for the same; and upon producing to them, or
either of them, a certificate of such, his appearance and declaration, shall and may have and receive such pardon made and
passed to him in due form.[1]

MESSRS. HOWE.—We have seen your proclamation, and as
it is a great curiosity, think it deserves some notice; and lest
no one else should deign to notice it, will make _{Answer to Howes}
a few remarks upon what was designed for public   Proclamation.
benefit.   In this rarity we see slaves offering liberty to free
Americans; thieves and robbers offer to secure our rights

[1] Upcott, iv. 417

and property; murderers offer us pardon;—a perjured Tyrant, by the mouth of two of his hireling butchers, "commands" all the civil and military powers in these independent States, to resign all pretensions to authority, and to acknowledge subjection to a foreign despot, even his mock majesty, now reeking with blood and murder. This is truly a curiosity, and is a compound of the most consummate arrogance and folly of the cloven-footed spawn of despairing wretches, who are laboring to complete the works of tyranny and death. It would be far less wicked, and not quite so stupid, for the Grand Turk to send two of his slaves into Britain, Howelizts and W. Howoldozt, to command all the Britons to acknowledge themselves the slaves of the Turk, offering to secure their rights and property, and to pardon such as had borne arms against his Sublime Highness, upon conditions of their making submission within "sixty days."

Messieurs Howe and W. Howe, pray read your proclamation once more, and consider how modest you appear; and reflect on the infinite contempt with which you are viewed by the Americans, and remember the meanest freeman "scorns the highest slave."

We do not, however, suppose you are such idiots as to expect your proclamation will meet with any thing but contempt from these independent States; you have had too much experience of their wisdom and valor to hope for any thing else; but as you have failed to subjugate the Colonies, (and as our haughty masters have told the nation you would "bring them to obedience,") this proclamation is to furnish a puff in the place of victory; thereby to support the dying hopes of those miserable wretches who are wishing for our destruction. So that George and his slaves, while they are gaping for the tidings of our being conquered, will, instead thereof, receive your conquering proclamation, commanding us to submit! Truly, if we had any pity for tyrants or their tools, we should pity you; but, to be honest, we sincerely despise you, and all your abettors, without the least mixture of fear, esteem, or compassion. except that which is due to the greatest criminals.

Before concluding, we will give you some good advice, and some information, which we had thought of issuing by way of proclamation, but it may suffice in this place. We advise you, and each of you, jointly and separately, to make the best of your way to Britain; and if your master should frown upon his wicked servants for not having done more wickedly, you may perhaps escape with your necks; and if not, you will perhaps only be hanged, and that may preserve you from a worse punishment in America.—And now for information, (which you seem very much to want:) Know ye, the States of America are now completing an army raised for the whole war, consisting of eighty-eight battalions, viz., sixty-four thousand and sixty-four men, who are to be reinforced if necessary from the well-formed militia in the States, which may be three hundred and forty-six thousand. This will be something of an object; but add to this vast army our resource by sea, (the captures this year are estimated at not less than two millions sterling;) and consider our rapid progress in arms and all the implements of war; can *you* suppose, can even the button-making idiot of Britain imagine these United States, with the glorious prize of liberty in their hands, and the most animating prospect of every felicity that Heaven can bestow, will resign themselves, their posterity, and all that is great and good into the devouring jaws of hellish tyrants?

You are no doubt pleased with being reinforced by a few dastardly Tories at New York; and we sincerely wish every wretch who deserves that name was with you. We would inform you, that we have assurance from Europe, that several nations are preparing to revenge past injuries received from Britain, and that his Tyrantship will have full employ very soon, without troubling the States of America. In concluding, let us advise you to prepare for your latter end that you may be proper objects for a pardon.[1]

THERE was a large forest, inhabited by a few sheep. In

---

[1] An American, in the Boston Gazette, December 30.

the neighborhood was a nation of mastiff dogs, another of
foxes, another of wolves, and another of boars.   The sheep

A Fable.   were protected by the dogs till they increased to a
great multitude. After a bloody war, in which they
were saved by the dogs from both the foxes and the wolves,
the sheep imagined themselves to be a very mighty people,
and some old stinking rams told them it was not proper that
the dogs should any longer rule over them.   The dogs had
bit them they said, and intended to bite them more severely.
And so the sheep proclaimed themselves a commonwealth of
free people.   Yet while they complained how the dogs had
oppressed them, they boasted with the same breath, that
so greatly had they prospered, that in twelve years they were
become a match for the world, though it was evident that
before that time they could not defend themselves against the
foxes only.   The dogs, upon this, resolved to bring them
back to obedience, but the sheep implored the foxes, the
wolves, and the boars to attack the dogs, which they gladly
performed; and while the best mastiffs were in the country
of the sheep, these different tribes so violently attacked their
old formidable enemies the dogs, that they utterly broke their
strength, and ruined them as a people.   But the sheep did not
long boast of their profound politics; the foxes, the wolves, and
the boars poured in upon them, and soon rendered them the
most abject and miserable of all animals.

THE MORAL

is this.   The Americans are, in reality, as defenceless as
sheep; it is impossible they can, for several centuries, constitute an empire; they want many requisites.   The English
are generous, brave mastiffs; the French have always been
sly, ravenous foxes, the Spaniards cruel wolves, when they
conquer, and the Dutch mere wild boars, wherever they
can effect a settlement.   Amboyna and all their settlements
witness this.   But though, for the fable's sake, I suppose
the conquest of the mastiffs, I trust that event is yet very
distant; and that half a million of determined fighting

sheep, with all their ingratitude, (a circumstance infinitely more to be feared than the strength of their horns,) will never effect so unworthy a purpose. And let me add, there is a circumstance in the natural history of the sheep which greatly resembles American courage. When you go near a flock of sheep, a few will at first run, then the whole body of them will draw up in a line like soldiers; will watch your motions; will seem as if they felt vastly bold, aye, and will stamp their feet on the ground in a menacing manner; but let a mastiff walk up to them, and half a million of these determined threateners, will instantly take to their heels, and fly off in the greatest fear and confusion.[1]

DECEMBER 1.—SINCE the rebels abandoned Fort Lee, they have been hurrying through the Jerseys, closely followed by Cornwallis and his *magic lights*. The arch-rebel Washington is now at Brunswick, but how long he will remain the devil only knows, (for the Lord won't have any thing to do with him.) Yesterday we heard that our friends were coming on, and, in that event, we shall soon lose the company of the Congress *tatter de mallions*, which certainly most of the people here (Brunswick) do not feel sorry for. * * * * * * *

Ned has just come in from Bonum, by the back road, and says that the troops are now passed through that town, and will soon be here.[2]

DECEMBER 2.—YESTERDAY, on the appearance of the enemy at Brunswick, General Washington ordered a retreat to Princeton, where we arrived early this morning. We are in a terrible situation, with the enemy close upon us, and whole regiments of Marylanders and Jerseymen leaving us. To-morrow we go to Trenton, where the general is determined to make a stand. * * * A Tory from Monmouth lower county, was brought in here to-day by a party of the Pennsylvania boys. He mistook them for the reg'lars, and came quite into camp without perceiving his mistake. This afternoon, after

---

[1] "Britannicus," in the Middlesex Journal, December 26. [2] Carver. †

taking off his breeches and giving him an absolution, by set-
ing him on the ice, (to cool his loyalty,) they set him to work
bringing in fagots. He seems pleased with his new office,
knowing that he got off easy. Notwithstanding General
Stirling deprecates severity to the infernal Tories we catch,
they get absolution often.[1]

WHEN Governor Trumbull recommended to the house-
holders in Connecticut, who were not obliged to do military
The duty, to form themselves into companies, choose
Married Regiment. their own officers, and equip themselves for the
defence of these States, a number of aged gentlemen in the
town of Waterbury embodied themselves, and nominated
their own officers, who were honored with commissions. When
the regiment of militia, to which they belong, was ordered to
New York, agreeable to a late resolve of the general assembly,
this company was the first that marched and reached the
place of rendezvous. It is now at Rye, and consists of twenty-
four men; their ages added together, are a thousand years;
they are all married men, and when they came from home
left behind them their wives, with an hundred and forty-nine
children. One of them is fifty-nine years of age, and is the
father of nineteen children, and twelve grandchildren;
fourteen of his own children are now living. A worthy
example of patriotism.—Let others go and do likewise.[2]

MR. WASHINGTON has ordered the people of New Jersey
to burn and destroy all the hay and corn which they cannot carry back into the country. This, among other enormities of the like kind, will ruin many farmers in that
province and desolate the country. And yet this is the man,
who has the assurance to accuse others of devastation and
mischief. Rebels are hopeful reformers.

So great is the rage of fighting among the Presbyterian
preachers, that one of them has taken no less than seven
different commissions, in order to excite the poor deluded

Clift's Diary.   [2] Pennsylvania Evening Post, February 25, 1777.

men who have taken up arms, they know not why, to stand forth with an enthusiastic ardor, against their King and the constitution.

Two or three members of Congress, one or two of them worse than nothing, and the other involved in debt, have realized great sums, which they have remitted to Holland and some of the European banks; where, it is supposed, they mean to retire when the desperate game they are now playing can be no longer maintained. This is plunder upon their country, under the infamous pretence of patriotism and public virtue. Charity itself cannot wish that men with such illgotten goods, acquired at the expense and ruin of a once happy and flourishing country, should ever be able to enjoy them in peace and security.[2]

THIS morning, at Charleston, South Carolina, John Roberts, a dissenting minister, was seized on suspicion of being an enemy to the rights of America, when he was tarred and feathered; after which, the populace, whose fury could not be appeased, erected a gibbet on which they hanged him, and afterwards made a bonfire, in which Roberts, together with the gibbet, was consumed to ashes.[2]

DECEMBER 12.—SINCE last Sunday, we have all been at the laboring oar, from the generals to the privates. Early in that day we heard that Cornwallis was coming in three different ways.[3] Knowing our weak situation, he *Americans Retreat to Trenton Falls.* made a forced march to come up with us, and was within two miles of Princeton, when Lord Stirling began his retreat with two brigades. Boats from every quarter were collected, and our stores, together with the troops remaining at Trenton, were immediately conveyed over the Delaware. On Sunday morning, having every thing over, we crossed the Delaware, and took our quarters about half a mile from the river. About eleven o'clock the enemy came marching down with all the pomp of

---

[1] Gaine's Mercury, December 2.   [2] Upcott, iv. 419.
[3] Clift's Diary.

war, in great expectation of getting boats, and immediately pursuing; but of this we took proper care, by destroying every boat, shallop, &c., we could lay our hands on. They made forced marches up and down the river, in pursuit of boats, but in vain. This is Thursday; the enemy are much scattered, some in Trenton, directly opposite; from that on their left to Bordentown and Burlington, on the river banks. They are at least twelve thousand strong, determined for Philadelphia, for which purpose they are transporting flat-bottomed boats from Brunswick to Trenton by land.[1]

DECEMBER 13.—THIS morning, about eleven o'clock, General Lee was taken prisoner at Baskenridge, in New Jersey, by Colonel Harcourt with a party of light horse.

General Lee taken Prisoner. The sentry placed at the door of the house at which General Lee was stopping, saw the troopers coming on the run, and at first supposed them to be ours; but soon perceived his mistake by their swords, which are more crooked than ours. His piece not being loaded, he charged; they rode up to him and said, "Don't shoot; if you fire we will blow your brains out." General Lee cries out, "for God's sake, what shall I do?" The lady of the house took him up stairs, in order to hide him between the chimney and the breastwork over the fireplace, but he could not, the place being so small. The enemy at this time firing in at the windows, the captain gave orders to set fire to the house. The general seeing no way of escaping, sent down he would resign himself. They fired three times at the messenger, but missed him. The general came down without his hat or outside coat, and said, "I hope you will use me as a gentleman; let me get my hat and coat." The captain said, "General Lee, I know you well; I know you are a gentleman; you shall be used as such. I know you too well to suffer you to go for your hat and coat," and ordered him to mount. Upon which they went off, carrying with them the general and a Frenchman, left the baggage, wounded one of the aide-de-camps, and one or two of

---

[1] Extract of a letter from Trenton Falls, in the Freeman's Journal, December 31.

the guard. There were but thirteen men with the general. He was about four miles from his division, and a mile out of the road.[1]

Intelligence of General Lee's unguarded situation was given to the enemy last night, by an inhabitant of Baskenridge, personally known to the general, and who had made great pretensions of friendship for the American cause, though at heart the greatest villain that ever existed. This Judas rode all the preceding night to carry the intelligence, and served as a pilot to conduct the enemy, and came personally with them to the house where the general was taken.

The enemy showed an ungenerous, nay, boyish triumph, after they had got him secure at Brunswick, by making his horse drunk, while they toasted their king till they were in the same condition. A band or two of music played all night to proclaim their joy for this important acquisition. They say we cannot now stand another campaign. Mistaken fools! to think the fate of America depended on one man. They will find ere long that it has no other effect than to urge us on to a noble revenge.[2]

[1] The following is said to be an authentic copy of a letter sent by General Lee to Captain K——y, after his being taken prisoner:—

SIR,—The fortune of war, the activity of Colonel Harcourt, and the rascality of my own troops, have made me your prisoner. I submit to my fate, and hope that whatever may be my destiny, I shall meet it with becoming fortitude; but I have the consolation of thinking, amidst all my distresses, that I was engaged in the noblest cause that ever interested mankind. It would seem to me, that Providence had determined that not one freeman should be left upon earth; and the success of your arms more than foretells one universal system of slavery. Imagine not, however, that I lament my fortune, or mean to deprecate the malice of my enemies; if any sorrow can at present afflict me, it is that of a great continent apparently destined for empire, frustrated in the honest ambition of being free, and enslaved by men whom unfortunately I call my countrymen. To Colonel Harcourt's activity every commendation is due; had I commanded such men, I had this day been free; but my ill fortune has prevailed, and you behold me no longer hostile to England, but contemptible and a prisoner! I have not time to add more; but let me assure you that no vicissitudes have the power to alter my sentiments; and that, as I have long supported those sentiments in difficulty and in dangers, I will never depart from them, but with life.—*Middlesex Journal*, February 20, 1777.

[2] Freeman's Journal, December 31, 1776, and January 14 and 21, 1777.

DECEMBER 14.—A CORRESPONDENT gives the following receipt to make a *patriot:*—Take two drachms of reason and six ounces of resolution; half a pound of eloquence and a pound of logic; three grains of truth and a pound of falsehood; stir them up together in a quart of opposition, with the necessary ingredients of poverty and distress; strain out all the pernicious juice of principle or honesty, and leave the dregs of treachery to settle at the bottom. Thus, after being boiled in the heat of ministerial vengeance, you will have a MODERN PATRIOT. N. B.—If the least use is made of that attracting weed called *pension*, the compound will instantly dissolve.[1]

SATURDAY morning last, (7th,) Sir Peter Parker, with seventy sail of men-of-war and transports, came into Narra-

British Fleet at Rhode Island.

ganset Bay, from New York, and anchored above the harbor of Newport. On Sunday they landed a body of troops, under the Generals Clinton and Percy, who took possession of the town, the inhabitants having previously determined that the place was not defensible against the enemy's shipping. The few troops we had on the island retreated to Bristol, leaving behind them some pieces of artillery. By the best accounts yet received, the enemy's troops do not consist of more than five thousand men; among them are a number of Hessians, some horse, and many invalids. They are intrenching, it is said, at a place called Meeting House Hill, three miles distant from Bristol ferry.

From the first appearance of the fleet, the militia and independent companies of the State have been in motion, and are since joined by a large body of troops, with some companies of artillery from the neighboring States. The readiness and zeal manifested on the occasion, by the troops of Rhode Island and her sister States, reflect on them the highest credit, and we hope will prove a happy presage of their success, should the enemy attempt to gain a lodgment in Providence, or penetrate the country.

We hear the enemy's troops were escorted into Newport

---

[1] Middlesex Journal, December 14.

by a set of well-known infamous Tories, who have long infested that town, and who may yet possibly meet with the fate justly due to their atrocious villanies.[1]

Some time ago a most excellent *coup de main* was executed at Guilford, in England, by Monsieur Masteau, a professor of fireworks, who had for some evenings exhibited specimens of his infernal abilities, in divers rockets, horizontal wheels, flying pigeons, &c., in a field adjoining the town, enclosed all round with a high wall.

M. Masteau's Affair.

As this was to be the last night, Monsieur, with all the *politesse* and address imaginable, applied to every family in town, begging them to take tickets "for the most august, superb, and grand exhibition of fireworks ever seen in the kingdom," assuring them he did not mean to get a penny by it, but did it purely to blaze his own reputation, and to testify his gratitude for the many honors he had received from the inhabitants of Guilford. He proposed to display a most surprising specimen of his art, by showing them forts and castles in the air, firing cannon, with ships under sail attacking them —being an exact representation of Sir Peter Parker's action with the Americans at Charlestown. After a series of manœuvres between the ships and castles, he told them that they would all blow up together—when the air would be filled with rockets and flying fiery dragons.

These wonderful promises drew a vast concourse of people to the place; and when all his tickets were come in, proclamation was made at the door, "that Monsieur, out of his great regard for the poorer sort, would admit them at two-pence each;" which soon introduced the whole *canaille* into the field; when Monsieur, recollecting something material left at his lodging, stepped home to fetch it—having first ordered his tyro to let off two rockets during his absence; then locking the whole company into the field, he set off with the key in his pocket.

The two rockets being let off, and Monsieur not returning,

[1] Freeman's Journal, December 24.

the company began to grow clamorous, when the deputy attempted to fire other pieces, but to his great surprise, not one would fire, and on examination proved to be only paper cases, without a grain of composition within side. It is impossible to describe the indignation of the deluded multitude, who had now been locked in nearly an hour; and it was some time before they could get out, which was at last effected by breaking open the door, when they were informed that the Monsieur had been met three miles from the town, on a dog-trot for London.[1]

DECEMBER 21.—SOME ministers of the established church of Scotland, are said to be such staunch friends to America, that since the declaration of war against the Americans, they have neglected to pray for his Majesty. One of them at Edinburgh having neglected it, the clerk, or, as he is there called, the precentor, being more loyal than the pastor, entertained the audience as follows: After sermon he took out of his pocket a paper, which he read, "The prayers of this congregation are desired for Janet Brown, an aged pauper, under great distress both of body and mind, and for King George," which sent the congregation home in a laugh.[2]

DECEMBER 26.—GENERAL WASHINGTON, finding it absolutely necessary to rouse the spirits of the army, which have been sorely depressed by the long series of disasters which have attended us for almost the whole of this month, resolved to attempt surprising a considerable body of Hessians, quartered at Trenton, consisting of about nineteen hundred, and a detachment of British light horse. The plan was as spiritedly executed as it was judiciously concerted, and terminated in fully answering the warmest expectations of its projectors. Yesterday morning, orders were given for a large part of the army to have three days' provisions ready cooked, and forty rounds a man, and to be ready to march by three

Battle of Trenton.

[1] New York Gazette, January 13, 1777.
[2] Pennsylvania Journal, April 23, 1777.

o'clock in the afternoon; accordingly the farthest brigades marched by two o'clock. About eleven o'clock at night it began snowing, and continued so until daybreak, when a most violent northeast storm came on, of snow, rain, and hail together.

Early, the American army, which did not exceed twenty-four hundred men, crossed the Delaware with several companies of artillery, and thirteen field-pieces, and formed in two divisions; one commanded by General Greene, the other by General Sullivan, and the whole by General Washington. The attack began about seven o'clock by the van-guard of Sullivan's division, who attacked the Hessians' advanced guard, about a mile from the town. These they soon drove, when the whole pushed with the utmost vigor for the town, which they immediately entered. General Greene's division attacked the town on the other side at the same time. The Hessians did as much as could be expected from people so surprised, but the impetuosity of our men was irresistible; fifteen minutes decided the action, and the enemy threw down their arms and surrendered prisoners of war. They consisted of three regiments of grenadiers and fusileers, and were equal to any troops the Prince of Hesse could boast of. The troop of British dragoons, without waiting to be charged, scampered off with the utmost expedition. Could the brigade under Colonel Ewing have landed below the town, as was intended, the light horse must inevitably have been taken, as well as a considerable number of the Hessians who got off; but the violence of the wind was such, and the quantity of ice so great, that he found it impossible to cross. Our success, though not complete, was great. The men behaved with the utmost bravery. Finding that their guns did not generally go off, owing to their having been exposed to the snow and rain for six hours, they charged bayonets, and, with three cheers, rushed like bloodhounds upon the Hessians, who, astonished at their fury, fled or threw down their arms; and it was owing to the ardor of the attack that so little blood was shed. The army returned the same day, and, notwithstanding a continual pelting for twelve hours, of a most violent rain, hail, and snow-storm, we had only two men frozen to death. Luckily they found some hogsheads of rum at Trenton, large draughts of which alone preserved the lives of many. The soldiers behaved exceedingly well with respect to plundering, considering they were animated by revenge for past insults, exasperated by the injuries done their messmates taken at Fort Washington, and animated by every incentive that could work upon the license of a successful army. The general gave the Hessians all their baggage, and they have since gone to the western counties of Pennsylvania, with their packs unsearched. They were amazed at the generosity of the general, so opposite to their own conduct, and called him a very good rebel.

The enemy who lay at Bordentown soon had the alarm, which was communicated to all the parties along the river, who, after remaining under arms the whole day, in the evening marched off, leaving us to take possession of Bordentown, Mount Holly, and Burlington.[1]

On the Hessian standards taken at Trenton, were engraved these words:—" Nescit Pericula," a fearlessness of danger, which was not displayed in the battle where the standards were surrendered to the American arms, and which hath drawn on the timid Hessian and his vaunting motto, the following epigram :

> The man who submits without striking a blow,
> May be said, in a sense, no danger to know;
> I pray then, what harm, by the humble submission,
> At Trenton was done to the standard of Hessian ?[2]

Freeman's Journal, January 21.   [2] Freeman's Journal, February 11, 1777.

CHAPTER IX.

JANUARY 1.—HIS Majesty intends to open this year's campaign with ninety thousand Hessians, Tories, Negroes, Japanese, Moors, Esquimaux, Persian archers, Laplanders, Feejee Islanders, and light horse. With America to be Subdued. this terrific and horrendous armament, in conjunction with a most tremendous and irresistible fleet, he is resolved to terminate this unnatural war the next summer, as it will be impossible for the rebels to bring an equal number in the field. His Majesty has also the strongest assurances that France will cooperate with him in humbling his seditious subjects; and as his admiral and general are still extending the arms of mercy for the gracious reception of those who will yet return to their duty and allegiance, for Heaven's sake, ye poor, deluded, misguided, bewildered, cajoled, and bamboozled Whigs! ye dumbfounded, infatuated, back-bestridden, nose-led-about, priest-ridden, demagogue-beshackled, and Congress-becrafted independents, fly, fly, oh fly, for protection to the royal standard, or ye will be swept from the face of the earth with the besom of destruction, and cannonaded in a moment into nullities and nonentities, and no mortal can tell into what other kind of quiddities and quoddities.[1]

IT is confidently reported in London, that the Congress have devolved all their power upon Mr. Washington, and appointed him dictator, in example of the Romans. The Washington appointed Dictator. reason, if the fact be true, is very apparent. They find themselves in a slippery situation, and are glad to throw

---

[1] Extract of a letter from London, in the Freeman's Journal, March 22.

their burden upon the first simpleton of consequence that would take it. Washington has now no mean character to support. He must be the *first* or *last* of men, who would accept power upon such terms. But as the Congress are desperate, so is this gentleman. As the first instance of this protectorship, he has ordered all persons to take an active part in his concerns, and for the support of his authority, under pain of confiscation of all their properties.[1]

RAN away, from St. James's, an old servant called Common Sense and Honesty, formerly belonging to his late Majesty,

Honesty run away from St. James's. George the Second, and by him imported from Hanover. He served the old King faithfully, and was of great service in procuring him the esteem and affection of all his subjects; but being constantly made a laughing stock by the Lords Bute and Mansfield, since his Majesty's demise, he took the resolution suddenly to absent himself from court. His present owner, it is said, is very indifferent whether he ever returns or not, having, by the arts and misrepresentations of these noblemen, and others, taken a prejudice against him; but some of the people who knew the old King and the regard he had for his useful servant, have authorized the printer to promise five thousand pounds reward to any person who shall bring him back to the palace, and prevail upon him to continue only one month longer in his Majesty's service.[2]

JANUARY 5.—AMONGST the worthies who have joined, or

Pennsylvanians joined Howe. put themselves under the protection of Howe and company, at Trenton, we find the names of the following noted personages, viz.:

John Allen, Esq., (son of the celebrated rhetorical, impartial, learned judge, whose memory will outlive the five mile stone,) late a member of the Philadelphia Committee of Observation, Inspection, &c.

Andrew Allen, Esq., (brother to Jack,) late a member of Congress, one of the Pennsylvania Committee of Safety, and,

---

[1] Gaine's Mercury, February 3.
[2] From the London Gazette, October 10; See Freeman's Journal, March 22.

at the same time, a sworn advocate for George III., of Britain, and his creatures.

William Allen, Esq., (brother to Andrew,) late a lieutenant-colonel in the Continental service, which station he resigned —not because he was totally unfit for it, but because the Continental Congress presumed to declare the American States Free and Independent, without first asking the consent, and obtaining the approbation of himself and wise family.[1]

Joseph Galloway, Esq., late a member of the Congress, Speaker of the Pennsylvania Senate, and printer of a public newspaper in Philadelphia.[2]

JANUARY 7.—On the second instant, intelligence was received by express, that the enemy's army was advancing from Princeton towards Trenton, where the main body of the Americans were stationed. Two brigades *Battle of Princeton.* under Brigadier-Generals Stephen and Fermoy, had been detached several days before, from the main body, to Maidenhead, and were ordered to skirmish with the enemy during their march, and to retreat to Trenton, as occasion should require.

[1] Freeman's Journal, February 4 and March 15.
[2] These lines are the thoughts of a few minutes, which, if severe enough, "Print them egad."

Gall'way has fled, and join'd the venal Howe,
To prove his baseness, see him cringe and bow;
A traitor to his country, and its laws,
A friend to tyrants, and their cursed cause.
Unhappy wretch! Thy interest must be sold,
For continental, not for polish'd gold;
To sink the money, thou thyself cried down,
And stabb'd thy country, to support the crown.

Go to and fro, like Lucifer on earth,
And curse the Being that first gave thee birth;
Away to Scotland, and thyself prepare,
Coal dust and brimstone is their only fare;
Fit materials for such Tory blood,
Who wrong their country, and deny their God;
There herd with Bute, Mansfield, and his brother,*
Bite, twist, sting, and poison one another.

* Murray, " confidential Secretary to the Pretender."
VOL. I.—24

A body of men under command of Colonel Hand, were also ordered to meet the enemy, by which means their march was so much retarded as to give ample time for our forces to form, and prepare to give them a warm reception upon their arrival. Two field-pieces, planted upon a hill, at a small distance above the town, were managed with great advantage, and did considerable execution for some time; after which they were ordered to retire to the station occupied by our forces on the south side of the bridge, over the little river which divides the town into two parts, and opens at right angles into the Delaware. In their way through the town, the enemy suffered much by an incessant fire of musketry from behind the houses and barns. Their army had now arrived at the northern side of the bridge, whilst our army were drawn up, in order of battle, on the southern side. Our cannon played very briskly from this eminence, and were returned as briskly by the enemy. In a few minutes after the cannonade began, a very heavy discharge of musketry ensued, and continued for ten or fifteen minutes. During this action, a party of men were detached from our right wing, to secure a part of the river, which, it was imagined, from the motions of the enemy, they intended to ford. This detachment arrived at the pass very opportunely, and effected their purpose; after this the enemy made a feeble and unsupported attempt to pass the bridge, but this likewise proved abortive. It was now near six o'clock in the evening, and night coming on, closed the engagement. Our fires were built in due season, and were very numerous; and whilst the enemy were amused by these appearances, and preparing for a general attack the ensuing day, our army marched, at about one in the morning, from Trenton, on the south side of the creek, to Princeton. When they arrived near the hill, about one mile from the town, they found a body of the enemy formed upon it, and ready to receive them; upon which a spirited attack was made, both with field-pieces and musketry, and, after an obstinate resistance, and losing a considerable number of their men upon the field, those of them who could not make their escape, surrendered prisoners of war. We immediately marched on to the centre

of the town, and there took another party of the enemy near
the college.   After tarrying a very short time in the town,
General Washington marched his army from thence, towards
Rocky Hill, and they are now near Morristown, in high spirits,
and in expectation of a junction with the rest of our forces, sufficiently seasonable to make a general attack upon the enemy,
and prevent, at least, a considerable part of them from reaching their asylum in New York.   It is difficult precisely to
ascertain the loss we have sustained in the two engagements,
but we think we have lost about forty men killed, and had near
double the number wounded.   In the list of the former are
the brave Colonel Hazlet, Captain Shippen, and Captain Neal,
who fell in the engagement upon the hill near Princeton;
amongst the latter was Brigadier-General Mercer,[1] who received seven wounds—five in his body, and two in his head,
and was much bruised by the breech of a musket, of which
bruises he soon after died.   The loss sustained by the enemy
was much greater than ours, as was easily discovered by viewing the dead upon the field, after the action.   We have near a
hundred of their wounded prisoners in the town, which, together with those who surrendered, and were taken in small
parties endeavoring to make their escape, amount nearly to the
number of four hundred, chiefly British troops.   Six brass
pieces of cannon have fallen into our hands, a quantity of ammunition, and several wagons of baggage.   A Captain Leslie
was found amongst the dead of the enemy, and was this day
buried with the honors of war.   A number of other officers
were also found on the field, but they were not known, and
were buried with the other dead.   According to information
from the inhabitants of Princeton, the number which marched
out of it to attack our army, amounted to seven thousand men,
under command of General Cornwallis.   This body, as soon
as they discovered that they were out-generaled by the march
of General Washington, being much chagrined at their disappointment, (as it seems they intended to have cut our army to
pieces, crossed the Delaware, and have marched immediately,

[1] Hugh Mercer.

without any further delay, to Philadelphia,) pushed with the
greatest precipitation towards Princeton, where they arrived
about an hour after General Washington had left it; and imagining he would endeavor to take Brunswick in the same
manner, proceeded directly for that place. Our soldiers were
much fatigued, the greatest part of them having been deprived
of their rest the two preceding nights; otherwise we might,
perhaps, have possessed ourselves of Brunswick. The enemy
appear to be preparing to decamp and retire to New York, as
they are much disgusted with their late treatment in New
Jersey, and have a great inclination to rest themselves a little
in some secure winter-quarters.[1]

[1] Pennsylvania Journal, February 5. Gaine, in his paper of January 13, gives
another account of this battle:—Several skirmishes between the King's troops
and the rebels have lately happened in the Jerseys. But the most distinguished
encounter occurred on the 3d instant, near Princeton. The 17th regiment, consisting of less than three hundred men, fell in with the rebel army of between
five and six thousand, whom they attacked with all the ardor and intrepidity of
Britons. They received the fire from behind a fence, over which they immediately leaped upon their enemies, who presently turned to the right about with
such precipitation as to leave their very cannon behind them. The soldiers instantly turned their cannon, and fired at least twenty rounds upon their rear; and
had they been assisted with another regiment or two, the rebels would have found
it rather difficult to make good their retreat. This has been one of the most
splendid actions of the whole campaign, and has given a convincing proof that
British valor has not declined from its ancient glory. Of Colonel Mawhood, their
gallant commander, and of his conduct in the affair, too many encomiums cannot
be said. The loss was about twenty killed, and eighty wounded, of the troops.
Of the rebels above four hundred were killed and wounded. Among their slain
were eleven officers. Mr. Mercer, (one of the rebel officers, since dead,) when
he was taken up by our people, asked how many the numbers were who had thus
attacked him, and upon being told, he cried out with astonishment, "My God;
is it possible? I have often heard of British courage, but never could have
imagined to find such an instance as this!"

Another account says, that the 17th regiment just before they charged the
rebels, deliberately pulled off their knapsacks and gave three cheers; then broke
through the rebels, faced about, attacked, and broke through a second time.
Colonel Mawhood then said, it would be prudent, as they were so few, to retire;
upon which the men, one and all, cried out, "No, no; let us attack them again;"
and it was with great difficulty their colonel could induce them to retreat; which
at length they performed in the utmost order.

To the honor of this brave regiment, both as soldiers and as men, not one of
them has ever attempted to plunder, nor encouraged it in others.

JANUARY 9.—THE enemy have abandoned Elizabethtown. Our people have entered it and taken thirty Waldeckers and fifty Highlanders, and about thirty baggage wagons fully loaded. The enemy who had all the Jerseys, are now only in possession of Amboy and Brunswick. This is a great reverse in the course of a fortnight, to the British power. Whether they mean to collect their whole force at Brunswick, and give us battle, or whether they mean to push for Staten Island, and abandon the Jerseys entirely, is matter of doubt. We shall make a move towards them to-day, with a view to avail ourselves of circumstances. The enemy appear to be panic-struck in the extreme. God prospers our arms in an extraordinary manner. There is to be an eclipse of the sun to-day; we mean, if possible, to attack the Germans as soon as it begins, and take the advantage of their ignorant superstition.[1]

ADMIRAL GAYTON has taken upon him publicly to declare, in opposition to the author of Common Sense, and from his own knowledge, that when he was in America forty years since, "there never had been a man-of-war of any kind built in New England."[2] It is but just that the public should be informed, that in the year 1690 a fourth-rate ship-of-war was launched at New Castle, in Piscataqua River: and in the year 1696 another, whose force is not remembered. The former was the Falkland, and the latter the Bedford Galley.

It is not probable that Admiral Gayton had any knowledge of these ships having been built here, so that he cannot be charged with falsehood, but it is hoped if he should publish any thing further relating to this country, he will express himself not quite so positively, especially if he undertakes to prove a negative.

The evidence of the above facts depends on an original manuscript letter from Mr. Emerson, formerly minister of

[1] Extract of a letter from Morristown, New Jersey, in the Freeman's Journal, January 28.
[2] See Essex Journal, of December 26, 1776.

New Castle, to the late Mr. Prince, and is to be found among
the collection of manuscripts relating to the history of New
England, made by fifty years' industry of that worthy gentleman, unless it has been pilfered or destroyed by the Saracen-
like barbarity of the late occupiers of the Old South meeting-
house in Boston, in an apartment of which those valuable
manuscripts were deposited.[1]

JANUARY 19.—GENERAL HOWE has discharged all the
privates, who were prisoners in New York; one-half he sent
to the world of spirits for want of food—the
other he hath sent to warn their countrymen
of the danger of falling into his hands, and to convince
them by ocular demonstration, that it is infinitely better to
be slain in battle, than to be taken prisoners by British brutes,
whose tender mercies are cruelties.[2]

Sufferings
of American
Prisoners.

The following account of the sufferings of these unfortunate
men was obtained from the prisoners themselves:—As soon as
they were taken they were robbed of all their baggage, of
whatever money they had, though it were of paper, and could
be of no advantage to the enemy, of their silver shoe-buckles,
and knee-buckles, &c., and many were stripped almost naked
of their clothes. Especially those who had good clothes,
were stripped at once, being told that *such clothes were too
good for rebels.* Thus deprived of their clothes and baggage
they were unable to shift even their linen, and were obliged to
wear the same shirts for even three or four months together,
whereby they became extremely nasty; and this of itself was
sufficient to bring on them many mortal diseases.

After they were taken, they were in the first place put
on board the ships and thrust down into the hold, where
not a breath of fresh air could be obtained and they were
nearly suffocated for want of air. Particularly some who
were taken at Fort Washington, were first in this manner
thrust down into the holds of vessels in such numbers,
that even in the cold season of November they could

---

[1] Freeman's Journal, January 14.   [2] Freeman's Journal, February 18.

scarcely bear any clothes on them, being kept in a constant sweat. Yet these same persons, after lying in this situation awhile, till the pores of their bodies were as perfectly opened as possible, were of a sudden taken out and put into some of the churches in New York; without covering or a spark of fire, where they suffered as much by the cold as they did by the sweating stagnation of the air in the other situation; and the consequence was, that they took such colds as brought on the most fatal diseases, and swept them off almost beyond conception.

Besides these things, they suffered extremely for want of provisions. The commissary pretended to allow half a pound of bread and four ounces of pork per day; but of this pittance they were much cut short. What was given them for three days was not enough for one day; and in some instances, they went for three days without a single mouthful of food of any sort. They were pinched to that degree, that some on board the ships would pick up and eat the salt which happened to be scattered there; others gathered up the bran which the light horse wasted, and ate it, mixed with dirt and filth as it was. Nor was this all, both the bread and pork which they did allow them was extremely bad. For the bread, some of it was made out of the bran which they brought over to feed their light horse, and the rest of it was so muddy and the pork so damnified, being so soaked in bilge water in the transportation from Europe, that they were not fit to be eaten by human creatures; and when they were eaten, were very unwholesome. Such bread and pork as they would not pretend to give their own countrymen, they gave to our poor sick, dying prisoners.

Nor were they in this doleful condition allowed a sufficiency of water. One would have thought that water was so cheap and plentiful an element, that they would not have grudged them that. But there are, it seems, no bounds to their cruelty. The water allowed them was so brackish and withal nasty, that they could not drink it, till reduced to extremity. Nor did they let them have a sufficiency even of such water as this.

When winter came on, our people suffered extremely for want of fire and clothes to keep them warm. They were confined in churches where there were no fireplaces, that they could make fires even if they had wood. But wood was only allowed them for cooking their pittance of victuals; and for that purpose very sparingly. They had none to keep them warm even in the extremest of weather, although they were almost naked, and the few clothes that were left upon them were their summer clothes. Nor had they a single blanket or any bedding, not even straw, allowed them till a little before Christmas.

At the time those were taken on Long Island, a considerable part of them were sick of the dysentery, and with this distemper on them were first crowded on board the ships, afterwards in the churches in New York, three, four, or five hundred together, without any blankets, or any thing for even the sick to lie upon, but the bare floors or pavements. In this situation that contagious distemper soon communicated from the sick to the well, who would probably have remained so, had they not in this manner been thrust in together without regard to sick or well, or to the sultry, unwholesome season, it being then the heat of summer. Of this distemper numbers died daily, and many others, by their confinement and the sultry season, contracted fevers and died of them. During their sickness, with these and other diseases, they had no medicines, nothing soothing or comfortable for sick people, and were not so much as visited by the physician by the month together.

Nor ought we to omit the insults which the humane Britons offered to our people, nor the artifices which they used to enlist them in their service and fight against their country. It seems that one end of their starving our people was to bring them, by dint of necessity, to turn rebels to their own country, their own consciences, and their God. For while thus famishing they would come and say to them, "This is the just punishment of your rebellion. Nay, you are treated too well for rebels; you have not received half you deserve or half you shall receive. But if you will enlist into his

Majesty's service, you shall have victuals and clothes
enough."

As to insults, the British officers, besides continually curs-
ing and swearing at them as rebels, often threatened to hang
them all; and on a particular time, ordered a number, each man
to choose his halter out of a parcel offered, wherewith to be
hanged; and even went so far as to cause a gallows to be
erected before the prison, as if they were immediately to be
executed. They further threatened to send them all into the
East Indies, and sell them there for slaves. In these, and
numberless other ways, did the British officers seem to rack
their inventions to insult, terrify, and vex the poor prisoners.
The meanest upstart officers among them would insult and
abuse our colonels and chief officers.

In this situation, without clothes, without victuals or drink,
and even water, or with those which were base and unwholesome, without fire, a number of them sick, first with a contagious and nauseous distemper; these, with others, crowded by
hundreds into close confinement, at the most unwholesome
season of the year, and continued there for four months without blankets, bedding, or straw; without linen to shift, or
clothes to cover their bodies. No wonder they all became
sickly, and having at the same time no medicine, no help of
physicians, nothing to refresh or support nature, died by scores
in a night; and those who were so far gone as to be unable to
help themselves, lay uncared for, till death, more kind than
Britons, put an end to their misery.

By these means, and in this way, fifteen hundred brave
Americans, who had nobly gone forth in defence of their injured, oppressed country, but whom the chance of war had
cast into the hands of our enemies, died in New York, many
of whom were very amiable, promising youths, of good families—the very flower of our land. And of those who lived to
come out of prison, the greater part, as far as I can learn, are
dead and dying. Their constitutions are broken, the stamina
of nature worn out, they cannot recover—they die. Even the
few that might have survived, are dying of the small-pox.
For it seems that our enemies determined that even these,

whom a good constitution and a kind Providence had carried through unexampled sufferings, should not at last escape death, just before their release from imprisonment infected them with that fatal distemper.

To these circumstances we subjoin the manner in which they buried those of our people who died. They dragged them out of their prisons by one leg or one arm, piled them up without doors, there let them lie till a sufficient number were dead to make a cart load; then loaded them up in a cart, drove the cart thus loaded out to the ditches made by our people when fortifying New York; there they would tip the cart, tumble the corpses together into the ditch, and afterwards slightly cover them with earth.

* * * * While our poor prisoners have been thus treated by our foes, the prisoners we have taken have enjoyed the liberty of walking and riding about within large limits, at their pleasure; have been fully supplied with every necessary, and have even lived on the fat of the land. None have been so well fed, so healthy, so plump, and so merry as they; and this generous treatment, it is said, they could not but remember. For when they were returned in the exchange of prisoners, and saw the miserable, famished, dying state of our prisoners, conscious of the treatment they had received, they could not refrain from tears.[1]

But it is not the prisoners alone who have felt the effects of British humanity. Every part of the country through which they have marched, has been plundered and ravaged. No discrimination has been made with respect to Whig or Tory; but all alike have been involved in one common fate. Their march through New Jersey has been marked with savage barbarity. But Westchester witnesseth more terrible things. The repositories of the dead have ever been held sacred by the most barbarous and savage nations. But here, not being able to accomplish their accursed purposes upon the living, they wreaked their vengeance on the dead. In many places, the graves in the church-yards were opened, and the

[1] Connecticut Journal, January 30.

bodies of the dead exposed upon the ground for several days. At Morrisania, the family vault was opened, the coffins broken, and the bones scattered abroad. At Delancey's farm, the body of a beautiful young lady, which had been buried for two years, was taken out of the ground, and exposed for five days in a most indecent manner. Many more instances could be mentioned, but my heart sickens at the recollection of such inhumanity. Some persons try to believe that it is only the Hessians who perpetrate these things, but I have good authority to say that the British vie with, and even exceed the auxiliary troops in licentiousness. After such treatment, can it be possible for any persons seriously to wish for a reconciliation with Great Britain? [1]

To the melancholy picture already exhibited of the brutal behavior of the Britons, (who vainly boast being ever preeminent in mercy,) aided by Hessian and Waldeck mercenaries, in New York and New Jersey, it gives us pain to add that they have not only outraged the feelings of humanity, to many people who were so unhappy as to fall into their hands, particularly the fair sex, but have degraded themselves beyond the power of language to express, by wantonly destroying the curious water works at New York, an elegant public library at Trenton, and the grand orrery, made by the celebrated Rittenhouse, which was placed in the college at Princeton, a piece of mechanism which the most untutored savage, staying the hand of violence, would have beheld with wonder, reverence, and delight! Thus are our cruel enemies warring against liberty, virtue, and the arts and sciences. "*How are the mighty fallen.*" [2]

JANUARY 24.—AT a crisis when America is invaded by one of the most powerful fleets and armies that ever the world beheld arrayed in order of battle; when the hand   An Appeal. of tyranny is uplifted to fell the glorious plant of liberty, which our ancestors have cherished from the earliest ages as the tree-of life; when war, with all its horrors, is in-

---

[1] Freeman's Journal, February 18.   [2] The same, January 28.

vading this once happy land, and every sacred right is at stake; when every filial and affectionate sentiment should engage us to step forth in support of those who have been the guardians of our tender years, or the sweet companions of our halcyon days, must not that soul be frozen even to apathy that is not roused by such important and irresistible impulses! Our country, our lives, our liberties, our parents, our children, and our wives, &c., are the sacred pledges for which we are now contending. We stand on the brink of a precipice, from which we cannot advance without the noblest exertions of virtue, unanimity, and fortitude. A single false step may precipitate us from the enjoyment of the inestimable blessings of liberty, peace, and independence, to the abyss of slavery and woe. But, on the contrary, whilst we are animated by the glorious cause we are engaged in; whilst we with cheerfulness embark in the defence of the most valuable of sublunary blessings; whilst we are united in our sentiment, vigilant in our duty, and active in our operations, we need not dread the thunder of cannon, nor tremble at the names of heroes arrayed in all the splendor of a corrupt court, or crowned with the faded laurels which have been plucked by the hand of tyranny.

Such, my countrymen, is the present state of America; such the consequence of slumbering in the arms of peace, whilst your enemy is at your gates; and such the glorious reward of those who nobly stand forth and oppose the progress of a mercenary army, more venal than a court favorite, more savage than a band of Tartars, and more spiritless than the sorry, sooty sons of Afric, when opposed by men animated by liberty and the sacred love of their country.

Should any one among you require the force of example to animate you on this glorious occasion, let him turn his eyes to that bright luminary of war, in whose character the conduct of Emillus, the coolness of a Fabius, the intrepidity of a Hannibal, and the indefatigable ardor and military skill of a Cæsar, are united. Let not the name of Brutus or Camillus be remembered whilst that of Washington is to be found in the annals of America. Great in the cabinet as in war, he shines with unrivalled splendor in every department of life; and

whilst his abilities as a statesman and a general excite our wonder, his disinterested patriotism and domestic virtues command
universal veneration.   When sent out by Governor Dinwiddie
to order the French to desist from their encroachments on Virginia, view him in the early period of life, traversing in the
service of his country the dreadful wilds of America, through
nations of savages, with no other attendant but an interpre-
ter.   Behold him at the head of a handful of his gallant countrymen, engaged for many hours with more than treble the
number of French, at the Meadows, where the fire first ceased
on the side of the enemy, who previously proposed a parley;
and though surrounded by numbers, yet, a stranger to the impulses of fear, he capitulated on the terms of retiring with the
honors of war.   Follow him to that tremendous scene which
struck a universal panic in the bravest of the British troops,
when, as aide-de-camp to the intrepid Braddock, amidst the
dreadful carnage of that day, he was engaged in giving out
the orders of that unfortunate general with a coolness that
marked the hero, and at length brought him off the field of
battle, after he had received his mortal wound.   Again, behold him exchanging the din of arms for the calmer scenes of
life, still active in the service of his country in the senate, until the impending storm, which is now bursting on America,
called him forth as the guardian protector of his country.
Behold him abandoning the delights of peace, the enjoyment
of affluence, and the pleasures of domestic felicity, and entering with ardor upon a military life again.   Let imagination
paint him at the head of a few raw, undisciplined troops, destitute of arms and ammunition, besieging an army of veterans
supported by a powerful navy; consider with what unparalleled fortitude he withstood the difficulties that surrounded
him on every side; behold him embracing the earliest opportunities of driving the enemy from their advantageous post,
and obliging them to abandon the long persecuted town of
Boston.   Again, survey the plains of Long Island, whither he
flew like a guardian angel to protect and bring off his brave
troops, surrounded on every side by a host of foes, and with
a conduct unparalleled in history, secured their retreat across

a river of which the enemy's ships were in full possession. Surely Heaven interposed in behalf of America on that day, by permitting such numbers to escape with glory from such a superior force! Behold his glorious struggles on the heights of Harlem, and at the White Plains, counteracting the best concerted plans of the ablest generals of the age; in thought attend him, (if thought does not lag behind,) when, as it were, he bounded from the White Plains to the Jersey shore, covering the retreat of his men from Fort Lee, and throwing himself with them before the enemy, and with the scattered remains of his disbanded army, now amounting to only three thousand men, checking at every step the progress of the British army, and often halting to offer battle to numbers vastly superior to his own. Gracious Heaven! can any Virginian—his countrymen, or can any American who regards him as the saviour of the States, reflect on his situation at that juncture without horror? Would he not rather share his fortunes for the rest of the war, than hazard the salvation of his country by a short enlistment, at the end of which his general might be left without an army to support him? Yet, even in such a situation, his calmness and intrepidity never forsook him, but he appeared still greater in proportion to the dangers that surrounded him. At length, when the enemy flattered themselves with the pleasing expectations of a speedy accomplishment of their darling wish, we behold him by *coup de main* dissipating the fears of his country, and striking terror into troops who, the day before, conceived themselves on the eve of a triumph. Whilst each effeminate son of peace was revelling in luxury, his active mind was employed in preparing for scenes equally glorious to himself, and terrible to his enemies. Success attended this matchless enterprise, and Philadelphia, with the rest of America, hailed him her deliverer and guardian genius.

Such, my countrymen, is the general who directs the military operations of America; such the glorious leader of her armies; such the hero whose bright example should fire every generous heart to enlist in the service of his country. Let it not be said you are callous to the impressions of such noble considerations, but, by following his glorious example, show yourselves worthy of possessing that inestimable jewel, Liberty, and reflect that you have nothing to dread whilst you are engaged in so glorious a cause, and blessed with a Washington for a leader.[1]

JANUARY 25.—THE following proclamation was this day published by the Lord Protector, Mr. George Washington:

"Whereas several persons, inhabitants of the United States of America, influenced by inimical motives, intimidated by the threats of the enemy, or deluded by a proclamation issued the 30th of November last, by Lord *Washington's Proclamation.* and General Howe, styled the King's Commissioners for granting pardons, &c., (now at open war, and invading these States,) have been so lost to the interest and welfare of their country, as to repair to the enemy, sign a declaration of fidelity, and in some instances have been compelled to take the oaths of allegiance, and engage not to take up arms, or encourage others so to do, against the King of Great Britain: And whereas it has become necessary to distinguish between the friends of America and those of Great Britain, inhabitants of these States, and that every man who receives protection from, and is a subject of any State, (not being conscientiously scrupulous against bearing arms,) should stand ready to defend the same against hostile invasion: I do, therefore, in behalf of the United States, by virtue of the powers committed to me by Congress, hereby strictly command and require every person, having subscribed such declaration, taken such oaths, and accepted such protection and certificate, to repair to head-quarters, or to the quarters of the nearest general officer of the Continental army or militia, (until further provision can be made by civil authority,) and there deliver up such protection, certificate, and passports, and take the oath of allegiance to the United States of America; nevertheless, hereby granting full liberty to all such as prefer the interest and protection of Great Britain to the freedom and happiness of their country, forthwith to withdraw themselves and families within the enemy's lines. And I do hereby declare, that

[1] Freeman's Journal, April 12.

all and every person who may neglect or refuse to comply with this order, within thirty days from the date hereof, will be deemed adherents to the King of Great Britain, and treated as common enemies of these American States."

'Tis hardly possible to read over this miserable proclamation without pity and astonishment. That Mr. Washington, who

Loyal Criticism.

once was esteemed a gentleman, should forfeit that character by becoming the tool of an impracticable ambition, is a matter of commiseration; but, that he should be so contaminated by the vice of his associates as to lose all regard to the common forms of morality, all dignity of sentiment, and decency of conduct, was not to have been expected from a man who owned the least pride, or felt the least consciousness of virtue. His desperate situation may be his apology, but it cannot be his excuse. He might have been mistaken in respect to his notions of civil polity; but he could not have been deceived in those actions and ideas of moral turpitude, which is the disgrace of human nature. 'Tis an old and true observation, *Magistratus indicat Virum*, "the Ruler shows the Man;" and we have now nothing more to learn of this famous Mr. Washington.

He has the boldness to declare, that there are "some instances" of persons who "have been compelled to take the oath of allegiance." This is an absolute falsehood in fact, and he knew it was a falsehood; he knew such conduct was repugnant to the genius and spirit of the British nation, or he would have produced one instance to confirm his assertion. The bravery of Britons, which sooner or later will make him tremble, disdains any but voluntary professions of allegiance, and above all things, despises the dastardly subterfuges of falsehood and slander.

The next material circumstance in this Proclamation, is sufficient to make an honest man shudder. It may be styled, a Proclamation for the encouragement of Perjury. Mr. Washington "strictly commands and requires every person," who has taken a solemn oath of Allegiance to the King, and called God to witness the truth and sincerity of it, to repair to him or his officers, and take another solemn oath, and call

God to witness the sincerity and truth of his adherence to the cause of rebellion. Such an impious disregard, such a flagrant violation of all that is serious and sacred among men, has rarely been seen in any age, country, or profession.

For the honor of human nature, it may be said, that it was left for rebels to their King and destroyers of their country, to give a public sanction to *Wilful Perjury*.

'Tis no wonder that a principle of this kind should be attended with a suitable practice. Mr. Washington grants by this proclamation "full liberty" to all such as prefer the protection of Great Britain to his own, "forthwith to withdraw themselves and families within the enemy's lines." This is only a trap to discover those who are not affected to the rebellion; and even this mean idea has been followed by a conduct of which a common Turk would have been ashamed. Doctor Brown, of Newark, in the Jerseys, relying not merely upon Mr. Washington's word as a gentleman, but upon his public faith pledged in the foregoing paper as a public man, immediately wrote to him, desiring leave to withdraw himself and family to New York, pursuant to his proclamation. Instead of complying with the Doctor's wishes, he sent a party of his rebels to drag him away to Morristown. He is now confined there in jail, his family is almost distracted, and all his property seized. So much for the public faith of Mr. Washington!

He seems indebted for the last cruel idea of his proclamation to the worthy author of "Common Sense," and the "American Crisis." This gentleman is for seizing all the property of people who refuse to join in his measures, for the sake of the spoil; and has the confidence to declare, that such a seizure would enable his rebellious adherents to carry on the war for two years longer. 'Tis to be hoped, for the honor and safety of America, that the good people of this country will give an exact account of him and some of his associates in half the time. It is every man's interest, who has any thing to lose, to take care of a person who has the impudence to profess himself a public robber and destroyer, and can call this unheard of cruelty and devastation by the name of "soft resentment." However, if men who can encourage perjury by proclamation, and plunge thousands of families into irretrievable ruin, only for the purpose of answering their dark ambition; if men who can have the consummate boldness to break their public faith, and, calling the gentle government of Britain, tyranny, can become the most insolent and outrageous tyrants themselves; if such can possibly arrive at the rule of this once happy country, it will be the interest of every one who loves the enjoyment of liberty more than the sound, to retire from America as speedily as he can. In such an event, (which, however, is not likely to happen,) he would escape the anarchy, riot, and bloodshed, which these "unprincipled impostors" sooner or later would spread over the land, and which would then become the vengeance of Providence itself on this most ungrateful and unnatural rebellion.[1]

JANUARY 26.—LAST evening, the little theatre in John street, in New York, was opened, with the celebrated burlesque
John Street Theatre.
entertainment of Tom Thumb, written by the late Mr. Fielding to ridicule the bathos of several dramatic pieces that at his time, to the disgrace of the British stage, had engrossed both the London theatres. The characters were performed by gentlemen of the navy and army. The spirit with which this favorite piece was supported by the performers, proves their taste and strong conception of the humor. The performance convinces us that a good education and knowledge of polite life, are essentially necessary to constitute a good actor. The play was introduced by a prologue written and spoken by Captain Stanly. We have great pleasure in applauding this first effort of his infant muse, as replete with true poetic genius. The scenes, painted by Captain De Lancey, have great merit, and would not disgrace a theatre, though under the management of a Garrick. The house was crowded with company, and the ladies made a brilliant appearance.[2]

---

[1] New York Gazette, February 10.   [2] Gaine's Mercury, January 27.

THE defeat of the Hessians at Trenton, was primarily owing to a dispute which existed between the English and German troops. Colonel Rahl, apprehending Reason of the that he should be attacked by superior numbers, Success at Trenton. required of Lord Cornwallis a reinforcement. Two regiments, under Colonel Grant, were detached for that purpose. The English troops showed a reluctance to assist the Hessians. They halted a few hours, during which interval Colonel Rahl was defeated.

The disputes between the English and the Hessians troops originated from the following incident: An officer of the regiment of Losberg engaged some English officers at Princeton in a conversation respecting military discipline. An English officer, whether heated by liquor, or irascible through passion, replied to the German by throwing a punch bowl at his head. The insult was properly resented. But the seeds of discord being thus unhappily sown, a crop of evils ensued. The private men, adopting the quarrels of their officers, indulged themselves in frequent rencounters.[1]

FEBRUARY 1.—AN anonymous correspondent living in London, says: We have received, through the indefatigable assiduity of Lord Stormont, the English ambassa- Franklin to the dor at the court of France, a copy of Doctor King of the French Franklin's proposals[2] from the American Congress to the French court, which are as follows:

MAY IT PLEASE YOUR MAJESTY:—We, the most puissant, high and invincible of States of North America, have em-

---

[1] Pennsylvania Journal, June 25.

[2] Doctor Franklin, having been elected a commissioner from the Congress to conclude a treaty of amity with the French court, sailed for France on the 27th of October, and arrived at Nantz on the 13th of December, 1776. He at once proceeded to Paris, "where," says a correspondent, "he now engrosses the whole attention of the public. People of all ranks pay their court to him. His affability and complaisant behavior have gained him the esteem of the greatest people in this kingdom. Lord Stormont has represented him to the French ministry as a traitor to his country, and that it was a high affront to the King his master, to show so much favor to one of his rebellious subjects; but this is paid little regard to. Lord Stormont is fully employed in watching the Doctor's motions."—*Extract of a Letter from Paris*, February 1; Upcott, iv. 457.

powered our trusty and well-beloved Benjamin Franklin, one of the principal members of our Commonwealth, to make the following overtures of a treaty with your most christian Majesty, in behalf of, and for us the above States, upon the subsequent honorable principles and conditions.

That being now to our sorrow convinced of the dastardly and cowardly behavior of the army of this commonwealth, in not daring to face the troops of our once parent state, and at the same time sensible of having drawn God's curse and heavy displeasure upon us for our enormous ingratitude and disobedience towards our Mother country; we came to a resolution of applying to your Majesty's aid in this our sad inability and disappointment in striving against such power, that as your Majesty is styled "The Most Christian," for whose religion and laws we the Independents of America, as well as our ancestors, always had the most high and cordial esteem and reverence, as they are framed and calculated for the security and promotion of the purest and most extensive liberty, both religious and civil. We flatter ourselves that your arms may be more successful in this our just and laudable cause, so conformable to the laws of God and man. And should your most christian Majesty's arms prove victorious against those our cruel enemies, and we thereby be reinstated in the enjoyment of our most equitable rights, and reassuming, and once more clothing ourselves with that Heaven descended power which we exercised over said States, we shall condescend to requite and acknowledge your effort and expense in the said war and conquest, with giving you our permission and liberty to conquer also for your own use and dominion your ancient colony of Canada, which when there was no risk and resistance against us, we so justly and bravely invaded, and partly conquered, but at the appearance of the troops of our late parent State, we so heroically evacuated again, of which the bearer, Mr. Franklin, is a living instance, having escaped out of a window, without even breaking his neck, owing to the assistance of his guardian spirit, who probably intends him for a more conspicuous and exalted death, as a reward for his shining public virtues.

You shall have our sovereign consent and permission also to conquer both the Floridas, which were exchanged for the territories on the Mississippi, which, with the province of Quebec, the British nation, at a considerable expense of blood and treasure, conquered for us last war, as a small return for the inestimable benefits which they had derived from our commerce and friendship.

As another instance of our acknowledgment for these your signal services, we the aforesaid most powerful States surrender you the full property and dominion of the British West India islands, which are now, and ever have been, dependent on these States for the common necessaries of life, and are therefore naturally subordinate to them, and at their control and disposal.

As a further motive and encouragement, we also covenant and engage, that such sums of money in our own specie shall be transmitted and delivered into your most christian Majesty's coffers, as shall be adequate to the expense you may incur in assisting us, and as shall appear equal to the gratitude and dignity of these States to give. We lastly permit our subjects to carry on trade with yours, as long as it suits their conveniency and interests.

These our most gracious concessions, we hope, will induce you to accept our offers, and most amply satisfy and reimburse you for the troubles and difficulties you may undergo in conquering our said enemies, and reinstating us in the possession and dominion of the countries which have been discovered and protected at the expense of the British nation, and we have a just right and claim to by virtue of our charters granted us by said nation, and by the laws of God and nature.[1]

LORD STORMONT, whose time is chiefly employed in circulating reports to discredit the Americans, having in a very serious manner lately told a French nobleman, that six battalions in Washington's army had laid down their arms, the nobleman applied to Doctor

A Bon Mot.

---

[1] Upcott, iv. 455.

Franklin, to know whether the story was a truth, (*une vérité*,) to which the Doctor answered, "*Non, Monsieur, ce n'est pas vérité, c'est seulement un Stormont.* No, Sir, it is not a truth, it is only a Stormont." This answer was afterwards handed about amongst the wits of Paris, and the word Stormont has since become the cant phrase for a lie.[1]

FEBRUARY 6.—It may be relied on as a matter of fact, that when the enemy took possession of Newport, in Rhode Island, Prescott's Barbarity. a person who lived on the island, and had been a lieutenant of a privateer, was taken up and carried before Lord Percy, Sir Peter Parker, and Colonel (or as some call him) General Prescott. Says Prescott, "What are you?" "I have been a lieutenant of a privateer." "A lieutenant of a privateer, ha! Damn your blood, one of the damn'd thieves," and immediately made up to him and hit him a knock in the jaws, and said he should be hanged. He told the colonel he, too, had had prisoners in his power, and always had used them well; and even when he himself had short allowance the prisoners had a full allowance of provisions. "Yes, damn you, I have been a prisoner among you and know how I was treated;" and hit him another knock. Lord Percy desired the colonel not to proceed in that way, as he was a prisoner; the colonel told the prisoner he should be chained neck and heels, and be fed with nothing but oatmeal and wetel, and while he lived his life should be miserable, and hit him another knock, which Lord Percy again disapproved of, and ordered him to be put into prison, which he said was enough without blows or irons.

We shall leave it to our readers to make their own reflections on this treatment, and to determine from it the character of Colonel Prescott, and whether it does not indicate him to be a blustering coward: for according to an established maxim, the brave are always generous, and treat with humanity those whom the fortune of war has made their prisoners.[2]

[1] New York Journal, September 8.
[2] Pennsylvania Journal, February 19.

THE characteristic virtue of the natives of Rhode Island is liberality, and it should seem (at least it is hoped) Heaven favors this sequestered isle. It were a pity human blood should stain the most beautiful spot in all America, where, till the commencement of the unhappy war, the inhabitants lived in all that reciprocal friendship, that harmony and happiness, which minds undisturbed by ambition, or uninfluenced by prejudice, so fully and amply enjoy.[1]

A CORRESPONDENT thinks the following new catechism will amply repay an attentive perusal:[2]

What is war?—It is the curse of mankind, the mother of pestilence and famine, and the undistinguishing destroyer of the human species. A New Catechism.

How is war divided?—Into offensive and defensive.

What is the chief end of offensive war?—Sometimes it is to regain by the sword what had been unjustly taken away from the rightful possessor; but, for the most part, it is to gratify the ambition of a tyrannic prince, by subjecting to his arbitrary will a people whom God had created free, and giving their hard-earned possessions to support him in luxury, idleness, and sensuality.

Are there any instances of such princes?—Yes, many, both in ancient and modern times. History is filled with the wicked lives and miserable deaths of tyrants. The present King of Great Britain, whose history is not yet completed, is a living example of such a prince. He carried an offensive war into the East Indies, and deprived many thousands of those innocent people of their lives and properties, that he might snuff the spices of the east, and repose his sluggard limbs on the sofa of a nabob. He is now carrying an offensive war into America, without one specious plea for so doing, most wickedly aiming at the absolute disposal of that extensive country and all its numerous inhabitants; for this purpose he has spread desolation and death through their peaceful habitations, pursuing his iniquitous designs with every aggravated species of obstinacy, cruelty, and horror.

[1] Upcott, iv. 455.   [2] Brasher's Journal.

What·may be said of such a prince?—That he looks upon mankind as created only for his use, and makes their misery his support; that the spirits of thousands, who have fallen a sacrifice to his ambition, cluster around the polished points of his imperial crown, and daily cry aloud to Heaven for justice; that his throne is built of the bones of his fellow creatures, and rests on the skulls of the slain; that his unhallowed feasts are sprinkled with human blood, and that the groans of widows and orphans attend him with innumerable curses at every rising sun.

What will be the probable end of such a prince?—That history will do justice to his memory, in spite of all the fawning sycophants of his court, and hand his name to posterity with infamy and detestation; that whilst his royal carcass fattens the common worms of the earth, his miserable soul shall give an account to God for the wanton slaughter of his creatures, whose blood will most assuredly be required at his hands; and that the vaults of hell shall ring with, *Hail, thou great destroyer of the human species!*

What is a defensive war?—It is the taking up arms to resist tyrannic power, and bravely suffering present hardships, and encountering present dangers, to secure lasting liberty, property, and life to future generations.

Is a defensive war justifiable in a religious view?—The foundation of war is laid in the wickedness of mankind. Were all men virtuous, just, and good, there would be no contention, or cause of contention, amongst them; but as the case is far otherwise, war is become absolutely necessary, as many other things are which are only the product of the weaknesses or iniquity of men. Even the invaluable blessings of a constitutional government would be unnecessary incumbrances, were there no open violence or secret treachery to be guarded against. God has given to man wit to contrive, power to execute, and freedom of will to direct his conduct. It cannot be, therefore, but that some will abuse these great privileges, and exert these powers to the ruin of others. The oppressed will then have no way to screen themselves from injury but by executing the same powers in their defence, and it is their duty so to do. If it were otherwise, a few miscreants would tyrannize over the rest of mankind, and make them abject slaves of oppression and pensioners of their will. Thus it is that a just defensive war is not only necessary, but an indispensable duty, and consistent with religion, accommodated as it must be to our present imperfect state of existence.

Is it upon these principles that the people of America are now resisting the arms of England, and opposing force by force?—Strictly so. The Americans had nothing in view but to live peaceably and dutifully in a constitutional submission to Great Britain. They suffered patiently, for a long time, many unjust encroachments of power, being loath to offend their rulers by a too strict attention to every right, till at last the designs of the court became too evident to be mistaken, and they were pushed to the distressing necessity of choosing one of two evils, viz., either to enlist themselves and their unborn posterity the avowed unconditional slaves of a corrupt and wicked administration, or to brave the horrors of war in a noble contest for liberty and life. They have wisely determined on the latter; and after solemnly appealing to God and the world for the justice of their cause, they are prosecuting the war under the favor of Heaven, and with the most promising hopes of success. Supported by the equity of their principles, they have surmounted the greatest difficulties, and exhibited instances of bravery not exceeded by the heroes of antiquity—and may Heaven prosper their virtuous undertaking.

But it has often been said that America is in a state of rebellion: tell me, therefore, what is rebellion?—It is when a great number of people, headed by one or more factious leaders, aim at deposing their lawful prince, without any just cause of complaint against him, in order to place another on his throne.

Is this the case of America?—By no means. They have repeatedly declared, with all sincerity, that they were ever ready to support, with their lives and fortunes, the present King of Great Britain on the throne of his ancestors, and only requested in return the enjoyment of those inestimable rights which the British Constitution confirms to all its subjects, and without which the boasted freedom of that constitution is but a solemn mockery, and an empty name.

To whom has the British court committea the conduct of the present war?—To Lord and General Howe.

Who are these gentlemen?—They are the brothers of a Colonel Howe, who fought bravely by the side of the Americans in a former war, and fell in battle; who, by his amiable character, endeared himself to those people so much, that they lamented his fate with unfeigned sorrow, and erected, at their own expense, a costly monument to his memory. But these gentlemen, with unrelenting hearts and sacrilegious hands, have defiled their brother's monument with the blood of those whose affection reared it to his honor, and plunged their murderous weapons into bosoms glowing with love and esteem for their mother's son.[1]

What progress have the English made in subduing America?—Very little. They got possession of Boston by the tacit consent of its inhabitants, but could not hold it long. They were but tenants at will, strictly speaking, for their landlords turned them out without any warning, and distrained upon certain military stores, &c., although they had sat there at a rent of about five hundred pounds per day.

What did they next?—They took Staten Island, where there was nothing to oppose them, and a part of Long Island, by an exertion of almost their whole force against a small part of the American army, and then ferried themselves over to the city of New York; from thence they crept into the Jerseys,

---

[1] Lord Viscount George Howe was the eldest son of Sir E. Scrope, second Lord Viscount in Ireland. He arrived at Halifax in the summer of 1757, having under his command five thousand British troops, who had been despatched from England to assist in the expedition against the French. In the next year he was with Abercrombie at the renowned attack on Ticonderoga, and at the first fire of the French, who were posted in the woods a short distance westward of the fort, he fell mortally wounded. "In him the soul of the army seemed to expire." His kindly disposition, bravery, and many virtues, endeared him to the soldiers; and Massachusetts, as a "proof of her love and esteem for his gallantry and daring," erected a monument to his memory in Westminster Abbey. At the time of his death he was thirty-three years of age.

and taking advantage of a critical period, when the American army was disbanded by the terms of enlistment, and before a new force could be raised, they heroically advanced to the banks of the Delaware, well knowing there was nothing to oppose their progress.   On the banks of the Delaware they set them down, settled, as they thought, for the winter season, and plundered the adjacent country.   In the mean time these extraordinary conductors of the war published a wonderful and gracious proclamation, offering such protection as they could afford to all those who would accept of it, upon the easy terms of absolute, unconditional submission.   But the Americans, whose resources are endless, soon found a spirited militia to supply the place of the disbanded troops until a new army could be raised.   This militia crossed the Delaware in a snow storm at midnight, and after marching ten miles, very uncivilly attacked the enemy before they had breakfasted, and drove them from the banks of the Delaware in the utmost consternation, and with a loss of twelve hundred men.   The American army then recrossed the Delaware and suffered the enemy to return to their post, where they anxiously waited the arrival of an expected reinforcement.   But the American general, by a stroke of policy above their comprehension, once more passed the river with his army, and kindled a few fires in the night near their station ; and whilst they were foolishly gazing at the beauty of the curling flames, he marched on, attacked, routed, and entirely defeated the said reinforcement.   The shattered remains of General Howe's army are now close confined in Brunswick, where they are doing penance on salt meat and musty biscuit.

Where are injustice, obstinacy, and folly united in one character in an eminent degree?—In George the Third. He is unjust, because he endeavors to gain by force what is denied him by the laws of the realm over which he presides, in direct violation of his coronation oath, and pursues his unconstitutional claims to the effusion of human blood ; he is obstinate, because he refuses to hear the humble petitions and modest reasonings of an oppressed people, and will not yield to the forcible convictions of truth ; and his folly is conspicuous in quarrelling with a people who loved and honored him, who were the chief supporters of his crown and dignity, and a never-failing source of increasing wealth.

Who is the soggiest man in the world?—Lord Howe.

Who is the weakest?—General Howe.

Who is the greatest liar upon earth?—Hugh Gaine, of New York, printer.[1]

Who is the most ungrateful man in the world?—Governor Skinner.[2]

Why do you call him governor?—Because when Lord and General Howe thought that they had conquered the Jerseys, they appointed him lieutenant-governor of that State. Skinner assumed that title over one-tenth part of the said State, and continued his usurpation for six weeks, five days, thirty-six minutes, ten seconds, and thirty hundred parts of a second, and then was deposed.

Why is he called ungrateful?—Because he has joined the enemies of his country, and enlisted men to fight against his neighbors, his friends, and his kinsfolk; because he has endeavored to transfer the soil that gave him bread from the rightful possessors to a foreign hand; because he is doing all he can to defraud the fruit of his body of their just inheritance; and because, to gain present ease and transitory honors, he would fasten the chains of slavery on three millions of people and their offspring forever.

Who is the best man living?—His Excellency General Washington, to whom the title of Excellency is applied with the greatest propriety. He has left a peaceful habitation and an affluent fortune to encounter all the dangers and hardships of war, nobly stepping forth in the defence of truth, justice, and his country. In private life he wins the hearts and wears the love of all who are so happy as to live within the sphere of his action. In his public character he commands universal respect and admiration. Conscious that the principles on which he acts are indeed founded on virtue, he steadily and

[1] And editor of the New York Gazette and Weekly Mercury.
[2] Cortlandt Skinner.

coolly pursues those principles, with a mind neither depressed by disappointments nor elated by success, giving full exercise to that discretion and wisdom which he so eminently possesses. He retreats like a general and acts like a hero. If there are spots in his character, they are like the spots in the sun, only discernible by the magnifying powers of a telescope. Had he lived in the days of idolatry, he had been worshipped as a god. One age cannot do justice to his merit, but the united voices of a grateful posterity shall pay a cheering tribute of undissembled praise to the great asserter of their country's freedom.[1]

FEBRUARY 18.—OUR cruel enemies are still in possession of Newport, Rhode Island, but by all appearances they will not infest it three weeks hence. Percy, the person so famous for his *well*-ordered retreat from Lexington, is, since Clinton's departure, chief commander on the island, and makes head-quarters at Mr. Levy's house, near the parade. By the best accounts that can be collected, their numbers do not exceed three thousand ; they give out five or six thousand. From two or three of their late villanous papers it may easily be discovered they are not unacquainted with the art of lying. One of them contains an address to Clinton, signed by four hundred and forty-four of the inhabitants, welcoming him to the island, desiring his protection, swearing allegiance to George the Third, acknowledging him as their true and lawful sovereign, and expressing their surprise at the strange infatuation of a deluded people, who are led into the present rebellion by the art of a few designing men.

By the most authentic information, one-half of the signers were induced to put their names to the address by the persuasions of the principal Tories, who, by the assistance of all the powers of darkness and the father of liars at their head, in order to carry their point, gave out that Philadelphia was in their possession, and Connecticut had, to a man, laid down their arms and sworn allegiance to George the Third.

British at Newport, R. I.

[1] Pennsylvania Journal, February 19.

There are one hundred flat bottom boats building with all expedition in the different parts of Rhode Island. The other day two or three scows with soldiers went from Providence to quarter at Tiverton. Their appearance in passing through Bristol ferry caused a general alarm on the island, and set the Hessians to retreating with the utmost precipitancy with their baggage, into the town. There is no doubt but that six thousand troops could dispossess these sons of Belial with the greatest ease; a trial of which we expect very shortly. Doctor H——r's death and false character was lately published in one of their papers. May it be the fate of every Tory scoundrel that now infests this once happy land, to make his exit out of America before the present month is closed.[1]

AT the adjourned superior court lately held at Hartford, in Connecticut, the following persons were convicted of the following crimes, viz. : Moses Dunbar, of Waterbury, convicted of having a captain's commission from General Howe, and enlisting men to serve in the ministerial army—sentenced to suffer death, but the time of his execution is not fixed upon. The Reverend Roger Viets, of Simsbury, convicted of aiding and assisting Major French, and a number of other prisoners, in making their escape, and holding a traitorous correspondence with the enemy—sentenced to pay twenty pounds to the State, and suffer one year's imprisonment. Gurdon Whitmore, of Middletown, found guilty of high treason by the jury, but an arrest of judgment being pleaded in his favor, a final determination of the trial was put off till March next. At the same time the Reverend Mr. Nichols, of Waterbury, was tried for treasonable practices against the United States, and acquitted.[2]

Connecticut Criminals.

FEBRUARY 27.—By a passage from the London papers it appears that the mildness of the Massachusetts government, and the generosity of the Whigs to the Tories, is attributed altogether to timidity, and an apprehension that the cause of the Americans is gone. "It is now

Massachusetts Lenity.

[1] Pennsylvania Evening Post, March 8.   [2] Upcott, iv. 453.

very common," says the passage referred to, " to see the friends
of government walking arm in arm in the streets of Boston,
unnoticed ; and they hold meetings and visit one another,
which they have not done since General Gage's army came
among them.   In short, it is said they are very much dis-
heartened."   It seems, then, that the Tories are allowed more
liberty under the present government than they were in Gage's
time, which is undoubtedly true; but then all is owing to fear.
It is in this manner our enemies construe all we say and do.
The humanity with which we have treated those who have
fallen into our hands by the fortunes of war, is ascribed to the
same principle of fear, and has been returned by the most barbarous treatment of the subjects and friends of the United
States, who have fallen into their hands—even the sailors on
voyages of mere trade.   They have been murdered in a system-
atical way, by crowding them together in cells and dungeons,
and gradually starving them.   This is not high painting ; it is
literally true.

But we may venture to say, it is not the interest of our
enemies to treat us in this manner.   If gratitude will not,
prudence ought to teach them better.   Did the impartial
world know all the circumstances, and the unexampled provo-
cations we have met with, they would admire us as much for
our moderation and mildness, as for our bravery and love of
liberty.[1]

MARCH 1.—A DESERTER from the rebel army at Westchester,
who came into New York this morning, says that the Congress
troops are suffering extremely for food and rum ;   State of the
that there is not a whole pair of breeches in the   American Army.
army, and that the last news from Mr. Washington's camp
was, that he had to tie his up with strings, having parted with
the buttons to buy the necessaries of life.   There is a great
plenty of rag money, but since old Franklin went to France,
there is no one left to argue it into the favor of the Jerseymen,
who, though justly called republicans, are not willing to give

[1] Freeman's Journal, March 4.

even bad provisions for Congress notes, or mere rebel promises
to pay.   At a *frugal* dinner lately given by the under officers
in Heath's command, (supposed to be in honor of his *demand*
at Fort Independence,[1]) but seven were able to attend ; some
for the want of clean linen, but the most of them from having
none other than breeches past recovery.[2]

MARCH 4.—THIS day at noon, " His Excellency Thomas
Wharton, jun., Esq., President of the Supreme Executive Council of the Commonwealth of Pennsylvania, Cap-
tain-General and Commander-in-Chief in and over
the same," was proclaimed at the court house in Philadelphia,
in the presence of a vast concourse of people, who expressed the
highest satisfaction on the occasion by unanimous shouts of
acclamation.

*Thomas Wharton
Inaugurated.*

[1] This refers to the attempt made in January, 1777, to take Fort Independence,
and thus secure a passage into New York island.   About four thousand militia, in
four divisions, under Generals Heath, Wooster, Parsons, and Lincoln, were destined for the service.   General Heath was commander-in-chief.   All met on the
heights about and near Kingsbridge.   The fort had but a trifling garrison, which
could have made no effectual resistance had a vigorous push been made; and the
men were in spirits for the attempt.   In this way only could it be carried, was
defence attempted, as the Americans had no other artillery than three field-pieces.
With these they fired a number of shots at eighty or one hundred Hessians, and a
few light horse, who collected on the York side of Harlem River.   The Hessians
were thrown into a momentary confusion, but soon formed again.   General Heath
demanded a surrender of the fort, and threatened in case of non-compliance.
The threat was disregarded.   The troops were now employed chiefly in picking up
Tories, in foraging, and in taking stores that had been in the possession of the
enemy, till more artillery could arrive from Peekskill, which a council of war had
agreed to send for.

About nine days from the first appearance of the Americans before the fort,
the artillery came to hand, and consisted of one brass twenty-four pounder and
two howitzers.   The twenty-four pounder was fired twice when the carriage
broke; and a few shells were thrown without any execution.   A great number of
teams were then employed in carrying off forage.   The British, who had been reinforced during these delays, sallied out, but were repulsed.   Soon after the
Americans retired.   General Heath's conduct was censured by men of sense and
judgment, who were with him on the expedition.   It was fraught with so much
caution, that the army was disappointed, and in some degree disgraced.   His
summons, as he did not fulfil his threats, was idle and farcical, and tended to bring
on all of them the ridicule of their enemies.—*Gordon*, ii. 181.

[2] Smythe's Diary, 51.

The procession began at the state house, and was conducted in the following order, viz. :—Constables with their
staves; Sub-Sheriffs; High-Sheriff and Coroner; His Excellency the President and Vice-President; Members of the Supreme Executive Council; Sergeant-at-Arms; the Honorable
Speaker of the House—Clerk of the House on his left hand;
Members of the General Assembly; gentlemen members of
the Council of Safety, and the Navy Board. These dined together at the city tavern, where an entertainment was provided
by order of the House; the members of Congress then in the
city, and the general officers of the army of the United States
of America, being also present.

After dinner the following healths were drank, under the
discharge of cannon, &c. :—1. The United States of America.
2. The Congress. 3. The Commonwealth of Pennsylvania.
4. General Washington, and the Army of the United States
of America. 5. The Navy of the United States. 6. The
Friends of Liberty in all parts of the world. 7. Perpetual
union and strict friendship among the States of America. 8.
The Arts and Sciences. 9. Agriculture. 10. Trade and Nav-
igation. 11. The memory of the brave patriots, of all ranks,
who have gloriously fallen in their country's cause. 12. May
every American know his true interest. 13. May Justice,
Firmness, and Humanity, ever characterize Americans. 14.
May human Knowledge, Virtue, and Happiness, receive their
last perfection in America. 15. May every private consideration give way to the means of our public defence. 16. General Lee, and all our friends in captivity. 17. Doctor Franklin.

The bells of the city were rung, and the whole was conducted with the utmost decency, and no accident happened of
any kind.[1]

RAN away from Isaac Harris, living in Pittsgrove, Salem
County, Pennsylvania, an English servant man, named William
Blackmore; about twenty-two years of age; five feet five, or
six feet high; light complexion, light straight hair; a very

[1] Freeman's Journal, April 5.

clumsy fellow, turns the toe of his right foot very much out in his walk; very much addicted to swearing and getting drunk; he has run away several times, and has an iron collar round his neck, marked I. H. and W. B., which he wears under his shirt, but may be easily discovered. Had on, when he went away, a brown cloth coat with blue sleeves, a light colored cloth jacket, leather breeches, and blue stockings. All recruiting officers are requested not to enlist him. He will endeavor to get to the ministerial army if he has opportunity, as he is a great Tory. Whosoever takes up and secures the said servant in any gaol so that his master may have him again, shall receive six dollars and reasonable charges paid if brought home.[1]

MARCH 6.—DAY before yesterday, departed this life, in the fifty-sixth year of his age, the Reverend Samuel Auchmuty, D. D., Rector of Trinity Church in New York, a gentleman greatly beloved and respected.

He was born at Boston, in the province of Massachusetts Bay, and educated at the college of Cambridge, in the same colony, where he took the usual degrees in the liberal arts. He devoted himself early to the sacred ministry, and soon after his ordination was fixed as assistant minister of Trinity Church and catechist, in the year 1748; in which stations he continued till 1764, when, on the death of the late worthy Doctor Barclay,[2] he was chosen Rector. About this time the degree of Doctor in Divinity was conferred on him by the University of Oxford.

Samuel Auchmuty.

During his residence in New York, which was twenty-nine years, he discharged the pastoral duties of his function with assiduity and fidelity; of which, the respect showed to him by the inhabitants, and the flourishing state of the Episcopal congregations in the city when our public troubles broke out, are incontestable proofs.

Firmly and conscientiously attached to the doctrines and discipline of the Church of England, he was indefatigable in promoting her interests; yet without any of that narrow spirit

[1] Pennsylvania Journal, March 12.   [2] Henry Barclay, D. D.

of bigotry, which is the disgrace of religion. His sentiments were generous and enlarged, which led him to prize
merit wherever he found it, and this disposition and conduct
will ever command the approbation of the rational and virtuous part of mankind, and succeed where bigotry will assuredly fail.

Christianity never appears more amiable or winning than
when accompanied with that easy-tempered cheerfulness
which rectitude and benevolence of heart naturally inspire.
In this he greatly excelled, and it gave him many advantages
to serve the cause of religion.

Few men ever possessed a more humane, benevolent, and
compassionate heart. He often melted into tears at the sight
of distress, which never sought his aid in vain. He was a
liberal, sympathizing friend to the indigent and afflicted, a
zealous promoter of every institution or scheme that could
contribute to the welfare of mankind, and was never more
happy than when alleviating the misfortunes of others, or employed in some office of benevolence and friendship.

Such a temper and disposition must necessarily endear him
to his intimate acquaintances, and enable him to shine in
the more tender connections of social life. He was indeed a
sincere, warm friend, a most affectionate, tender husband and
father.

Those who were unfriendly to the Church of England and
to the British Constitution could hardly be well affected to him,
considering his station and principles. Yet no man had a
more placable, forgiving disposition under injuries or ill usage.
He pitied those misguided people; but as for malice, it found
no harbor in his bosom. He practised the Apostolic rule,—
Let not the sun go down upon your wrath.

During the troubles which have involved this country
in its present calamities, he took that part, as may be easily
supposed, which duty, truth, and reason pointed out. Unshaken in his loyalty to our gracious sovereign, and in his
attachment to the Constitution, he spurned the breath of
popular applause where conscience forbid him to receive it.
This drew upon him much persecution, which, with the distress

he felt for the miseries of this country, greatly impaired his constitution; the case could scarcely be otherwise with a person of his extreme sensibility.

His ill state of health obliged him to reside in the country the greatest part of last summer, and when New York was reduced by his Majesty's forces in September, he applied repeatedly to the rebels, in whose hands he was, for leave to return, which was as often denied. This obliged him to come away privately, and exposed him to such hardships, while making his escape, that his constitution was reduced still lower. With difficulty he got there; but how was he shocked on viewing the ruins of so great a part of the city consumed by the fire in September! especially those of Trinity Church, that ancient and once venerable edifice. The sight drew floods of tears from him; and although he lost by the fire, private property to the amount of some thousands of pounds, yet the destruction of Trinity Church, and of so much of the property belonging to its corporation, which has been estimated at forty thousand pounds, affected him much more.

When the King's troops penetrated into Jersey, his family was set at liberty to return. His spirits seemed to revive, his health to mend, and he and his friends indulged themselves in the pleasing expectation of peace and happiness at last, after struggling through so much disquietude, anxiety, and persecution. But alas! these flattering hopes were soon blasted! His lungs had been weakened by constant exertions in preaching, and other parochial duties: a severe cold which he caught at a funeral, and could never wholly get the better of, weakened them still more, and greatly injured his voice. On Tuesday, February twenty-fifth, he was seized with a bilious fever, which, by the assistance of physic, was removed in a great measure, yet left him exceedingly weak, and the disorder settling on his lungs, finally carried him off in a few days.

On his death-bed he behaved with that patience, calmness, and fortitude which became a Christian, and which a well-grounded hope of immortal happiness inspires. In his last moments he retained the perfect use of his understanding and reason, and joined fervently in prayer about four hours before he expired. He died without a struggle or a groan.

To-day his remains were interred in the chancel of St. Paul's church—a church which was built under his inspection, consecrated by him to the service of Almighty God, and where he preached his last sermon on Sunday, February twenty-third, two days before he was seized by his last illness.

Blessed are the dead which die in the Lord, for they rest from their labors, and their works do follow them.[1]

MARCH 8.—THIS day, between the hours of twelve and one o'clock, Brint Debadee, a soldier belonging to the tenth Pennsylvania regiment, was shot upon the commons in Philadelphia, pursuant to the sentence of a general court-martial. Brint Debadee Shot. This unhappy man was in his twenty-fourth year, in the vigor of life, and it is hoped his untimely and dreadful end will be a warning to others, who, when they desert, not only defraud their officer and abuse their country, but are also guilty of the dreadful and heinous crime of perjury. Of his past misconduct he appeared very sensible, and behaved in his last moments with great resignation and calmness, declaring that he sincerely forgave all his enemies, and hoped that his example would be serviceable to some of his thoughtless brother soldiers. He was attended by the Rev. Mr. Coombe, and the Rev. Mr. Rogers. The last gentleman, being a chaplain in the service, delivered to the soldiers present a pathetic address, suitable to the melancholy occasion.[2]

MARCH 9.—YESTERDAY, the British, supposed to be about three thousand, came out from Amboy, and posted themselves on Punk Hill. They brought artillery and a number of wagons, as if to forage, though there Skirmish at Punk Hill, New Jersey. were none left in that neighborhood worth notice. General Maxwell, with the troops under his command, was on a rising ground to the northward, in plain view, though at a good distance. The enemy were too well situated to be attacked.

[1] Gaine's Mercury, March 10. [2] Pennsylvania Evening Post, March 8.

Maxwell sent a party to the left to amuse them, while his real design was to the right, on the heights towards Bonamtown. He sent a strong party that way to examine their lines, if they had any, and to fall in near the end of them, that he might fall on their flank; this was performed by part of Colonel Potter's battalion of Pennsylvania militia, and part of Colonel Thacher's New England troops. Colonel Cook, of the Pennsylvanians, had been ordered from Matuchin to come down on Carman's Hill, and keep along the heights till he met the enemy. About half a mile lower down, between Carman's Hill, and Woodbridge, the two parties being joined, met a strong advanced party of the enemy. On the first firing, Colonel Martin and Lieutenant-Colonel Lindley were sent to support them; they all behaved well and kept their ground till they were supported from the main body, which immediately marched that way. The enemy also sent out a reinforcement, but on another regiment of Americans being sent on the left to cut them off from their main body, the party gave way in great confusion, and the flame catching their main body, all went together. Our people pursued them and took a prisoner and a baggage wagon close in their rear, a good way down in the plain ground. Bonamtown lay too near on the right, and a plain, open ground towards Amboy, to pursue far. They left four dead on the field, and we took three prisoners. By the quantity they carried off in sleds and wagons, it is supposed they had near twenty killed, and twice that number wounded.

General Maxwell says that by a soldier taken prisoner, he learns that General Howe was at Bonamtown during the engagement, till he saw his troops make the best of their way home, when he thought it was time for him to go.[1]

MARCH 15.—I am no prophet, nor the son of a prophet, yet I believe in the prophecies of the Old and New Testaments, and also in some other prophecies; nor can I forbear thinking

---

[1] Extract of a letter from Haddonfield, New Jersey, in Pennsylvania Journal, March 19.

there is something prophetic and important in the number *seven*—else why do the holy scriptures hold out the number seven so frequently, and so remarkably? There we may read that God rested from his work the ^{Behman's Seven.} seventh day, that the seventh day is the Sabbath, of the seventh year of release, of seven times seven being the year of the jubilee, of seven vials, seven trumpets, seven golden candlesticks, and of the seven spirits of God. In civil story, too, the number seven is distinguished. Witness the seven wonders of the world, seven wise men of Greece, and the seven champions of Christendom. Seven days make a week; the seventh son is of course a doctor, and nine sevens form the grand climacteric year. If there should be, indeed, any peculiar significancy in the number seven, which I believe no one will be hardy enough to dispute, the oftener that number occurs in any subject, especially in dates and eras, the more significant and important must be the subject, date, or era; from hence the importance of the present year, in which three sevens unite, may be fairly deduced.

I have been led to these reflections by a tradition which hath been handed down from the first settlement of New England: that when three sevens should meet in the date of the year, the American colonies would become independent States; and a prophecy that was some years ago published—that in the year 1777 there would be war throughout Europe. Whether appearances favor this last prophecy or not, let those say who are better acquainted with the European States than I am, and know how the war between the United States of America and Great Britain will affect them; but a great number of circumstances concur to countenance the prophecy respecting the establishment of American Independency, which are too obvious to be mentioned.

I cannot, however, leave this subject without acknowledging my great obligations to an ingenious gentleman, who is deeply read in prophecies, for furnishing me with the following prophecy, which relates directly to my subject, and had escaped my observation. Alexander Pedan, an eminent Scotch divine, not more remarkable for his piety and suffer-

ings than his spirit of prophecy, hath left it on record, that
when three sevens should meet, a star of the first lustre and
magnitude would fall from the crown of Great Britain. Most
prophecies are delivered in enigmatical terms, which time only
can develop. However, may we not conjecture that the noted
divine, Alexander Pedan, had in idea the present year? And
does it require much skill in enigmatical learning to see
through these prophecies, and to conclude, with a degree of
confidence, that this very year, 1777, will be the grand jubilee
of American Freedom and Independency?

May He that holdeth the seven stars in his right hand accomplish the prophecy! Thus devoutly wisheth and prayeth
Behman.[1]

A CORRESPONDENT in London says, that since the ministry
have not been able, by their arms, to reduce America, a pro-
A scheme to reduce jector has delivered to them a scheme which will
the Americans. soon bring the rebels to an unconditional submission; and it is confidently reported that administration have
with great avidity adopted it, and mean to carry it into execution by contract, proposals for which having already been
received from two Englishmen and eleven Scotchmen. It is
that sixty thousand barrels of lamp black be immediately
bought in Russia, Prussia, or Scotland, and that it be sent on
or before midsummer day to the respective colonies; that
commissioners be appointed in every such colony to *paint* the
faces, and every other part of the bodies of the Americans as
black as negroes; and that soon after this operation they shall
be sold, as negroes are, at public auction, twenty in a lot, to
the Creole planters of Jamaica, Barbadoes, Antigua, &c., and
that the money arising from such sales be principally applied
in improving his Majesty's loyal but barren kingdom of Scotland, and the remainder in pensions to North, Bute, Mansfield,
the two Howes, the Minden hero, Governors Dunmore, Tryon,
and their heirs for three lives, and five pounds a year to every
Bostonian in Brompton Row, who will return thither and be
the negro drivers.[2]

---

[1] Freeman's Journal, March 15.   [2] Pennsylvania Journal, July 23.

MARCH 17.—LAST night, a detachment of the Queen's rangers, and New York companies, with twenty of the Hessian troops, and a subaltern, under the command of Captains John Branden and Archibald Campbell, Fight at Ward's House. were ordered out from New York to attack a party of the rebels at De Lancey's Mills, in Westchester county ; but they having intelligence of the movement of our detachment, fled to the house of Stephen Ward, about nine miles north from Kingsbridge, where the party attacked them, about nine o'clock at night, killed between forty and fifty, and took twenty-seven prisoners, amongst whom were a major, a captain, (wounded,) and a forage-master. They brought off at the same time twenty-four head of cattle, and four horses, part of which the rebels had robbed the friends of government of that day. Our loss would have been very inconsiderable, had it not been for the death of the brave Campbell, who, after the villains had begged for quarters, went into the house, and was immediately shot through the heart. We had five privates killed on the spot, and six wounded, one of whom is since dead.[1]

MARCH 20.—THIS morning, a young woman passing an evacuated house in Woodbridge, New Jersey, saw through the window a drunken Hessian soldier, who had straggled from his party. There being no men within less than a mile of the town, she went home, dressed herself in man's apparel, and armed with an old firelock, returned to the house, entered it, and took the Hessian prisoner, whom she soon stripped of his arms and was leading off, when she fell in with the patrol guard of a New Jersey regiment, stationed near Woodbridge, to whom she delivered her prisoner.[2]

MARCH 27.—THE American post at Peekskill, New York, since the removal of the militia of the Eastern States, has been in a manner in a defenceless situation, there being only part of two regiments stationed there, Attack on Peekskill, N. Y. under the care of General McDougal, amounting to about two

[1] Gaine's Mercury, March 24.   [2] Freeman's Journal, April 26.

hundred and fifty men. The enemy having received intelligence of this, formed an expedition thither with a view to take or destroy the stores belonging to the continentals, that were deposited there. Accordingly, on Sunday last, 23d, they appeared with a frigate, four transports, and several other small vessels, in the bay, and landed about one thousand men, with several pieces of cannon. General McDougal not thinking it prudent to hazard a battle with such an unequal force, and not having seasonable advice of the enemy's movement, was under the necessity of destroying the stores in order to prevent their falling into their hands, and retired about two miles into the pass in the Highlands, carrying with him his baggage and military stores, his advanced guard being stationed at Courtlandt's house, in the valley. The enemy the same day took possession of the village, and remained close in their quarters until the next day in the afternoon, when a party of them, consisting of about two hundred men, possessed themselves of a height a little south of Courtlandt's. The general having received a reinforcement from Colonel Gansevoort's [1] regiment of about eighty men, under the command of Lieutenant-Colonel Willett,[2] permitted them to attempt to dispossess the enemy from that eminence.

Colonel Willett having accordingly made the necessary disposition, advanced with his small party with the greatest firmness and resolution, and made the attack. The enemy instantly fled with the greatest precipitation, leaving three men dead on the field, and the whole body, panic-struck, betook themselves to their shipping, embarking under cover of the night; and by the last accounts they had sailed down the river. Before they embarked, they gave out that they intended to stop at Tarrytown, on their way down, and attempt to destroy our magazine of forage at Wright's mills. Upon their evacuating the place, General McDougal took possession of his former quarters, and detached a party of men to watch their motions. The enemy on this occasion have been exceedingly disappointed, as they have not been able to carry off any stores left be-

---

[1] Peter Gansevoort, Jr.   [2] Marinus Willett.

hind by our men, and no other stock than about forty sheep, and eight or ten head of cattle, with which they were supplied by our good friends, the Tories. Never did troops exhibit more firmness and resolution than did our army on this occasion. Notwithstanding the disparity of numbers was great, and the measure absolutely necessary, it was with the utmost reluctance they retired to the pass. As usual, these heroes of Britain have burnt some houses, plundered the inhabitants of what they could conveniently take with them, frightened the women and children, and raised the spirits of their Tory brethren in that quarter; but which, alas! as is always the case when unnaturally elevated, are now again proportionately depressed.[1]

A British officer in this expedition gives another account of it:—On Saturday last and the two following days, an important enterprise was effected upon a large magazine, which the rebels had formed at Peekskill, near British account of the Highlands, under the conduct of Colonel the Attack on Peekskill. Bird and Major Hope, assisted by Lieutenant Durnford of the Engineers, with only five hundred men. The troops were embarked on board four transports on Saturday, with every precaution of secrecy as to their destination, and proceeded up the North River under the convoy of the Brune frigate, Captain Ferguson, and an armed galley. They came upon the rebels, almost unapprised of the adventure, on the Sunday afternoon, who soon ran away from their post, (though they were at least equal to the troops in number,) with the greatest precipitation. Before they quitted the spot, they set fire to the mills up Gregory's Creek, in which were stored above five hundred barrels of flour, and eighty hogsheads of rum, also to two large storehouses containing an immense quantity of military stores; and to their forage yard, with all the hay, straw, and corn. They likewise staved a great number of hogsheads of rum, during the approach of the ships.

Immediately upon landing, the troops advanced to the ex-

---

[1] Connecticut Journal, April 2.

ecution of their design, and burnt and destroyed the whole magazine, the barracks, the workshops, storehouses, and all the appurtenances of this principal deposit of military furniture and stores, which the rebels had been forming for a long time with the greatest expense and labor. Besides the barracks, which were exceedingly well constructed, and several other buildings, above one hundred and fifty new wagons were committed to the flames, together with a vast collection of intrenching tools, carpenter's tools, and an immense quantity of beef, pork, flour, rice, and biscuit, all in casks, and above four hundred hogsheads of rum. Many casks of tallow, boxes of candles, hogsheads of molasses, about a dozen casks of coffee, some boxes of chocolate, chests of arms, artillery stores, thirty casks of nails, twenty boxes of grape shot, and a large quantity of bar and slit iron, were either conveyed to the ships, or entirely destroyed. The camp equipage, belonging to McDougal, who commands the rebels in that quarter, was in part destroyed, and in part brought away, with some officers' uniforms, and colors. In the conflagration, which with such a collection of combustible matters may be easily imagined to have been prodigious, a large quantity of bark for tanning, and of leather for shoes and other purposes, was consumed. In short, the destruction was complete and effectual, scarce any thing escaping that could be of use either to the troops or to the rebels. Several sloops and boats were likewise destroyed, and others brought off laden with some of the most valuable articles. A fine twelve-pounder, which the rebels had placed there, was dismounted, and left without its trunnions. The whole affair was carried on with the utmost spirit and harmony, and to the honor of the soldiers it may be said, that not one of them, among the streams of rum that run about in every quarter, was in the least disordered in his duty. They only expressed their disappointment in not having had a brush with the rebels. Nothing could exceed the cool intrepidity and precautions of the commanding officers throughout the enterprise, nor the alacrity and vigor of the whole party. Not a man was lost or hurt upon the occasion. The sailors performed their part with equal spirit, and as British seamen are used to do. The loss of the rebels cannot be easily calculated; their disappointment and want, in consequence of it, may be more easily guessed at, and the more, as that loss is now irreparable.[1]

MARCH 31.—THIS day, James Molesworth, a spy, was executed on the commons near Philadelphia. It appears by sundry evidences, and his own confession, that he had been sent from New York to procure pilots for conducting the British fleet up the river Delaware.[2]

[1] Gaine's Mercury, March 31.   [2] Upcott, v. 15.

CHAPTER X.

APRIL 1.—THE pasteboard dollars of the Congress are now refused by the hottest among the rebels themselves. One, who was a member of a committee to punish those who might refuse them, was lately punished for refusing them himself; and, in short, every one is putting them off from himself, in exchange for almost any thing that can be got for them.[1]

Yesterday, a Connecticut parson, with a parcel of the rag money in one of his moccasins, was taken at Kingsbridge and brought into New York. He was this morning obliged to chew up all the money, and declare, in the presence of a large assemblage of people, that he will not again pray for the Congress, or their doer of dirty work, Mr. Washington; on the conclusion of which he was set at liberty, with orders not to go above the third line. He is an obstinate hypocrite, but will now have plenty of time for psalmody and repentance, which latter, I *veouw*, he stands much in need of.[2]

APRIL 5.—LAST Thursday, a party of rebels, under the command of one George Babcock, came into the house of Mr. Charles Slocum, at North Kingston.[3] His son coming to the door, was immediately collared by one of the banditti. Young Slocum clenched with him, and would soon have made him repent his rashness, had it not been for the interference of the rest of the gang. His father, seeing the scuffle, came out of the house to interfere in behalf of his son, when the infamous Babcock discharged a pistol at him. The ball entered a little below his heart, and he died in

Affair at North Kingston, R. I.

---

[1] Upcott, iv. 463.   [2] Smythe's Journal.   [3] In Rhode Island.

about three hours. Not content with the misery they had already occasioned to this unhappy family, they took both his sons and dragged them before their assembly, who, in their clemency, permitted them to return under a strong guard to attend the funeral of their murdered father. The mourning relatives were accordingly escorted to the grave by this unfeeling clan, who immediately upon their return home, carried both the young men off to Providence jail. This unparalleled barbarity is said to be occasioned by the information of some villain that has escaped from Newport.

Every breast susceptible of the miseries of its fellow creatures must feel for this unhappy family—a husband murdered! a number of orphan children deprived of him to whom they were wont to look up for support; and to complete the tragic scene, two sons, whose presence at home might in some measure have alleviated the loss of their parent, are likewise torn from their wives, expecting soon to share the same cruel fate. And all this performed by men who have decorated their standard with the specious names of *Liberty* and *Justice*.[1]

APRIL 14.—DAY before yesterday, General Lord Cornwallis, Generals Grant and Matthews, with the first battalion of grenadiers, one battalion of light infantry, a detachment of the guards, the light horse, two battalions of Hessians, and the Yagers, commanded by Colonel Donop, marched from New Brunswick, in New Jersey, between eight and nine o'clock at night, in order to surprise a large body of the rebels stationed at Boundbrook, seven miles distance from that city, commanded by a General Lincoln. The expedition was conducted with so much secrecy that scarce any of the inhabitants knew of the departure of the troops till Sunday morning. They avoided the roads, and got close to the rebel intrenchments before day; heard the sentinels cry " All's well," and were ordered to lie on their arms till the rebels should fire their morning gun. The order being given for the attack, their troops rushed on with their

Skirmish at Boundbrook.

usual intrepidity, and put the rebels to flight, killed upwards
of one hundred, took seventy-three prisoners, (among whom
was one of Lincoln's aide-de-camps, one captain, one lieutenant, and a man in irons, sentenced by the rebels to be shot,)
three brass cannon, a quantity of arms, two wagons loaded
with ammunition, a number of horses, one hundred and twenty head of cattle, sheep, hogs, &c., besides destroying three
hundred barrels of flour, several hogsheads of whiskey and
New England rum, with sundry other articles that the flourishing States cannot very well spare. The troops returned on
Sunday forenoon, and the rebels crawled back to Boundbrook
on their departure. Our loss was one man killed, and two
Yagers wounded.

Many of the friends of government availed themselves of
the confusion the rebels were thrown in by the above disaster,
and came into Brunswick with the troops ; several of the rebels embraced the same opportunity, and brought in their arms.

It is said that the rebel general had not time to collect his
clothes, his safety requiring his utmost dexterity and swiftness.

The prisoners were brought to New York to-day, and are
lodged in gaol with their wretched brethren.[1]

THE late proclamation, issued by Sir William Howe, we

---

[1] Upcott, v. 19.   The following is another account of this action:—"On Saturday, the 12th instant, Lord Cornwallis, with the Generals Grant and Matthews,
with a body of British troops, and Colonel Donop with a detachment of Hessians,
surprised a large body of the rebels at Boundbrook, about seven miles from Brunswick, New Jersey, under the command of one *Benjamin Lincoln*, late secretary to
the conventions and congresses of Massachusetts Bay, and a forward person in
all the rebellious proceedings of that colony.   The troops lay upon their arms till
daybreak, and commenced the attack upon the rear of the rebel quarters, who
made so weak a resistance as only to wound slightly four of the soldiers.   Above
one hundred of the rebels were killed, eighty-five taken prisoners, among whom
was a fellow who passed for Lincoln's aide-de-camp, and two others under the
style of officers.   The rebels taken have been brought to town, and are the most
miserable looking creatures that ever bore the name of soldiers, being covered
with nothing but rags and vermin.   Three brass field-pieces, muskets, ammunition,
camp equipage, papers, several horses, near two hundred head of cattle, with
sheep, hogs, rum, flour, bread, &c., were chiefly brought away, and the rest, such
as the rum and salted provisions, being very bad, were destroyed."—*Gaine's
Mercury*, April 21.

hear, has been read to the several corps in the rebel army, by their respective leaders, who strove to show them that the design of it was to lead them to bondage and destruc-   Hugh Gaine's
Facts and
tion, to alienate them from their allegiance to Mes-   Criticisms.
sieurs *John Hancock, Samuel Adams,* and the other members of the Congress, and to bring them out of their present state of happiness and freedom. Many and wonderful were the speeches made upon this occasion, all founded upon an evident fear lest their poor deluded followers should see and think for themselves. Their fear seems to have been just ; for many, in following their own senses, have quitted the desperate and wicked cause they have been engaged in, and have brought in (some of them at least) two or three muskets apiece, for which they have been handsomely paid in *silver* dollars.[1] Some whole companies have come in, and particularly from the northward. A party of them who came up a few days since from Amboy, in order to join the royal provincials, were astonished to see any ships in New York harbor, as it had been industriously reported among the rebels that they were all sailed for England, and that the troops were to quit the colonies as soon as fresh ships could arrive to carry them home. A very few weeks will convict these impostors of their numberless falsehoods.

Several men-of-war, and above one hundred transports, are stationed in the North River. The East River is crowded with merchantmen, prize-vessels, and ships of all sorts.

A correspondent remarks, that whilst most of the other seaport towns and colonies groan under the dearness of provisions, and the common necessaries of life, New York is supplied, at very little more than the usual rate in this season of the year, with every species of food and all kinds of clothing and dry goods.

The Philadelphia newspapers are stuffed with continual false accounts of skirmishes and other exploits of their ragamuffins in the Jerseys, in which they always obtain most wonder-

---

[1] The Congress paper dollars are now used for papering rooms, lighting pipes, and other conveniences.—*Carver.*

ful and "never-to-be-heard-of-victories." The following may
serve for a specimen, taken from the *Pennsylvania Journal*
of the second of April. In a skirmish, which is stated to have
happened near Quibbletown on the twenty-fourth of March,
they say the British " must have lost some men, as they were
seen carrying them off in the time of action, which happened
within half a mile of their breastworks. We had two rifles
broke, but not a man hurt in this skirmish ; an evident proof,
that Providence shields the just and brave, (they mean themselves,) for we forced them from an advantageous wood, where
they were posted behind trees and our people entirely exposed
in an open field. The troops that were engaged with ours
were British and not Hessian. Our whole party did not
exceed one hundred and thirty, and the enemy not less than
three hundred men." What opinion must these people have
of their followers, when they suppose them capable of believ-
ing such enormous falsehoods as these?

Some days ago, the daughter of Mr. Jonathan Kniffin, of
Rye, in Connecticut, was murdered by a party of rebels near
or upon Budd's Neck. She was carrying some clothes to her
father in company of two men who had the charge of a herd
of cattle. They were fired upon by the rebels from behind a
stone wall. The poor young woman received a ball in her
head, of which she instantly died. The men escaped unhurt.
They plundered her dead body of its clothes, cut one of her
fingers almost off in order to take a ring, and left the corpse
most indecently exposed in the highway. Such are the advocates of this cursed rebellion ! Yet the officer (so called) who
commanded the party, and who is said to be a colonel among
the rebels, gloried in the exploit, and swore it was better to kill
one woman than two men ; adding, moreover, that he would
put both man and woman to death, who should presume to
cultivate their farms or their gardens in the neighborhood of
Rye this spring.[1]

THREE men-of-war have sailed up the Delaware, and an-

[1] Gaine's Mercury, April 14.

chored off Reedy Island. This has thrown all the rebellious
part of Philadelphia, with the congress at their head, into the
utmost perturbation. Handbills have been distributed to
implore the people to assemble in arms against the troops of
their sovereign, but it won't do. The people begin to see the
baseness and villany of their leaders, and think it high time to
take care of themselves. Some of the New England and other
people who do not belong to the province, have attempted to
burn the city, and actually did set it on fire in two places.
This has induced the Quakers and other inhabitants to mount
guard every night for the preservation of their property from
destruction by these lawless incendiaries.[1]

APRIL 18.—THE committee appointed by Congress some
time ago to inquire into the conduct of the British troops in
their different marches through New York and   Report on the
New Jersey, have to-day reported :—That in every   Ravages of the British.
place where the enemy has been, there are heavy complaints
of oppression, injury, and insult, suffered by the inhabitants,
from officers, soldiers, and Americans disaffected to their country's cause.

The committee found these complaints so greatly diversi-
fied, that as it was impossible to enumerate them, so it appeared exceedingly difficult to give a distinct and comprehensive
view of them, or such an account as would not appear extremely defective when read by unhappy sufferers or the country in general. In order, however, in some degree to answer the
design of their appointment, they determined to divide the object of their inquiry into the following parts, and briefly state
what they found to be the truth upon each.

First :—*The wanton and oppressive devastation of the
country, and destruction of property.*

The whole track of the British army is marked with desola-
tion, and a wanton destruction of property, particularly through
Westchester county, in the State of New York, the towns of
Newark, Elizabethtown Woodbridge, Brunswick, Kingston,

---

[1] Gaine's Mercury, April 21.

Princeton, and Trenton, in New Jersey. The fences destroyed, houses deserted, pulled in pieces or consumed by fire, and the general face of waste and devastation spread over a rich and once well-cultivated and well-inhabited country, would affect the most unfeeling with compassion for the unhappy sufferers, and with indignation and resentment against the barbarous ravagers.

It deserves notice, that though there are many instances of rage and vengeance against particular persons, yet the destruction was very general and often undistinguished; those who submitted and took protections, and some who were known to favor them, having frequently suffered in the common ruin. Places and things which from their public nature and general utility should have been spared by civilized people, have been destroyed or plundered, or both. But above all, places of worship, ministers, and other religious persons of some particular Protestant denominations, seem to have been treated with the most rancorous hatred, and at the same time with the highest contempt.

Second :—*The inhuman treatment of those who were so unfortunate as to become prisoners.*

The prisoners, instead of that humane treatment which those taken by the United States experienced, were in general treated with the greatest barbarity. Many of them were kept near four days without food altogether. When they received a supply, it was insufficient in quantity, and often of the worst kind. They suffered the utmost distress from cold, nakedness, and close confinement. Freemen and men of substance suffered all that a generous mind could suffer from the contempt and mockery of British and foreign mercenaries. Multitudes died in prison. When they were sent out, several died in being carried from the boats on shore, or upon the road attempting to go home. The committee, in the course of their inquiry, learned that sometimes the common soldiers expressed sympathy with the prisoners, and the foreigners more than the English. But this was seldom or never the case with the officers ; nor have they been able to hear of any charitable assistance given them by the inhabitants who remained in or resorted to the city of New York, which neglect, if universal, they believe was never known to happen in any similar case in a Christian country.

Third :—*The savage butchery of those who had submitted, and were incapable of resistance.*

The committee found it to be the general opinion of the people in the neighborhood of Trenton and Princeton, that the British, the day before the battle of Princeton, had determined to give no quarter. They did not, however, obtain any clear proof that there were general orders for that purpose, but the treatment of several particular persons at and since that time, has been of the most shocking kind, and gives too much countenance to the supposition. Officers wounded and disabled, some of them of the first rank, were barbarously mangled or put to death. A minister of the gospel, who neither was nor had been in arms, was massacred in cold blood at Trenton, though humbly supplicating for mercy.[1]

Fourth :—*The lust and brutality of the soldiers in abusing women.*

The committee had authentic information of many instances of the most indecent treatment and actual ravishment of married and single women ; but such is the nature of that most irreparable injury, that the persons suffering it, though perfectly innocent, look upon it as a kind of reproach to have the facts related, and their names known. Some complaints

---

[1] The following circumstances relative to the death of the Reverend Mr. Roseburgh, chaplain to a battalion of the Pennsylvania militia, who was killed at Trenton, on the evening of the second of January, are given in the affidavit of the Reverend George Duffield:—" As a party of Hessian Jagers marched down the back of the town after the Americans had retreated, they fell in with him, when he surrendered himself a prisoner; notwithstanding which, one of them struck him on the head with a sword or cutlass, and then stabbed him several times with a bayonet, whilst imploring mercy and begging his life at their hands." This account was given by a Hessian, who said that he had killed him, (save only that he did not know Mr. Roseburgh's name, but called him a *damn'd rebel minister*,) and that Cortlandt Skinner, and several other officers who were present at the relation of the fact, highly applauded the perpetrator for what he had done. After he was thus massacred he was stripped naked, and in that condition left lying in an open field, till taken up and buried near the place by some of the inhabitants.—*Pennsylvania Evening Post*, April 29.

were made to the commanding officers on this subject, and one
affidavit made before a justice of the peace, but the committee
could not learn that any satisfaction was ever given, or punishment inflicted, except that one soldier in Pennington was kept
in custody for part of a day.

On the whole, the committee are sorry to say that the cry
of barbarity and cruelty is but too well founded; and as in
conversation those who are cool to the American cause, have
nothing to oppose to the facts but their being incredible and
not like what they are pleased to style the generosity and clemency of the English nation, the committee beg leave to observe
that one of the circumstances most frequently occurring in the
inquiry, was the opprobrious, disdainful names given to the
Americans. These do not need any proof, as they occur so
frequently in the newspapers printed under their direction, and
in the intercepted letters of those who are officers, and call
themselves gentlemen. It is easy, therefore, to see what must
be the conduct of a soldiery greedy of prey, towards a people
whom they have been taught to look upon, not as freemen
defending their rights on principle, but as desperadoes and
profligates, who have risen up against law and order in general, and wish the subversion of society itself. This is the
most charitable and candid manner in which the committee
can account for the melancholy truths which they have been
obliged to report. Indeed, the same deluding principle seems
to govern persons and bodies of the highest rank in Britain;
for it is worthy of notice that not pamphleteers only, but
King and Parliament, constantly call those acts *lenity*, which
on their first publication filled this whole continent with resentment and horror.[1]

APRIL 20.—To THE TORIES.—WANTED for his Majesty's service, as an assistant to his Excellency General Howe and
Hugh Gaine, printers and publishers of the New York Gazette, a gentleman who can lie with ingenuity.

Enquire of Peter Numbskull, collector and composer of

[1] Pennsylvania Evening Post, April 24.

lies for their Excellencies at New York. N. B.—A good hand will receive the honor of knighthood.[1]

A CORRESPONDENT in England says :—An American priva-teer was some time since taken by one of our frigates. She car-ried the continental colors, which are thirteen red and white stripes ; but it was observed that this privateer had but twelve stripes in his colors. On being asked the reason, he answered that since we had taken the province of New York, the Con-gress had a province less ; and that whenever they lost any of the provinces, it was their orders to cut away one of the stripes from their colors, so that there should be no more stripes than provinces.

A gentleman, who was a prisoner in America, has brought to Whitehaven, a Boston almanac for the year, in which the days of his Majesty's birth, accession, &c., are not marked as usual, but the particular days relative to Oliver Cromwell in-stead of them. The year is denoted by the " first of American Independence, which began July 4, 1776." [2]

APRIL 30.—LAST Friday, the twenty-fifth instant, twenty-six sail of British ships appeared off Norwalk Islands, stand-ing in for Cedar Point, where they anchored at four o'clock P. M., and soon began landing troops. Attack on Danbury, Conn. By ten o'clock they had landed two brigades, consisting of up-wards of two thousand men, and marched immediately for Danbury, where they arrived the next day at two o'clock in the afternoon.

The handful of continental troops there were obliged to evac-uate the town, having previously secured a part of the stores and provisions. The British, on their arrival, began burning and destroying the stores, houses, provisions, &c.

On their appearance, the country was alarmed. Early the next morning Brigadier-General Silliman, with about five hun-dred militia, (all that were collected,) pursued them. At Read-

[1] Pennsylvania Journal, April 30.
[2] Low's Astronomical Diary ; Upcott, v. 21.

ing he was joined by Major-General Wooster, and Brigadier-General Arnold. The heavy rain all the afternoon retarded the march of the Americans so much that they did not reach Bethel (a village two miles from Danbury) till eleven o'clock at night, much fatigued, and their arms rendered useless by being wet. It was thought prudent to refresh the men and attack the enemy on their return. Early the next morning, (which proved rainy,) the whole were in motion. Two hundred men remained with General Wooster, and about four hundred were detached under General Arnold and General Silliman, on the road leading to Norwalk. At nine o'clock A. M., intelligence was received that the British had taken the road leading to Norwalk, of which General Wooster was advised, and pursued them. He came up with them about eleven o'clock, when a smart skirmishing ensued, in which General Wooster, who behaved with great intrepidity, unfortunately received a wound by a musket ball through the groin, which it is feared will prove mortal. General Arnold, by a forced march across the country, reached Ridgefield at eleven o'clock, and having posted his small party, (being joined by about one hundred men,) waited the approach of the British, who were soon discovered advancing in a column, with three field-pieces in front and three in rear, and large flank guards of near two hundred men in each. At noon they began discharging their artillery, and were soon within musket shot, when a smart action ensued between the whole, which continued about an hour, in which the Americans behaved with great spirit; but, being overpowered by numbers, were obliged to give way, though not until the enemy were raising a small breastwork, thrown across the way, at which General Arnold had taken post with about two hundred men, (the rest of our small body were posted on the flanks,) who acted with the greatest spirit. The general had his horse shot under him, when the enemy were within about ten yards of him, but luckily received no hurt; recovering himself, he drew his pistol and shot the soldier who was advancing with his fixed bayonet. He then ordered his troops to retreat through a shower of small and grape shot. In the action the British suffered very considerably, leaving about thirty dead and wounded on the ground, besides a number unknown buried. Here we had the misfortune of losing Lieutenant-Colonel Gold, one subaltern, and several privates killed and wounded. It was found impossible to rally our troops, and General Arnold ordered a stand to be made at Saugatuck bridge, where it was expected the enemy would pass.

At nine o'clock on the morning of the 28th, about five hundred men were collected at Saugatuck bridge, including part of the companies of Colonel Lamb's battalion of artillery, with three field-pieces, under command of Lieutenant-Colonel Oswald, a field-piece with part of the artillery company from Fairfield, sixty continental troops, and three companies of volunteers from New Haven, with whom Generals Arnold and Silliman took post about two miles above the bridge. Soon after the enemy appeared in sight, their rear was attacked by Colonel Huntington, (commanding a party of about five hundred men,) who sent to General Arnold for instructions, and for some officers to assist him. General Silliman was ordered to his assistance. The enemy finding our troops advantageously posted, made a halt, and after some little time wheeled off to the left and forded Saugatuck River, three miles above the bridge. General Arnold observing this motion, ordered the whole to march directly for the bridge, in order to attack them in the flank, General Silliman at the same time to attack their rear. The enemy, by running full speed, had passed the bridge on Fairfield side with their main body, before our troops could cross it. General Silliman finding it impossible to overtake them on their route, proceeded to the bridge, where the whole were formed. They marched in two columns, with two field-pieces on the right, the other on the left of the enemy, when a smart skirmishing and firing of field-pieces ensued, which continued about three hours. The enemy having gained the high hill of Compo, several attempts were made to dislodge them, but without effect. Having landed a number of fresh troops to cover their embarkation, which they effected a little before sunset, they weighed anchor immediately, and stood across the Sound for Huntington, on Long Island. Our

loss cannot exactly be ascertained, no return being made ; it is
judged to be about sixty killed and wounded. Among the
killed are one lieutenant-colonel, one captain, four subalterns,
and Doctor David Atwater, of New Haven, whose death is
greatly lamented by his acquaintance. Among the number
wounded are Colonel John Lamb, (of the artillery,) Arnah
Bradley, and Timothy Gorham, volunteers from New Haven,
though not mortally.

The enemy's loss is judged to be more than double our
number, and about twenty prisoners. They behaved, on this
occasion, with their usual barbarity, wantonly and cruelly
murdering the wounded prisoners who fell into their hands,
and plundering the inhabitants, burning and destroying every
thing in their way.[1]

The following is Gaine's account of this affair :—" In consequence of information received of the rebels having collected
large magazines at Danbury, in Connecticut, a
detachment of two hundred and fifty men from
each of the following regiments, fourth, fifteenth, twenty-third,
twenty-seventh, forty-fourth, and sixty-fourth, a subaltern's
command of dragoons, three hundred of Governor Brown's
corps, and six three-pounders, under the command of Major-
General Tryon, and Brigadier-Generals Agnew and Sir William Erskine, proceeded up the East River, and on Friday
evening last, at six o'clock, landed at Compo Point, near Norwalk. The debarkation being completed about ten, the troops
got in motion, and after a march of twenty-five miles, arrived
without opposition at Danbury, at three o'clock on Saturday
afternoon. The remainder of that day, and part of next morning, were employed in destroying the stores, which were found
to exceed their expectation. At nine o'clock they began their
march back to the shipping, and proceeded without interruption until they approached Ridgefield, where they found a
body of the rebels, under the command of Mr. Arnold, who
had fortified the entrance of the town, which they carried after
small opposition, with considerable loss on the side of the reb-

Gaine's Account.

[1] Connecticut Journal, April 30, and Pennsylvania Journal, May 14.

els, the rear repulsing another body, who attacked them at the
same time, under Mr. Wooster. The troops continued their
march next morning at four o'clock, the rebels firing on their
flanks and rear, but from such a distance as to do them but
little injury. About half a mile from the ships where the
troops halted, part of the rebel army, which consisted of at
least four thousand, kept up a heavy fire from behind stone
walls, whilst two columns made a show of attacking; but part
of the detachment charged them with fixed bayonets, and put
them to a total rout, with considerable slaughter. The troops,
after remaining some time upon the ground, embarked with
the greatest regularity and order, without further interruption
from the rebels, who never showed themselves more.

"The spirit and firmness shown by the troops on this occasion, does them infinite honor.

"The loss sustained was fourteen men killed, ten officers and
eighty men wounded, most of them slightly." [1]

We are here presented with an account of the Danbury
expedition from two different sides; by which it appears, that
the English paid dear for their entertainment in Connecticut;
but if we may judge of Mr. Gaine's modesty in telling a
story from the account he gave of the action at Princeton in

[1] Pennsylvania Journal, May 14. The following account was sent by another
hand:—

Governor Tryon, whose bloodthirsty, thievish disposition, and beggarly circumstances, impel him to rob and plunder for subsistence, having collected a
gang of thieves and starved wretches from among the British troops and Tories,
came over from Long Island on the 26th ultimo, and landed at Compo, between
Norwalk and Fairfield; from thence they beat through the woods to Danbury,
where they found a quantity of provisions, some of which they eat, and some they
destroyed, and some they attempted to carry off; but a number of people collecting, alarmed their guilty fears, and caused them to flee back with precipitation,
through thick and thin, wet and dry, rough and smooth, leaving bag and baggage, about fifty killed and forty taken prisoners, eighteen or twenty of whom are
now in jail in New Haven. Thus ended the glorious expedition of the freebooter
Tryon. The poor rogue found such good picking while Governor of New York,
that his head aches beyond conception to get possession of that government
again; but he must gnaw his trencher a great while before that time arrives.
We expect another visit from these hungry bellies in a short time, and it may be
proper enough to keep a good look out.—*From a Connecticut Paper.* See *New
York Gazette*, May 19.

January last, where he says (speaking of the British troops) "that they had ten killed, and a few wounded;" when it is an uncontroverted fact, that we buried one hundred and four regulars who were killed outright, and left fifty wounded at Princeton, besides above two hundred taken prisoners; we have, by a comparison of their accounts of the two affairs, good reason to think they have paid such a price as that a few more of those bargains would lower the stock of Howe & Co., so that they would be obliged to keep close, or beat a retreat.[1]

THE EXPEDITION TO DANBURY.

A "royal attack and feat," under the command of General Tryon, to destroy the stores of beef, pork, and rum.

SCENE.—NEW YORK.

Without wit, without wisdom, half stupid and drunk,
And rolling along arm in arm with his punk,
The gallant Sir William,[2] who fights all by proxy,
Thus spoke to his soldiers, held up by his doxy:

"My boys, I'm a going to send you with Tryon,
To a place where you'll all get as groggy as I am;
And the wounded, when well, shall receive a full gill,
But the slain be allowed just as much as they will.
By a Tory from Danbury I've just been informed,
That there's *nobody there, so the place shall be storm'd.*"

TRYON.

If there's nobody *there*, sir, and nobody *near it*,
Two thousand will conquer the *whole*, never fear it.

[JOE GALLOP-AWAY,[3] *a refugee Tory, with several others.*]

JOE.

Good soldiers, **go fight**, that we all may get rich.

SOLDIERS.

Go get you a halter.   *   *   *   *
Get out, and go live in the woods upon nuts,
Or I'll give you my bayonet plump in your ——
D'ye think you contemptible thief-looking crew,
That we fight to get beef for such rascals as you?

---

[1] Pennsylvania Journal, May 14.
[2] General Sir William Howe, whose irregularities are now pretty well known.
[3] See page 369, ante.

TRYON.

Come on, my brave boys, now as bold as a lion,
And march for the honor of General Tryon;
My lads, there's no danger, for this you may know,
That I'd let it alone if I thought it was so.

SCENE.—CONNECTICUT. TROOPS LANDED.

TRYON.

In cunning and canting, deceit and disguise,
In cheating a friend, and inventing of lies,
I think I'm a match for the best of my species,
But in this undertaking I feel all in pieces;
So I'll fall in the rear, for I'd rather go last;—
Come, march on, my boys, let me see you all past;
For his Majesty's service (so says my commission)
Requires that I *bring up* the whole expedition.

SCENE.—DANBURY. TROOPS ARRIVED.

TRYON.

Come, halloo, my lads, for the day is our own,
No rebels are here; not a soul in the town;
So fire all the houses, and when in a blaze,
We'll honor the King with a shout of huzzas.

[*A noise among the soldiers.*]

TRYON.

In his Majesty's name, what's this mutinous jargon?

SOLDIERS.

We came to get drunk, sir, for that was the bargain!

IRISH SOLDIER, DRUNK.

Huzza for the Congress—the Congress and toddy.

TRYON.

You scoundrel, I'll run you quite through the body.

SECOND IRISH SOLDIER.

By the head of St. Paddy,
I care not a louse for King George nor his daddy.

THIRD IRISH SOLDIER.

What plenty is here! Oh what eating and drinking!
Who'd stay in New York, to be starving and ——.

FOURTH IRISH SOLDIER.

The rebels, huzza! in a hat full of rum.

FIFTH IRISH SOLDIER.

Come let us drink bumpers, Jack,—out of a drum.

SCOTCH SOLDIER.

Laird Bute and his clan are a bundle of thieves.

ENGLISH SOLDIER.

Lord North and his gang are a kennel of slaves.

WELSH SOLDIER.

And a Welshman, prave poys, never harbors with knaves.

ALL.

Then let us go over,
Who'd stay to be starv'd, that might thus live in clover?

[*They Sing.*]

Let freedom and love be the glee of our song,
Let America flourish—the Congress grow strong,
And brave Washington *conqueror* all the day long.

[*A consultation of officers.　At a distance, houses and stores on fire.*]

TRYON.

I wish I was back, for I'm woefully scar'd,
The light will be seen and the noise will be heard,
And the rebels will gather so thick in ou way,
That whether we run for it or whether we stay,
The fate of the whole will be doubtful -and then—

[*A sudden alarm; an officer in a fright gallops about crying*]

To arms, to arms, to arms,—ten thousand men
Are pouring from the clouds—ten thousand more
Are got between the army and the shore,
Ten thousand women too.

TRYON.

Run, run; stop, stop,
Here, help me on my horse before I drop.

[*Enter an officer from New York.　To* TRYON.]

OFFICER.

The King hath promised, sir, you shall be *knighted.*

TRYON.

The devil take the King—for I am so frighted—

OFFICER.

But, sir, you must attend to what I've said.

TRYON.

Why, then, the King must knight me when I'm dead.

OFFICER.

But I bring orders, sir, which say "*you must*"—

TRYON.

Aye, *must* or *not*, I'll have a gallop first.

[*Sets off with the whole after him.*]

SCENE.—THE SHIPPING.

[*Troops on board.* TRYON *surrounded with Surgeons.*]

TRYON.

My belly's full of balls—I hear them rattle.

SURGEON.

'Tis only, sir, the echo of the battle.

TRYON.

Do search me over—see where 'tis I'm wounded.

SURGEON.

You are not hurt, sir.

TRYON.

Then I am confounded;
For as I stood, not knowing what to do,
Whether to fight to fly, or to pursue,
A cannon ball, of two and thirty pound,
Struck me just where Sir Peter [1] got his wound;
Then passing on between my horse's ears—

SURGEON.

Compose yourself, good sir—forget your cares,
You are not slain—you are alive and well.

TRYON.

Between my horse's ears, and down he fell,
Then getting up again,

SURGEON.

Dear sir, compose,
And try to get yourself into a doze;
The hurt you've got is not so dangerous deep,
But bleeding, shaving, patience, time, and sleep,
With blisters, clysters, physic, air, and diet,
Will set you up again, if you'll be quiet.

[1] Sir Peter Parker.   See page 258, ante.

TRYON.

So thick, so fast, the balls and bullets flew,
Some hit me here, some there, some thro' and thro'—
And so by thousands did the rebels muster
Under Generals Arnold and old Wooster,
That let me, let me, let me, let me but
Get off alive—*farewell Connecticut.*[1]

MAY 3.—MAJOR-GENERAL DAVID WOOSTER died this day, of the wounds he received in the late affair at Danbury, in Connecticut. He was born at Stratford, in that State,

General Wooster.

on the second of March, 1710–'11, and was educated at Yale College, where he graduated in the year 1738. Soon after the Spanish war broke out in 1739, he was employed, first as lieutenant, and then as captain, of the armed vessels built by Connecticut for a Guarda Coasta. After this he engaged in the military service of this country, and was a captain in Colonel Burr's regiment, in the expedition against Louisburg in 1745.

After the reduction of that place, he was sent to France, with a part of the prisoners taken there, and from thence went to England, where he received the honor of a captaincy on the establishment, in Sir William Pepperell's regiment. During the peace which soon followed, he received his half pay, and was chiefly employed in his private affairs. When the war with France was renewed in 1755, he was soon thought of as a gentleman qualified for a higher sphere of command, and served his country as colonel and commandant of a brigade to the end of the war.

From the first rise of the present controversy with Great Britain, in 1764, though his interest as a half-pay officer might have apologized for him, if he had observed a perfect neutrality, yet so fully convinced was he of the ruinous measures of the British court, and so jealous was he for his country's rights, that regardless of his private interest, he took an open and decisive part, and avowedly espoused the cause

[1] "Comus," in the Pennsylvania Gazette, May 14, and Pennsylvania Evening Post, May 22.

of America, and persisted in that line of conduct to the day of
his death. As soon as hostilities were commenced in the
Lexington battle, the General Assembly of Connecticut set
about raising an army, and Colonel Wooster, from his approved abilities, well-known courage, and great experience, was
appointed to the chief command. The same summer he was
appointed a brigadier-general in the continental service. Honored with these commissions, he first commanded the troops
sent to guard New York, where it was expected that part of
the British army, which came over in 1775, would land. In
the latter part of that campaign, he, with his troops, went into
Canada, and assisted much in the reduction of St. John's, Montreal, &c., and after General Montgomery's death, had the chief
command in that province. He returned home in the summer
of 1776, and not long after was appointed first major-general
of the militia of Connecticut.

He had been out the whole of the last winter, at the head
of a body of men raised by the State for its own security,
and was but lately returned, when on Saturday the 26th of
April last, he received the news that the enemy, in a large
body, had landed at Compo. He immediately set off for Fairfield, leaving orders for the militia to be mustered and sent forward as fast as possible. When he arrived at Fairfield, finding
General Silliman had marched in pursuit of the enemy with
the troops then collected, he followed on with all expedition,
and at Reading overtook General Silliman, with the small body
of militia, of which he of course took the command, and proceeded that same evening to the village of Bethel. Here it was
determined to divide the troops, and part were sent off under
Generals Arnold and Silliman, the rest remained with General
Wooster, and them he led by the route of Danbury, in pursuit
of the enemy, whom he overtook on the Sabbath, about four
o'clock, near Ridgefield. Observing a part of the enemy who
seemed to be detached from the main body, he determined to
attack them, though the number of his men was less than two
hundred; he accordingly led them on himself with great spirit
and resolution, ordering them to follow him. But being inex-
perienced militia, and the enemy having several field-pieces,

our men, after doing considerable execution, were broken and
gave way. The general was rallying them to renew the attack, when he received the fatal wound. A musket ball from
the distance of fifty rods, took him obliquely in the back,
broke his back bone, lodged within him, and never could be
found. He was removed from the field, had his wounds
dressed by Doctor Turner, and was then conveyed back to
Danbury, where all possible care was taken of him. The surgeons were from the first sensible of the danger of the case,
and informed the general of their apprehensions, which he
heard with the greatest composure.

The danger soon became more apparent, his whole lower
parts became insensible, and a mortification, it is thought,
began very early. It was designed to carry his remains to
New Haven, to be interred there, but that being found impossible, they will be interred at Danbury.[1]

MAY 5.—This day, Earl Percy, the hero of Lexington,
weary of the American war, though covered with laurels, sailed from Newport, in Rhode Island, for England, in a ship
mounting fourteen guns only. The command devolves on
General Prescott.

A person belonging to *the nest of pirates at Providence*
presents his compliments to Sir Peter Parker, at Newport.
Should Sir Peter attempt an expedition up the bay, he might
possibly find that a *nest of pirates* would prove as fatal to his
breeches as the *nest of hornets* on Sullivan's Island, which Sir
Peter so very imprudently disturbed.[2]

It is now thought, says a writer in London, that General
Washington will hold the two posts of Protector and General,
in imitation of the redoubtable hero of republicanism, Oliver
Cromwell, who was, many years after he was raised to the
Protectoral chair, his own generalissimo. And the former
will doubtless regard the orders of Congress, as Oliver did those
of the Rump Parliament.—*The writer of this article is cer-*

[1] Connecticut Journal, May 14.   [2] See page 258, ante.

*tainly entirely ignorant of the characters of General Washing-
ton and Oliver Cromwell.*[1]

MAY 6.—WE have often had occasion to observe, that
lying and misrepresentation, to the greatest extent, is a necessary part of the ministerial plan of operation *Strictures on the*
against us. They have given us a thousand proofs *Tory Press.*
of this, and continue to give new ones every day, to the utter
disregard of truth or justice, sincerity, honor or honesty.

The original design of the court of Great Britain, in their
contest with America, was so base and treacherous, and so
utterly inconsistent with the principles of the English Constitution, that they were obliged to have recourse to every artifice, in order to deceive the people of England, and even their
own emissaries who were not yet so abandoned and hardened
in villany, as heartily to co-operate in the destruction of the
English Constitution, which had so long been the boast and
glory of the nation, had raised it to its highest degree of opu-
lence and splendor, and had been the distinguishing characteristic of England from every other nation. In speculation, one
would have thought it impossible to persuade Englishmen, or
any of those who were real friends to them, to lend a helping
hand to the destruction of that revered Constitution, which
it had been the work of ages to form and establish; a Constitution which secured the freedom and property of the people,
gave the King as much power as any wise man could wish to
have, or as any wise people could, with safety to themselves,
possibly trust in the hands of their supreme magistrate. He
had an almost unlimited power to do good, and was only restrained from doing evil, and becoming a tyrant in stead of a
father to his people. But a wicked and abandoned court
and ministry were not content with this. They had broke
through every moral and religious restraint, and run into
boundless extravagance and expense, which no honest income
was sufficient to support; and in defrauding the public, by
betraying the trust reposed in them, and converting the na-

[1] Pennsylvania Evening Post, May 27 and June 10.

tional revenues to their own use, they knew they were liable
to be called to a severe account and punishment, and could
not be screened even by the King himself, under a Constitution, where the law was above him, and bound him as well as
his subjects. They knew that under a government where the
King is arbitrary and makes his will the supreme law, they
could, by keeping in his favor, effectually secure themselves
from being called to account for the most atrocious and treasonable breaches of trust they could possibly be guilty of;
they therefore, with much application and artful contrivance,
formed a deep-laid design to destroy the Constitution, by
making the King absolute, and the people slaves.

To execute this design, they found means to draw in a formidable combination, partly of men in similar circumstances
with themselves, and the rest, such as had a greater relish for
the advantages they might expect under a despotic prince,
than in a government where every member, from the highest
to the lowest, was under the restraint of law. It was no difficult matter to seduce the King himself to enter into this combination, and promote the design with all his power and influence. He was not of a disposition to resist so strong a temp-
tation as appeared in the offer of unlimited power; and as
little doubtful of his qualifications to exercise it with propriety
as Phæton was of his ability to drive the chariot of the Sun.
Such were the motives of the King and his ministry for their
conduct respecting America. But it was necessary to deceive
the people, and pretend other motives for this conduct, in order to conceal these. To this end, the expedient of lying and
deception was adopted, and has been continually appropriated
by the ministry and all their emissaries, both in Europe and
America, to serve their purposes upon all occasions.

Whenever we have had an opportunity to examine any accounts they have published, either from England or America,
we have found them either absolutely false, or grossly misrep-
resented; we have, therefore, reason to suppose they have had
the same disregard to truth in those accounts we have not had
the means of examining, as we have found in others.

The following paragraphs, lately published, are illustrations of these observations :—" *The New Yorkers, we are informed, are exasperated to the highest degree against the Congress, and the army acting under their orders ; and declare, that when they act against the rebels, they will neither give nor receive quarter.*"

Who are the persons here styled New Yorkers? The city of New York, that rueful scene of ruin, violence, and distress, is inhabited at present by a few sorts of people, viz. :

1. A crew of bloody murderers and base robbers, sent by the King of Great Britain to enslave the Americans, and plunder them of their property.

2. A still more infamous and execrable herd of Tory natives and former inhabitants of New York, who, with unparalleled folly and villany, have joined the foreign enemies of their country in promoting its destruction, in entailing upon it and even their own posterity, endless slavery and subjection to a tyrant's will. And all this for the despicable consideration of a little present emolument, or perhaps only the delusive hopes even of that ; or from the basest cowardice, which, to shun a lesser evil, has plunged them, loaded with guilt, into a greater.

3. A number of poor, helpless, or indigent people, who, unable to remove, or having nothing to lose, have remained in New York, and been forced to submit to every imposition of an insolent, tyrannical enemy.

4. A number of honest, worthy men, who have unfortunately fallen into the enemy's hands, and because they had acted as friends to their country, as they were in duty bound to do, have not only been detained as prisoners, but treated with every kind of insult, cruelty, and inhumanity. These four sorts make up the present inhabitants of the city of New York.

As to the two first, we have no doubt of their rancor, malice, and cruelty ; they have repeatedly given unquestionable proofs of it, and they never had, or ever will have, a disposition to give quarter to any honest man that has had the misfortune to fall into their hands, or even to treat him with humanity. And it is not improbable, that at a time when they thought to carry all before them—that all was quite over with us, that we were entirely in their power and should be obliged to ask for quarter, which they were determined to refuse, they might have made such a declaration, that they would neither give nor receive quarter, in order to give a color of reason and equity to their barbarous treatment of our people. At this time they did not imagine they should ever be in our power, and have occasion to ask that quarter for themselves which they refused to us. But the tables being turned since they made that declaration, we may be assured their humor of refusing quarter has subsided, and they would receive it now with as much humility as they possessed of haughtiness and cruelty when they refused it to us. But their behavior having left them no room to hope for it, there remains only to them a fearful looking for of judgment and retribution. Meanwhile their number is become so small, their strength so weak, their distress and anxiety so great, that their very existence seems to have become a curse, and those they have most injured can hardly wish them to be more miserable than they really are.

" *By a letter received from Rhode Island, we have advice that an engagement lately happened near that place between seven privateers, fitted out by the colonists, and four King's frigates, when, after a warm contest, one of the privateers was sunk, and the others were beat off.*"

This engagement of the vessels we do not remember to have heard of, and believe it to be no more than a fiction, invented to make their principals think they were still going on with mischief, and had done more than it has been in their power to do ; though we must do them the justice to own, they do as much as they can.

" *We hear that government has received advices by the way of Holland, from New York, which give an account of some further advantages gained over the rebels, and that several despatches had passed between Lord and Sir William Howe and the ruling powers of the Congress, but that nothing decisive had been resolved on when these advices came away.*"

This, of their negotiation with the Congress, &c., is a *lie* throughout, devised, probably, in part for the same purpose as the last mentioned, and partly to amuse the opposite party in England, to whom the ministry pretended that Sir William and Lord Howe were sent out principally with a view to accommodate differences, and effect a reconciliation between Great Britain and America ; though the full powers of these famous commissioners extended no farther than to the grant of pardons, if they thought proper, to such of the Americans as should consent to unconditional submission to the authority of the King and Parliament of Great Britain, and to be bound by laws of their making, in all cases whatsoever.

"*We hear that of the thirty nurses that lately took care of the sick in the Philadelphia hospital, no less than twenty-seven of them died in one week.*"

The death of twenty-seven of the thirty nurses in the Philadelphia hospital, is probably a wilful mistake. That it is not true is certain. If the account had been, that of thirty sick persons who had been prisoners at New York, twenty-seven had died under the care of the nurses in the Philadelphia hospital, we might have believed the relation to be true ; because it is well known that those poor prisoners were generally starved to death, or from want of food and through barbarous usage in many respects, died in nearly the above proportion, after they were released in exchange for prisoners in our hands, who were well kept, and returned in health and good order.

There are many other articles in the English papers, and from them republished in American papers, that ought not to appear in any of our papers without proper notes to guard the unwary reader from deception and false impressions.[1]

MAY 8.—A CORRESPONDENT has offered the following query and remarks to General Howe :—" If with thirty thousand men you conquered two towns and one village in *one* year, how many years will it be before you A Question for General Howe. will be able to conquer and occupy all the towns and villages on the continent of America ? "

It is incumbent upon your excellency to answer this ques-

---

[1] "O.," in the New York Journal, September 15.

tion immediately, in order that the few recruits whom you
have enlisted by your late proclamation, in which you have
offered them the forfeited property of the Whigs, may know
exactly how many *hundred years* they must wait before you
eject the Whigs, and give them the peaceable possession of
their estates.

Oh, fie, Sir William ; fie, for shame ! Such proclamations become a general at the head of a powerful and victorious army, and a whole country *almost* prostrate at his feet, and
not the poor, contemptible chief of a vanquished, blockaded,
half-starved, half-naked, half-rotten, half-paid, mongrel banditti, composed of the sweepings of the jails of Britain, Ireland, Germany, and America. Oh, fie ; Sir William ! Blush,
blush for your proclamation !

Carleton, Burgoyne, Howe,
Bow——Wow——Wow ! [1]

SOME days ago a villain was taken up at Peekskill, in New
York, in whose custody were found eighty-eight counterfeit
Connecticut forty shilling bills, and one of thirty
Counterfeiting. dollars, Continental currency, badly done, being
paler and fainter impressed than the true ones. Those of Connecticut are done on copper-plate, and not easily to be distinguished from the true ones, but from that circumstance ; the
true ones being done off at the common printing press. Another of these adventurers, with two thousand seven hundred
pounds of counterfeit money about him, is secured at Peekskill.

It seems they are tempted to follow this desperate employment by the terms offered in the following advertisement
taken from H. Gaine's Gazette of the 14th of April last,
viz. :

" Persons going into the other colonies may be supplied
with any number of counterfeited Congress notes for the price of
the paper per ream. They are so nearly and exactly executed
that there is no risk in getting them off, it being almost impos-

---

[1] " A Tar," in the Pennsylvania Evening Post, May 8.

sible to discover that they are not genuine. This has been proved by bills to a very large amount, which have been successfully circulated. Inquire for Q. E. D., at the coffee house, from eleven P. M., to four A. M., during the present month." [1]

MAY 12.—THE rebels have industriously reported, and even had the assurance to publish in some of their newspapers, that the King's troops employed in destroying the magazine at Danbury, "behaved with great barbarity, wantonly and cruelly murdering the wounded prisoners who fell into their hands, and plundering the inhabitants, burning and destroying every thing in their way." That this is a most audacious falsehood, fabricated to delude the weak and credulous into a state of desperation, the inhabitants of the country from Norwalk to Danbury can, if they *dare*, sufficiently testify. The country people know that not the least plunder was committed either upon their goods or cattle, even where the houses were abandoned; that the soldiers paid for every article they wanted; and that neither man, woman, nor child received the least injury or molestation from the army, except the rebels who attacked them, or were found in arms. They accomplished the object for which they entered the country, and then returned, in the utmost order, to the place of embarkation.

The Danbury Expedition.

For the same inflammatory purpose, the following article, taken from the Connecticut Journal of the thirtieth of April, was evidently composed: " A member of Congress, in a letter dated April fifteenth, 1777, writes to his friend in this town, (New Haven,) that an extract of a letter from England to the commissioners, (Doctor Franklin, &c., in France,) mentions, that the British ministry intends totally to destroy the New England States, and make slaves of the southern." So we see what we poor people of New England have to depend on. A certain old gentleman would be puzzled to exceed this story in impudence or falsehood. The author at least must have had his full inspiration to invent it. [2]

---

[1] Pennsylvania Evening Post, May 13.   [2] Gaine's Mercury, May 12.

MAY 24.—YESTERDAY, General Parsons having received information that the British had collected, and were collecting large quantities of forage at Sag Harbor, on Long Island, together with about two hundred of the continental troops who had previously rendezvoused at Sachem's Head, in Guilford, embarked on board a number of whale boats, commanded by Lieutenant-Colonel Meigs, to destroy it. At about six o'clock in the afternoon they arrived at the beach, on the side of Plumgut, and transported their boats about fifty rods over the beach, when they again embarked, and landed several miles from Sag Harbor, where (after leaving a suitable guard to protect the boats) they marched with such secresy as not to be discovered till within a few rods of the sentry. They soon set about destroying the forage, &c. As the enemy stationed there were entirely off their guard, the troops met with little opposition. An armed schooner of twelve guns, which lay not far from the shore, kept an incessant fire on them, but happily did them no damage. The Americans returned the fire with their small arms, but whether with effect is not known; five or six of the enemy on shore were destroyed, and three or four made their escape; the others were made prisoners. The Americans then set fire to the hay, (about one hundred tons,) which was on board transports, and on the wharves, and entirely destroyed it, with ten transport vessels, mostly sloops and schooners, and one armed vessel of six or eight guns, two or three hogsheads of rum, &c. They then returned to Guilford, having performed their expedition in twenty-four hours.[1]

Attack on Sag Harbor.

A LATE letter from England says :—" Mr. Rigby has proposed in the cabinet a scheme for adjusting all disputes with America. His plan is to decide the quarrel after the Roman fashion, by single combat. Mr. Rigby offers himself as the champion of England; he will box Wash-

Rigby's Plan.

---

[1] Connecticut Journal; see Barber's Connecticut, 217.—*Return of Prisoners taken at Sag Harbor*:—1 captain, 2 commissaries, 3 sergeants, 53 rank and file, 10 masters of transports, 27 seamen; in the whole, 90. The Americans brought off fifty muskets. One of the commissaries above mentioned, is Mr. Joseph Chew, formerly of New London, in Connecticut.

ington, Lee, or Putnam.   This is at least as good a mode of reconciliation as that projected by the Howes.[1]

MAY 29.—GENERAL G——Y, from Amboy, to-day, says the
rebels in Philadelphia are very unsettled in their minds, and
are mostly friendly to government, although their   An Advisory
situation prevents their acting so. In the evening   Petition.
before the meeting at the State house on the tenth instant, a
gentleman who reached Amboy a short time before G——y
left, passing the hour at Mrs. D——'s, where a cheerful party
of *out-of-door-rebels* had met, amused himself in preparing the
following advisory petition to the Congress, which was highly
applauded, and forthwith voted to be sent to old Thomson:[2]

LOW AND LOUSY BEGGARS, REBEL TAILORS, LAWYERS, PIMPS, PAR-
SONS, AND COBBLERS:—Since by your machinations you have led
us into difficulty with our just and gracious King George the
Third, and now have left us at the mercy of a worse than lord
protector, we humbly *veouw* we will see you all to the devil before we'll continue our allegiance to you or your pious Connec-
ticutian tricks, either by love, labor, or lying; for which last we
are in constant expectation of a judgment. And we further
advise and declare, that if you don't " disband, and at once return to the peaceful employments " discerning nature hath
pointed out for you, (you, W., to your ink and horn book;
you, A., to your cheating; you, H., to your goose, and you,
D., to your wax,) you must expect to receive unseasonable
things at unseasonable hours.

We have been misled by the knaves among you, bewrayed
by the dirtiest of you, and soporated by the stupidity of all
of you, until we know not where to go, are unclean, and
are become mere tools in your hands, and without the least
spark of the ancient freedom of Britons. Therefore, beware!
Get home ! Get out of debt, and make your wives happy, and
leave the affairs of kingdoms to those your God has placed
over you.[3]

WILLIAM STONE, a traitor and spy, who was convicted of

[1] Pennsylvania Evening Post, May 15.   [2] The Secretary of Congress.
[3] Smythe's Journal, 61.

having a commission from General Howe, and endeavoring to enlist men to serve in the ministerial army, was executed at Hartford, in Connecticut, pursuant to the sentence of a court-martial.[1]

JUNE 2.—THIS day, came on the trial of Mather Byles, late minister of the gospel in Boston, charged with being an enemy to the United States; when, after a fair and candid examination of evidences, the jury returned their verdict, that he, Mather Byles, is and has been since the nineteenth of April, 1775, inimically disposed towards Massachusetts and the other United States, and that his residence in the State is dangerous to the public peace and safety. He was then delivered into the custody of a proper officer, who conducted him to the Honorable the Board of War, there to be dealt with agreeable to a late act for such persons made and provided.[2]

Mather Byles.

THE American republicans, like the rebels of all ages, from their *justice, peaceloving, and mercy,* pretend to have the especial favors of God, and none of the devil's, on their side, and for this reason we rarely see a proclamation from the rebel camp, without a pious sentence bringing

Washington forbids Gaming.

[1] Pennsylvania Evening Post, June 10.

[2] Pennsylvania Evening Post, June 17. MATHER BYLES, D. D., was born in Boston on the 26th March, 1706. He was educated at Harvard College, from which institution he graduated in 1725. He became a distinguished minister and loyalist, and for his political principles was separated from his people, to whom he was never afterward united. In 1776 he was denounced in town meeting as inimical to his country, and obliged to enter into bonds for his appearance at a special court, at which he was found guilty, as appears from the above. When brought before the board of war, by whom he was respectfully treated, his sentence seems to have been altered; and it was directed that he should be confined to his own house and there guarded. After a few weeks the guard was removed; a short time after, a guard was again placed over him, and again dismissed. Upon this occasion he observed, that "*he was guarded, regarded, and disregarded.*" The substance of the charges made against him was, that he continued in Boston with his family during the siege; that he prayed for the King and the safety of the town. His literary merit introduced him to the acquaintance of many men of genius in England. The names of Pope, Lansdowne, and Watts are found among his correspondents. He died July 5, 1788.—*Curwen.*

up the rear. The late orders given by the head rebel at Morristown, in the Jerseys, a copy of which is printed in all the rebel prints, is a greater illustration of this Yankee piety than any yet come out. In it Mr. Washington forbids card playing under the penalty of a court-martial, ostensibly for the reason that it is wicked and brings a disgrace on the officers, but in reality to enlist the parsons and other old women stronger in the cause of rebellion.

Old De Heister used to say, "Isht dakes de veek to fool der Deutsche, isht dakes de day to fool de Anglees, isht dakes der tyfel to fool de rebel, but *all* together couldn't fool de Lord." So it is with Mr. Washington:—However easily he may bait old Witherspoon, Billy Livingston, Jacky Jay, and some of the other pious ones, who are hanging on the rear of his *moral* forces ; when the time comes, he'll find he can't "fool the Lord" with pretended piety or Presbyterian general orders.[1]

JUNE 3.—A writer in London, says :—A young fellow named Dawkins, who was some time since tried at Chelmsford assize, and transported for stealing cheese, &c., has, we hear, just sent

---

[1] Carver, 113. The following are the orders referred to by this writer:—

HEAD-QUARTERS, MORRISTOWN, May 8, 1777.

GENERAL ORDERS :—As few vices are attended with more pernicious consequences in civil life, so there are none more fatal in a military one than that of gaming, which often brings disgrace and ruin upon officers, and injury and punishment upon the soldiery. And reports prevailing, which it is to be feared are too well founded, that this destructive vice has spread its baneful influence in the army, and in a peculiar manner, to the prejudice of the recruiting service, the Commander-in-chief, in the most pointed and explicit terms, forbids all officers and soldiers playing at cards, dice, or at any games, except those of exercise or diversion, it being impossible, if the practice be allowed at all, to discriminate between innocent play for amusement and criminal gaming for pecuniary and sordid purposes.

*   *   *   *   *   *   *   *   *

The commanding officer of every corps is strictly enjoined to have this order frequently read, and strongly impressed upon the minds of those under his command.

Any officer or soldier, or other person belonging to, or following the army, either in camp, in quarters, on the recruiting service, or elsewhere, presuming, under any pretence, to disobey this order, shall be tried by a court-martial, etc.— *Pennsylvania Evening Post*, May 13.

a letter to his mother, informing her the American Congress
have presented him with a captain's commission. He says
several other Essex patriots, who like him were torn from their
dearest connections, and banished for their firm attachment to
the cause of Liberty, now rank high in the American army.[1]

JUNE 9.—ABRAHAM PATTEN, a spy from the rebel army,
was executed at Brunswick, New Jersey, last Friday, between
                       eleven and twelve o'clock. He had agreed to
Abraham Patten. give a grenadier fifty guineas to carry four letters
to Washington and Putnam; the soldier took the cash, and
carried the letters to his Excellency Lord Cornwallis, wherein
was proposed on a certain day to set fire to Brunswick in four
places at once, blow up the magazine, and then set off a rocket
as a signal for the rebels to attack the town. At the gallows
he acknowledged all the charges brought against him, and said
he was a principal in setting fire to New York, but would
not accuse any of his accomplices. The said Patten formerly
lived in New York and has left a wife and four children at
Baltimore in Maryland.[2]

JUNE 13.—THIS day the Assembly of Pennsylvania resolved, that Mr. Parker, Colonel Coats, and Mr. Whitehill, be
a committee to purchase a coach and present the same to the
Honorable Mrs. Washington, the worthy lady of his Excellency General Washington, as a small testimonial of the sense the
Assembly have of his great and important services to the
American States.

JUNE 14.—THE committee appointed to purchase a coach
to be presented to the Honorable Mrs. Washington, reported,
that they had bought a very elegant one, and, in the name of
the House, had presented it to that lady, by whom it had been
politely accepted.[3]

CONGRESS this day resolved that the flag of the United States

---

[1] Pennsylvania Ledger, October 29.   [2] Upcott, v. 35.   [3] Same, v. 37.

be thirteen stripes, alternate red and white ; and that the union
be thirteen stars white in a blue field, representing a new con-
stellation.[1]

JUNE 17.—A MEMORIAL was lately transmitted from England to Sir Joseph York, at the Hague, to be presented to the
States-General. The memorial complains of the Sir Joseph York at
conduct of the States for permitting the Ameri-   the Hague.
cans to be supplied, through the means of their subjects, with
such warlike stores as have been prohibited by proclamation.
Sir Joseph York delivered the memorial to the monthly president of the assembly, who, after laying it before the assembly,
returned to the ante-chamber, in which Sir Joseph was waiting.
Sir Joseph requested an answer. The president informed him
that the memorial was then under consideration. Sir Joseph
wished the assembly to be informed " that unless a categorical
answer was returned to the memorial, he should quit the
Hague immediately." The president delivered this message
to the assembly, and soon returned with the following retort :
" I am desired by the States-General to acquaint your excellency that there are not any gates to the Hague."

A gentleman just returned from making the tour of France,
says :—" From Dunkirk to Brest, from thence to Bordeaux to
Bayonne, then through Toulouse to Marseilles, and lastly,
through Lyons and Dijon to Paris, I met neither men nor
women, in high or low stations, but were friends to the Americans." [1]

A CORRESPONDENT in London says :—When the Congress
had declared for Independence, a new mode of government
was consequently the first object to be considered, and Adams
had himself prepared almost a complete code of laws ; but
many were rejected, though with great caution, and an explanation' of each particular impropriety, from a dread of too
much offending that great man, who, to make use of an expression in a letter received some time since in America, was

[1] Pennsylvania Journal, Sept. 3.   [2] Pennsylvania Evening Post, June 17.

"so clever a fellow, and so dangerous a v——n, that it was no man's interest to quarrel with him."[1]

JUNE 25.—THIS day, the *Senator's Remembrancer*, a curious performance of Mr. John Stewart, of London, consisting of fourteen copper-plate prints, done on white satin, and most elegantly framed and gilt, presented to the public by Doctor Benjamin Franklin, were placed in the council chamber at Philadelphia. This performance is dedicated by the author to Doctor Franklin.[2]

<small>Senator's Remembrancer.</small>

JUNE 30.—ON Sunday morning, the 22d, the British left Brunswick, in Jersey, apparently with an intention to embark; they gave out that they were going to Philadelphia by water, but their real design was to draw General Washington from the mountains above Quibbletown, and force a general engagement. Their policy, however, was not an overmatch for our prudence. Light parties harassed him, but not in such numbers as to produce any considerable action. Great part of our army, however, had left the mountains, and General Lord Stirling was posted at the short hills with about one thousand men.

<small>Affairs in Jersey.</small>

On Thursday morning, General Howe having reinforced his army with all the marines that could be spared, began his march towards the American camp. By accounts of deserters and others, his numbers were from twelve to fourteen thousand. He met with Lord Stirling's party early in the morning; a smart engagement ensued, and the Americans stood their ground manfully for a considerable time; but the amazing superiority of numbers obliged them to retreat; and, the enemy having flanked them, they lost two pieces of cannon with a number of men. No return having yet been made, the exact number of killed, &c., cannot be ascertained. The British continued near the place of engagement that day, and are now at Westfield. The Americans are encamped in the old spot, only large bodies are posted at all the passes, and in some advanta-

[1] Upcott, v. 43.   [2] Pennsylvania Evening Post, June 28.

geous places below the mountains. It is suspected that the
enemy would force our camp if possible ; but to attack us in
the mountains is a thing devoutly to be wished for by every
one that desires to see the destruction of the British army.

We must not omit to mention a little affair that happened
in the engagement. The fire growing hot, and our men
beginning to retreat, a British officer singly rode up to a cannon that was playing on the enemy, and with his pistols and
hanger forced every man from it ; then seeing Lord Stirling,
he cried, " Come here, you damned rebel ; and I will do for
you." Lord Stirling answered him by directing the fire of four
marksmen upon him, which presently silenced the hardy fool
by killing him on the spot.[1] Our men recovered the field-
piece, which their want of small arms obliged them to
abandon.[2]

GENERAL HOWE, in a letter to Lord George Germaine,
gives the following account of the above :—

Having established a corps sufficient to the defence of
Amboy, the army assembled at Brunswick on the 12th of
June.

The enemy's principal force being encamped upon the
mountains above Quibbletown, with a corps of two thousand
men at Princeton, it was thought advisable to   Howe's Move-
make a movement in two columns from Bruns-   ments in Jersey.
wick on the 14th, in the morning, leaving Brigadier-General
Mathew with two thousand men to guard that post. The first
division, under the command of Lord Cornwallis, advanced to
Ailsborough, and the second to Middle Bush, under the command of Lieutenant-General De Heister, with a view of drawing on an action, if the enemy should remove from the mountain towards the Delaware ; but on finding it to be their intention to keep a position which it would not have been prudent

---

[1] The person who was killed in attempting to take the cannon in the affair of
Lord Stirling, was the Honorable Mr. Finch, son of the Earl of Winchelsea, who
came out this spring as a volunteer. After he fell, his horse came over and was
taken by our army. Finch was buried with great pomp by General Howe.—*Pennsylvania Journal*, July 16.

[2] Pennsylvania Journal, July 2.

to attack, I determined without loss of time to pursue the principal objects of the campaign, by withdrawing the army from Jersey ; and, in consequence of this determination, returned to the camp at Brunswick on the 19th, and marched from thence to Amboy on the 22d, intending to cross to Staten Island, from whence the embarkation was to take place.

Upon quitting the camp at Brunswick, the enemy brought a few troops forward, with two or three pieces of cannon, which they fired at the utmost range, without the least execution, or any return from us; they also pushed some battalions into the woods to harass the rear, where Lord Cornwallis commanded, who soon dispersed them with the loss of only two men killed and thirteen wounded ; the enemy having nine killed and about thirty wounded.

The necessary preparations being finished for crossing the troops to Staten Island, intelligence was received that the enemy had moved down from the mountain, and taken post at Quibbletown, intending, as it was given out, to attack the rear of the army removing from Amboy ; that two corps had also advanced to their left, one of three thousand men and eight pieces of cannon, under the command of Lord Stirling, Generals Maxwell, and Conway, the last said to be a captain in the French service; the other corps consisted of about seven hundred men, with only one piece of cannon.

In this situation of the enemy, it was judged advisable to make a movement that might lead on to an attack, which was done on the 26th, in the morning, in two columns ; the right, under the command of Lord Cornwallis, with Major-General Grant, Brigadiers Mathew and Leslie, and Colonel Donop, took the route by Woodbridge, towards Scotch Plains; the left column where I was, with Major-Generals Sterne, Vaughan, and Grey, Brigadiers Cleveland and Agnew, marched by Metuchin meeting-house, to join the rear of the right column in the road from thence to Scotch Plains, intending to have taken separate routes about two miles after the junction, in order to have attacked the enemy's left flank at Quibbletown. Four battalions were detached in the morning, with six pieces of cannon, to take post at Bonam-Town.

The right column having fallen in with the aforementioned corps of seven hundred men, soon after passing Woodbridge, gave the alarm, by the firing that ensued, to their main army at Quibbletown, which retired to the mountain with the utmost precipitation. The small corps was closely pushed by the light troops, and with difficulty got off their piece of cannon.

Lord Cornwallis, soon after he was upon the road leading to Scotch Plains from Metuchin meeting-house, came up with the corps commanded by Lord Stirling, whom he found advantageously posted in a country much covered with wood, and his artillery well disposed. The King's troops, vieing with each other upon this occasion, pressed forward to such close action, that .the enemy, though inclined to resist, could not long maintain their ground against so great impetuosity, but were dispersed on all sides, leaving behind three pieces of brass ordnance, three captains and sixty men killed, and upwards of two hundred officers and men wounded and taken.

His lordship had five men killed, and thirty wounded. Captain Finch of the light company of the guards was the only officer who suffered, and to my great concern, the wound he received proving mortal, he died on the 29th of June, at Amboy.

The troops engaged in this action were the 1st light infantry, 1st British grenadiers, 1st, 2d, and 3d Hessian grenadiers ; 1st battalion of guards, Hessian chasseurs, and the Queen's Rangers. I take the liberty of particularizing these corps, as Lord Cornwallis, in his report to me, so highly extols their merit and ardor upon this attack. One piece of cannon was taken by the guards, the other two by Colonel Mingerode's battalion of Hessian grenadiers.

The enemy was pursued as far as Westfield with little effect, the day proving so intensely hot that the soldiers could with difficulty continue their march thither ; in the mean time it gave opportunity for those flying to escape by skulking in the thick woods until night favored their retreat to the mountains.

The army lay that night at Westfield, returned the next

day to Rahway, and the day following to Amboy. On the 30th, at ten in the forenoon, the troops began to cross over to Staten Island, and the rear guard, under the command of Lord Cornwallis, passed at two in the afternoon, without the least appearance of an enemy.

The embarkation of the troops is proceeding with the utmost despatch, and I shall have the honor of sending your lordship further information as soon as the troops are landed at the place of their destination.[1]

GENERAL HOWE'S LETTER.

The substance of Sir W.'s last letter from New York, versified.

> As to kidnap the Congress has long been my aim,
> I lately resolv'd to accomplish the same ;
> And, that none, in the glory, might want his due share,
> All the troops were to Brunswick desir'd to repair.
> > Derry down, &c.
>
> There I met them in person, and took the command,
> When I instantly told them the job upon hand ;
> I did not detain them with long-winded stuff,
> But made a short speech, and each soldier look'd bluff.
>
> With this omen elated, towards Quibbletown
> I led them, concluding the day was our own ;
> For, till we went thither, the coast was quite clear,—
> But Putnam and Washington, d——n them, were there !
>
> I own I was stagger'd, to see with what skill
> The rogues were intrench'd, on the brow of the hill ;
> With a view to dismay them, I show'd my whole force,
> But they kept their position, and car'd not a curse.
>
> There were then but two ways,—to retreat or attack,
> And to me it seem'd wisest, by far, to go back ;
> For I thought, if I rashly got into a fray,
> There might both be the Devil and Piper to pay.
>
> Then, to lose no more time, by parading in vain,
> I determin'd elsewhere to transfer the campaign ;
> So just as we went, we return'd to this place,
> With no other diff'rence,—than mending our pace.

---

[1] Upcott, v. 55.

Where next we proceed, is not yet very clear,
But, when we get there, be assur'd you shall hear;
I'll settle that point, when I meet with my brother,—
Meanwhile, we're embarking for some place or other.

Having briefly, my lord, told you,—how the land lies,
I hope there's enough—for a word to the wise;
'Tis a good horse, they say, that never will stumble,—
But, fighting or flying,—I'm your very humble.[1]

WHEREAS a certain William Howe, alias General Howe, alias Sir William, alias any thing or nothing, has lately gone off, greatly in debt to sundry persons in New Jersey and other parts of the continent, and has not left wherewithal to make payment for the same; this is therefore to caution all persons not to trust him on any account, as they will certainly lose their money. Said Howe is charged with having, in company with one Cornwallis, not yet taken, broken into several houses in New Jersey, and stolen and carried off many valuable effects; likewise with being concerned in counterfeiting the currency of this continent, and of having starved to death several good subjects of the States, while he was chief jailer at New York. He is a very ill-looking fellow, and is an indented servant to a certain George Whelp, alias Guelph, alias King George.

Whoever will secure said Howe in any of the jails of this continent, or will give notice where he is to the American army, shall be handsomely rewarded.

N. B.—He was lately seen skulking about Amboy, Westfield, and Spanktown, in the Jerseys, and has not since been heard of. Should he attempt to practice any more of his villanies, 'tis hoped all persons will be on their guard to apprehend him.[2]

[1] Upcott, v. 45.　　[2] Pennsylvania Evening Post, July 10.

CHAPTER XI.

JULY 1.—THE movements of the American army in the north, since the commencement of the war, have been, with The Northern Army. one or two exceptions, but a series of disgraceful defeats, or more disgraceful retreats. The only satisfaction those who have been taken have enjoyed, is the kind treatment of General Carleton, who has lately been deprived of his commission for his *kindness* to rebels ; while the reward of those of us who have managed to escape, has been the hardest of poor fare, and a continual suffering, the usual attendant upon bad generalship and still worse internal mismanagement. * * * * We are now at Ticonderoga, and to-day General Burgoyne, whose army has been hovering Burgoyne's Proclamation. around us and in sight for the few days past, has put forth a pompous proclamation, which is probably intended to frighten us into desertion or a surrender.[1] It is as follows :

By John Burgoyne, Esq., Lieutenant-General of his Majesty's armies in America, Colonel of the Queen's regiment of light dragoons, Governor of Fort William, in North Britain, one of the Representatives of the Commons of Great Britain in Parliament, and commanding an army and fleet employed on an expedition from Canada, &c., &c., &c.

The forces entrusted to my command are designed to act in concert, and upon a common principle, with the numerous armies and fleets which already display in every quarter of

Extract of a letter from John Hawk to his wife, dated Ticonderoga, July 1, 1777.

Eng^d by A.H. Ritchie

Guy Carleton

America, the power, the justice, and, when properly sought, the mercy of the King.

The cause in which the British arms are thus exerted, applies to the most affecting interests of the human heart ; and the military servants of the crown, at first called forth for the sole purpose of restoring the rights of the constitution, now combine with love of their country, and duty to their sovereign, the other extensive incitements which spring from a due sense of the general privileges of mankind. To the eyes and ears of the temperate part of the public, and to the breasts of suffering thousands in the provinces, be the melancholy appeal, whether the present unnatural rebellion has not been made a foundation for the completest system of tyranny that ever God, in his displeasure, suffered for a time to be exercised over a froward and stubborn generation.

Arbitrary imprisonment, confiscation of property, persecution and torture, unprecedented in the inquisitions of the Romish church, are among the palpable enormities that verify the affirmative. These are inflicted by assemblies and committees, who dare to profess themselves friends to liberty, upon the most quiet subjects, without distinction of age or sex, for the sole crime, often for the sole suspicion, of having adhered in principle to the government under which they were born, and to which, by every tie, divine and human, they owe allegiance. To consummate these shocking proceedings, the profanation of religion is added to the most profligate prostitution of common reason ; the consciences of men are set at naught ; and multitudes are compelled not only to bear arms, but also to swear subjection to an usurpation they abhor.

Animated by these considerations ; at the head of troops in the full powers of health, discipline, and valor ; determined to strike where necessary, and anxious to spare where possible, I, by these presents, invite and exhort all persons, in all places where the progress of this army may point, and by the blessing of God I will extend it far, to maintain such a conduct as may justify me in protecting their lands, habitations, and families.

The intention of this address is to hold forth security,

not depredation to the country. To those whom spirit and principle may induce to partake of the glorious task of redeeming their countrymen from dungeons, and re-establishing the blessings of legal government, I offer encouragement and employment; and upon the first intelligence of their associations, I will find means to assist their undertakings. The domestic, the industrious, the infirm, and even the timid inhabitants, I am desirous to protect, provided they remain quietly at their houses; that they do not suffer their cattle to be removed, nor their corn or forage to be secreted or destroyed; that they do not break up their bridges or roads; nor by any other act, directly or indirectly, endeavor to obstruct the operations of the King's troops, or supply or assist those of the enemy. Every species of provision brought to my camp, will be paid for at an equitable rate, and in solid coin.

In consciousness of Christianity, my royal master's clemency, and the honor of soldiership, I have dwelt upon this invitation, and wished for more persuasive terms to give it impression; and let not people be led to disregard it, by considering their distance from the immediate situation of my camp. I have but to give stretch to the Indian forces under my direction, and they amount to thousands, to overtake the hardened enemies of Great Britain and America; I consider them the same wherever they may lurk.

If, notwithstanding these endeavors, and sincere inclinations to effect them, the frenzy of hostility should remain, I trust I shall stand acquitted in the eyes of God and men in denouncing and executing the vengeance of the State against the wilful outcasts. The messengers of justice and of wrath await them in the field; and devastation, famine, and every concomitant horror that a reluctant but indispensable prosecution of military duty must occasion, will bar the way to their return.[1]

JULY 2.—THE following answer to Burgoyne's proclamation was written by a young officer, and designed for the soldiers in the American army:

[1] Pennsylvania Evening Post, August 21.

To John Burgoyne, Esquire, Lieutenant-General of his Maj-
esty's armies in America, Colonel of the Queen's regiment
of light dragoons, Governor of Fort William in North
Britain, one of the Representatives of the Commons of
Great Britain, and commanding an army and fleet em-
ployed on an expedition from Canada, &c., &c., &c.

MOST HIGH, MOST MIGHTY, MOST PUISSANT, AND SUBLIME
GENERAL.

When the forces under your command arrived at Quebec,
in order *to act in concert and upon a common principle with*
the numerous fleets and armies which already dis-
play in every quarter of America the justice and   Answer to
Burgoyne.
mercy of your King, we, the reptiles of America, were struck
with unusual trepidation and astonishment.   But what words
can express the plenitude of our horror when the *Colonel of the*
Queen's regiment of light dragoons advanced towards Ticonderoga.   The mountains shook before thee, and the trees of the
forest bowed their lofty heads ; the vast lakes of the north were
chilled at thy presence, and the mighty cataracts stopped their
tremendous career, and were suspended in awe at thy approach.
Judge, then, *oh ineffable Governor of Fort William in North*
Britain, what must have been the terror, dismay, and despair
that overspread this paltry continent of America, and us its
wretched inhabitants.   Dark and dreary, indeed, was the prospect before us, till, like the sun in the horizon, your most
gracious, sublime, and irresistible proclamation opened the
doors of mercy, and snatched us, as it were, from the jaws of
annihilation.

We foolishly thought, blind as we were, that your gracious
master's fleets and armies were come to destroy us and our
liberties ; but we are happy in hearing from you (and who
can doubt what you assert ?) that they were *called forth for*
the sole purpose of restoring the rights of the constitution to a
froward and stubborn generation.

And is it for this, oh sublime *lieutenant-general,* that you
have given yourself the trouble to cross the wide Atlantic,
and with incredible fatigue traverse uncultivated wilds ?   And

we ungratefully refuse the proffered blessing? To restore the rights of the constitution you have called together an amiable host of savages, and turned them loose to scalp our women and children, and lay our country waste—this they have performed with their usual skill and clemency, and we yet remain insensible of the benefit, and unthankful for so much goodness!

Our Congress have declared Independence, and our Assemblies, as your highness justly observes, have most *wickedly* imprisoned the avowed friends of that power with which they are at war, and most PROFANELY compelled those, whose consciences will not permit them to fight, to pay some small part towards the expenses their country is at in supporting what we call a necessary defensive war. If we go on thus in our obstinacy and ingratitude, what can we expect but that you should, in your anger, *give a stretch to the Indian forces under your direction, amounting to thousands, to overtake and destroy us;* or which is ten times worse, that you should withdraw your fleets and armies and leave us to our own misery, without completing the benevolent task you have begun, *in restoring to us the rights of the constitution.*

We submit, we submit, *most puissant Colonel of the Queen's regiment of light dragoons, and Governor of Fort William in North Britain!* We offer our heads to the scalping knife and our bellies to the bayonet. Who can resist the force of your eloquence? Who can withstand the terror of your arms? The invitation you have made in the *consciousness of Christianity, your royal master's clemency, and the honor of soldiership,* we thankfully accept. The blood of the slain, the cries of injured virgins and innocent children, and the never-ceasing sighs and groans of starving wretches now languishing in the jails and prison ships of New York, call on us in vain, whilst your sublime proclamation is sounded in our ears. Forgive us, oh our country! Forgive us, dear posterity! Forgive us, all ye foreign powers who are anxiously watching our conduct in this important struggle, if we yield implicitly to the persuasive tongue of the most elegant *Colonel of her Majesty's regiment of light dragoons.*

Forbear then, thou magnanimous *lieutenant-general!* Forbear to denounce vengeance against us! Forbear to *give a stretch to those restorers of constitutional rights*, the *Indian forces under your direction*.—Let not *the messengers of wrath await us in the field, and devastation, famine, and every concomitant horror*, bar our return to the allegiance of a prince, who, by his royal will, would deprive us of every blessing of life, with all possible clemency.

We are *domestic*, we are *industrious*, we are *infirm and timid;* we shall *remain quietly at home, and not remove our cattle, or corn, or forage*, in hopes that you will come at *the head of troops in the full powers of health, discipline, and valor*, and take charge of them for yourselves. Behold our wives and daughters, our flocks and herds, our goods and chattels.—Are they not at the mercy of our Lord the King, and of his *lieutenant-general, member of the House of Commons, and governor of Fort William in North Britain*? [1]

PROCLAMATION.

By John Burgoyne, and Burgoyne John, Esquire,
And grac'd with titles still more higher;
For I'm lieutenant-general too,
Of George's troops both red and blue.
On this extensive continent;
And of Queen Charlotte's regiment
Of light dragoons the colonel:
And governor eke of Castle Will.
And furthermore, when I am there, ⎫
In House of Commons I appear,   ⎬
(Hoping ere long to be a Peer,)   ⎭
Being member of that virtuous band
Who always vote at North's command;
Directing, too, the fleet and troops
From Canada as thick as hops;
And all my titles to display,
I'll end with thrice et cætera.

The troops consign'd to my command,
Like Hercules to purge the land,
Intend to act in combination
With th' other forces of the nation,

[1] A, B, C, D, etc., etc., in the New York Journal, September 8.

Displaying wide thro' every quarter
What Briton's justice would be after.
It is not difficult to show it,
And every mother's son must know it,
That what she meant at first to gain
By requisitions and chicane,
She's now determin'd to acquire
By kingly reason, sword, and fire.
I can appeal to all your senses,
Your judgments, feelings, tastes, and fancies;
Your ears and eyes have heard and seen
How causeless this revolt has been;
And what a dust your leaders kick up,
In this rebellious civil hick-up,
And how upon this curs'd foundation ⎱
Was rear'd the system of vexation, ⎰
Over a stubborn generation.
But now inspir'd with patriot love,
I come th' oppression to remove;
To free you from the heavy clog
Of every tyrant-demagogue,
Who for the most romantic story,
Claps into limbo loyal Tory,
All hurly burly, hot and hasty,
Without a writ to hold him fast by;
Nor suffers any living creature
(Led by the dictates of his nature)
To fight in *green* for Britain's cause,
Or aid us to restore her laws:
In short, the vilest generation,
Which in vindictive indignation,
Almighty vengeance ever hurl'd
From this, to the infernal world.
A Tory cannot move his tongue,
But whip in prison he is flung,
His goods and chattels made a prey
By those vile mushrooms of a day.
He's tortur'd too, and scratch'd, and bit,
And plung'd into a dreary pit,
Where he must suffer sharper doom
Than e'er was hatch'd by Church of Rome.
These things are done by rogues, who dare
Profess to breathe in freedom's air.
To petticoats alike and breeches,
Their cruel domination stretches,
For the sole crime, or sole suspicion,
(What worse is done by th' inquisition!)

Of all still adhering to the Crown,
Their tyrants striving to kick down,
Who by perverting law and reason,
Allegiance construe into treason.
Religion, too, is often made
A stalking horse to drive the trade,
And warring churches dare implore
Protection from th' Almighty pow'r;
They fast and pray: In Providence,
Profess to place their confidence;
And vainly think the Lord of all
Regards our squabbles on this ball;
Which would appear as droll in Britain
As any whim that one could hit on:
Men's consciences are set at nought,
Nor reason valued at a groat;
And they that will not swear and fight,
Must sell their all, and say good night.

By such important views there prest to,
I issue this my manifesto.
I, the great knight of *De la Mancha*,
Without Squire Carleton my Sancho,
Will tear you limb from limb asunder,
With cannon, blunderbuss, and thunder;
And spoil your feath'ring and your tarring,
And cag you up for pickl'd herring.
In front of troops as spruce as beaux,
And ready to lay on their blows,
I'll spread destruction far and near;
And where I cannot kill, I'll spare;
Inviting, by these presents all,
Both old and young, and great and small,
And rich and poor, and Whig and Tory,
In cellar deep, or lofty story,
Wher'er my troops at my command,
Shall swarm like locusts o'er the land,
(And they shall march from the North Pole,
As far at least as Pensecole,)
So break off all their communications,
That I can save their habitations;
For finding that Sir William's plunders,
Prove in the event apparent blunders,
It is my full determination,
To check all kinds of depredation;
But when I've got you in my pow'r,
Favor'd is he, I last devour.

From him who loves a quiet life,
And keeps at home to kiss his wife,
And drinks success to King Pigmalion,
And calls all Congresses Rabscallion,
With neutral stomach eats his supper,
Nor deems the contest worth a copper,
I will not defalcate a groat,
Nor force his wife to cut his throat;
But with his doxy he may stay,
And live to fight another day;
Drink all the cider he has made,
And have to boot, a green cockade.
But as I like a good Sir Loin,
And mutton-chop whene'er I dine,
And my poor troops have long kept lent,
Not for religion but for want,
Whoe'er secretes cow, bull, or ox,
Or shall presume to hide his flocks;
Or with felonious hand eloign
Pig, duck, or gosling from Burgoyne;
Or dare to pull the bridges down,
My boys to puzzle or to drown;
Or smuggle hay, or plough or harrow,
Cart, horses, wagons, or wheel-barrow;
Or 'thwart the path, lay straw or switch,
As folks are wont to stop a witch,
I'll hang him as the Jews did Haman,
And smoke his carcass for a gammon.

I'll pay in coin for what I eat,
Or Continental counterfeit;
But what's more likely still, I shall
(So fare my troops) not pay at all.

With the most Christian spirit fir'd,
And by true soldiership inspired,
I speak as men do in a passion,
To give my speech the more impression.
If any should so hardened be, ⎫
As to expect impunity,   ⎬
Because *procul a fulmine*,   ⎭
I will let loose the dogs of hell,
Ten thousand Indians, who shall yell,
And foam and tear, and grin and roar,
And drench their maukesins in gore;
To these I'll give full scope and play
From Ticonderog to Florida;

They'll scalp your heads, and kick your shins,
And rip your guts, and flay your skins,
And of your ears be nimble croppers,
And make your thumbs tobacco stoppers.

If after all these loving warnings,
My wishes and my bowels' yearnings,
You shall remain as deaf as adder,
Or grow with hostile rage the madder,
I swear by George and by Saint Paul,
I will exterminate you all.
Subscribed with my manual sign,
To test these presents,

JOHN BURGOYNE.[1]

JULY 4.—THIS day, being the Anniversary of American Independence, when the thirteen United States publicly
Independence cele- and gloriously threw off the shackles forged by
brated in Boston. George the Third, the British tyrant, and nobly reassumed those rights which God and nature bestowed on man, the same has been noticed by every mark of joy. In the forenoon, the Reverend Mr. Gordon, of Roxbury, at the desire of the assembly sitting at Boston, preached an excellent discourse from 1 Kings xii. 15. After which the General Court having given previous orders for making every preparation for drinking success to the Thirteen United States, sent an invitation to General Heath, and the officers of the Continental army and navy; Colonel Crafts and the officers of the train; Colonel Hichborn, of the independent company; Colonel Hatch, the officers of the militia, and many other gentlemen. While the Congress, and other toasts were drank, the guns at Fort Hill, Castle Island, Hull, and the vessels of war in the harbor, fired a grand salute. Also a detachment of Colonel Crafts' regiment of artillery in Congress street, gave thirteen discharges from brass cannon and with powder, both manufactured in the State of Massachusetts. The independent company and the militia, in conjunction with the train of artillery, made a very martial appearance, manœuvred and performed their

[1] "A New Jerseyman," in the New York Journal, September 8.

firings in view of the General Court, to their full acceptance,
and the approbation of the spectators at large.

In the evening Colonel Crafts illuminated his park on the
common, threw several shells, and exhibited a number of fireworks. The cheerful appearance of the gentlemen and ladies
in the park, and the pleasantness of the eve, closed with
universal satisfaction the joys of the day, which so conspic-
uously appeared in the countenances of every true friend of
America.[1]

WE hear that the young ladies of Amelia county, in Virginia, considering the situation of their country in particular,
and that of the United States in general, have entered into a resolution not to permit the addresses of any person, be his circumstances or situation in life what they will, unless he has
served in the American armies long enough to prove by his
valor that he is deserving of their love.[2]

JULY 5.—YESTERDAY, being the first anniversary of the Independence of the United States of America, was celebrated
Independence in Philadelphia with demonstrations of joy and
celebrated in
Philadelphia. festivity. About noon all the armed ships and
galleys in the river were drawn up before the city, dressed in
the gayest manner, with the colors of the United States and
streamers displayed. At one o'clock, the yards being properly
manned, they began the celebration of the day by a discharge
of thirteen cannon from each of the ships, and one from each
of the thirteen galleys, in honor of the thirteen United States.

In the afternoon an elegant dinner was provided for Congress, to which were invited the president and the supreme
executive council, and speaker of the assembly of the State,
the general officers and colonels of the army, and strangers of
eminence, and the members of the several continental boards
in town. The Hessian band of music, taken in Trenton the
twenty-sixth of December last, attended and heightened the
festivity with some fine performances suited to the joyous

---

[1] Pennsylvania Evening Post, July 24.   [2] Pennsylvania Journal, July 16.

occasion; while a corps of British deserters, taken into the service of the continent by the State of Georgia, being drawn up before the door, filled up the intervals with *feux de joie.* After dinner a number of toasts were drank, all breathing Independence, and a generous love of liberty, and commemorating the memories of those brave and worthy patriots who gallantly exposed their lives, and fell gloriously in defence of freedom and the righteous cause of their country.

Each toast was followed by a discharge of artillery and small arms, and a suitable piece of music by the Hessian band.

The glorious fourth of July was reiterated three times, accompanied with triple discharges of cannon and small arms, and loud huzzas that resounded from street to street through the city. Towards evening several troops of horse, a corps of artillery, and a brigade of North Carolina forces, which was in town on its way to join the grand army, were drawn up in Second street, and reviewed by Congress and the general officers. The evening was closed with the ringing of bells, and at night there was a grand exhibition of fire-works (which began and concluded with thirteen rockets) on the commons, and the city was beautifully illuminated. Every thing was conducted with the greatest order and decorum, and the face of joy and gladness was universal.

Thus may the fourth of July, that glorious and ever memorable day, be celebrated through America by the sons of freedom, from age to age, till time shall be no more. Amen and amen.[1]

JULY 7.—FRIDAY last being the first anniversary of the glorious formation of the American empire, when thirteen colonies, driven by necessity, threw off the yoke and rejected the tyranny of Great Britain by declaring themselves free, independent, and sovereign States, the same was commemorated by every demonstration of joy. Ringing of bells ushered in the day. At sunrise, American colors were displayed from all the forts and batteries, and vessels in the harbor. The Charleston regiment of militia, com- Independence celebrated in Charleston, S. C.

---

[1] Pennsylvania Journal, July 9.

manded by the Honorable Colonel Charles Pinckney, and the
Charleston artillery company, commanded by Captain Thomas
Grimball, were assembled upon the parade, and reviewed by his
Excellency the President, who was attended upon this occasion
by his honor the Vice-President and the honorable members of
the privy council. At one o'clock the several forts, beginning
with Fort Moultrie, on Sullivan's Island, discharged seventy-
six pieces of cannon, alluding to the glorious year 1776, and
the militia and artillery fired three general volleys. His Excellency the President then gave a most elegant entertainment
in the council chamber, at which were present all the members
of the Legislature then in town, all the public officers, civil
and military, the clergy, and many strangers of note, to the
amount of more than double the number that ever observed
the birthday of the present misguided and unfortunate King
of Great Britain. After dinner the following toasts were
drank, viz. : "1. The free, independent, and sovereign States
of America. 2. The great council of America—may wisdom
preside in all its deliberations. 3. General Washington. 4.
The American army and navy—may they be victorious and invincible. 5. The nations in friendship or alliance with America. 6. The American ambassadors at foreign courts. 7. The
fourth of July, 1776. 8. The memory of the officers and soldiers who have bravely fallen in defence of America. 9. South
Carolina. 10. May only those Americans enjoy freedom who
are ready to die for its defence. 11. Liberty triumphant. 12.
Confusion, shame, and disgrace to our enemies—may the foes
to America (slaves to tyranny) humble and fall before her. 13.
May the rising States of America reach the summit of human
power and grandeur, and enjoy every blessing." Each toast
was succeeded by a salute of thirteen guns, which were fired
by Captain Grimball's company from their two field-pieces,
with admirable regularity. The day having been spent in
festivity, and the most conspicuous joy and harmony, the
evening was concluded with illuminations, &c., far exceeding
any that had ever been exhibited before.[1]

[1] Pennsylvania Journal, July 30.

JULY 9.—THIS night, General Prescott, who has held the command of the British forces on Rhode Island, since the departure of Earl Percy, was taken prisoner at his quarters, and carried off by a party of Americans. The following particular account of the manner of his taking, is by a gentleman from Rhode Island :—Lieutenant-Colonel Barton,[1] of Warren, in Rhode Island, is a young gentleman of about twenty-three or twenty-four years of age, of a martial and enterprising disposition, who has signalized himself on several occasions, particularly in attacking and driving the noted pirate, Wallace, and a party of his men, from an island near Newport, which they had been robbing and plundering ; and in an expedition last fall, to Long Island, attacking a number of Tories, and bringing them prisoners to New Haven. He was then a captain, having refused a higher post till he had done more to deserve it ; and in the body of forces lately raised by the State of Rhode Island for fifteen months, was appointed lieutenant-colonel in Colonel Stanton's regiment, stationed at Howland's ferry, on the west side of the river.

General Prescott taken by Colonel Barton.

Here Colonel Barton happening to see a deserter from the British army in Newport, who gave him a particular account of the place where General Prescott kept his head-quarters, formed a scheme to surprise and bring him off. It being communicated to and approved of by the commanding officer, Colonel Barton selected and engaged about forty men to go with him on a secret expedition by water in five batteaux. When they were prepared and got to the shore he told them his design, acknowledged it was hazardous, and probably could not be executed without the loss of life to some of those engaged in it ; that for his part he was determined to risk his, which would be at least as much exposed as any of theirs ; but if any of them were unwilling to engage in the enterprise, they were then at full liberty to decline it, and he should not have the worse opinion of any person for so doing ; that he desired no man with him who did not go willingly, and would freely hazard his life to render his country an important service, and

---

[1] William Barton, born May 26, 1748, died October 22, 1831.

obtain honor to himself. On putting the matter to their
choice, they unanimously resolved to go with him.

They then set off with muffled oars, crossed the bay, passed
Bristol ferry, where the British have a fort, undiscovered, and
went to Warwick Neck on Providence side, near the east side
of the island, where the British have several forts but no ships,
as they would be exposed to the guns in our forts. They passed
the enemy's redoubts on the east side, and when they came to
the west, which is guarded all along by the enemy's ships-of-
war, they passed between them and the shore till they came
opposite to the house where General Prescott kept his head-
quarters. Here they landed, about five miles from Newport,
and three-quarters of a mile from the house, which they approached cautiously, avoiding the main guard, which was at
some distance. The colonel went foremost, with a stout, active negro close behind him, and another at a small distance ;
the rest followed so as to be near, but not seen.

A single sentinel at the door saw and hailed the colonel ;
he answered by exclaiming against and inquiring for rebel
prisoners, but kept slowly advancing. The sentinel again
challenged him, and required the countersign ; he said he had
not the countersign, but amused the sentry by talking about
rebel prisoners, and still advancing till he came within reach
of the bayonet, which, he presenting, the colonel suddenly
struck aside and seized him. He was immediately secured
and ordered to be silent, on pain of instant death. Meanwhile, the rest of the men surrounding the house, the negro,
with his head, at the second stroke forced a passage into it,
and then into the landlord's apartment. The landlord at first
refused to give the necessary intelligence ; but on the prospect
of present death he pointed to the general's chamber, which
being instantly opened by the negro's head, the colonel calling
the general by name, told him he was a prisoner. He replied
he knew it, and rising from his bed, desired time to put on his
clothes. The colonel told him to put on his breeches, and the
rest of his clothes should be carried with him, at the same time
handing his slippers from the bedside. Meawhile the general's
aide-de-camp got out of the window in his shirt, but was there

secured by some of the party, who all went off by the same way they came, carrying with them the general, his aide-de-camp, and the sentinel.

The general was desired to run, but he said he was an old man and could not. He was told that they would help him, and accordingly a stout man taking him under the arm on each side, enabled him to run. As they went through a field of barley, the stalks very much annoying the general's naked legs, he exclaimed, "Gentlemen, do you mean to kill me?" One of them replied, "No, we do not intend to kill you, but to exchange you for General Lee, and after that we do not care how soon the devil has you."

They all embarked in their boats, and rowing back the same way they came, passed all the enemy's ships and forts undiscovered. When they passed the last fort, the general exclaimed, "And is it possible that I am a prisoner of war! Yes, I see I am; but when you set out with me, I had no doubt but that I should have been rescued, and you all have been made prisoners."

When the boats had got almost to Warwick Neck, a sky rocket was sent off, and immediately alarm guns were fired from all the ships and forts on and about the island, and there appeared to be such a general confusion and consternation, that it was thought one thousand men could have taken them all prisoners. From Warwick Neck a flag was sent for the general's clothes.

Thus was this general officer, in the midst of the British army and navy, where he was commander-in-chief, made prisoner, together with his aide-de-camp and the sentinel that guarded his door, by the bravery and judicious conduct of this young colonel and his gallant followers, without the loss of a man, or the fire of a gun, though they did not expect to have accomplished their design without resistance and a pursuit from the enemy, for both of which they were prepared. In the planning and execution of this enterprise, Colonel Barton has given a noble proof of his zeal and ability to render the most important services to his country. In comparison to this action, how contemptible was that of Colonel Harcourt,

for which the King, his master, was in raptures, and lavished
upon him such extravagant encomiums,—his surprisal, with a
large force, of General Lee, unguarded, several miles distant
from his army, and betrayed by an ungrateful wretch, on
whom he had just before been conferring great and unmerited
favors.[1]

JULY 17.—By an express from the northward we learn
that the American forces, under the command of General St.

Ticonderoga Abandoned. Clair, abandoned Fort Ticonderoga and the adjoining lines, on the morning of the 6th instant,
and are now encamped in the vicinity of Moses Creek. A
letter from an officer at that place, written this day, gives
the following account of the retreat and its consequences:—
The retreat from Ticonderoga will be a matter of speculation

[1] Pennsylvania Evening Post, August 7:—A writer in Providence, Rhode Isl-
and, gives the following account of this expedition: July 12.—Thursday evening
last, a party of thirty-eight men of the troops belonging to this State, under the
command of Lieutenant-Colonel William Barton, of this town, accompanied by
Major Adams, of the train, Captain Phillips, Lieutenants Porter and Babcock, and
Ensigns Stanton and Wilcox, went in five boats from Warwick Neck, with a view
to take Major-General Prescott, commander-in-chief of the British and foreign
troops on Rhode Island, whose head-quarters were then at a house about four
miles from Newport. The colonel and his party, after passing the enemy's ships
and guard boats, landed about twelve at night, and with "infinite address and
gallantry" got to Prescott's quarters undiscovered. A sentinel at the door hailed
but was immediately secured, and the party instantly breaking the doors and
entering the house, took the general in bed. His aide-de camp leaped from a
window in his shirt, but was taken a few rods from the house. The party soon
after returned to their boats with the prisoners, and some time after they had put
off, the enemy fired rockets from their several posts, as signals for an alarm, but
too late, the bird had fled. The prisoners were landed about daybreak at Warwick
Neck.

On receiving the intelligence at Providence, a coach was immediately sent,
and the general; with his aide-de-camp, attended by Colonel Barton and some
other officers, arrived in that town at twelve o'clock. This bold and important
enterprise must reflect the highest honor on Colonel Barton and his little party.
*A lieutenant-colonel of the horse, with at least seventy light dragoons, took Major-
General Lee, (betrayed by a Tory,) five miles from his troops. A lieutenant-colonel
of foot, with only thirty-eight privates and six officers, has taken a chief commander, when almost encircled by an army and navy.—Pennsylvania Evening
Post,* July 29.

in the country, and the accounts different and confused, a true state of facts will therefore be very satisfactory without doubt.

We were deceived with respect to the strength of the enemy, and our own reinforcements. The enemy have practised a piece of finesse which has too well answered their purpose; they have so conducted that all hands in the United States believed they had drawn their force from Canada to the southward, and designed only to garrison their posts in the northern world; the consequence of this belief has been the ordering eight regiments, destined for Ticonderoga and its environs, to Peekskill, and little attention has been paid to this department. The enemy's condition in Canada has been represented as miserable, confused, scattered and sickly; this has been the general opinion in camp and country, and our situation has been thought perfectly safe.

Our force consisted of about four thousand, including the corps of artillery, and artificers who were not armed, a considerable part of which were militia; we could bring about three thousand fit for duty into the field. General Burgoyne came against us with about eight thousand healthy, spirited troops, with a lake force consisting of three fifty-gun ships, a thunder mounting eighteen brass twenty-four pounders, two thirteen-inch mortars, a number of howitz, several sloops, gun-boats, &c., &c.

Their strength being so very superior to ours obliged us to tamely sit still and see them erect batteries all around us, without hazarding a sally. Two batteries were erected in front of our lines, on higher ground than ours; within half a mile on our left they had taken post on a very high hill overlooking all our works; our right would have been commanded by their shipping and the batteries they had erected on the other side of the lake. Our lines at Ticonderoga would have been of no service, and we must have inevitably abandoned them in a few days after their batteries opened, which would have been the next morning; we then should have been necessitated to retire to Fort Independence, the consequence of which, I conceive, would have been much worse than the mode adopted; for the

moment we had left Ticonderoga fort, they could send their
shipping by us, and prevent our communication with Skenesborough; then the only avenue to and from Fort Independence
would have been by a narrow neck of land leading from the
mount to the Grants. To this neck they had almost cut a road;
a day more would have completed it. A few troops stationed
at Ticonderoga, would have prevented our communication
with Lake George, as our own works would have been against
us. Their shipping would have destroyed our connection with
Skenesborough, and their main body might have been placed
on this neck of land, which, by a few works, might have prevented all supplies and reinforcements; we might have stayed
at the mount as long as our provisions would have supported
us; we had flour for thirty days, and meat sufficient only for a
week. Under these circumstances General St. Clair, on the
sixth instant, called a council of war, and an evacuation was
unanimously agreed upon as the only means of saving the army
from captivity.

It was necessary also that our retreat should be precipitate,
as the communication was almost cut off, and they would soon
be apprised of our designs. It was therefore determined to
send the baggage and sick in boats to Skenesborough, and for
the army to march by land from the mount to that place,
being forty miles. At the dawn of day we left Fort Independence, and I cannot say the march was conducted with the
greatest regularity; the front, which was the main body, marched thirty miles to a place called Castleton, about twelve
miles from Skenesborough; the militia halted three miles in
the rear of the front, and the rear guard, commanded by Colonel Francis, being joined by Colonels Warner and Hale, halted at Hubbardton, about a mile and a half in the rear of the
militia. As the march was severe, the feeble of the army had
fallen in the rear, and tarried at Hubbardton with the rear
guard. This body in rear might consist of near a thousand
men. Before I proceed further it may be necessary to give you
the enemy's dispositions after they were advised of our retreat:
A large body, at least two thousand, were detached to pursue
our main body and harass our rear; all the gun boats and some

of their shipping were sent after our baggage, came up with it at Skenesborough and took it. The ninth regiment, commanded by Lieutenant-Colonel Hills, was ordered to run down South Bay, and land and march on a by road to Fort Ann, and take that before our troops could reach it; the remainder of the army went on to Skenesborough, except a garrison at Ticonderoga.

The body of the enemy sent to harass our rear, came up with it the next morning at Hubbardton, which was then commanded by Colonel Warner; by the exertions of the officers our little army formed and gave them battle, which continued about twenty-five minutes very severe, when our party were overpowered with numbers and gave way. The loss on both sides was considerable; as our people took to the woods and are daily coming in, it is impossible to ascertain our loss. Colonel Francis, a worthy, brave officer, after signalizing himself, was shot through, and expired instantly; Colonel Hale is missing. It is natural to ask why was not Colonel Warner reinforced? Let me tell you; orders were sent to Colonel ———, who commanded the militia, to go to the assistance of the rear guard, but before they arrived, the action was over and our people dispersed. Our main body being now twelve miles from Skenesborough, and hearing that a large body of the enemy were arrived there, and knowing that a large body were in our rear, the general imagined if we pursued our route, that we must engage both in front and rear under great disadvantage; and to pursue his plan in first retreating, which was to save the army, he though prudent to file off to the left, and before we reached Hudson River, we marched one hundred and fifty miles; in this march we picked up about thirty prisoners, part British, part Waldeckers, and part Canadians. The party of our men who were at Skenesborough, retreated to Fort Ann; they were twice attacked by the ninth regiment, and both times repulsed them. They took a Captain Montgomery and a doctor, and would probably have taken the whole regiment had their ammunition held out. This is a candid statement of facts, and for this conduct we are told our country calls us either knaves or cowards; I conceive they

ought to be grateful to our general, for had we stayed we very
certainly should have been taken, and then no troops could have
stood between the enemy and the country. Our affairs now
are not desperate in this quarter, as they would certainly have
been ; we have destroyed Fort George and its appendages, and
shall soon be able, I hope, to make head against our enemies,
as we are gathering strength and re-collecting ourselves.[1]

ON the late alarm occasioned by the evacuation of Ticonderoga, a number of the Stockbridge Indians marched with
the militia of that county, and were stationed
with Generals Nixon and Fellows, between Fort
Edward and Fort Ann. On the eighteenth of July, General
Fellows sent out five of them on a scout to Skenesborough ;
the next day before sunset they returned with six prisoners,
consisting of two regulars and four Tories. The account being
somewhat entertaining, we shall give it to the public nearly in
their own words, as related by Abraham, who commanded the
party. He says : " We passed the creek, and went within a
mile or two of Skene's house, where we lay down in a thick
spot of woods, by the side of the road. It was not long before there came along two regulars driving a number of horses ;
we jumped up and seized them ; the regulars were so very
much frightened that they made no resistance ; neither could
they speak plain. We found by the noise there were a number more behind driving cattle. One of our prisoners called
to the sergeant for help ; upon this we thought it wise to make
the best of our way into the woods. Our prisoners attempted
to get away from us ; we were therefore obliged to make them
feel that our hatchets were heavy. I told them, " If you will
behave like prisoners, we will use you well ; but if you don't,
we must kill you." After this they behaved well, and did
every thing we bid them. On our way to our encampment,
we thought we would take in with us as many Tories as we
could find ; and in order to find them out, we gave our prisoners their guns, taking out the flints. When we came near a

Stockbridge Indians.

[1] Pennsylvania Evening Post, August 9.

house, we told our prisoners, " you must keep before us, and if you see any men you must cock your guns and present them at them, and demand who they are for, the King or country." They did so, and the Tories answered they were for the King, or they should have moved off long ago. They seemed to be glad to see the regulars, and told them, " You are our brothers." I knew one of the Tories as soon as I came in sight of him ; I therefore put my hat over my face for fear the fellow should know me till the red coats had done their duty. After he had in a most strong manner declared he was for the King, I asked him further, " Will you be true to the King, and fight for him till you die ? " " O yes," said the Tory. Upon this he discovered his error, knew me, and immediately said, "What King do you mean ? I mean King Hancock." " Ah," said I ; " we have found you out ; we don't know kings in America yet ; you must go along with us."

When they came near the camp, their war-cry was heard and answered by the rest, who went out to meet them. The prisoners were delivered to General Nixon, and sent to head-quarters.[1]

JULY 27.—GENERAL BURGOYNE is at Fort Edward, and has with him about six thousand regulars, three or four hundred Indians, and about two hundred Canadians. The frequent injuries and horrible actions committed Murder of
Jenny M'Crea. by his scouting parties on single unarmed men and defenceless women, are sufficient to give every man a thorough detestation of their whole conduct ; and were not the Tories' hearts made of more than iron hardness, it would inspire them with a desire of ridding this world of such a set of villains as their army is in general composed of. Several of our officers and soldiers have been inhumanly shot as they passed from one fort to another unarmed, and scalped while yet alive. It would take too much time to enumerate every action of this kind. One instance which happened yesterday, during a skirmish, may serve for the whole. A young lady, by the name of Miss

[1] Pennsylvania Journal, September 3.

Jenny M'Crea, of a good family, and some share of beauty, was, by some accident, at Fort Edward when the enemy attacked the picket guard. She and an old woman were taken by the savages, who generally serve as an advance guard or flanking parties to the regulars, (the latter of whom were drawn up on a hill just above the fort,) and then, with a barbarity unheard of before, they butchered the poor innocent girl, and scalped her in the sight of those very men who are continually preaching up their tender mercies, and the forbearance of their more than Christian King. Is not this sufficient to congeal the heart of humanity with horror, and even oblige a Tory of liberal sentiments to curse the cause which approves or winks at such worse than hell-like cruelties?

The unfortunate maid's corpse was brought to Snook Hill last night, together with a young lieutenant, a Mr. Van Rachter, of Brunswick, who is also scalped, and will be interred to-day. What renders this affair more remarkable is, that Miss M'Crea has a brother an officer in the British service, now at New York, and she herself leaned to that side of the question; but thus they treat their friends as well as their enemies. The young lady has also a brother a senior surgeon in our hospital, a worthy, sensible young fellow, who will not forget the injury, but revenge it tenfold.[1]

[1] Pennsylvania Evening Post, August 12. Another writer in the same paper gives the following account:—In retreating from Fort Edward the Americans brought off the grain and forage, and destroyed what they could not remove. Many families fled; those that would not come away, relying on General Burgoyne's proclamation, were killed, scalped, or inhumanly butchered by the Indians, without any discrimination of Whigs or Tories. A Miss M'Crea, who was to have been married to one Jones, a Tory, who had joined the enemy, and whom she daily expected to bring her off, was dragged by the savages out of her house, shot twice through her body, her clothes torn off her back, and left scalped in the bushes. This brutal scene was transacted by four Indians, under cover of three hundred British regulars, drawn up at a small distance, and in sight of an advanced party of Americans, who could give her no assistance. Several families have been murdered and scalped by the Indians; man, wife, and five or six children, and their negroes. Many families have fallen a sacrifice to their credulity in Burgoyne's proclamation, which promised protection to all who remained peaceably and quiet at their houses with their stock, &c.

AUGUST 1.—AT a meeting of the Common Hall, of Williamsburg, in Virginia, to-day, to take into consideration the arrival of General Washington's lady, they came to the following resolutions:—*Resolved unanimously*, That the most respectful testimony be presented to her on the occasion, of the high sense this hall entertains of General Washington's distinguished merit, as the illustrious defender and deliverer of his country.

Resolved unanimously, That a golden emblematical medal be prepared, to be presented to the general's lady, as the most suitable method of carrying that design into execution; and that the mayor be desired to form the device, and agree with some proper persons to execute the same.

Resolved unanimously, That the freedom of this city be presented to General Washington through his lady, and that the mayor be desired to wait upon her with the same, and with a copy of these several resolutions.[1]

AUGUST 5.—THIS morning, about eleven o'clock, arrived at Williamsburg, in Virginia, from the seat of Burwell Bassett, Esquire, in New Kent, Lady Washington, the amiable consort of his Excellency General Washington. Upon her arrival she was saluted with the fire of cannon and small arms, and was safely conducted to Mrs. Dawson's, in the city, and intends setting out for the northward in a few days.[2]

AUGUST 7.—YESTERDAY, about nine o'clock, an engagement ensued between a part of the militia of Tryon county, under the command of General Herkimer, and a party of savages, Tories, and regulars, a short distance from Fort Stanwix. It lasted till three o'clock in the afternoon, when the British thought proper to retire, leaving General Herkimer master of the field. Unluckily, however, the general and some valuable officers got wounded or killed in the beginning. But this did in nowise intimidate the ardor of the men, and the general, although he had two wounds, did

Lady Washington.

Siege of Fort Schuyler.

---

[1] New York Journal, September 8.   [2] Same.

not leave the field till the action was over. He seated himself on a log, with his sword drawn, animating his men.

About one o'clock, Colonel Gansevoort[1] having received information of General Herkimer's march, sent out Lieutenant-Colonel Willet,[2] with two hundred men, to attack an encampment of the British, and thereby facilitate General Herkimer's march. In this the colonel succeeded, for after an engagement of an hour he had completely routed the enemy, and taken one captain and four privates. The baggage taken was very considerable, such as money, bear skins, officers' baggage, and camp equipage; one of the soldiers had for his share a scarlet coat, trimmed with gold lace to the full, and three laced hats.

When Colonel Willet returned to the fort, he discovered two hundred regulars in full march to attack him. He immediately ordered his men to prepare for battle, and having a field-piece with him, Captain Savage so directed its fire as to play in concert with one out of the fort; these, with a brisk fire from his small arms, soon made these heroes scamper off with great loss. Colonel Willet then marched with his booty into the fort, having not a single man killed or wounded.

General St. Leger, who commands the enemy's force in that quarter, soon after sent in a flag to demand the delivery of the fort, offering that the garrison should march out with their baggage, and not be molested by the savages; that if this was not complied with, he would not answer for the conduct of the Indians, if the garrison fell into their hands; that General Burgoyne was in possession of Albany. Colonel Gansevoort, after animadverting on the barbarity and disgraceful conduct of the British officers, in suffering women and children to be butchered as they had done, informed the flag that he was resolved to defend the fort to the last, and that he would never give it up as long as there was a man left to defend it.[3]

[1] Peter Gansevoort.   [2] Marinus Willet.
[3] Pennsylvania Evening Post, August 19 and 21:—St. Leger continued the siege until the 22d of August, when he suddenly retreated.

A GENTLEMAN, who lived some years in Philadelphia, informs us, that during all his residence in that city, he never saw a person begging in the streets. This happy circumstance is owing to the following wise and useful institution: There is a building near the city called the Veteran House, which he describes to be about the size of the London Foundling Hospital, with large gardens adjoining. Into this house, all persons not being able to procure employment, are received, and put to work at their respective trades, the house supplying them with tools, materials, and every other requisite. They are likewise found in lodging, clothes, provisions, &c., and paid the customary price for their work, one shilling a day being deducted out of their earnings for the support of the foundation. Those who through laziness do not earn the stipulated sum, receive proper punishment. Persons who cannot give an account how they maintain themselves are compelled to work in the Veteran House. Might not, says our correspondent, similar institutions in this kingdom, especially in London, where, notwithstanding the excessive heighs of the poor's rate, every street swarms with beggars, be attended with very happy consequences?[1]

Veteran House at Philadelphia.

AUGUST 17.—YESTERDAY is to be remembered on account of a signal victory the militia, under the command of General Stark, obtained over a body of the King's troops, commanded by Colonel Baum, some account of which is here given by one who was himself in the action. It seems that General Burgoyne had detached this corps, consisting of about fifteen hundred men, chiefly Waldeckers and Brunswickers intermixed with some British troops and Tories, a motley compound, to penetrate as far as Bennington, and further if it should be found practicable, with a view to increase the number of his friends, to disperse his protections in the country, to procure for his army provisions, and to wreak his wrath and vengeance on those who had disregarded his calls of mercy, and slighted with indignity his proffered protection. Colonel Baum had advantageously posted his corps

Battle of Bennington.

[1] Upcott, v. 123.

within about five miles of Bennington meeting-house, where in different places they made breastworks for their own security. This digression was of such ill tendency, and savored so much of presumption, that General Stark, who was at that time providentially at Bennington, with his brigade of militia from New Hampshire State, determined to give him battle. Colonel Simond's regiment of militia in Berks county was invited to his assistance; and a part of Colonel Brown's arrived seasonably to attend on the action, and some volunteers from different towns, and Colonel Warner, with a part of his own regiment, joined him the same day. The general, it seems, wisely laid his plan of operation, and Divine Providence blessing us with good weather, between three and four o'clock P. M. he attacked them in front and flank in three or four different places, at the same instant, with irresistible impetuosity. The action was extremely hot for between one and two hours; the flanking parties had carried their points with great ease, when the front pressed on to their breastwork with an ardor and patience beyond expectation. The blaze of the guns of the contending parties reached each other, the fire was so extremely hot, and our men easily surmounting their breastworks, amidst peals of thunder and flashes of lightning from their guns, without regarding the roar of their field-pieces, that the enemy at once deserted their covers and ran; and in about five minutes their whole camp was in the utmost confusion and disorder, all their battalions were broken in pieces, and fled most precipitately; at which instant our whole army pressed after with redoubled ardor, pursued them for a mile, made considerable slaughter amongst them, and took many prisoners. One field-piece had already fallen in our hands. At this time our men stopped the pursuit, to gain breath, when the enemy being reinforced, our front fell back for a few rods for conveniency of ground, and being directed and collected by Colonel Rensselaer, and reinforced by Major Stanton, renewed the fight with redoubled ardor. They fell in upon the enemy with great impetuosity, put them to confusion and flight, and pursued them about a mile, making many prisoners. Two or three more brass field-pieces fell into our hands, which are supposed to be the whole of what they brought out with them. At this time darkness came upon us, and prevented our swallowing up the whole of this body. The enemy fled precipitately the succeeding night towards the North River, and, unless they should be met with by a party of our army there, may have reached there without any further molestation. Governor Skeene, in surprise and consternation, took horse and fled.

This action, which redounds so much to the glory of the Great Lord of the heavens, and God of armies, affords the Americans a lasting monument of the Divine power and goodness, and a most powerful argument of love to and trust in God. Our loss is about forty or fifty killed, and more wounded. The enemy's loss is greater, and many more wounded. Their baggage fell into our hands. The number of prisoners taken is said to be about six hundred. Two of their colonels were amongst the prisoners and mortally wounded. A number of inferior officers have also fallen into our hands, and in particular the general's aide-de-camp. A good number deserted and joined us. This victory is thought by some to equal any that has happened during the present controversy; and, as long as prudence, moderation, sobriety and valor, are of any estimation amongst the United States, will not fail to endear General Stark to them. It is the opinion of some, if a large body of militia was now called to act in conjunction with the northern army, the enemy might be entirely overthrown. May all be concerned to give God the glory, whilst we commend the good conduct of the officers and soldiers in general on so important an occasion.

There is adjoining Pittsfield, in Massachuetts, a place called Jericho. From this place forty men marched, under Colonel Brown, for Bennington; on their way eighteen of them deserted and went over to the enemy. After the battle, fifteen of the eighteen were found dead upon the field. The remaining twenty-two were in the action, signalized themselves by their bravery, and came off unhurt. May all villains and traitors meet a similar fate to that of the fifteen.[1]

[1] Account by "a gentleman who was present in the action."—*Pennsylvania Evening Post*, September 4.

AMONG the many brave militia who were in the action yesterday, at Bennington, the Reverend Mr. Allen, of Pittsfield, ought not to be omitted. At the commencement of the action, he marched up within a few yards of the enemy's breastworks, and demanded a surrender of the same in the name of the Congress, on which he received a shower of balls, accompanied with the epithet of a "damn'd bold Yankee." Mr. Allen, however, soon returned at the head of the Pittsfield militia, and was one of the first over the breastwork.

Thomas Allen.

[The above account reminds the printer of another he received from a private gentleman immediately after the battle of Bennington, which places Mr. Allen's conduct in a different point of view, and shows it to have arisen solely from a sudden impulse of humanity, which hurried him, contrary to the opinion and advice of his friends, into a total disregard of his own personal safety. On finding the superiority of our troops, and that the enemy had no probable means of escape, just before the onset he threw himself between the two armies, called to the enemy, reminded them of their situation, pathetically exhorted them, from a regard to justice to their country, and to their own safety, to surrender, and prevent the effusion of blood. While he was speaking, with his hat in his hand, a number of balls were fired at him, several of which went through his hat ; on which he retired, joined in the attack of the enemy, and was among the foremost to enter their intrenchments.][1]

AUGUST 23.—YESTERDAY morning, before daybreak, a body of rebels, under the command of Messrs Sullivan, Smallwood, and De Bourg, landed in two divisions upon the west end of Staten Island. By the acknowledgment of some of their officers, now prisoners here, their number was at least two thousand. One division of them soon fell in with a part of the New Jersey volunteers, which brigade was posted, in small detachments, along the side of the island, from

Sullivan's descent on Staten Island.

[1] New York Journal, September 22.

Decker's ferry to the point opposite Perth Amboy, a distance of fifteen miles. The rebels, greatly superior in numbers, had the fortune with success to engage the detachments that were commanded by Lieutenant-Colonel Laurence, and Lieutenant-Colonel Barton, who were both made prisoners, with several other officers, and a considerable number of men. They then marched down to Decker's ferry, where they burned about thirty-five tons of hay, and set fire to a barn. As soon as the alarm had reached head-quarters, Brigadier-General Campbell marched with the 52d British and 3d battalions of Waldeck, leaving a regiment of Anspack to guard the camp and redoubts. Upon the approach of the regular troops, the rebels instantly marched off with all speed. In the mean time Brigadier-General Skinner had collected those of his corps which had been dislodged from their stations, and detached Major Tympany, with twenty-five men, to gain information of the route which the enemy had taken. The major came up with a number of them at the house of Doctor Parker, which they were plundering. He attacked them immediately, killed several, and took the rest prisoners; among the killed was Mr. Smallwood's brigadier-major.

It was now known that the rebels on this side had gone off towards Richmond; they were eagerly pursued, and on the road beyond that village an account was received from Lieutenant-Colonel Dongan, that his post had been attacked by the second division of the enemy, and obliged to retire, (which they did with very little loss,) towards Lieutenant-Colonel Allen, who had himself very seasonably retired, and taken post on a height near Prince's Bay, where Lieutenant-Colonel Dongan had joined him. A large body of the rebels had twice made a show of attacking them, but finally declined it, and marched off towards the Old Blazing Star. Those two gallant officers soon determined to pursue them, and now gave information to Brigadier-General Skinner that they were on the way, and requested orders which were immediately despatched to them, to proceed, and at all events to attack the enemy as soon as possible, informing them at the same time, that their brother volunteers from the right were coming up with all speed to join them, and that the regular troops, with General Campbell, were at hand to support them. These orders were executed with equal spirit and success. Notwithstanding a great disparity of numbers, these new troops attacked the rear of the enemy, consisting of Smallwood's and other corps that are foremost in reputation among the rebels, with an intrepidity and perseverance that would have done honor to veterans. A considerable number of the enemy were killed, and about three hundred taken prisoners, including twenty-one officers, viz., one lieutenant-colonel, three majors, two captains, ten lieutenants, three ensigns, one surgeon, and one officer wounded. By this time General Campbell had got up one piece of cannon with a detachment of the artillery. That piece was soon followed by two or three more, and a well-directed fire of round and grape shot had a great effect on the rebel boats, and on those of their people who had got over to the Jersey shore. Our loss, in the whole affair, is five killed, seven wounded, and eighty-four missing. Among the wounded were Lieutenant-Colonel Dongan[1] and Major Barnes, both officers of distinguished bravery.

The rebels, by this attempt, have, indeed, got a good deal of plunder, chiefly from the inhabitants, of which they may possibly be ready to boast, for they have often boasted of exploits which honest men would deem a disgrace; and they have reason on this occasion to blush for their conduct.[2]

An American who took part in this expedition gives the following account: About eleven o'clock last night (August 23)
American
Account.
I returned to Hanover[3] from an excursion from Staten Island. Thursday, at four o'clock in the afternoon, the division marched from this place, and arrived at Elizabethtown; at ten in the evening moved down to Hal-

---

[1] Lieutenant-Colonel Edward Vaughan Dongan died of his wounds soon after the action. He was the commandant of the third battalion of New Jersey Volunteers; the youngest son of Walter Dongan, Esq., late of Staten Island; was bred to the law, and supported a most amiable character. He was in his twenty-ninth year, and left a young distressed widow to lament the death of an affectionate husband. Their only child died a few hours before him.—*Gaine's Mercury.*

[2] Gaine's Mercury, September 1.   [3] In New Jersey.

sted's Point, where there were boats collected, and at daybreak the division had completely crossed.   Colonel Ogden
with his own regiment, Colonel Dayton's, and about one hundred militia, crossed at the same time at the Old Blazing Star.
General Sullivan moved with General Deborre's brigade to
attack Colonel Barton's regiment that lay at the New Star.
General Smallwood, with his brigade, moved in another column to the Dutch church, to attack Colonel Buskirk's regiment; and Colonel Ogden marched in another column to
attack Allen's, Laurence's, and Dongan's regiments, that lay
about the Old Star.   General Smallwood's guide, instead of
bringing him in the rear of the regiment, led him in full front
of them; they formed on the east side of the bridge, and the
general was moving over in a solid column to attack them;
but the enemy, unwilling to be shot at, retreated to their
lines in the northeast part of the island.   Instead of Buskirk's,
it was a British regiment, which retreated so precipitately
that the general took their stand of colors, burnt seven small
armed vessels and a large barn full of forage.   The general
being ordered not to go any farther than that place, joined
General Sullivan at the New Star, who had in a little time
settled the matter with Colonel Barton's regiment, they
being but few in number, and the greatest poltroons I ever
saw.

   They made a show of fighting, but did not stand to receive
our fire; we took about thirty of them, and their colonel.
Colonel Ogden's party advancing with the utmost precipitation, drove the cowardly enemy before them, took Colonel
Laurence, three captains, six subalterns, one doctor, and eighty
privates.   General Sullivan marched the division to the Old
Star, and got them all over except the rear guard, which the
enemy advanced upon and took.   The bravery of the little
party commanded by Major Stewart would do honor to the
first troops in the world; they were posted behind a hedge,
and kept up such a blaze upon the enemy, that they were
forced to retreat every time they advanced; the little party,
consisting of not more than fifty men, having bravely maintained their post and expended their ammunition, Major Stew-

art, whose gallant behavior would do honor to the first of characters, told his party that he had too great respect for their bravery to sacrifice them, that he would surrender himself and give those that could swim an opportunity to get off; they all pulled off their hats, and begged of him not to surrender; that some of them had two cartridges left, that they would fire them, and stand by him till they were cut to pieces. They were, however, obliged to surrender, and Stewart, fixing a white handkerchief on the point of his sword, walked as coolly as if he had been going to shake hands with a friend; many of the party got over the river. The action was grand, though horrid. I plainly saw the whole. We have lost three majors, some captains, subalterns, stragglers, and in all one hundred and twenty-seven privates.

By a gentleman from Albany, we are favored with the following anecdote: At the late battle between General Herkimer and the enemy at Oneida Creek, there was a friendly Indian, with his wife and son, who distinguished themselves remarkably on that occasion. The Indian killed nine of the enemy, when having received a ball through his wrist that disabled him from using his gun, he fought with his tomahawk. His son killed two, and his wife on horseback, fought by his side, with pistols, during the whole action, which lasted six hours.[1]

AUGUST 25.—YESTERDAY morning (Sunday) part of the Continental army, amounting to about ten thousand men, with his Excellency General Washington at their head, marched through Philadelphia, and proceeded over the Schuylkill to the southward. This day General Nash's brigade of North Carolinians and Colonel Proctor's regiment of artillery have also passed through the city, and are to pursue the same route in order to join our most illustrious general.[3]

[1] New York Journal, September 15.   [2] Pennsylvania Journal, Sept. 3.
[3] Pennsylvania Journal, August 27. General Washington, in a letter of August 23, says, "I expect this evening to encamp within five or six miles of Philadelphia. To-morrow morning it will move again; and I think to march it

EARLY this morning the people of Liverpool, in England, received the account of General Burgoyne and his brave forces having taken the fortress of Ticonderoga from the provincials, a place fortified so well both by art and nature as to imprint an idea in the minds of many that it was impregnable. But what task is too hard, what dangers so great, or what obstacles too difficult for British seamen and soldiers to surmount at any time, but more especially when commanded by a Howe or a Burgoyne? This welcome news diffused·a universal joy through all ranks of people. And in celebration of this glorious event, colors were displayed on the public buildings and on the ships in the docks and harbor. The bells rang, the cannon planted on the batteries, and in other parts of the town, were, at intervals, discharged; at noon, the invalids quartered there, were drawn up before the Exchange, and fired three volleys, by way of *feu de joie*, and this evening sky-rockets and other fireworks have been exhibited.[1]

AUGUST 26.—THE governor and the council of New Jersey have confined James Parker, one of his Britannic majesty's nominal council of that quondam province, and Walter Rutherford, both gentlemen of very large Disaffected Jerseymen. landed estates, which they seem determined to secure by such a neutrality of conduct as to stand equally fair with both contending parties in the final result of the conflict. Having evinced their disaffection, or at least want of affection to the present government, by repeatedly refusing to take the oaths of abjuration and allegiance prescribed by law, (as a test to try all suspicious and doubtful characters,) and hence become proper objects for the purpose; they are to be kept in durance until the honorable John Fell, a real councillor of New Jersey, and Captain Wynant Van Zandt, a young gentle-

through the city without halting. I am induced to do this from the opinion of several of my officers and many friends in Philadelphia, that it may have some influence on the minds of the disaffected there, and those who are dupes to their artifices and opinions. The march will be down Front and up Chesnut-streets, and I presume about seven o'clock."—*Official Letters,* ed. 1795, v. 2, p. 144.

[1] Gaine's Mercury, October 18.

man of great magnanimity and merit, (both kidnapped by the
Tories in the county of Bergen, carried to New York and
there imprisoned,) shall be set at liberty.

The governor and council have also confined a number of
other disaffected inhabitants, chiefly of Bergen county, to
be released, for an equal number of honest citizens stolen and
imprisoned in like manner, being determined in the future
thus to retaliate, till the enemy shall think proper to discontinue that infamous part of their infamous system.[1]

EXCLUSIVE of the *natural* character by which mankind are
distinguished from each other, there is, in most men, a *second-
ary* or *artificial* character, through which they
present all their actions to the world. I call it
artificial, because it is neither produced nor supported by any
principle, and is no more than the fashion under which the actors suppose they appear to the most advantage.

*Burgoyne's
Instructions to
Colonel Baum.*

This taste is formed very early in life, and frequently by
accident either of company or education. Some men are
pedantic, and with them every phrase must be technical;
others are foppish, and *their* descriptions are always intended to be light and novel; but Burgoyne's turn, or artificial
character, is that of a mountebank, in which every thing must
be *wonderful*. In his proclamation, which has already been
in most of the papers, he has handed himself out under as
many titles as a High German doctor, and given as wonderful a detail of enterprises as is to be found in Waltho Van Clut-
terbank's harangue.

The same pompous complication opens his instructions to
Lieutenant-Colonel Baum. "The object (says he) of your
expedition is to try the affections of the country, to disconcert
the councils of the enemy, mount Reidesel's dragoons, to complete Peter's corps, and—to obtain large supplies of cattle,
horses, and carriages."

From this catalogue of orders we may infer, that the instant Burgoyne got into the country, he was at loss how to

---

[1] Pennsylvania Evening Post, August 26.

go *on*, and perhaps by this time he is at as great a loss how to get *out;* that his dragoons were on foot, his army incomplete, and unfurnished with horses and carriages : but the grand secret, and that which engrosses his first thought, and occupies his first line, is "*to try the affections of the country.*" A mountebank may sometimes hit upon the right disease, and Burgoyne has here given a proof of it; for unless America turns a traitor to herself, *his* efforts will be in vain. The second article in the orders is very judiciously placed, viz., *to endeavor to disconcert our councils;* very happily thrown in ! Because it shows us the necessity of attending firmly to business, and the danger of employing our ingenuity to evade or perplex it.

After this introduction of general heads, he lays down the route, the manner of conducting it, with directions for the treatment of the inhabitants. "*All possible care* (says he) *is to be used to prevent plundering.*" This seems a very extraordinary order to be given to a plundering party, but is perfectly consistent when we understand that plundering a *country* for *stores* or *supplies* is the general's perquisite, and plundering houses, that of the men. Burgoyne's orders are to bring in *one thousand three hundred horses at least, with all the saddles and bridles that can be found, together with all the wagons, carriages, draft oxen, and cattle fit for slaughter;* for these no money was to be paid, but receipts were to be given, and those to such only as had complied with the terms of his manifesto. Had Burgoyne made the sweep of horses, saddles, bridles, cattle, &c., which he was in hopes of, he would at least have pocketed thirty or forty thousand pounds, *by taking those articles from the country without paying for, and charging them to the treasury as if he had purchased them;* the receipts and the pretended distinction of persons serving as a mask to cover the fraud. As this plundering in the wholesale was the business the party was sent upon, no wonder they were forbidden to spend their time in dividing themselves into parties to rob hen-roosts and cider-cellars, or stealing blankets, breeches, and petticoats.

"As you will," say the instructions, "have *persons with*

you perfectly acquainted with the abilities of the country, it may perhaps be advisable to *tax* the several districts with the portions of the several articles, and limit the hours for the delivery ; and should you find it necessary to move before such delivery can be made, *hostages* of the most *respectable* people should be taken to secure their following you the ensuing day."

Of all the unjust modes of taxation hitherto proposed by our enemies, this is the most summary and the most pernicious. A stranger to the country is to be informed by strangers to him, of the circumstances of the inhabitants ; and upon such information a *tax* is to be imposed, for the immediate payment of which the most *respectable people* are to be seized as hostages and carried into captivity ! Take care, Americans, how you admit men who practise such wicked methods of taking your property, and such cruel ways of enforcing your compliance.

"You will," say the instructions, "use all possible means to *make the country believe* that the troops under your command are the advanced corps of the army, and that it is intended to pass Connecticut on the road to Boston. You will likewise *insinuate* that the main army from Albany is to be joined at Springfield, by a corps of troops from Rhode Island."

No real, lasting good, Sir John Burgoyne, can come of lying, and if no credit is to be given to your declarations, you cannot expect that any will be given to your proclamation, but that the inhabitants, in all places, will look upon the latter and upon all others which either you or General Howe may put out, as farragoes of threats and delusions, to deter or dissuade them from removing their property till you or he may send parties to plunder and fetch it off. This is the true intent and meaning of all your proclamations.

There is something prophetically pensive towards the conclusion of the instructions. "It is highly probable," he says, "that the corps under Mr. Warner, now supposed to be at Manchester, will retreat before you ; but should they, contrary to expectation, be able to collect in great force and post themselves advantageously, it is left to your discretion to attack them or not; *always bearing in mind* that your corps is *too valuable* to let any considerable loss be hazarded on this occasion." *Poor unfortunate John Burgoyne!*

The general, in the next paragraph of his instructions, gives a kind of triumph over his qualmish apprehensions, and putting on the soldier, assures Colonel Baum, that should the rebels attempt to interrupt him, he, General Burgoyne, "will make *such a movement* as shall put the rebels between two fires." A wonderful piece of firework indeed!—and shows that *one real fire* of ours is better than *two of his* contriving; for the event of this double-barrelled scheme has been, that the colonel and his party are defeated,' near a thousand of them made prisoners, and, they say, poor General Burgoyne is gone STARK MAD.²

SEPTEMBER 1.—WE are credibly informed that Burgoyne, the chief and director of the King of Great Britain's band of thieves, robbers, cut-throats, scalpers, and murderers of every denomination, now infesting the northern and western frontiers of several of the American United States, has not only discontinued the reward he had offered and given to the savage Tories, Indians, Britons, Hessians, Brunswickers, Waldeckers, and other profligate scum of the human race, now in his service, for the scalps they brought him, from the murdered and half murdered inhabitants, but has strictly prohibited, for the future, under a severe penalty, the practice of scalping. It must not, however, be supposed, that the chief of the ruffian band was so weak as to be in the least influenced to this prohibition by any motive of compassion or humanity; his inducements were purely political. He had found by experience, that his rewards lessened the number of his emissaries, who not only scalped some of his Tory friends, concealed among the inhabitants, but also scalped one another; and that a scalping party of a lieutenant, and about thirty men, he lately sent ·out, with a large number of Indians, were by the latter all killed and scalped, none of the party having been since seen or heard of, and the lieutenant's hair, which was remarkably full,

---

¹ Colonel Baum was mortally wounded in the action with General Stark.
² Pennsylvania Evening Post, August 28.

bushy and red, being known.   We had intelligence by several
persons, that Burgoyne had laid aside his usual practice of
scalping, and strictly forbid it for the future, but we did not
before know his reason for the prohibition.   It is not improbable
he might be apprehensive, that some of the dexterous hands
about him, might take an opportunity, one time or another,
and slip off his own night-cap.[1]

SEPTEMBER 2.—LORD MULGRAVE, in the Ardent man-of-war,
took the other day, on his cruise in the English channel, a
Dutch vessel, with three hundred barrels of gunpowder on
board, no part of which could be found in her bill of lading.
On board her likewise were several French officers of distinction, and a German count, disguised as common mariners, who
were discovered, it seems, by one of them being heard to speak
elegant French.   Finding they could no longer conceal themselves, they went down into the cabin, and soon after came on
deck dressed in their French uniforms, denied that they were
bound to America, and insisted on being released as officers
of the King of France.   Lord Mulgrave, however, refused to
release them, but told them if they expected to be treated like
gentlemen, they must honorably confess the errand on which
they were going, for that he was convinced their intended
voyage was to join the rebel forces of America.   This had the
desired effect, for it extorted from them a confession that they
had each of them received commissions from the Congress,
and on landing at Boston were to have been invested with
separate commands of great consequence.[2]

SEPTEMBER 5.—GENERAL WASHINGTON, our great and illustrious commander, the prop and glory of this western world,
Washington's issued this day at Wilmington, the following
General Orders. orders, which cannot too much be admired on account of the virtuous and noble sentiments they contain:—

GENERAL ORDERS.—From every information of the enemy's
design, and from their movements, it is manifest that their

[1] Pennsylvania Journal, September 10.   [2] Pennsylvania Ledger, Nov. 26.

aim is, if possible, to possess themselves of Philadelphia. This is with them a capital object; 'tis what they last year strove to effect, but were happily disappointed. They made a second attempt at the opening of this campaign; but after vast preparation and expense for that purpose, they abandoned their design and totally evacuated the Jerseys. They are now making their last effort. It seems they first intended to come up the Delaware, but from the measures taken against them in the river, judged the enterprise that way too hazardous. At length they have landed on the eastern shore of Maryland and advanced some little way into the country, but the general thinks they will again be disappointed in their views, should they push their design against Philadelphia, on this route. Their all is at stake. They will put the contest on the event of a single battle. If they are overthrown they are utterly undone—the war is at an end. Now, then, is the time for our strenuous exertions; one bold stroke will free the land from rapine, devastation, and burnings, and female innocence from brutal lust and violence. In every other quarter the American arms have been of late rapidly successful; great numbers of the enemy have fallen in battle, and still greater numbers have been taken prisoners. The militia to the northward have fought with a resolution that would have done honor to the oldest soldiers—they bravely fought and conquered, and glory attends them. Who can forbear to emulate their noble spirits? Who is there without ambition to share with them the applause of their countrymen and of all posterity, as the defenders of liberty, and preservers of peace and happiness to millions in the present and future generations?

Two years we have maintained the war and struggled with difficulties innumerable, but the prospect has since brightened and our affairs put on a better face. Now is the time to reap the fruits of all our toils and dangers; if we behave like men this third campaign will be our last. Ours is the main army. To *us* our countrymen look for protection; the eyes of all America and Europe are turned upon us, as on those by whom the event of war is to be determined; and the general assures his countrymen and fellow-soldiers, that he believes the critical, the important time is at hand, which demands their most spirited exertions in the field.

Here glory waits to crown the brave. Peace, freedom, and happiness will be the rewards of victory. Animated by motives like these, soldiers fighting in the cause of innocence, humanity, and justice, will never give way, but with undaunted resolution press on to conquest. And this the general assures himself is the part the American forces, now in arms, will act, and thus acting he will insure them success.[1]

SEPTEMBER 8.—By intelligence from the grand army, we learn that General Washington's head-quarters were at Wilmington on the first instant, and the main body of the army encamped on the heights, on the environs of the town; that strong parties of light troops and militia were advancing towards the enemy; that frequent skirmishes ensue, though of but little consequence.

Situation of the Main Armies.

That the enemy landed about four miles below the head of Elk, and in a day or two advanced their van to Grey's Hills, where they remained inactive. That their cavalry suffered very much during the voyage for want of forage, (having on board only enough for three weeks, whereas they were out six weeks;) many of them died before they were landed, and many more have been ruined by being turned into corn-fields, so that we may presume Mr. Howe will not be in a capacity to act *vigorously* very soon. Deserters come in daily, and our people frequently pick up small parties of prisoners. The American army is in high health and spirits, and eager for action.

We hear from Poughkeepsie, that about a week ago, seven Tories were committed to jail there, charged with robbing several houses, and putting the families in fear. It is said, when taken, they were all painted and dressed like Indian men, but that five of them proved to be women, three of whom are a mother and two daughters. Thus do the infernal designs and proceedings of the court of Great Britain

[1] Pennsylvania Journal, September 10.

assimilate to their own character all those who espouse their cause; not only seducing them to become base, treacherous thieves, robbers, murderers, &c., but divesting them of humanity, and converting them into savages and perfect devils in human shape.[1]

SEPTEMBER 11.—WE have had a severe time of it to-day. Early in the morning the commander-in-chief receiving intelligence that the British were advancing in two columns from their camp at Kennet Square, made a proper disposition to receive them. The first attack was made by Knyphausen, on a party of Americans under General Maxwell, who had crossed the Brandywine, and posted himself in an elevated position on both sides of the main road. In this affair the Americans twice repulsed the British, but the latter receiving a strong reinforcement, General Maxwell was obliged to give way and retreat across the river.

Brandywine.

About four o'clock in the afternoon the action became general, and continued very severe until dark, when the British stopped the pursuit, and the Americans retired to Chester, where they are now encamped.[2]

---

[1] New York Journal, September 8.

[2] Clift's Diary. The following account is given in the journal of a British officer:—"At four o'clock in the morning the army moved in two columns; that under General Howe and Lord Cornwallis to the left, and crossing the river Brandywine. Some miles above the direct road and Shad's Ford, came on the right flank and rear of the enemy, who were posted there in great strength, having several batteries and many cannon on exceeding strong ground. Whilst this manœuvre was performing, the column under the commands of Generals Knyphausen and Grant, marched by the usual road to Shad's Ford, and attacked several posts the enemy had on the south side of the Brandywine; these being driven across the river, the cannon were drawn up to the most advantageous situations, and a heavy cannonade kept up. As soon as it was perceived that General Howe had attacked the rebels, the troops passed the river, stormed the batteries, and took their cannon. The rout of the enemy then became general. They were pursued as long as daylight and the fatigued condition of the troops would permit, General Howe's column having marched seventeen miles the day before the engagement. We took ten pieces of cannon, a royal howitzer, several ammunition wagons, &c. It was difficult to ascertain the number of the enemy killed, as they were scattered over a great extent of ground."—*Pennsylvania Ledger*, December 6.

SEPTEMBER 17.—As the rebels have in their newspapers
favored the public with General Burgoyne's orders to Lieutenant-Colonel Baum, it might be interpreted mali-

Retort on the
Rebels.

ciously should we refuse to commit to print any
pieces of elegance of their commanders which may fall into our
hands. For this reason I send you a copy of some orders for
the Jersey militia which we picked up in a late excursion.
I hope no invidious comparisons will be drawn between this and
General Burgoyne's, for though the latter, to give him his due,
writes in a pretty style, and plausibly enough as to military
matters, his performance falls infinitely short of that energy,
that precision, that sublimity which grace the composition of
the Jersey Brigadier. The candid public must consider, that
probably poor Burgoyne has not had those advantages of education which have refined the sentiments and expressions of
the elegant writer of the following orders. I give them in the
original spelling. Probably the brigadier strove to adapt his
orthography to the genius of his troops:—

"*Mendon Sep.* 5 1777.

"Sir you are to keep one man allways with an order already writ to Impres any Horss on the way he shall want that
upon the first appearance of the enemy's coming to attack you
or yours you are to dispatch the man and tell him to come the
nighest road direct to me or my house and he is to call to
every man woman and child he sees and desire them to call
upon all men to push down whare the enemy is and give them
battle. But he is not to stop to tell his story but call out as
he rides along and tells his story he is to ride six or seven
miles an ower if they have no guns or Ammunison they are
to carry pitchforks flailes stones or such weapons as they chuse
or think best. But if any man is afraid to goo to battle that
hath no gun he is immediately to set out as a Common Cryer
towards the back country and desire everyone he sees to come
down to the help of the Lord against the mighty and I will
keep a becon out so that if you with what will turn out nigh
by can keep the enemy in play a few howers I will be down
with 1000 or 1500 men. Shew this letter to all men you see

and send Coppys of it to all the militia officers you can that
live within 15 or 20 miles of the Lines and Shores.—This gentlemen I have writ to the commanding officers down at the
shore therefore I desire all men old and young as they regard
their lives & properties and all that is dear to them when
they hear the a Larm that they a quip themselves as well as
they can and march immediately towards the enemy whare I
will meet them.   Let every man as soon as he is ready stop
for no company.   But call as they see to come along & they
are to send word by some of thare family that cant fight to
their next neighbor of the a Larm—and cursed is he that is well
& will not turn out when this a Larm comes.

WILLIAM WINDS, B. G.[1]

SEPTEMBER 20.—YESTERDAY, about noon, the two armies
met near Stillwater, and a most obstinate and bloody battle
ensued.   The advanced parties of the Americans,   Battle of
which were composed of Morgan's riflemen and   Stillwater.
Dearborn's infantry, received the first fire of the enemy, and
a little after two o'clock the action became general.   The right
wing of the British forces was commanded by Burgoyne in
person, the left by Phillips and Reidesel, and the centre, covered
by Frazer and Breyman, was supported by the savages, Canadians, and renegade Provincials and Tories.   Never was more
bravery or determination shown.   For upwards of three hours
the blaze from the artillery and small arms was incessant, and
sounded like the roll of the drum.   By turns the British and
Americans drove each other, taking and retaking the field
pieces, and often mingling in a hand to hand wrestle and fight.
Scammell[2] fought like a hero, leading his regiment where the
fire was the hottest, and did not leave his post until he was
wounded and taken off the field.   The British artillery was
well served, and worked with sad havoc among our poor fellows, who are the more to be wept, for their gallantry and devotion to their country.   The cannon of the British was lost to
us only for the want of horses to draw them off.   Arnold

---

[1] Pennsylvania Ledger, November 19.   [2] Alexander Scammell.
VOL. I.—32

rushed into the thickest of the fight with his usual reckless-
ness, and at times acted like a madman. I did not see him
once, but S. told me this morning that he did not seem
inclined to lead alone, but as a prominent object among the
enemy showed itself, he would seize the nearest rifle-gun and
take deliberate aim.

During the action a party of our men got up into some
trees, and as the clouds of smoke opened, poured in upon the
enemy single shot. In this manner several of the officers were
killed or wounded. One of Brook's regiment says he silenced
two fellows with laced coats, and it is said that Burgoyne had
a narrow escape.[1]

At sundown the action was less furious, and a little after
dark a greater part of the two armies retired from the field.
Some of our men did not come off until near midnight. In
the midst of so much destruction, it is a wonder how any of
them escaped; "but it is in this cause," as old Emerson used to
say about the hens that laid every day in the year but Sunday,
"*Providence is with 'em.*" [2]

SEPTEMBER 22.—YESTERDAY, the British having received
intelligence of the situation of General Wayne, and his design
of attacking their rear, should they attempt to
pass the Schuylkill, a plan was concerted for surprising him, and the execution intrusted to Major-General
Gray. The troops for this service were the fortieth and fifty-
fifth regiments, under Lieutenant-Colonel Musgrave, and the
second battalion of light infantry, the forty-second and forty-
fourth regiments, under the general. This last detachment
marched at ten o'clock last night, the other at eleven. No
soldier of either were suffered to load; they that could not
draw their pieces, took out the flints! The general knew
nearly the spot where the rebel corps lay, but nothing of the
disposition of their camp. He represented to the men that
firing would discover them to the enemy, kill their own
friends, and cause a confusion favorable to the escape of the

General Gray attacks Wayne.

---

[1] Letter from General Enoch Poor.   [2] Churchill Papers.

rebels, and perhaps productive of disgrace to the British. On the other hand, by not firing, they would know the foe to be wherever fire appeared, and a charge insured his destruction; that amongst the enemy, those in the rear would direct their fire against whoever fired in front, and consequently destroy each other.

General Gray marched by the road leading to the White Horse, and took every inhabitant with him as he passed along. About three miles from camp he turned to the left, and proceeded to the Admiral Warren,[1] where, having forced intelligence from a blacksmith, he came in upon the out sentries, pickets, and camp of the rebels! The sentries fired and ran off, to the number of four, at different intervals; the picket was surprised, and most of them killed in endeavoring to retreat. On approaching the right of the camp, the line of fires were perceived, and the light infantry being ordered to form to the front, rushed along the line, putting to the bayonet all they came up with, and overtaking the main herd of fugitives, stabbed great numbers, and pressed on their rear till it was thought prudent to order them to desist. The forty-fourth regiment, advancing in line likewise, closed up in support of the light infantry, putting to the sword such of the rebels as in the heat of the pursuit had escaped that corps, whilst the forty-second came on in a third line as a reserve. Upwards of two hundred were killed, many more wounded. Seventy-one prisoners were brought off; forty of them being badly wounded were left at different houses on the road. The British loss consisted of Captain Wolfe, and one or two men killed; Lieutenant Hunter, and five men wounded! It was about one o'clock this morning when the attack was made, and the rebels were then assembling to move towards the King's forces.[2]

SEPTEMBER 25.—To-DAY, as a party of Captain Emmerick's new corps of chasseurs were bathing near Kingsbridge, in New York, he suddenly beat to arms, when they, with the

---

[1] White Horse and Admiral Warren were two taverns on the Lancaster road. Washington's camp on the 16th of September, was situated between them.

[2] Gaine's Mercury, December 1.

greatest spirit imaginable, flew to their firelocks, and appeared naked, in order to have attacked any enemy that might be at hand. This so pleased the captain, that he presented each man with a dollar, and gave them his thanks for their alertness.[1]

SEPTEMBER 26.—LAST night, the royal army, under the command of his Excellency Sir William Howe, Knight of the
British Army
enters
Philadelphia. Bath, marched from their encampment, near the Swedish ford, in two grand divisions, one by the Falls of Schuylkill, the other by the road to Germantown, and formed their camp at and near those places. This morning a large detachment, under the command of the Right Honorable the Earl Cornwallis, entered Philadelphia, marched through Second street, and after placing the proper guards, encamped to the southward of the town.

The fine appearance of the soldiery, the strictness of their discipline, the politeness of the officers, and the orderly behavior of the whole body, immediately dispelled every apprehension of the inhabitants, kindled joy in the countenances of the well affected, and has given the most convincing refutation of the scandalous falsehoods which evil and designing men have been long spreading to terrify the peaceable and innocent. A perfect tranquillity now prevails in the city; numbers who have been obliged to hide themselves from the former tyranny and to avoid being forced into measures against their conscience, have appeared to share the general satisfaction, and to welcome the dawn of returning liberty.[2]

[1] Pennsylvania Ledger, October 29.   [2] Rivington's Gazette, November 8.

CHAPTER XII.

OCTOBER 1.—IT is unnecessary to say a word of the spirit and numbers of the people of America—of their attachment to their liberty—of the extent and nature of their country—of their resources—and the interest all De Lisle's Letter. the powers in Europe have in maintaining the independence of the American States, to show the absolute impracticability of Great Britain's ever subduing this country. I should not despair of the final success of the Americans in the present war, if they were at this time expending their last pound of powder, and their last ounce of ball. Desperation would supply the want of every thing. No force can subdue the hearts of these people; and nine-tenths of them, I am sure, are determined in their opposition to the government of Britain. It is inconceivable to see the exertions of these young republican States. They have done wonders. All the force of the monarchy of Britain in the last war with France, did not produce from the whole continent of America, half the exertions which we sometimes see here in a single State; and yet these republics have as yet put forth but a small part of their strength. I expect to see them, before the close of the war, upon a footing with the oldest monarchies in Europe: and if I was not sure that a love of conquest was incompatible with a love of liberty, I should think they would make some of them tremble from their foundations.

Every part of the conduct of Great Britain, and of her generals and armies, shows the power of this country, and the absolute impossibility of conquering it. Why has the court of Britain meanly solicited all the courts of Europe to withhold aid of all kinds from the Americans? Why has she bought up twenty thousand foreigners to assist in the reduction of America? Why did she send an army of forty thousand men across the ocean for that purpose last year? Why has the King of Britain proclaimed a fast, and called upon the Almighty to enter into an alliance with him, to assist in conquering his rebellious subjects? Surely all this has been done because they dreaded the power and resources of America.

I believe in no war with the powerful monarchy of France did Britain ever negotiate with more expense—stood more for foreign alliances—lie more for internal support—or fast and pray with more seeming devotion than in the present war with America. An uninformed spectator, from a view of these things, would suppose that the only object of Britain in the prosecution of the war, was not to suppress a rebellion in America, but to defend herself from being subjugated by her American colonies.

But the conduct of her generals in America is all of a piece with the conduct of the court. Read their letters to the British ministry. Observe with what caution they land, how slowly they advance and how circumspectly they march through the country. Their modes of attack and defence in all their battles and skirmishes with the Americans from their own accounts of them, show that they are aware of the skill, and fear the courage, of their generals and armies. Their stratagems (of which they boast) confess that they are contending with a regular army, and not with an undisciplined mob. Even their shouts of victory and the high encomiums they publish of the gallant behavior of their officers and soldiers, declare that they fight with a formidable enemy. The inhumanity of their generals, the insolence of their officers, and the rancor of their soldiers towards the Americans, are all testimonies of the strength of this country. They indicate hatred which can only be exercised towards equals or superiors. The exchange of letters and prisoners between the British and American generals, are further acknowledgments on the behalf of the former, of the stability of the power from whence the latter derive their authority. In spite of all the pains the

British generals have taken to destroy the credit of the paper money emitted by the Congress, they have given a sanction to its validity by sending it out from New York to support their prisoners among the Americans. The indiscriminate ravages to which the professed royalists or Tories are exposed in common with the republicans or Whigs, show that the British army believe that a great majority of the people of America are opposed to them, and that all professions of attachment to them are hypocritical, and intended only to save property. But the British generals have gone still farther in declaring by their conduct, that the Americans are invincible. They have, in some measure, thrown down their arms as useless in the present controversy, and have attempted to subdue their enemies by the perfidious arts of a court. They have attempted to surprise the Congress into a negotiation, only for the purpose of deceiving them. They have published proclamations for the encouragement of desertions in the army, and defection among the citizens of America. They have hired printers to traduce the Congress and the army; and to complete all, they have made and attempted to circulate large quantities of counterfeit continental money among the Americans; aiming thereby, at one blow, to cut their sinews of war. Their folly in this manœuvre exceeded their villany; for they weekly advertised their money for distribution, in a New York paper.

I am not so sanguine as some of my friends, as to the issue of the present campaign. But I rest satisfied at all times, that the loss of a battle or of a town will detract nothing, finally, from the Americans; and that the acquisition of victories and of territory will serve only to weaken General Howe's army, and to accelerate the period when America shall establish her freedom and independence, upon the permanent foundation of public virtue and military knowledge.[1]

OCTOBER 2.—A CORRESPONDENT in Paris says:—" When

---

[1] Extract of a letter from a French gentleman, who "has been near two years in America, and has been introduced to the first characters on the continent. His real name must be a secret. The name by which he has chosen to be known to the public," is DE LISLE.—*New Jersey Gazette*, January 7, 1778.

Doctor Franklin appears abroad, it is more like a public than a private gentleman, and the curiosity of the people to see him is so great, that he may be said to be followed by a genteel mob. A friend of mine paid something for a place at a two-pair-of-stairs window to see him pass by in his coach, but the crowd was so great that he could but barely say he saw him."

Doctor Franklin.

We are well assured that Dr. Franklin, whose knowledge in philosophical sciences is universally allowed, and who has carried the powers of electricity to a greater length than any of his contemporaries, intends shortly to produce an *electrical machine*, of such wonderful force that instead of giving a slight stroke to the elbows of fifty or a hundred thousand men, who are joined hand in hand, it will give a violent shock even to nature herself, so as to disunite kingdoms, join islands to continents, and render men of the same nation strangers and enemies to each other; and that by a certain chemical preparation from oil, he will be able to smooth the waves of the sea in one part of the globe, and raise tempests and whirlwinds in another, so as to be universally acknowledged for the greatest physician, politician, mathematician, and philosopher, this day living.[1]

OCTOBER 4.—THIS morning, before daybreak, (the weather being foggy,) the rebels attempted, with all their force, in six columns, to penetrate on the outposts of our army; they began their attack with three of them on the second light infantry and the fortieth regiment at the end of Germantown, where they were so warmly received that they did not make the least impression for the space of two hours; at length being overpowered with numbers, and risking to be surrounded if longer opposition was made, our two battalions thought it expedient to retire. These columns imagining victory was about to declare in their favor, two of them came into the village, while the third filed off obliquely to our left. Colonel Musgrave having judiciously thrown himself with six companies of the fortieth, into a square house of

Battle of Germantown.

---

[1] New Jersey Gazette, December 31.

Mr. Chew's, checked one of the two columns that had followed him, while the other pushed into Germantown. The one at the house immediately invested and riddled it with musketry, grape and cannon shot for a full hour, British Account. the colonel defending it most gallantly, killing them by dozens from the windows of every face; but, upon the forty-fourth regiment advancing into the village, supported by the seventeenth, and driving all before them as far Mr. Chew's mansion, both these columns retired precipitately, and would have been totally demolished if the fog had not made it hazardous for so small a body to pursue so rapidly, as it might have done had the weather been clear; the other column, that had filed off towards our left, being drove shortly after by the thirty-third, forty-sixth, and sixty-fourth regiments. Two other columns, that had attacked and obliged the pickets of our right to fall back on their respective corps, were, in their turn, defeated, upon the first light infantry, fourth, fifth, fifteenth, thirty-seventh, forty-ninth, and fifty-fifth regiments attacking them; and the Hessian Yagers repulsed and beat back the column which attacked their post. It now began to clear up, and the commander-in-chief having perceived a large body (that had rallied) forming itself on Chestnut hill, (apparently to retard our pursuit,) his excellency ordered Major-General Gray to advance upon it with the seventeenth, thirty-third, forty-fourth, forty-sixth, and sixty-fourth regiments, directing the other corps to follow as fast as possible to sustain; but the rebels did not think proper to maintain that ground, retiring precipitately upon the approach of this small corps; and although we pursued for nine miles, till three in the afternoon, we were never able to come up with any considerable body. Thus Mr. Washington's army, consisting of upwards of twelve thousand men, was totally dispersed by a few British battalions, and the Hessian Yagers, (the rest of our army having never had an opportunity of engaging,) and would not only have been cut up had the morning been bright, but all their artillery, &c., must unavoidably have fallen into our hands.[1]

[1] Gaine's Mercury, November 10.

OCTOBER 5.—DIED at the American camp, near Pawling's mill, this evening, Major Edward Sherburne, aide-de-camp to Major-General Sullivan. He received the mortal wound, of which he died, yesterday at the battle of Germantown, after having given the most striking evidence of his bravery and good conduct. He was in the severest of the fire for near two hours before he received the fatal wound which forced him from the field; and during the whole time behaved with such uncommon firmness, as the love of freedom only can inspire. This promising youth sprung from one of the most reputable families in New Hampshire, entered the service of this country, as a volunteer, at the commencement of the war, and served as such till the last campaign, when he was appointed aide-de-camp to General Sullivan, with whom he has ever since served with great credit and reputation. He was in most of the actions since the war commenced, and ever showed the same coolness and bravery which he discovered in the late action. He endured with great constancy the pains occasioned by his wound, and departed this life with a heroic firmness, which well witnessed the satisfaction he felt in suffering for his much injured country.[1]

OCTOBER 6.—THIS day the fortresses Clinton and Montgomery, on the North River, in New York, fell into the hands of the British, under the command of Sir Henry Clinton. A gentleman who was in Fort Montgomery when it was taken, gives the following particulars of the event:—On Saturday night, we had advice that a large number of ships, brigs, armed vessels, &c., had arrived at Tarrytown, where they had landed a considerable body of men, supposed to be about one thousand, and had advanced towards the plains. Colonel Lutlington being posted there with about five hundred militia, they sent in a flag to him requiring him to lay down his arms and surrender himself and men prisoners of war. Whilst he was parleying with the flag they endeavored to surround him, which he perceiving, ordered his men to retreat. The British then returned to their shipping, and the

---

[1] New York Packet, October 23.

next morning we had advice of their being under sail, and coming up as far as King's Ferry. In the afternoon they landed a large body of men on the east side of the river to draw our attention that way, but they re-embarked in the night and next morning landed on the west side.

On Sunday night his Excellency Governor Clinton, who then commanded at Fort Montgomery, sent out a party of one hundred men, under the command of Major Logan, across the Dunderburg, to watch the motions of the enemy. This party returned in the morning, and reported they had seen about forty boats full of men land below the Dunderburg. The governor sent out another small party of about twenty-eight men, under the command of Lieutenant Jackson. On the road that leads to Haverstraw, two or three miles below Fort Clinton, they fell in with a concealed part of the enemy, who ordered them to club their muskets, and surrender themselves prisoners. They made no answer, but fired on the enemy and hastily retreated. They returned the fire and pursued our people half a mile, but they all got back to the fort without losing a man, though within five rods of the enemy before they were discovered. Upon this intelligence one hundred men were immediately sent off, under Colonel Brown, who fell in with the enemy about two o'clock in the afternoon, when a smart engagement ensued, but the enemy being of much superior force, our people were forced to retreat.

At the same time it was thought proper to send some of the artillery, with a field-piece, to occupy an eminence commanding the road that leads to Orange Furnace, with a party of men to defend it. They were attacked soon after, and our field-piece did great execution; but it soon bursting, our men retreated, and an engagement of small arms was kept up a good while. Most of our men got within the breastworks, when the attack became general on both forts. At the same time the enemy's shipping came in sight, but the wind being light, and the tide against them, none of the vessels could come up, except the galleys and armed sloops, which fired upon us, but did no execution; we, in return, fired upon them, and believe did them some damage.

The enemy continued a vigorous and incessant attack upon the forts; but notwithstanding their utmost efforts, they were many times repulsed and beaten back from our breastworks with great slaughter. But the smallness of our numbers, (being in both forts but about five hundred,) which required every man to be upon continual duty, and obliged him to unremitted exertions, fatigued our people greatly; while the enemy, whose number was supposed to be at least four thousand, continued to press us with fresh troops.

About four o'clock they sent in a flag, demanding in five minutes a surrender of the forts; and ourselves prisoners of war; or that they would put us all to the sword. An answer was returned by Colonel Livingston, acquainting them that we were determined to defend the forts to the last extremity. The action was renewed with fresh vigor on both sides, and continued till the dusk of the evening, when they stormed our upper redoubt, which commanded the fort, which after a severe struggle, and overpowering us with numbers, they got possession of; and we were obliged to give way. At the same time they stormed and got possession of Fort Clinton, in which were none but militia, who nobly defended it, till they, like the garrison at Fort Montgomery, were obliged to give way to superior force.

The darkness of the evening much favored the escape of our people, the greatest part of whom, with almost all the officers, by some means or other got off, and joined our army, or returned to their places of residence. How those who were so unfortunate as to fall into the hands of the enemy, were treated by them, we have not heard, but have reason to think it was with a cruelty suitable to the wickedness of the cause in which the British are engaged.[1]

---

[1] New York Journal, May 11, 1778. Gaine, in his paper of the 11th of October, gives the following account sent by an officer in the British army:—I have now the pleasure to felicitate you on our taking the forts Montgomery and Clinton by storm. It was effected last night. The garrisons in both places consisted of twelve hundred rebels. Of our detachment, we lost Mungo Campbell, Lieutenant Colonel of the 52d, and Major Sill of the 63d. Major Grant, of the New York Volunteers, was killed a little before the attack, which was commanded by Colonel Mungo Campbell. My old acquaintance, George Turnbull, late captain in the

OCTOBER 11.—ON Tuesday last, departed this life, at his house on Staten Island, aged seventy-two years, the Reverend Mr. Richard Charlton, missionary from the Society for the Propagation of the Gospel in Foreign Parts. Richard Charlton. This worthy clergyman was born in Ireland, and received his education in Trinity College, Dublin. He came over to this country soon after he entered into holy orders; and was the first missionary of New Windsor, on Hudson River. From thence he moved to New York, being chosen assistant minister of Trinity Church, and catechist; in which station he continued several years, before his appointment as the missionary of Staten Island, in 1747, where he remained ever since.

Sincere and steady in friendship, charitable to the distressed, and hospitable to all, he was deservedly esteemed and respected. Amidst the confusions of the present rebellion, his loyalty was unshaken; his attachment to the Constitution, in church and state, unalterably firm. The great increase of his congregations, during his incumbency for thirty years at Staten Island, was an evidence of the assiduity with which he discharged the duties of his office; and the tears which were plentifully shed over his remains at the grave, by the members of his flock, were a sure indication that they considered themselves as having lost, in him, a common father and friend.[1]

Royal American Regiment, was ordered to take the command of Grant's corps. He has acquired great honor, being the first that entered Fort Montgomery, after losing one officer and eight privates. Sir Henry Clinton, who himself narrowly escaped the enemy's grape-shot, in consideration of his very gallant behavior, has appointed him Lieutenant-Colonel Commandant of the New York Volunteers, in the room of the brave Major Grant. The gallant Count Gabrouski,* lately arrived from England, has died of his wounds. Amongst the prisoners is Colonel William Allison, of the Drowned Lands, whose son was killed in the fort. This person is a member of the provincial congress for the State (as it is termed) of New York. Also young William Livingston, late of New York, in the profession of the law. A great part of the twelve hundred rebels, who garrisoned the forts Montgomery and Clinton, or were not killed or prisoners, made their escape, as it was very dark when the forts were taken. The forbearance and humanity shown by all the troops to the rebels after they became their conquerors, was astonishing; and savored of that benign temper which ever characterizes the army of Great Britain.

[1] Gaine's Mercury, October 11.

* This was a Polish nobleman, who entered the British service as a volunteer.

OCTOBER 14.—YESTERDAY, General Vaughan, having under his command a large body of British, who have committed various acts of vandalism, in their passage up the North River, landed a number of men at Esopus, marched up to the defenceless town of Kingston, about two miles from the river, and immediately set it on fire. The conflagration was general in a few minutes, and in a very short time that pleasant and wealthy town was reduced to ashes; one house only escaped the flames. Thus by the wantonness of power the third town in New York for size, elegance, and wealth, is reduced to a heap of rubbish, and the once happy inhabitants (who are chiefly of Dutch descent) obliged to solicit for shelter among strangers; and those who lately possessed elegant and convenient dwellings, obliged to take up with such huts as they can find to defend them from the cold blasts of approaching winter. We learn that the inhabitants saved the best part of their movable property; but some lost the greatest part of their temporal all. 'Tis said the enemy took little plunder, being told that Governor Clinton was at hand with fifteen hundred men, but unluckily not so near as to save the town. They burnt several houses at Rhynbeck Flats, and proceeded as far as Livingston Manor, where they burnt a few more. Our troops are now up with them. It is hoped they will be able to put a stop to these depredations. Britain, how art thou fallen! Ages to come will not be able to wipe away the guilt, the horrid guilt, of these and such like deeds, lately perpetrated by thee.[1]

(margin note) Burning of Kingston.

---

[1] New York Packet, October 23. A Philadelphia paper gives the following notice of this expedition:—" By express from New York, we have the following intelligence:—That General Sir Henry Clinton, after his successes on the North River, had detached General Vaughan with two thousand men towards Albany; that at Esopus, about fifty miles this side of Albany, General Vaughan had fallen in with a very large party of rebels, and had entirely defeated them; had taken between thirty and forty pieces of cannon, with all their stores, baggage, &c.; that the rebels having fled to the houses at Kingston and fired upon the royal army from the windows, General Vaughan had set fire to it and laid it in ashes; that from Esopus he had proceeded on to join General Burgoyne, and in a few days we hope to hear of the two generals having formed a junction at Albany."— *Pennsylvania Ledger*, October 29.

OCTOBER 17.—GENERAL BURGOYNE having been defeated in a second trial on the field at Stillwater,[1] and finding himself encircled without the least chance of escape, to-day surrendered to the Americans. General Gates, in a letter to his wife, written from Albany three days after the surrender, says:—

The voice of fame, ere this reaches you, will tell how greatly fortunate we have been in this department. Burgoyne and his whole army have laid down their arms, and surrendered themselves to me and my Yankees. Thanks to the Giver of all victory for this triumphant success. I got here the night before last, and the army are now encamped upon the heights to the southward of this city. Major-General Phillips, who wrote me that saucy note last year from St. John's, is now my prisoner, with Lord Petersham, Major Ackland, son of Sir Thomas, and his lady, daughter of Lord Ilchester, sister to the famous Lady Susan, and about a dozen members of Parliament, Scotch lords, &c. I wrote to T. Boone, by Mr. Fluck, an engineer, whom I permitted to pass to Canada, and who goes immediately from thence to England. I could not help, in a modest manner, putting him in mind of the *fête champêtre* that I three years ago told him General Burgoyne would meet with if he came to Amercia. If Old England is not by this lesson taught humility, then she is an obstinate old slut, bent upon her ruin. I long much to see you, and have therefore sent the bearer to conduct you to Albany by the way of Reading, where you will be received and entertained by Mrs. Potts. Before you leave Reading, you must take advice whether to come by Nazareth or Bethlehem; after that your road up the country by Van Camp's, through the Minnisinks, to Hurley and Esopus, is plain, and well known to the bearer. Don't let Bob's zeal to get to papa, hurry you faster than, considering the length of your journey, you ought to come. If you come by Bethlehem, there is a Mr. Oakley, who holds an office under Mifflin, who will provide you with every thing you may have occasion for, and will introduce you to Madame Langton, and the bishop, and Mrs. Ilsley, &c. Perhaps you may get ruffles to your apron; if they are not finished I desire you will bespeak them.

[1] On the 7th of October.

Tell my dear Bob not to be too elated at this great good
fortune of his father. He and I have seen days adverse, as
well as prosperous. Let us through life endeavor to bear
both with an equal mind. General Burgoyne has promised
me to deliver any letters I please to commit to his care in England. I think to send a few to some principal men there.
Perhaps they may have a good effect for both countries. I
would fain have the mother reconciled to her child, and consent, since she is big enough to be married, to let her rule and
govern her own house.

I hope Lady Harriet Ackland will be here when you arrive. She is the most amiable, delicate little piece of quality
you ever beheld. Her husband is one of the prettiest fellows
I have seen, learned, sensible, and an Englishman to all intents
and purposes; has been a most confounded Tory, but I hope to
make him as good a Whig as myself before he and I separate.
You must expect bad and cold days up the journey, therefore
prepare against it. I thank God I am pretty well; have had
a bad cold, with loss of appetite from being continually harassed with so much business; but I hope to find some rest in
winter and much comfort in yours and Bob's company. I will
try to get some good tea for you from some of the English officers. Accept my tenderest wishes for your health and safety,
and assure my dear Bob how much I am interested in his welfare. Heaven grant us a happy meeting.[1]

OCTOBER 18.—ON the morning of the seventh instant, General Burgoyne invited General Frazer to breakfast with him.
In the course of their conversation, Frazer told
General Burgoyne that he expected in a day or
two to be in Albany. "Hold," said General Burgoyne, " the
owners of the land (meaning the militia) are come out against

Anecdote of
Burgoyne.

---

[1] Gates Papers, New York Historical Society. Rivington, in his paper of
November 1, says:—"As no accounts, properly authenticated, of the situation of
the northern army, have yet been brought to New York, the printer entreats the
public to excuse his inserting any of the reports that have been circulated, until
he may be warranted by intelligence derived   immediately from General Burgoyne."

us. We cannot proceed any farther so fast as we have done."
The same day the second battle at Stillwater was fought, in
which the militia acquitted themselves like veterans, and the
whole British army was routed.[1] The consequence of this defeat is the glorious Convention of Saratoga, which was signed
yesterday. A French officer who has served under General
Gates during the campaign, says: "When dere be no more
militia in dis country, I be one very great Tory."[2]

OCTOBER 23.—LAST night, was received at Cambridge, in
Massachusetts, a confirmation of the important intelligence,
that the British Lieutenant-General, Burgoyne,   Rejoicings at
with upwards of five thousand men at his com-   Cambridge.
mand, submitted themselves prisoners of war to the Honorable
Major-General Gates, commander of the American army in the
northern department. In consequence of which the colleges
were beautifully illuminated; and to-night the town of Cambridge was universally illuminated in high taste and elegance.
A bonfire was made upon the common, where were fired a
number of cannon, answered by musketry from the troops stationed in Cambridge, in honor to General Gates.

A number of principal gentlemen, both of the town and
army, spent an agreeable evening in company, where the following toasts were drank, with the discharge of cannon: 1.
The brave Major-General Gates, who with effect said to the
vaunting General Burgoyne, "Hitherto shalt thou come and
no farther." 2. General Washington, and his army. 3. May
every minion general intruding upon American rights and innocence, meet with the fate of Burgoyne. 4. May tyrant
princes submit to superior American souls. 5. May the wisdom of Congress ever be superior to the policy of Britain. 6.
Complete establishment to American independence. 7. May
American bravery and honesty rise superior to Britannic artifice and fraud. 8. May generous harmony forever firmly
unite the States of America. 9. Freedom to the whole world.

[1] In this action General Frazer was killed.
[2] Pennsylvania Packet, September 5, 1778.

The rejoicings were introduced by the discharge of thirteen cannon, in honor to the thirteen United States of America.[1]

YESTERDAY morning, about fifteen hundred Hessians, under the command of Count Donop, came down from Philadelphia to Red Bank[2] in order to take the fort, under the command of Colonel Greene, belonging to Rhode Island. About four o'clock in the afternoon the attack was begun by a most furious cannonade, which held a quarter of an hour; the Hessians then rushed on to storm the fort, and got into the old part of the works, when they thought it was all their own, and gave three cheers, but were soon obliged to retreat out of it in the utmost hurry. The galleys at the same time kept up a constant fire on them, which did great execution; and in about three-quarters of an hour's attack they ran off with the greatest precipitation, leaving behind them, dead, about ninety persons. Among them was a lieutenant-colonel and four captains; and from a good authority we are assured that the enemy buried one colonel and twenty-one privates between the fort and Cooper's Ferry, and carried over not less than two hundred wounded. The enemy left on the field, wounded, Count Donop,[3] his brigade-major, a lieutenant, and about eighty privates; the brigade-major and lieutenant are permitted to go into Philadelphia, and most of the privates have died of their wounds.

While the enemy was attacking the fort, the Augusta, of sixty-four guns, the Roebuck, of forty-four, two frigates of thirty-two, the Merlin of eighteen, and their large galleys came through the lower *chevaux-de-frize*, and kept up a great firing, in order to draw off the galleys from giving any assistance to the fort; but they were mistaken. The Augusta, in going down in the evening got aground. Early this morning all the galleys and floating batteries began the attack, when an incessant fire was kept up on both sides; so that the very elements

Attack on Red Bank.

---

[1] Boston Gazette, and Upcott, v. 83.
[2] Situated at the junction of the Delaware and Schuylkill Rivers.
[3] He died soon after the action.

seemed to be on fire. At eleven o'clock the Augusta was set on fire, and at twelve she blew up with an astonishing blast. One of our people was killed in a galley by the fall of a piece of timber, and we were so near that some of our powder-horns took fire and blew up. The engagement still continued ; but the Roebuck fell lower down, and the Merlin, of eighteen guns, ran aground, and at three o'clock the enemy set fire to her, when the engagement ceased, the enemy falling still lower down. Thus ended two glorious days. The commodore with his boats went on board the wrecks, and took out much plunder, and brought off two of their cannon, one an eighteen, the other a twenty-four pounder.[1]

THE two following advertisements lately appeared, one in the Carolina, and the other in the Virginia newspaper, which show the humanity and great consistency of conduct of the sons of freedom, as the Americans are pleased, in several of their writings, to style themselves :—" Ran away, the tenth instant, a lusty negro, named Bob ; the said fellow is outlawed, and I will give ten pounds for his head, severed from his body, and forty shillings if brought alive."

The second advertisement breathes the same infernal spirit, viz. :—" Ran away from the subscriber, a negro fellow named Zeb, aged thirty-six ; as he is outlawed, I will pay twenty pounds currency, to any person who shall produce his head, severed from his body, and five pounds if brought home alive." [2]

By the most cruel treatment, they make these poor people desperate, and fly from misery ; then they are proclaimed, and exposed to be murdered for a reward. The real friends to liberty should be consistent in all their proceedings! [3]

THIS day departed this life, at New Lots, in the township of Flatbush, in King's county, Long Island, Elbert Hegeman, Esq., in the ninety-first year of his age. Few men ever possessed a more humane, benevolent, and compassionate heart; he was no less remarkable for his piety

Elbert Hegeman.

---

[1] New Jersey Gazette, December 5.   [2] Signed John Mosely.
[3] Rivington's Gazette, October 25.

than his benevolence, and exhibited to us a remarkable instance of his attention to the divine laws of his Creator, having read the Bible through no less than three hundred and sixty-five times.[1]

OCTOBER 28.—BY a gentleman from Baltimore, we learn that last week a *feu de joie* was celebrated there, on account of the rebel army having retaken possession of Philadelphia, but that, nevertheless, the inhabitants would not believe it, nor would the militia, as was expected, turn out in consequence of it.   Indeed, for some weeks past, the rebel army in the country round here have been very busy in celebrating their *feux de joie* on the different accounts their leaders have pretended to receive, of victories obtained by their northern army over General Burgoyne.   These finesses, intended to delude the country, and to keep up the sinking spirits of their army, cannot last long, but must in the end, render their general officers contemptible in their own army, and exasperate the whole country against them.[2]

Burgoyne's Defeat.

OCTOBER 29.—THIS morning President Hancock took leave of the Congress in the following speech :—" Gentlemen, Friday last completed two years and five months since you did me the honor of electing me to fill this chair.   As I could never flatter myself your choice proceeded from any idea of my abilities, but rather from a partial opinion of my attachment to the liberties of America, I felt myself under the strongest obligations to discharge the duties of the office, and I accepted the appointment with the firmest resolution to go through the business annexed to it in the best manner I was able.   Every argument conspired to make me exert myself, and I endeavored by industry and attention to make up for every other deficiency.   As to my conduct, both in and out of Congress, in the execution of your business, it is improper for me to say any thing.   You are the best judges.   But I think I shall be forgiven, if I say I have spared no pains,

Hancock leaves Congress.

---

[1] Rivington's Gazette, November 8.   [2] Pennsylvania Ledger, October 29.

expense, or labor, to gratify your wishes, and to accomplish the views of Congress. My health being much impaired, I find some relaxation absolutely necessary, after such constant application; I must therefore request your indulgence for leave of absence for two months. But I cannot take my departure, gentlemen, without expressing my thanks for the civility and politeness I have experienced from you. It is impossible to mention this without a heartfelt pleasure. If in the course of so long a period as I have had the honor to fill this chair, any expressions may have dropped from me that may have given the least offence to any member, as it was not intentional, so I hope his candor will pass it over.

" May every happiness, gentlemen, attend you both as members of this House and as individuals; and I pray Heaven that unanimity and perseverance may go hand in hand in this House; and that every thing which may tend to distract or divide your councils may be forever banished." [1]

DEACON LOUDON[2] has taken upon himself to give in his *extraordinary* Packet a garbled account of the late squabble among the Congress rapscallions, which terminated in British account of Easy John's leaving the chair. As this produc- Hancock's Speech. tion is calculated to mislead the public, we are happy to present to our readers a statement by an eye-witness, who has been watching the Congress since it left Philadelphia:

" As soon as the rebels learned that the British fleet was at the head of the Chesapeake, a motion was made in the Congress for an adjournment to some place ' at least one hundred miles from any part of God's kingdom where the British mercenaries can possibly land,' which, after some rapturous demonstrations, was carried *nem. con.* Immediately the Congress commenced the retreat, leaving old nosey Thomson[3] to pick up the duds and write promises to pay (when the Congress should return) the Congress debts. In the flight, as in the rebellion, Hancock, having a just apprehension of the vengeance which awaits

---

[1] Gordon, ii. 296:—On the 1st of November, Congress elected Henry Laurens to the chair, made vacant by Hancock's resignation.

[2] Editor of the New York Packet.   [3] Charles Thomson.

him, took the initiative and was the first to carry out the letter of the motion of his associates.

"In four days they met at York. At the opening of the session, the President, having performed his journey on horseback, and much more like an express than a lord, was unable to take his seat, and for several days the chair was filled by a *pro tempore*. On the return of Hancock, he gave many indications of the intense fright he had experienced, and was observed to assume the chair with more than usual care and quiet seriousness; whether from soreness or a desire for the further remove of the Congress, his best friends could not tell.

"Out of this silent discontent murmurs soon sprung, and one day before the dinner hour of the Congress, he offered a motion that 'this body do adjourn until the troops under the Howes, now pursuing the freemen of America, retire altogether from the State of Pennsylvania.' This was not adopted. Hancock then arose and delivered the following, which is a fair specimen of rebel eloquence, and 'much to the *pint*,' as the Yankee parsons say :—

"BRETHREN, FREEMEN AND LEGISLATORS :—It's now more'n two years sence you done me the honor of puttin' me in this seat, which however humbly I have filled I was determined to carry out. It's a responsible situation, and I've been often awaken'd of nights a hearin' them reglars a comin' for my head. I can't bear it. It's worked on me, and already I feel as though I was several years older than I was. My firmness, which has made up for all my other infirmities, has been the cause of many heartburnings, which I am sure the candor of those among you who don't like it, will pass over. As to the execution of business, I have spared no pains, and shall return to my family and folks with that satisfaction. In taking leave of you, my brethren, let me wish that we may meet soon under the glories of a free, but British government."

After requesting the Congress to pass around his chair and shake his hand, the afflicter of his country retired, satisfied as usual with himself and the Congress, who, with equal satisfaction, welcomed his departure.[1]

[1] Rivington's Gazette Extraordinary, December 21.

NOVEMBER 8.—AT Edmonton, in England, on Wednesday last, a gibbet was erected, under which a load of wood was laid, and from the gibbet hung a figure, with a mask for a face, and on its breast a label, with this inscription: "Washington, General of the Americans:" and in the evening the gibbet, and the general, were reduced to ashes.[1]

NOVEMBER 19.—THIS day the Hessian Lieutenant-General Philip De Heister, died at Cassel, in Germany, in the sixty-first year of his age. His death was occasioned by an inflammation of his lungs, which carried him off in four days.[2]

NOVEMBER 20.—THE martial spirit which at present shines forth amongst the inhabitants of New York city, reflects the highest honor upon them, and is at once a proof of their loyalty and gratitude. Ever since the arrival of the King's troops, the greatest harmony and most cordial friendship have subsisted between them and the citizens, nor has the martial law been a grievance to any. None have been required to take arms, not even the most apostate amongst those who have taken the benefit of the proclamation and come to the city for protection. How different the prospect if we look where "fraud prevails, and impious men bear sway," and where the wretched inhabitants have been dragged to the field to fight against the most glorious constitution in the universe. The indulgence of the commander-in-chief has prompted the principal gentlemen, inhabitants of this city and refugees from other provinces, to form themselves into independent companies, twenty of which are nearly completed.

New York City.

Last Monday, several companies of them paraded on the fields, at the upper end of Broadway, headed by the Worshipful David Matthews, Esq., and made a very fine appearance. These companies, together with the militia, will greatly add to the strength of the city, and relieve the King's troops, who may be employed elsewhere.[3]

Matthew's Independent Companies.

---

[1] Rivington's Gazette, Jan. 3, 1778.   [2] New Jersey Gazette, March 4, 1778.
[3] Rivington's Gazette, November 22. In the same paper, Rivington continues:—"Every loyal heart must have been delighted with the first appearance

THIS day arrived at Boston, in Massachusetts, under an escort of American light dragoons, the Honorable John Hancock, Esq., President of the American Congress, and first major-general of the militia of that State. By his coming into town sooner than was expected, he avoided some public marks of respect which would otherwise have been paid him; his arrival was made known by ringing the bells, the discharge of thirteen cannon of Colonel Craft's park of artillery on the common, the cannon on the fortress on Fort Hill, and the shipping in the harbor. The independent and light infantry companies paid him their military salutes. He received the compliments of gentlemen of all orders; and every indication was given of the sense the public has of his important services to the American cause.[1]

John Hancock.

NOVEMBER 22.—A GENTLEMAN in the American army gives the following account of the late movements of the British forces on and about the Delaware and Schuylkill Rivers:

About the 12th of October, the British erected a battery near the mouth of the Schuylkill, in order to prevent our boats going into that river, and then landed a large body of troops on Province Island opposite Fort Mifflin, with intention to erect batteries against that fort.

Siege of Fort Mifflin.

In the night they threw up one battery within point blank

of some of our volunteer companies at the parade on Monday last. So spirited a beginning gives us reason to flatter ourselves that the whole will soon be complete; and as the body of the militia are subject to the same tour of duty, every individual must be induced by the motives of greater regularity, to associate under some of the different captains, appointed by his Excellency Governor Tryon. When the several companies are filled we shall be able to boast of a militia, (as they will be united by the noblest motives, the interest of their country and constitution,) whose only contention will be to be most forward in promoting the safety and good of the public.—A band of brothers connected by such ties must tend to awe the attempts of an enemy from without, and to frustrate the machinations of villains (if any such there be) within. To add to the satisfaction of the public, we have the pleasure of acquainting them, that the colonel and lieutenant-colonel of the volunteer battalion appointed by his Excellency Governor Tryon, are men of approved abilities, uniting the fortitude and resolution of the officer, with the milder virtues of the citizen."

[1] Pennsylvania Ledger, January 7, 1778.

shot directly opposite to the fort, which was attacked the next day by the galleys, who kept up so warm a fire on them for two hours, that one captain, one lieutenant and ensign, with about eighty men, came on the bank with a flag, clubbed their muskets, and surrendered themselves prisoners; but a large body of fresh men coming in through the meadows to rescue them, they were fired at from the block house at Fort Mifflin, and many of those who had submitted, thinking it was them, ran off; that fifty-six privates with Lieutenant Finch and Ensign Hankey were brought off. On the next day the galleys attacked the battery again, but without any effect. The enemy now threw up another battery on the hospital wharf, from which they fired red hot shot, and kept up a firing every day of shells and red hot balls, but to little purpose, having since their first firing to the 9th November killed but two men and wounded a few, though they had thrown some thousand shot and shells. On Monday, the 10th of November, the enemy had completed five batteries, one on the hospital wharf above mentioned, one on the wharf below that, and three others, one just above the fort, another right opposite, and the third a little below the fort. From all these, about seven o'clock in the morning, they began a most furious cannonade, with shot, shells, and carcasses, not throwing less than fifteen hundred of them a day. Tuesday morning they began in the same manner, when Captain Treat of the artillery, a brave officer, with two others, were killed, and several wounded; and in the evening Colonel Smith, who commanded the fort, was brought off wounded. Three of the enemy's ships came up the same morning a little above Mantua Creek, where we had thrown up a small battery, but had that day no guns in it, and kept a continual fire on it for some hours, without the least damage to the battery. Wednesday and Thursday the cannonade of shells, &c., was kept up most violently, which tore the stockades, barracks, &c., all to pieces, and dismounted and broke many of our guns. Friday the fire was also very hot, and the Vigilant galley, which had been cut down and carried sixteen twenty-four pounders, got behind Hog Island designing to get up to Fort Mifflin, but could not do it that day. Saturday the 15th we got three guns in the battery mentioned above, and that morning the Somerset of sixty-four guns, the Isis, and another fifty-gun ship, two large frigates, and a galley they brought from New York came up within reach of Fort Mifflin, when the battery began firing on them. This drew the fire from all the men-of-war, which was incessant; so that from the cannonade on the fort and the fire from the enemy, there was one continual roar of cannon. The wind was high, and directly against the galleys, which prevented them from getting to action for some time. In the afternoon the Vigilant got through close up to Fort Mifflin and fired most furiously on it. The commodore sent over six galleys to attack her; but she lay so covered by the enemy's batteries that it could not be done to any purpose. The other galleys with the floating batteries, were engaged with the ships; and such a cannonade, I believe, was never seen in America. It continued till the evening, when all the ships fell down and the firing ceased except from the Vigilant and the batteries on Province Island against Fort Mifflin, which was by this time torn all to pieces, having scarce a stockade standing, the block houses almost beat down, and every gun dismounted or broken. It now being found impossible to defend it any longer, Major Thayer, who for some days had so bravely defended it, about eleven o'clock at night set fire to the remains of the barracks and brought off his garrison. Thus fell Fort Mifflin after a close siege of near one month, in which time we had on board the galleys only thirty-eight men killed and wounded.

Sunday and Monday the enemy were quite still, and on Tuesday the 18th, in the morning, a large number of transports with troops from New York came up to Billingsport and landed their men; and General Cornwallis came over from Pennsylvania with a number more, in order to attack the fort at Red Bank, where we had not men sufficient to hold a siege. In council it was thought best that it should be evacuated, and on Thursday evening the fort was blown up, and the garrison, with the ammunition, went off.

Our little fleet was now to be preserved; and in consultation with the land and sea officers, it was agreed that it should, if possible, pass by Philadelphia and go up the river. Accordingly, on Wednesday night, the commodore ordered the thirteen galleys to pass close under the Jersey shore, which they all did without a shot being fired at them. It being quite calm, the top-sail vessels could not attempt it. Friday morning, before day, it still being calm, the brig Convention, Captain Rice, the schooner Delaware, Captain Eyres, with six of the shallops, set off to get by, which they all did, through an exceeding hot fire of shells and shot, except the Delaware and one shallop, which were run aground and set on fire. Finding that all the troops were gone, and that there was no wind to carry the continental vessels by, it was thought better to set them on fire, than to let them fall into the enemy's hands; and the same morning before day, the brig Andria Doria, the xebecks, Repulse and Champion, the sloops Racehorse and Champion, with the two floating batteries and three fire-ships, were accordingly set on fire and destroyed.[1]

DECEMBER 1.—WE hear from London, that a treaty is to be concluded with Russia for taking thirty-six thousand Russians into pay; and with the King of Prussia, but the Russians for America. contents are not known. It is not for a body of his troops; but twelve thousand more Hessians, Wurtemburgers, Palatines, and Mecklenburgers, are agreed for. Four and twenty new regiments are to be raised in England and Ireland of five hundred men each, so that the army in America, next campaign, will not be short of eighty thousand men.[2]

IT is observable that at the opening of every campaign in the spring, the British plunderers, and their Tory emissaries, announce the total reduction of America before the Hortentius. winter. In the fall they find themselves as remote from their purpose as they were in the spring; and then we are threatened with innumerable hosts from Russia and Germany, who will utterly extirpate us the ensuing summer, or reduce us to the most abject submission. They have so beat this beaten track, that for mere sake of variety, I would advise

---

[1] New Jersey Gazette, December 5.   [2] Same.

them to explore a new road; and not compel us to nauseate a
falsehood, not only because we know it to be one, but for its
perpetual repetition without the least variation or alternity.
According to custom, therefore, the new lie (that is the old lie
reiterated) for next summer is, that we are to be devoured,
bones and all, by thirty-six thousand Russians; besides something or other that is to be done to us by the King of Prussia.
What this is to be, is still a profound secret; but as it will
doubtless be something very extraordinary, and it being impossible to conceive what else he can do to us, after we are swallowed by the Russians, he is probably, by some political
emetic or other, to bring us up again. I should think, in common complaisance to human reason, that absurdities so gross,
and figments so destitute of probability, could only deceive
those who choose to be deceived. The Empress of Russia,
though a sovereign in petticoats, knows too well that the true
riches of a nation consist in the number of its inhabitants, to
suffer such a number of her inhabitants to be knocked in the
head in America, for the sake of facilitating the frantic project
of a more southern potentate in breeches, deluded by a blundering ministry, and the universal derision of Europe. It is her
interest (and I shall wonder if ever princes proceed upon any
other principle, before the commencement of the millennium)
to have America dismembered from Great Britain, which must
of necessity reduce the naval power of the latter, and make
Russia a full match for her on the ocean. And as for the King
of Prussia, considering that there never was any love lost between him and the family of Brunswick, and that he has long
been jealous of the maritime strength of Britain, these artifices
of fraud might, with equal plausibility, have introduced the
Emperor of Japan as entering into leagues and alliances with
our late master at St. James. It is nothing but an impudent
forgery from first to last, and merely fabricated to restore to
their natural shape and features, the crest-fallen countenances
of the Tories, and if possible, to intimidate the genuine sons of
America. The utmost they can do, they have already done;
and are this moment as far from any prospect of subjecting us
to the dominion of Britain, as they were in the ridiculous hour

in which General Gage first arrived in Boston. This is no secret with those who have the management of their armies in America, how greatly soever the nation itself may be deluded by the pompous accounts of their progress. But whatever becomes of Old England at last, these gentlemen are sure of accumulating immense wealth during the war; and are therefore determined to keep up the delusion as long as possible. Burgoyne is the only one of any distinction, who has virtue enough to own the truth; and I am credibly informed, that he has frankly declared, that he was most egregiously deceived in the Americans, that he had been led to believe they would never come to bayoneting, that they behaved with the greatest intrepidity in attacking intrenchments, that although a regiment of his grenadiers and light infantry displayed, in an engagement with Colonel Morgan's battalion of riflemen, the most astonishing gallantry, Morgan exceeded them in dexterity and generalship, and that it was utterly impossible ever to conquer America.[1]

DECEMBER 9.—A CORRESPONDENT in London writing under this date, says:—"The account of General Burgoyne's treaty with Mr. Gates, arriving when the two Houses of Parliament were sitting, and in the warmth of high debate, the friends of government were much confounded and staggered by such a shock; but you cannot imagine how furiously, illiberally, and indecently opposition triumphed on the occasion, opening and roaring like so many bull dogs against administration. The King, God bless him, for we never had a better one, and no other nation had ever so good a one, who feels every calamity and misfortune of his people, was greatly affected; but, with that magnanimity which distinguishes his character, he soon declared that such a cause could never be given up, that this loss must be retrieved by greater and more vigorous exertions, and that he would even ' *sell Hanover and all his private estate, before he would*

"Burgoyne's Defeat" at London.

----

[1] Hortentius, (Governor William Livingston,) in the New Jersey Gazette, December 24.

*desert the cause of his loyal American subjects, who had suffer-
ed so much for him.'*

" In two or three days the nation recovered from its surprise,
and now is ready to support the King and his ministers in the
proper and vigorous use of such means as are adequate to the
great end of reducing the revolted colonies to a constitutional
subordination. Many in both Houses of Parliament have
spoken to this effect with great spirit, and one member of the
Commons, Mr. Cambridge, said that he would part with reluctance with one shilling in the pound towards raising another
army of ten thousand men for America, yet he would cheerfully pay twelve shillings in the pound towards an additional
army of sixty thousand men." [1]

DECEMBER 10.—On the night of the fourth instant, the British army, distressed for want of " elbow room," marched from
Philadelphia with an avowed intention of obliging
the American army to quit their post at Whitemarsh, and driving them back into the country. Early on Friday morning, they posted themselves strongly on the heights
of Chestnut hill, about two miles in front of the right wing of
our army. While they lay here, General Irvine, with a body
of militia, attacked a party of their light troops which were a
little advanced in front of their encampment. The skirmish
was pretty warm, and the enemy being reinforced, our militia
were obliged to retreat in some confusion. Unfortunately
General Irvine was wounded in the hand and thrown from his
horse, by which means he was made prisoner. The enemy had
a number killed and wounded, among the latter was Sir James
Murray, a captain of the light infantry. Having reconnoitred
our right sufficiently, and not liking its appearance of strength,
on Saturday night they silently filed off to our left, leaving a
party behind them to keep up their fires. On Sunday morning they took post on Edge Hill, in front of our left. In the
afternoon, Colonel Morgan with his light corps fell in with a
large body of the enemy, attacked them with spirit, and did

Skirmish at Whitemarsh.

[1] Pennsylvania Ledger, March 7, 1778.

great execution. Burgoyne's grasshoppers[1] galled them extremely. The next day the enemy suddenly retired, and before
we could expect such a thing from these braggadocios, they
were on full march for Philadelphia.

This expedition has only served to discover the weakness
and cruelty of the British army. Whenever they marched it
was in the night; whenever they halted they took post on the
strongest grounds; wherever they came they plundered the
miserable inhabitants without respect of persons. Those merciful considerations which should influence us in our treatment
of our worst enemies, found no place among them. The poor,
the widow, the fatherless children were stripped of their all,
even without leaving them bread to eat, or clothes enough to
cover them. Did they who talk of British mercy and protection but see those unhappy sufferers![2]

DECEMBER 31.—THE neglect of some of the people of Jersey
and Pennsylvania, to supply clothing and necessaries to the
army at Valley Forge, in accordance with the late requisition
made by General Washington, creates much comment.[3]

Among the suggestions for relief is the following by Governor Livingston, published in this day's gazette:—"I am afraid
that while we are employed in furnishing our
battalions with clothing, we forget the county　Hortentius.
of Bergen, which alone is sufficient amply to provide them
with winter waistcoats and breeches, from the redundance and
superfluity of certain woollen habits, which are at present applied to no kind of use whatsoever. It is well known that the
rural ladies in that part of New Jersey, pride themselves in an
incredible number of petticoats; which, like house furniture,
are displayed by way of ostentation, for many years before
they are decreed to invest the fair bodies of the proprietors.
Till that period they are never worn, but neatly piled up on
each side of an immense escritoire, the top of which is deco-

---

[1] These are two light three-pounders, made of wrought iron, and manageable
with a very few hands. They were taken at Saratoga.
[2] New Jersey Gazette, December 24.　　　[3] Letter of Francis Mercer.

rated with a most capacious brass-clasped Bible, seldom read. What I would, therefore, humbly propose to our superiors, is to make prize of these future female habiliments, and, after proper transformation, immediately apply them to screen from the inclemencies of the weather those gallant males who are now fighting for the liberties of their country. And to clear this measure from every imputation of injustice, I have only to observe, that the generality of the women in that county, having for above a century *worn the breeches*, it is highly reasonable that the men should now, and especially upon so important an occasion, make booty of the petticoats." [1]

[1] New Jersey Gazette, December 21.

END OF VOLUME I.